Structured Finance and Insurance

Founded in 1807, John Wiley & Sons is the oldest independent publishing company in the United States. With offices in North America, Europe, Australia, and Asia, Wiley is globally committed to developing and marketing print and electronic products and services for our customers' professional and personal knowledge and understanding.

The Wiley Finance series contains books written specifically for finance and investment professionals as well as sophisticated individual investors and their financial advisors. Book topics range from portfolio management to e-commerce, risk management, financial engineering, valuation, and financial instrument analysis, as well as much more.

For a list of available titles, visit our Web site at www.WileyFinance.com.

Structured Finance and Insurance

The ART of Managing Capital and Risk

CHRISTOPHER L. CULP

John Wiley & Sons, Inc.

Published by John Wiley & Sons, Inc., Hoboken, New Jersey.
Published simultaneously in Canada.

For general information on our other products and services or for technical support, please
contact our Customer Care Department within the United States at (800) 762-2974, outside
the United States at (317) 572-3993 or fax (317) 572-4002.

Designations used by companies to distinguish their products are often claimed by
trademarks. In all instances where the author or publisher is aware of a claim, the product
names appear in Initial Capital letters. Readers, however, should contact the appropriate
companies for more complete information regarding trademarks and registration.

Wiley also publishes its books in a variety of electronic formats. Some content that appears
in print may not be available in electronic books. For more information about Wiley
products, visit our web site at www.wiley.com.

Library of Congress Cataloging-in-Publication Data:
Culp, Christopher L.
  Structured finance and insurance : the ART of managing capital and risk /
by Christopher L. Culp [et al.].
      p. cm.—(Wiley finance series)
  Includes bibliographical references and index.
  ISBN-13: 978-0-471-70631-1 (cloth)
  ISBN-10: 0-471-70631-0 (cloth)
  1. Asset-backed financing. 2. Securities. 3. Risk management. 4. Risk
(Insurance). I. Title. II. Series.
  HG4028.A84C85 2006
  658.15'5—dc22
                                                            2005019905

Printed in the United States of America.

10 9 8 7 6 5 4 3 2 1

Contents

Wherefore ART Thou?
The Importance of Principle-
Based Structured Finance

Whenever I get a chance to speak to one of Chris's MBA classes at the University of Chicago, I enjoy the look on his students' faces when I start spouting Shakespeare's views on risk management and corporate finance. For practitioners of structured finance and alternative risk transfer (ART), many of his quotes are quite instructive. For example:

> Eye of newt, and toe of frog,
> Wool of bat, and tongue of dog,
> Adder's fork, and blind-worm's sting,
> Lizard's leg, and howlet's wing,—
> For a charm of powerful trouble,
> Like a hell-broth boil and bubble.

Macbeth's witches truly appear to be our first structured finance specialists. At least that is what some may conclude when reading about the efforts of managers and their financial advisers to practice structured finance and ART as a sort of alchemy—turning debt into insurance, taking liabilities off balance sheet, or accelerating earnings to cover known losses. We can't "bid farewell to magic" (*Tempest*, Act V, Scene I), but we can establish the fundamentals on which the proper solutions are structured to address fundamental capital and risk management issues.

In Parts One and Two of this book, Chris lays out the building blocks of finance and risk management drawing on corporate finance theory and applied research that has been developed over the past 30 years. These tools are then sharpened in Parts Three and Four as we move from theory to applications involving project finance, securitization, and the convergence between insurance and capital markets solutions such as catastrophe bonds and committed capital. Chris brings together two different worlds—the world of corporate finance and the world of insurance—and explains how the tools, while they may look different, are based on the same fundamentals.

These worlds are complicated on their own. When practitioners bring them together they often create Byzantine structures to address accounting, regulatory, tax, and corporate finance drivers that might lead even the most astute shareholder or analyst to proclaim:

> Sir, I am vexed;
> Bear with my weakness; my old brain is troubled.
> (*Tempest*, Act IV, Scene I)

This is why simple principles are important. Shakespeare's entreaty "To thine own self be true" (*Hamlet*, Act I, Scene III) can be used by any manager to question whether the structured transaction is a means for obscuring or addressing underlying risks. Structured transactions—whether they securitize assets, cover difficult-to-insure risks, or access capital markets investors more efficiently—are of questionable value if management cannot explain clearly why considerable time and resources were spent to structure such solutions.

Often, the decision to structure a solution is a type of "To be or not to be" question. Does management of an airline company believe its shareholders wish it to be in the transportation business or the fuel speculation business? To what degree should the future oil price be hedged, for how long, and at what cost? Chris explains the fundamental principles to answer these questions and goes one step further by explaining the confusion shareholders face if they do not know or understand management's risk management strategy.

Of course, it is because companies can never be "secure from worldly chances and mishaps" *(Titus Andronicus)* that risk management has a role. It is equally important that risk managers understand that shareholders expect management to take risks. Without taking risk, management cannot create value. It is the balancing act between risk and ruin that Chris concentrates on in such detail by keeping our attention focus on both capital and risk management.

To some financial advisers, ART transactions once appeared as the perfect means to address both core and noncore risks. It was thought that one master insurance policy could cover both insurance and financial risks.

Management could use structured insurance transactions as a kind of "cookie jar" to dip into whenever they needed just the right amount of earnings to cover unexpected losses. Chris points out (for example, in Chapters 23 and 24) how this could occur if management and its financial advisers did not apply two important principles:

1. ART transactions should not be used to cover core business risks.
2. ART transactions should not allow management a cookie jar to obscure the true reasons for unexpected losses.

When ART transactions are transparent, are focused on noncore risks, and avoid creating cookie jars for management, we get back to the fundamental purpose of these products.

In the coming years, we will see insurance and capital markets applications come closer together as capital markets investors and insurance underwriters will accept a common language for risk and risk analysis. In Chapter 22, Chris describes why and how capital markets investors have been tapped to take on insurance-based risks through catastrophe bonds and how insurance underwriters have learned to appreciate that they can participate in the recovery of their clients if they provide capital instead of insurance after an insurable event.

To bring these two markets together into effective and responsible structures, it is important to understand how they differ. Students of corporate finance and risk management require this understanding in order to avoid concluding that an insurance or financial solution is just "a rose by any other name." The characteristics of a debt obligation or the payment of an insurance premium are critically important differences that Chris describes using common sense and clarity. Hopefully, structured finance practitioners as well as future risk managers will read these chapters carefully and understand that:

> You are a councillor. . . .
> Use your authority. If you cannot,
> give thanks you have lived so long. . . .
> (*Tempest*, Act I, Scene I)

Structured solutions are a critical element in our sophisticated financial and insurance markets. Used properly, they provide firms with greater financial flexibility and shareholders with greater confidence that management is focusing on the firm's core business rather than being exposed to unmanageable risks. Chris helps to bring needed clarity to the profession

of structured finance and the responsibility management has to ensure that
shareholders understand the value that structured transactions can create
for the firm.

    Shakespeare put this best when he admonished us to "Leave not wrack
behind." Had he been able to read Chris's book, he may even have added
that structured finance was "such stuff as dreams are made on."

TOM SKWAREK
Swiss Re Capital Solutions

---

*Mr. Skwarek is Managing Director and Head of Swiss Re's Corporate Capital Solu-
tions Group. He manages this business from London. The thoughts expressed
herein are his alone and do not necessarily represent those of Swiss Re or any of its
clients.*

Preface

This is a book about how structured finance and structured insurance—a.k.a. alternative risk transfer (ART)—can help corporations achieve their corporate financing and risk management objectives in an integrated and comprehensive fashion. Structured finance is the use of nontraditional financing methods to raise funds in a way that also alters the firm's risk profile in the process. Structured insurance or ART is the use of nontraditional risk finance and risk transfer techniques to manage risk in a way that also affects the firm's capital structure and/or weighted average cost of capital. They are two sides of the same coin.

Convergence between insurance and capital markets has been a buzzword for at least a decade. And slowly but surely, each year the worlds of insurance, derivatives, and securities do become progressively more integrated. The trend toward convergence in insurance and capital markets is much more fundamental, however, than just increasing product or institutional similarities. The *real* convergence is between *corporation finance* and *risk management*. It is convergence in a way of thinking.

Unfortunately, one area in which the markets are still badly behind is cross-disciplinary communication. Insurance and derivatives practitioners still speak largely different languages, and even the most similar concepts in the two worlds are often not recognized as being essentially the same thing. This book is intended to help address that by putting both ART and capital markets into the single common denominator and unifying framework of the theory and practice of modern corporation finance.

ORGANIZATION OF THE BOOK

Part One lays a basic foundation about capital, risk, corporation finance, and risk management that is intended to serve as a theoretical backdrop for the more practical discussions in the rest of the book. This firm grounding on first principles of corporate finance and risk management is now even more important than ever, not just so that firms can continue to pursue the most efficient and customized solutions to their risk and capital management problems but also so that firms can avoid the pitfalls of engaging in structured transactions the wrong way, for the wrong reasons, or both.

From the failure of Enron in 2001 to the very recent investigations into structured insurance products like finite risk (see Chapter 24), one might conclude that structured solutions are or are about to be on the wane. One could, of course, have drawn a similar conclusion about derivatives in the 1990s or high-yield debt in the 1980s, and both of those markets are still going strong. The fundamental economic forces that have led more and more firms to pursue integrated financing and risk management tools in the structured finance and insurance markets are not going away. If anything, the recent controversy simply makes it all the more important that the range of these products and solutions be fully understood *in the underlying context of what economic and financial objectives those products are intended to accomplish.*

After developing our basic foundations in Part One, Part Two provides a brief review of *traditional* risk transfer methods—insurance, reinsurance, derivatives, and credit protection products in both the (re)insurance and derivatives worlds. Parts Three and Four then examine the main processes, products, and solutions in the structured finance and structured insurance/ART markets today.

In Part Five, a number of experts have been kind enough to share their thoughts on some of the more specific issues and topics facing participants in both markets today. The order in which the guest essays appear roughly corresponds to the part of the text with which they are most closely associated.

A "REVISION"?

Technically and strictly speaking, this book is the second and revised edition of my 2002 text *The ART of Risk Management: Alternative Risk Transfer, Capital Structure, and the Convergence of Insurance and Capital Markets* (John Wiley & Sons). However, the overlap between this book and that one is fairly minimal. Part of the difference owes to our decision to add a Part Three on structured finance that was not in the prior book. And part owes to new products, case studies, and examples that have occurred in the past five years.

Mainly, however, the substantial revision is a result of my own learning process. As I continue to work closely year after year with both corporations that use structured finance and ART products as well as with firms that provide these solutions, I continue to gain more insight from my clients and colleagues about how this market fits into the broader theory and practice of corporate finance. Hopefully, this "edition" of the book is more streamlined in how it connects the theory to the practice, as well as being more comprehensive and up to date in its product coverage.

TARGET AUDIENCE AND BACKGROUND OF READERS

This book has a conceptual orientation toward the use of structured finance and insurance by nonfinancial corporations and thus will be primarily of interest to corporate risk managers, treasurers, and CFOs, and those on the sell side who deal with corporates, including (re)insurers, insurance brokers, and investment bankers. Professional services firms and regulators with an interest in learning more about where insurance meets derivatives and where both meet the theory and practice of corporate finance should also find some useful material here. Financial institutions, asset managers, collateralized debt obligation (CDO) collateral managers, investors, and others might benefit from getting a bit of the corporate perspective, but only for that reason.

Importantly, this is *not* a book aimed at financial engineers. This book is based on the MBA course I offer at the University of Chicago's Graduate School of Business with the same title as the book. That class deliberately gets into *nothing* concerning issues like cash flow waterfall modeling in CDOs, optimizing attachment points for risk management, term structure modeling, and the like. The reason is that there are other classes at Chicago that *do* cover those specific areas. My class is intended to be a conceptual and institutional course that connects the theory of corporate finance with the practice of risk management and structured products, and this book has the same broad goals and exclusions as the class.

No prior background in insurance or reinsurance is assumed. Part Two provides you with the basic background to both of those worlds. Some background in basic swaps and options will prove useful, but also is not strictly essential. The critical prerequisite here is a basic fundamental grounding in corporate finance. If you have that, the rest of the material is fairly self-contained.

There are some mildly technical sections and several places where mathematical notation is used extensively. If this bothers you, feel free to read around the equations—you won't lose out on that much. The math here is not proofs or demonstrations of key points, but is instead included mainly to help clarify certain concepts and ideas. It is, in short, optional.

ACKNOWLEDGMENTS

I have been lucky to have learned so much from those with whom I have worked, and that list has now grown far too long to give everyone the proper thanks they deserve by name. With apologies to those whom I have not listed, I would like to single out a few exceptions.

For their comments on chapters, lengthy conversations, thoughtful feedback, and blunt constructive criticism, I am grateful to Keith Bockus, Stuart Brown, Valerie Butt, Don Chew, Kevin Dages, Greg Ehlinger, Paul Forrester, Ken French, Richard Green, Al Harris, J. B. Heaton, Steve Kaplan, Barb Kavanagh, Andie Kramer, Mort Lane, Alastair Laurie-Walker, Claudio Loderer, Andrea Neves, Paul Palmer, Tom Skwarek, Jeff Summerville, Paul Wöhrmann, and Heinz Zimmermann.

I would also like to thank two different groups of my former students collectively. First, the last two years of students in my Chicago Graduate School of Business MBA class on structured finance and ART have given me good feedback on the manuscript, my lecture notes, and the content of the course and the book, as well as a lot to think about. Reading their term papers has been enjoyable and instructional for me and has made me wish that I could give far more As than I am able to award.

Separately, I have had the great pleasure for several years of working closely with Swiss Re on a seminar that we call "Risk and Capital Management." We offer this seminar in the United States and in Europe exclusively to Swiss Re clients and Swiss Re personnel, and we cover pretty much the contents of Parts One and Four of this book in a two amazingly full days. The dialogue that occurs between attendees at these events is of the highest quality. I can tell immediately that I am in front of a room full of very senior people who have spent a huge amount of time thinking about this subject and exploring what the market has to offer. I have had a lot of fun playing facilitator in those forums, and I feel like a kid in a candy store in what I learn from them, for which I am obviously grateful.

In that same connection, I am especially grateful to Tom Skwarek, who when he is not busy quoting Shakespeare's views of risk management is always willing to take the time to help me broaden my understanding of the structured insurance market and to push the boundaries of how theory and practice meet in this world. I keep waiting for the day when he sends me the note that he's sick of getting my e-mails and tells me to go away, but he hasn't yet. And for that, I am deeply grateful. I have learned much from our discussions.

A special word of thanks is in order to all of those colleagues who contributed guest essays to this book. As with the prior edition, their contributions make this a vastly more interesting and useful book than if the text were mine alone. Their expertise and knowledge are matched only by their dedication and willingness to contribute.

Finally, a brief personal word of thanks to all the friends and family who have helped me get through this seemingly never-ending project. Although this book is technically a second edition, it has taken far longer to complete than any of my prior works. As a direct result, the entire rest of my life has been thoroughly disrupted and put on hold. I am very blessed to have clients that are willing to go away for a few months and still be there when I resurface, and friends and family who seem to know exactly when to call or stop by as well as when not to do so. I am deeply appreciative to all of you—you know who you are.

Bill Falloon and Pamela van Giessen at John Wiley & Sons, Inc., were patient with me beyond all expectations of reasonableness. I lost count of the number of deadlines that I missed, and I am grateful to both of them for not having a contract put out on my life. Aside from their patience and understanding, it's also a pleasure to work with people who care more about publishing a good book than just ticking off an item on a production checklist.

Notwithstanding all the help, cooperation, feedback, and comments I have received, the usual disclaimer applies, and I alone am responsible for all remaining errors and omissions. In addition, any opinions I have expressed herein are mine alone and are not necessarily those of any of my clients or any institution with which I am affiliated.

CHRISTOPHER L. CULP

Chicago, Illinois
November 2005

One

Integrated Risk and Capital Management

CHAPTER 1

Real and Financial Capital

A firm is essentially a transformation function (held together as a "nexus of contracts") that takes certain inputs and transforms them into outputs.[1] In this transformation process, *capital* has two altogether distinct conceptual meanings. The first is the traditional notion of capital as a factor of production—some kind of asset that helps a firm transform inputs into widgets. In order to finance the required investments in such capital and to disperse the risks of the firm's assets among a pool of investors, firms issue securities. These securities are *also* referred to as capital.

The two concepts are, of course, related—*too* related, unfortunately, despite representing different sides of the traditional corporate balance sheet. It is precisely this close connection that can lead to a fairly significant amount of confusion, especially when it comes to discussing the relation between risk and capital in a practical capital management exercise such as capital budgeting. A banker, for example, is quite likely to define capital budgeting as the allocation of capital to business units. The role played by risk in that exercise is in computing some risk-adjusted return on capital at risk that serves as the hurdle rate or performance measure for these attributions of risk capital to business risks. A corporate treasurer faced with a capital budgeting problem, by contrast, will more likely faithfully compute the net present values of all projects under consideration in order to decide which ones to pursue as new investments in hard assets. Risk comes into the picture through the weighted average cost of capital—itself a risk-adjusted measure of expected returns—used to discount the future risky cash flows on the investment project.

Neither perspective is wrong per se. In fact, we'll see in Chapter 5 the conditions under which the two approaches imply *the same decision rule* for whether to accept a new investment project. Clearly, though, the potential for confusion is enormous. Our sole objective in this introductory chapter is to eliminate those sources of confusion by introducing the concepts of capital in a careful, systematic way—specifically, by considering the relationships of the market values of both real capital and financial capital to the market value of the firm. Not surprisingly, we will conclude that they are equal!

In the process of showing this result, we also accomplish two other objectives. First, we provide a quick review of how corporate securities can be viewed through an "options contract lens." Second, we develop the notion of an economic balance sheet for a firm—a concept that will be very simplistic in this chapter, but which will play an important role and become increasingly complex as we move forward through Part One and the rest of the book.

REAL CAPITAL AND THE VALUE OF THE FIRM

A *real asset* is any asset that can be consumed or used directly.[2] The ability of people or organizations to consume or use a real asset is what gives that asset its value.[3] More colloquially, we sometimes say that real assets have value because we can either eat them, give them to someone else to eat, or use them to produce something edible.

A *real capital asset*—or just *real capital*—is a specific type of real asset that contributes to the production of a sequence of goods or services over time. What distinguishes a real capital asset from any other real asset is mainly the time dimension. Real capital is involved in medium- and long-term production, whereas real *non*capital assets are often consumed immediately. A large dump truck is a real capital asset, for example, whereas an apple is a real *non*capital asset intended more for immediate consumption. Other examples of real capital include plants, equipment, patented production processes and technologies, and the like.

A *firm* is a collection of real assets held together through a nexus of contracts between various parties, including laborers and capitalists, contractors, customers, and the like. What gives the firm its value is the cash flow that the assets owned by and entrusted to the firm may produce over time. Myers (1977) usefully suggests that the market value of the real assets of the firm—denoted $A(t)$ at any time t—be divided into two components:[4]

$$A(t) = V^A(t) + V^G(t) \tag{1.1}$$

where $V^A(t)$ = time t market value of the firm's assets in place
$V^G(t)$ = time t market value of the firm's growth opportunities

Assets in Place

A firm's assets in place at time t are those real capital assets that the firm has already bought and paid for with prior investments. The current market value of assets already in place is equal to the discounted present value (PV) of the future net cash flows on those assets plus the firm's current-period net cash flow from operations, or

$$
V^A(t) = \overbrace{\sum_{j=1}^{\infty} \frac{E[X(t+j)]}{1+E[R^A(t,\ t+j)]}}^{\text{Discounted Expected PV of Future Net Cash Flows}} + \overbrace{[X(t)-I(t)]}^{\substack{\text{Current Net}\\\text{Operating Cash Flow}}}
$$

$$
= \underbrace{\sum_{j=0}^{\infty} \frac{E[X(t+j)]}{1+E[R^A(t,\ t+j)]}}_{\text{Market Value of Assets in Place}} - I(t)
$$

(1.2)

where $X(t+j)$ = time $t+j$ net cash flows on current assets

The future expected net cash flows are discounted at the rate of capitalization appropriate to the risk of the stream of future net cash flows—that is, at the expected return on current assets over the relevant time period, $E[R^A(t, t+j)]$.

In equation (1.2), net cash flows X are aggregated across all parts of the firm. We include in these quantities, moreover, any noncapital or other operating income and expenditures so that the value of current assets in place is an exhaustive representation of all the firm's current and future cash flows excluding only the cash flows from growth opportunities (to be discussed shortly). We will retain this assumption through this book unless we explicitly state otherwise.

We can also view the firm as a portfolio or bundle of specific projects or business units. If the firm has U such units and the cash flows from these projects are all mutually exclusive and exhaustive relative to the representation in equation (1.2), then we can rewrite the current market value of the firm's assets in place as the sum of the market values of the projects or operating divisions of the firm, any of which is denoted $V_j^A(t)$ at time t:

$$
V^A(t) = \sum_{u=1}^{U} V_u^A(t) = \sum_{u=1}^{U} \sum_{j=0}^{\infty} \frac{E[X_u(t+j)]}{1+E[R^A(t,\ t+j)]} - I_u(t)
$$

(1.3)

where $X_u(t + j)$ = time $t + j$ net cash flows on current assets in business unit u

$I_u(t)$ = time t investment expenditure on assets in business unit u

Growth Opportunities

Myers (1977) defines growth opportunities as future opportunities the firm will have to acquire or develop an asset. If the firm decides to make a subsequent investment expenditure, the current growth opportunity will become a future asset in place. Otherwise, the growth opportunity will expire worthless. Growth opportunities may be either strategic decisions the firm faces that have value in their own right or actual future investment opportunities that can be identified today.

As an example, suppose the firm in question is a pharmaceutical company. At some future date $t + j$, the firm has the opportunity to begin developing a new drug that will be designated "Project Q." The firm will incur a series of known future investment expenditures to develop the drug over time, but we treat this sequence of expenditures as a single expenditure made at time $t + j$ equal to the discounted present value of all future investment expenditures for the drug's development. Denote this investment expenditure as $I_Q(t + j)$ at time $t + j$. If the firm undertakes the project, its net present value will be

$$\overbrace{\sum_{k=1}^{\infty} \frac{E[X_Q(t + j + k)]}{1 + E[R^A(t + j, \ t + j + k)]}}^{\substack{\text{Discounted Expected PV} \\ \text{of Future Cash Flows}}} - \overbrace{I_Q(t + j)}^{\substack{\text{PV of All Investment} \\ \text{Expenditures}}} \tag{1.4}$$

where future cash flows come from drug sales revenues, patent licensing revenues, and so on. Alternatively, the firm may decide not to incur the investment expense and to forgo the project. The value at time $t + j$ of Project Q to develop the drug thus is

$$\max\left\{\sum_{k=1}^{\infty} \frac{E[X_Q(t + j + k)]}{1 + E[R^A(t + j, \ t + j + k)]} - I_Q(t + j), \ 0\right\} \tag{1.5}$$

Growth opportunities are more commonly known as *real options* because of their call option–like features that are apparent in equation (1.5). Specifically, any particular growth opportunity can be viewed as a call option on the value of a future asset in place with a strike price equal to the investment expenditure required to develop or acquire that asset. We generally associate real options with strategic asset acquisitions or with latent and intangible assets, such as intellectual property.

The market value of a growth opportunity at any time t is just the time t price of the real option that can be exercised at time $t + j$. The market value of all K growth opportunities the firm has identified is just the sum of all the real option prices corresponding to each of the K future projects, decisions, or opportunities:

$$V^G(t) = \sum_{k=1}^{K} V_k^G(t) \tag{1.6}$$

Value of the Firm

The market value of a firm is equal to the market value of its real capital, which, in turn, is just the sum of the market values of the firm's assets in place and growth opportunities:

$$V(t) = A(t) = V^A(t) + V^G(t)$$

$$= \underbrace{\sum_{u=1}^{U} \sum_{j=0}^{\infty} \frac{E[X_u(t+j)]}{1 + E[R^A(t,\ t+j)]} - I_u(t) +}_{\substack{\text{Market Value of Assets in Place in} \\ \text{U Operating Divisions}}} \underbrace{\sum_{k=1}^{K} V_k^G(t)}_{\substack{\text{Market Value of K} \\ \text{Growth Opportunities}}} \tag{1.7}$$

FINANCIAL CAPITAL AND THE VALUE OF THE FIRM

A *financial asset* is just a claim on the cash flows generated by one or more real assets. Financial assets come in numerous forms and are created for a variety of reasons, all of which are intended in some way to assist individuals in the consumption, production, and/or exchange of real assets or to assist corporations in some aspect of their business activities.

When a financial asset is issued by a corporation, we call that asset *financial capital* for the corporate issuer. Corporations generally issue financial capital for several reasons. The first and most obvious function of financial capital is raising funds to help the issuing firm finance its investments by exchanging a claim on the future cash flows of the firm's real assets for current cash. In addition, issuing financial capital pools investments in the firm's assets to diversify the risks of those assets across multiple investors. Financial capital, of course, also carries the same benefits of other financial assets, such as facilitating a change of control of a bundle of assets (e.g., a firm) without forcing the real assets to be exchanged.

As was the case with real capital as compared to real assets, the main distinction between financial capital and financial assets is generally the perceived longer-term nature of the latter. In addition, financial capital involves *some* degree of risk in the business enterprise for investors in such claims. In that manner, the firm both finances its operations *and* spreads the risk of its investments across multiple investors whenever it issues financial capital.

Basic Forms of Financial Capital

Securities issued as financial capital by a corporation represent claims on the future net cash flows of that business enterprise and come in essentially two different forms: *equity* and *debt*. We will discuss a wide range of hybrids that fall somewhere between the textbook definitions of equity and debt, but we save that discussion for later (Chapter 14).

Equity and debt capital are distinguished along principally two dimensions. The first is governance. For the most part, holders of a firm's common stock and certain types of preference shares are the only claim holders who can take an active role in the firm's management and operations.[5] The second distinction concerns the nature of the claim itself, which in turn affects the risk/reward profile of the two types of securities.

Equity is known as a *residual claim* because it gives holder a claim on the net cash flows of a firm remaining *after* the firm has paid all of its fixed claims and bills. For publicly listed and traded firms, the most basic form of equity claim is common stock, which is essentially a proportional interest in the firm's residual net cash flows. Common stock is generally a "perpetual" security—it has no stated date on which the corporate issuer buys back the security for a defined price. Equity also comes in the forms of preferred stock or preference shares, shares in a general or limited partnership, and the like. Equity holders of a firm can earn income from their claims by reselling them or waiting for the firm to close its doors and pay a liquidating dividend. In addition to these two ways of turning shares into a capital gain (or loss), some firms also choose to compensate their equity claim holders with periodic cash distributions or dividends.

The second type of financial capital that a firm can issue to raise cash—called *debt*—is a loan in which the firm promises to repay principal and/or interest according to some predetermined schedule.[6] Unlike equity, the maximum payoff on debt is stated explicitly in the debt contract, so that debt holders do not receive a higher payoff when the firm is more profitable. In return for less of an upside, debt holders also bear less business risk than equity holders because they are paid off before equity holders. That does not mean that debt bears no business risk. As the risk of a default on debt rises, the expected return on the debt will rise accordingly to induce creditors to continue holding the debt. The closer to default, the more the debt begins to look like equity even despite having a specified maximum payoff.

Unlike common equity shares, debt generally does have a stated maturity date. Accordingly, debt holders usually earn income from their claims according to the schedule of any interim interest payments promised over the life of the debt and the principal repayment promised at maturity. Debt may also contain early redemption options for either issuers (i.e., callable debt) or investors (i.e., puttable debt), in which principal is payable on the early redemption date. In addition, like equity, debt holders can also earn income prior to redemption by selling their claims to other investors or if the firm becomes insolvent and enters liquidation.

Interest paid to holders of debt securities is similar in spirit to dividends paid to equity holders. As a practical matter, however, there are two key differences. First, unlike dividends, interest on debt is defined in advance for the whole term of the debt contract.[7] Second, because debt holders have priority over equity holders in receiving cash distributions, interest on debt is payable *before* any dividends can be disbursed to equity holders.

Seniority, Priority, and Subordination

In the event that the value of the firm's assets is below the promised payments on the fixed claims the firm has issued, we know that equity holders receive nothing and debt holders receive a pro rata distribution of the remaining assets. Most corporations, however, have a richer variety of securities than just a single class each of debt and common stock.

The concept of *priority* refers to the preference given to certain claim holders when the firm becomes insolvent and the proceeds from the liquidation of a firm's assets must be distributed. The *seniority* of a claim refers to the priority of claim holders. Alternatively, the *depth of subordination* of a security is the inverse of its seniority—that is, the most deeply subordinated securities have the lowest seniority and the lowest priority in the event of insolvency. In general, the higher the depth of subordination of a given class of security, the greater the default risk of the security for a given market value of assets. The reason is that claim holders with a given priority cannot receive any payments in the event the firm becomes insolvent until all claim holders senior to them are paid off first.

Exhibit 1.1 illustrates the related concepts of priority, subordination, and seniority in financial capital. The exhibit depicts the economic balance sheet of a firm at time t that owns assets that back financial capital in the form of debt and equity. The financial capital of the firm is shown on the right side of the economic balance sheet in the order of increasing seniority/priority (i.e., decreasing depth of subordination/increasing risk) from bottom to top. Although we continue to ignore any corporate securities apart from plain-vanilla debt and equity, we now allow for multiple classes and depths of subordination within each category.

The lowest-priority claimant on a corporation is always the holder of some type of equity or residual interest in the firm. In fact, equity claims are sometimes called "soft" claims because their seniority in the capital structure of the firm adjusts to the other securities that the firm issues so as to remain the most junior claim outstanding. The most junior and softest claim is usually common stock, the class of equity that receives nothing in the event of insolvency unless all other security holders have first been made whole.

Senior to common stock but junior to all else is preferred stock or preference shares. Preferred stock is another type of equity, but with features more closely resembling debt such as a stated maturity date and often limited voting rights. Dividends on common stock cannot be paid until dividends on preferred stock have been paid. But at the same time, preference shares are equity and not debt, thus implying that the preferred dividend is discretionary. Whereas the failure of a corporation to make a promised interest payment on debt is an event of default, the preferred stock dividend can usually be suspended without triggering default provisions.[8]

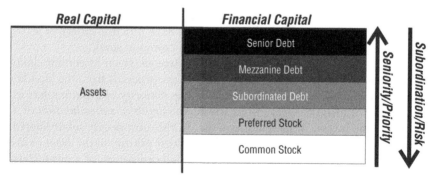

EXHIBIT 1.1   Seniority/Priority/Subordination of Financial Capital

Debt as a type of financial capital often has several levels of subordination, with the lowest priority going to subordinated or junior debt and the highest to senior creditors. An unsecured senior creditor to a firm is the holder of an unsecured debt claim that is the most senior unsecured security in the firm's capital structure. (We will deal with secured debt in Part Three of the book.) Senior debt often comes in the form of bank loans made directly by commercial banks to corporations.

Subordinated debt is debt in which the lenders receive a pro rata share of the cash proceeds from liquidated assets after senior lenders have been paid off. It is possible to have multiple levels of subordinated debt, often held by different types of firms. Banks, for example, may hold a firm's senior subordinated (senior sub) debt, and public or institutional investors may hold the same firm's junior subordinated debt.

In terms of credit risk and external credit ratings, the most junior tranche of subordinated debt is generally two rating levels below the senior tranche. Although this makes junior sub debt relatively much riskier than senior debt, the *absolute* risk of the debt depends on the overall risk of the firm. For a start-up or a highly leveraged and thinly capitalized firm, subordinated debt may well be "junk."[9] But for a well-capitalized AAA-rated issuer, junior sub debt might well still carry a AA+ or AA rating.

Capital Structure

The capital structure of a corporation is, very simply, the relative mixture of fixed and residual claims that a firm issues. We can examine a firm's mixture of fixed and residual claims in terms of either stocks or flows.

If we adopt a stock perspective of capital structure, we think in terms of ratios of outstanding debt to equity or to total financial capital *at any given point in time*. The capital structure of a firm is essentially the mixture of debt and equity issued by a firm, together with the subordination and maturities of those claims.

The most common way of describing a firm's capital structure if we adopt a stock perspective in lieu of a flow perspective is the *leverage ratio*, or the percentage of the firm's total financial capital that is in the form of fixed rather than residual claims. A leverage ratio of .30 or 30 percent, for example, means that 30 percent of the capital structure of the firm is comprised of fixed income obligations, with the remaining 70 percent in the form of equity claims. We can evaluate these ratios, moreover, in terms of either book or market values depending on what we are trying to accomplish.

Alternatively, the firm's capital structure can also be described in terms of flows. If we think of capital structure in terms of *flows of funds*, we will tend to focus on variables like dividend payout ratios and interest service coverage ratios. Or we can think of capital structure in terms of *flows of securities issued*, which indicates a firm's preference for issuing different types of claims to manage risk or finance new investments.

Capital Structure and Organizational Form

Fama and Jensen (1983a, 1983b, 1985) define four types of organizations, distinguished principally by the nature of the financial capital claims they issue and by the governance model for the firm—more specifically, the relationship between who holds the financial capital claims issued by the firm and who governs the firm.

First, an *open corporation* issues residual claims usually in the form of unrestricted common stock. Common stock entitles each shareholder to a proportional claim on the net cash flows or value of the assets of the firm. If the firm has issued N shares, each shareholder will receive $S(T)/N$ upon liquidation of the firm on date T or a similar proportional dividend payment in any preliquidation period that the firm pays dividends.

Shares issued by open corporations can be freely bought and sold in a secondary market once they have been issued. Although the owner of a share is recorded at the securities registrar for the issuing company, the investor alone can decide when to buy or sell it. The company's permission is usually not required for a transfer of share ownership to occur.[10]

Second, a *closed corporation* or *proprietorship* also issues residual claims in the form of equity shares, but the equity of a closed corporation usually *cannot* be bought and sold freely. In proprietorships, equity shares usually take the form of partnership shares or interests. These interests are often obtainable only by managers of the firm and cannot usually be sold or transferred to just anyone, unlike common stock which *can* be freely bought and sold by about anyone with the cash to buy it. In limited partnerships, equity shares may not be conditional on management responsibilities, but are still usually bought and sold under highly restrictive conditions that tend to limit the number of potential partners to a prespecified group of investors with whom the company wants to deal.

The third type of Fama/Jensen organization is a *financial mutual* or *syndicate*. The residual claimants in these types of firms are also the customers of the firms. Shares in an open-end mutual fund or real estate investment trust (REIT), for example, represent pro rata claims on the assets in which the fund or trust invests the proceeds it receives from share sales. But the only reason the fund/trust has collected funds from investors in the first place is to reinvest these funds on behalf of investors in some specific asset class or investment program. This may seem like circular logic, when in fact it is merely evidence that the residual claimants of the firm are also its *users*.

Shares in some financial mutuals are listed for trading in organized markets, whereas others are available only through private negotiations or auctions. A share in a country club, for example, is a share in a mutual in which the share purchasers also use the facilities of the club. In this case, the purchaser likely must obtain the membership share directly from the club and its governing members, must meet certain membership criteria, and may not necessarily sell her membership to the average man on the street without permission of the other governing members.

Finally, *nonprofits* are organizations that have no residual claimants per se. The closest thing are the donors and supporters who provide operating cash flows directly. Instead of receiving a residual claim on the net cash flows of the nonprofit, donors receive an intangible residual claim on the fruits of the nonprofit's labors.

The choice of organizational form has a strong relationship to the firm's capital structure. Remember that issuing financial capital is a way for a firm not only to raise money, but also to pool investment in the firm so that the business risk of the firm is dispersed among a group of investors. The risk-bearing attributes of securities issued by different firms often relate to the organizational form chosen. Because an open corporation, for example, has achieved a separation of ownership and control, equity is intended mainly as fund-raising device. Because it also allows investors to share in the risks and rewards of the business, it will be priced accordingly. But because equity ownership is separated from direct managerial control, the risks of equity do not play an incentive role. On the contrary, these risks can give rise to conflicts between security holders and management when the latter does not act in the best interests of the former.

A small partnership, by contrast, is often characterized by more consolidation of ownership and control. Equity in a partnership thus serves not just as a means of raising funds, but also to give the partners of the firm an ongoing incentive to invest their own time and effort in keeping the firm as profitable as possible.

Value of the Firm . . . Again

The combined value of all the firm's securities at any time t—denoted $W(t)$—is just the sum of the market values of the debt and equity claims issued by the firm, regardless of the maturity structure and subordination of those claims. The total market value of the firm's financial capital at time t thus is

$$W(t) = [S(t) + \delta(t)] + [D(t) + \rho(t)] \tag{1.8}$$

where $S(t)$ = time t market value of the firm's equity or share capital outstanding at the end of time $t - 1$

$\delta(t)$ = dividends paid at time t to shareholders

$D(t)$ = time t market value of the firm's debt outstanding at the end of time $t - 1$

$\rho(t)$ = interest paid at time t to creditors

Provided that the aggregate value of all financial claims exhaustively represents all the firm's cash flows arising from its assets in place and growth opportunities, the combined wealth of the securities issued by the firm must equal the combined value of the firm's assets. Combining equations (1.1) and (1.8) thus leads us to conclude that

$$V(t) = A(t) = W(t) \tag{1.9}$$

In other words, *the market value of the firm is always equal to the market value of the real assets held by the firm, which in turn is also equal to the market value of the aggregate financial capital issued by the firm.*

Note that equation (1.9) is a tautology and it *always* holds, provided *only* that the financial claims issued by a firm exhaustively represent all the cash flows on the assets owned by the firm. To see why this is indeed the case, we can utilize an options-theoretic perspective. This also provides a good chance early in the book to review the most rudimentary option structures at a level sufficient for even readers with limited background to digest the references to options later in the book.

FINANCIAL CAPITAL THROUGH AN OPTIONS LENS

Financial claims derive their value solely from the cash flows of the portfolio of real assets held by the firm issuing those claims. As long as the firm issues at least one residual class of security to absorb fluctuations in the value of its real assets, the sum of the market prices of all financial capital claims will always exactly equal the mark-to-market value of the firm's real capital. We can use options theory to verify this is indeed the case—and to provide us with a quick review of options theory at a level that should be more than adequate to digest later references to options in this book.

For concreteness in what follows, consider a firm that issues common stock and zero coupon debt that matures on date T with a total face value of FV. Suppose the debt is divided into senior and subordinated classes with face values of X and Y, respectively, so that $FV = X + Y$. For simplicity, assume that $A(T)$ indicates the market value of the firm's net assets on date T, where we define net assets as the firm's real assets less any current liabilities due at T other than debt. Further assume the firm liquidates its real assets on date T at the market price of $A(T)$ for cash and costlessly redistributes that cash to investors in its three classes of securities.

Debt

Senior debt is a fixed claim on the cash flows of the firm that pays X to investors as long as the firm's net assets are sufficient to cover that outlay. If $A(T) < X$, senior creditors to the firm receive as a group a pro rata distribution of whatever cash was obtained from liquidating the firm's net assets for $A(T)$. The payoff to senior debt when it matures thus can be written logically as

$$D^{sr}(T) = X - \max[X - A(T), 0] \qquad (1.10)$$

Viewed through an option product lens, senior debt thus can be viewed as the combination of a riskless loan of X plus a *short* put on the firm's assets struck at X. The payoff to senior debt holders is shown graphically as a function of $A(T)$ in Exhibit 1.2.

The interpretation of senior debt is fairly intuitive. If the firm is doing well and $A(T)$ is relatively high, bondholders receive their fixed commitment X in full but never participate in the firm's profitability with payoffs

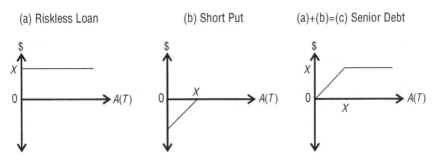

EXHIBIT 1.2 Value of Zero Coupon Senior Debt at Maturity

above that amount. But if the firm's assets fall below X so that the firm is in default, senior creditors as a group will receive whatever is left.

Subordinated debt, in turn, is a fixed claim on the cash flows of the firm that pays Y to investors as long as the firm's net assets are sufficient to cover that outlay. But because subordinated debt is junior in capital structure to senior debt, the junior creditors receive nothing until senior debt has been completely retired. Full repayment of the subordinated debt thus requires that the firm have assets worth at least $X + Y$ to cover both payments.

By analogy to senior debt, we can view the *gross* payoff to subordinated debt as a riskless loan of $X + Y$ plus a short put on the firm's assets struck at $X + Y$. The *net* payoff, of course, must also take into account that part of that gross total has been set aside for senior creditors. So, we must subtract the value of the senior debt from the gross payoff on the subordinated debt to get the net payoff to junior creditors:

$$D^{sub}(T) = (X + Y) - \max[(X + Y) - A(T), 0]$$
$$- \{X - \max[X - A(T), 0]\}$$
$$\rightarrow D^{sub}(T) = Y - \max[(X + Y) - A(T), 0] + \max[X - A(T), 0] \qquad (1.11)$$

The payoff to subordinated debt in (1.11) is shown graphically in Exhibit 1.3, which readers will recognize as the payoff on a long or bullish vertical spread consisting of a riskless loan Y, a long put struck at X, and a short put struck at $X + Y$. As before, the payoff is again intuitive if you look at the graph. For asset levels below X, subordinated debt receives no payment at all because all the firm's assets have gone to pay off senior debt. For asset values above X but below $X + Y$, junior creditors get a pro rata portion of their total claim on the firm. And for assets with values above $X + Y$, junior debt is fully repaid and reaches its maximum cash inflow of Y.

Comparing the payoffs of senior and subordinated debt in equations (1.10) and (1.11) and in Exhibits 1.2 and 1.3, we can see that the put written by senior debt holders has essentially been purchased by junior creditors. This is the essence of subordination and seniority. The long put essentially puts a "wall" between subordinated debt and senior debt that cannot be crossed in the event that the firm is insolvent, thus guaranteeing that subordinated debt holders cannot try and make a claim on assets of the firm when assets are below the face value of senior debt.

Further reinforcing this concept, we can see that the wall separating junior and senior creditors—the put struck at X—disappears when we aggregate the total value of all outstanding debt issued by the firm:

$$D(T) = D^{sr}(T) + D^{sub}(T) = FV - \max[FV - A(T), 0] \qquad (1.12)$$

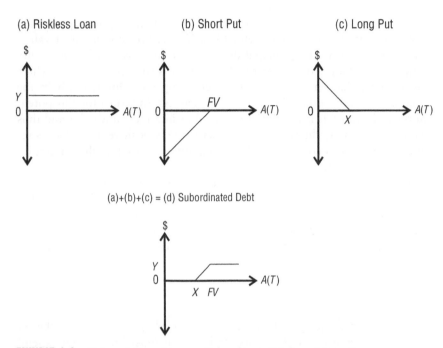

EXHIBIT 1.3   Value of Zero Coupon Subordinated Debt at Maturity

So, debt *as a whole* has the payoff of a cash loan of $X + Y$ plus a short put struck at $X + Y$. The long put struck at X helps us determine how junior and senior creditors split this total among themselves, but it does not affect the total.

Equity

Common stock is a residual claim on the net cash flows of the firm. Common stockholders thus get a payoff at T equal to gross proceeds of the liquidation of the firm's assets minus all the bills the firm has yet to pay, including repaying senior and junior creditors. Common stock is a limited liability contract, so in the event that the firm's assets are not sufficient to cover a full repayment of debt, equity is simply worthless. The payoff to common stockholders as a group thus is

$$S(T) = \max[A(T) - FV, 0] \tag{1.13}$$

So, equity can be viewed as a long call with a strike price equal to the book value of all outstanding debt, $FV = X + Y$. For any net asset values $A(T)$ that are above the principal due on the two classes of bonds, equity holders as a group gain dollar for dollar. This is the "residual" on which equity holders have a claim, and its potential upside is limited only by the potential increase in the value of the firm's assets. In return for this potential reward, equity is last in line from a subordination standpoint and thus has no value unless the residual net asset value is positive after debt is repaid. The payoff in equation (1.13) on equity as a group is shown graphically in Exhibit 1.4.

Conceptually, we can think about the value of equity from both gross and net standpoints, just as we did with subordinated debt. On a gross basis, equity gets the value of the remaining assets of the firm $A(T)$ when the firm goes into liquidation on date T. But payments on all claims senior to equity must be subtracted from this total to get the net payoff to equity. So, equity has a payoff of

$$S(T) = A(T) - \{FV - \max[FV - A(T), 0]\} \qquad (1.14)$$

In other words, equity holders get all the cash proceeds from the en masse liquidation of the firm's assets but then must immediately spend $X + Y = FV$ to repay all debt holders. The expression in equation (1.14) is equivalent to the payoff on a call option we wrote in equation (1.13).[11]

The Value of the Firm

Just as our put option struck at X acted as a wall between junior and senior debt to preserve seniority, the put option struck at FV in the payoffs for debt and equity shown in equations (1.12) and (1.14) now acts as a similar wall to separate equity holders as a class from debt holders as a

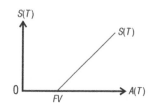

EXHIBIT 1.4 Value of Equity on Debt Maturity Date

class for subordination purposes. Recall from before that this wall went away when we added the values of sub and senior debt to get the total market value of debt. Similarly, if we now add the values of total debt and equity to get the total value of all outstanding financial capital issued by the firm, the wall again vanishes, leaving us with

$$W(T) = A(T)$$

As was the case within the debt class of securities, the same thing is true for the firm as a whole—how we apportion payments between security holders does not affect the total that we have to apportion.[12] Exhibit 1.5 shows the result graphically.

All of our examples have focused on the date that debt matures. If we look at any other date, all the relations explored still hold, although the graphs are not as pretty. Nevertheless, the above results hold for all time periods.

We have also been ignoring dividends and interest on debt. But if we now add those back, we can confirm our earlier assertion in equation (1.9) that the value of the firm is equal to the value of all financial capital issued by the firm *and* the value of the firm's real assets:

$$W(t) = [S(t) + \delta(t)] + [D(t) + \rho(t)] = A(t) = V(t) \qquad (1.15)$$

As we said earlier—and now we can see why—equations (1.8) and (1.15) are a tautology. Absolutely the only assumption we need to make for these equations to hold true is that the firm's financial capital must include at least one residual claim. If the firm issues only debt, then you can see the residual value of the firm's remaining assets will never balance out. But with at least one equity claim, the equity security always absorbs whatever residual market value is left over after debt holders are repaid.

ECONOMIC BALANCE SHEET OF THE FIRM

With these concepts in hand, we can now write down the economic balance sheet of the firm, sometimes called the mark-to-market balance sheet of the firm. We must emphasize that this is not an accounting concept. In particular, items that we would consider "off balance sheet" under accounting rules will show up on the firm's economic balance sheet.

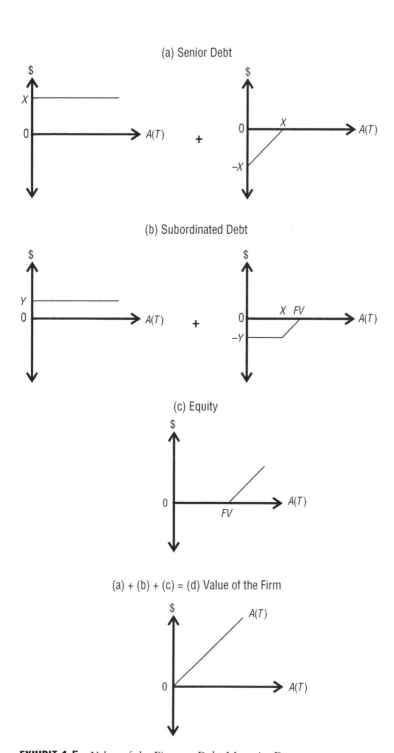

EXHIBIT 1.5 Value of the Firm on Debt Maturity Date

Assets	Liabilities and Equity
A(*t*)	D(*t*)
	S(*t*)

EXHIBIT 1.6   Economic Balance Sheet of the Firm

Our uses of certain terms like "financial capital," moreover, are economic. Accountants would define financial capital as shareholders' equity plus depreciation and retained earnings, whereas the economic definition of financial capital is the sum of the market values of all the firm's debt and equity securities.

The economic balance sheet for a firm that issues a single class each of debt and equity is shown in Exhibit 1.6. This shows the fundamental relationship between real and financial capital—namely, that the market values of the two must be equal and that this is the market value of the firm. This economic balance may seem a simple construct now, but we will make extensive use of it later when things are not so simple.

CHAPTER 2

Risk and Risk Management

Until the early 1990s, most people seem to have adopted the same approach to defining risk and risk management that Justice Potter Stewart took when faced with the task of defining pornography: "I'll know it when I see it." Perhaps nowhere was the knowledge gap wider than between insurance and capital markets. Each had its own definitions of risk, its own transactions to help firms manage risk, its own special skill sets for risk analysis (actuarial analysis in insurance versus econometrics and stochastic calculus in derivatives), and its own vocabulary for selling risk management to corporate clients. A meaningful intellectual exchange about risk and risk management was more likely to have occurred between a corporate treasurer and a Jack Russell terrier than between insurance and derivatives sales reps.

Nonfinancial corporations paid the price of this lack of integration between two otherwise similar worlds. They essentially had little choice but to treat insurance and financial risks and risk management solutions as completely distinct—they were, after all, repeatedly told to do so both specifically and by example. With no good reason to do otherwise offered by either insurance companies or derivatives dealers, the segregated worlds of risk thus became the standard way of thinking at corporations.

In recent years, this has all begun to change. The vocabularies that once separated two otherwise similar industries have become both less cryptic and less important, and cross-industry awareness of the concepts, tools, and definitions of risk and risk management have grown. Indeed, the existence of this book is predicated on an integrated demand curve in the corporate sector for insurance and financial risk and increasingly integrated supply curves in the structured finance and alternative risk transfer space that occupies the middle ground between derivatives and insurance.

Nevertheless, confusion still abounds about what is meant by terms like risk and risk management. Regardless of industry bias or prior background, this chapter thus attempts to level the playing field and create a common risk vocabulary that will be used through the rest of the book. In addition, we distinguish here between methods of risk management—risk *finance* versus risk *transfer*, in particular.

FINANCIAL VERSUS NONFINANCIAL RISKS

Risk can be defined as any source of randomness that may have an adverse impact on the market value of a corporation's assets net of liabilities, on its earnings, and/or on its raw cash flows. Developing a common understanding of what is meant by the term *risk* at the conceptual level is no trivial task. Simply making a list of the ways a firm can lose money is actually not so hard—but also not so helpful. We need instead to make a list of risks in a way that helps the firm *manage* those risks.

To begin with, let us set forth some important distinctions between risks that we will address here:[1]

- *Financial risk*—a financial event that can give rise to unexpected reductions in a firm's cash flows, value, or earnings, the amount of which is determined by the movement in one or more financial asset prices.
- *Peril*—a natural, man-made, or economic situation that may cause a personal or property loss.
- *Accident*—an unexpected loss of resources arising from a peril.
- *Hazard*—something that increases the probability of a loss arising from a peril.

We discuss each of these concepts in turn.

Financial Risks

A financial risk is a source of potential unexpected losses for a firm that will arise because of some adverse change in market conditions, the financial condition of an obligor to the firm, or the financial condition of the firm itself. Financial risk can impact a company's cash flows, accounting earnings, and/or value (i.e., asset and liability market values). Importantly, the amount of money a firm loses from financial risks that are realized usually depends on the behavior of one or more market-determined prices. There are five primary types of financial risk.[2]

Market Risk Market risk arises from the event of a change in some market-determined asset price, reference rate such as the London Interbank Offered Rate (LIBOR), or index, usually classified based on the asset class whose price changes are impacting the exposure in question. Common forms of asset class-based market risk include interest rate risk, exchange rate risk, commodity price risk (through input purchases or output sales), and equity price risk.

Apart from the market risk factors that influence the value of an exposure, the market risk of an exposure can also be characterized based on *how* those risk factors impact its value. In this context, market risk generally is classified by using a colorful argot known as "fraternity row—delta, gamma, vega, theta, and rho, which indicate (respectively) the sensitivity of the value of a position or exposure to changes in underlying prices, the rate of change in underlying prices, the volatility of underlying prices, the passage of time, and the discount rate. Market risk also includes *basis risk*, or the risk that differences in assets and liabilities can give rise to imperfectly correlated price changes, in turn creating a mismatch between assets and liabilities.

Funding Risk   Funding risk occurs in the event that cash inflows and current balances are insufficient to cover cash outflow requirements, often necessitating costly asset liquidation to generate temporary cash inflows. Most firms, both financial and nonfinancial, have liquidity plans designed to manage funding risks. The well-publicized failures of firms like Drexel Burnham Lambert Group, Inc. and MG Refining & Marketing, Inc. (a subsidiary of the German giant Metallgesellschaft AG) occurred largely due to funding problems and have increased corporations' attention to this risk.

The distinctions between pure funding risk and market risk are subtle, as the two are clearly related. Market risk can be viewed as the risk of changes in the *value* of a bundle of cash flows when adverse market events occur. But value is just defined as the discounted net present value (NPV) of *future* cash flows. Funding risk is based on the risk of cash flows *when they occur in time*. For the purpose of comparing liquidity risk at one time to liquidity risk at another, discounting to an NPV serves no purpose. On the contrary, all that is relevant is cash balances *per period*. Market risk, by contrast, deals with cash flow risks in *any* period, because *all* future cash flows ultimately affect the current NPV of the asset or liability in question.

Despite the distinction, market price fluctuations almost always characterize the exposure associated with funding risk. Although the triggering event is a cash funding shortfall, the amount of the shortfall itself and the economic consequences of the shortfall are usually determined by movements in market prices.

Market Liquidity Risk   Market liquidity risk is the risk that volatile markets will inhibit the liquidation of losing transactions and/or the establishment of new transactions to hedge existing market risk exposures. Suppose a firm has negotiated an agreement with a bank to purchase British pounds for deutsche marks three months from now. If the British pound experiences a massive and rapid depreciation vis à vis the Dmark—as happened in September 1992 when the European Monetary System's exchange rate mechanism imploded on "Black Wednesday"—the currency purchase agreement will rapidly decline in value.

The firm in this case may attempt to neutralize its original agreement or enter into an offsetting contract. If the agreement is left unhedged or the counterparty to any offsetting contract defaults, volatility may be so high that a new hedge cannot be initiated at a favorable price, even using liquid exchange-traded futures on pounds and Dmarks. The firm's market risk is thus exacerbated by market liquidity risk.

The *exposure* the firm faces—the size of its potential loss—will be based on the amount of the market-driven change in the sterling/Dmark rate. Consequently, we treat this risk as financial in nature.

Credit Risk Credit risk is the risk of the actual or possible nonperformance by an obligor to the firm. Credit risk usually comes in four forms: *presettlement* risk arises from the potential for an obligor to default on a transaction prior to the initiation of the settlement of that transaction; *settlement* risk is specifically associated with the failure of a firm during the settlement window, or the time period between the confirmation of a transaction and the final settlement of that transaction; *migration* or *downgrade* risk is the risk that the increase in the market's perception of a default at a firm causes a decline in the value of the claims issued by that firm; and *spread* risk is the risk that deteriorations in general corporate credit quality will affect the claim issued by a given firm.

The distinctions in these four types of credit risk are best illustrated by a simple example. Suppose Wolfram owns a lyre and issues a claim that entitles its holder to receive his lyre one month hence for the prenegotiated price of 10 gold coins. Assume moreover that at the time the claim is issued, everyone agrees that Wolfram has no possibility of being unable to deliver his lyre. Suppose the value of this claim is worth one gold coin today and that the current market price of lyres is 10 gold coins.

Consider now that Tannhäuser buys the claim from Wolfram and that both payment and delivery are to occur in a month. If Wolfram informs Tannhäuser that he cannot deliver the lyre one hour before the exchange is due to occur, Tannhäuser may experience a presettlement loss. Specifically, suppose the market price of lyres has risen to 15 gold coins, and Wolfram informs Tannhäuser that there is no lyre and gives Tannhäuser his one gold coin back. But if Tannhäuser still wants a lyre, he must now enter into a new lyre purchase agreement at the new and higher price. Tannhäuser thus incurs a five gold coin replacement cost presettlement credit loss.

Settlement risk, by contrast, arises after the transaction has entered the settlement process and one party defaults. Suppose a month has passed and Tannhäuser pays Wolfram the 10 gold coins, but Wolfram *then* informs Tannhäuser that he has no lyre to sell and he is keeping the 10 gold coins. In that case, Tannhäuser incurs a settlement credit loss of 10 gold coins, *and* has no lyre to show for it.[3]

Both presettlement and settlement risk involve the actual default by Wolfram to Tannhäuser. But credit risk may also occur in the form of migration or downgrade risk, arising not from an actual default but by an increase in the market's perception of the *probability* a default will occur. To continue the example, suppose Tannhäuser no longer wishes a lyre but that Venus is in need of one. Tannhäuser may sell the claim to Venus. But if Venus now suspects that Wolfram may not be able to deliver the lyre when the full month passes, she likely will pay Tannhäuser less than he paid Wolfram for the original claim whose value was based on the market's original assessment of Wolfram's creditworthiness. In other words, Tannhäuser will experience a capital loss on the claim even though Wolfram has not actually defaulted. The mere increase in the market's perception that he might is enough to reduce the value of the claim.

Finally, Tannhäuser may receive less for the claim than he paid when he sells it to Venus if the market's perception of *all* corporate credit risks has gone up. This is sometimes called "spread risk" in reference to the default credit spread over the risk-free rate at which cash flows on risky corporate claims must be discounted. Spread risk may be affected by firm-specific credit concerns (i.e., migration risk) or by more systematic default risk premiums in the sense of Fama and French (1993).

Legal Risk   Legal risk is the risk that a firm will incur a loss if a contract it thought was enforceable actually is not. The Global Derivatives Study Group (1993) identified several sources of legal risk for innovative financial instruments that are often associated with risk management, including conflicts between oral contract formation and the statutes of frauds in certain countries and jurisdictions, the capacity of certain entities (e.g., municipalities) to enter into certain types of transactions, the enforceability of so-called close-out netting, and the legality of financial instruments. In addition, unexpected changes in laws and regulations can expose firms to potential losses, as well.

Legal risk is classified here as a financial risk because this particular incarnation of risk results in losses that usually are driven in size and economic importance by changes in market prices. A netting agreement that is unenforceable in insolvency, for example, could lead to cherry-picking losses whose total amounts are based on market price movements. Suppose, for example, that Firm Wotan has an agreement with Firm Siegfried to swap a fixed cash flow of $10,000 quarterly in exchange for receiving from Siegfried a payment equal to the total interest that Siegfried, in turn, receives on a loan portfolio currently equal to, say, $10,000. With a netting agreement in place, if Firm Siegfried fails, no cash flow occurs on the agreement. If a netting agreement is in place and is held to be unenforceable, Firm Siegfried may try to cherry-pick Firm Wotan by demanding the $10,000 Wotan owes Siegfried while simultaneously refusing to pay the $10,000 Siegfried owes Wotan.

The amount of risk borne by Firm Wotan in this example depends on the value of Siegfried's own loan portfolio. If Siegfried's loans are floating-rate and the interest rate rises, Siegfried may then owe Wotan $15,000. But without a binding netting agreement, Wotan might never see that money, either.

Perils, Accidents, and Hazards

A peril is a natural, man-made, or economic situation that can cause an unexpected loss for a firm, the size of which is usually *not* based on the realization of one or more financial variables. A peril thus is essentially a nonfinancial risk. An accident is a specific negative event arising from a peril that gives rise to a loss, and is usually considered unintentional. A hazard is something that increases the probability of a peril-related loss occurring, whether intentional or not.

The distinctions among these three concepts are perhaps best understood by way of an example. Consider the peril to a firm of having its employees sustain on-the-job injuries. A related accident would be the unintended opening of a valve on some storage tank at a firm. A hazard could be alcohol or drugs that make an employee more likely to open the valve, the presence of corrosive chemicals in the tank that dissolve the valve seals, and the like.

Different types of perils that firms typically face in their business operations include the following, with some examples offered in each case by way of a definition:[4]

- *Production*—unexpected changes in the demand for products sold, increases in input costs, or failures of marketing.
- *Operational*—failures in processes, people, or systems.
- *Social*—adverse changes in social policy (e.g., political incorrectness of a product sold), strained labor relations, changes in fashions and tastes, etc).

- *Political*—unexpected changes in government, nationalization of resources, war, and so on.
- *Legal*—tort and product liability and other liabilities whose exposures are *not* driven by financial variables.
- *Physical*—destruction or theft of assets in place, impairment of asset functionality, equipment or mechanical failure, chemical-related perils, energy-related perils, and so on.
- *Environmental*—flood, fire, windstorm, hailstorm, earthquake, cyclone, and so on.

Outreville (1998) provides some examples of hazards that increase the probability of loss for different perils:

- *Human*—fatigue, ignorance, carelessness, smoking.
- *Environmental*—weather, noise.
- *Mechanical*—weight, stability, speed.
- *Energy*—electrical, radiation.
- *Chemical*—toxicity, flammability, combustibility.

It is quite impossible to list and classify all the different perils and related accidents or hazards that may face all firms. Nevertheless, some are significant enough that they warrant further discussion.

Production Perils and Business Continuity Risks Production-related perils cover any perils that threaten a firm's ability to carry out its normal business activities as expected, usually resulting from changes to the supply or demand for the firm's product or to the physical production process. Shocks to a firm's cost or demand functions, for example, can precipitate a loss of value owing to production risks. Three other production-related perils include customer loss risk, key employee overdependency, and supply chain risk.

At the core of risks facing a business is the risk that the business can lose its customers, either because a competitor attracts them away or because they no longer demand the products and services the firm is selling at the prices it is quoting. Customer loss risk thus encompasses pricing risk, or the risk that firms misestimate either the level or the structure of prices for their customers.

The importance of customer retention has been vividly illustrated by the recent boom in Internet commerce. To a start-up Web company, its ability to accurately assess customer value is everything. Only when those values can be compared accurately to the cost of customer acquisition can the business truly be valued. For this reason, attention to customer loss risk and customer valuation has perhaps never been higher.

Nevertheless, customer loss risk is just as important—perhaps the real core risk of operating a profitable business—for *all* types of firms. An airline must worry about customer loss just as much as an online bookstore. And a consulting firm must be as attentive as an airline. If either the demand curve shifts inward for exogenous reasons or available substitutes for the good or service being sold become relatively more attractive, the business is in trouble.

Many nonfinancial firms also face risks from adverse events that may occur at any point along a physical supply chain, the chain that connects inputs to the firm's production process to its outputs. Problems may arise at any juncture in this supply chain. Consider, for example, a firm that grows wheat, mills it into flour, and exports the flour to bread makers around the world. Problems could arise at origination from disease, bad weather, insects, vandalism, or any number of other factors that prevent the crop from being grown and brought in according to schedule (both time and quantity). At the transformation stage, equipment breakdowns could occur, contamination of the grain is a possibility, and losses of product during transportation are a consideration. And so on. In short, the firm faces some form of inventory or product risk at every stage here.

A third major production-related peril faced by virtually all firms is the risk of a loss to their brand name capital or reputation that can translate into reduced revenues, increased expenses, and fewer customers—hence its classification as a type of production peril. Reputation risk can arise when a firm acts negligently, or is simply *perceived* to act negligently—for example, Exxon following the *Valdez* oil disaster along the Alaskan coast.

Reputation risk can also arise from the poor public relations management of external crises, whether or not the crises are the direct fault of the company. A plane crash resulting from weather, for example, can still impose major adverse reputation effects on both the airline and the aircraft manufacturer if the public relations dimension of the disaster is not handled properly.

Finally, reputation risk can arise when a firm simply fails to honor its commitments. An insurance company that regularly tries to avoid paying out claims even when the claims are unambiguous and legitimate, for example, will quickly find itself short of customers.

Operational Perils Operational risk has been defined by the International Swaps and Derivatives Association (ISDA), British Bankers' Association (BBA), and Risk Management Association (RMA) as "the risk of loss resulting from inadequate or failed internal processes, people, and systems or from external events." (ISDA/BBA/RMA 1999) Examples of losses that can be attributed to operational risk include failed securities trades, settlement errors in funds transfers, stolen or damaged physical assets, damages awarded in court proceedings against the firm, penalties and fines assessed by member associations or regulators, irrecoverable or erroneous funds and asset transfers, unbudgeted personnel costs, and negligence or fraud.[5]

Operational perils can also sometimes be considered as a type of financial risk if the operational losses are driven by market, credit, or liquidity risks. The failure of Barings Bank to catch the huge position buildup by rogue trader Nick Leeson was in some sense an operational risk management failure. It was a failure of processes (i.e., internal audit and control), people (i.e., Leeson was defrauding the firm and others); and systems (i.e., a consolidated global position-keeping system would have revealed Leeson's rogue positions). But in the end, Barings went bust because Leeson's positions went underwater as a result of their market risk. Operational risk management may have failed to catch the process, personnel, and systems problems, but market risk sank the firm.

CORE VERSUS NONCORE RISKS

The *core* risks facing a firm may be defined as those risks that the firm is in business to bear and manage so that it can earn returns in excess of the risk-free rate. *Noncore* risks, by contrast, are risks to which a firm's primary business exposes it but that the firm does not necessarily need to retain in order to engage in its primary business line. The firm may well be exposed to noncore risks, but it may not wish to *remain* exposed to those risks. Core risks, by contrast, are those risks the firm is literally in business *not* to get rid of.

Core and noncore risks are sometimes today called business and financial risks, respectively. A major distinction between core and noncore risk thus is not surprisingly driven purely by information. Those factors about which a firm perceives itself as having some comparative informational advantage will be those factors on which the business concentrates for its core business cash flows. Risks about which the firm has comparatively less information will be those risks more likely to be hedged, diversified away, insured, or controlled in some other fashion.

The distinction between core risk and noncore risk clearly rests on a slippery slope. Not only does it vary from one firm to the next, but it also depends not on the quality of information the firm actually has, but rather on the firm's *perceived* comparative advantage in digesting that information. Perceptions, of course, can be wrong. Businesses fail, after all, with an almost comforting degree of regularity. Without business failures, one might tend to suspect the market is not working quite right. Accordingly, the preponderance of actual business failures clearly means that some firms thought they had a better handle on information than they did, whether that information concerns their competitors, their costs, or market demand for their products.

Slippery though the slope may be, it must be traversed. Every firm should identify the risks to which it is subject and then classify those risks as core or noncore. And this classification will differ firm by firm. Indeed, sometimes the same type of firm may classify the same risk in different ways. Some airlines choose to hedge their jet fuel price risk, for example, whereas others do not. Those airlines that do hedge must believe their core risks include flying planes without crashing them, selling as many seats as possible, and the like, but do not include jet fuel price risk. Airlines that do not hedge their jet fuel price risks, by contrast, clearly seem to believe that part of their business means bearing jet fuel price risk.

RISK MANAGEMENT ALTERNATIVES

A major purpose of distinguishing among risks along the lines discussed in the previous sections is to help a firm develop a risk management strategy for how to handle different types of risks. How a firm chooses to deal with any given risk is called the firm's *retention decision* for that risk. For any given risk facing the firm as a part of its normal business—core or noncore, financial or nonfinancial—the firm essentially has three strategic alternatives for its retention decision: *retain, neutralize,* or *transfer* the risk in question. Exhibit 2.1 illustrates this decision.

Any particular firm may choose different solutions for different risks, *and* the solution may also depend on the severity and likelihood of occurrence of the risk event, as well. These concepts are absolutely fundamental to understanding the remainder of this book, so let's be precise in getting our definitions down early.

Risk Retention and Risk Finance

The *retained risk* or *risk retention* of a firm is the agglomeration of risks to which the firm is naturally exposed in the conduct of its business that the firm decides to bear rather than to try to internally neutralize or shift to another market participant. A risk retention may be either *planned* or

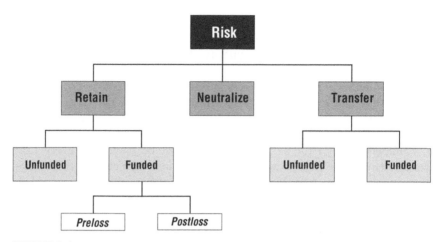

EXHIBIT 2.1   Risk Management Alternatives

unplanned. The latter arise from a failure of the firm to identify its risks or to manage them properly, and we won't pay much attention to those sorts of risks here. For now, let's stay focused on planned retentions.

The deliberate decision to retain a given risk is essentially a determination by the firm's shareholders that they are willing to absorb any realized losses arising from the risk in question. A core factor to firms in making this determination will, of course, be the benefit/cost trade-off—namely, whether the expected benefit of retaining the risk is above the expected cost at the margin. The benefit is the return or revenue that the firm might earn by bearing the risk, and the cost is the potential loss.

Funded and Unfunded Retentions   As shown in Exhibit 2.1, a firm's retained risks may be either *funded* or *unfunded.* Whether a retention is funded or unfunded relates to how the firm will pay for any realized economic losses. The funding of a planned retention pertains to the timing of when the economic loss is realized on a cash basis. A funded retention is a retained risk for which the firm has set aside specific funds or sources of funds in advance of the risk event translating into a realized loss.

If a firm decides to retain a specific risk and not to fund it, that simply means the firm plans to pay for its losses out of pocket when those losses occur. In that case, the firm can either use its current free cash reserves, divert funds away from planned investment spending, or issue new securities—assuming the loss is not so large as to deprive the firm of its capacity to do the latter.

For a variety of reasons that we will explore later, a firm may opt instead to fund its retention of certain risks at certain levels. In this case, the firm literally sets aside cash or a source of raising the cash to pay for all or part of a loss in the event that a loss occurs.

Preloss versus Postloss Funding As Exhibit 2.1 shows, a funded risk retention may be funded on a *preloss* or *postloss* basis. This distinction relates entirely to when the cash is actually raised to pay for the loss in question, should that loss occur. Preloss financing is cash raised in advance of the loss event, whereas postloss financing arrangements allow firms to prenegotiate a means of raising cash specifically to cover a loss in the event the loss occurs *but not before*. Setting aside cash in a dedicated reserve to cover a possible future loss is an example of preloss financing, whereas negotiating a line of credit on which the firm can draw following a loss is a form of postloss finance.

In all cases here, the firm's equity share capital must eventually absorb the loss. Whether or not to fund a retention—and if so, how—does not change that fact. For that reason, we generally refer to any kind of contract or structure that firms use to address their planned retentions as *risk finance* (as opposed to risk transfer, to which we will return later in this chapter).

Note carefully that risk finance is *not* an accounting practice. In the sense we have defined it, a firm's motivation for preloss or postloss funding a retention *is totally economic*. It may or may not be the case that the firm still has to recognize the loss in current income after taking into consideration the proper accounting for the risk financing arrangements the firm has chosen, but it does not matter. When a firm engages in *legitimate* risk financing, we're assuming it has a reason to do so that is unrelated to accounting and related instead to its liquidity or cash flows.

Risk Neutralization[6]

Risk neutralization occurs when a firm is able to reduce or eliminate its exposure to a risk without seeking the assistance of another firm, as would be required if the risk were being transferred. The firm retains the risk but does not bear the adverse consequences of the retention because of some other action taken by the firm. We can consider these other actions as falling into two categories discussed below.

Risk Reduction, Prevention, and Control If a firm does not wish to retain a source of risk to which its business naturally exposes it, one alternative always available to the firm is *risk reduction*. We can define risk reduction as the process by which a firm reduces either the probability of suffering an unexpected loss or the severity of such a loss without engaging in risk transfer. Risk reduction thus includes any activities in which the firm acts *essentially on its own* to reduce the risks to which it is naturally exposed.[7]

Some risks, for example, can be eliminated through the advancement of technology or the use of research. A firm that faced significant product liability risks from distributing spoiled foods, for example, would have benefited significantly from the development of refrigeration technologies.[8]

Risk reduction also includes prevention and control whereby a firm adopts prudential *ex ante* measures to reduce either the probability that a risk becomes an adverse outcome or loss or the consequences of that loss should it occur. Frequent maintenance inspections performed by qualified personnel, for example, help airlines reduce the risk of crashes. Similarly, a credit risk limit system that prohibits a firm from trading with non-investment-grade counterparties can help to reduce the risk of unexpected credit losses.

Risk Consolidation   When total risk risk is reduced by aggregating multiple risks, the process can be called *risk consolidation*. One way that a firm can reduce its risks through consolidation simply involves the principle of diversification. In the context of corporate hedging, we sometimes refer to this as *balance sheet hedging*, or the process by which a firm deliberately reduces one risk exposure by adding another risk exposure that is negatively correlated with the first. A farmer, for example, can choose to grow one crop that thrives on low rainfall and another than requires a lot of rainfall instead of putting all of her eggs into one basket or the other.

Consolidating risks inside the single portfolio we know as "the firm" can be beneficial for some firms even if the benefit from diversification is not significant. Specifically, probabilistic inference is often more reliable when performed at the portfolio level. Thanks to the central limit theorem, we know that the distribution of the expected loss approaches normal as the number of different losses combined in the same portfolio rises—no matter what the shapes of the component loss distributions. If you are, say, an insurance company setting insurance premiums equal to expected losses, this increased precision can be an important source of risk reduction. Similarly, firms that include expected loss estimates in capital budgeting decisions as investment costs would also find the higher precision arising from aggregation to be desirable.

Risk Transfer

Risk transfer is the explicit process by which the adverse impacts of a risk are shifted from the shareholders of one firm either to one or more individuals or to the shareholders of one or more other firms. The risk to be transferred can be systematic or idiosyncratic, financial or nonfinancial, and either core or incidental to the primary business of the firm dealing with the original risk. About the only limitation on what risk or bundle of risks can be transferred is the ability to define the risk in a contract to which both the original party and at least one counterparty can agree on terms of trade.

Counterparties to Risk Transfer Agreements   Risk transfer by necessity requires at least one willing counterparty to assume the risk(s) that the original firm is attempting to reduce. The motivations for counterparties to enter into risk transfer arrangements are essentially threefold. First, firms with opposite risk exposures may seek risk transfer with one another—for example, a farmer wishing to protect a forward crop sale against price declines and a miller wishing to guard against price rises on a similar forward purchase. Second, in liquid markets for traded assets, speculators may agree to risk transfer as part of their efforts to exploit a perceived informational advantage or trading opportunity. Finally and most commonly, firms can engage in risk transfer with a risk transfer specialist.

Risk transfer specialists are, quite literally, specialists in the supply of financial products designed to facilitate risk transfers. For many such firms, promoting risk transfer is a business line and perceived source of economic profits. Yet, risk transfer specialists are not always—or even often—specialists in risk bearing. In many cases, an insurance company "reinsures" or "retrocedes" a large portfolio of the risks that it assumes when it writes insurance contracts (see Chapters 8 and 9). Similarly, most derivatives dealers seek to run a "matched book" in which a risk assumed in one contract is offset by another such contract. And when a matched book does not naturally result from the demands of different firms seeking risk transfer, the derivatives dealer may well turn to another risk management mechanism to deal with its residual risk.

Risk transfer specialists are thus often active *users* of risk transfer contracts. As said, insurers buy insurance actively. And derivatives dealers are in turn active users of derivatives. In many cases, risk transfer specialists also rely on the other methods by which firms can deal with risk explored in this chapter. Insurance companies first seek to reduce their risks through consolidation, and *then* turn to reinsurance. Derivatives dealers likewise rely strongly on prevention as well as consolidation to keep their own risk profiles in line with their risk tolerances.

The common features of risk transfer specialists thus do not really concern the tastes of their managers and security holders for assuming risk. Instead, risk transfer specialists tend to have some other comparative advantage(s). A risk transfer specialist, for example, generally faces lower search costs than individual firms seeking risk transfer (often called end users), thereby enabling those specialists to identify offsetting risk transfer demands among a customer base more easily than if, say, the Swiss chemical company had to go out and find for itself a firm that wanted to go long the Brazilian real against the Swiss franc.

Not surprisingly, the largest derivatives dealers thus are those firms with a large number of customers and a significant depth of information about those customers, such as commercial and investment banks. Depth of customer information is important for several reasons. First, dealers assume credit risk on the transactions into which they enter, and some expertise in identifying and managing such risks is essential in order for a dealer to survive. Second, better derivatives dealers are those that have enough information about their customers' needs to anticipate their demands for often-customized risk transfer solutions. Similarly, organized financial exchanges that list derivatives for trading must have extensive information about what it is exactly that customers want to trade.

Apart from economies of scope, depth, and breadth of customer information, a risk transfer specialist must also appear to be fully creditworthy to be a reliable counterparty in a risk transfer contract. A firm seeking to transfer its risks must have full confidence that the risk transfer specialist will be around to honor its commitments. An insurance company perceived to lack funds to pay off claims will not likely get many buyers of a new policy, and so, too, will derivatives dealers. Perceived creditworthiness is correlated with the credit rating assigned to the risk transfer specialist. Generally, it is difficult for a firm with below a single-A credit rating to maintain an active risk transfer business.

In addition, risk transfer specialists typically have significant amounts of equity capital, both in absolute terms and as a proportion of their capital structures. Excessively leveraged firms and firms with low market values of equity generally do not fare well as derivatives dealers or insurance providers.

A good reputation is also an essential characteristic of any true risk transfer specialist. Holistic risk transfer solutions like corporate mergers and acquisitions generally focus on a whole spectrum of risks bundled with the firm's operating profits. Risk transfer solutions, by contrast, are essentially transactional, undertaken one contract at a time to realize the benefits of tailoring and customizing risk transfer needs to risk transfer mechanisms. Because of the transactional nature of the risk transfer business, the commercial reputation of the counterparty is critical. Firms seeking risk transfer solutions are, of course, quite focused on the price of that risk transfer—much more on this later in Parts Three and Four. But assuming that competition keeps prices of comparable transactions roughly in line, reputation plays a critical secondary role in helping end users identify an appropriate risk transfer counterparty. Similarly, satisfied customers tend to engage in significant repeat business once a relationship to a risk transfer counterparty is established.

Although risk transfer specialists need not have a comparative advantage in risk bearing to be successful intermediaries, some probably do. This does not necessarily mean those firms are better informed or better price forecasters, but rather that it is sometimes more efficient for a certain combination of risks—and here we must be talking about idiosyncratic or diversifiable risks—to be combined in the same portfolio rather than left in the market separately. This "optimal risk packaging" argument can be true for one of two reasons.

First, we know from the most basic principles of financial economics that there can be diversification benefits to be achieved when certain risks are combined. The lower the correlation, the more the benefit to having the risk borne in the same portfolio under the same layer of capital.

Second, some risks when combined facilitate better risk management than when left separate. Thanks to the central limit theorem, the expected loss on a portfolio of multiple loss exposures is distributed normally when the number of exposures increases—no matter what the underlying distributions of losses look like for each component risk. The result is that a firm that consolidates the multiple exposures will be able to estimate the expected portfolio loss with greater precision than any individual risk. Expected loss is an important component of risk capital allocation and/or risk transfer pricing (see, e.g., Appendix C), thus making it advantageous and efficient to exploit these benefits of risk consolidation when practical to do so.

Types of Risk Transfer   Risk transfer can, of course, be accomplished in many different ways. In some cases, risk transfer is as simple as the sale of an asset or extinguishment of a liability. A Swiss chemical company that owns a factory in Mexico and is concerned about the risk of an adverse change in the price of the peso that could reduce its effective profits to be repatriated, for example, could simply sell the factory to, say, a German chemical company. In so doing, the risk of fluctuations in the peso are transferred from the Swiss firm to the German purchaser of the factory. The asset sale, however, also transfers all other risks *and revenues* to the purchaser of the factory. Risk transfer thus is a consequence of the sale of the factory, but only in certain situations is it likely to be a motivation.

In exploring structured finance, we will see a lot of examples later where asset or liability divesture is indeed undertaken with risk transfer as at least a partial objective. But it is important to recognize this is not the only way to manage risk. As an alternative, firms can simply enter into contracts whose payoffs are positive at the same time the firm experiences a loss on some other part of its enterprise portfolio. Such transactions can generally be distinguished along three dimensions:

1. Indemnity versus parametric risk transfer contracts.
2. Limitation of liability.
3. Funded versus unfunded risk transfer solutions.

Indemnity versus Parametric Risk Transfer Contracts An *indemnity* contract is a contract that makes a reimbursement to a firm for economic damage actually sustained. A *parametric* contract, by contrast, generates a cash flow based on movements in one or more market-determined asset prices, interest rates, or index values. Insurance is a classic form of indemnity contract, whereas derivatives are the archetypical parametric risk transfer contracts.

As we will discuss at length later in Part Two, there are numerous trade-offs between indemnity and parametric risk transfer structures. The important thing to recognize is that if they are properly designed, *both* can be effective solutions for a firm that is seeking risk transfer without also undertaking an asset or liability divestiture.

Limitation of Liability Another distinction we will see in Part Two between insurance and many types of derivatives is that insurance cannot in principle ever be the source of a net profit for a firm, but neither can insurance ever require firms to incur a new liability. The maximum payoff on an indemnity contract is the damage sustained by the buyer of the contract, thus implying that the best-case scenario for the contract purchaser is to break even . Similarly, the minimum payoff is zero—the contract in and of itself is limited liability and guarantees that its purchaser will not have to write an additional check later to its risk transfer counterparty.

In this sense, insurance is similar to option contracts. But futures, forwards, swaps, and other derivatives are not always limited liability. On the contrary, they can lead to huge losses. In principle, if the derivatives are being properly used, any large losses would be offset with gains elsewhere at the firm. But this is true only in principle. In reality, parametric contracts like forwards and swaps have no limitation on liability for their users.

Funded versus Unfunded Risk Transfer Solutions A fully funded risk transfer solution is a structure in which risk is shifted from one firm to one or more counterparties so as not to expose the risk protection buyer to any risk of nonperformance by its counterparties, such as the risk of a counterparty default or disputed payment.[9] In other words, the cash has been set aside in advance of any loss and has been de facto pledged to collateralize any payments on the risk transfer arrangement. In some cases the funds are even set aside de jure as actual collateral held in trust for the risk protection buyer, and in still other cases the funds may simply be paid up front to the risk protection buyer.

An unfunded risk transfer solution, by contrast, involves contingent payment obligations by the risk transfer counterparties. The performance on these transactions is secured only by the ability and willingness of the counterparties to pay.

Insurance and reinsurance are almost always unfunded. Derivatives generally are unfunded or partially funded through the posting of collateral or other credit enhancements. A fully funded transaction, by contrast, would be a structured note (see Chapter 16) or the actual sale of a risky asset.

Whether or not a risk transfer solution is funded is important not just because of the credit risk of the transaction itself. The funding status of a transaction also has an impact on its cash flow profile and on the funding profile of the risk protection buyer. We will discover, for example, that unfunded risk transfer may be a substitute for issuing new equity in some ways because it enables the firm to absorb larger losses at a given level of debt and profitability—just as equity would do. But unlike equity and other financial capital, unfunded risk transfer usually does not put any new cash into the hands of the risk protection seeker and thus impacts the financial strategy of the firm only through its market capital structure, not through its liquidity or funding profile.

CHAPTER 3

Leverage

When all investors and agents of firms have access to the same information, when they have equal access to securities markets, when capital markets are perfect, and when a firm's investment decisions are taken as a given, Modigliani and Miller (1958) showed that changes in the firm's capital structure and financial policies cannot influence the value of the firm. The value of a firm and its weighted average cost of capital (WACC) are determined independently of how much debt a firm issues, how much cash the firm pays out as dividends, how much risk the firm retains, and all other financial considerations. In other words, the value of the firm is independent of its *financial* capital. Appendix A reviews these four M&M assumptions and the three associated celebrated M&M irrelevance propositions in more detail for the uninitiated.

When the four M&M assumptions do not hold, the financial policies of a firm can and often will affect the value of the firm's real assets and the market value of the firm itself. That is what we want to consider in this chapter, with specific attention to how *leverage* may affect the value of a firm. Related to this is the notion of *debt capacity*, or the ability of a firm to increase its leverage by borrowing more without causing a lot of problems.

To analyze the economic effects of leverage on the value of a firm, we consider the benefits and costs of debt to a firm. Those benefits and costs of levering up are also the basis of the *trade-off theory of optimal capital structure*. The concept of an optimal capital structure is the idea that for some firms, a specific set of financing decisions will lead to a maximum value of the firm—and, by extension, that all other financial decisions will lead to a lower market value of the firm. In the case of the trade-off theory, a firm realizes its maximum market value at any given time when its market leverage ratio of debt to equity just equates the costs of issuing new debt to the benefits of issuing new debt at the margin. The empirical evidence supporting this theory, however, is quite mixed. On the one hand, the various benefits and costs of debt that we explore in this chapter do seem to play some role in influencing corporate decisions. On the other hand, several testable implications of the theory are at odds with the extant empirical evidence. Fortunately, this need not bother us too much.

There is a huge number of potential theories of optimal capital structure when the M&M assumptions do not hold. Our task here is neither to summarize all of these theories nor to pick favorites. Instead, our purpose in Part One is merely to lay a sound foundation of economic principles and corporate finance theory that may help explain some of the benefits and costs of the products and solutions discussed later in the book. To do this, we do not need to run a full horse race of competing theories of optimal capital structure. We need to understand only the basic factors that seem to play a role in influencing actual corporate financing decisions.[1]

We may thus question the trade-off theory as a prescription for firms to pursue a single, specific target leverage ratio. But that does not mean firms should ignore the benefits and costs of leverage in making their financial and risk management decisions—on the contrary! So, the remainder of this chapter explores those benefits and costs of debt, the implications of those benefits and costs for pursuing a target leverage ratio, and implications of the benefits and costs of debt for risk management.

BENEFITS OF LEVERAGE TO THE VALUE OF THE FIRM

In this section, we explore the reasons that a firm might benefit from adding debt to its capital structure. These benefits apply to an all-equity firm considering its first dollar of borrowings, as well as to firms that are already leveraged. The benefits of debt, of course, may differ depending on how much existing debt a firm already has.

Debt Tax Shield

The impact of taxes on capital structure has been analyzed by Modigliani and Miller (1963), Miller (1977), Miller and Scholes (1982), DeAngelo and Masulis (1980), and many others.[2] Because many countries allow firms to deduct interest payments from their corporate taxes but do not allow a similar deduction for retained earnings or dividends paid, there would seem to be a natural bias, all else equal, toward debt.

Suppose a corporation's income or earnings are taxed at the rate of τ_c per annum. The firm's tax shield from debt is the present value of the tax savings generated by making interest payments on debt in lieu of dividend payments to equity holders or retained earnings. This present value is typically calculated with a discount rate equal to the firm's cost of debt capital, with the argument for this being that the risk associated with the tax shield is equivalent to the risk of the debt that generates that tax shield.

If all the M&M assumptions hold with the exception of the existence of a corporate tax on income, the value of a leveraged firm at any time t can be redefined:

$$V(t) = V^E(t) + T(t) \tag{3.1}$$

where $V(t)$ is the value of a leveraged firm at t, $V^E(t)$ is the time t value of the same firm financed with only equity, and $T(t)$ is the present value of the tax shield at time t.[3] Assume that the leveraged firm has a core amount of debt outstanding with a market value of $D(t)$ at time t. The present value of the tax shield is then equivalent to an annuity. If a firm's cost of debt capital at time t is $R^D(t)$, then the present value of a firm's tax shield from debt is

$$T(t) = \frac{\tau_c[D(t) \cdot R^D(t)]}{R^D(t)} = \tau_c D(t) \tag{3.2}$$

which, substituting into equation (3.1), implies that the value of the leveraged firm is just

$$V(t) = V^E(t) + \tau_c D(t) \tag{3.3}$$

Taken in isolation, equation (3.3) thus implies an optimal capital structure of 100% debt.

The preceding analysis, however, is incomplete. A corporation is essentially just a legal association of numerous parties, ranging from employees to residual and fixed claimants to customers. A corporation, in other words, does not have a mind of its own nor a purse of its own. The purse, in particular, really belongs to the claimants on the firm. In this sense, the objective of a corporation should not be to minimize the corporate taxes it pays, but rather the total taxes paid by bondholders and stockholders. These taxes include taxes the claimants pay indirectly through corporate taxes on earnings *and* personal taxes paid by claim holders directly on the cash flows generated by the securities they hold.

A firm with positive net earnings in a financial reporting and tax period may either retain those earnings or pay them out to investors in the form of dividends or interest payments. If profits are retained, they are taxed at the corporate tax rate τ_c. If profits are instead fully distributed to debt holders, the profits escape corporation taxation *but* are subject to personal taxation as income for holders of the debt securities. And if profits are paid to equity holders in the form of dividends or capital gains, they are subject to *both* the corporate tax rate *and again* to taxation as personal income of equity holders.

If the equity distribution comes entirely in the form of dividends, then the personal tax rate is the same whether the income is received as dividends or as interest on debt. But if the equity distribution involves capital gains and there is a tax on such capital gains, then the personal tax rate paid by stockholders will differ from that paid by bondholders. Accordingly, we denote τ_{pE} and τ_{pD} to be the personal tax rates for equity and debt claimants, respectively.

Assume that annual net cash earnings $X(t)$ are fully retained or fully disbursed to either stockholders or bondholders; that is, $X(t)$ is not split. Table 3.1 illustrates the tax consequences of these three scenarios.[4]

If the firm chooses a capital structure to minimize total taxes, the firm must choose the mixture of debt and equity that maximizes income net of all taxes. Miller (1977) showed that the relative gain to a firm with a core amount of debt $D(t)$ has a gain from leverage as follows (per dollar of earnings):

$$G_L(t) = \left[1 - \frac{(1-\tau_c)(1-\tau_{pE})}{(1-\tau_{pD})}\right] D(t) \tag{3.4}$$

Note that M&M is a special case of equation (3.4). When all taxes are zero, $G_L(t) = 0$. When capital gains taxes do not exist and $\tau_{pD} = \tau_{pE}$, equation (3.4) simplifies to an analogue of the equation (3.3) we saw earlier when only corporations were taxed—that is, $G_L = \tau_c D(t)$. With capital gains taxes and different personal and corporate tax rates, however, an optimal

TABLE 3.1 Corporate and Personal Taxation of Corporate Income

	$X(t)$ Retained by Firm as Earnings	$X(t)$ Paid as Interest to Bondholders	$X(t)$ Paid as Dividends to Stockholders
Corporate Tax	$X(t)\tau_c$	0	$X(t)\tau_c$
Posttax Corporate Income	$X(t)(1-\tau_c)$	$X(t)$	$X(t)(1-\tau_c)$
Personal Tax	0	$X(t)\tau_{pD}$	$X(t)(1-\tau_c)\tau_{pE}$
Income Net of All Taxes	$X(t)(1-\tau_c)$	$X(t)(1-\tau_{pD})$	$X(t)(1-\tau_c)(1-\tau_{pE})$

leverage amount is now implied (all else being equal) that is not 100 percent debt. Equation (3.4) together with the bottom row of Table 3.1 provide firms with a guideline for how to determine what that optimal capital structure is.[5]

Reducing the Agency Costs of Free Cash Flows

With imperfect capital markets and asymmetric information, the need for security holder "principals" to monitor their manager "agents" gives rise to costs, the most obvious type of which is the cost incurred by principals to monitor and measure agent behavior and to control that behavior through compensation, rules, policies, and the like. If the actions of agents can be only partially observed by principals, the potential for agents to pursue their own agendas at the expense of their principal masters is even greater. A related agency cost is the cost that agents sometimes incur to demonstrate that they will not take certain actions adverse to principals' interests. Such "bonding costs" may be incurred either as a substitute for direct monitoring or as a way of paying principals back when the actual behavior of agents deviates from behavior consistent with the interests of residual claim holders.

A particular form of agency cost is associated with the temptation that a firm's managers may face to divert the firm's free cash flows—cash flow in excess of current investment requirements assuming the firm accepted every positive net present value (NPV) project—away from productive investment activities toward negative NPV projects that benefit the firm's managers but not necessarily the firm's security holders.

Managers are believed to like free cash flow because it enhances their consumption of perquisites. Jensen (1986) and Stulz (1990) argue that a problematic perquisite that managers may choose to pursue is the consumption value of making new investments, even when they may be in questionable projects with declining or negative NPVs. Whether a genuine mistake or a desire to flex their managerial muscles, this overinvestment in bad projects is a direct consequence of too much free cash flow and hence a direct agency cost of equity. Jensen (1986) uses the oil industry in the 1970s to make the point. Unchecked, managers are simply presumed to prefer investing money than leaving it sitting idle, even when idle money earns the risk-free rate and bad investments *cost* the firm.

So, the solution to the agency cost of free cash flow would, all else equal, seem to be for the firm to *disgorge* that free cash flow. A firm could accomplish this by paying a higher dividend to stockholders or repurchasing stock. When monitoring costs are positive, information asymmetric, and agency conflicts acute, however, disgorging free cash in the form of dividends and share repurchases will not necessarily satisfy equity holders. Managers are, after all, still in control of any *future* free cash flows. They could announce a "permanent" dividend increase, but that creates problems of its own because the decision can later be reversed.

Jensen (1986) suggests that a better solution to the free cash flow problem—a solution that, unlike a higher dividend or share repurchase, *cannot* be reversed later by managers—is issuing debt. The need to service the debt constrains future free cash flows. And to avoid the cash inflow associated with a new debt issue in the *current* period, a firm simply issues debt through an exchange offer of existing equity for new debt. Debt thus replaces some equity in the firm's capital structure without creating a current cash inflow, and at the same time creates a disciplining mechanism for managers on their future investment and perquisite consumption decisions.

Encouraging Timely Liquidation Decisions

Harris and Raviv (1990) argue that debt has the benefit of forcing firms to make better liquidation decisions. If debt exists and a default occurs, then investors get to decide whether to keep the firm in operation or liquidate its assets. Without debt, managers make this decision, and will tend to err on the side of continued operation, even when the assets of the firm are more valuable if liquidated and placed into alternative use.

Corporate law, moreover, increasingly requires managers to act in the interest of creditors rather than shareholders when the firm is near insolvency. The creditors of Rhythms NetConnections, Inc., for example, considered the firm to be in a so-called zone of insolvency and thus asked the company to halt its cash drains and wind up its operations before a default occurred (Pacelle and Young 2001). Similar actions occurred at other telecom firms in mid-2001 as creditors either sought to get firms to pay them off prior to bankruptcy or sought to change the investment strategies of the firms to lower-risk initiatives.[6]

COSTS OF LEVERAGE

The present value of the tax shield for many corporations in countries with the personal taxation of capital gains provides a strong incentive to have at least some debt. This benefit declines as the firm becomes more and more leveraged given that at some point it will become increasingly hard to induce investors to hold debt. Nevertheless, what we have seen thus far would, in isolation, imply that most firms should be extremely highly leveraged.

In this section, we see why this is not always the case by looking at the costs to a firm of incurring additional indebtedness.

Expected Costs of Financial Distress

When capital markets are imperfect, information is asymmetric, and/or investors do not all share equal access to markets, insolvency—or even the approaching possibility of insolvency—can impose significant costs on a firm's security holders. As we shall see, debt can substantially increase these expected costs of financial distress, especially for high levels of leverage.

Expected costs of financial distress include two components: the probability that financial distress will be encountered, and the actual costs of financial distress. We explore how each of these may be affected by debt in a firm's capital structure. But we first begin with a brief discussion of why insolvency is itself costly.

Costs of Financial Distress   The idea that financial distress is costly is hardly a controversial one. Just ask any manager or shareholder in a firm that went under. The failure of a firm, however, is not really the cost of financial distress. Of course the managers and security holders in a firm prefer that the firm's assets generate positive net cash flows and have a market value as high as possible. But that isn't the question. The question about which we care is whether financial distress creates losses for the firm as a legal entity.

In an M&M world, financial distress does not have any adverse impact on a firm's security holders above and beyond the adverse impact associated with a decline in the value of the firm's assets. When a firm's assets no longer have a market value sufficient to pay the bills and service the firm's debt, the firm closes. The assets of the firm, however, are not destroyed. They are simply sold and redeployed into another productive part of the economy. The M&M assumptions assure us that all assets can be sold for their fair market prices (symmetric information and equal access) and that the sale of the assets and distribution of the cash proceeds to the firm's security holders occurs costlessly (perfect capital markets).

Even in an M&M world, insolvency can, of course, affect the *relative* prices of financial capital claims issued by the firm. A very small shortfall of assets below the face value of the firm's debt will leave equity holders penniless and result in a near-total recovery for debt holders, and this probably won't make equity holders too happy. Similarly, the employees of a firm that closes will probably be none too thrilled at having to go find new jobs, possibly a new place to live, a new set of co-workers and carpoolers, and so on. But again, in an M&M world, all of this is costless, so even workers are not harmed by the failure of the firm per se.

When we relax the M&M assumptions, however, financial distress begins to impose costs on the firm itself. The costs of financial distress have been subject to extensive discussion and study by academics and practitioners alike for many years. These costs range from straightforward transaction costs to more subtle opportunity costs.

A major cost of financial distress, of course, is the legal fees that formal insolvency proceedings can precipitate. Even if the insolvency of a corporation is not contested or disputed by some interested party, the distribution of the firm's assets is never costless—not even close. And the costs of the insolvency are still borne by the now-defunct legal fiction that used to be a corporation. That means that even if the assets of the firm can be liquidated at a fair price, the debt holders of the firm will never see *all* of that money because the often-substantial fees associated with the insolvency itself get subtracted before debt holders get repaid.

The assumption that the receiver of an insolvent firm can liquidate or sell the assets of the old firm at fair market prices in a non-M&M world is also extremely questionable. If the receiver engages in a hasty or panic liquidation in particular, the old firm's debt holders will be lucky to recover anything close to the fair value of the firm's old assets. And if the receiver takes its time and tries to wait for fair prices, the result may be delays of several years before debt holders experience their recovery, whatever the final amount may be.

The degree to which a firm may experience distress costs in the form of asset sales below market prices will depend to some extent on the type of assets the firm holds. A firm whose assets consist primarily of assets in place that have liquid secondary markets and relatively homogeneous attributes will probably experience minimal asset degradation through depressed-price sales. Conversely, a firm with a high degree of intangible assets, latent assets, and growth opportunities may expect to incur fairly substantial losses on the sales of assets at below-market prices.

A potentially greater cost of financial distress can arise at some firms *prior to* their actual insolvency and closure. If a firm experiences liquidity problems prior to insolvency, for example, it may begin liquidating assets in a desperate effort to generate cash, and it may be willing to do this at well below fair market values. Firms that enter periods of financial distress also may encounter severe perception problems that can adversely affect their reputations, franchise values, sales relationships, ability to negotiate long-term contracts, and the like.

Perhaps the greatest cost of financial distress is the distraction that it creates for senior management. Financial distress forces managers into a crisis management mode and, in extreme cases, into an almost bunker mentality. Even if the managers are able to avert catastrophe and keep the firm operating, who knows how many positive net present value (NPV) investment opportunities went unexploited when the firm was liquidity constrained and preoccupied with saving itself. To put it simply, a major cost of financial distress is just preventing managers from doing the job that the firm opened its doors to do in the first place.

Debt and the Likelihood of Insolvency   Debt in a firm's capital structure can increase the probability of encountering distress, thus increasing expected distress costs and giving rise to a significant cost of issuing new debt beyond a certain leverage ratio.

For a given market value of assets, a higher face value of outstanding debt increases the likelihood that the firm will encounter financial distress. Recall from Chapter 1 that equity can be viewed as a call option on the assets of the firm with a strike price equal to total outstanding debt repayment obligations. Increasing a firm's leverage is tantamount to increasing the strike price on equity's call. For a given asset value, the probability that the equity call will expire out-of-the-money—that is, that the firm will be insolvent—is higher for higher strike prices. With positive financial distress costs, the expected costs of distress are thus higher for firms with more outstanding debt, thus implying a negative relation between book leverage and firm value, all else equal.

We can see this clearly on Exhibit 3.1. Suppose we consider two firms that hold identical assets. Both firms issue one class of debt. Literally the only difference between the firms is how much they borrow, or their book leverage. Suppose Firm Ravel issues debt in the amount of $FV(Ravel)$ and that Firm Debussy issues debt in the amount of $FV(Debussy)$, such that $FV(Ravel) < FV(Debussy)$—that is, Ravel is less leveraged than Debussy. Exhibit 3.1 shows on the x-axis the possible market values of the assets held by the two firms on the date that the bond issues by both firms mature. The y-axis on the left shows the value of the two firms' total equity on that date, and the y-axis on the right is the probability density function for the firm's assets when the debt matures, denoted $f(A)$.

The curved line in Exhibit 3.1 is the probability density function corresponding to the right y-axis. Overlaid on top of this distribution are the market values of equity for Ravel and Debussy. For both firms, equity is worthless unless the value of the firm's assets exceeds the face value of debt issued by the firm. In other words, Firm Ravel becomes insolvent for any asset value below $FV(Ravel)$, and similarly Firm Debussy for asset values below $FV(Debussy)$. From the exhibit, we can easily see that the

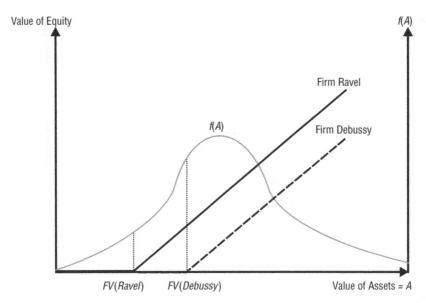

EXHIBIT 3.1 Leverage and Financial Distress

probability of insolvency is higher for Firm Debussy by recognizing that the area under the curve $f(A)$ is greater for Debussy than for Ravel.[7] This area, of course, represents the cumulative probability of encountering financial distress. So, all else being equal, more debt means a higher probability of insolvency; more debt means that a higher market value of assets is required to keep the firm afloat.

We also turn the preceding analysis around to say that firms with riskier assets should be expected to have less leverage, all else equal. Exhibit 3.2 illustrates, now with the two firms Mozart and Salieri. Both firms have FV debt outstanding, but now the firms hold different real assets. The expected values of the assets held by the two firms are fairly close, but a comparison of the solid and dashed black lines (Mozart and Salieri, respectively) easily reveals that Firm Mozart is riskier, both in the sense of a higher variance of asset values and a higher cumulative probability of default. If there are any benefits to issuing debt (e.g., tax), Firm Salieri should be able to exploit more of those benefits before expected distress costs become too high. In other words, all else being equal, Firm Salieri has a much higher debt capacity than Firm Mozart.

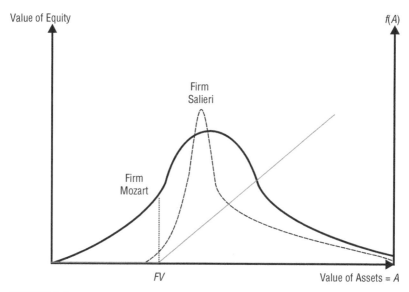

EXHIBIT 3.2   Risk, Leverage, and Debt Capacity

Debt, Distress Costs, and Deepening Insolvency   Debt can also increase a firm's expected costs of financial distress if managers of the firm wrongfully and fraudulently issue new unpayable debt. Most obviously, this can affect the probability that the firm will encounter distress for the same reasons discussed in the previous section. But wrongfully incurred debt can also harm the corporation by increasing the actual *costs* of financial distress.

The idea that wrongfully incurred debt can raise the costs of distress for a firm is known in the legal world as the doctrine of *deepening insolvency*. To be perfectly accurate, this is *one* notion of the doctrine of deepening insolvency. The other notion holds that the amount of damage to a corporation can be measured as a function of the amount of wrongfully incurred debt. Heaton (2004) explains in detail why this latter definition of deepening insolvency is problematic and can create highly distorted incentives when adopted as a legal doctrine.

Heaton (2004) also makes a strong case, however, why the first notion of deepening insolvency is a sensible one, supported both by the empirical evidence and by a body of case law that is nicely consistent with the basic tenets of modern corporate finance (unlike the second interpretation, which seems to disregard modern corporate finance). As an example of how the courts can interpret deepening insolvency correctly, Heaton cites the following case law ruling, which is also just a good characterization of the deepening insolvency problem itself:

> *When brought on by unwieldy debt, bankruptcy . . . creates operational limitations which hurt a corporation's ability to run its business in a profitable manner. . . . [D]eepening insolvency can undermine a corporation's relationships with its customers, suppliers, and employees. The very threat of bankruptcy, brought about through fraudulent debt, can shake the confidence of parties dealing with the corporation, calling into question its ability to perform, thereby damaging the corporation's assets, the value of which often depends on the performance of other parties. . . . In addition, prolonging an insolvent corporation's life through bad debt may simply cause the dissipation of corporate assets. These harms can be averted, and the value within an insolvent corporation salvaged, if the corporation is dissolved in a timely manner, rather than kept afloat with spurious debt. (267 F.3d at 349-50, quoted in Heaton, 2004, pp. 20–21)*

Agency Costs of Debt

When a firm is financed entirely with equity, the only agency costs the firm is likely to find troublesome are conflicts between shareholder principals and manager agents. The agency costs of free cash flow discussed earlier in this chapter are an example. In addition, managers who are excessively risk-averse may reject positive NPV investment projects if they are too risky out of fear of losing their jobs if the firm encounters financial distress.

The moment that a firm introduces debt into its capital structure, however, additional agency costs can arise. Specifically, equity and debt holders face very different incentives to take on certain investment projects, and this can give rise to conflicts between debt and equity. Similarly, introducing multiple layers of subordination into the debt category can exacerbate this problem.

Underinvestment in Growth Opportunities   We saw earlier that debt (and dividends of stock repurchases) can be a solution to the overinvestment problems associated with free cash flows. In this section, we explore how the very same debt that mitigates overinvestment can lead to the opposite problem of underinvestment. Specifically, when a firm has what Myers (1977) calls a "debt overhang," equity holders may not want management to pursue all positive NPV investments because the benefits of the investments inure mainly to creditors at the same time the equity holders bear most of the risks and costs of the projects.

As we noted in Chapter 1, the current value of a firm's real assets—following Myers (1977)—is best viewed as the sum of the current values of the firm's assets already in place and the discounted present value of its future growth opportunities:

$$V(t) = A(t) = V^A(t) + V^G(t) \qquad (3.5)$$

where $V^A(t)$ and $V^G(t)$ denote current assets and growth opportunities, respectively. Recall that growth opportunities are real options where the strike price is equal to the future investment outlay, and the intrinsic value, if exercised, is the NPV of the project. An unsurveyed piece of land, for example, is a growth opportunity whose true value cannot be determined until the land has been explored for mineral rights, oil and gas deposits, and the like. And in some cases, the true value of the project is not known until well after the investment expenditure is made; for example, investing in the development of a new drug often occurs decades before the pharmaceutical company really knows how much value the drug has in terms of product sales and patent revenues. It is this timing of the investment in the growth opportunity that presents us with our problem.

A simple example will help illustrate the "agency cost of a debt overhang."[8] Consider a pharmaceutical firm with no current assets— $V^A(t) = 0$—and one growth opportunity whose time t value we will denote as $V(t)$ for simplicity. To exploit the growth opportunity, the firm will have to invest $I(t + 1)$ million in research and development (R&D). If and only if the firm makes this investment, the firm will have the new drug as an asset. The value of the drug will depend on numerous random factors such as demand, whether a natural cure is found for the disease in question, and the like. This value will be revealed at time $t + 1$ and is denoted $V(t + 1)$.

Although we will stick to a simple two-period example, the timing of the revelation of information will be important in the cases that follow. In all of these, the firm decides at time t whether to issue new securities to raise the funds it may require for the R&D spending. At time $t + 1$ several things happen. First, the true state of nature is revealed so that the firm knows the true NPV of investing in the new drug, equal to $V(t + 1) - I(t + 1)$. Having observed this value, the firm then makes the actual investment if it so chooses.

Now let's consider several cases. First, suppose the firm has no debt and issues new equity at time t in an amount sufficient to cover the potential investment expenditure of $I(t + 1)$. In this case, the firm always make the optimal investment decision. If $V(t + 1) - I(t + 1) < 0$, the firm does not make the R&D investment. The value of the firm and the value of equity are both worthless. But for any $V(t + 1) > I(t + 1)$, the firm does make the investment, with the resulting profits accruing to equity holders.

Now suppose the firm issues FV of debt specifically to help fund the R&D spending on the new drug. Note, however, that the firm cannot issue riskless debt. Although the firm knows the true NPV of the drug project before it has to make its investment decision in the drug, it does not know what the drug will be worth when it originally issues debt. If $V(t + 1) - I(t + 1) < FV$, debt will experience at least a partial default.

If the debt issued by the firm matures after the true value of the drug is revealed but before the investment decision must be made, the firm still pursues the right investment criterion; that is, the firm's shareholders will instruct management to develop the drug as long as $V(t + 1) - I(t + 1) > 0$, as it should be. If $V(t + 1) - I(t + 1) > FV$, debt holders are fully repaid and equity keeps the remaining profits. If $V(t + 1) - I(t + 1) < FV$, debt holders still are better off if the firm accepts the project than if it does not as long as $V(t + 1) - I(t + 1) > 0$. In that case, bondholders will receive a partial repayment equal to $V(t + 1) - I(t + 1)$. Although not enough to fully repay them, it is still preferred to the alternative of receiving nothing. Shareholders will not oppose this, moreover.

Now suppose, however, that debt matures before the state of nature is revealed. In other words, the shareholders of the firm now must consider whether to pay off the debt before the true NPV of the drug is known. In this case, shareholders will benefit from the project only if the revenues from the drug exceed the investment cost plus the debt service obligation— that is, if $V(t + 1) - FV - I(t + 1) > 0$. If $V(t + 1) < FV + I(t + 1)$, the investment outlay will exceed the market value of the outstanding equity shares even if the project has a positive NPV. In other words, shareholders now care about whether $V(t + 1) - FV - I(t + 1) > 0$ and not whether the project has a positive NPV—that is, $V(t + 1) - I(t + 1)$. If shareholders control the firm's investment decisions, they will thus reject certain positive NPV projects, resulting in what we call underinvestment.

Conflicts between Equity and Debt Holder   Recall from Chapter 2 that we can view equity as a European-style long call option and debt as a riskless loan plus a short European-style put option, both written on the firm's net assets and maturing on the date that the firm's debt matures. We can make use of these options characterizations to examine the incentive problem more closely.

As a long call, equity holders are long the company's assets *and* long volatility. As a result, this gives equity holders a preference for higher-volatility investment projects as the firm becomes financially weaker. As the firm approaches insolvency, equity holders begin to consider huge investment risks. Because volatility is symmetric, these higher risks mean higher probabilities for both high and low project returns. But because equity holders have limited liability, they have little or nothing to lose and everything to gain from such investments.

The short put that is part of debt's position creates different incentives. The creditor-writers of this put are long the firm's assets, just like equity. But unlike the stockholders, writers of the short put have a *short* volatility position. All else being equal, they prefer investment projects with *low* volatility. The reason is that their promised fixed repayment is the best they can ever do. In contrast, higher asset volatility increases the risk to debt holders of a partial or total default without any additional compensating upside.

You may recall from an introductory options course that the sensitivity of the price of an option to changes in the volatility of its real asset values, moreover, reaches its maximum when the equity option is just at-the-money—right at the point when equity is worthless but the firm's creditors still get fully repaid. This means that disagreement over the firm's investment strategies will become increasingly severe as the firm approaches and enters financial distress.

We saw in Chapter 2 that the value of the firm is equal to the market value of its total securities, which in turn is equal to the market value of the firm's assets in place plus growth opportunities. The unique investment rule that maximizes the value of the firm is the market value rule that managers should choose investments that maximize the sum of shareholder and bondholder wealth. For reasons just mentioned, however, debt and equity may both at different times try to influence management to pursue a different investment rule—one that maximizes the value of *either* debt *or* equity instead of the sum of the two. Firms can try to mitigate this risk by adding protective covenants to bonds and the like, but not without cost.[9]

Companies may also face credibility problems persuading the market that the firm is indeed maximizing its total value and not pursuing the interest of one group of security holders at the expense of another. If the firm's managers cannot credibly convince outside investors that its investment strategy is intended to maximize the value of the whole firm, then investors may not be willing to pay a full fair price for the firm's securities. Fama (1978, p. 42) summarizes the problem nicely:

> *[T]he essence of the potential problems surrounding conflicting stockholder-bondholder interests is that . . . it will be difficult for the stockholders to resist the temptation to try to carry out an un-*

expected shift from a rule to maximize [the value of the firm] to the rule that maximizes stockholder wealth. . . . To maximize [the current market value of the firm], the wealth of its organizers, the firm must convince the market that it will always follow the investment strategy maximize [the combined value of all securities]. The market realizes that the firm might later try to shift to another strategy and it will take this into account in setting [the current prices of the firm's securities]. To get the market to set [current security prices] at the value appropriate to the strategy maximize [the combined value of all securities], the firm will have to find some way to guarantee it will stay with this strategy. The important point is that the onus of providing this guarantee falls on the firm. In pricing a firm's securities, a well-functioning market will, on average, appropriately charge the firm in advance for future departures from currently declared decision rules. The firm can only avoid these discounts in the prices of its securities to the extent that it can provide concrete assurances of its forthrightness.

OPTIMAL CAPITAL STRUCTURE?

As noted earlier, the trade-off theory of optimal capital structure implies that a firm's optimal capital structure exists at some leverage ratio that exactly equates the marginal benefit of debt to its marginal cost. Specifically, let $V^E(t)$ denote the value of an all-equity firm. Then let $B(t)$ and $C(t)$ represent the present values of the benefits and costs of debt, respectively, as of time t. Both $B(t)$ and $C(t)$ are functions of the firm's time t leverage ratio. The total market value of the firm at any time t thus is

$$V(t) = V^E(t) + B(t) - C(t) \qquad (3.6)$$

Define $L(t) = D(t)/V(t)$ to be the firm's market leverage ratio at any time t. The value of the firm attains its maximum where the first-order condition of equation (3.6) with respect to $L(t)$ is satisfied:

$$\frac{\partial V(t)}{\partial L(t)} = 0 \Rightarrow \frac{\partial B(t)}{\partial L(t)} = \frac{\partial C(t)}{\partial L(t)}$$

which occurs at $L^*(t)$. Issuing one more dollar of debt after $L^*(t)$ is reached will cause a loss in firm value because the cost of the next dollar of debt exceeds its benefit. Conversely, gains in firm value can be realized at all debt levels below $L^*(t)$ because the addition of one more dollar of debt has benefits that exceed the costs of debt in present value terms. A financial capital structure that yields $L^*(t)$ thus maximizes the value of the firm.

Exhibit 3.3 illustrates the optimal capital structure and leverage ratio graphically. The x-axis is the firm's market leverage ratio, and the y-axis represents the market value of the firm as a function of the company's leverage. For now, think of the market value of the firm as the sum of the market values of all the securities issued by the firm. We will consider firm value in the context of the value of the assets held by the firm in the next section.

The horizontal line in Exhibit 3.3 at $V^E(t)$ is the value of an all-equity firm. The heavy dashed line at the top of the figure is the value of an all-equity firm grossed up by the present value of the benefits of debt (e.g., tax shield, reduced agency costs of free cash flow, etc.). The heavy solid curve below the dashed curve is then the value of the firm as a function of its leverage defined as the all-equity value of the firm $V^E(t)$ *plus* the present value of the benefits of debt and *minus* the present value of the costs of debt (e.g., expected financial distress costs, underinvestment, etc.).

Comparative Statics

For small leverage ratios, the costs of debt tend to be small. In fact, both expected distress costs and the agency costs tend to remain small for a

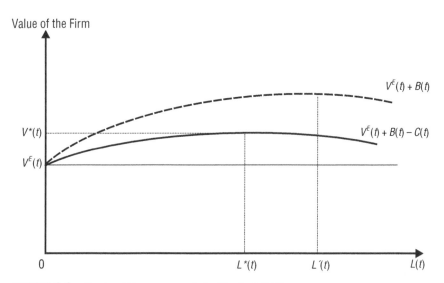

EXHIBIT 3.3 Optimal Leverage and the Trade-Off Theory

large range of leverage ratios, but past a certain point those costs rise quickly for even small increases in the firm's proportion of debt to equity. The present value of the benefits of debt—especially the tax shield—has value to the firm, by contrast, and rises quickly for even small levels of debt. The benefit of the tax shield and the other benefits of debt thus start to get overwhelmed by the costs of debt when the firm's leverage ratio exceeds $L^*(t)$. So, the value of the firm is maximized at exactly that point— that is this firm's optimal capital structure.

Contrast the optimal leverage ratio with point $L'(t)$. From Exhibit 3.3, leverage ratio $L'(t)$ appears to be the point where the marginal benefit of debt is highest, ignoring the cost of debt. For a firm that faces no prospects of financial distress and no agency costs of debt, *this* would be the leverage ratio that maximizes the market value of the firm's financial capital. This reminds us that the optimal capital structure depends strongly on the exact nature of the functions $B(t)$ and $C(t)$ and that these functions will differ for each individual firm.

Take careful note, moreover, that $B(t)$, $C(t)$, and $L(t)$ are subscripted by time and are defined in *market value terms*, not book terms. Very small changes in the firm's activities or financial markets can change this leverage ratio quickly, and this need not accompany a new offering of securities. Suppose, for example, that a AAA-rated oil company computes its benefits and costs of debt and its optimal leverage ratio at a time when oil prices are high, stable, and expected to remain that way. Then suppose oil prices decline precipitously and unexpectedly.

The impact of an unexpected decline in oil prices could have several effects. If the firm has not hedged or insured its exposure to oil price fluctuations, the price decline will reduce its cash flows and cause an immediate decline in present and future expected profitability. This erodes the current market value of the firm's existing equity and thus increases the firm's market leverage ratio. If there is no other impact on the firm than this, the firm will find itself having to retire some of its existing debt (or conduct an exchange offering of debt for equity) in order to remain at its capital structure maximum.

In addition, significant unanticipated price fluctuations may actually shift the curves $B(t)$ and $C(t)$ themselves, in which case $L^*(t)$ also changes. Depending on the relative magnitudes of the shifts in $L^*(t)$ and $L(t)$, this could force the firm to retire existing debt or possibly to issue new debt in order to try to remain at its optimum.

Clearly, firms wishing to pursue an optimal capital structure for trade-off theory reasons could be in for a rough ride consisting of frequent adjustments to their outstanding securities. Returning to Exhibit 3.3, the total value to the firm of pursuing an optimal capital structure of leverage ratio $L^*(t)$ is given by the vertical distance between the value of the leveraged firm $V^*(t)$ and the value of the all-equity firm $V^E(t)$. If this quantity does not well exceed the transaction costs and operational hassles of constantly fine-tuning the firm's financial capital structure, then pursuing a capital structure optimum may not be worth the trouble.

Implications for the Value of the Firm's Real Assets

We saw in Chapter 1 that the value of a firm—equal to the value of its total financial capital or outstanding securities—is also equal to the market value of the real assets owned by the firm. This relation holds as a tautology. So, if some specific mix of securities maximizes the value of the firm and the value of the firm is also equal to the value of the assets the firm owns, the optimal capital structure must *also* maximize the *value* of the real assets of the firm.

Needless to say, the capital structure of the firm does not somehow transform the firm's actual assets. Clearly the plants and equipment do not mutate when the firm's leverage ratio changes! Yet, our economic balance sheet of the firm will still balance anyway. The reason is simply that the benefits and costs of leverage that we have been discussing in this chapter also affect the *value* of the firm's assets.

Recall from Chapter 1 our original definition of the market value of the firm's assets as the sum of the market value of the firm's assets in place plus the present value of the firm's growth opportunities:

$$V(t) = \overbrace{\underbrace{\sum_{j=0}^{\infty} \frac{E[X(t+j)]}{1+E[R^{WACC}(t,\,t+j)]} - I(t)}_{\substack{\text{Discounted PV of Expected} \\ \text{Cash Flows on Assets in Place}}} + \underbrace{V^G(t)}_{\substack{\text{Present Value of} \\ \text{Growth Opportunities}}}}^{\text{Market Value of Real Assets}}$$

$$= \overbrace{\underbrace{S(t)}_{\text{Stock/Equity}} + \underbrace{D(t)}_{\text{Debt}}}^{\text{Market Value of Financial Capital}} \quad (3.7)$$

If some specific combination of stock and debt on the right-hand side of equation (3.7) yields a single value of the firm $V^*(t)$ that is higher than all other values of the firm for all other possible mixtures of equity and debt, then the optimal capital structure also leads to a maximum value of the firm's assets as given on the left-hand side of (3.7). In other words, if we begin with a mixture of debt and equity that is not the optimum and then shift the firm's leverage ratio to its optimum, the value of the firm will rise to $V^*(t)$ and the market value of the real assets owned by the firm will rise by the same amount.

Looking at equation (3.7), there are only three possible ways that changing the firm's leverage ratio could increase the value of the firm's assets:

1. By increasing the firm's current and/or expected future net operating cash flows (either by increasing cash inflows/revenues or by decreasing cash outflows/expenditures).
2. By increasing the present value of the firm's growth opportunities.
3. By decreasing the firm's weighted average cost of capital.

Any of these three effects will show up on the left-hand side of the firm's economic balance sheet.

Consider, for example, a firm that faces benefits and costs of debt at any time t that are a function of the firm's ratio of debt to equity at time t denoted $L(t)$, and suppose these benefits and costs can be represented by the functions $B(t)$ and $C(t)$ in Exhibit 3.3.[10] Now suppose the firm has a current leverage ratio of $L'(t)$.

As we can see on Exhibit 3.3, this leverage ratio represents the level of indebtedness for the firm that maximizes the present value of the debt tax shield—that is, the point at which one more dollar of debt would no longer translate into a tax savings for the firm. At this level of debt outstanding, however, the expected costs of financial distress have been rising at an increasing rate for a while now. This leverage ratio thus does *not* maximize the value of the firm.

Just because leverage ratio $L'(t)$ does not maximize the value of the firm, however, does not mean that the firm's assets are no longer equal in value to the firm's outstanding securities.

Exhibit 3.4 shows the economic balance sheet of the firm. In Panel (a), real and financial capital values are shown for a suboptimal leverage ratio $L'(t)$. Evidently, the left-hand and right-hand sides still balance. In Panel (b), we consider the same firm, now supposing that its leverage ratio is $L^*(t)$. As Exhibit 3.3 shows, this now is the optimal leverage ratio consistent with a value of the firm $V^*(t)$ that is the "global maximum." At no other level of leverage will the firm's value be this high or higher. Panel (b) of Exhibit 3.4 shows that the values of the firm's real and financial capital are equal, as they were in Panel (a). But now the *total values* of both the firm's real and financial capital are higher than in Panel (a).

Of course we could just as easily have subsumed the definitions of functions $B(t)$ and $C(t)$ into our existing definitions of the values of assets in place and growth opportunities instead of having afforded them separate

Panel (a) Suboptimal Capital Structure

Assets	Liabilities and Equity
$V^A[L'(t)]$	$D'(t)$
$V^G[L'(t)]$	$S'(t)$
$B[L'(t)]$	
$-C[L'(t)]$	

Panel (b) Optimal Capital Structure

Assets	Liabilities and Equity
$V^A[L^*(t)]$	$D^*(t)$
$V^G[L^*(t)]$	$S^*(t)$
$B[L^*(t)]$	
$-C[L^*(t)]$	

EXHIBIT 3.4   Economic Balance Sheet of Firm

entries on the firm's economic balance sheet. Consider, for example, a firm that is vulnerable to the agency costs of a debt overhang at any leverage ratio above $L^*(t)$. Let $V_G^*(t)$ denote the present value of the firm's growth opportunities at time t assuming that all positive NPV growth opportunities are accepted in the future when they should be. In other words, $V_G^*(t)$ is the present value of all the firm's real options to undertake future strategic opportunities or investments, assuming "optimal exercise behavior." That just means that firms reject only those projects for which $V_G^*(\tau) - I(\tau) < 0$ at whatever time τ the investment decision must be made. The market value of the firm's total assets thus is maximized at the leverage ratio $L^*(t)$, the particular mix of debt and equity that promotes an optimal investment policy consistent with $V_G^*(t)$.

With agency costs of debt, the firm may pass up some of those positive NPV projects at leverage ratios above $L^*(t)$. At leverage ratio $L'(t) > L^*(t)$, for example, equity does indeed prompt management to reject certain positive NPV investments. The value of the firm's growth opportunities thus is $V_G'(t) < V_G^*(t)$. The underinvestment cost of the debt

Panel (a) Suboptimal Capital Structure

Assets	Liabilities and Equity
$V^A[L'(t)]$	$D'(t)$
$V^G[L'(t)]$	$S'(t)$

Panel (b) Optimal Capital Structure

Assets	Liabilities and Equity
$V^A(t)$	$D^*(t)$
$V^{G\,*}(t)$	$S^*(t)$

EXHIBIT 3.5 Economic Balance Sheet of Firm with Potential Underinvestment in Growth Opportunities

overhang in present value terms thus is our total cost of debt at leverage ratio $L'(t)$:

$$V_G{}^*(t) - V_G(L'(t))$$

This is the amount by which the firm's current assets are being inefficiently deployed at leverage ratio $L'(t)$. This is also the amount by which the sum of the market values of the firm's debt and equity are underpriced. Alternatively, we can think of this as the gain that would accrue to the security holders of a firm that bought out the corporation and then adopted optimal capital structure $L^*(t)$.

This situation is depicted in Exhibit 3.5. In Panel (a), the firm has too much debt and thus is penalized with a market value of growth opportunities below what it should be. Panel (b) shows the economic balance sheet of a firm that has less debt and thus exercises its real option growth opportunities optimally. The firm in Panel (b) has a market value that exceeds the market value of the Panel (a) firm by $V_G{}^*(t) - V_G[L'(t)]$—that is, by exactly the amount of the present value of forgone positive NPV investment projects that the overly leveraged firm would reject and that the optimally leveraged firm would not.

CHAPTER 4

Adverse Selection and Corporate Financing Decisions

Increasing amounts of evidence suggest that, in addition to the benefits and costs of leverage explored in Chapter 3, some firms' corporate financing decisions are heavily influenced by the presence of "adverse selection" costs (Fama and French 2002, 2004). Specifically, investor concerns about the financial health of a firm arising from the inability of investors to verify costlessly the quality of the firm's investment decisions can cause investors to demand a discount on the corporate securities issued by that firm. As a result, firms will tend to eschew such financing methods in favor of securities that can be offered at a cost of capital more commensurate with the true risk profile of the firm. In addition, firms will attempt when possible to use their corporate financing and capital structure decisions to try to signal their true financial health, thereby reducing the adverse selection costs of issuing securities in certain markets.

Recall from Chapter 3 that a firm's capital structure and financing decisions cannot affect the value of the firm under the four assumptions of perfect capital markets, symmetric information, equal access to security markets, and given investment strategies. (See Appendix A for more details.) Although we allow for the violation of any of the first three assumptions and wish to build on what we saw in Chapter 3, our focus in this chapter will be primarily on a violation of the symmetric information assumption. This assumption is perhaps best summarized in the classic article by Fama (1978): "Any information available is costlessly available to all market agents (investors and firms), and all agents correctly assess the implications of the information for the future prospects of firms and securities" (Fama 1978, 273). Asymmetric information thus means that not everyone has costless access to the same information at the same time and/or that not everyone agrees on how a new piece of information will impact security prices.

The study of asymmetric information and its numerous impacts on economic activity led to the award of the 2001 Nobel Prize in Economic Sciences to George Akerlof, Michael Spence, and Joseph Stiglitz. As you would guess, the academic literature on asymmetric information has grown quite voluminous over time. And we saw examples of it already in Chapter 3 when we examined the agency costs of debt. Fortunately, our task in this chapter is a little more tractable. We focus here on one specific aspect of asymmetric information called adverse selection. We begin with a characterization of the adverse selection problem itself and then turn to see how it can impact capital structure and corporate financing choices.

ADVERSE SELECTION AND MARKETS FOR LEMONS

When the buyer of a good or service does not know the true value of the good or service but the seller does know its true value, adverse selection can occur. The buyer generally will only be willing to pay a price that reflects the *expected* value of the good or service. Because sellers know the true quality of what they are selling, this price will be too low for a provider of a high-quality good, and the sellers of those high-quality goods will not enter into transactions. Only the sellers of low-quality goods will be willing to transact at the price that buyers would initially offer. Knowing this, however, buyers adjust their expectations, assuming that only the poor-quality goods will be brought to market, and thus reduce their offering price to the price of the bad good. This becomes a self-fulfilling prophecy, resulting in only bad goods being bought and sold.

The classic, original application of adverse selection is insurance markets, and we will indeed return in Chapter 8 to discuss adverse selection in the specific context of insurance. In this chapter, we focus our attention on adverse selection in the markets for corporate securities. But first let's go through the basic idea again, this time in a little more detail.

In his Nobel Prize–winning article "The Market for 'Lemons,' " Akerlof (1970) explored the situation where a good has several quality grades that cannot be verified at the time of purchase by a buyer. As a result, as he put it, "a structure is given for determining the economic costs of dishonesty" (Akerlof 1970, 488). The applications of his ingenious model are as far-reaching today as when he wrote the paper.

Because of the importance of understanding Akerlof's "lemons problem" for later discussions in this book, we present a simplified version of his model here to illustrate the exact nature of the problem. Specifically, consider a market for used cars that contains two types of cars: good cars and bad ones, where the latter are called lemons. Suppose there are equal proportions of good cars and lemons available for sale in this market.

The true value of a car is known to the seller who contemplates bringing the car to the market. Good cars should be worth $100 and lemons worth only $50. Buyers, however, cannot tell the difference and have no way to ascertain whether the car is good or is a lemon until after they own it. (Even in today's world of vehicle identification number [VIN] databases and CarFax, this is probably still true!) Buyers do know, however, the *proportions* of good cars and lemons.

Knowing only the proportions of good cars and lemons, a buyer comes to the market with an initial price proposal for a car equal to her expected price given quality:

$$E(p) = \frac{1}{2}\$100 + \frac{1}{2}\$50 = \$75$$

At this price, sellers of good cars will not deliver their cars into the market—to do so would be to take an immediate $25 loss. Sellers of lemons, by contrast, would regard the $75 price proposal as a great deal!

Although buyers cannot differentiate between qualities of cars, they do know that sellers know the true quality and will abide by profit-maximizing behavior. Buyers thus know that $75 is not an equilibrium price that will clear the market. Knowing that only lemons will be sold at that price, buyers update their expectation to reflect the fact that only lemons will be sold:

$$E'(p) = 1 \times \$50 = \$50$$

So, the equilibrium price that clears the market is $50 per car, but only lemons are sold at this price.

This is a simplification of Akerlof's model, but the basic economics are the same. When information is asymmetric across car buyers and sellers, we essentially get a self-fulfilling feedback loop—buyers expect lemons, will pay only a lemons price, and, as a result, get only lemons. Akerlof likens the problem to a type of Gresham's law in which lemons drive good cars out of the market.

In fact, in Akerlof's more general model, he shows situations in which the problem becomes so severe that there is a failure to trade anything at all: "[I]t is quite possible to have the bad driving out the not-so-bad driving out the medium driving out the not-so-good driving out the good in such a sequence of events that no market exists at all" (Akerlof 1970, 490). We won't take his model to that extreme here, but it is a potential outcome of severe information asymmetries.

ADVERSE SELECTION IN SECURITIES MARKETS

Myers (1984) and Myers and Majluf (1984) argue that when information is asymmetric across corporate insiders and public investors in the firm's securities, the market for those securities will behave like a market for lemons. The information is asymmetric about the true quality of the firm's real capital investments. Accordingly, investors assume that managers of a firm are going to the market for new funds only when they have bad news about an investment. This depresses the price that outsiders are willing to pay for the new securities, which in turn creates a self-fulfilling prophecy that indeed leads managers to issue new securities mainly when they are overpriced.

In other words, investors believe that a firm will issue new stock only when it is overpriced, so they are willing to pay only a discounted price for the new stock assuming that it is overpriced, and that discount induces insiders of the firm to issue stock only when it is overpriced. Our self-fulfilling prophecy has come true.

Myers (1984) argues that the immediate implications of this analysis are twofold. First, the cost of external finance is not purely the cost of issuing securities (e.g., underwriting costs)—in addition, external finance can lead to underinvestment in growth opportunities of the kind discussed in Chapter 3.

Second, if external finance is required, safer securities are preferred to risky ones; the managers of the firm first prefer to issue riskless or low-risk debt, then risky debt, then hybrids, and last of all outside equity. The reason is that riskier securities have prices that are more sensitive to the revelation of information. The price impact on a security when the true value of the firm is revealed thus is greater the riskier the security. Or, turning the logic around, the more the revelation of information may impact the value of the security, the bigger its initial discount will be. The best way to finance a new investment project under conditions of adverse selection thus is to issue securities whose values are least sensitive to the ultimate revelation of information to the market, regardless of what that information is. In other words, the safer the security, the less the adverse selection discount will be and the less its price will change to incorporate the revelation of private information when that information is revealed. In the limiting case of riskless debt, the value of the debt will not change at all based on the revelation to the market of the true value of the investment project.

Pecking Order Theory of Optimal Capital Structure

If we take the Myers/Myers and Majluf application of Akerlof's model to securities markets to its logical extreme, the result is a four-part pecking order that firms follow in making their financing decisions:

1. Firms always prefer internal finance to external finance.
2. Firms have target dividend payout ratios that are adapted to investment opportunities, but dividends are relatively "sticky" (i.e., firms try to avoid sudden and large changes in their dividend policies).
3. Because of sticky dividend policies and unexpected changes in profitability and investment opportunities, internal cash flows may be greater or less than required investment outlays. When there is a net cash flow surplus, firms use the surplus to pay off debt or investment in liquid securities. When there is a net cash flow deficit, firms draw down net cash balances and liquidate their investment portfolios of marketable securities.
4. If external financing is required, firms issue the lowest-risk security first. In other words, firms prefer to issue securities in the following order: senior or low-risk debt, mezzanine and subordinated (i.e., risky) debt, hybrid debt-equity securities, and equity.

This pecking order leads to two different implications about the relation between a firm's value and its financing decisions. The first is the obvious one—the theory predicts that the financing choices and security issuance decisions made by firms should conform to the pecking order given. The second is an implication of the first and relates more to the firm's optimal capital structure in the sense discussed in Chapter 3. Specifically, Myers (1984) contends that variations in a firm's leverage should be driven by the firm's cumulative need for external financing—that is, by the cumulative net cash flows on the firm's investments over time. Whereas the trade-off theory explains leverage changes based on the benefits and costs of debt, the pecking order theory attributes leverage changes only to the firm's cumulated financing deficit of investment expenditures minus retained earnings.

Empirical Evidence

As with the trade-off theory, empirical support for the undiluted pecking order theory is mixed. Because the theory has implications both for the financing decisions of firms and for the variations in the leverage of firms, it makes sense to summarize the evidence along these two dimensions separately.

Evidence from Firms' Financing Decisions   When it comes to examining the financing decisions of firms, much of the empirical literature is based on the traditional event study methodology in finance of examining announcement effects of new securities offerings. Specifically, abnormal stock returns are analyzed to determine whether the announcement of a particular security offering is interpreted as "good news," "bad news," or "no news."

In support of the pecking order theory, the announcements of new equity issues tend to be followed by large negative abnormal returns.[1] Announcements of new preferred stock issues also result in stock price declines, and there is a strong negative effect for low-rated preferred stock.[2] Firms that repurchase their stock, as expected, tend to have stock price increases following the repurchase announcement.[3] Exchange offers also adhere to the expected pattern. Exchanges of debt for equity yield higher stock prices, whereas exchange offers that increase outstanding equity yield lower stock prices.[4]

Evidence also suggests that convertible debt is viewed more as equity than as debt. Consequently, convertible debt issues result in negative stock price responses,[5] with highly rated convertibles engendering a larger negative reaction than low-rated ones.[6]

Contrary to the model's predictions, however, is evidence that the announcement effect of new nonconvertible debt issues does not depend on the relative riskiness of the debt.[7] In addition, Fama and French (2004) find that, contrary to the pecking order theory, most firms issue or retire equity each year, the issues are large, and these issues are not typically by firms "under duress."

Evidence from Firms' Capital Structures and Leverage Ratios   The evidence on capital structure and leverage is equally mixed. For the most part, increases in debt that do not involve reductions in equity produce weak stock price responses that generally are not distinguishable from zero.[8] In other words, issuing debt appears to have no real impact on firms' stock prices.

Consistent with the pecking order theory, Eckbo and Masulis (1995) find that commercial banks are a dominant source of external finance in all major industrialized countries. Smith (1986a) and James (1987) further find significant and *positive* stock price responses to the announcement of new bank loans—virtually the *only* security type that is viewed as good for firm value. But this is consistent with *both* models—with the trade-off theory because bank loans are debt, and with the pecking order theory because bank loans are the highest form of external finance in the pecking order, and with the proper monitoring may not be susceptible to the information asymmetry that creates adverse selection problems for the issuance of public securities.

Also consistent with the pecking order theory, Shyam-Sunder and Myers (1999) find strong evidence that firms' internal financing deficits are responsible for variations over time in corporate leverage. Fama and French (1998) find, moreover, that changes in leverage and dividend payouts do tend to convey valuable signals about profitability.[9] Rajan and Zingales (1995) and Fama and French (1998) also both conclude that high leverage and increases in leverage tend to be bad news for firm value, as the pecking order theory predicts in contrast to the trade-off theory. Fama and French (1998, 2002) find that the negative relation between debt and firm value persist even after controlling for earnings, dividends, investment, and R&D. And Fama and French (2002) observe that profitability is strongly negatively correlated with leverage.

Frank and Goyal (2004) find evidence of long-run leverage ratios to which deviations in actual firm leverage revert. Deviations from the long-run trend are absorbed primarily by changes in leverage, not net equity. This is supportive evidence for both the trade-off and pecking order theories.

But the evidence is hardly uncontroversial. Barclay and Smith (1996), for example, find that the relationship between a firm's leverage and an earnings increase is negative, suggesting that larger earnings increases are associated with firms that have relatively less debt. Similarly, Fama and French (1999) find that debt has more benefits for firms when they are mature and have established track records. This is consistent with the agency cost stories about debt in the trade-off theory more than with the pecking order theory.

Finally, Frank and Goyal (2003) find that the financing deficit of a firm is tracked more closely by issues of new equity than by a firm's leverage. Fama and French (2002) also find that small, less-leveraged growth firms have the largest new equity issues. These firms should have high low-risk debt capacity, so this is a troubling result for the pecking order theory, as well.

IMPLICATIONS OF ADVERSE SELECTION IN SECURITIES MARKETS

The pecking order theory may not have much empirical evidence supporting it as a cohesive stand-alone theory of how corporations finance themselves, but there can be little question that asymmetric information does indeed affect certain firms' financing choices. Many of the products and solutions we discuss in Parts Three and Four seem to be particularly consistent with the basic economic forces underlying the pecking order theory, at least anecdotally.

The pecking order theory as originally framed by Myers (1984), moreover, is not the only way to view the impact of asymmetric information on securities markets. In the pure pecking order theory, firms cannot rectify the information asymmetry that is at the root of the pecking order in their financing alternatives. In reality, firms appear instead to seek out financing alternatives that try to either minimize their adverse selection costs or send a signal to the public investors responsible for imposing those costs in an effort to make public securities offerings less costly.

We consider next some alternative implications of adverse selection problems—implications that are not part of the pecking order theory per se, but that may go further toward explaining observed corporate financing patterns. Importantly, evidence against the pecking order as a stand-alone theory of optimal capital structure is not necessarily evidence against any of the six implications discussed next. In fact, some of the same evidence that indicts the pecking order actually *supports* the following statements—see Fama and French (2004).

1. When a firm must raise external funds, it will prefer to do so from suppliers of capital that are relatively better informed about the true quality of the firm's business.

In the traditional pecking order model, the extent to which a given security is mispriced depends *only* on the riskiness of the security. The information that insiders possess, moreover, is presumed to be completely unavailable to outside investors. But this ignores some important features of securities markets. Fama and French (2004) summarize this point particularly well:

> *Myers (1984) and Myers and Majluf (1984) do not allow for equity issues that do not have an asymmetric information problem. One story for our results is that there are important ways to issue equity that avoid this problem. If so, the pecking order, as the stand-alone model of capital structure proposed by Myers (1984), is dead: financing with equity is not a last resort, and asymmetric information problems are not the sole (or perhaps even an important) determinant of capital structures. This does not mean the asymmetric information problem disappears. But its implications become quite limited: firms do not follow the*

pecking order in financing decisions; they simply avoid issuing equity in ways that involve asymmetric information problems. (p. 3)

As we will see in Parts Three and Four of the book, a number of structured finance and insurance transactions are essentially substitutes for traditional debt and equity issues. One important feature that distinguishes them is the way in which they are issued. Because structured finance and alternative risk transfer (ART) transactions both raise funds for a firm and significantly alter the firm's risk profile, the due diligence process looks quite different for these products than for normal securities.[10]

Consider, for example, the contingent capital deals we discuss in Chapter 15. In these deals, a major insurance company—usually rated AA or AAA—precommits to purchasing a corporation's preferred stock or subordinated debt at a fixed price upon exercise by the corporation, which is possible only after some exogenous triggering event has occurred. The triggering event is generally included to mitigate moral hazard problems. These providers of contingent capital, moreover, retain an appreciable amount of the securities on their own balance sheets and do not merely re-sell the securities in the market.

As you would expect, the due diligence that precedes such a deal is careful and time-consuming, and far surpasses the information contained in a credit rating. Part of that due diligence involves a general credit risk review of the corporation. But part involves an analysis of the firm's intended use of the funds so that an exogenous trigger can be chosen that both mimics the company's specific fund-raising goals *and* is beyond the control of the firm's management.

In addition, providers of ART tend to view the products and solutions they supply as much more of a partnership with the firm than banks and investment banks, which are generally motivated by transactions rather than by overarching business relationship management. For this reason, ART suppliers are more likely to have a big-picture view of the overall core business of a firm and thus may be less likely to assign too much weight to the performance of any individual project.

That the corporate insiders may through this process be able to rectify some of the adverse selection problems they would encounter by making an otherwise equivalent issue of unsecured public bonds or preferred stock is extremely plausible.

2. Firms will attempt to raise funds from relatively better-informed investors not just to reduce the adverse selection costs of a new securities issue, but also to signal the true quality of their investment portfolio to relatively less-informed investors. This "delegated monitoring" role has shifted in recent years away from banks toward insurance companies.

Unsecured senior loans made to corporations by commercial banks have long been thought to help reduce the costs associated with asymmetric information. Commercial banks serve a role as delegated monitors of the investment activities of their borrowers. By providing borrowers with monitoring and outside discipline, banks encourage their borrowers to undertake only positive net present value projects.[11] If the loan is later rolled over, the bank traditionally would reevaluate the credit risk of the firm, thus giving the borrower an ongoing incentive to undertake only positive net present value projects and investments. When a loan is rolled over, a positive signal thus is sent to other creditors. In that manner, "informed" bank debt makes other sources of less-informed public debt viable.[12] Not surprisingly, small firms and high-risk start-up ventures in particular build financial market reputations by first acquiring bank-monitored debt and only later move on to acquire arm's-length public or privately placed debt.[13]

The advent of credit derivatives, credit insurance and synthetic reinsurance, and other credit risk mitigation structures discussed in Part Two, however, has greatly diminished the ability of public security holders and junior creditors to rely on the credit extension and rollover decisions of senior creditors as a signal of the firm's true credit quality. Because it is impossible for these junior creditors and bondholders to know when a senior creditor is hedged, the value of the signal sent by the loan renewal is diminished to virtually zero. What does it mean, after all, to observe a senior bank creditor roll over a loan *on which it bears no credit risk?* The guest essay by Harris and Kramer (Chapter 31) explores how the failure of Enron greatly exacerbated this problem and probably spelled the end of the era of delegated monitoring by banks.

As will be discussed at several stages later in this book, one of the more interesting recent developments in financial markets is the apparent replacement of banks as delegated monitors with well-informed insurance and reinsurance companies. Despite the fact that many insurance and contingent capital solutions involve relatively junior claims, these claims are nevertheless highly dependent on ongoing monitoring by their provider. Remember, these transactions blend fund-raising and risk transfer, and it is the latter that generally keeps the capital providers' ongoing attention.

Although the junior nature of the claim makes the claim more sensitive to the revelation of private information, it also makes the claim riskier for the capital supplier. In the particular case of (re)insurers, this makes them all the more inclined to gather additional information about borrowers—information that convinces the lenders to accept a junior position in the securities capital structure but that *also* reduces the sensitivity of the claim to the information asymmetry.

So, although the role of banks as delegated monitors has waned in recent years, it may well be that insurance and reinsurance companies are stepping in to replace them.

3. Firms will utilize structured financing methods when the structuring process can successfully mitigate adverse selection and moral hazard concerns.

Part Three is dedicated to structured finance. Without wishing to front run that section of the book, we note here only that a major reason underlying structured financing solutions may well be the desire by firms to reduce adverse selection costs. Specific examples include project finance, trade finance, and receivables securitizations.

The reasons that the structuring process may help reduce the informational asymmetries that give rise to adverse selection costs are at least twofold. The first concerns the structuring process itself. As we will see in Part Four, structuring usually involves the significant use of credit enhancements and outside credit protection by what we have called "the new delegated monitors"—for example, an AAA wrap provided to the senior tranche of an asset-backed security. By focusing the attention of a greater number of informed parties on a careful analysis of the quality of the firm's assets, it seems less likely that a lemons problem could arise. Moral hazard, of course, may take its place to the extent that investors fear the firm is "reverse cherry-picking" only its worst credits to securitize. But again, the disproportionate attention to structured deals from external monitors like rating agencies, swap counterparties, and insurance companies should ameliorate that, as well.

A second possible motivation for structured finance deals concerns the so-called noise of the firm's assets and investments. Suppose for simplicity that a firm has a portfolio of risky assets and considers issuing new securities to finance a new capital investment project. The lemons problem will arise whereupon investors in the new securities worry that the firm will seek outside funds only when it has private information about the poor quality of the planned investment.

Now suppose instead that the new investment is financed through a project finance structure in which the new investment is placed on its own inside a highly transparent special purpose entity (SPE). The SPE contains only the single capital project and no other assets. As we will see in Chapter 21 (and as J. Paul Forrester discusses in his guest essay in Chapter 32), project finance includes multiple layers of subordination; numerous guarantors, insurers, and monitors; and a large number of credit and liquidity support provisions. As already discussed, it is much less likely that financiers of the project financed in this manner would demand the same adverse selection discount that an investor in the firm's unsecured debt would demand on the same project when commingled with the rest of the firm's assets.

The value of removing an asset or project into a structured financing conduit depends, of course, on the other assets the firm is holding. If the firm is holding only Treasuries, for example, removing the project for separate financing almost certainly will not reduce the firm's all-in borrowing costs. But if the firm is holding primarily intangibles, then removing a tangible project for separate financing could help the firm avoid the same adverse selection discount that is associated with its unsecured debt.

4. Firms will benefit from utilizing financing methods that integrate risk management and funding solutions into the same product.

A primary tenet of the pecking order theory is that firms will prefer to issue lower-risk securities. Their adverse selection discount will be lower because they have less potential for a large adverse price swing when the true information about the firm's investments is revealed.

Products in which corporate financing and risk management goals are integrated may be appealing to firms facing significant information asymmetries, as well. These securities and assets may not have lower price variance, and the pecking order theory by itself thus would argue for firms to avoid such offerings. But because the firm's use of these products reduces its overall risk, the sensitivity of the firm's overall performance to the outcome of a single investment project may be significantly reduced. This has the same effect as issuing low-risk securities—it reduces the impact of the revelation of the true information on the outside investors in these integrated risk and capital transactions.

5. The greater a firm's adverse selection costs of new security offerings, the more attention the firm will pay to liquidity and funding risk management. Firms with a large quantity of latent or intangible assets and real options will be even more inclined to manage their per-period net cash flows either through hedging or through the use of preloss financing structures like finite risk or contingent capital.

Myers (1984) notes that in some situations, firms may maintain a stock of external debt to keep enough cash in current assets to finance their investments, but in that case the firm does everything it can to make the debt as low-risk as possible. He postulates that their rationale is both to minimize expected costs of financial distress (see Chapter 3) and to maintain "financial slack" in the form of reserve borrowing power. In other words, issuing debt that is reasonably low-risk or not issuing debt at all keeps the firm's debt capacity positive, especially for the subsequent issue of more low-risk debt.

The desire to preserve financial slack and avoid underinvestment problems affects a firm's risk management strategy in addition to its capital structure. We will return to this issue in Chapter 7.

6. *Firms facing significant adverse selection costs will try to utilize other forms of signaling (apart from structured finance or borrowing from relatively better-informed investors) to try to reduce the adverse selection discount on its public securities offerings.*

In the pecking order theory, asymmetric information leads to over- and underinvestment problems, and the firm's capital structure emerges as a means of addressing the costs associated with these problems. The net cash flows of the firm thus dictate its capital structure. Other models with asymmetric information at their root, by contrast, take the firm's net cash flows and real investments *as given* and then examine how capital structure decisions can be used to signal the quality of the firm's investments to a less-informed capital market. These signaling theories are complementary to and not substitutes for the pecking order theory.

In an early model, Leland and Pyle (1977) consider a single entrepreneur seeking additional equity financing for a project about which the entrepreneur is better informed than the would-be investors. Although investors cannot observe the true value of the project, they *can* observe the amount of money the entrepreneur commits to the project. Not surprisingly, investors' willingness to pay more for their share of the project rises as the entrepreneur's investment in the project rises. The entrepreneur's insider investment decision thus sends a signal to less-informed market participants about the unobservable investment project.

Miller and Rock (1985) develop a signaling model for dividends in which the investment expenditures and external financing of a firm are held fixed and external investors cannot accurately assess current and future expected operating cash flows of the firm. Recall that under M&M, dividend policy is irrelevant because, in the absence of surplus operating cash flows, new equity or debt must be issued to finance the higher dividend, which in turn depresses the value of outstanding securities by the amount of the increased dividend. But operating cash flows cannot be observed by outsiders, while the dividend paid by the firm can help reveal or signal when a firm *truly* has a surplus operating cash flow.

In the Miller and Rock model, a higher-than-expected dividend signals higher-than-expected net operating cash flows. Conversely, a higher-than-expected external financing or new security issue signals lower-than-expected operating cash flows. In other words, announcements of higher-than-expected dividends are positive signals that should increase the value of outstanding residual claims, and announcements of new securities issues are negative signals that should depress stock prices. The empirical evidence is broadly consistent with these predictions.[14]

Ross (1977) develops a signaling model in which higher debt levels are a signal to the market of higher-quality investments. The intuition is simple enough. Firms with riskier investment projects have higher expected costs of financial distress than sound firms *for any level of debt*. Firms with safer investments can afford to issue more debt to distinguish themselves from bad firms as long as the increase in the marginal expected cost of financial distress associated with the higher debt level is more than offset by the adverse selection costs (i.e., the amount of underpricing of the firm's securities) avoided by sending an informative signal.[15]

CHAPTER 5

Capital Budgeting, Project Selection, and Performance Evaluation

apital budgeting is the process by which corporations decide what investments to make in long-term real capital assets and investment projects and how to finance those investments with the proceeds from newly issued or existing financial capital claims. Most firms undertake a serious capital budgeting exercise at least annually. When a firm's funds are limited and its capital budget constrained by an unwillingness or inability to issue new securities, the capital budgeting process is also sometimes called *capital rationing* or *capital allocation*.

Embedded into a firm's capital budgeting process is a firm's *project selection* methodology, or the rules that a company applies to help determine whether a given investment opportunity will add value to the firm and its security holders and should thus be undertaken. When a firm has sufficient funds or is willing to issue new securities to finance some or all of its potential investments, project selection usually involves some kind of decision rule that tells the firm whether to accept or reject a given investment opportunity based on either a comparison of some measure of the project's value or return to a hurdle rate or on some absolute measure of the project's value contribution to the firm. In the face of capital rationing, project selection also requires the firm to develop a methodology for choosing among several competing opportunities, all of which may potentially be value-enhancing for the firm.[1]

Performance evaluation is the process by which firms try to assess how well a given capital budget and/or a specific project or business unit is performing or has performed. Performance evaluation has several purposes. First, it is the means by which firms assess the ongoing value of existing projects and businesses—or lack thereof. In this sense, performance evaluation is how firms decide when to pull the plug on existing projects and divisions—or, perhaps, when to expand them. Second, performance evaluation is also used by some firms to implement performance-based compensation and other incentive schemes designed to address agency problems in the firm and to prompt senior managers to pursue only those capital budgets and projects that result in shareholder value creation. When both performance evaluation and project selection rules are explicitly connected to maximizing the value of the firm, the whole exercise is popularly known as *value-based management* (VBM).

Project selection and performance evaluation are essentially *ex ante* and *ex post* versions of the same problem. Not surprisingly, the basic metrics used to evaluate the potential value added by a project initially are extremely similar to the metrics a firm will use to consider the performance and value added by a project on an ongoing basis. The primary difference is that project selection will always involve *expectations* (e.g., expected returns, expected cash flows, etc.), whereas the latter will involve actual performance data.

These related concepts lie at the heart of how a firm conducts its primary business—deciding which strategic opportunities to pursue, which assets to invest in, when to invest in upgrading a losing business, when to shut that business down, and so on. Less obvious, however, is why these topics are relevant to a firm's risk and capital management process generally and to its structured finance and insurance programs more narrowly. Although the connection may be less apparent, it exists and is quite important.

Risk capital is the amount of financial capital that a firm needs to set aside in order to reserve against losses arising from one or more specifically identified risks. As we discuss again in Chapters 6 and 7, equity risk capital can be a substitute for risk transfer, and funds obtained from debt set aside against risks are known as pre- or postloss risk finance. We also discuss risk capital again in detail in Appendix C.

The purpose of *this* chapter is confined to examining the traditional capital budgeting process of a firm in which projects are selected and their performance evaluated and how risk enters into that process. This chapter is essential if you plan to dig into the issue of risk capital in Appendix C. Otherwise, the chapter should be used as yet another illustration of the relations between capital and risk.

ACCOUNTING METRICS FOR PROJECT SELECTION AND PERFORMANCE MEASUREMENT

In this section, we summarize some of the popular project selection and performance measurement criteria that are derived solely from book accounting data. Despite their popularity, these measures are not derived from "first principles" corporate finance and thus do not provide any guarantee that decisions made based on these measures will lead only to value maximization of the firm. Indeed, in some cases, these criteria can lead to highly distorted decisions that *erode* firm and/or shareholder value.

We include a discussion of these metrics not merely as a point of intellectual interest, but rather because so many firms continue to rely on these rules today. Ours is not to question corporations wedded to the rules, but rather to make sure that those corporations using these measures understand fully the consequences of their use.

Earnings and EPS Growth

The earnings statement is a necessary evil of accounting—a required summary disclosure of the profitability of a firm and its businesses. Analysts and investors watch earnings and earnings growth like hawks, and firms are often penalized severely for deviating from earnings targets or expectations.

Many firms, moreover, actively focus on earnings as a criterion for *ex ante* project selection and *ex post* performance evaluation. At a firmwide level, many corporate managers remain seduced by the allure of steady earnings growth as a measure of financial strength. A high price-earnings (P/E) ratio is still considered a distinguishing feature of a firm's balance sheet. And within the firm, earnings or earnings per share (EPS) attributed to specific business lines and projects often affect—directly or indirectly—decisions by the firm about continued investment or reinvestment in those enterprises.

At least four good reasons suggest that earnings and EPS are not good variables on which a firm should base its project selection and performance evaluation decisions. First, earnings are quite sensitive to accounting rules. Such rules may change over time, differ across otherwise-similar international jurisdictions, and propagate significant debates over interpretation—see Chapter 30 by J. Paul Forrester and Benjamin S. Neuhausen.

A second problem with earnings is that they do not take into account the true economic effects of investment spending. Accounting considerations like depreciation and amortized cost can make it hard to tell the true *cash flow* impact of investments in fixed real capital assets. In addition, earnings estimates often do not treat investments in working capital properly—investments that can significantly affect the profitability and risk of a firm. This is perhaps most obvious when we look at the trade receivables a firm may have outstanding. Suppose, for example, that a firm called Circuit Village buys a large number of consumer electronics from a firm called Stony for resale, for which Stony sends Circuit Village a bill for $1 million. That remains a receivable up to and until the time Circuit Village pays the bill. If Stony has $2.5 million in sales revenues booked, its earnings will show the $2.5 million in revenues, but its available cash on hand is only $1 million. In general, a firm whose receivables are growing will have overstated revenues and earnings relative to the true cash position of the firm.

This leads us to identify the third shortcoming of earnings: their failure to reflect risk and the value of risk management on the balance sheet. The cash position of the firm is important not just because it is a better measure of the firm's true profitability. It also better accounts for the firm's risk. In the earlier example, Stony has reported $2.5 million in sales revenue, but has $1 million in working capital tied up to fund its receivables. All else being equal, this can affect the firm's debt capacity as working capital needs begin to eat up the firm's entire free cash flow. The $1 million receivable already reflected as earned income for the firm, moreover, is subject to the credit risk of a default by Circuit Village.

A firm that has purchased trade credit insurance (see Chapter 10) from an AAA-rated insurance company will have lower earnings than a firm that remains exposed to a default by the original counterparty—lower by the cost of the insurance. But this reflects the fact that this firm has *locked in* its risk position through the purchase of insurance. The firm that did not purchase trade credit insurance has higher reported earnings, but the *earnings at risk* for that firm are also much higher. Yet earnings are earnings, and this risk may not be clearly understood by all investors. Although insurance lowers earnings, it also makes the number reported much more representative of the true risk profile of the firm.

Finally, earnings estimates do not reflect the time value of money or the firm's cost of capital. A firm may generate earnings growth and still be eroding the value of its assets and securities if its investments in new assets are generating returns below the firm's cost of capital.

Suspicions about earnings as a measure of a firm's profitability reached epic proportions following the demise of Enron, a firm preoccupied to the point of obsession with maintaining earnings growth and a high P/E target.[2] That the firm managed to do so while experiencing substantial contemporaneous negative cash flows—ultimately spelling the end for the firm—is a case in point of the fallacy of a pure earnings target for a firm's operating decisions. Admittedly, Enron is the reductio ad absurdum version of this story—but the basic theme is all too familiar in today's corporate C suites and boardrooms.

Return on Investment and Return on Assets

Nonfinancial corporates first turned to *return on investment* (ROI) as a solution to the problems discussed in the previous section with a pure earnings target. Separately, financial institutions long considered *return on assets* (ROA)—a close cousin of ROI—to be the holy grail of project selection and performance evaluation. In both cases, the solution was—and remains—unsatisfactory and does not eliminate the basic problem of judging economic viability based on potentially inappropriate accounting data.

For a given capital project over a specific accounting reporting period, ROI is usually measured as[3]

$$\text{ROI} = \frac{\text{Net Operating Income}}{\text{Assets}} \tag{5.1}$$

where both net operating income and assets are measured in book terms. Net operating income is essentially income less expenses for the accounting period (generally one year), excluding one-time specific events and charge-offs. Assets are measured as the average book value of assets over the accounting period.

The book ROI computed in equation (5.1) is often compared to a hurdle rate when used for project evaluation purposes, and the hurdle rate is generally the firm's weighted average cost of capital (WACC). Comparing a static accrual accounting aggregate to a market-determined expected return demanded by investors, however, can lead to some strange decisions and need not guarantee the acceptance of only projects that maximize the value of the firm.

The numerous shortcomings of using ROI for project evaluation are well-known.[4] First, ROI typically understates the true economic value of a project in early years and overstates the value of a project in later years. Because it relies on average book value of assets, the undepreciated asset base decreases steadily over time, thus giving rise to this appearance of inferior performance early and superior performance late in the life of the project *even when net operating income is unchanged.*

Second, ROI is highly sensitive to the level of the initial investment. Consider two firms with similar projects. In fact, suppose expectations about profitability are identical for the two projects, and that the cash flows on the two projects are the same as well. The only distinction between the projects at the two firms is the beginning investment base. The firm with a larger investment base will have a lower project ROI early in the life of the project, purely because of the overhang of undepreciated assets weighing down the denominator in equation (5.1). Yet, in an economic sense, this is a sort of sunk cost fallacy; because assets in previous periods are already committed and in place, they should not affect the decision about whether to take on a new project.

Third, ROI fails to account for the true economic risks and rewards of off-balance-sheet items. Even if the impact of those items hits the income statement, it will not be included in the firm's accounting assets.

Fourth, ROI makes no attempt to control for the relative risks of investment projects. Two projects with identical investments and identical expected profits will have the same ROI, even though one project may exhibit much higher variance of profitability over time. As long as the firm is producing an unconstrained capital budget, this won't matter. But if the firm is forced to ration/allocate capital, ROI does not allow the firm to distinguish properly between the two alternative projects.

Finally, ROI measures the profitability of a project to the company and makes no effort to control for leverage, the source of financing for the project, or returns to specific investors in the project.

Return on Equity

As noted in the previous section, ROI attempts to quantify the return on a project, strategy, or business line from the perspective of the company. In an effort to better quantify the benefits of a project, strategy, or business to the equity holders of a firm, many companies turned away from ROI and toward *return on equity* (ROE):

$$\text{ROE} = \frac{\text{Net Operating Income}}{\text{Shareholders' Equity}} \qquad (5.2)$$

ROE as shown in equation (5.2) is related to ROI shown in equation (5.1) as follows:

$$\underbrace{\frac{\text{Net Operating Income}}{\text{Equity}}}_{\text{ROE}} = \underbrace{\frac{\text{Net Operating Income}}{\text{Assets}}}_{\text{ROI}} \times \underbrace{\frac{\text{Assets}}{\text{Equity}}}_{\substack{\text{Accounting} \\ \text{Leverage}}} \qquad (5.3)$$

ROI and ROE may have begun as competing alternatives for project selection and performance evaluation, but today they are generally used together in different applications. Corporations often use ROI to analyze the performance and evaluate investments in existing business units and operating divisions. ROE, by contrast, is usually used to evaluate company-wide performance or to evaluate investments in new stand-alone projects that require separate investor financing.

ROE has all the same shortcomings as ROI. In addition, ROE is unduly sensitive to leverage. Consider, for example, a specific project being considered by a firm with an optimal leverage ratio of 50 percent. If the new project is financed with any other mixture of securities than half debt and half equity, the firm will be pulled away from its optimal capital structure and experience a loss of market value as a result.

Not only is this capital structure effect not addressed in the ROE calculation, but ROE-based project evaluation can actually create perverse incentives. If the return on a project is greater than the cost of debt capital, the firm may choose to fund the project with suboptimally high levels of debt in order to increase the ROE. Such apparent increases in ROE are the result of the positive interest spread. Nowhere is the adverse impact of this financial policy on the firm's capital structure subtracted from the ROE, nor is the impact of higher leverage on risk and on the expected return on equity explicitly considered.

DISCOUNTED CASH FLOW METHODS WITH NO RISK ADJUSTMENT

Metrics used by firms for project assessment and performance evaluation need not rely only or primarily on accrual accounting estimates of a firm's financial condition over some reporting period. As an alternative, firms may rely instead on *discounted cash flow* (DCF) metrics for project selection and evaluation. These methods all rely on *actual per-period cash flows*, not earnings, income, revenues, expenses, and other purely accounting aggregates.

DCF or Market ROI, ROA, and ROE

Instead of looking at the return on a project using accrual net income as the basis for quantifying the return, we can look instead at a more economic measure of return—the *market* ROI, which can be defined for the holding period from t to $t + T$ as

$$\text{ROI} = \frac{CF(t,\ t+T) + A(t+T) - A(t)}{A(t)} \tag{5.4}$$

where $CF(t, t+T)$ = cash flows between t and $t+T$
$A(t+T)$ = market value of assets at end of period $t+T$
$A(t)$ = market value of assets at beginning of period t

If we are comparing market to book ROI, then we would choose a holding period for the investment in equation (5.4) that is the same as the accounting period used in equation (5.1).

When applied to individual assets, equation (5.4) is more commonly known in financial economics as the *holding period return* of that asset. Generalized to a project, strategy, or business unit, market ROI is the so-called economic return.

As with book ROI, firms may be tempted to use expected market ROI as the basis for project selection when compared to a hurdle rate such as the firm's WACC—that is, accept projects with a market ROI above the firm's WACC and reject projects otherwise. Far preferable to the book ROI for measuring the economic performance of an asset, market ROI still will prove deficient as the basis for project selection. Its primary shortcoming is the failure to account for risk.

As before, we can define market ROA and ROE comparably, but again with the same deficiencies that we get when jumping from book ROI to market ROI.

Internal Rate of Return

The *internal rate of return* (IRR) on a project is the return that equates the present value of the discounted net cash flows on the project to exactly zero. The IRR is extremely appealing to many firms as a base criterion for project selection and performance evaluation for several reasons. First, it has the natural interpretation as the break-even return for that project; if the project has a return below the IRR then the project has lost money. Second, unlike ROI and ROE, the IRR of a project uses DCF analysis and thus relies on cash flows rather than account period averages.

For a project with expected net cash flows of $X(t + j)$ in any year $t + j$ and T years during its useful life, the IRR or yield of the project is the rate IRR that satisfies the following equation:

$$\text{NPV} = \sum_{j=1}^{T} \frac{E[X(t+j)]}{(1+IRR)^j} - I(t) = 0 \qquad (5.5)$$

A project with an expected net cash flow of $1 per year for the next 50 years that requires a $10 current investment outlay, for example, has an IRR of about 9.91 percent per annum.

The practical use of an IRR for project selection is generally for comparison to a hurdle rate—as in our prior examples, usually the firm's WACC. Any project with an IRR less than the firm's WACC should be rejected on the grounds that it costs the firm more in financial capital to finance the project than the project is expected to return. Conversely, projects for which IRR exceeds WACC should be accepted.

The IRR decision rule is significantly better than the ones we have seen thus far because it does, in fact, sometimes lead to value-maximizing decisions. Nevertheless, the IRR rule still ultimately fails us as a reliable and consistent means of project selection. The situations when the IRR rule will lead firms to accept the wrong project usually involve either mutually exclusive projects or capital rationing. Specifically, IRR can be useful when looking at the economic viability of a project *totally in isolation*, but IRR can lead to problems when we use it to compare one project with another one. Interested readers can consult Fama and Miller (1972) for a more detailed explanation. Peterson and Fabozzi (2002) provide some good worked examples that nicely illustrate the problems of using IRR.

NET PRESENT VALUE RULE

The primary tool in use for the past several decades in corporate capital budgeting exercises is the net present value (NPV) rule. Under the M&M assumptions, the NPV rule guarantees that the only projects a firm accepts are those that will increase shareholder value. Even when the M&M assumptions are abandoned, the broad NPV framework is usually still salvageable and preferable to the available alternatives, if for no other reason than its simplicity and intuitiveness.

The NPV rule says that a firm should accept only those projects with nonnegative NPVs. We saw in Chapter 1 that the NPV of an asset in place is just the discounted expected gross present value of the cash flows on that asset minus the investment expenditure. For assets that require ongoing maintenance expenditures, we include the present value of all future expected outlays either in the current investment expense or as subtractions from future revenues on the project.

Consider an investment project that generates a sequence of net cash flows from time $t + 1$ to the end of its useful economic life, time T. Using the same notation as in Chapter 1, this sequence of net cash flows is denoted $X(t + 1), \ldots, X(t + T)$. Suppose the project also requires an up-front investment expenditure of $I(t)$. We can write the project's NPV as:

$$\text{NPV} = \sum_{j=1}^{T} \frac{E[X(t + j)]}{1 + E[R(t, \ t + j)]} - I(t) \qquad (5.6)$$

The term $E[R(t, t + j)]$ is the appropriate expected return that we will use as a risk-adjusted discount rate specific to cash flows occurring at time $t + j$.

Most good corporate finance texts will satiate any demand you have for a discussion of practical questions surrounding the use of the NPV rule, and there are far too many such issues even to begin discussing them here. Nevertheless, some very broad additional commentary is appropriate. In particular, we consider the major practical challenges of implementing the NPV rule both for the *expected cash flows* in the numerator of equation (5.6) and for the *discount rates* in the denominator.

Forecasting Expected Cash Flows

Populating the NPV calculation for any given project with expected cash flow data is really the meat of the problem. There is not much to say about the theory of doing this. It's the practice that is the hard part—two parts art, and only one part science.

One of the big challenges to keep in mind when coming up with an expected cash flow estimate for a project is that the NPV rule is expressed explicitly in terms of cash flows, not accounting data. Yet accounting data is likely where most of the data exists from which we must draw our expected cash flow forecasts. Caution must be exercised when translating data from accounting and earnings formats into per-period cash inflows and outflows. A machine that costs $1 million, for example, might be expensable over the next decade using straight-line amortization of cost. Earnings thus would show the expense for the machine as around $100,000 per year for the next 10 years. But if the machine was bought and paid for in full today, the NPV must include the full $1 million cash outflow today. Indeed, accounting measures like earnings before interest and taxes (EBIT) and earnings before interest, taxes, depreciation, and amortization (EBITDA) have historically performed quite poorly as proxies for actual net cash flows.[5]

Coming up with a good forecast of the cash revenues from a project is often the easy part. True, the forecasts might not be very precise, but at least there is probably some basic agreement on what is being forecast.

Costs, in contrast, are more challenging to model and forecast. There are more than a few pitfalls of which to beware. First, beware expenses associated with projects for which the firm enjoys an *economy of scope*. Defined as the reduction of average costs for a firm when the same input can be used for multiple outputs, economies of scope are often associated with infrastructure, information technology (IT) projects, general overhead expenditures, and the like. Accountants tend to try to allocate all of those shared expenses across any projects or business units that rely on them. NPV analysis of the project, however, should treat such items as cash outflows *only* if the acceptance of the project by the firm *genuinely increases cash outflow*.

To take an example, suppose a firm is considering investing in a new operating branch. If the branch is opened, the branch would utilize the firm's existing centralized general ledger and accounting system, which already has been bought and paid for. In order to include the new branch in the existing system, the firm will have to spend some money on systems integration. This is the only cash outflow that should be included in the NPV analysis of the branch. It may well be the case that the firm allocates a part of the total overhead associated with the system to the branch, but the company as a whole has already paid for the system. The *marginal* cash outflow is only the integration fees.

As a related matter, many firms are tempted to include sunk costs in an NPV calculation to try to recover some prior expenditure. The very definition of sunk costs, however, is that the money has been irreversibly spent already. No matter how tempting, such costs should not affect the evaluation of the new project's NPV.

Other costs that should be included but often are left out of the NPV calculation include opportunity costs (if the acceptance of the project denies the firm other opportunities), externalities to other parts of the firm (e.g., customers attracted to a new division at the expense of an old one), and so on. Firms should also remember to treat contributions to working capital associated with a project as cash outflows on that project. Recall equation (1.3) from Chapter 1 where we expressed the value of the firm as the sum of the values of the discounted expected net cash flows on all the firm's various projects. Clearly, in order for that expression to equal the true value of the firm, *all* of the firm's cash flows must be exhaustively included. We noted at the time, for example, the need to include operating cash flows. In the same way, short-term assets less short-term liabilities that constitute a firm's net working capital also must appear in that equation, both when that net working capital is invested (usually at the beginning of a project) and when it is recovered from a specific project.

Discount Rate Issues

Although we have considered the calculation of expected cash flows and the discount rate separately, we cannot ever separate the two issues entirely. In modern finance, there are always two ways to compute the present value of the expectation of a risky cash flow stream:

1. Compute the *actual* expected cash flow and discount at the appropriate *risk-adjusted* discount rate.

2. Model the expected cash flow *relative to a risk-free set of probabilities* and then discount at the *risk-free* rate.

We stick to the former approach in this book, both because it remains the most popular and because it conforms best with the data that most firms track and save. But both are possible. Not only is one approach no more theoretically sound than the other, but you should, in fact, get the same results both ways. If you don't, it's a problem with the data or the risk-adjustment methodology, *not* a problem with the underlying economic theory.

For many projects, small changes to the discount rate may well not affect whether the NPV is positive or negative. Some people thus question the time and attention often paid to the discount rate most appropriate for discounting the cash flows in equation (5.6). As we will see later in this section and again later in this chapter, however, serious attention to this issue *is* required. Specifically, a firm must answer six major questions related to the discount rate in order to use the NPV criterion appropriately for its capital budgeting process:

1. How should systematic risk be accounted for in risk-adjusted expected returns?
2. Is the risk of the project or the risk of the firm the right risk on which to focus?
3. Should time-specific discounting be used?
4. Should discount rates be pretax or posttax?
5. How can the benefits of specific financing strategies be incorporated into the analysis?
6. When the firm and/or project is affected by idiosyncratic risk that shareholders cannot diversify away, how should the discount rate be changed?

Systematic Risk and the Discount Rate In an M&M world, systematic risk is the only risk that matters. Accordingly, the way to compute the risk-adjusted expected return will depend on the relationship we assume between expected returns and systematic risk. Cochrane and Culp (2003) survey alternative methods of adjusting a risky cash flow stream for risk in equilibrium for the purpose of capital budgeting and/or risk management.

Perhaps the most common hurdle rate is still based on the old capital asset pricing model (CAPM). According to the CAPM, the expected return on any bundle of assets or cash flows can be expressed as

$$E(R) = R_f + \beta[E(R_m) - R_f] \qquad (5.7)$$

where R_f is the risk-free rate, R_m is the return on the market portfolio, and β is the covariance of returns on the assets or cash flows with the return on the market portfolio, reflecting how the systematic risk of the market is mirrored in the return on the specific assets in question.

Most studies and current texts claim that the most common way that firms actually measure their investment hurdle rates is by using the CAPM and some measure of beta (asset, firm, industry, etc.). Despite its popularity, however, the CAPM has been subjected to significant criticism. Fama and French (1992) provide a good survey of the shortcomings of the CAPM and why, despite the simplicity of the model, it may not make sense to use it for true cost of capital estimation.

The basic criticism of the CAPM is that other risk factors apart from the market are known as an empirical matter to provide explanatory power to expected returns. These factors include firm size (Banz, 1981); the ratio of a firm's book-to-market equity (Fama and French, 1992, 1993, 1995, 1996); labor income (Jagannathan and Wang, 1996); industrial production and inflation (Chen, Roll, and Ross, 1986); and investment growth (Cochrane, 1991, 1996).

One such popular alternative to the CAPM that accommodates additional risk factors is to use a multifactor model to determine expected asset returns:

$$E(R) = R_f + \sum_{j=1}^{N} \beta_j f_j \qquad (5.8)$$

where β_j is the "factor loading" of risk factor j on the asset bundle and where f_j is the jth "factor risk premium." Increasingly popular specific multifactor models used in cash flow discounting by corporations are the three- and five-factor models of Fama and French (1992, 1993).

Fama and French (1997) note that three problems complicate any efforts to extract a meaningful cost of equity from equation (5.8) by running the least squares regressions that the equation implies. The first and obvious problem is which model (i.e., what factors) to use. For some sense of how unsettled that debate is, see Cochrane (2001).

A second problem is time variation in the parameter estimates β_j. Movement over time in these parameter estimates indicates changes in the loadings of various risk factors on expected returns. This makes the practical estimation of these parameters a real challenge. One might try to use industry-level data instead of firm-level data, but doing so doesn't really improve things. Fama and French (1997) study, for example, estimates of factor loadings in their own three-factor model consisting of the market portfolio, size, and book-to-market factors, as described in Fama and French (1992, 1993). They find that parameter estimates obtained from a full sample from 1963 to 1994 are no more reliable than estimates obtained from the last three years of data.

A third problem is imprecision in the statistical estimation of the factors or factor risk premiums themselves. Taking only the excess return on the market as a risk factor, Fama and French (1997) find that the 1963–1994 average excess market return is statistically indistinguishable from any number in the range from just under 0 percent to just over 10 percent! Again, industry-level data and longer time series do not seem to help much.

So, where does this leave today's corporate treasurer seeking a good estimate of her firm's cost of capital? Unfortunately, not anywhere particularly pleasant. Indeed, CAPM estimates of cost of capital are still widely used not because graduate business schools have failed to communicate the failings of the model, but rather because there is no good and obvious alternative available. Indeed, perhaps the main strength of the CAPM approach—and, more generally, an approach to WACC determination that adheres to the original M&M model—is its internal consistency with its assumptions. As most of the remainder of Part One illustrates, the particular way that violations of M&M assumptions impact WACC can be so contentiously argued that a major case for using the CAPM is the very simplicity of its assumptions. In short, using CAPM and M&M approaches to WACC estimation allows us to avoid the "my assumptions are better than yours" kind of argument.

So, the CAPM and M&M frameworks remain the dominant—and probably the most tamper-proof—approaches for practical cost of capital estimation. With those models in hand, Fama and French (1997) rightly conclude, "[W]hatever the formal approach, two of the ubiquitous tools in capital budgeting are a wing and a prayer, and serendipity is an important force in outcomes."

Project Risk versus Firm Risk   When the M&M assumptions hold, M&M Proposition III tells us that the NPV of a project will never depend on the combination of securities that a firm issues to finance that project. In an M&M world, after all, the value of a project does not depend on the firm that owns the project. As such, the way a firm finances a particular project won't affect the fundamental value of that project. See Appendix A for a brief discussion and proof of this proposition.

Various adjustments can be made to the discount rate to reflect firm-specific variables if the M&M assumptions do not hold. An adjustment we will *never* make, however, is to use the actual mixture of securities issued to finance a specific project as the discount rate on that project. If the project is financed with 90 percent debt and 10 percent equity, advocates of this approach would compute a WACC under the assumption of 90 percent leverage. The danger here is that the financing mix that a specific project can support may well not be supportable by the firm as a whole, and we want to discount the cash flows of the project at a rate that will reflect the project's true risk *inside the firm.*

As a general rule and in an ideal world, the right discount rate to use in computing a present value is always the discount rate that best reflects the riskiness of the cash flow stream being discounted. For a project, this will almost always be the expected return on the project itself—or, equivalently, the expected return on the assets associated with the project. Even in a non-M&M world, using the expected return on assets is often the best starting point—*if you can do it.*

Very few firms in actual practice rely on expected asset returns for discounting project cash flows. The reasons are all practical. The sheer lack of data on most projects, for example, makes it extremely hard to estimate project-specific asset betas or other comparable systematic risk adjustments for specific projects. Even when you have the data, it may not be very good, leading to severe measurement problems in the actual econometric estimation exercise.

Instead, most firms opt to use their WACC as the hurdle rate for new investments, where the capital structure in place at the time of the project evaluation supplies the weights for the WACC calculation. We know from Chapter 2 that the value of the firm as a whole is just the value of all of its projects and assets. Accordingly, the firm's WACC will also be the expected return on all the firm's assets combined. In other words, the WACC is essentially the average expected return on the various projects and assets that the firm has in place. In a CAPM world, the asset beta for the whole firm is just the weighted sum of asset betas for all the assets in place that the firm already owns prior to the project being considered. If the firm has in place U projects or assets, any one of which is worth $V_u^A(t)$, the correspondence between the asset beta for the firm (as opposed to the project's asset beta) and the betas on the firm's securities is

$$\beta^A = \sum_{u=1}^{U} \frac{V_u^A(t)}{V(t)} \beta_u^A = \frac{D(t)}{V(t)} \beta^D + \frac{S(t)}{V(t)} \beta^S = \beta^{WACC}$$

As long as the risk of the project is approximately the same as the *average* risk of the firm's existing projects, the WACC can be used as a suitable discount rate in the NPV calculation. But you still have to be a bit careful. If the project beta differs significantly from the firm's asset beta, this can lead the firm to inappropriately adjust for risk in the project evaluation process. A firm that always compares the expected return on projects with its WACC will overinvest in projects that are riskier than the average risk of the firm's assets already in place and will underinvest in projects that are safer.

We also have to be careful if the project in question is extremely large and has cash flow characteristics or risks that sharply differ from the firm considering the project. In this case, the best approach may be to try to identify the WACC of a comparable firm—a firm that has a similar project in place as a major component of its business, or a firm that has a comparable risk profile to the project in question.

Time Variation in Expected Returns   The discount rates in equation (5.6) are specific to the timing of the cash flow being discounted. This can be an important issue if the expected returns on the project *or* the firm's WACC exhibit significant time variation—which they probably will. As before, however, we will be limited by the availability of data to do anything about this.

Suppose, for example, that we have a 10-year project with annual cash flows. In order to apply a different risk-adjusted discount rate to the cash flows in each year without assuming constant expected returns, we would need to run 10 regressions. Suppose we are estimating asset betas on the project in question or a comparable project. The 10 regressions would take the form:

$$R(t, t + k) = R^f + \beta_k[R^m(t, t + k) - R^f] + \varepsilon_{t,t+k}$$
$$k = 1, 2, \ldots, 10 \quad t = 1, \ldots, N(k)$$

Each regression would have $N(k)$ historical sample data points, and we would run one regression for each of our 10 time horizons—the first using annual returns, the second using two-year returns, and so on.

Now recognize that we usually need 30 or so data points to get a decent fit in a typical regression. If we don't want to run into the econometric problems associated with overlapping observations, that means we would need 30 years of data *just to estimate the annual beta*. For the 10-year beta, we would theoretically need 300 years of past data on the project or a comparable! Forget it.

So, we usually settle for a constant expected return calculation in which

$$E[R^{WACC}(t, t + j)] = E(R^{WACC}) \quad \forall_j$$

so that equation (5.6) invariably becomes

$$NPV = \sum_{j=1}^{T} \frac{E[X(t + j)]}{[1 + E(R^{WACC})]^j} - I(t) \qquad (5.9)$$

Pretax or Posttax Discounting   The M&M world assumes no taxes, and, hence, no tax shield for debt. In a non-M&M world, however, firms may be inclined to include debt in their capital structure in no small part because of the beneficial tax effect, and we want to take that into account explicitly.

If the corporate tax rate is denoted τ_c as in Chapter 3, the posttax WACC for the firm can be written as

$$E(R^{WACC}) = \frac{S(t)}{V(t)} E(R^S) + \frac{D(t)}{V(t)} E(R^D)(1 - \tau_c) \qquad (5.10)$$

We will almost never include this term in our formulas in this book, but that's just to make the formulas easier to read. You *do* want to adjust for taxes in practice.

Idiosyncratic Risks and the Discount Rate   An extremely important implication of the M&M assumptions that is central to the M&M irrelevance propositions is that only systematic risk should affect the expected return on any bundle of assets. This is the main reason that M&M Propositions I and II hold—that the expected return on a bundle of assets depends *only* on their systematic risks and thus does *not* depend on the firm that holds the assets. All firms holding the same bundle of assets thus should have the same WACC irrespective of whether they have the same capital structures and financing policies. In the context of this chapter, firms should evaluate projects entirely based on whether the risk-adjusted expected return of those projects is at least as great as the expected return on the assets underlying the project after controlling for systematic risks.

When one or more M&M assumptions are violated, an immediate implication is that idiosyncratic risks *can* matter. They are going to matter, moreover, for *equity*, not for debt; it is the shareholders of the firm who presumably cannot diversify away the idiosyncratic risks of either the project on its own or the project as it interacts with the rest of the firm. Consequently, it is equity holders who will demand a higher expected return for bearing stock exposed to those nondiversifiable risks.

One possible solution is to modify the firm's WACC to take into account the idiosyncratic risk premium borne by equity explicitly:

$$E(R^{WACC}) = \frac{D(t)}{V(t)} E(R^D) + \frac{S(t)}{V(t)} E * (R^S) \qquad (5.11)$$

where $E*(R^S)$ represents the expected return equity holders will now demand for bearing these extra risks that the project is imposing on the firm. Just where one might choose to get these risks and how one might incorporate them into the traditional expected return on equity is not obvious, but it *is* possible.

Adjusted Present Value Rule

M&M Proposition III reminds us that the financing strategy should not impact the firm's capital budgeting decision. But when the M&M assumptions do not hold, there can be benefits and costs associated with adding debt to a firm's capital structure. We already discussed those benefits and costs in Chapters 3 and 4.

One way to incorporate those benefits (and costs!) of a particular mix of securities is to try to adjust the WACC directly. We have seen in equation (5.10) how to do this to reflect the tax benefit of debt, but this approach sometimes proves more cumbersome when it comes to quantifying the impact of the other benefits and costs of debt that we discussed.

Alternatively, firms may prefer to use the adjusted present value (APV) rule instead of the NPV rule. The APV of a project is defined as

$$\mathrm{APV} = \overbrace{\sum_{j=1}^{T} \frac{E[X(t+j)]}{[1+E(R^A)]^j} - I(t)}^{\text{NPV to an All-Equity Firm}} + \overbrace{B(t) - C(t)}^{\substack{\text{PV of Net Benefits} \\ \text{of Debt}}} \qquad (5.12)$$

where $B(t)$ and $C(t)$ were defined in Chapter 3 as the present values of the benefits and costs of debt, respectively. Recall that this net benefit of debt is a function of the actual leverage the firm has in its capital structure and will include variables like the present value of the debt tax shield, expected costs of financial distress, agency benefits and costs of debt, and the like.

Interpreting equation (5.12), we can see that the APV of a project is just the NPV of the project to an all-equity firm plus the net benefit to debt finance. The latter are sometimes called the *financing side effects* of the project.

Notice that the discount rate used to compute the NPV for the project financed by an all-equity firm is not the expected return on the *project* assets, but rather the expected return on the assets of the firm. This is the same as the expected return on the stock of an unleveraged firm.

If we properly account for the benefits and costs of leverage, the APV of a project should be equal to the NPV of a project. As a practical matter, however, firms sometimes find it easier to incorporate the benefits and costs of debt through the APV approach than into the WACC in the NPV approach or into the expected cash flows of the project directly.

Strategic Net Present Value[6]

We saw in Chapter 1 that the firm's investment policy includes investments in real assets in place *and* growth opportunities. Growth opportunities can be viewed as real options, or call options on a future asset in place that must be financed with a future investment. Growth options are often a bit harder to value in practice than are assets in place. Because the future expected cash flows are uncertain, we need to make use of some kind of option modeling methodology to compute the current price of a growth opportunity.

The mere presence of growth opportunities at a firm does not change the spirit of the NPV rule. For growth opportunities, just like new assets in place, the value of the firm will rise only if the gross present value of the growth opportunity exceeds the investment outlay required to finance it.

Things get more complicated, however, when we recognize that real options are not limited to growth opportunities. Since Myers first introduced the term in 1977, there has been an increasing broadening of what constitute real options. The term *real option* has more recently come to mean a strategic alternative that a firm may face in its capital budgeting process. Many such real options are naturally occurring; that is, a firm has them whether it realizes it does or not. The identification of such real options plays a critical role in corporate strategic planning, capital budgeting, and revenue optimization.

To ignore real options from capital investment decisions is quite often to leave money on the table. Usually we just use an appropriate option pricing model and then add the value of the real option to the NPV of the project. The result is what some call the *strategic NPV*:

Strategic NPV = NPV + Value of Real Options

Populating the last term with numerical estimates is easier said than done, of course, but readers interested in confronting the devil in these particular details are referred to one of the many treatises available on real options. Here, we can content ourselves just to identify the strategic options that should be included in a firm's capital budgeting framework; we won't get into *how* to include them.

Probably the most basic and frequently occurring real options concern the timing of investment and production decisions or the *size* of investment and production decisions. We briefly review the major types of real options along these lines in the following sections.

The Option to Wait to Invest   One of the most basic real options is the waiting-to-invest option for capital-intensive investment projects. The reason this option is a basic one is that in its pure form—articulated by Ingersoll and Ross (1992)—the value of the option is based entirely on interest rate uncertainty and not on market price uncertainty. In other words, the option to wait when making an investment decision has value even when the cash flows on a project are totally known.

Ingersoll and Ross (1992) offer a simple example of why the NPV criterion alone is not enough for most corporations. Their example is reproduced here with few changes.

Suppose the one-year risk-free interest rate is 10 percent, and a capital investment is available that requires a one-time current investment outlay of $100. The investment will return $112 in one year. According to the NPV criterion, we accept the project:

$$\text{NPV} = \frac{\$112}{1.10} - \$100 = \$1.82 > 0$$

Now suppose the yield curve is inverted and the one-year interest rate one year from now is 7 percent, known today with certainty. Instead of taking the investment now, we could wait a year. If we wait a year, the NPV *today* for the investment taken in a year is

$$\text{NPV} = \frac{\dfrac{\$112}{1.07} - \$100}{1.10} = \$4.25 > 0$$

By waiting, we are clearly better off.[7]

Now let's consider interest rate uncertainty. To see the effect that even a little randomness can have on our capital budgeting decision, suppose first that the yield curve is flat and constant at 10 percent and you consider undertaking a project that yields $109 in a year for sure. Based on the NPV criterion alone, you reject the project:

$$\text{NPV} = \frac{\$109}{1.10} - \$100 = -\$0.91 < 0$$

Because the yield curve is flat, moreover, you will *always* reject this project—there is no value to waiting.

But now suppose there is *some* chance, however small, that the one-year rate will fall below 9 percent at some point in the future, however distant. Because the project might be valuable to undertake in the future, it is not worthless today despite what the NPV criterion alone tells us. That means the investment has *some* value today.

Similarly, what if the yield curve is flat at 7 percent today but interest rates fluctuate? The NPV of the project today is positive at that rate, but the fluctuation of rates means that we should not definitely undertake the project today. If the probability is high enough that rates will decline further in the future, it pays to wait.

Deferral Option   The waiting-to-invest option is a special case of the more general option to defer an investment expenditure. In the waiting-to-invest option just discussed, the only source of risk was the variability of the interest rate, or the discount rate used to calculate the project's NPV. When input and output price uncertainty and/or market, credit, and other event-driven risks subject the cash flows of the project to uncertainty, the deferment option becomes even more interesting.

Consider the variables that can affect the value of waiting to invest when the cash flows on the underlying project are uncertain. These variables include:

- *Gross present value of the project.* Other things being equal, the higher the gross present value of expected future cash flows on the project, the more valuable the deferral option.
- *Investment cost.* Other things being equal, the lower the investment cost of the project, the more valuable the deferral option.
- *Time until the opportunity to undertake the project disappears.* Other things being equal, the longer you have to decide whether to undertake the project, the more valuable the deferral option.
- *Uncertainty about project cash flows.* Other things being equal, the more uncertain you are about the value of the project, the more likely it will be that the project *is* valuable and, hence, the more valuable the deferral option.

This list of variables should look suspiciously like the underlying asset price, strike price, time to maturity, and volatility of the underlying asset in a traditional options sense. Accordingly, we can easily use appropriate option pricing techniques to add the value of the deferral option to the simple, static NPV of a project.

Abandonment Option   The option to abandon a current asset is the option to terminate all production and operations and sell the current asset for its market value. The abandonment decision thus is permanent unless the company repurchases its assets on the market after liquidating them.

Abandonment options are particularly common in capital-intensive industries, such as transportation and financial services. The capital intensity of investments is sufficiently high that even small declines in demand for the end product may imply a higher liquidation value of investments and assets than they would have if left in development or active production.

The abandonment option has as its underlying asset the value of the asset, assuming that it remains in continuing operations. The strike price of the option is then the value of the assets in the project if they are redeployed or sold on the open market. The option is then a put option on the asset if left in continuing operation. If the value of the asset in the current project falls below its redeployment or resale value, the option will be exercised and the asset abandoned.

Because the value of the abandonment option often depends on the value of the assets in an alternative use, the strike price for the abandonment option is generally an asset value itself. Rather than expressing the option as a put on the underlying asset of continued operational value, the abandonment option can also be viewed as the combination of an asset in its current use with the option to exchange that asset for its salvage value or alternative use. The two positions thus together constitute an option on the maximum of two asset values, where the two assets are, for example, the machines and equipment of a railcar factory under alternative use scenarios.

Time-to-Build Option   The time-to-build option combines the deferment option and the abandonment option. In the time-to-build option, capital investment expenditures are staged and coupled with the option to abandon the investment project at any time if new information is obtained that reduces the NPV of the project. The presumption is that information impacting the project's NPV is released gradually over time and that investment decisions can be linked to those information releases.

Each stage of an investment project can be viewed as a compound option, or an option on the project itself *plus* the subsequent options to abandon the project at any stage. Applications include any time-sensitive R&D, such as the pharmaceutical development of new drug products. Other applications include large-scale construction products and the venture capital financing of start-up industries.

The time-to-build option is more valuable when the assets acquired through staged investment decisions can be resold (as in the regular abandonment option), but this is not a requirement. Abandoning a staged investment project midstream can make sense even when no costs incurred to date can be recovered. Consider the example—popularized in Danny DeVito's classic speech in the film *Other People's Money*[8]—of the buggy whip industry just after the invention of the automobile. If you were in the middle of staged investment expenditures in a new buggy whip factory when the auto came along, abandonment might make sense even if no recoveries were possible. Any such situation where demand falls *structurally* rather than *cyclically* can give the time-to-build abandonment option value. Considering the option from a different perspective, structuring investment decisions in a staged fashion makes more sense the more variable the demand for the final product at the completion of the investment project.

Operating Scale Option to Alter   Sometimes the abandonment of an asset or current investment is a bit extreme, even if a contraction in demand for the product produced by an investment-intensive production process suggests a smaller scale than initially thought. Temporary shut-down decisions can even make sense in this situation.

Conversely, suppose demand for the product being produced is much higher than expected. In that case, you might wish to incur additional investment expenditures in order to *expand* your capacity and meet this newly arrived demand.

The option to expand or contract (including temporary shut-down and restart decisions) is known as the option to alter operating scale. Common applications of the option to alter operating scale include:

- Natural resource extraction, where extraction costs vary with extraction rates and where output prices vary significantly over time.
- Facilities planning, construction, and real estate development, especially in cyclical industries such as entertainment.
- Fashion- and fad-sensitive industries, including entertainment, fashion apparel, and food service.

The Switching Option   The option to switch can refer to switching either inputs or outputs in a production process. Input switching is common in industries where production inputs are flexible, such as electric power and rotated-crop farming. In the former case, for example, power can be generated using natural gas turbines, hydroelectric and pump storage facilities, fossil fuels, nuclear fuels, and the like. If the price of natural gas rises significantly with respect to the price of fossil fuels like coal, the ability to switch generation from gas turbines to coal-fired plants is a valuable option.

Output switching is valuable and common in industries whose outputs are characterized both by volatile demand and by small-batch production. An excellent example of the output switching option that is beneficial to the product buyer and easily accommodated by the seller is the option to switch aircraft types provided by Airbus Industrie.[9] When airlines want to purchase aircraft from Airbus, they enter into purchase agreements that obligate them to a *family* of aircraft, but not to a specific type. The purchase agreements may give the airline the option to buy planes for several years. Once exercised, there is still a manufacturing lead time required to produce the aircraft. For example, a purchase agreement might entitle the airline to a four-year option to buy a family of aircraft and an 18-month manufacturing lead time between the airline's decision to exercise its purchase option and the actual delivery.

One family is the Airbus A319/A320/A321 family, which differ primarily based on number of seats; for example, the A319 and A320 seat 120 and 150 people, respectively, but otherwise do not differ materially. Another aircraft family is the A330/A340 family, which differ mainly based on distance (i.e., the A330 can be used for short-haul or long-haul flights, whereas the A340 is primarily a long-haul aircraft).

The flexibility afforded the purchaser of Airbus aircraft is the option to defer investment. Not only can the airlines decide not to purchase at all, but they can choose the product they want *after* getting a better sense of their demand curves. This flexibility can be offered by Airbus because of Airbus' own output switching option created by its standardized production processes. Specifically, each family of aircraft comes off the same assembly line. Because the A330 and A340 are produced on the same production line, the cost of switching A330 and A340 to meet customer demand is next to zero. This greatly enhances the ability of Airbus to tailor its production decisions to the demands of its customers.

The switching option can be viewed in the two-asset case (e.g., the option for airlines to choose between the A330 and A340) as an exchange option or an option on the better of two assets. An option on the better of two assets has a value at expiration time $t + T$ of

$$\max[S_1(t + T), S_2(t + T)] = S_1(t + T) - \max[S_1(t + T) - S_2(t + T), 0]$$

or the value of one asset (net of its acquisition costs) minus the value of the option to exchange that asset for a second asset. In the Airbus example, $S_1(t + T)$ and $S_2(t + T)$ might denote the present values to an airline of an A319 order and an A320 order, respectively, both of which would depend on the demand for travel observed at time $t + T$. A higher demand would increase the value of $S_2(t + T)$.

Interactive Growth Option The option for interactive growth is an option where the staged investment in one project opens up opportunities for growth in other areas. Mergers and acquisitions, for example, are obvious examples of transactions with embedded options for interactive growth. When one oil company merges with another, the merger target conveys on the acquiring firm its current assets *and* its own real options. The investment in the merger thus enables the acquiring firm to acquire the target's real options, as well as its current assets.

To consider another example, suppose a minerals exploration firm owns some land that has never been surveyed or explored. The firm can invest in exploration to determine what other real options the firm has— for example, exploration for oil can identify an oil reserve, which upon discovery then conveys to the firm the asset plus all the real options the asset conveys.

SHAREHOLDER VALUE ADDED

The NPV rule—both in its simple and augmented strategic form—is a reliable and sound investment rule that controls for risk properly, is consistent with an investment policy that maximizes shareholder wealth and the value of the firm, and is practically feasible to implement. Some managers do not like this rule because it is not just a simple "hurdle rate," but rather relies on actual nominal dollar amounts. Nevertheless, the economic foundations and practical applications of the rule make it tremendously useful.

Conceptually, *shareholder value added* (SVA) is just a small additional step beyond the NPV rule. Like the NPV rule, SVA calculations begin with expected future net cash flows discounted at the appropriate cost of capital. SVA involves several features, however, that take it well beyond the NPV rule. First, SVA attempts to value the whole firm before and after a project or strategy in order to focus on the marginal contribution of risk and return to the firm associated with the contemplated project or strategy.

Second, SVA focuses on returns to shareholders rather than the wealth created for the firm as a whole.

As a theoretical matter, SVA treats the value of the firm just as we expressed it in Chapter 1, equation (1.7):

$$V(t) = A(t) = V^A(t) + V^G(t)$$

$$= \underbrace{\sum_{u=1}^{U}\sum_{j=0}^{\infty}\frac{E[X_u(t+j)]}{1+E[R^A(t,\ t+j)]} - I_u(t)}_{\text{Market Value of Assets in Place in U Operating Divisions}} + \underbrace{\sum_{k=1}^{K}V_k^G(t)}_{\substack{\text{Market Value of K}\\\text{Growth Opportunities}}} \quad (5.13)$$

As a practical matter, SVA analysis splits this into three more easily identifiable components. The distinction between the first two components—*net cash flows from operations* and *residual value*—is based entirely on the notion of a forecast or performance period that represents the time horizon for the project or investment strategy being analyzed (rather than the infinite sum of all remaining cash flows as we have been doing until now). The third component to be added to those first two is just the value of the firm's investment portfolio in liquid marketable securities. Provided that portfolio is unrelated to the operations of the firm, the cash flows on that portfolio will not show up in operating cash flows and thus are added separately.

Suppose we fix the forecast period at T periods, which we can assume is the length of the useful life of the project being evaluated. The net cash flow from operations is just valued as

$$\sum_{j=1}^{T}\frac{E[X(t+j)]}{[1+E(R^{WACC})]^j} \quad (5.14)$$

Comparing equations (5.14) and (5.13), we can express the firm's residual value as

$$\underbrace{\sum_{j=T+1}^{\infty}\frac{E[X(t+j)]}{E(R^{WACC})}}_{\text{Residual Value}} + V^G(t) \quad (5.15)$$

where $V_G(t)$ denotes the time t present value of all growth opportunities facing the firm. The value of the firm expressed in (5.13) can be rewritten in more SVA-friendly terms as

$$
V(t) = \overbrace{\sum_{j=1}^{T} \frac{E[X(t+j)]}{[1+E(R^{WACC})]^j}}^{\text{PV of Net Operating Cash Flows}} + \overbrace{\sum_{j=T+1}^{\infty} \frac{E[X(t+j)]}{E(R^{WACC})} + V^G(t)}^{\text{Residual Value}}
$$

$$
+ \underbrace{Z(t)}_{\substack{\text{PV of Marketable} \\ \text{Securities in the Firm's} \\ \text{Investment Portfolio}}}
\tag{5.16}
$$

SVA analysis often uses what is known as the perpetuity method as a short-cut to equation (5.16). We essentially assume that the forecast period T is also the value growth period of the firm, after which the firm invests in only zero NPV projects.[10] In that case we can compute the residual value component as a perpetuity equal to the expected annual net cash flow of the firm—let's denote that $\overline{X}$—which has a present value of

$$
\frac{E(\overline{X})}{E(R^{WACC})}
\tag{5.17}
$$

so that the value of the firm expressed in (5.16) becomes just

$$
V(t) = \overbrace{\sum_{j=1}^{T} \frac{E[X(t+j)]}{[1+E(R^{WACC})]^j}}^{\text{PV of Net Operating Cash Flows}} + \overbrace{\sum_{j=T+1}^{\infty} \frac{E(\overline{X})}{E(R^{WACC})}}^{\text{Residual Value}} + \overbrace{Z(t)}^{\substack{\text{PV of Marketable} \\ \text{Securities in the Firm's} \\ \text{Investment Portfolio}}}
\tag{5.18}
$$

From equation (5.18)—or from the more general (5.16) if you prefer—we then define shareholder value as just the value of the firm given in one of these equations minus the market value of its debt. Shareholder value added (SVA) is just the incremental value added to shareholders by a given forecast scenario. For any given year in the forecast period, SVA is just the *cumulative* present value of operating cash flows plus the residual value. Alternatively, SVA is often computed for a project or scenario as the discounted present value of the increase in net operating profits after taxes (NOPAT) minus the incremental cost of the investment.

SVA is often translated into a more user-friendly hurdle rate, called *threshold margin*. The threshold margin is just the minimum operating profit margin that a business must sustain in any period in order to maintain shareholder value that period. Any operating profit margin below this threshold margin will result in the firm incurring a net reduction in value, because operating margin will be below the firm's cost of capital.

ECONOMIC VALUE ADDED AND RESIDUAL INCOME

Economic value added (EVA[11]) is a close cousin to SVA—a specific case of SVA, in fact, originally developed by General Electric in the 1950s (Rappaport 1998). The EVA or residual income of a project is defined as the net operating profits after taxes (NOPAT) of the project minus an absolute capital charge for the investment required to finance the project:

$$EVA = NOPAT - I(t)[1 + E(R^{WACC})] \qquad (5.19)$$

where NOPAT and the WACC are generally annual—or, at least, annualized. A closely related concept in the EVA world is the concept of *economic profit* (EP). This is just the excess of the project's ROI above the cost of capital, adjusted by the total capital the project ties up:

$$EP = [ROI - E(R^{WACC})]I(t) \qquad (5.20)$$

The difference between the project ROI and the cost of capital is known as the *residual return on capital* (RROC) or the *EVA spread*.

Net operating profit (NOPAT) is, of course, also related to the project's ROI. In fact,

$$NOPAT = I(t)(1 + ROI) \qquad (5.21)$$

Substituting (5.21) into (5.19) gives us (5.20). And discounting these expressions by the cost of capital returns us to our familiar old friend, the project's NPV:

$$NPV = \frac{I(t)[ROI - E(R^{WACC})]}{1 + E(R^{WACC})} = \frac{EVA}{1 + E(R^{WACC})} \qquad (5.22)$$

In other words, the net present value of a project is equal to the present value of the economic value added to the firm from that project, discounted at the firm's WACC.

The preceding can be translated into a variety of decision rules.

Equation (5.20) tells us, for example, to accept or maintain only those projects with a positive EVA spread:

$$ROI > E(R^{WACC})$$

Or we express the rule in dollar amounts to say that a project should be accepted only if it has a positive EVA:

$$NOPAT - I(t)[1 + E(R^{WACC})] > 0$$

And, of course, we can restate the NPV criterion in EVA terms—accept a project only if

$$\frac{EVA}{1 + E(R^{WACC})} > 0$$

Implementation of the Theory

The preceding discussion is all nice and fine, but, of course, the proof of the pudding is in the eating. EVA, like SVA, is populated with accounting variables, and numerous tweaks and adjustments may be required to do a proper job of it. Consulting firms and software vendors earn a lot of money each year by helping firms do the required computations.

Rappaport (1998) usefully identifies three variants of EVA-like measures that have enjoyed fairly widespread use as the basis of project selection, performance measurement, and value-based management systems. The first is the original formulation proposed in the 1950s by General Electric that relies on residual income as the core driver of project selection and performance review. In this original formulation, the amount of invested capital—which, when multiplied by the cost of capital, yields the capital charge in equation (5.19)—is book value. By contrast, the specific version of EVA promulgated by Stern Stewart & Company—from whence the trademarked name "EVA" comes—replaces book capital with "economic book capital" in an effort to better capture the cash invested in the business or project that is not reflected in pure book capital. Finally, some firms focus primarily on the periodic *change* in EVA or residual income.

Common Criticisms

EVA is often criticized on the grounds that it is a short-term snapshot of the firm's financial condition. This is not entirely true. EVA merely collapses longer-term items into single entries. Grant (2003) notes that "economic profit (EVA) is the *annualized* equivalent of the firm's net present value." Some information may be lost in the simplification, but not enough to distort decision making—at least not solely for reasons associated with time.

Another potential problem with EVA analysis is its inability to handle growth options easily. One can modify EVA applications to develop analogues to strategic NPV, but they can seem a bit forced at times. If a firm wishes to account explicitly for real options and growth opportunities, the NPV framework is more naturally accommodating.

Perhaps the most significant problem with EVA analysis when applied to existing projects or a firm on the whole is its reliance on book value as a starting point against which shareholder value added can be compared. In both the traditional residual income and EVA implementations, the capital invested in a project or business is a sunk cost; it is not an estimate of expected future cash flows, but rather prior investment spending. Apart from representing a sunk cost, book capital numbers (adjusted or unadjusted) are also *noncash* charges that may or may not correspond closely to a firm's or project's actual cash flows.

Differences with SVA

Although SVA and the various versions of EVA we just discussed have fundamentally similar conceptual foundations, they are implemented fairly differently in practice. One important difference concerns the treatment of future time periods by the two approaches. In the SVA concept, there is a more explicit forecast period followed by a residual income term that reflects the cash flows beyond the forecast period. One could criticize SVA if the forecast period is too short and misses important longer-term cash flow developments. Yet the forecast period provides a more explicit breakdown and modeling of the per-period cash flows than does EVA and thus is slightly more general. Nevertheless, one must remember in both cases that a firm will generally trade at least some precision for tractability, especially if the loss of precision does not lead to downright erroneous investment decisions. The annualization simplification of EVA and the forecast period simplification of SVA are unlikely to change the "go/no go" decision for a project, but these issues may become more important in capital rationing when a firm is forced to choose between multiple projects—a situation when small differences may really count.

The major difference between SVA and EVA pertains to the way investments and real capital are reflected in the models. In the EVA model, capital is book or adjusted book capital, whereas the SVA approach uses the true present values of beginning and ending assets. In this sense, SVA computes value added relative to a forward-looking estimate of future cash flows and not relative to a sunk cost measure of past investment decisions. When book capital is used, the investment expenditures all precede the performance evaluation period. In this sense, SVA is a much more realistic depiction of the true economic benefits and costs of a project. SVA's reliance on investments made during the forecast period instead of those preceding it also makes SVA a much more reliable tool of analysis for use in *ex ante* project selection.

Change in Residual Income or Change in EVA

Although residual income and EVA both represent estimates of value added based on historical cost measures, the *change* in residual income or EVA, when properly measured, yields virtually the same information as SVA. Specifically, the change in EVA over a given year is equal to the SVA times the cost of capital for that year (Rappaport, 1998).

CASH FLOW RETURN ON INVESTMENT

Cash flow return on investment (CFROI[12]) is essentially a posttax IRR for a firm's existing assets. It is the rate that equates the present value of all future cash flows on those assets already in place to the investment cost of acquiring those assets. For project selection, one computes CFROI before the new project and then after the inclusion of the new project. When CFROI exceeds a firm's cost of capital after the inclusion of the cash flows on a new project, that project can be selected as a value-enhancing project.

CFROI is extremely similar to EVA. In fact, the only substantive difference occurs if the annualization effect of the EVA calculation somehow loses information that the CFROI calculation preserves. As a matter of pure theory, the metrics will lead to identical decisions (Grant 2003).

Look back at equation (5.21), where we defined the NOPAT of a project as its investment cost grossed up at the expected return on capital for the project. Rearranging the equation, we get

$$\frac{NOPAT}{(1+ROI)} = I(t) \qquad (5.23)$$

from which it is obvious that ROI is also the IRR for the project. Because NOPAT is an after-tax profit, the CFROI metric is identical to ROI in the EVA measurement system.

In EVA measurement, firms pursue those projects with nonnegative economic profits. Economic profit is positive when the EVA spread or residual return on capital is positive. As we can now see, this is equivalent in a CFROI framework to a firm pursuing a project only when its CFROI (IRR) exceeds the firm's WACC.

CHAPTER 6

Risk Transfer

Recall from Chapter 2 (see especially Exhibit 2.1) that firms can manage the risks they face in the normal course of their businesses (core and noncore risks alike) in one of three ways: retention, neutralization, and transfer. Our focus in this chapter is on risk transfer: when it makes sense and can benefit a firm, and how risk transfer is related to a firm's capital structure.

RISK TRANSFER AND EQUITY CAPITAL

In the early 1990s, a senior manager at a huge, globally active European bank was asked what his bank's philosophy was toward risk management. He is said to have replied, "Having enough equity to absorb any large loss." On the one hand, his statement was probably true for that bank and his logic reflects the essential correspondence between risk and capital—large amounts of equity capital to absorb losses make costly risk transfer programs less necessary and appealing, all else being equal. On the other hand, the absorption of large losses may not have been the *best* use of the firm's funds. The bank's equity holders didn't think so—the senior manager did not keep his job for long after making this apocryphal statement.

At a fundamental level, risk transfer and equity capital are essentially similar. All else being equal, more equity capital makes it less likely that a firm will encounter financial distress and thus accomplishes much the same thing as transferring those risks that expose a firm to possible ruin. But what about risks to which a firm may be exposed that are *not* catastrophic? And what if the firm's goal in managing risk is not merely the protection of capitalized net asset values, but rather the protection of its per-period earnings or cash flows? In the worst case, new equity may not actually work to help the firm accomplish its risk management objectives. Even in the best case, an additional equity cushion may work, but it may be overkill.

Risk transfer is much more "surgical" in nature than issuing new equity. True, additional equity will absorb losses the firm may take, but it will absorb *any* losses incurred by the firm no matter what the size or the source of risk (i.e., core or noncore). Risk transfer, by contrast, can be much more specifically tailored by a firm to specific loss levels, risk types, and the like. Transferring risk using derivatives or insurance thus can be accomplished *selectively*, whereas transferring risk to new equity holders cannot.

Yet many corporate treasurers still question the need for hedging and insurance, especially when the firm in question is already capital-rich and highly rated. The more costly the risk transfer solution, the less such firms will appreciate its benefits. Those costs are usually fairly transparent—for example, the cost of paying premium for insurance or options; the cost of forgone profits if using futures, forwards, or swaps; and so on. The benefits are less obvious, and it is to those benefits that we now turn our attention.

RISK TRANSFER AND THE VALUE OF THE FIRM

Under the same four M&M assumptions that guarantee independence between the value of the firm and its capital structure, the value of the firm is also independent of any deliberate actions taken by management to control risks through hedging or insurance purchasing. The reason is simple: Shareholders can manage risks *themselves.*

Consider a corporate farm whose business is selling corn to grain elevators and millers. Residual claimants that own the farm will find that the value of their cash flows and the value of the farm's assets are strongly and directly related to corn prices. When the price of corn rises, the farm's revenues rise, all else being equal. And conversely, falling corn prices mean decreasing farm revenues.

Under the M&M assumption of symmetric information, shareholders know the impact of corn price risk on their pro rata claim on the farm just as well as the farm's managers do. And under the M&M assumption of equal access, any individual shareholders can engage in financial transactions on the same terms as the farm itself—terms that include zero transaction costs under the perfect capital markets assumption.

The final M&M assumption is that investment decisions are taken as given. So, shareholders look at the investment decisions of the firm and its product market exposure to corn prices, and then determine *on their own* whether they want to bear corn price risk as a part of their investment portfolios. If not, shareholders can neutralize their corn price risk exposure quite easily by buying shares in a grain elevator or mill. Otherwise, they do nothing and diversify away their idiosyncratic risks as they normally would. In either case, the decision whether to manage the corn price risk *was made by the shareholder.*

All opportunities for risk management to increase firm value require the violation of one or more M&M assumptions. But even when those assumptions are violated, a firm whose managers adhere to the market value rule can benefit from risk management only in certain circumstances. Specifically, in order for risk transfer to add value to a firm, it must *either* reduce the firm's cost of capital *or* increase its expected future net cash flows.

In addition, we want to bear in mind that in a *non*-M&M world, firms may derive gains from managing the impact of risks on their earnings and/or per-period cash flows. That would never be the case in an M&M world,[1] but it *is* in reality. As we summarize next the various gains to a firm from engaging in risk transfer, we want to keep in mind that the appropriate risk management strategies for exploiting these gains will depend on whether the firm is seeking capital, earnings, or cash flow protection.

Reducing Expected Taxes

When a firm faces a *convex* corporate tax schedule, hedging can reduce expected tax liabilities and increase the firm's expected net cash flows. A convex tax schedule is one in which a firm's average tax rate rises as pretax income rises. This can occur because of progressivity in the corporate tax rate, the impact of the alternative minimum tax, tax carryforwards and tax credits, and other tax shields that defer taxation.

The basic intuition here is straightforward. Suppose a firm has two possible pretax earnings levels, X_1 and X_2, that may occur with any probability ρ and $(1 - \rho)$, respectively. Suppose further that the firm can lock in its earnings at level X^* for a cost C, where $X^* = E(X) = \rho X_1 + (1 - \rho)X_2$. Hedged earnings thus are locked in at $X^* - C$.

Associated with each level of earnings is a tax liability $T(X_j)$ where T is an increasing and convex function of X; that is, $T(X) \geq 0$ for all X, $\partial T/\partial X > 0$, and $\partial^2 T/\partial X^2 > 0$. If the firm locks in its earnings, its known tax liability is $T(X^*)$. Otherwise, the firm's expected tax liability is $E[T(X)] = \rho T(X_1) + (1 - \rho)T(X_2)$. By Jensen's inequality, we know that $T[\rho X_1 + (1 - \rho)X_2] < \rho T(X_1) + (1 - \rho)T(X_2)$ since $T(\cdot)$ is convex; that is, $T(X^*) < E[T(X)]$. Provided that $T(X^*) - E[T(X)] < C$, the tax savings from locking in earnings and avoiding the high tax rate on high earnings levels is less than the cost of hedging, and hedging thus can increase the firm's value.

To put things in plainer language, a firm facing a given change in earnings and a convex tax schedule will have a greater tax increase when earnings rise than the tax liability reduction that will occur if earnings decline by the same amount. Some firms would prefer to stabilize their earnings in order to avoid these disproportionate and unexpected large tax increases. Transferring risk is the obvious way to engage in such earnings volatility reduction.

Reducing Expected Financial Distress Costs

We discussed the expected costs of financial distress in Chapter 3. Hedging or purchasing insurance is often associated with the attempt by firms to avoid catastrophic losses that could expose the firm to positive distress costs and, in the extreme, to ruin. Firms that use risk transfer to mitigate the risk of ruin may seek to manage both their core and noncore risk exposures.

The objective of risk transfer undertaken for this reason generally is capital preservation, or, more concretely, the protection of a firm's net asset values.

Mitigating Underinvestment

If a positive net present value (NPV) project is rejected by the firm in the absence of a risk management program but accepted otherwise, then the benefit of risk transfer is fairly clear. As we discussed in Chapter 3, one reason firms may decline positive NPV projects owes to "debt overhang." (Myers 1977) If a firm has too much debt, shareholders may opt to reject positive NPV projects because the benefits of a successful project will go mainly to pay off debt holders, whereas the risks of an unsuccessful project affect primarily equity holders. We called this underinvestment, and this problem can be mitigated if hedging or insurance is used to increase the firm's debt capacity and decrease its effective leverage.

Underinvestment may also occur if a firm's cash flows are depleted and the costs of issuing new securities to finance the new project are prohibitive (Froot, Scharfstein, and Stein, 1993, 1994). In this case, a firm may hedge its cash flows to try to ensure that enough internal funds are always available to exploit all positive NPV investment opportunities.

Reducing Asset Substitution Monitoring Costs

If managers of the firm respond to shareholders more than to creditors and if costly monitoring mechanisms like bond covenants are not used, managers may choose excessively risky projects to the benefit of equity and at the expense of debt. If the firm can selectively hedge the volatility of net cash flows on projects with positive NPVs but with high risks, managers may be discouraged from taking on excessively risky projects when they result in the expropriation of bondholders to the benefit of stockholders.

Mitigating Excessive Managerial Risk Aversion

In general, when too much of a manager's wealth is tied up in his compensation package, his expected utility starts to depend on the value of the firm where he works. If the manager faces capital market imperfections or does not have equal access to the market, he may not be able to diversify away enough of these risks and thus may begin to behave more conservatively than security holders prefer. In an effort to keep the firm solvent and preserve his primary source of income, a manager might reject high-risk but high-NPV investment projects—again, underinvestment.

Selective hedging or insurance of catastrophic risks can help assuage managers' concerns in this regard and thus mitigate underinvestment.

Reducing Adverse Selection Costs

As we discussed in Chapter 4, new issues of debt and equity to public investors often occur at a discount owing to asymmetric information and adverse selection. Firms with high adverse selection costs can utilize risk transfer to lower their costs of capital.

One way that risk transfer can lower a firm's adverse selection costs and its cost of capital is to reduce the need for public securities issues. Risk finance will also do the trick if this is the goal, as we discuss later in this chapter and again in Chapter 7.

Risk transfer also reduces adverse selection costs if the adverse selection costs are themselves related to concerns about the performance of projects arising from noncore risks that can be insured or hedged. Consider, for example, an oil company looking to expand into the power business by generating power to be transmitted and distributed through a network of lines and transformers. Investors may worry that the transmission and distribution network is too susceptible to physical asset risks arising from weather, terrorism, vandalism, and the like and that management is better informed about the true nature of those risks than it has revealed to investors. By purchasing insurance, the company can assuage any concerns outsiders might have about these risks. In general, any time adverse selection costs arise over hedgeable or insurable risks, hedging or insuring those risks will reduce adverse selection costs and lower the cost of capital.

Finally, hedging and buying insurance reduce the amount of equity that the firm needs to hold in order to minimize its expected costs of financial distress. This equity capital may be subject to adverse selection costs (e.g., if it is obtained through a seasoned equity offering). By insulating the firm from shocks and reducing the equity the firm needs to hold to maintain a given risk level, risk transfer thus enables firms to escape the adverse selection costs that may have been incurred through the issuance of additional equity required in the absence of the risk transfer program.

Synthetic Diversification

At a closed corporation whose owners cannot fully diversify their idiosyncratic risks, shareholders may be *incapable* of holding diversified portfolios because so much of their wealth is tied up in their own firm. In this case, hedging can reduce the cost of capital by lessening the impact of idiosyncratic risks on the firm's manager/owners.

Enhancing the Quality of Earnings

The accounting treatment afforded to different risk transfer strategies is relevant to a very large number of corporate risk managers. If a firm successfully uses insurance and/or derivatives to reduce its risks but cannot show that in its financial statements, the hedging program may be of limited use. In other words, many firms have hedging objectives that are defined in terms of how their hedging strategies impact certain accounting aggregates, such as earnings.

We have to tread very lightly here and be extremely careful to distinguish between legitimate earnings-oriented motivations for engaging in risk transfer as compared to the far less legitimate practice of abusing risk transfer contracts for the purpose of misstating earnings and misleading investors. Earnings, remember, are just a proximate opinion about a firm's financial condition, as we explained in Chapter 5. The reason it is necessary to report earnings is that investors rarely have the ability to observe the firm's true cash flows. As such, earnings are a signal of the firm's true financial quality, albeit a noisy one.

Consider a firm whose per-period earnings have an average level of μ and are subject to two types of random shocks. Earnings shock ε_t reflects unexpected gains and losses arising from the firm's core business activities, and η_t denotes shocks to earnings arising from noncore risks. Earnings reported at time t thus can be written as

$$Y_t = \mu + \varepsilon_t + \eta_t$$

In turn, we can write the *volatility* of earnings as

$$\sigma_Y^2 = \sigma_\varepsilon^2 + \sigma_\eta^2 + 2\sigma_{\varepsilon\eta}$$

The only things that outsiders observe are the reporting earnings number, Y_t, and its volatility, σ_Y^2. With this framework in hand, we can now discuss several different ways that a firm can benefit from adopting risk transfer strategies that help improve the quality of earnings releases.

Catastrophic Protection Against Core Risks   In certain industries and at some firms, outsiders like analysts, security holders, rating agencies, and the like may penalize the firm for unexplained increases in reported earnings volatility based on the belief that these volatility increases are driven by ε_t—the firm's core business risks—that could expose the firm to costly financial distress and the risk of ruin.

Risk transfer products like insurance can be useful to such firms by putting a sort of floor on core business shocks. Catastrophic protection of that sort will at least persuade investors that despite the increase in core business risk, the firm's financial health will not be significantly jeopardized by that increase in risk.

Decreasing Adverse Selection Costs   High earnings volatility can raise the adverse selection costs of public securities offerings, as we discussed in Chapter 4. Because outsiders cannot distinguish between risk arising from hedgeable and insurable activities and risk arising from poor fundamental business decisions, they likely will assume the latter. This in turn depresses the prices at which the firm can issue new debt and equity securities.

Risk transfer can also make sense for firms when noncore risks contribute so much to total earnings volatility that outsiders are unable to assess the true quality of the firm's investment opportunities and core business operations. This is most likely to occur when the firm's noncore risks contribute significantly to the firm's reporting earnings volatility on their own (i.e., σ_η^2 is high) and when noncore shocks to the firm's earnings are positively correlated with core shocks (i.e., $\sigma_{\varepsilon\eta}$ is positive). In these situations, transferring the noncore risks of the firm to another market participant will reduce both noncore risk on its own and the contribution to total earnings volatility arising from the positive correlation between core and non-core risk. Outsiders will then be better able to assess the true business performance of the firm, thus reducing adverse selection costs.

Increasing the Ratio of Signal to Noise   Because the firm can insure against or hedge the risks that generate the non-core earnings shock η, we can describe the volatility of this component of earnings as noise. As we just discussed, firms may find it useful to use risk transfer products to reduce noise simply to give investors a higher-quality estimate of the firm's financial performance. But there may also be another reason.

Suppose we consider a firm in an industry that is generally performing poorly relative to expectations (e.g., telecom or Internet firms in the late 1990s). Suppose further that the firm in question happens to be one of the few firms in that industry whose primary business is going strong. High earnings volatility arising from noncore risks can obfuscate this strong performance and make the firm look like all the other dogs in the industry.

Telecommunications in the late 1990s is a perfect example of this problem. Most firms were relatively small with minimal cross-border activities and were performing poorly because of bad investments, unproven technologies, the failure of broadband markets to materialize, and the like. A handful of large multinational telecom firms generally avoided the risky and unproven technologies of the moment. Those firms, however, showed earnings volatility comparable to the small bad performers. In their case, it was often exchange rate fluctuations causing the problem. Hedging that exchange rate risk thus stripped out a significant amount of noise from their earnings and showed investors that their performance was in fact much stronger than would have appeared to be the case by looking at the industry as a whole.

As we noted in Chapter 4, a signal is useful only if bad types cannot imitate good types, and the telecom example is again a fruitful illustration of this idea. For those strong firms with high earnings volatility arising from noncore exchange rate risk, hedging reduced earnings volatility and revealed the true quality of those firms' businesses. Other firms could not imitate that behavior because they did not really have any material exchange rate risk. The smaller firms' risk was mainly bad performance in their core business, and this was not something those firms could eliminate—at least, not without basically closing their doors, which many eventually did.

Quality of Earnings, Not Earnings Management Earnings-based motivations for firms to engage in risk transfer may be economically legitimate. But extreme care should be taken not to confuse earnings *risk* management with earnings management. The former is the stabilization of earnings for one of the reasons already discussed—to reduce expected distress costs, to solve adverse selection problems, and to increase the quality of information contained in an earnings release. All of these reasons for earnings risk management represent an effort by a firm to improve the *quality* of its earnings.

"Earnings management," by contrast, is usually a pejorative term associated with firms attempting deliberately to smooth reported income and conceal the firm's true financial condition from outsiders. This is *not* an appropriate use of risk transfer products, needless to say.

Especially with recent controversies about earnings management at a fever pitch, firms must take great care not to stray across the line that separates legitimate earnings risk management from inappropriate earnings management. Invariably, the best way to do this is through extremely detailed disclosures. We will return to this issue again in Chapter 24.

RISK TRANSFER VERSUS RISK CAPITAL

Risk capital is financial capital allocated or assigned to absorb specific risks and/or to guarantee the performance on specific portfolios. Mechanically, risk capital is essentially cash set aside in a loss reserve with the specific purpose of providing a cushion against losses that may arise in a particular business line or asset/liability portfolio.

Risk capital and risk capital allocation have limited applications for nonfinancial corporations. Few corporate treasurers think about allocating capital to specific risks. As discussed earlier in this chapter, it is much more common for corporations to think about protecting net profits, cash flows, or earnings. Nevertheless, this focus by most corporates on variables other than capital does not change the fundamental relationship between risk capital and risk transfer acquired for capital preservation purposes. That relationship is relevant even to firms focused solely on earnings or cash flows, moreover, because the essential similarities of risk capital and risk transfer affect the relationship between the *costs* of these alternative sources of capital protection.

To explore the relations between risk capital and financial capital, we will use a modified version of the model presented by Merton and Perold (1993). Suppose we consider a company called Enterprise, Inc., that is a wholly owned subsidiary of a default-risk-free parent corporation—say, a bank. Enterprise contemplates buying a single risky loan on the secondary market with a face value of $100 million with one year remaining to maturity and a single remaining fixed interest payment of 20 percent. If the loan does not default, Enterprise will earn $120 million in principal and interest (P&I) on the loan over the next year. But because the loan is risky, the borrower may well default. In one default scenario (called "partial recovery"), the borrower defaults and Enterprise is able to recover 75 percent of the loan principal. In this scenario, Enterprise earns $75 million for the year. Alternatively, the borrower may default and pay no recoveries at all (called "total default"), in which case Enterprise has no earnings at all for the year. Finally, suppose the market price of the loan is currently $100 million.

Case I: External Credit Risk Transfer

Suppose the risk-free interest rate is 10 percent. Enterprise, Inc., decides to raise the $100 million it needs to buy the loan by issuing *default-risk-free* debt with a face value of $100 million. This creates a $110 million payment obligation in a year. But because Enterprise has borrowed at the risk-free rate, Enterprise now must "credit enhance" the note to guarantee the $110 payment obligation. Enterprise may obtain credit enhancement externally by buying insurance on the loan or may obtain the credit enhancement internally from the firm's equity investors. Let's consider the former situation first as our Case I.

Suppose Enterprise buys a type of credit insurance or guaranty that reimburses the firm dollar for dollar on any loss that occurs on its loan asset up to the face value of the asset of $110 million. The total cost is $5 million for this external credit protection or risk transfer. (We'll discuss actual credit insurance and guaranties later in Chapter 10.)

In the event of a default on the loan, the insurer makes a cash payment to Enterprise to cover the loss up to $110 million. That guaranty is itself an asset. Together, the loan and the guaranty ensure that Enterprise, Inc., *always* has adequate funds to repay its note holders fully, thus making the Enterprise debt free of default risk. The accounting and economic balance sheets of Enterprise, Inc., are shown in Exhibit 6.1. In this case, the two are the same.

Table 6.1 shows the various payoffs in the three scenarios. In the no-default scenario, Enterprise receives $120 million in P&I, $110 million of

(a) Accounting Balance Sheet

Assets		Liabilities and Equity	
Loan	$100	Riskless Note	$100
Guaranty	$5	Equity	$5

(b) Economic Balance Sheet

Assets		Liabilities and Equity	
Loan	$100	Riskless Note	$100
Guaranty	$5	Equity	$5

EXHIBIT 6.1   Balance Sheets for Enterprise, Inc., with External Financial Guaranty ($millions)
Source: Merton and Perold (1993).

TABLE 6.1 Payoffs after One Year with External Financial Guaranty ($millions)

	Assets			Liabilities/Equity	
Scenario	Loan	Guaranty	Guaranteed Loan	Note	Equity
No Default	$120	$ 0	$120	$110	$10
Partial Recovery	75	35	110	110	0
Total Default	0	110	110	110	0

Source: Merton and Perold (1993).

which goes to bondholders and $10 million of which goes back to the parent corporation as the sole equity holder in Enterprise, Inc. In either of the two default scenarios, the financial guaranty pays off up to $110 million, in which case note holders are always repaid *but* equity's residual claim is worthless. So, the financial guarantor as the external provider of credit enhancement bears all the credit risk of the loan participation, and Enterprise, Inc.'s parent corporation as its sole equity holder bears only the cost of the premium paid for the credit enhancement.

Case II: Credit Protection Provided by Parent Guaranty

Now suppose that instead of purchasing external credit protection for the loan, Enterprise instead seeks a guaranty for the repayment of its debt from its parent corporation—an *internal* credit enhancement provided by the sole equity holder of the firm. In this case, the parent corporation need not even make an explicit equity investment in Enterprise—its equity stake comes through its guaranty. We can see this in the accounting balance sheet for Enterprise shown in Panel (a) of Exhibit 6.2.

In this situation, the risk of nonperformance on the asset is borne completely by the parent company. If a default and partial recovery occurs, the parent will have to make a cash infusion of $35 million to enable Enterprise, Inc. to repay its note holders in full. And in the total default scenario, the cash payment from the parent will be the full $110 million required to pay off debt claimants.

Note in Exhibit 6.2 on the economic balance sheet in Panel (b) that the parent guaranty shows up on both sides of the balance sheet. That the guaranty is an economic asset is fairly obvious. Less obvious is that the credit enhancement is essentially a type of equity capital. Merton and Perold (1993) call this *risk capital*, which we discuss in Appendix C. But how did we know that the value of this credit enhancement was $5 million?

(a) Accounting Balance Sheet

Assets		Liabilities and Equity	
Loan	$100	Riskless Note	$100

(b) Economic Balance Sheet

Assets		Liabilities and Equity	
Loan	$100	Riskless Note	$100
Parent Guaranty	$5	Credit Enhancement	$5

EXHIBIT 6.2   Balance Sheets for Enterprise, Inc., with Internal Parent Guaranty ($millions)
Source: Merton and Perold (1993).

For our answer, note the payoffs to claim holders shown in Table 6.2. Because the cash flows for the parent corporation on the guaranty are *identical* to the cash flows on the external financial guaranty shown in Table 6.1, the credit enhancement (i.e., risk capital) in this case should have the same value as in the explicit guaranty of $5 million.

Case III: Credit Protection Provided by Investors in Default-Risky Debt

Now suppose that Enterprise, Inc., is willing to issue debt that is subject to default risk. In this case, a 10 percent note with face value of $100 million will no longer be riskless. So that it can return more than the 10 percent riskless rate, the note will issue at a discount to par of, say, $δ million. But if Enterprise, Inc., only raises $100 − δ million from note investors, it does

TABLE 6.2   Payoffs after One Year with Internal Parent Guaranty ($millions)

Scenario	Assets			Liabilities/Equity	
	Loan	Guaranty	Guaranteed Loan	Note	Equity
No Default	$120	$ 0	$120	$110	$10
Partial Recovery	75	35	110	110	0
Total Default	0	110	110	110	0

Source: Merton and Perold (1993).

TABLE 6.3   Payoffs after One Year with Risky Debt ($millions)

	Assets			Liabilities/Equity	
Scenario	Loan	Guaranty	Guaranteed Loan	Note	Equity
No Default	$120	$ 0	$120	$110	$10
Partial Recovery	75	35	110	75	0
Total Default	0	110	110	0	0

Source: Merton and Perold (1993).

not have enough to buy the loan. Clearly, the firm will have to issue new equity in the amount of δ million. Suppose Enterprise raises the additional funds by issuing stock to its parent.

Table 6.3 shows the cash flows in all three scenarios for the loan. The asset called "insurance" is the insurance provided by the holders of the risky debt. In the partial recovery scenario, for example, the loan is worth only $75 million, so note holders receive only $75 million. But we can view that $75 million as the $110 million value of a riskless note minus $35 million in insurance payments note holders make to the firm to cover the asset shortfall.

Notice in Table 6.3 that Enterprise's parent has exactly the same cash flows as the financial guarantor and as it would have had in the case where an explicit parental guaranty was offered. Accordingly, the value of the equity must be $5 million initially, thus making the debt worth $95 million upon issue with an expected return of 15.8 percent or $15 million on $95 million.

Exhibit 6.3 shows the accounting and economic balance sheets for

(a) Accounting Balance Sheet

Assets		Liabilities and Equity	
Loan	$100	Note	$95
		Equity	$5

(b) Economic Balance Sheet

Assets		Liabilities and Equity	
Loan	$100	Note	$100
Insurance	$5	Credit Enhancement	$5

EXHIBIT 6.3   Balance Sheets for Enterprise, Inc., with Risky Debt ($millions)
Source: Merton and Perold (1993).

Enterprise, Inc. Debt has an economic value of $100 million, as compared to a book value of $95 million. The difference arises from the fact that debt holders have now essentially sold asset insurance to the firm for its assets.

We know from Chapter 1 that we can view a risky bond as a riskless loan plus a short put option on the firm's assets. This short put is what we are calling asset insurance that the note holders have sold to the firm. Looking at Table 6.3, it may help to consider the risky bond in this manner as having two components whose payoffs are netted—the riskless note and an insurance contract that note holders have written. As the value of the loan declines, Enterprise note holders must pay more to the firm in loan insurance—equivalent to getting less of their P&I back. The additional $5 million in the value of the bond on the economic balance sheet shown in Panel (b) of Exhibit 6.3 is the insurance premium that the bondholders charge for providing the risk capital in this case. Not surprisingly, the value of this insurance is the same as the premium paid for the financial guaranty and the value of the credit enhancement when it was provided by the parent corporation (i.e., by equity holders rather than note holders).

CHAPTER **7**

Risk Finance

We encountered the term *risk finance* in Chapter 2. To repeat what we said there, risk finance is the process by which a firm tries to ensure that it has the adequate funds to survive a large unexpected financial loss arising from a risk that the firm has deliberately retained. *Preloss* risk finance represents funds that have been set prior to the loss, and *postloss* risk financing arrangements are funds that are raised after a loss—but on preloss terms—to help a firm weather the cash consequences of the loss.

A traditional example of preloss finance is funding a loss reserve, and nontraditional types of preloss finance include captives and captivelike structures, funded blended finite deals, and financial reinsurance. A traditional example of postloss finance is a draw on a credit or bank line, whereas nontraditional examples include contingent capital and unfunded blended finite deals. We will revisit all these nontraditional sources of risk finance later in this book.

Be careful to distinguish between the postloss financing of a retention and an unfunded retention. A retention is any risk that a firm retains; that is, if the risk translates into a loss, the shareholders of the firm (and perhaps other stakeholders in the firm, as well) ultimately bear the full force of that loss. An unfunded retention is a retention for which a company essentially sets aside no actual funds or sources of funds to help get through any loss arising from that retention. If the firm needs additional cash following such a loss, it can, of course, issue new securities or tap its retained earnings. But this is fundamentally different from a *funded* retention, in which the firm identifies either specific funds (in the case of preloss finance) or a specific source of raising additional funds (in the case of postloss finance) in order to cover any cash shortfalls arising from losses.

CASH FLOW DISTINCTIONS BETWEEN
PRE- AND POSTLOSS FUNDING

Preloss finance is the economic equivalent of establishing a loss reserve. When financed with equity, preloss finance is paid-in risk capital as discussed in Chapter 6. When financed with additional debt, preloss finance is just a means of liquidity management.

Although we will see in Chapters 23 and 24 that there are far better ways of prefunding a loss than with a reserve, for now a reserve is probably the best way to visualize a preloss funding structure. In short, the company wishing to earmark funds for a specific loss funds a reserve out of its current cash flows and retained earnings or by issuing new securities. Those funds are held until the risk event either does or does not occur. If it occurs, the funds are available to pay off the loss immediately. If the risk event does not translate into a loss, the reserve is freed or rolled forward to cover a new future risk event.

One of the most common methods firms use to fund their retained risks is indeed through the use of economic reserves. We use the term *economic reserves* to distinguish the concept from *accounting reserves*. Economic reserves are a type of preloss risk finance in which the firm takes cash that it already has and earmarks that cash for application to a future loss event. In the event the loss event does not occur, the reserve either is maintained and earmarked for the next such possible loss event or is released with the funds flowing back into the company's free cash flow.

Postloss finance is the economic equivalent to a firm buying a put option on its own debt. If a risk event translates into a future loss, the firm can exercise or draw down the facility and borrow at a prenegotiated rate, using the proceeds of the borrowing to finance the loss. If no loss occurs, the facility expires unused. In exchange for giving firms the right but not the obligation to incur new debt, the provider of postloss finance will charge the firm a *commitment fee*, the economic equivalent of a put option premium.

Exhibits 7.1 and 7.2 provide a concrete example of preloss versus postloss risk finance. In the examples, we assume that a firm is facing a potential loss sometime in a risk period spanning the next two years. If the loss occurs, the firm would like to finance that loss out five years with a new debt issue at a rate negotiated in quarter 0. When the facilities are negotiated, the firm knows only that *if* the loss occurs, it must make a $100 million payment in the same quarter as the loss. The firm does not know whether the loss will occur, nor in which quarter of the risk period the loss will occur. In the figure, *in*flows appear above the time line and cash *out*flows are below.

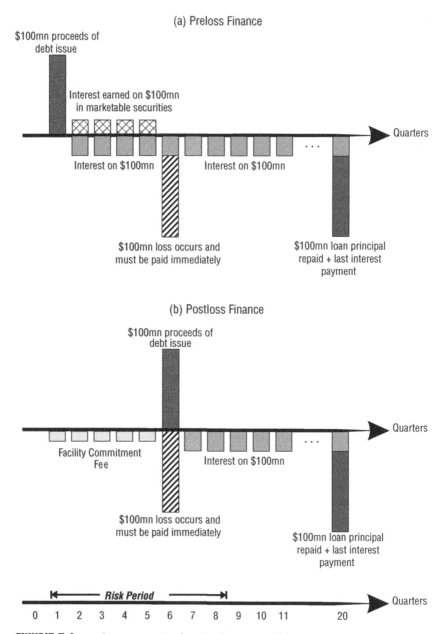

EXHIBIT 7.1   Preloss versus Postloss Risk Finance If the Loss Event Occurs

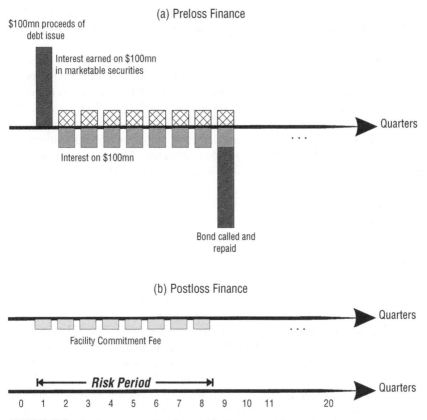

EXHIBIT 7.2 Preloss versus Postloss Risk Finance with No Loss Event

If the firm funds the retention on a preloss basis, depicted in Panel (a) of Exhibit 7.1, it will set aside $100 million in the first quarter in a loss reserve. To fund the reserve, the firm either diverts cash out of current cash balances (probably a part of working capital or retained earnings) or issues new debt. For comparability to the postloss structure, suppose the firm issues $100 million in debt in the first quarter. This provides the firm with the $100 million it will need to cover the expected loss if that loss occurs, and, in so doing, has allowed the firm to finance the loss gradually over the entire five-year term of the debt issue. In addition, the firm can invest the proceeds of the debt issue in highly marketable securities until the loss occurs, thus reducing its net interest expenses to the *spread* between the cost of its newly issued debt and the income on the marketable securities held. After the loss occurs, of course, the firm has used the $100 million and no longer earns any interest income to defray its ongoing interest expense.

In this example, the postloss financing structure allows the firm to issue new debt at any time up to quarter 8 with a fixed debt maturity of quarter 20. For this right, the firm pays a commitment fee up to the date on which the facility is drawn. As shown in Panel (b) of Exhibit 7.1, the loss occurs in quarter 6, at which time the firm draws down the entire $100 million facility and generates a cash inflow of $100 million to exactly offset its loss obligation that quarter. The commitment fee disappears thereafter, but the firm has now incurred a 3.5-year debt obligation.

Exhibit 7.2 shows the same two facilities, but now we assume the loss never occurs. In Panel (a), we see that the firm still has the new $100 million in debt set aside to cover the loss. Because the firm is at risk of a loss until quarter 8,[1] the proceeds of the debt issue cannot be used for other reasons during that period. Nevertheless, the firm is able to earn investment income on the reserve while the firm is still at risk, reducing its net cost of the facility to the spread between its own debt cost of capital and the interest earned on the marketable securities.

In the preloss finance case, what the firm does after the risk period is over depends on the kind of debt the firm has issued. If the firm issued a fixed five-year bond initially, then the risk reserve is simply reversed, thus giving the firm an additional $100 million in cash to use in its normal business operations. Alternatively, the firm may have chosen at time 0 simply to make the debt callable after the risk period ends. This is the case shown in Panel (a) of Exhibit 7.2.

Panel (b) of Exhibit 7.2 shows the cash flow profile of a postloss facility, again assuming the risk event never translates into a loss. The firm will now pay commitment fees over the entire risk period, at which point it simply allows the facility to expire undrawn.

IRRELEVANCE OF RISK FINANCE UNDER M&M

If the four M&M assumptions (see Appendix A) hold, firms should be indifferent between preloss and postloss funded retentions. Furthermore, firms should be equally indifferent between a funded retention and an unfunded retention. To see why, suppose the current time period is 0, and the firm in question faces a risk of loss. If the loss occurs, the firm would like to incur debt to finance the loss out to time T. If the loss occurs, suppose it will occur at time τ and require Z to be paid immediately.

Suppose all debt requires a single payment of interest at the end of the life of the bond so that all bonds issue at par. Suppose further that any proceeds of a bond issue intended to fund a future loss are held in interest-bearing assets that earn the same rate as the coupon rate on the debt itself until the loss occurs.

The price of a corporate bond issued at time t with a principal of $\$Z$ and a coupon of $R(t, T)$—both payable at time T when the bond matures—is

$$B(t, T) = \frac{Z[1 + R(t, T)]}{1 + R(t, T)}$$

where $R(t, T)$ is a non-annualized multi-period rate. We assume throughout that the coupon/discount rate fully reflects *all* the risks of the bond, including both interest rate risk and issuer default risk. We also assume for simplicity that the expectations hypothesis of the term structure of interest rates holds, so that

$$[1 + R(0, T)] = [1 + R(0, \tau)] \{1 + E_0[R(\tau, T)]\}$$

Case 1: Unfunded Retention

If the firm does not fund a retention, it will have to issue $\$Z$ in new debt when and if the loss occurs. If the loss occurs at time τ, the bond can be issued at the fair market price of

$$B(\tau, T) = \frac{Z[1 + R(\tau, T)]}{1 + R(\tau, T)} = Z \qquad (7.1)$$

The proceeds of the bond issue are immediately applied to the loss of Z at time τ. The firm then has until time T to come up with the principal repayment and the coupon, which has the same economic effect on cash flows as delaying the loss payment to date T.

The firm's expected funding rate on this strategy conditional on a loss occurring is just

$$\text{Expected Funding Rate} = E_0[R(\tau, T)]$$

Case 2: Preloss Funded Retention

Now suppose the firm fully funds its $\$Z$ retention on date 0 through date T. To do this, the firm purchases a T-period bond with face value $\$Z$ at time 0 at par. The \$Z proceeds of the bond issue are placed in a risk reserve that earns $R(0, \tau)$ until time τ.

When time τ arrives, if the loss occurs the firm takes \$Z from the reserve and pays for the loss. The proceeds of the bond issue up to this date have generated $ZR(0, \tau)$ in investment income, which is left in the reserve account until time T. The total investment income on the strategy at time T will be

$$ZR(0, \tau)[1 + R(\tau, T)]$$

At time T, the firm then repays principal and interest income in the amount

$$Z[1 + R(0, T)]$$

So, if a loss did occur, the firm's *net* cash flow on the preloss financing arrangement at time T is

$$ZR(0, \tau)[1 + R(\tau, T)] - Z[1 + R(0, T)]$$

The firm's expected funding rate in the event a loss occurs thus is

$$\text{Expected Funding Rate} = E_0[R(\tau, T)]$$

which is identical to our expected funding rate if we had not funded the retention.

Case 3: Postloss Funded Retention

For our third case, suppose the firm funds its retention on date 0 by purchasing a postloss financing arrangement—specifically, a European-style put option on a bond issued at time τ and maturing at time T with face value \$Z and coupon rate $R(\tau, T)$. Suppose the option has a strike price of K°. This gives the firm the right but not the obligation to issue new debt at time τ for fixed price K°, such that

$$K^\circ = \frac{1}{1 + R^\circ(\tau, T)}$$

In return for this right, the firm pays a commitment fee equal to $p(0)$ at time 0 that is nonrefundable.

If time τ arrives and the loss does not occur, the firm will not issue any new debt but will have incurred the commitment fee as a cost. If the loss does occur at time τ, the firm will compare the funding cost of a new debt issue with the fixed funding cost available through the postloss financing counterparty. If the market coupon rate $R(\tau, T)$ is below the fixed funding rate $R^\circ(\tau, T)$, the firm will leave the postloss funding facility undrawn and will issue new debt at the prevailing market coupon rate. Otherwise, the firm will borrow through the facility at the prenegotiated rate. The value of the postloss finance facility at time τ expressed in terms of funding costs thus is

$$\min[R(\tau, T), R^\circ(\tau, T)]$$

which is equivalent to

$$R(\tau, T) - \max[R(\tau, T) - R^\circ(\tau, T), 0] \tag{7.3}$$

The firm in this case is free to choose any fixed price K° at which it wants to be able to issue debt. But this will affect the commitment fee the firm must pay for this right. In an M&M world, the provider of the facility will set this commitment fee at the break-even point so that the price paid by the firm to the option writer will equal the discounted expected value of the facility. No matter what K° is chosen, the firm will get what it pays for in expected value terms in an M&M world; that is,

$$p(0) = \frac{E_0\{\max[R(\tau, T) - R^\circ(\tau, T)]\}}{1 + R(0, \tau)}$$

So, the expected funding rate under the postloss financing program inclusive of the commitment fee thus is

$$\text{Expected Funding Rate} = E_0[R(\tau, T)]$$

which is identical to our expected funding rate if we either had not funded the retention or had used preloss financing.

Note that our expected funding rate does not depend on the fixed coupon rate $R^\circ(\tau, T)$ to which our facility gives us access. A lower funding rate will benefit the firm by exactly as much as it raises the commitment fee.

There is one slight difference between this postloss finance structure and the preloss finance program or the unfunded strategy. In this case, the firm pays the commitment fee *even if there is no loss*. So, it would seem that this strategy is strictly more expensive, but this is not true. The option to issue debt at a fixed rate exists *independently* of whether there is a loss in this example. The commitment fee in an M&M world will reflect this possibility along with the potential for a profitable exercise of the option given a loss. As before, the commitment fee paid in the no-loss scenario is exactly equal to the value of issuing new debt with a floor on the firm's funding rate in the no-loss scenario.

Interpretation

The results just discussed should not surprise us. In an M&M world, we are merely reconfirming that there are no free lunches. A firm can borrow now to finance a loss later, borrow later to finance the same loss at then-current market prices, or enter into an option now to borrow later. In equilibrium, the expected borrowing cost to the firm will be the same in all three cases.

In an M&M world, funding a retention thus makes little sense. But again, this should not surprise us. One of the key assumptions in an M&M world is that the firm has unlimited access to the capital markets, and a loss event will not change that. In reality, this may well not be the case, which is why pre- and postloss finance can add value to the firm.

MOTIVATIONS FOR FUNDING A RETENTION

Knowing what we now know about pre- and postloss risk finance, let's drop the M&M assumptions and explore when and why such programs *can* add value to the firm. Because losses arising from a retained risk will ultimately be borne by the shareholders of a firm, the benefits to a firm of funding a retained risk are not immediately obvious. To the extent such benefits exist, they will be related to the firm's *cash flows*, not its total value. The reason is that the economic consequences of a loss will be priced into the firm's share capital *immediately upon the occurrence of a loss*. A firm thus cannot use risk finance to avoid the immediate impact of a loss on its market value.[2]

Preserving Financial Flexibility

A major reason why firms may wish to fund a retention on either a preloss or post-loss basis is to help them preserve what managers like to call *financial flexibility*. This is essentially excess cash and/or debt capacity that a firm retains "just in case." Sometimes firms like the extra cash to help cover unanticipated losses arising from unfunded retentions. In other situations a firm's goals are more specific (e.g., to ensure that the firm can meet a dividend target).

Funding a retention can help firms preserve financial flexibility by better planning for their cash flow needs. In the event that a large loss does occur, having set aside funds to cover that loss helps eliminate any worries the company might have about preserving liquidity. Many firms are willing to pay something purely for this level of comfort—just to know that following a large loss they won't be at the mercy of the market to replenish their cash coffers. This is especially true for firms with a high degree of intangible assets, whose traditional efforts to raise debt financing can already take considerable time and effort. The value of financial flexibility derived from prenegotiating such liquidity facilities should not be underestimated.

If the sole motivation for risk finance is financial flexibility, however, the firm won't be willing to pay very much for this right. And in fact, many such facilities aimed at giving firms financial flexibility—for example, straightforward letters of credit—do cost only a few basis points either in commitment fees or in the coupon rate of an up-front financing structure.

Reducing Adverse Selection Costs and Avoiding the Appearance of "Cookie Jars"

When a firm incurs a financial loss, the market value of its equity declines relative to the market value of its debt, and the market leverage of the firm rises. Given the costs of debt discussed in Chapter 3 and the adverse selection problems discussed in Chapter 4, issuing new debt and becoming more leveraged following the announcement of a loss can be interpreted by investors as "seriously bad news."

If the only issue were avoiding the adverse selection costs of public securities, we could not make the case that a firm should gravitate toward risk finance. A private placement with no connection to risk could be just as useful. But this is not the only issue. As noted in Chapter 4, firms will not only pursue sources of funding with low adverse selection costs, they will also when possible try to secure funding that signals their credibility to the rest of the market.

One reason that public securities issued by a firm may be viewed as lemons and may trade at an often deep discount to fair value owes to *credibility* that a firm has in how it spends its money. Credibility problems are exacerbated by so-called cookie jars—places that the firm may squirrel away cash for a stated purpose later, but for which investors have no reason to believe the funds will be used as promised. Indeed, this is the main reason that risk financing tools like reserves don't work half the time—it's too easy for a firm to reverse a reserve for reasons having little to do with why it was created.

Credibility is created when the word *risk* in the phrase *risk finance* becomes a binding feature of the contract. As we will see later in Part Four of the book, for example, some risk financing transactions involve pre- or postloss funding *that is specifically conditioned on a risk trigger.* This is very different from putting funds in a reserve or establishing a new unrestricted, unpledged letter of credit and then simply promising that the funds will be used to finance a specific loss. In the case of true risk finance, the company *is unable* to access the funds in question—whether already on deposit or contingent—until a specific loss event has occurred.

Risk finance thus can be beneficial to firms with credibility problems by essentially allowing them to create the equivalent of actual cash reserves or contingent reserves *credibly.* The credibility of such structures comes from the way they incorporate risk into the financing program *explicitly.* Some risk finance structures state specific risk scenarios under which the firm can get access to the money. Other risk financing products allow the firm to draw them down essentially at any time, but the amount of the cash inflow depends on the losses that have occurred. And there are products that have risk restrictions both on the trigger and on the payout.

Indeed, one reason that lines of credit and earmarked reserves are not *true* risk finance is that neither is contractually conditioned on the occurrence of a risk event. A loss reserve can be reversed for reasons having nothing to do with the underlying risk that served as the initial justification for the reserve in the first place. Similarly, lines of credit can essentially be drawn at will. There is no guarantee a firm will draw on the line just to generate the cash flows it needs to fund a retention that has become a loss. On the contrary, credit lines often contain material adverse change (MAC) clauses that *prevent* their drawdown if the firm's financial condition has deteriorated significantly.

We will return to this issue with examples and more discussion later. Suffice it to say for now that *true* risk finance can reduce adverse selection costs by *strictly* conditioning a firm's leverage on the occurrence of certain risk events.

Mitigating Underinvestment Problems

Recall from Chapters 3 and 4 that with too little internal funds, underinvestment may occur when a firm is forced to reject positive NPV projects because funds are unavailable to make the investment expenditures required to finance new projects or future anticipated growth opportunities. Such problems are most likely to occur if the investment is required at a bad time for the firm, such as immediately following a large depletion of the firm's internal funds.[3]

Underinvestment is most likely to arise in connection with rising expected costs of financial distress. Specifically, if a firm enters a period of financial distress, it may be very difficult for the firm to issue new debt or equity securities without incurring a significantly higher cost of capital as a result of adverse selection problems and heightened credit risk concerns. This, in turn, could force a firm to reject a positive NPV project.

Issuing securities before the distress period kicks in, however, may not impose the same costs on the firm. True, there will still be some adverse selection problem—investors will assume that securities issued today are being used to fund a reserve against a future loss. Nevertheless, if the firm is not actually in financial distress, the adverse selection discount may be much lower prior to the loss. In this way, a firm can prefund a loss without incurring significant adverse selection costs.

Although a clear potential benefit of preloss financing is avoiding the heightened costs of distressed debt financing, the even bigger benefit comes if the costs of external finance are so high following a depletion of funds that the firm is forced actually to reject positive NPV projects. To illustrate, consider a chemical firm Spock that has three possible R&D projects for new chemical development that cost €100 million, €200 million, and €400 million, respectively.[4] Assume these are mutually exclusive projects that yield riskless discounted net cash flows of €200 million, €1,000 million, and €450 million, respectively. The resulting project NPVs are shown in Table 7.1. This example is adapted from Froot, Scharfstein, and Stein (1993).

From Table 7.1, Firm Spock clearly prefers Project 2, where a €200 million expenditure results in a €800 million NPV. Nevertheless, the NPVs of all three projects are positive, thus suggesting that Spock will undertake all three projects if it possibly can.

Now suppose that Firm Spock's current net income plus depreciation plus retained earnings is €250 million, but that Spock faces potential product liability from a chemical spill. If the spill occurs, Firm Spock must immediately pay €100 million in product liability and damages. To keep the example simple, assume that Firm Spock *cannot* issue new debt or equity following an announcement of a chemical spill. Table 7.2 shows the net impact of the two scenarios on Spock's capital budget.

TABLE 7.1 Capital Budget for Firm Spock's Chemical Production (€ millions)

	Investment Expenditure	Discounted Cash Flows	NPV
Project 1	€100	€ 200	€100
Project 2	200	1,000	800
Project 3	400	450	50

TABLE 7.2   Firm Spock's Project Acceptance Decisions (€ millions)

Scenario	Free Cash Flow	Project(s)	Investment	NPV
No Spill	€250	2	€200	€800
Spill	100	1	100	100

From Table 7.2, it is clear that the chemical spill could deplete internal funds so much that the firm will be forced to choose a suboptimal investment program. In other words, the firm suffers underinvestment because it forgoes an additional €800 million in NPV terms purely because its free cash flows are too low to fund the project and the market would not allow a new securities offering.

Funding the retention of chemical spill–related product liability risk could help the firm avoid this problem. Preloss funding would require the firm to set aside €100 million in a period prior to the loss, and postloss funding would give the firm a facility to draw down €100 million following the loss. In either case, funding the retention adds value to the firm by guaranteeing that an unexpected loss will not deplete the firm of cash flows it needs to undertake positive NPV projects. The source of this value added is the inability of the firm to borrow at a fair market price following a loss.

Readers may recognize that the example and situation are strongly reminiscent of the classic model in Froot, Scharfstein, and Stein (1993). Their model is a common rationale for corporate uses of derivatives and insurance—namely, to reduce cash flow volatility and mitigate underinvestment when external finance has deadweight costs. As here, those deadweight costs could arise from adverse selection, agency costs of debt, disportionately increasing expected distress costs, and so on. Interestingly, what we see here, though, is not as strong as what Froot, Scharfstein, and Stein argue. In their opinion, true risk transfer is a solution to the underinvestment problem. We agree that risk transfer will solve this particular underinvestment problem, but we can also see now that it may be a bit extreme. All that is required to mitigate underinvestment problems in the face of costly external finance is risk finance.

PART TWO

Traditional Risk Transfer

CHAPTER 8

Insurance

In Chapter 2, we consider traditional insurance and reinsurance as a form of risk transfer. We begin with insurance and a discussion of insurance as a type of legal contract. We then discuss how insurance premiums or rates are established by insurance companies in a process known as *rate making*. As part of that discussion, we review the various methods by which insurance companies attempt to use rate making and contract design to mitigate the problems of *moral hazard* and *adverse selection* endemic to insurance markets. The chapter then concludes with a discussion of typical insurance companies—how they are organized, how they operate, and how they manage their capital using technical reserves.

INSURANCE PRODUCTS AS CONTRACTS

A traditional insurance contract is generally a contract in which one party pays a fixed price to an insurance company for the right to receive compensation following the occurrence of a specific adverse event. The compensation is intended to reduce the economic damage sustained by the insurance purchaser as a result of the occurrence of the adverse event. This is, of course, a highly generic definition that could describe almost any risk transfer contract, such as a put option. As we have seen in Chapters 1 and 6, it's no accident that the basic features of insurance and options are similar—both are just types of contingent risk capital, as we defined that term in Chapter 6. So the first issue we want to consider is what specifically makes something insurance as opposed to something else. (Kramer also considers this question in Chapter 28.)

The word *contract* is key in answering that question. Insurance emerged originally as a legal contracting device in the tradition of English common law. As a result, insurance is often distinguished from other risk transfer arrangements by legal aspects of the contracts themselves and what kinds of obligations they create. In addition, insurance is an industry steeped in decades of tradition with its own vocabulary and commercial practices. Over the years, certain features that now are integral features of insurance contracts have evolved purely by convention. Although these features lack the same legal basis as the others, they nevertheless deserve discussion. In the sections that follow, we discuss the essential features of insurance, from the perspectives of both how they evolved as common law contracts and how they have come to be known through industry custom and practice.

A word of warning, however, before we proceed. Namely, the characteristics of insurance that are often used to differentiate *traditional* insurance from alternative risk transfer (ART) and derivatives continue to evolve. Many of these characteristics, moreover, are highly subjective, especially across national boundaries. As a result, there is no consistent litmus test for determining what is and is not an insurance contract. In many countries, moreover, the definition of insurance may also depend on what the definition is being used for—for example, a contract deemed insurance for *tax* purposes may not be deemed insurance for *accounting* purposes. So, when in doubt, it's always a good idea to check with local experts and authorities about whether a product is insurance for some specific purpose, such as tax or regulatory compliance.

Of all the characteristics of insurance discussed in this chapter, moreover, only one of them is truly unique to insurance. That is the feature of "insurable interest," and even that has been losing ground as a necessary feature of insurance in recent case law in some countries. So the attributes of insurance discussed here should be interpreted more as historical guidelines than hard-and-fast rules. Or, as economists like to say, the following are necessary but not sufficient conditions for a contract to be considered in insurance, although even that is changing for certain of the criteria.

Insurable Interest

To have an insurable interest means that the purchaser of an insurance contract must be at risk to sustain some economic loss as a precondition for receiving compensation under insurance of that risk. A firm that has an insurable interest in property, for example, could sustain direct and material damage by the loss or degradation of the property asset. Or a firm with an insurable interest in professional liability must be capable of sustaining direct and material damage from the professional misconduct or negligence of its agents.

Insurable interest is required for a contract to be considered classical insurance as opposed to, say, an option contract.[1] Recall from Chapter 2 that we defined traditional derivatives as being "parametric" contracts. This means that the payoff on a typical derivatives transaction is defined by reference to some market parameter, such as an asset price or interest rate. That payoff may or may not be exactly the same as the actual economic damage sustained by the purchaser of risk protection. At the same time, the risks transferred in a derivatives contract need not be risks to which the derivatives counterparties are naturally exposed. In a typical pay fixed/receive London Interbank Offered Rate (LIBOR) interest rate swap, for example, the end user need not have a natural exposure to rising LIBOR as a precondition of doing the swap. If LIBOR rises relative to the fixed swap rate, the fixed rate payer is entitled to a net payment from the swap counterparty regardless of whether the fixed-rate payer has sustained any economic damage from the interest rate increase. This would be impossible in a traditional insurance contract.

Aleatory Contracts, the Trigger, and the Benefit Amount

Insurance contracts are known as *aleatory* because their value to either or both parties depends on some random or uncertain future event. In an aleatory contract, moreover, the value of the obligations of the two parties may be unequal *ex post*. Traditional insurance is aleatory because the insurance provider's obligation depends on a future loss event, whereas the insurance purchaser owes a fixed premium to the insurance company that is independent of future losses.

The two essential features of traditional insurance contracts that make them aleatory are the *trigger* and the *benefit amount*. In plain language, the benefit amount is what the insurance purchaser gets if the insurance contract pays off, and the trigger determines when she can get it. In order for the contract to be aleatory, the trigger and/or benefit amount of the insurance contract must be based on some uncertain event *where the uncertainty has not been fully resolved at the policy's inception*.

There's a lot going on here, so let's proceed methodically and discuss in more detail some of the definitions we've just tossed out.

Insurance Trigger An insurance contract specifies very clearly the nature of the risk, hazard, or peril that can trigger the contingent payment promised by the insurance company to the insurance purchaser. All insurance contracts have at least one specific trigger, unless that trigger is pulled (i.e., the risk event in question has occurred), the insurance purchaser cannot file a claim to receive compensation from the insurance provider. Not surprisingly, a contract is not an insurance contract unless the risk on which the trigger is based exists for the insurance purchaser *at the inception of the contract*. We'll return to discuss what this means shortly when we tackle the issue of differentiating between what we call *retrospective* and *prospective* insurance coverage.

Some insurance is highly specific to a certain enumerated risk, hazard, or peril. Examples include property damage insurance triggered by fire or flood, health insurance linked to particular medical problems (e.g., dental or ophthamological coverage), or casualty insurance linked to injuries sustained in automobile accidents. Other insurance structures may be more comprehensive in nature, such as a general homeowner's policy protecting property for essentially any damage not willfully imposed by the policyholder or general medical coverage applying to any treatments not arising from preinsurance health problems.

Insurance Benefit Amount   The benefit amount of an insurance contract may be either fixed or variable. A *valued contract* is an insurance contract that pays a fixed amount if the triggering event occurs. A regular life insurance contract, for example, pays a fixed amount following the triggering event of the death of the insured. A *contract of indemnity*, by contrast, has a contingent payment that is proportional to the economic loss incurred by the insured party. A small loss thus results in a small payment, whereas a large loss results in a large payment, subject to the important constraint than the insured cannot recover more on the insurance contract than the actual economic damage sustained. A *full indemnity contract* is one that restores the insurance purchaser to exactly the same condition as before the adverse triggering event.

Consider an example in which the insurance purchaser is a homeowner, the insurable interest is the value of the owner's house, and the insurance is tied to the specific triggering event of a fire. Suppose the value of the house is currently $1 million. The homeowner can buy two insurance contracts. In the first—a valued contract—the insurance purchaser pays premium for the right to receive, say, $400,000 in the event of a fire. The $400,000 benefit amount is fixed at the inception of the contract and does not depend on how much damage the fire did, although the $400,000 is payable only if a fire does, indeed, occur.

The second contract—an indemnity contract—pays the homeowner an amount equal to the damage sustained from the fire relative to the current price of the house ($1 million) in return for receiving premium—almost certainly not the same premium amount that was payable for the valued contract. Exhibit 8.1 shows the payoffs to the valued and indemnity contracts following a fire as a function of the value of the house after the fire has done its damage. (As in earlier chapters, payoffs are gross payoffs and do not represent net-of-premium payoffs.)

Consider first the valued contract. If there is no fire, there is no payoff on the contract and its net value to the homeowner is just the premium paid. In the event there is a fire, however, the homeowner receives $400,000. As long as the fire damage does not cause the value of the house to fall below $600,000, the owner of the value contract actually receives a higher payout than the actual sustained damage. (This is unusual—more on this in a minute.) But for a decline in the value of the house below $600,000, the gross payoff on the insurance is insufficient to compensate the owner for the damage sustained.

Now consider the indemnity contract. In the case of no fire, the payoff is again zero—the triggering event has not occurred, and the insurance buyer has not sustained any fire-related damage. But in the event of a fire, the value of the indemnity contract is exactly equal to the decline in the value of the house. Whether the house declines in value to $999,999 or to $1, the homeowner receives the difference between the initial value of the house ($1 million) and that new value.

Comparing the two contracts, it is clear that for damage to the house in excess of $400,000, the indemnity contract is preferable *ex post*. And conversely, a valued contract would likely be preferred by a homeowner who has a small kitchen fire that causes slight decline in value but still constitutes a triggering event under both contracts. The homeowner, however, does not know the amount of damage that will occur *ex ante*. The premiums on the two policies, moreover, will not be the same—the indemnity contract will provide greater protection for more extreme disasters and thus will be more expensive. So, it is not clear *ex ante* which contract a homeowner would choose.

Note in Exhibit 8.1 that the valued contract is equivalent to a binary put option (see Chapter 11) on the house, whereas the indemnity contract is equivalent to a traditional put option on the property struck at $1 million. Importantly, however, two important differences separate the options we have discussed earlier and these insurance contracts. The first is the existence of an insurable interest; the insurance purchaser had to own the house and be at risk of sustaining actual damage from a fire in order to purchase either insurance contract shown in Exhibit 8.1. The second is that the exercise value of these options does not depend just on their intrinsic value, but also on the occurrence of the triggering event. A decline in the value of the house arising from, say, a flood would send these options into-the-money, but in a nonexploitable way. In order for the insurance contracts to be "exercised," they must be in-the-money *and* a fire must have occurred.

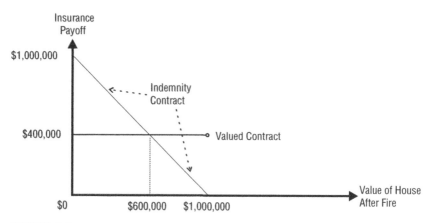

EXHIBIT 8.1   Payoffs of Insurance Contract Following House Fire

We said earlier in this chapter that insurance is intended to reimburse purchasers for all or part of the damage they sustain. Yet the example we just reviewed clearly shows the possibility for the homeowner to make money on a valued contract for fires that impose less than $400,000 in damage. The reason this looks a bit strange is that we generally don't see valued contracts in situations like this. Valued contracts are mainly used to insure objects or events with highly subjective values that are hard to quantify using some mutually acceptable set of objective criteria. Examples include exotic art, the human life, and so on. By preagreeing to a fixed benefit payment, the need to determine a valuation *ex post* is avoided. Although valued insurance plays a significant role in the insurance world, we will find little opportunity to discuss it in this book. Unless otherwise explicitly stated, all subsequent references to traditional insurance should be presumed to mean indemnity insurance contracts.

Prospective and Retrospective Insurance versus Retroactive Contracts
Because the benefit amount is fixed in a valued insurance contract, the only uncertainty in such a contract is whether the trigger has been pulled. A fixed-payoff valued contract is thus generally not an insurance contract if the trigger has already been pulled at the time the policy is negotiated and executed. The Art Institute of Chicago, for example, may not purchase valued insurance on a Degas that has already been destroyed in a fire.

If the benefit amount is variable and the contract is an indemnity contract, however, the value of the insurance contract may be uncertain and dependent on future events *even if the trigger has already been pulled.* In order to be insurance, it need only be the case that the *benefit amount* remains uncertain *and* possibly equal to zero.

A *prospective* insurance contract is a contract that is negotiated between the insurance buyer and seller before either the trigger event has occurred or the benefit amount is known. *Retrospective* coverage, by contrast, is negotiated *after* the trigger event but *before* the benefit amount is known. In both cases, the contract is still aleatory because the value to the purchaser and the liability to the seller remain uncertain and dependent on some future event.

An example may help distinguish prospective and retrospective risk. Consider a chemical company. A prospective risk for the company could be the risk that one of its trucks crashes and spills chemicals into a water supply system. The firm could then face liability risk arising from property and/or casualty claims. A similar retrospective risk could occur if the firm's truck has already spilled chemicals, but the firm has not yet been found out. The liability has been incurred, but the question of whether the firm will actually have to make liability payments remains unresolved. In either case, it would be legitimate for the chemical company to purchase an insurance contract on its liability risk.

What is *not* allowed is *retroactive* coverage. To continue the example, if a chemical company has already been sued for a spill and the verdict has been rendered that the firm is liable for, say, $1 million in damages, the chemical spill is no longer an insurable event for the firm. *The loss is known and is no longer a risk, and the insurance is no longer an aleatory contract.*

Exhibit 8.2 may help clarify the distinctions among these concepts. In all three panels of the exhibit, let us define the coverage period as the period of time during which the insurance purchaser may sustain economic damage as a direct result of the triggering event. Suppose the insurance is for property damage to a building following an earthquake.

Panel (a) of Exhibit 8.2 depicts a prospective insurance contract in which the insurance is purchased before the quake. Suppose in this case that the quake damaged the building, but that damage is not detected until a month after the quake when the building falls and the civil engineers determine that the quake made the building structurally unsound. The property owner should have no trouble filing a legitimate claim with the insurance company a month following the quake.

Panel (b) depicts a retrospective policy. The example we just explored probably would not qualify for retrospective coverage. In that example, the structural damage was sustained at the time of the quake and the only delay is the detection of the damage. But suppose instead that the owner of a small coffee shop on the first floor gets worried after the quake that the

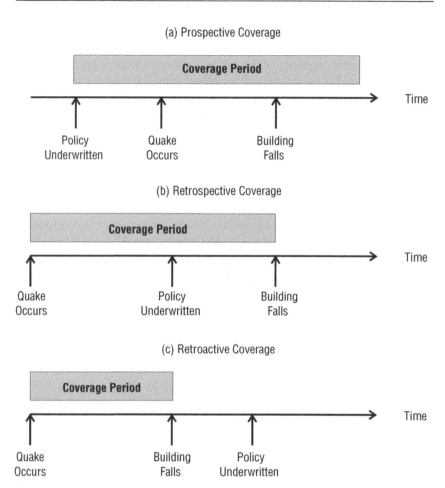

EXHIBIT 8.2   Prospective versus Retrospective versus Retroactive Coverage

building might fall. If we continue to define the quake as the trigger, a new policy that protects the coffee shop from the building's subsequent collapse would be fine.

We might ask why the coffee shop owner should not just buy plain old property insurance prospectively in this situation. She could, although she would have to be very careful to make sure that earthquake-related damage is not excluded from the prospective property insurance policy through some "preexisting condition" clause.

What would *not* be fine is for either the building owner or the coffee shop owner to buy insurance after the building has fallen. True, the exact amount of the structural damage may not be known, but the damage *will be positive* and it can be estimated. It is no longer subject to *future randomness*, except possibly the randomness associated with damage measurement—a thin reed on which to rest a claim that the contract is aleatory and dependent on a future risk. This situation is depicted in Panel (c) of Exhibit 8.2, where the trigger event and the risk period both predate the contract execution.

Blurred Boundaries   The distinction between retrospective coverage and retroactive coverage is sometimes murky. Suppose a company has been sued by its shareholders for misstating its accounting earnings. The suit has been filed, but the case has not yet been argued or decided. Can the company buy insurance on the outcome of the case? Technically, yes, because the verdict of the jury trial will determine the liability and the damages amount, and it is possible that the company will be found not to be liable.

Now suppose the same company has been sued and found to be liable, but there is an open question of what damage the firm's misstatement inflicted on shareholders. Now the purchase of insurance might be a tougher problem for the firm. In order to qualify as a legitimate aleatory insurance contract, the company must essentially be able to argue that the amount of damages remains unknown. And as a commercial consideration, it would help greatly if the company can still maintain that zero damages is a legitimate possible outcome of the trial. If there is a real possibility that the firm is liable for something that did not result in damage (e.g., the firm's share price skyrocketed despite inflated earnings numbers), then insurance may be a possibility. If not, best to ask a lawyer. In *all* cases, when in doubt, best to ask a lawyer on matters such as these.

Definition of the Trigger   The definition of the trigger has a lot to do with whether we consider a program retrospective or prospective. If we define the insurance trigger as the *occurrence of damage* arising from a specific risk event, then we have tied the trigger to a positive benefit amount. In this case, both retrospective and prospective insurance policies would involve triggers that have not been pulled at the time the policies are negotiated. If we instead define the trigger to be *only* the occurrence of a risk event that *might* lead to a future loss, then the distinction between retrospective and prospective is significant.

It doesn't really matter which way we go. What matters is that we are clear about what we mean in the policy language *and* that the contract is aleatory. What you choose to call it to get to that end result is a matter of vocabulary choice and pedagogy.

Due Consideration for Risk Transfer

A legitimate traditional insurance contract must transfer some portion of the risk from the purchaser of the insurance to the insurance provider or seller, in return for which some consideration must be conveyed to the insurance seller by the purchaser. The consideration is, of course, the premium, and legitimate insurance should involve a premium amount that is reasonable relative to the amount of risk that the contract transfers.

Keeping in mind that a true insurance contract must be aleatory, that also implies that *some* risk is being transferred. Paying $10 million in premium for a property insurance policy that has a maximum payout of $10 million, for example, would fail the test of due consideration for risk transfer and would not involve any transfer of risk.

The real challenge in interpreting this particular feature of insurance—and it has led to some very heated recent controversies—is in how to determine how much risk transfer is enough and what is an appropriate consideration for that risk transfer. There are absolutely no uniformly agreed upon accounting, legal, or regulatory checklists to answer either question.

For many years, the accounting industry has relied on an informal heuristic known as the "10/10 rule" to make the determination of whether a contract contains a sufficient risk transfer for a given premium payment to qualify as insurance. Under this rule, a contract can be considered insurance if the insurance company has at least a 10 percent chance of losing at least 10 percent of its premium. A series of controversies in the past few years has led many accountants to adopt the same type of heuristic, but at the stricter "20/20" level. Even this, however, is still just a heuristic and has no foundation in statute, case law, regulation, or the like.

We will return to discuss this issue again in significantly more detail in Chapter 24.

"Utmost Good Faith"

Unlike most traditional commercial or financial transactions, insurance has also historically required the contract to be of utmost good faith. Also known as the principle of *uberimae fidei*, this means that the standard of honesty applied to an insurance contract is *higher* than the standard applied to ordinary commercial or capital market transactions.

The principle of utmost good faith requires adequate information disclosures by both the insurance purchaser and the insurance company. Insurance purchasers are typically held to a standard of disclosure commensurate with their expertise—for example, corporate risk management professionals will be scrutinized more for disclosure violations than individuals will be. The insurance purchaser can violate the disclosure obligation under utmost good faith in one of three general ways: breach of warranty, misrepresentation, or concealment.

Breach of Warranty   A warranty is a statement by the insured that is a material part of the conditionality of the insurance contract. An *affirmative warranty* is a condition that exists on the date the statement is made; for example, the purchaser of automobile insurance claims she has not had an accident in the prior year, or the purchaser of health insurance indicates that he has not been diagnosed with a terminal illness. A *promissory warranty* is a condition that will exist on all or part of the policy period; for example, the purchaser of theft insurance commits to maintain a burglar alarm in working order, or the purchaser of fire insurance will keep a charged fire extinguisher on the premises at all times.

Noncompliance with a warranty is grounds for an insurer not to pay. Warranties are discouraged by courts, however, except in cases where the insurance purchaser is a risk management professional. *Representations* are preferred by courts, and place a higher burden of proof on the insurer.

Misrepresentation   A misrepresentation is an untrue fact or opinion, usually given in response to due diligence questions asked by the insurer.

Misrepresentation *of a fact* is grounds for nullification of the insurer's obligation even if the information is both *incorrect* and *immaterial*. The misstated fact does not have to be connected to the loss from which a claim arises. John Smith, for example, buys auto insurance and replies "no" when asked by the insurer if any driver under the age of 18 is permitted to use the car. John Smith lets his 16-year-old daughter Jane drive the car regularly. If the car is in an accident, the insurer may have grounds not to pay *even if John was driving and not Jane.*

Misrepresentation *of an opinion* can be grounds for nullification of the insurer's obligation to pay only if the information presented by the insured was *material* and *intentionally misleading*. Suppose our friend John Smith now buys life insurance. The insurer asks John Smith if he is in good health, to which he replies "yes" despite having an *undiagnosed* terminal illness. In order to later deny a claim on the grounds of misrepresentation, the insurer must prove that Smith knowingly gave an incorrect opinion *and* that if he had given the correct opinion, it would have affected the design or offering of the policy.

Concealment   A misrepresentation involves the commission of an error concerning information about the insured. Concealment, on the other hand, is an error of omission. In order to void the policy, the concealment must be shown to be *intentional* and *material*. Suppose, for example, that internal tests at a drug company have shown that a new cure for AIDS works but, as a side effect, kills everyone with blood type O+. If this fact is knowingly concealed when the drug company purchases product liability insurance, the insurer could later argue that the policy is null and void on the grounds that the drug company intentionally concealed from the insurer a test result that certainly would have affected the insurance decision.

Offer and Acceptance

Like most contracts, insurance must be an agreement of offer and acceptance—that is, both parties must confirm that they agree to the terms of the deal. This may seem innocuous, but it is a useful reminder to us that a lot of the issues we have just discussed can be resolved bilaterally by the two counterparties, provided both are acting in good faith on truthfully disclosed and complete information.

One major implication of this is that a contract may be considered insurance even if the underlying trigger is a risk that is not universally recognized or supported with objective data. In 1971, for example, Cutty Sark whiskey distillers offered a £1 million reward for the capture of the Loch Ness Monster. To insure the payoff, Cutty Sark purchased insurance from Lloyd's. The premium was £2,500 and covered the risk that the monster would be apprehended between May 1, 1971, and April 30, 1972. To eliminate doubts about the viability of the contract, it contained the following language: "As far as this insurance is concerned the Loch Ness Monster shall be deemed to be: (1) in excess of 20 feet in length, (2) acceptable as the Loch Ness Monster to the curators of the Natural History Museum, London" (Outreville, 1998).

Not Contrary to Public Interest

Although the offer and acceptance principle gives the insurance company and purchaser of coverage a lot of latitude in defining the risk that the contract is transferring, the contract must also be deemed not contrary to the public interest. Although this is yet again an ambiguous turn of phrase, it leaves wide open the door for contracts to be excluded from the definition of insurance if they are used to facilitate illegal activities, such as money laundering or deliberately and maliciously misleading investors about the true financial condition of a firm.

Unilateral Performance Obligation

Many commercial contracts are *bilateral*—performance may be forced on either party if challenged in a court. A binding bilateral agreement that Fox Mulder sell his "I Want to Believe" poster to Dana Scully in return for a cash payment of $100 by Scully to Mulder, for example, is enforceable against either party in the event the agreement is broken. If Scully pays, Mulder must deliver the poster. And if Mulder delivers, Scully must pay.

Insurance contracts, by contrast, are often *unilateral*. A court will enforce the contract in one direction only. As long as the insurance purchaser has made the premium payment, enforcement will typically constitute action forcing the insurance company to honor its commitment to pay. If a purchaser has stopped making premium payments, the insurance company can, of course, consider the policy terminated. But, like options, no one can force the purchaser "to exercise."

Suppose, for example, our old pal John Smith buys marine insurance for his boat against damage to the hull arising from collisions. Even if he is in good standing on his premium payments, he is not *required* to make a claim in the event of an accident. If John Smith happens to be having an intimate evening alone on the lake with his mistress when a collision occurs, for example, he may well not want the paperwork arising from an insurance claim to be mailed to his home address. No court would force him to do so. In this sense, the contract is unilateral.

Adhesion

Insurance companies usually are responsible for drafting their own contracts. In a contract of adhesion, the contract writer is responsible for clarity and nonambiguity. So, if the contract language is unclear, a contract of adhesion forces the drafter to assume the responsibility. In other words, the presumption is that the insurance purchaser is correct when in doubt.

This is sometimes called the *ambiguity rule* of insurance. If an insurance provision is ambiguous, the court will usually hold for the benefit of the policyholder.

Subrogation Rights

Insurance contracts also often include the right of *subrogation* for the insurer. Subrogation is a common law term that applies when the insured loss is caused by a party other than the insurance purchaser. Under common law, the party damaged has the sole right of recovery against the party that inflicts the damage. Subrogation is the transfer of that right of recovery from the insurance purchaser to the insurer.

Subrogation helps enforce the principle of indemnity that prevents the insured party from collecting more than one payment on a single economic loss. Suppose, for example, that a homeowner purchases fire insurance and then experiences a major loss from a fire that is determined to be arson. Subrogation gives the insurer rather than the homeowner the exclusive right to pursue a claim on the arsonist for a recovery—at least up to the amount paid by the insurer on the claim.

In the absence of a subrogation right, it might be possible for the homeowner to collect twice on the fire—once from the insurer and once through a legal claim on the arsonist. This ability, in turn, can create a moral hazard, whereby the homeowner agrees to pay a large sum to the arsonist to torch the house—or simply agrees not to pursue the arsonist with a claim. Especially if the insured value of the house is above its market value at the time of the fire, then both the arsonist and the homeowner can make a substantial gain on such an arrangement in the absence of clearly defined subrogation rights for the insurance provider.

Annual Term

The final characteristic of insurance worth noting is not a feature of insurance contracts as much as it is a result of the type of insurance *contracting* that has emerged over the years. Namely, traditional insurance policies almost always have a one-year duration or term.

The main reason is that insurance has historically been a brokered industry, and brokers are compensated based on commission. The annual renewal or renegotiation of insurance helps guarantee that brokerage commissions occur every year, even on repeat customers who make no material changes to their coverage.

INSURANCE PRICING

Insurance companies use at least three different terms to describe the prices of the contracts they provide. The *premium* is the total price paid for a particular policy. The *rate* is the price *per unit of coverage*. And the *rate on line* (ROL) is the premium divided by the total policy limit. Consider, for example, an automobile liability and collision insurance policy on which a driver pays $1,000 per year. The policy entitles the insurance purchaser to reimbursements of up to $500,000 in damages relating to auto damages or liability to other drivers in the event of one or more accidents. In this case, the premium would be $1,000, the rate would be $1 for every $500 in damage, and the ROL would be 0.2 percent.

In general, the premium on an insurance contract is the sum of three variables: the "pure premium," the "premium loading," and the "markup."

$$\text{Total Premium} = \text{Pure Premium} + \text{Load} + \text{Markup}$$

The last term—the markup—is the amount that an insurer can add to the premium as a profit margin. This amount depends on how competitive the insurance industry is—the more competitive, the lower the markup. We will ignore this term for the remainder of this section so that we can focus on the more interesting practical issues of insurance pricing—known in industry parlance as the *rate making* process.

Determining the Pure Premium

If all four M&M assumptions hold, the pure premium of an insurance contract—also called its *actuarially fair premium*—should be equal to the expected loss of the insurer (or, equivalently, the expected benefit amount paid to the insurance buyer). Recall in Chapter 6, we saw that the "fair price" of contingent risk capital was equivalent to the price of net asset insurance or an option on the firm's net assets struck at the forward price of those net assets. Here we are saying the same thing in "insurance-speak." The actuarially fair price of an insurance contract is that price at which the insurance purchaser gets exactly what he is paying for.

A Simple Example   Suppose we consider N identical private airlines, each of which owns a single plane. As long as the airplane remains operational, each firm will have earnings per year of e°. But if the airplane breaks or crashes and goes out of commission, the airline will suffer a loss of exactly L. That may occur with a probability of π. The insurance seller and purchaser agree on the magnitudes of both π and L. The insurance company offers a contract in which the airline can pay Q in premium in order to obtain a payment of L in the event that the airplane breaks or crashes. The premium on the contract thus is Q, and we can define the rate as q such that $Q = qL$.

The earnings of any given airline can be examined in two states of the world: the no-accident state that occurs with probability $(1 - \pi)$ and the accident state that occurs with probability π:

No-accident state: $e^{NA} = e^o - Q$
Accident state: $e^A = e^o - Q + L - L$

So, an airline that purchases insurance has fully protected itself by giving up Q in *both* states of the world in return for eliminating the possibility of a catastrophic loss in the accident state.

The total underwriting income of the insurance company is NQ. In turn, the insurer expects to pay out L in losses with probability π on each of the N policies, so that its expected payout or loss is $N\pi L$. With perfect competition and symmetric information, a competitive equilibrium will ensure that

$$Q = \pi L$$

or

$$q = \pi$$

In other words, the actuarially fair insurance rate is equal to the probability that a loss will occur, provided all four M&M assumptions hold.

Pure Premium More Generally   Suppose an insurance company offers N policies. If the insurer has provided L_j in coverage on policy j (i.e., the benefit amount of j is L_j), the actuarially fair price of policy j is just

$$q_j = E(L_j) = \int L_j dL_j$$

and in aggregate for N policies written is

$$Q = \sum_{j=1}^{N} E(L_j) = \sum_{j=1}^{N} \int L_j dL_j$$

Most insurance companies do not attempt to solve this directly for each policyholder and policy line. Instead, consider a portfolio of policies offered in a single line and suppose that the same price is offered to all purchasers of this policy. Define the following variables:

n = number of losses incurred by a claimant in the policy period
E = exposure units
L = dollar losses = nE

Some further concepts that insurers like to use:

f = average frequency of loss = n/E
S = average severity of loss = L/n

Then the price per unit of coverage can be expressed as

$$q = f \times S = (n/E) \times (L/n) = (L/E)$$

With symmetric information, using actual data to populate the above expression and estimate the pure premium for a given policy line would be trivial. Asymmetric information, however, greatly complicates our task. We shall return to that issue shortly.

Premium Loading

Loading is added to pure premium to get the final premium and is intended to reflect administrative costs and expenses, the costs of hedging or reinsurance (see Chapter 9), and the cost of providing related services. These related services may include:

- *Loss adjustment expenses.* Adjustment is the process by which an insurance company investigates the veracity of a claim, usually by sending an adjuster to inspect the damage relative to the claim filed.
- *Underwriting expenses.* These are the expenses incurred with maintaining a full underwriting business. Some of these expenses will be directly attributable to the business line in question, but many of the costs of underwriting are shared overhead and fixed costs.
- *Investment expenses.* As we will discuss later in this chapter, an insurance company is an asset management organization—it invests premium in assets to fund future claims. The investment management process can be costly, and these expenses may be passed back to customers through loading.

Other expenses will be evident when we discuss the operation of insurance companies later in this chapter.

Load is often computed by insurance companies as a proportion of the total premium charged. Consider, for example, a line of automotive insurance policies offered by a Swiss insurance company in the local market. Suppose the pure premium collected from each policy holder is 100 Swiss francs per annum and that loading on the policy line is proportional to the total premium at the rate of 40 percent per annum. In other words, the cost to the insurer of providing the insurance is about 40 percent of the total price of the insurance. The price charged by the insurance company to a customer thus will be around 166 Swiss francs per year. Of that amount, about 60 percent (or CHF100) will cover the insurer's expected loss and the remaining 40 percent (or CHF66) will cover the insurance company's expenses.

But is the assumption that loading is proportional to premium realistic? For some insurance services, premium is a good and nondistorting measure because the services are provided at a cost that truly is highly correlated to the underlying underwriting volume. But for certain costly services related to adjustment and loss control, proportionality makes less sense. On the one hand, an increase in premium that reflects an increase in the expected size or frequency of claims would increase the insurer's adjustment and loss control activities. On the other hand, the insurer will not increase adjustment and loss control unless the total number of claims is expected to fall, implying a *negative* relationship to premium.

Optimal loading occurs where the expected marginal reduction in the cost of claims equals the expected marginal spending on variables like loss control and adjustment. At the same time, of course, the insurer is pursuing an optimal number of policies to achieve economies of scale and risk pooling in its underwriting portfolio.

Many firms assume that an approximately proportional relationship exists between claim costs and optimal spending on adjustment and loss control. The ratio of claims adjustment costs to claims payments thus should be relatively stable within a given coverage line. By extension, the ratio of claims adjustment costs to premiums and the ratio of claims payments to premiums should also be stable. So when optimal cost amounts have been allocated to the writing and servicing of insurance, the *target loss ratio*—the ratio of claim costs to premium—should be stable.

Some insurance companies pursue a stable target loss ratio as a policy target. After defining a representative period of time called the "risk period," usually the same as the length of the policies outstanding in a given policy line, the firm then sets a target ratio of expected claims payments to premium received—denoted R—given an optimal level of spending on adjustment, underwriting, loss control, and so on. The firm then periodically estimates the ratio of actual claims payments to premium received, denoted r. Current rates are then adjusted by the amount $(r - R)/R$. If an insurance company defines a target loss ratio of 65%, for example, suppose actual losses over a risk period yield $r = 70\%$. A firm adjusting rates to target loss ratios then will raise its premiums by 7.7 percent (= 0.70 − 0.65/0.65).

Target loss ratios, however, can vary significantly across coverage lines. Claims processing costs for health insurance in a group plan, for example, should be well below claims processing costs for medical malpractice liability insurance. In addition, target loss ratios tend to ignore all of the incentive effects embedded in insurance pricing that we discussed earlier. It may be a useful guideline for insurance companies, but it is probably not a sufficiently robust pricing rule to maximize the value of the firm over time.

Asymmetric Information and Insurance Pricing

As a practical consequence of the insurable interest doctrine and the indemnity aspect of insurance, insurance contracts tend to be associated with firm-specific risks, hazards, or perils. Indemnity contracts, moreover, have contingent payments based on firm-specific economic losses incurred. Because the purchaser of insurance must be at risk to suffer direct economic damage before engaging in an insurance transaction, insurance thus poses two potential problems to a classical insurer that are not found in markets for parametric risk transfer contracts like derivatives.

Called *moral hazard* and *adverse selection*, both of these classical insurance problems are a result of asymmetric information between the insurer and insured. Moral hazard problems arise from *hidden action*. Specifically, insurers cannot perfectly observe the risk management activities of insurance purchasers. Insurance, in turn, affects those risk management activities—if risk management is costly, the existence of insurance may mitigate a firm's incentives to manage its risks proactively and preventively. So, insurance may lessen the insurance purchaser's attention to risk management, and the insurer is unable to observe that—and, in consequence, cannot directly adjust insurance prices to reflect the true risks and incentives faced by the insurance purchaser.

Adverse selection, by contrast, arises from *hidden information*. We have already seen and discussed adverse selection in Chapter 4 at some length. In an insurance context, adverse selection occurs when insurers cannot distinguish inherently good risks from bad ones. Insurers will tend to assume the worst, which may yield insurance prices that are too high for low-risk types and too low for high-risk types. In turn, the extreme case occurs when insurers expect this outcome, set prices assuming only the bad types will insure, and thus essentially guarantee that only the bad types will indeed insure.

Moral hazard and adverse selection have a significant impact on the structure of insurance markets and the design of insurance contracts. Although we have touched on these fundamental issues of asymmetric information already in Part One, some more specific attention is warranted as to how these two problems manifest themselves in insurance markets.

MORAL HAZARD AND INSURANCE CONTRACT DESIGN

When the purchaser of insurance can take actions that impact either the probability of incurring an insurable loss or the size of that loss *and* asymmetric information prevents the insurer from perfectly observing those actions of the insured, the problem of moral hazard can arise.

Most people are familiar with the usual, cynical examples of this phenomenon in personal insurance markets—the insured home owner who burns the house down; the insured auto owner who leaves the keys in the car, abandons it in a bad part of town, and then claims it was stolen. And without proper attention to contracting issues, these can indeed be problems.

Much more common, however, is the impact that insurance has on even well-intended individuals and on cost-minimizing corporations. If risk management and risk prevention are at all costly, then insurance will reduce the amount spent on risk management. As long as an insurance company can observe this, the price of the insurance will adjust to reflect the new probability of a loss. But when the insurance company *cannot* observe the purchaser's risk management activities, it must try to address moral hazard through nonprice mechanisms in the design of the insurance contracts. Several commonplace features of insurance are directly traced to the moral hazard problem.

Policy Limits

A very common way both to mitigate moral hazard and to limit an insurance company's own maximum risk is to include a policy limit in the insurance contract. This establishes a maximum amount that the insurance company will pay. Policy limits may be defined on a per-loss or per-occurrence basis, in aggregate over the life of the policy, or in other ways. To find an insurance policy without a limit is quite rare.

Aggregate Annual Limit   The most straightforward type of limit is a fixed aggregate limit that applies to the whole life of the policy—a year per our earlier discussion. To illustrate this concept, let's return to the homeowner buying fire insurance in Exhibit 8.1. Now suppose the indemnity contract is chosen, and the insurance company includes an aggregate policy limit of $500,000 per year. We assumed before that the current value of the house was $1 million and that the policy payoff was calculated relative to that amount. Assuming that is still true, Exhibit 8.3 shows the payoff on the same policy with a limit of $500,000 per year. For all losses in value attributable to the fire *up to* $500,000, the policy reimburses the homeowner dollar for dollar. But any loss in excess of $500,000 is retained by the homeowner, thereby giving the homeowner a stronger incentive to engage in fire prevention and risk management.

Exhibit 8.3 is the payoff on a short vertical spread in option parlance. In this example, the policy is equivalent to a long put option struck at $1 million and a short put option struck at $500,000, both of which have a maturity date equal to the policy term and an underlying asset defined as the postfire value of the house.

Per-Occurrence or Per-Loss Limits   Policy limits can also apply on a per-occurrence or per-loss basis. This limits the amount that the insurance company owes *on any single claim*. Such limits are commonly associated with insurance contracts that cover risks that have a reasonable likelihood of causing more than one claim per year. Per-occurrence limits are usually found in combination with aggregate annual limits. The two complement one another to mitigate moral hazard; one type of limit generally is not a replacement or substitute for the other.

To keep our previous example going, a property insurance policy triggered by fire might have an annual aggregate limit of $500,000 and a per-loss limit of $250,000. This means that the insurance company will not pay out more than $500,000 in claims *per year* but will not pay more than $250,000 *per fire*. If a fire occurs and destroys the house, for example, the policy would pay $250,000, not the full limit of $500,000. But if two fires occur and each causes $200,000 of damage, the home owner can collect a total of $400,000 because neither fire exhausts the per-risk or aggregate policy limit.

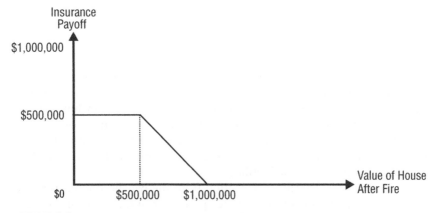

EXHIBIT 8.3   Property (Fire) Insurance with $500,000 Aggregate Limit per Year

Other Limits   Insurance companies concerned about moral hazard can get quite creative in defining new ways of limiting their liability and encouraging better risk management on the part of the insurance purchaser. Some limits are more intended to accomplish the former, whereas others are more clearly directed at the latter.

Health insurance policies often contain a *lifetime coverage limit*, for example, that puts a maximum liability on a single insurance purchaser. Such a policy may also still have annual limits and possibly per-occurrence limits. A lifetime coverage limit does not do much to mitigate moral hazard, but it doesn't hurt. Instead, lifetime limits are more likely driven by a desire to mitigate adverse selection. In the event that the insurer fails to identify a purchaser who poses an incredibly high ongoing risk to the insurer, a lifetime limit will cap its maximum liability.

As another example, insurance may contain *sublimits* or *inner limits* that are directed at certain specific risk types. Dental insurance, for example, may pay for the cost of regular preventive teeth cleanings subject only to an annual limit, but might place a per-risk sublimit on payments related to, say, maxillofacial surgery.

Reinstatement   Some insurance policies (mostly reinsurance, as we will encounter in Chapter 9) include a provision that allows an insurance contract to be restored to its full amount relative to the limit following a large loss. This almost always requires the payment of additional premium and thus is not a free option. Without reinstatement, a large loss that exhausts a policy limit early in a policy year will force the insurance purchaser to essentially go through the rest of the year uninsured. In this sense, reinstatement—even when it is costly—can provide insurance purchasers with an additional level of comfort.

Deductibles

By capping the total amount of a loss that an insurance company must pay, policy limits discourage insurance purchasers from throwing all caution to the wind and abandoning prudential risk management. Policy limits, however, apply either to single catastrophic losses or to a pattern of multiple smaller losses. Either way, they may not be adequate to encourage firms to incur the costs of managing the risks of encountering *small* losses. For that, insurance companies use deductibles.

A deductible is literally a deduction from the benefit amount that the insurance company owes the insurance purchaser in the event of a loss. If the deductible exceeds the loss, no payment occurs either way. If the loss exceeds the deductible, the payout to the insurance buyer is equal to the loss *less* the deductible.

Straight Deductibles A *straight deductible* is a fixed amount. It can be applied annually or per loss, just like the policy limits discussed earlier.

To see how a straight deductible works, return again to the homeowner buying indemnity insurance against damage from a house fire. Assume the policy has a $500,000 annual limit and that the house is worth $1 million before the fire. Now suppose the policy has an annual deductible of $125,000. Exhibit 8.4 shows the payoff on such an insurance contract. The policy now pays the difference between $875,000 and the postfire value of the house up to a total payout of $500,000. The first $125,000 in losses are absorbed by the homeowner.

The gray line in Exhibit 8.4 shows for comparison the original policy with no deductible. In the no deductible case, the homeowner receives the maximum insurance payment if the value of the house declines to $500,000. With the deductible, the homeowner receives the maximum payout of $500,000 only if the house declines in value to $375,000.

The insurance contract still resembles a short vertical spread, but now the long put option is struck at $875,000; it is out-of-the-money by the amount of the deductible. With a large enough deductible, the insured party has some incentive to engage in protective actions such as installing

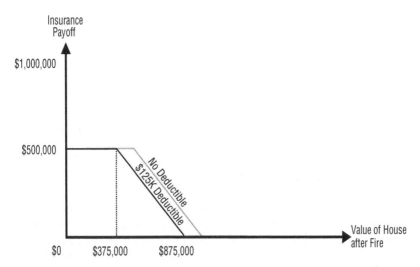

EXHIBIT 8.4 Property (Fire) Insurance with $500,000 Aggregate Limit and $125,000 Deductible per Year

smoke detectors, buying fire extinguishers, and the like. In addition, the deductible lowers any return to arson on the part of the insured.

Disappearing Deductibles   A disappearing deductible is an alternative to a straight deductible that becomes smaller as the economic damage sustained becomes larger. Such a deductible results in the following contingent liability for the insurer following an occurrence of the triggering event underlying the policy:

$$(L - D)(1 + \zeta)$$

where L is the aggregate economic loss or damage sustained, D is a fixed deductible amount, and ζ is a "recapture factor" that turns the fixed deductible into a disappearing one.

Consider in our ongoing example that the fire insurance policy has a fixed deductible D of \$125,000 and a recapture factor ζ of 10 percent. Suppose the aggregate annual loss from fire to the home is only \$150,000. The insurance company then owes

$$(\$150,000 - \$125,000)1.10 = \$27,500$$

The remaining \$122,500 of damage is retained by the insurer as a deductible at that loss level. But for a much larger loss of \$500,000, the insurance company then owes

$$(\$500,000 - \$125,000)1.10 = \$412,500$$

leaving the homeowner with only \$87,500 in retained losses.

Franchise Deductibles   A *franchise deductible* specifies a minimum threshold for losses before any payments are made. When payments are made, however, the *entire loss* is payable by the insurer. The franchise deductible may either be a fixed or percentage number, may be per-occurrence or aggregate, and may be used in conjunction with straight deductibles (in which case the benefit payment still reflects the straight deductible amount).

A franchise deductible essentially acts like a *second trigger* on a traditional insurance contract. The first trigger requires that the specified risk event has occurred and that the insurer owes a positive benefit payment to the insurance purchaser. With a franchise deductible, the second trigger must also be pulled before any benefit payment is made, but the amount of the benefit payment does not depend on this second trigger.

To see how it works, suppose now that our homeowner's policy has an annual limit of $500,000, no straight deductible, and a franchise deductible of $375,000. Exhibit 8.5 shows the payoff on this contract as a heavy gray line. The dashed black line, by comparison, is the payoff on a traditional insurance policy with a $500,000 limit and no deductible. The payoff on the policy with the franchise deductible is discontinuous where the value of the house following a fire has declined to $625,000. If the value of the house is $625,001 after the fire, the loss is only $374,999 and the franchise deductible is not satisfied. The policy thus pays nothing. But if the house were to lose just one more dollar of value and decline to $625,000 because of the fire, the policy would immediately pay out $375,000. And for every dollar of additional loss, the benefit amount would grow dollar for dollar up to the limit of $500,000.

Options aficionados will recognize the payoff in Exhibit 8.4 as the payoff on a down-and-in barrier put option. The "barrier" or "instrike" is defined as $625,000, and the strike price is $1 million. Unless the barrier is crossed, the option is not exercisable. But once this second trigger has been pulled, the option can be exercised at its normal intrinsic value.

Co-Insurance Provisions

Policy limits and deductibles are designed essentially for insurance purchasers to retain some risk at both extremes—for small, early losses and for large, catastrophic ones. Insurance may also involve a *co-insurance* provision that requires an insurer to pay only some fraction of the total

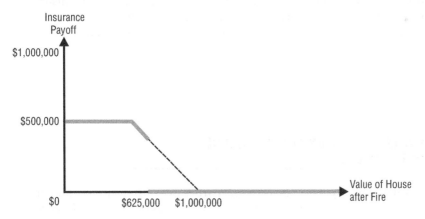

EXHIBIT 8.5 Property (Fire) Insurance with $500,000 Aggregate Limit and $375,000 Annual Aggregate Franchise Deductible

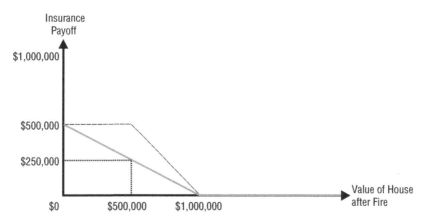

EXHIBIT 8.6   Property (Fire) Insurance with $500,000 Aggregate Limit and
50 Percent Co-Insurance

insured loss and leaves the remainder of the loss to be paid by the insured
party. Co-insurance provisions also may require that this uninsured portion of the exposure be retained to prevent the insured party from seeking coverage for the co-insured amount under another policy from
another insurance provider. The retention thus forces the policyholder to
engage in some prudent risk management and discourages fraudulent or
malicious claims.

Exhibit 8.6 shows our now-familiar fire insurance policy with no deductible, a $500,000 aggregate annual limit, and a 50 percent co-insurance
provision. Shown in gray, the payoff on this option forces the insurance
purchaser to bear 50 cents of every dollar lost. The limit on this policy is
now reached only if the house is completely destroyed, as compared with
the original policy (whose payoff is the black dashed line) that reaches its
limit when the house sustains $500,000 in damage.

Yet again, we can interpret the program in options lingo. We have in
this case bought *half* of a put struck at-the-money at $1 million.

ADVERSE SELECTION AND INSURANCE
CONTRACT DESIGN

Informational asymmetries between parties seeking insurance and those
providing it can also give rise to adverse selection problems. We encountered adverse selection already in Chapter 4. In the insurance context, adverse selection occurs when the insurer cannot tell the true risk type of the

insurance purchaser and gets stuck with too many bad risks at the rate levels it charges.

In the extreme, adverse selection in insurance can lead to a lemons problem such as we saw in Chapter 4. When an insurer cannot distinguish between a good insurance risk and a lemon, the rate charged will be based on some average across both types of customers. This pooled price will be too high for good risks, thus guaranteeing that only bad risks buy insurance. The goal for the insurer thus is to develop a contract design or pricing mechanism that helps it to distinguish good from bad insurance risks. Rothschild and Stiglitz (1976) and others have proposed various price/coverage combinations to help insurance companies resolve this problem.

In practice, insurance companies rely heavily on a process known as *classification* to help mitigate adverse selection problems. Classification is the process by which an insurance company classifies individuals or corporations in certain risk categories and then rates those categories. Insurance companies traditionally use one of four rating methods for their determination of an actuarially fair rate that covers their expected payments to a given risk classification group, each of which is discussed briefly: individual, judgment, class, and merit ratings.

Individual Ratings

Individual ratings are assessed *per individual, per company,* or *per policy* and are usually based on the actual loss experience of the insurance purchaser for the risk underwritten in the policy. This presumes that loss experience data is stable and representative of future loss experiences. Individual ratings also require either significant amounts of high-quality historical data on loss experience at the policyholder level or on aggregate loss experience that the insurer is comfortable can be applied to the policyholder in question.

Individual ratings are usually adopted either when an insurer has very good information about the true risk profile of a specific policyholder or when an insurer has an extremely large portfolio of homogenous loss exposure units. In that case, the insurer is essentially relying on the central limit theorem, which says that the larger the number of policies, the more the distribution of average losses converges to a normal distribution. So, the insurer really needs data only on the mean and variance of losses in order to come up with a fairly reliable estimate for the pure premium, which we saw earlier is the expected loss. Remember, however, that the variance of losses on any given policy can be huge even if the average policy is priced properly.

Judgment Ratings

When information and/or historical data are lacking about the loss experience of a given insurance purchaser, the subjective judgment of the insurance company's rating division is usually the primary determinant of the rate. Like individual ratings, judgment ratings are assessed on a *per policy* basis.

Judgment ratings are sometimes called *expert systems* and can involve varying degrees of formality. Sometimes the career experience of the rating personnel is deemed adequate. In other cases the insurance company may develop elaborate models that attempt to predict or approximate the loss experience of a given policy.

Judgment ratings apply most commonly to exotic risks that are difficult to quantify with objective criteria and existing historical data.

Class Ratings

Class ratings are assigned to groups of people or companies rather than assessed on a per-policy basis. Class rating typically involves three key components: defining classes for a given risk, classification of policyholders into the proper class rating, and determining the proper rate for each class.

In defining the classes for a given policy line, classes must be large enough to facilitate adequate risk pooling and averaging *within the class* so that the average policy risk within a given class can be covered by the class rating. Ideally, classes should be defined so that risk is relatively homogeneous within a given class. The insurance company can then diversify its overall risk exposure across classes and policy lines. In addition, members of a class should have a causal relationship with the claim exposure.

When it comes to classifying individual policyholders, mitigating adverse selection is the foremost goal. But insurance companies should not forget moral hazard, as well. A firm that knows it is being classified as a low-risk type may engage in less risk management than is desired, and this must also be taken into account in the classification process.

With the right amount and quality of data, classification is often done using principal components analysis, which is a type of regression analysis that seeks to associate a given loss experience with the underlying classes of risk that generate that loss experience. Subjective judgment is also more important than many insurers like to admit in the classification process. Especially where such subjective judgments are involved, care must be taken not to violate antidiscrimination laws and any egalitarian principles adopted by the insurer or in the insurer's policy regime.

Finally, the assignment of ratings to classes is largely an empirical exercise given loss frequency and severity within each class. In the absence of data, judgment comes into play.

Residential property insurance against fire-related damage is often subject to class ratings. Fire insurance classes are based upon variables like type of occupancy; mobility (i.e., whether the risk is a stationary object like a building or personal property); quality of local fire protection; construction type and materials; and amount of insurance purchased.

Automobile collision and liability insurance is also often class-rated. The pure premium rate p^* is set so that

$$p^* = p^°(\alpha + \beta)$$

where $p^°$ = base pure premium
α = primary adjustment factor
β = secondary adjustment factor

The base pure premium will be determined from variables such as the model and make of the car being insured and the territory of its principal use. The primary adjustment factor then attempts to incorporate information about who is using the car and why—number of drivers, age and sex of driver(s), primary use(s) of car, and so on. Finally, a secondary adjustment is made to reflect additional information relevant to the risk of the policy that is not directly related to the insured car and driver, such as total number of cars being insured, make and model of all cars together, and the like. Points assessed against drivers in an auto safety program also often enter through the secondary adjustment.

Merit Ratings

A merit rating system is a hybrid between an individual and a class rating system. Merit ratings begin with a group classification and a class rating. As the actual loss experience of the insured is revealed, the rate is changed to address the actual risk profile of the individual insurance purchaser. In this manner, merit ratings dynamically discourage moral hazard and mitigate adverse selection.

Three common forms of merit ratings include *schedule ratings, retrospective ratings*, and *experience ratings*. In a schedule rating regime, a schedule lists average characteristics for a given type of risk. Credit or deficiency points are then assigned to individuals or firms with a loss experience above or below the average. Schedule ratings are heavily reliant on judgment to determine whether the entire class rating should be changed or just the individual rate.

In a retrospective ratings system, a class rating is used to assess the initial premium, but the final premium paid is adjusted for actual loss experience *ex post*. Experience or prospective ratings, in contrast, are based on the actual past experience of the insured and the expectation of future loss experience.

As noted earlier, most residential fire insurance is class-rated. An exception is U.S. commercial fire insurance sold to large organizations; that is merit-rated using a scheduling approach. The U.S. *Commercial Fire Rating Schedule* specifies the rating procedure. First, an on-site inspection is undertaken to classify the property in terms of construction, occupancy, protection systems, and the like. The schedule rate then is determined by the information gathered from the on-site due diligence plus the addition of charges to reflect ways that the property is riskier than comparable properties in the area or the subtraction of charges to reflect ways that the property is less risky than comparable properties in the area.

A *bonus-malus* (B-M) rating system is a specific kind of merit rating approach that is explicitly designed to mitigate moral hazard and adverse selection. A *no-claims bonus scheme*, for example, sets the initial rate at a deep discount with the expectation of no claims. If over the life of the policy there are any claims at all, the future discount is forfeited. An *up/down scheme*, by contrast, places a policyholder in an initial category based on past loss experience and future expected losses. Each claim-free period allows the policyholder to migrate from the current class rating to a higher class rating, whereas each claim moves the policyholder to a lower rating. Movements into new categories may involve a change of more than one class and may not be symmetric for up and down moves.

The first up/down B-M system was used in Switzerland in 1963 in auto insurance and was a one-up/three-down system (Outreville, 1998). The system involved 22 premium classes, with class 1 being the lowest risk and lowest premium. Each claim-free period moved the insured down one class, whereas each claim moved the insured up three classes.

Considerations in Choosing a Rating System

In today's social and business environment, the age-old process of classification undertaken as part of insurance companies' rate-making processes requires careful attention from the insurer to several additional issues. Depending on the company, its location, and its aggressiveness, some of these issues may be deemed less important than others.

Commercial Considerations in Rate Making Insurance companies are businesses, and, as such, must set rates in a manner that is consistent with the interests of their security holders. Profit maximization in rate making is consistent with the market value rule that leads to maximization of firm value. But a number of issues can affect an insurance company's long-term profits. Some of these variables are:

- *Simplicity.* The most efficient or profit-maximizing rate structure is often too complex for consumers. Profits can be higher for a firm if a simpler yet suboptimal rate structure is adopted in place of one that is just too complex for consumers to follow.
- *Stability.* Given that many firms and individuals rely on insurance to help increase the predictability of their long-term consumption and production choices, too much rate volatility can undermine the benefits of the insurance program.
- *Responsiveness.* New information about the underlying risk should be incorporated into rates as quickly as possible.
- *Loss control.* Rates should reward mitigants and penalize accelerants of moral hazard.
- *Classification costs.* Classification itself is costly and increases the premium loading. All else being equal, the benefits of more efficiently priced risk must be compared to potential reductions in underwriting volume coverage associated with higher premium loadings.

Noncommercial Considerations Social and political considerations in the classification and rate-making process relate to the perception and operation of the insurer as part of a society's risk culture. Often influenced by regulatory considerations, the reputational impact of a pricing policy on the commercial operations of a firm cannot be dismissed.

The role played by insurance companies in some countries and societies goes well beyond the role of a normal for-profit corporation whose sole goal is pursuit of the market value rule and the maximization of the combined wealth of its security holders. Insurance of some kinds and in some places is still viewed as a type of right or entitlement—a public good, as it were. In such regimes, the following factors may play a role in insurance rate-making, whether or not the insurance company likes it:

- *Adequacy.* The rate structure must be enough to sustain the insurance company, given the perceived social costs of an insurance company failure.

- *Reasonableness.* The profit margin of the insurer should be positive but reasonable.
- *Equitableness.* The rate must not be unfairly discriminatory.

Relying too much on noncommercial considerations like these, however, can be dangerous. It interferes with the operation of the price system, which has long been recognized as far superior to other methods of resource allocation.

Consider, for example, the equitableness issue, which is essentially a veiled argument against price discrimination. Price discrimination occurs when different prices are charged to different groups of customers. Yet we know this is often efficient. When airlines charge higher prices to last-minute business travelers, they are merely relying on the fact that last-minute business travelers have a stronger intensity of demand for travel. Yes, the result is inequitable—two people in adjacent seats on the same plane may well be paying a fare that differs by a substantial amount. But this inequitability is hardly discriminatory, unless you consider discrimination against business travelers as a type of social discrimination.

Bigger problems arise when the risk of insurance purchasers is correlated with some sociopolitical variable like religion, race, or gender. Consider, for example, health insurance. Premiums are likely to be higher for policyholders who live in public housing, because, unfortunately, public housing in many cities is still dominated by drug lords and gangs and exhibits higher crime rates than other urban locales. In many cities, a disproportional number of minorities live in public housing. An insurance company that charges higher rates to people in public housing is thus at risk of being accused of discriminating against minorities.

This problem, of course, works in both directions. On the one hand, an insurance company may simply be using classification by location to price its risk and deter adverse selection. This is *correlated with* race, but not *driven by* racial discrimination. But on the other hand, an insurance company that wishes to discriminate racially could easily hide behind this correlation as a defense. And there is no easy way for outsiders to tell the difference.

INSURANCE COMPANIES

Insurance is provided by insurance companies or *primary carriers*. In some cases, a single risk is insured by more than one insurance company. Historically, the lead or primary insurance company would put its name at the top of a "slip" and then solicit other insurance companies to join in sharing the risk to be assumed. These firms would place their names underneath the lead insurer on the slip. The process by which an insurance company assumes risk thus came to be known as *underwriting*, and the lead insurer was called the *lead underwriter*.

Insurance Companies and Lines

Underwriters are also sometimes called carriers because they carry certain types of insurance policy coverage or *lines*. Within Lloyd's (which will be explained in the next subsection), underwriters are separated according to whether their primary product offerings are marine, nonmarine, aviation, or motor. Non-Lloyd's commercial insurance companies are usually distinguished based on whether they are life or nonlife carriers, and, in the latter case, whether they are mainly property and casualty or liability carriers.

A *monoline* insurer is an insurance company that underwrites only a single type of risk, such as credit risk. (See Chapter 10.) A *multiline* insurer, by contrast, offers products that cut across more than one type of risk, hazard, or peril.

Historically, insurance has been divided into *marine* and *nonmarine* coverage lines. Ocean marine insurance includes hull, cargo, freight, and liability risks. Nonmarine insurance then can be divided into *life* and *nonlife* products. Life insurance provides financial protection to a beneficiary in the event of premature death and includes a wide range of products such as term life, whole life, endowment life, variable life, and universal life. Nonlife, nonmarine lines are often separated based on the target population of insurance customers. There is one common division, along with examples of specific coverage offered to each group:[2]

- *Individual insurance* includes health and travel insurance.
- *Household insurance* includes home, renter's, and auto insurance.
- *Business insurance* includes property, liability, credit, crime, and errors and omissions (E&O) insurance.
- *Employee benefits insurance* includes group health and life, disability, workers' compensation, and unemployment insurance.

Business insurance, in particular, has many different variations depending on the nature of the risk, hazard, or peril the firm wishes to transfer to an assuming insurer. Following are some of the most common types of business insurance and some examples of the risks, hazards, and perils these business insurance products typically cover:

- *Professional indemnity (PI)*—liabilities arising from failures in business processes, negligent commercial conduct, and inaccurate information inadvertently supplied to customers.
- *Crime and fidelity*—fraud, theft of firm resources, malicious damage and sabotage, and employee collusion.
- *Directors and officers (D&O)*—failure to manage assets or finances of the firm responsibly, failure to maintain confidence or growth in the firm, negligent misstatements and accounting fraud, actions taken beyond the scope of authority, misappropriations of funds or property, and breach of statutory or fiduciary duty.
- *Property damage (PD)*—physical damage to property and equipment, and damage to information technology systems.
- *Product liability*—damages for which the insurance purchaser is liable arising from distribution or sale of a product resulting in damage to its customers.
- *Business interruption (BI)*—increasing working costs due to exogenous events, disruption of production, and interruption of service provision.
- *Errors and omissions (E&O)*—literally a catchall remainders policy to cover miscellaneous liability, damage arising from computer viruses and malicious code, terrorism, and the like.

Insurance Company Structures

Three types of companies typically provide insurance contracts to firms wishing to use insurance as a risk transfer mechanism. *Stock insurance companies* are open corporations, whereas *mutual insurance companies* are mutuals in which the policyholders insured by the company are also its owners. Finally, *cooperative insurance companies* are formed in conjunction with some cooperative movement, often in conjunction with organized labor or a trade association. Cooperatives may be organized as a stock or mutual and are usually distinguished from pure stock or mutual companies based on their mission statement and operating principles. A cooperative insurer might, for example, give policy preference to members of the trade union with which it is affiliated.

The evolution of ART and the integration of risk and capital management have led to significant and renewed interest in the organization and design of insurance companies—especially special-purpose insurance mutuals formed specifically to serve the needs of single firms or small groups. We will return to this issue again in some detail in Chapter 23.

In only one forum are individuals allowed to supply commercial insurance, and that forum is Lloyd's, operating since it was founded by Edward Lloyd in 1688 as Lloyd's Coffee House. Lloyd's has more than 30,000 members or "Names" that are grouped into nearly 500 "syndicates." Members are admitted as Names only if they deposit certain funds in trust and satisfy a minimum net worth requirement. Upon admission to membership, Lloyd's members are granted the right to underwrite insurance as individuals but face unlimited personal liability in any such underwritings.

Lloyd's is especially attractive to insurance purchasers wishing to underwrite an unusual or exotic risk exposure. Whether insurance for undiscovered environmental liabilities, kidnap and ransom (K&R), or an aborted treasure hunt in the South Pacific, Lloyd's has the reputation for offering coverage on just about anything that can be defined in insurance terms. To get coverage from Lloyd's, a firm brings its insurance need to a Lloyd's broker. The broker then declares the need of the insurance purchaser on a "slip" and solicits syndicate signatories to the slip to provide cover for the risk. Importantly, Names do not underwrite risks directly; syndicates underwrite slips and allow Names to underwrite only as a group through their syndicate.

Typical Insurance Company Operations

An insurance company is a company. Like all companies, the operation of the business involves various operating divisions that interact to provide a single set of core business lines. We review the main operating divisions of a typical insurance company in the sections that follow.

Product Design and Development   Product design and development is one of the most important areas of insurance company operations. This is part and parcel of the insurance company's core business. It essentially involves an assessment of demand, engineering the product or solution to meet the demand, evaluation of risk management and pricing for the new product, and advocacy of the new product line with senior management.

Production and Distribution   With very few exceptions, insurance companies rarely market their own products. When an insurance company does its own marketing, this is called *direct writing*. A very recent trend toward direct writing has been observed in the auto insurance area, but for the moment this remains a relatively uncommon practice. (One cannot help but wonder if recent controversies over insurance brokerage activities may tilt the scale more toward direct writing in the future.)

Insurance companies rely on two key distribution entities to sell their products to customers. The first is an *agent*, an authorized representative of an insurance company. An agent may be exclusive to a single insurance company or an independent representative of several insurance companies. All agents can solicit business, but only some can bind the company in a contract. Agents also often oversee premium collection, loss claims administration, and adjustment. Agents are typically associated with personal insurance.

Commercial insurance, by contrast, is generally distributed through *brokers* like Marsh, Aon, Willis, and Jardines. A broker acts as a representative of customers in their search for the right insurance company and policy. Large brokers often provide highly integrated services across all aspects of the insurance and risk management business.

Apart from managing any direct writing of the business, the production and distribution center of an insurance company focuses mainly on management of a sales force (including agents) and liaison with brokers.

Product Management   The central feature in the operation of an insurance company is the product management function, which includes rate making, underwriting, claims adjustment, and settlement. The rate making division is responsible for implementing the pricing structures discussed earlier in this chapter. This involves a considerable amount of statistical and actuarial research on products, risk types, and customer types. Ultimately, the rate making division is responsible for classification. Typical rate making groups also engage in some risk management as well as an analysis of the funding profile and costs of an insurance line.

The objective of the underwriting process is the determination of which policies are worth writing. This is not loss avoidance as much as an effort to avoid the misclassification of risks. Underwriting thus is essentially in charge of monitoring and controlling moral hazard and adverse selection. Staff underwriting functions include the formulation of general underwriting policies, the review of rating plans and reinsurance, and so on, whereas line underwriting functions include evaluations of proposed policies, analysis of information that comes from the producer (i.e., the sales agent), classification, and determination of final coverage and rate.

Finally, claims adjustment and settlement is the division that administers the claims processing cycle. The claims processing cycle at a typical insurance company is:

- *Reporting*—policyholder notifies insurance company of loss and provides proof of loss.
- *Processing*—verification of valid coverage, assignment to an adjuster, and estimation of loss reserve (see later in chapter) and loss adjustment expense.
- *Adjustment*—investigation of veracity of claim and loss evaluation, followed by suggested adjustment to claim if appropriate.
- *Settlement*—actual discharge of payment obligations to customer.
- *Recording*—loss reserve allocation (see later in chapter), subrogation and arbitration, and reinsurance (see Chapter 9).

Services and Administration   Like any other corporation, insurance companies also have the necessary services divisions like legal affairs, internal audit, employee training and education, human resources, and the like. Albeit cost centers rather than revenue-producing business units, these divisions are essential parts of the insurance company enterprise.

Finance and Investment   The financial side of an insurance company is unique and critically important to the operation of the firm. The responsibilities of this division include all the usual corporate treasury functions, such as liquidity and capital structure management. In addition, the finance and investment arm of an insurance company is also responsible for the asset-liability management (ALM) activities of the firm, which includes investing premium revenue in assets to fund subsequent policy payouts. We will return to discuss these activities in the next major section of this chapter.

Risk Management   The risk management function of an insurance company is among its most important operating divisions. The division is responsible for the identification, measurement, control, reporting, and oversight of the insurance company's risks. Activities in which risk management may be heavily involved include new product approval, limits administration, liaison and integration with finance and investment activities for ALM, risk capital allocation, and the like.

RESERVE AND ASSET-LIABILITY MANAGEMENT AT INSURANCE COMPANIES

Ostensibly, the core business of an insurance company is its liabilities—the policy lines that the firm underwrites. In reality, some contend that offering insurance is merely the excuse used by insurance companies to justify their involvement in asset management. The truth is probably somewhere in between.

In return for providing insurance contracts, insurance companies receive premiums. The total premium collected by an insurance company then can be used to pay off claims arising from its contingent liabilities. But because claims do not necessarily arrive in the same time period (e.g., year) that premium is collected, insurance companies must utilize *technical reserves*. How insurance companies manage their technical reserves is an important determinant for their demand for reinsurance as discussed in the next chapter, so some background discussion here is warranted.

Need for Reserves

If insurance pricing is always correct, then the average loss on a portfolio of policies will always be covered by the premium collected. Being right about the average, however, does not protect the insurer from the risk of potentially extreme payment obligations away from the mean. Being right about the average in present value terms, moreover, does not mean the insurer does not bear risk associated with large claims arriving earlier than expected. For these reasons, insurance companies rely on reserves. Reserves are the means by which an insurance company engages in preloss risk finance as discussed in Chapter 7.

It's also quite possible that pricing is wrong, in which case the pure premium plus load will not cover the average claim plus costs of administering a policy line. In this sense, reserves can be a "fudge factor" for getting the premium calculation wrong in the rate-making process.

Methods of Reserve Management

Technical reserves at an insurance company must be viewed differently from the concept of reserves introduced in Chapter 6. For an insurance company, its technical reserves are *liabilities*. The premium an insurance company collects is usually invested in assets that back those technical reserve liabilities, and the technical reserves of the firm then represent the future claims expected on insurance contracts the company has offered.

Insurance companies utilize one of two reserve management methods for financing the claims arising from their liabilities.[3] Under the *capitalization method* of reserve management, an insurance company invests its premium collected in assets and then uses those assets plus the return on those assets to finance subsequent insurance claims. Firms using the capitalization method usually attempt to keep assets funded by premium collections linked to the technical reserves of the liabilities for which premium was collected. If premium is collected on a property damage line, for example, the assets acquired with that premium are usually earmarked to back the technical reserve liabilities of the property damage line. Technical reserves at firms using the capitalization method tend to be medium- or long-term, as are the assets invested to back the corresponding liabilities.

The *compensation method* of reserve management, by contrast, is a pay-as-you-go system in which all premiums collected over the course of a year are used to pay any claims that year arising from any business lines. Under this method, no real attempt is made to connect assets with technical reserves. All premium collected is used to fund mainly short-term assets, and those assets collectively back all technical reserves for all insurance lines.

The type and maturity of investments made by insurance companies of their technical reserves depends on the reserve management method and the nature of the claims for which reserves are held. In the compensation method, reserves are usually short-term, and thus usually backed by money-market–like assets. The capitalization method usually involves a longer gap between premium collection and claims payments. Firms adopting the capitalization method thus usually invest in assets like fixed income securities (government, corporate, and agency), securitized products, real estate, and common stocks.

Types of Technical Reserves

Whether using the capitalization or compensation method, insurance companies writing nonlife business lines typically have three main types of reserves: unearned premium reserves, equalization reserves, and loss reserves.[4] Reserves can also be differentiated as either *retrospective* or *prospective* in the sense that we defined these terms earlier in this chapter. Specifically, retrospective reserves apply to a policy line that has already been underwritten but for which claims have not yet been filed, and prospective reserves are allocated to policies to be underwritten in the future.

Unearned Premium Reserves   In most traditional nonlife insurance lines (e.g., liability and property), policy coverage lasts one year and premium is payable at the beginning of the policy year. Although premium is collected in advance, it is *earned* only as time passes if a claim has not occurred. *Unearned* premium is premium that has been collected that may still need to be used to cover an as yet unsubmitted claim. The *unearned premium reserve* (UPR) is thus the proportion of premium that must be set aside to honor future expected claims.

Suppose, for example, that a firm writes a one-year fidelity policy on July 1 and collects \$100,000 in premium for writing that policy, but suppose the firm's financial reporting and fiscal year ends on December 31. In this case, only \$50,000 of the premium is considered earned at the end of the year. Unearned premium reserves may be calculated gross or net of commissions paid to insurance brokers and distributors and other expenses.

For accounting purposes, three calculation methods are generally allowed in most major countries (Outreville, 1998). The *half-yearly method* assumes that all policies are written at the midpoint of the calendar year. Policies are presumed to be issued at a constant rate every week or month over the liability period. At the end of the year, 50 percent of all premiums written defines the level of the UPR.

The *semimonthly method*, by contrast, assumes an even and constant distribution of policies during the month *and* that all policies are written in the middle of a month. For any given month k in a 12-month policy/liability period, the unearned premium reserve for policies expiring in month k is computed as

$$UPR_k = \frac{x_k}{24} \sum_{j=1}^{N_k} Q_{j,k}$$

where Q_j is the premium collected on the jth policy of N_k total policies expiring in month k, and where x_k is the number of semiannual periods that have elapsed up to the midpoint of the month. For January, $x_1 = 1$; for

February, $x_2 = 3$; . . . ; for December, $x_{12} = 23$. The total UPR is then the sum of the UPRs across policy months for all policy months in the policy year, or

$$UPR = \sum_{k=1}^{12} UPR_k = \sum_{k=1}^{12} \frac{x_k}{24} \sum_{j=1}^{N_k} Q_{j,k}$$

Finally, the *pro rata temporis* method allows the insurer to calculate the UPR on a daily basis. This assumes, of course, that the insurance company has the resources and data to accomplish this task. The *pro rata temporis* method, however, is not always recognized and allowed by local authorities and regulators.

Regardless of the method chosen, UPR can be calculated based on gross or net premiums—that is, before or after deducting commissions and expenses from the gross premium received. This can substantially affect the reserve number.

If an insurance company has unlimited access to capital, it really won't care whether expenses are included in the UPR calculation. But this is rarely the case. As discussed in Chapters 4 and 6 for nonfinancial corporates, capital tends to be scarce for almost all firms, if only because firms usually incur adverse selection costs to go and get it. But especially if the insurance company in question is capital and/or liquidity constrained, the additional amount of money that must be tied up in a reserve account purely to cover expenses that have been passed through to customers is fairly ridiculous. Nevertheless, many regulatory regimes around the world do not allow insurance companies to deduct expenses when they compute their UPRs.

Equalization Reserves   Some countries permit insurance companies to use equalization reserves to smooth their reported earnings with respect to changes in acquisition and underwriting expenses. In countries like Japan, this is permitted for all policy lines, whereas some other countries permit insurance companies to use equalization reserves only for specifically enumerated risks; for example, Denmark permits the use of equalization reserves to smooth the impact of expense changes on earnings, but only related to storm and hail insurance policy lines. The size of an equalization reserve is usually proportional to the variance of expenses.

Loss Reserves The technical reserves an insurance company maintains to honor any future claims—known or unknown—above the unearned premium is called the *loss reserve*. Loss reserves may be set aside for losses that have been reported and adjusted, reported but not adjusted, or incurred but not reported (IBNR), or for loss adjustment expense (LAE).

CHAPTER 9

Reinsurance

Insurance companies rarely retain all of the risks they underwrite. Some of the risks are neutralized through diversification across policyholders and policy lines, but many of the risks that primary carriers do not wish to retain are transferred to other firms using insurance. When an insurance company buys insurance, this is known as *reinsurance*.

The importance of reinsurance for this book goes well beyond its role in providing a means by which primary insurers can lay off their undesired risks. Reinsurance companies tend to be bigger and involved in a more comprehensive range of financial activities than primary carriers. They also tend to be relatively less regulated. As a result, reinsurers are increasingly providing direct protection to corporate clients. Reinsurance companies also tend to dominate the alternative risk transfer (ART) market space.

THE BASICS

An insurance company that buys insurance is called a *cedant*. The outward transfer of risk by the cedant to the reinsurance company is called a *cession*, and the taking up or inward transfer of risk by the reinsurance company is called an *assumption*. In return for taking up the risk originally borne by the cedant, the reinsurance company receives a premium from the cedant. This process is illustrated in Exhibit 9.1, in which a solid arrow indicates a fixed cash flow, a dashed arrow indicates a contingent cash flow, and a dotted arrow indicates the flow or transfer of risk. The rectangle with the rounded edges indicates an insurance company (later in the book this will more generally represent any provider of insurance or derivatives risk transfer). The light gray shading indicates the cedant, and the darker gray indicates the protection provider (i.e., reinsurer). The shading is specific to the transaction.

When a reinsurance company buys insurance on a reinsured risk, the outward transfer of risk is called a *retrocession* and the reinsurance company

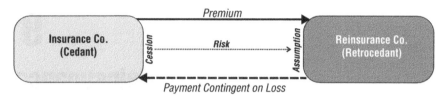

EXHIBIT 9.1   Reinsurance

buying the reinsurance protection is called the *retrocedant*. The reinsurance company that assumes the risk in a retrocession is called the *retrocessionaire*. The retrocession process is shown in Exhibit 9.2. Note that in this example, the original reinsurer is now shaded light gray and the original insurer is unshaded to emphasize that we are focusing here on the retrocession arrangement and not the primary reinsurance coverage, as in Exhibit 9.1.

For the rest of this chapter, we will not distinguish between reinsurance and retrocession since the mechanics and structure of the transactions used are too similar to warrant separate analysis. As a practical matter, however, the reinsurance and retrocession (or just "retro") markets are very different. They are comprised of different firms, and they have dramatically different liquidity and pricing—retrocession being both harder to obtain and significantly more expensive.

Reinsurance companies typically are very well capitalized, have a relatively high credit rating, and are internationally active firms with large, diversified portfolios of underwriting exposure. The top 20 reinsurers in 2003 based on net reinsurance premiums written (NRPW)—both life and nonlife—are listed in Table 9.1.

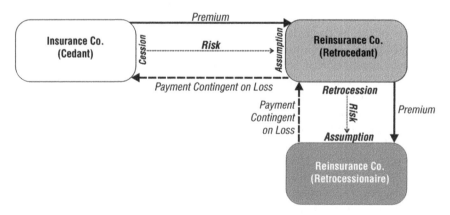

EXHIBIT 9.2   Reinsurance and Retrocession

TABLE 9.1 Top Global Reinsurance Companies in 2003

Ranking	Rating as of 8/1/2003	Company	Domicile	NRPW ($mns)	CR (%)	ASF ($mns)
1	AA–	Munich Re	Germany	$21,343.3	108.3%	$19,965.1
2	AA	Swiss Re	Switzerland	11,352.1	105.2	7,414.1
3	A	Lloyd's	U.K.	6,808.6	98.6	14,142.7
4	AA–	Allianz	Germany	4,046.4	107.2	34,628.2
5	AA–	Hannover Re	Germany	3,965.5	99.0	2,255.1
6	AAA	General Re	U.S.	3,617.4	104.7	4,095.1
7	AA	European Re	Switzerland	2,779.0	101.0	210.5
8	AA–	Employers Re	U.S.	2,550.9	171.8	4,876.1
9	AAA	National Indemnity Co.	U.S.	2,526.4	54.0	15,732.1
10	BBB+	SCOR	France	2,273.3	128.7	844.8
11	—	Gerling Global Re	Germany	2,247.7	106.6	589.9
12	AA	Transatlantic Re	U.S.	2,219.8	102.1	1,545.9
13	AA–	Everest Re	U.S.	2,119.2	98.8	1,494.0
14	AA–	GE Frankona Re	Germany	1,977.4	102.5	—
15	AAA	Cologne Re	Germany	1,950.9	114.7	969.8
16	AA–	Tokio Marine & Fire	Japan	1,941.7	49.1	18,584.5
17	AA	XL Re	Bermuda	1,857.9	94.8	—
18	A	Converium	Switzerland	1,670.5	87.8	—
19	AA	Swiss Re Germany	Germany	1,645.6	109.8	1,408.5
20	AA–	E+S Re	Germany	1,514.2	99.8	883.0

NRPW—net reinsurance premiums written; CR—combined ratio; ASF—adjusted shareholder funds.
Source: Standard & Poor's, *Global Reinsurance Highlights Special Edition* (Reactions, 2005).

The last three columns in Table 9.1 show various measures of size and profitability commonly used in the (re-)insurance world. NPRW is a measure of gross underwriting volume or throughput. This is the (re-)insurance industry analogue to a sales figure.

The combined ratio (CR) of a (re)insurance company is a measure of its profitability. The CR is defined as the sum of net losses incurred plus net underwriting expenses divided by net premium earned. (See Chapter 8 for a discussion of earned vs. unearned premium.)

Finally, the adjusted shareholder funds (ASF) is a measure of the surplus (equity) of the company. The number reflects the difference between the market value of the company's assets and its liabilities, inclusive of equalization reserves (see Chapter 8).

RISKS OF WRITING PRIMARY INSURANCE

Writing insurance exposes an insurance company to at least three distinct types of risk. We need to understand these before we can appreciate the role of reinsurance. We also return to this discussion in later chapters as we examine certain ART products whose purpose is specifically aimed at helping firms manage certain of these risks.

Underwriting Risk

Underwriting risk is the risk that claims filed on a policy line exceed the total premium collected for that policy line. Underwriting risk may occur if an insurance company has calculated the pure premium incorrectly, in which case the premium collected per policy will be too low relative to the size of an average claim. In this case, the insurance company incurs underwriting losses on the policy line on average.

Another source of underwriting risk, of course, is that any given claim may be well above the average. Even if the insurance company has collected adequate premium to cover the average claim, enough very large claims may still impose an underwriting loss on the insurer if its loss reserves are inadequate.

Investment Risk

Investment risk is the risk that the assets the insurance company has purchased to fund its reserves (policy liabilities) decline in market value before the corresponding claims are filed. In this case, the insurance company may have made its premium calculations perfectly correctly and set aside exactly the present value of future claims in unearned premium reserve (UPR) and loss reserves. But if these reserves are funded with, say, shares in a hedge fund and the hedge fund tanks, the cash invested to fund the reserve will be inadequate to pay claims when they arrive.

Timing Risk

Timing risk is the risk that claims arrive at a faster rate than expected. Even if the insurance company has properly reserved against claims and has invested in low-risk assets that have not experienced any investment losses, timing risk can still be a problem.

To see why, suppose the annual risk-free interest rate is 5 percent and that the insurance company funds its liabilities using only risk-free assets. (We assume this so we don't get timing risk mixed up with investment risk.) Suppose further than the insurer writes a one-year policy with an expected claim of $100 and a policy limit of $1,000. If the claim occurs, the insurer expects that it will occur in the last month of the policy. With no premium loading, the pure premium would be $95, or the $100 expected claim discounted back to the present at the riskless rate. The insurer thus receives $95 in premium, invests the proceeds in riskless securities, and expects those securities to be worth $100 when the claim for $100 is filed.

Now suppose the $100 claim is filed on the very next day. Clearly, the insurance company will take a $5 loss in order to pay the claim. This is not underwriting risk per se because the insurance company's estimate that an expected claim will be $100 has proven correct. Nor is this investment risk, because the assets set aside to fund the claim have not experienced any kind of capital loss. The loss is purely related to the insurer's incorrect assumption about when the claim will arrive.

This example is highly stylized. We will return again in Chapter 24 to this problem and be more realistic at that time. For now, it is enough to recognize the basic nature of the risk that incorrect timing assumptions can pose to the insurance company.

MOTIVATIONS FOR PURCHASING REINSURANCE

Traditional reinsurance is insurance purchased by insurance companies to cover their underwriting risks. Insurance companies can engage in reinsurance and retrocession for a wide variety of reasons, some of which are discussed in the following subsections. Note that these structures would not make sense in an M&M world. But when capital markets are imperfect and information asymmetric, *all* can make sense in at least some circumstances.

Increased Underwriting Capacity

Perhaps the most obvious potential benefit of reinsurance is the creation of additional underwriting capacity for the cedant or retrocedant. By transferring risk to the reinsurer or retrocessionaire, the cedant or retrocedant reduces its risk for a given level of insurance liabilities, thus making room for more such liabilities.

Capacity can be inadequate for a primary carrier or reinsurer along two dimensions. *Large-line capacity* is an insurer's ability to absorb an extremely large (i.e., catastrophic) loss on a single policy. In many situations, a policy may be attractive for an insurer, but only up to a certain amount of losses (or, as we shall see later, only between certain loss layers). In order to underwrite the policy, the insurance company needs to know *ex ante* that it will not have to retain all of the underwriting risk. Reinsurance can provide insurers with precisely this assurance.[1]

Separately, some insurers lack *premium capacity*, or the ability to write a large volume of policies in the same business line. Total premiums written by a primary carrier are constrained by the equity capital of the insurance company, sometimes called the firm's *surplus*. Of concern in this case is the ability of the insurer to weather a large number of possibly small losses rather than a single massive claim. But the fundamental rationale for reinsurance is essentially the same as in the large-line capacity case—"renting the balance sheet" of another insurance company as synthetic equity so that the primary carrier or reinsurer can provide all the policies that it would like to write.

Increased Debt Capacity

Reinsurance is risk transfer and contingent risk capital in the sense of Chapter 6. As such, it has the same impact on the firm's capital structure (although not necessarily the same impact on cash flows or earnings) as if the firm issued additional equity. As we saw in Chapter 3, this in turn increases the firm's debt capacity.

Reducing Underinvestment Problems and Enhancing Liquidity

As we saw in Chapter 8, cash held in UPRs is like paid-in risk capital as discussed in Chapter 6 and Appendix C. These funds are tied up and not available for other uses by the firm. In the extreme, this can lead to under-investment problems.

As we will see later, some types of reinsurance involve a cession of premium as well as risk to the reinsurer. This can reduce a firm's required UPR, thereby freeing up liquid funds for other uses. At the same time, ceding or retroceding premium and liabilities also increases the cedant or retrocedant's surplus by taking funds out of a reserve escrow and returning them to retained earnings.

Reduced Earnings and Cash Flow Volatility

When the diversification of risks in a policy line is inadequate, earnings and cash flows can be strongly influenced by small underwriting losses. Like other firms, insurance companies may wish to reduce that volatility of earnings and/or cash flows to avoid underinvestment problems, to increase the quality of information conveyed in a noisy earnings release, or just to facilitate internal cash management and capital budgeting activities. Reinsurance can be used to effect synthetic diversification and thus reduce the sensitivity of earnings and cash flows to highly correlated adverse underwriting results.

Reduced Expected Financial Distress Costs

The need for some carriers to secure catastrophic protection usually arises from low-frequency, high-severity events such as natural disasters, major industrial accidents, multiple accidents arising from a single peril or hazard, and the like. As explained in Chapters 3 and 8, high-severity losses of this kind can cause the market value of a firm's assets to approach or perhaps fall below the face value of the firm's outstanding liabilities, both in a capital structure sense and in a technical loss reserves context.

Reinsurance can create an additional layer of synthetic equity capital that reduces the expected costs of financial distress by reducing the probability that the firm will encounter financial distress.

Information Acquisition

The reinsurance process is extremely information-intensive. Accordingly, the information acquired by a reinsurer during the underwriting process can be quite extensive and potentially valuable. Like banks doing credit checks on their customers, reinsurers engaging in due diligence of prospective cedants may acquire information that enables them to better serve their insurance company client again in the future. In addition, the reinsurer may also require valuable market intelligence, information about its competitors, pricing information, and the like.

A purchaser of reinsurance may also find some benefits from this information transfer for reasons discussed in Chapter 4. Namely, the better informed other providers of capital are, the lower the adverse selection costs of capital obtained from that counterparty. In this sense, reinsurance obtained from a highly rated and respected counterparty can also send a positive signal to other capital providers, thus again reducing a firm's adverse selection costs associated with new securities issues.

Run-Off Solutions

Reinsurance can help primary carriers or reinsurers economically discontinue a policy line without actually having to sell or retire outstanding policies. Suppose, for example, that a primary carrier decides that the risks of providing marine coverage are too high and beyond its shareholders' risk tolerances. The firm can really only leave the business by terminating any new marine underwritings and then allowing its outstanding contracts to wind down. *Or* the carrier could purchase reinsurance, thereby synthetically eliminating the entire business line virtually overnight.

FACULTATIVE VERSUS TREATY REINSURANCE

Reinsurance contracts can take one of two forms—*facultative* or *treaty*. A facultative reinsurance contract covers a single risk and insurance policy. In other words, the reinsurer and insurer negotiate separate facultative contracts for each policy the primary carrier wishes to reinsure. Consequently, facultative reinsurance is extremely flexible and can have terms fully customized by the two parties to the contract. Facultative reinsurance is commonly used for the reinsurance of extremely large or catastrophic risks, very unusual or exotic risks, or specific risks that are not core business line risks for the ceding insurance company.

Treaty reinsurance, by contrast, involves the reinsurance of a group of policies that fall within general guidelines defined by the cedant and reinsurer (or retrocedant and retrocessionaire). In treaty reinsurance, the reinsurer cannot refuse any specific risk or policy in the business line or policy group as long as that policy falls within the predefined parameters of the treaty itself. Because treaties have broad terms negotiated in advance, this type of reinsurance is popular for insurance carriers wishing to reinsure a large number of similar policies, a whole business line, or a fairly traditional set of risks.

Facultative reinsurance is generally subject to larger potential moral hazard and adverse selection problems than treaty reinsurance because the risk, hazard, or peril underlying a facultative reinsurance is very specifically defined. Accordingly, facultative reinsurance generally involves a more in-depth due diligence exercise on the part of the reinsurer. Facultative reinsurance is also more time-consuming to negotiate and more expensive than treaty reinsurance.

Risk-sharing arrangements between the insurance provider and purchaser in classical insurance programs are defined on a policy-by-policy basis. Because reinsurance treaties involve the inclusion of more than one policy, however, the sharing of risk can be accomplished in a number of different ways. All risk-sharing arrangements in treaty reinsurance fall under either the *proportional* or the *excess of loss* (XOL) designation. Specific types of proportional and excess of loss treaties are discussed in the sections that follow.

PROPORTIONAL REINSURANCE TREATIES

Proportional reinsurance involves the sharing of risks between the cedant and reinsurer (or retrocedant and retrocessionaire) on a proportional basis. The proportionality may be defined in fixed or variable terms. The proportion of risk shared usually also acts as the proportion of premium collected that is divided between the two firms, as well as the proportion of any loss adjustment expense (LAE) that must be allocated in the reinsurance program.

Quota Share Treaties

Reinsurance treaties that allocate risk, losses, premium, and loss adjustment expenses on a fixed-percentage basis are called *quota share treaties* (QSTs). A quota share treaty defines a common ratio when the original treaty is bound. This percentage is immediately used to cede a fixed proportion of premium collected from the cedant to the reinsurer, in return for which the reinsurer will bear the same proportion of subsequent claims and LAEs.[2] To compensate the cedant for the expenses incurred in originating the primary policies, the reinsurer also pays a *ceding commission* to the cedant.

Exhibit 9.3 illustrates the mechanics of a QST using what is called a *policy distribution diagram*. The x-axis represents a rank ordering of all the policies underwritten by a primary carrier in a single policy line arranged from the lowest policy limit to the highest. Each point on the

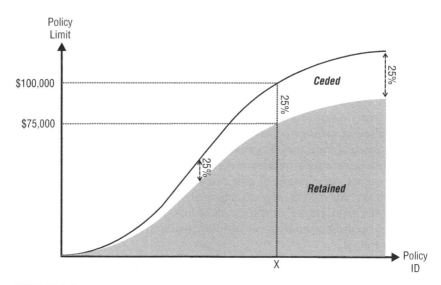

EXHIBIT 9.3   Quota Share Treaty

x-axis thus corresponds to some specific insurance policy. The y-axis then shows the policy limit or total coverage corresponding with each individual policy. Although we ordered the policy holders on the x-axis by increasing order of their policy limits, this need not have been the case. As long as we correctly associate each policy with this limit, we can present the x-axis in any order we like.

The QST depicted in Exhibit 9.3 specifies a reinsurance cession percentage of 25 percent. That means that the primary carrier cedes 25 percent of all premium to the reinsurer, and the reinsurer in turn absorbs 25 percent of all expenses and claims. The gray shaded area in the exhibit indicates the proportional retention by the primary insurer in this case.

Consider, for example, Policy X, which has a limit of $100,000. With a 25 percent cession, that means that the primary carrier is liable for up to $75,000 in claims from the holder of Policy X. In turn, the carrier keeps only 75 percent of the premium. The reinsurer receives the balance of the premium in return for paying 25 percent of all expenses and up to $25,000 in claims.

Note carefully that the percentage sharing rule functions like co-insurance discussed in Chapter 8; that is, the insurer and reinsurer split claims 75/25 for every dollar in claims filed. Looking at the diagram, it would be tempting to conclude that a $75,000 claim from the holder of Policy X would be paid entirely by the primary carrier. But a QST allocates claims liability *per dollar*, not in a way that depends on the order in which the claims were filed. A $75,000 claim thus will require the primary carrier to pay $56,250 on the retained 75 percent, but the reinsurance company will pick up the remaining $18,750.

QSTs are frequently used by insurance companies seeking either increased debt and underwriting capacity through reduced UPRs or additional diversification to reduce cash flow and earnings volatility. As concerns the latter, the practice in which two primary carriers essentially exchange whole portions of their insurance portfolios with one another to increase the diversification of both firms' underwriting businesses is known as a *reciprocity treaty*. A QST can be a useful mechanism to accomplish a reciprocity cession.

Surplus Share Treaties

A reinsurance treaty that allocates risk, losses, and premium on a fixed-dollar, variable-percentage basis is called *surplus share treaty* (SST). Although a treaty rather than a facultative reinsurance structure, the net retention of the cedant in a surplus share treaty is explicitly stated as a separate monetary amount for each policy or group of like policies. Because the dollar amount of the retention is fixed per policy or group, the percentage of each policy retained by the cedant varies from policy to policy or group to group.

Exhibit 9.4 shows a policy distribution diagram again, this time with an SST that defines a retention level of $75,000 across all policies.[3] All policies up to Policy Y would be 100 percent retained by the cedant under this SST because their coverage limits are below $75,000. For policies with higher limits than that, the limit relative to the fixed retention of $75,000 defines the proportional allocation rule. Policy X, for example, has a $100,000 limit. With a $75,000 retention, that means that the ceding insurer pays $75,000 in total claims, keeps 75 percent of the premium, and absorbs 75 percent of the expenses. For a policy with a limit of $110,000, the cedant would retain $75,000 in claims liability and keep 68.2 percent of premium and expenses. And so on.

An SST is effective in creating large-line capacity for the cedant, but it provides little UPR relief because of the focus on large policy exposures. Note also that adverse selection problems can be significant with surplus treaties because the cedant can choose the retention on each policy. Accordingly, the cedant will tend to cede the bad business and retain the good business. Although the surplus share is a treaty, the adverse selection problems thus are more akin to facultative reinsurance than to a QST.

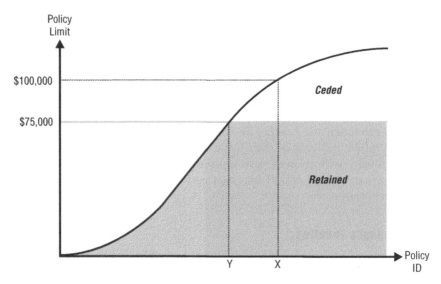

EXHIBIT 9.4   Surplus Share Treaty

EXCESS OF LOSS REINSURANCE

Proportional reinsurance like quota and surplus share treaties always involves *some* cession of premium and *some* allocation of losses to the reinsurer. In an *excess of loss* (XOL) *treaty*, by contrast, the order in which the
losses occur and the total amount of those losses affect the reinsurer's contingent liability. The reinsurer's obligations are based not on fixed or variable percentages of policy limits, but rather on actual claims received.
Small losses thus are retained by the cedant, and only losses over a certain
amount are paid by the reinsurer.

An XOL reinsurance treaty defines *attachment points* for the cession
of any given layer of losses to a reinsurer. The notation "*A* XS *Y*" (read "*A*
excess *Y*") means that a capital provider is supplying up to A of insurance, but only after the firm has already sustained total losses of Y. A
reinsurance program that covers the *A* XS *Y* loss layer thus provides a
maximum reimbursement of A to the primary carrier, but only to cover total losses from Y to $A + Y$. In this case, the lower attachment point is Y
and the upper attachment point is $A + Y$.

Consider a policy line where claims range from $0 to the maximum
loss in which every policyholder files a claim up to their limit. Suppose
there are 10,000 policies, each with a limit of $1,000, so that the maxi-

mum liability of the primary carrier (before reinsurance) is $10 million. Assume the primary carrier is comfortable retaining the first $2 million in claims but would like to reinsure all the rest. Finally, suppose that all the policies being reinsured cover the same calendar year, and that all reinsurance is purchased for the same period.

There are any number of ways that the primary carrier could design a XOL reinsurance treaty, two of which are shown in Exhibit 9.5. In Program 1 in Exhibit 9.5, a single reinsurer has agreed to a cession of the $8mn XS $2mn loss layer. In writing XOL notation, the units are often assumed known, so that we could also write the reinsurance layer here as just $8 XS $2. This means that the primary carrier will pay all claims up to $2 million, and the reinsurer will pay all remaining claims. If only $2 million in claims are submitted during the year, the reinsurer has no liability.

In Program 2 on Exhibit 9.5, the primary carrier has purchased reinsurance for all losses above $2 million, but this time the cedant has gone to three different reinsurance companies for three different layers. Program 2 is known as a *vertically layered* XOL reinsurance program because the liabilities of three reinsurers depend on the order in which the

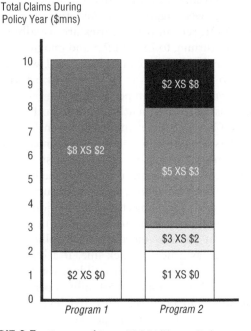

EXHIBIT 9.5 Excess of Loss (XOL) Treaty Reinsurance

claims are submitted over the policy year. Suppose, for example, that $5 million of claims are submitted during the policy year. The first $2 million are paid by the ceding underwriter. One reinsurance company then is liable to cover the $1 million in losses that occur between the $2 million and $3 million attachment points. The remaining $2 million in losses is paid for by the second reinsurer. In this example, the third reinsurer has no liability.

This is quite common for a number of reasons. Some reinsurers specialize in writing certain types of layers (e.g., layers with low or high attachments points). Diversification needs of reinsurers also may dictate their demand for accepting certain layers. And, of course, this can also affect the pricing of different layers quoted by different reinsurers.

The pricing of XOL treaties is generally a flat rate for the whole reinsurance treaty and usually involves some LAE sharing. Premium is allocated between the cedant and reinsurer both in terms of actual claims submitted and on a ratable basis over time.

Aggregate versus Per-Occurrence Programs and Limits

In the example just given, we assumed that the attachment points and reinsurance policy limits were aggregate, cumulative, and annual. This need not be the case. XOL reinsurance treaties are usually written on a per-occurrence basis. Returning to Exhibit 9.5 and imagining that the program is now a per-occurrence XOL program, Program 1 would require the reinsurer to provide up to $8 million in coverage toward $10 million in total damages *per risk event* rather than per annum.

XOL programs quite frequently contain both aggregate and per-occurrence limits. Consider the example shown in Exhibit 9.6 in which a property insurer has provided up to $10 million in coverage to two buildings. Suppose the insurer wishes to retain the first $2 million liability on each building and reinsure the rest. In this case, the insurer goes to a single reinsurer to reinsure both exposures, and the reinsurer agrees to provide $8 XS $2 in *aggregate* coverage, subject to a $4 million per occurrence limit. The reinsurer thus will provide up to $8 million in annual cover on each building, but will not pay any more than $4 million on any single loss, shown in Exhibit 9.6 as a heavy black line. If a hurricane destroys both buildings, resulting in claims on each building for $10 million, the reinsurer's maximum liability is capped at $4 million per building.

The definition of an occurrence or risk event can get quite contentious in such situations, as the tragic events of September 11, 2001, illustrated. Using those events but keeping the numbers in our example,

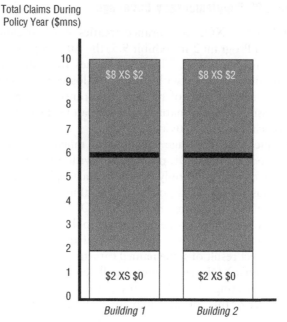

Total Claims During
Policy Year ($mns)

EXHIBIT 9.6 Aggregate versus Per-Occurrence Limits

suppose that each building is one of the Twin Towers. Both were destroyed when terrorists flew airplanes into each building. In our example, this would cause maximum damage of $10 million to each building. If we define the airplane strike to each building as a separate event or occurrence, the reinsurer would be liable for a payment of $4 million on each building. But if we define the "terrorist attack" to be a single event or occurrence, the reinsurer would be liable for only $4 million *total*. How the event is defined thus potentially doubles the liability of the reinsurer in this case.

Swiss Re, Chubb, and Allianz petitioned the New York courts to have the September 11th attacks classified as a single terrorist attack rather than two attacks to the separate buildings. In Swiss Re's case, this would have limited its liability to $3.6 billion, whereas a finding that the events of that horrible day were two events for insurance purposes would have doubled Swiss Re's price tag. On September 26, 2003, the Second District Court upheld the earlier District Court opinion and held that the events of 9/11 were a single occurrence for insurance purposes.

Catastrophic XOL Supplementary Coverage

The highest layer in XOL reinsurance treaties is often called the *catastrophic layer*. In Program 2 in Exhibit 9.5, the catastrophic layer is the $2 XS $8 layer shaded in black. The name comes from the extremely low probability usually associated with cumulative losses reaching this layer. In addition, in the specific area of property insurance, the catastrophic loss layer is often associated with natural disasters and catastrophes like earthquakes or tropical cyclonic activity.

Catastrophic XOL coverage functions in much the same manner as per-risk or per-occurrence XOL treaties, but with a few differences. First, the catastrophic coverage not only covers a catastrophic *layer* as in Exhibit 9.5, but the catastrophic XOL policy itself is almost always tied to a specific catastrophe as a triggering event. The XOL treaty shown in Exhibit 9.5 is essentially a blanket property damage policy, whereas a true catastrophic XOL policy would pay claims only if the property damage was sustained as a direct result of some named catastrophic event like a tornado. Second, catastrophic XOL reinsurance usually contains a co-insurance provision, rarely protecting more than 90 percent of the losses. Third, catastrophic insurance of this sort also may involve a deductible.

Aggregate XOL or Stop Loss Treaties

An *aggregate excess of loss treaty* applies to a predetermined aggregate loss arising from a policy portfolio. Aggregate XOL treaties are designed to cover a large number of *small* losses arising on multiple policies in the same policy year and thus are essentially the opposite of catastrophic XOL treaties.

Consider a primary carrier that writes homeowner's insurance and takes out per-occurrence XOL reinsurance on its homeowner insurance portfolio for $1,000,000 XS $125,000. But suppose the policy year is characterized by a large number of $100,000 claims, all of which will fall below the $125,000 lower attachment point in the per-occurrence reinsurance treaty. The carrier may wish to purchase aggregate XOL reinsurance for, say, $500,000 XS $500,000. Without the aggregate treaty, 10 claims of $100,000 each would cost the carrier $1 million, because no single claim would be covered by the per-occurrence treaty. But with the aggregate XOL reinsurance treaty in place, the cedant would be liable for only the first $500,000 in claims. The remaining five $100,000 claims would be covered by the aggregate treaty, even though no single claim is covered by any of the per-occurrence treaties.

Aggregate XOL treaties do not usually specify risks or perils as triggers and thus can include *any* claims arising on a book of underwriting business. As such, aggregate treaties are a highly effective means by which insurers can reduce their earnings and cash flow volatilities by locking in a maximum loss amount.

The versatility of these treaties also makes them quite expensive. In addition, to prevent the underwriter from being inattentive to the risk of its book, aggregate treaties usually include reasonably significant co-insurance provisions.

Optional Reinstatement

As discussed in Chapter 8, some primary insurance contracts and many reinsurance contracts allow for the purchaser to pay additional premium in order to restore an exhausted limit. Like insurance, reinsurance generally lasts for only a year. One way the reinsurers offer multiyear structures is through optional reinstatement. At the end of the year, the cedant may pay additional premium to restore the policy limit *and* extend the policy for another year. This does not offer the insurance purchaser protection from rising rates like a true multiyear contract would, but it does at least give the reinsurance purchaser some comfort that reinsurance capacity will still be there in a year, even if the limit for the first year has been exhausted.

*N*th Loss Excess Treaties

Insurers and reinsurers historically consider the number of very large claims per policy period to be limited. In particular, the belief is that the sixth largest claim in a typical insurance pool will be about the same value each year, with only the top five losses representing extraordinarily large or catastrophic events and varying dramatically from year to year. Six claims thus should define a reasonable expectation of a worst-case payout during a policy year for an insurer. In some reinsurance pools, the magic number is the third or fourth loss.

An Nth loss excess reinsurance treaty is a reinsurance treaty that covers the top *N* losses during the policy period. It is essentially a pure bulk capacity vehicle used by some primary carriers to increase the depth of their underwriting lines and raise the policy limits they can offer.

HORIZONTAL LAYERING AND BLENDED COVER

We described traditional XOL treaties as vertically layered. When more than one reinsurance company reinsures different loss layers for the same underlying risk, the term *vertical* refers to the fact that the liability of each insurer depends on the total amount of aggregate or per-occurrence losses.

Reinsurance programs may also be *horizontally layered*. In a horizontally layered reinsurance program, more than one reinsurance company provides coverage for the same layer of losses, simply splitting the bill. A program that is both horizontally and vertically layered is called a *blended cover*.

Exhibit 9.7 illustrates the three types of XOL reinsurance programs for a single policy line with a maximum payout of $10 million per year. White represents a retention by the cedant, and different shades of gray and black indicate different reinsurance companies.

In the vertically layered program, three different reinsurers provide coverage based solely on the amount of cumulative losses. In the horizontally layered program, two reinsurance companies together provide full coverage in the $8 XS $2 layer. For every dollar in claims above the $2 million deductible/retention, each reinsurer must contribute 50 cents. And finally, the blended cover illustrates two reinsurers dividing all claims above $2 million up to $8 million and then a third reinsurer providing separate $2 XS $8 catastrophic coverage.

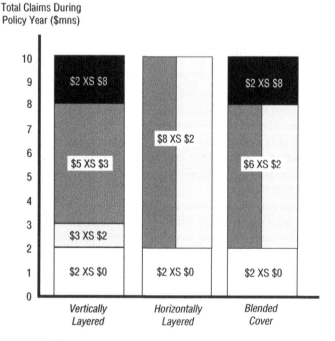

EXHIBIT 9.7   Vertically versus Horizontally Layered XOL Treaties

SYNDICATION

Reinsurance deals are often syndicated. A lead underwriter will take charge of the treaty negotiations, but will not underwrite all the risks. Instead, the risks are shared horizontally (or perhaps vertically or in a blended cover) across all syndicate members. The terms of risk sharing across syndicate members are agreed upon before the reinsurance policy is bound with the cedant.

Do not confuse a syndicated deal with a deal in which a single fronting reinsurer wishes to prearrange reinsurance on a deal. To see the difference, consider a primary carrier that seeks to acquire $100mn XS $10mn in reinsurance.

Reinsurance company Barenboim proposes a syndicated program to the cedant in which Barenboim will be the syndicate leader and lead underwriter and will assume up to $20 million in losses in the $100mn XS $10mn layer. Reinsurance companies Abbado, Boulez, Rattle, and Solti all agree to join the syndicate, each taking a $20 million slice of the $100mn XS $10mn layer.

In the syndicated deal, the cedant will deal primarily with Barenboim. The other reinsurers likely will delegate much of the due diligence and original credit risk evaluation (but not all) to Barenboim. Barenboim may also be responsible for dealing with the broker(s), doing most of the paperwork and administration, and the like. Expenses will be shared with syndicate members, of course.

Importantly, Barenboim is taking no risk on the deal apart from its $20 million slice of the coverage. To ensure this, all the policies will be bound with the cedant at the same time, and claims will be processed separately. This means that the cedant is exposed to the credit risk of all five reinsurance companies.

Now consider a deal proposed by reinsurance company Haitink in which Haitink will reinsure the entire $100mn XS $10mn layer. Haitink tells the cedant that it lacks more than $20 million in capacity and won't do the deal unless it can reinsure the other $80 million exposure, either horizontally or vertically. Haitink then goes out and procures $20 million in horizontally layered coverage from Abbado, Boulez, Rattle, and Solti. Once Haitink has provisional retrocession agreements in place, it will bind the original deal. Haitink is thus acting as a *fronting reinsurer* on the whole amount but retains only $20 million of the total loss exposure.

From the cedant's perspective, dealing with Haitink in the second deal will be essentially similar to dealing with Barenboim in the syndicated deal on an administrative basis. But the credit risk of the two deals is not the same. In the syndicated deal, the ceding primary carrier is at risk from a default or nonpayment by *all five* reinsurance companies, whereas in the second deal the cedant bears credit risk entirely to Haitink. If Rattle is unable to pay its $20 million share of a $100 million claim, for example, the cedant loses that $20 million to credit risk in the syndicated deal. In the second deal, Haitink is still obliged to pay that $20 million to the cedant.

The pricing of the two programs also may not be the same. The syndicated deal is 100 percent reinsurance, whereas the second proposal requires Haitink to retrocede 80 percent of its reinsurance cover in the retrocession market. Retrocession costs, however, will be passed on to the cedant in the premium loading on Haitink's $100mn XS $10mn reinsurance coverage. If retrocession costs exceed reinsurance rates, the cedant could well pay more for the second deal. But if Haitink is AAA-rated and Barenboim, Abbado, Boulez, Rattle, and Solti are all rated below AAA, the cedant might be willing to pay the higher cost in order to deal with the higher-rated player.

CHAPTER 10

Credit Insurance and Financial Guaranties

In this chapter we explore how traditional (re)insurance products can be used to help firms manage the risk of losses sustained following credit defaults. The products we examine include traditional credit insurance and financial guaranties (in several different forms and under several different names). We also discuss a noninsurance product that is very closely related to credit insurance—bank letters of credit. We will then compare and contrast the various solutions and conclude with a discussion of some of the recent controversies surrounding certain of these products.

CREDIT INSURANCE PRODUCTS

Insurance and reinsurance contracts can be used to transfer credit risk in much the same way that traditional insurance can be used to transfer nonfinancial risks like property and casualty losses. The contracts generally are indemnity contracts with all the usual features of insurance—deductibles, policy limits, subrogation rights, and so on. The triggering event may be defined very broadly as the default by a specific obligor on *any* financial obligation to the credit protection buyer, or may be defined more narrowly in terms of the nonperformance of specific obligations.

Trade Credit Insurance

Much of the market for traditional credit insurance is aimed at insuring against *trade credit* losses. Trade credit is extended between corporations engaged in commercial enterprises with one another and may involve financial obligations or obligations to deliver goods and services. Suppose, for example, that Stony Electronics sells audio/video (A/V) equipment to Circuit Town. If Circuit Town pays for the A/V equipment in advance and Stony has 45 days to deliver the equipment, Stony is the *obligor*, Circuit Town is the *obligee*, and the *obligation* is the delivery of A/V equipment. If Circuit Town is concerned that Stony may not make its required deliveries, Circuit Town can purchase trade credit insurance that will reimburse the firm for some or all of the cost required to replace the defaulted A/V equipment deliveries.

Suppose instead that Stony makes delivery of A/V equipment immediately to Circuit Town and invoices Circuit Town for payment within 45 days of delivery. In that case, Stony is now the obligee bearing the risk that Circuit Town will not pay its bills completely as a financial obligor on a commercial transaction. To manage this risk, Stony might purchase trade credit insurance from an insurance company that would cover Circuit Town's cash payment obligation in the event of a default.

Mechanics of Trade Credit Insurance   Exhibit 10.1 illustrates the mechanics of trade credit insurance more generally. Note that we adopt the same conventions as in Chapter 9—the light gray shaded box is the purchaser of credit protection, and the dark gray box with rounded edges is the provider or seller of that protection. Solid lines are firm cash flows, and

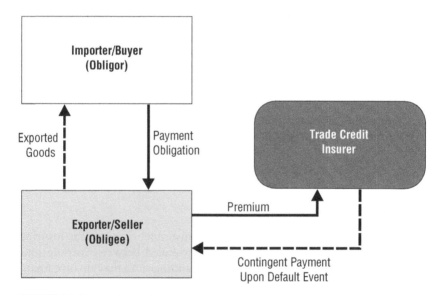

EXHIBIT 10.1   Trade Credit Insurance

dashed lines are structures including the transfer of goods and services or payments contingent on default events.

In this particular example, the obligor is an importer buying goods from a foreign exporter/seller obligee. Because we assume the importer is the obligor and the exporter the obligee, the delivery of goods must occur prior to the cash settlement of the invoice, thus creating credit risk for the exporter/seller on the cash payment leg of the commercial transaction. The exporter pays a premium to the insurance company and in turn receives protection that will cover the importer's required payment in the event the importer does not make that payment.

The coverage provided to the obligee in this example likely has the usual features of traditional insurance, including a deductible and policy limits. The trade credit insurer also will retain subrogation rights. This means if the importer receives goods and does not make its required payment to the exporter, the insurance company reimburses the exporter for the full amount of the defaulted payment. The insurer then has a claim on the importer and keeps any recoveries that it can extract from the importer, including proceeds realized from the sale of the goods the importer received from the exporter. If the importer is actually insolvent, the insurer retains a pro rata claim on the remaining assets of the company in any insolvency proceeding. The importer might, of course, make a partial payment to the exporter, in which case the insurer is liable to the exporter for only the unpaid amount and has subrogation rights on only the unpaid part of the obligation.

Trade Credit Insurance versus Factoring   Trade credit insurance is a popular means by which corporations manage the credit risk of their receivables in Europe, but it has never generated the same level of interest in the United States.[1] U.S. corporations have preferred to use a method of credit risk management known as *factoring* instead.

When the credit-sensitive receivables of a firm are factored, they are essentially sold to a third party known (not surprisingly) as a factor. The factor then becomes responsible for collecting on the receivables. The price that the factor pays to the original obligee for the receivable is at a discount to the face value of the receivable by the amount of the expected recovery. Factoring is shown in Exhibit 10.2 using the same trade finance example as in the previous section.

A significant difference between factoring and trade credit insurance is that factoring generally occurs after an event of default on the original receivable. This is not true in Europe, where factoring involves the sale of both performing and nonperforming receivables. In the United States, factoring pertains mainly to nonperforming receivables. In other words, factoring is not really insurance against a possible future default. The benefit of factoring

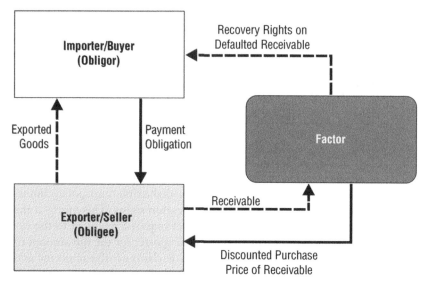

EXHIBIT 10.2   Factoring Trade Credit Receivables

is that the obligee avoids the costs and hassle of trying to extract a recovery from the obligor. In addition, the discounted price at which the receivables are sold to the factor by the obligee locks in the expected recovery for the obligee. If actual recoveries are less than expected, the receivables will be at a bigger discount to par and the obligee will have avoided this risk of loss. Conversely, if recoveries are higher than expected, the factor keeps that gain. Either way, the obligee has removed the risk of deviations between actual and expected recoveries; this is essentially the quantity for which a factor is providing insurance, *not* the risk of a default in the first place.

Financial Guaranties

A financial guaranty is a form of credit insurance in which the beneficiary may be fully or partially reimbursed following an event of default on a financial obligation. There are two very different forms of financial guaranties that both enjoy widespread prevalence in the market today—so-called *pure financial guaranties* and *wraps*. The two different forms of guaranties are discussed next.

Pure Financial Guaranties   Pure financial guaranties are, with a few exceptions, essentially financial or credit (re)insurance policies in which the credit protection purchaser is the beneficiary of the policy. Exhibit 10.3

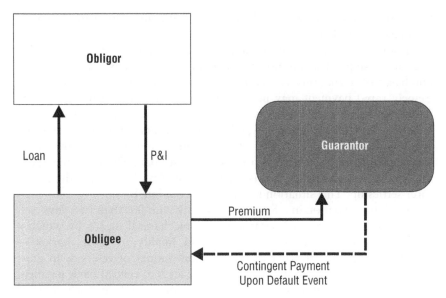

EXHIBIT 10.3   Financial Guaranty

shows the cash flows on a simple financial guaranty. The reference asset in this example is a loan made by the insurance purchaser (the obligee in the loan) to the loan obligor. In the event the obligor fails to make required principal and interest (P&I) payments, the loan will go into default and the guarantor will reimburse the obligee for the present value of the remaining P&I payment obligations (subject to any deductible and limit).

In a typical financial guaranty, the guarantor will retain subrogation rights on the original obligor. If a default occurs and a claim on the guarantor is made by the obligee, the guarantor has the right to attempt recovery on the amount for which the guarantor is liable. This right of recovery depends, of course, on whether the obligor made a partial payment. In other words, as explained in Chapter 8, subrogation passes on the right of recovery from the obligee to the guarantor but only for amounts that have not already been paid; subrogation rights are limited to the amount the guarantor has actually paid out on the guaranty.

Although pure financial guaranties are designed to pay off claimants immediately, the term *immediate* is relative in the insurance world. A traditional property/casualty insurance policy may take 30 to 90 days to pay, depending on the length of the adjustment process. A pure financial guaranty, by contrast, generally pays off anywhere from 3 to 10 business days following a claim. But what if the purchaser of a guaranty wants payment even faster than that?

Insurance companies are limited in their capacity to make irrevocable and final cash payments to policyholders in under two days.[2] If a corporate purchaser of a guaranty is seeking to protect its equity capital base, extremely rapid payment may not be required. But if the firm requires the funds immediately for cash flow risk management, a guaranty will usually include a *bank wrap*. Specifically, when a loss occurs that activates the trigger, a bank will accept a transfer of the payment obligation from the (re)insurance company as collateral for a short-term loan. The bank then pays the claimant immediately, and is repaid a few days later when the (re)insurer settles up. This situation is depicted in Exhibit 10.4.

Bank participation in a financial guaranty with less than two days' settlement is often necessary because of the mechanical means by which a funds transfer achieves irrevocability and finality in most markets— namely, through the transfer of central bank money or reserves. In most countries, only banks are permitted direct access to central bank payment systems and to maintain reserves with the central bank. In such systems, insurance companies and nonbank clients must settle their accounts through a bank. In the absence of a bank wrap, this adds time to the settlement process.[3]

Wraps   A *wrap* is a financial guaranty in which the purchaser of the insurance is not the beneficiary of the policy. The wrap purchaser is usually the issuer of a bond or other credit-sensitive obligation. In the event of a default on principal or interest by the issuer, the wrap provides for the unconditional and irrevocable guarantee of payments to the holders of the obligation. A wrap is essentially the same thing as a *financial surety bond*.

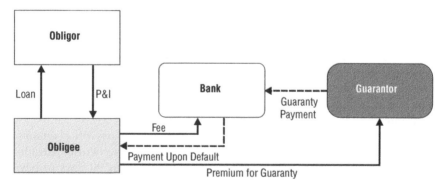

EXHIBIT 10.4   Financial Guaranty with Bank Wrap

In a traditional surety situation, a *principal* has some obligation to an *obligee*, usually involving the delivery of goods or the provision of services. The obligee, however, may be concerned about the creditworthiness of the principal and may demand that the principal post a surety bond to guarantee performance on its obligation. The principal makes a premium payment to a *surety* (usually an insurance company), which then issues a surety bond to the obligee that is payable by the surety in the event of default by the principal. A typical surety situation is shown in Exhibit 10.5.

Commercial surety bonds have historically been used to bond the performance of the provider of a good or service. They are extremely common in the United States in construction projects, for example. A general contractor is often required to post surety to the developer to guarantee its performance on the project. In the event that the general contractor cannot complete the project, the surety bond is drawn down by the developer and the proceeds used to hire a new general contractor. Surety bonds are also common in trade finance.

Principals in a purely financial transaction may also be requested to post a surety bond to the obligee, in which case the products are known as financial surety bonds. A wrap is really just another name for a financial surety bond, where the surety is a financial guarantor and the obligation being bonded is the principal and interest (P&I) on a bond issue. Exhibit 10.6 illustrates.

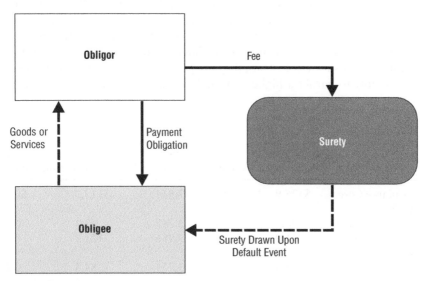

EXHIBIT 10.5 Surety Bond

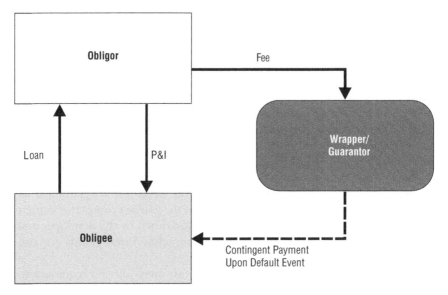

EXHIBIT 10.6 Bond Wrap

A significant amount of bond wrapping is done by the big New York monoline insurers: Ambac Assurance Corp., Financial Security Assurance, Inc. (FSA), Financial Guaranty Insurance Co. (FGIC), and MBIA Insurance Corp. Table 10.1 shows some key summary statistics for the top wrappers at year-end 2003. All of these monolines are rated AAA/Aaa at present.

Most monoline bond wraps are not intended to serve as a pure substitute for credit insurance. Instead, they are generally used as credit enhancements mainly to garner a higher external rating (and lower cost of funds)

TABLE 10.1 Top Monoline Bond Wrappers, Year-End 2003 ($billions)

	Total Net Par Exposure	Total Capital	Total Assets	Gross Premium Written per Annum	Net Income
Ambac Assurance Corp.	$425.9	$4.526	$7.354	$115.3	$0.598
Financial Guaranty Insurance Co. (FGIC)	206.7	1.835	2.747	42.4	0.178
MBIA Insurance Corp.	541.0	6.083	9.986	122.3	0.669
Financial Security Assurance (FSA)	294.4	2.104	3.754	84.3	0.263

Source: S&P 2004 Bond Insurance Book.

on the debt being wrapped. In essence, a monoline is leasing out its own balance sheet for a fee to the issuer of the bond. (The credit rating of a guaranteed obligation is almost always the credit rating of the guarantor, assuming that the guaranty is unconditional, irrevocable, and covers all P&I.) Wraps are very popular for credit enhancing municipal bonds and structured securities.

LETTERS OF CREDIT

A *letter of credit* (LOC or L/C) is a banking product that is a popular alternative to credit insurance. An LOC may be posted by an obligor or principal to an obligee in order to guarantee performance on a financial obligation to that obligee. In the event of a default, the obligee may draw on the LOC. LOCs have long been used in trade finance. A bank might issue an LOC, for example, to an importer that is payable to any foreign exporter selling goods to the importer. In the event that the importer defaults on a payment for goods received, the exporter can draw on the LOC. Exhibit 10.7 provides an example of the cash flows on a typical LOC.

An LOC functions a bit like a performance bond. It contains general terms like the maximum amount that may be drawn against it and the

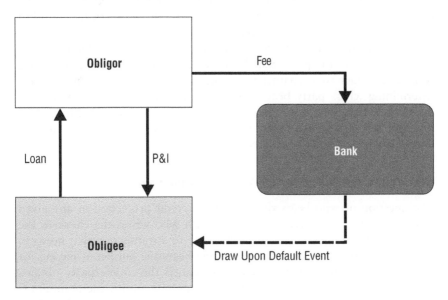

EXHIBIT 10.7 Letter of Credit

term, usually under a year. The LOC may also contain certain specific provisions dictating how the LOC can be used (e.g., only if the buyer defaults on a payment obligation for goods sold) and to whom the LOC can be presented (e.g., only the seller) in a specific trading deal. Most letters of credit, moreover, are irrevocable, although some revocable letters of credit do exist and function more like credit lines than performance bonds.

An irrevocable LOC is economically and functionally equivalent to a financial surety bond or a wrap.

WHO BEARS THE COST OF ACQUIRING CREDIT PROTECTION?

Notice in comparing Exhibits 10.1, 10.3, 10.6, and 10.7 that the obligee is always the beneficiary of credit protection but is *not* always the firm that writes the check to the credit protection provider. In traditional credit insurance or a pure guaranty (Exhibits 10.1 and 10.3, respectively), the premium is paid to the guarantor by the credit protection buyer, or the obligee in the guaranteed transaction. But in the wrap and LOC shown in Exhibits 10.6 and 10.7, by contrast, the premium/fee is paid to the guarantor *by the obligor* in the guaranteed transaction. From this distinction, one might question why a credit protection buyer would ever want to get insurance or a financial guaranty (for which it must pay) when it could instead demand an LOC or a wrap from the obligor that has an identical payoff but for which the obligor pays the premium.

In reality, the party who writes the check to the credit protection buyer is not necessarily the party that bears the economic cost. Specifically, we want to consider two separate points in this section. First, as mentioned, determining which party bears the economic cost of the credit protection does not necessarily depend on who writes the check for the credit protection fee. Second, we want to consider which party—obligor or obligee—does actually bear the cost of credit protection.

Who Writes the Check versus Who Bears the Cost

The question of who bears the cost of the credit protection in any given transaction does not have much to do with who writes the check to the guarantor. In commercial practice, the party to a transaction that needs to have its performance guaranteed generally bears the burden of paying for any credit protection or credit enhancement. If the counterparty obtains credit protection by buying insurance or a pure guaranty, the premium is generally reflected in a higher interest rate received by the obligor on the underlying transaction.

For concreteness, suppose investor Bogart makes a $100 cash loan to firm Cagney. At the end of a year, Cagney owes Bogart the $100 principal back plus a single interest payment. The market interest rate is 5 percent, or $5 on a principal of $100. Suppose that the cost of guaranteeing Cagney's payment to Bogart is $2, regardless of whether that guaranty is obtained in the form of a pure guaranty or a wrap. If a wrap is used, Cagney spends the $2 on the wrap and then has a P&I obligation to Bogart of $105. Cagney's total funding cost is $7, or the $5 interest cost plus the $2 cost of the wrap.

Now suppose instead that Bogart buys a guaranty directly for $2. In that situation, Bogart will demand a 7 percent interest rate on its loan to Cagney. Cagney's obligation to Bogart then is $107, which includes principal ($100), regular interest ($5), and a reimbursement for the cost of credit protection ($2). As in the case of the wrap, Cagney's total funding cost is again $7.

In both cases, Cagney bears the cost of posing a credit risk to Bogart and the resulting cost of Bogart's credit protection.

Note, however, that the party posing the credit risk is not always the party that bears the cost of credit protection. All that we are saying is that *the same party bears the cost of credit protection regardless of whether a wrap or guaranty is used.* Who writes the check for the credit protection thus is not necessarily indicative of who pays for it.

Who Bears the Cost?

In reality, it is not so easy to determine whether the credit protection buyer or the obligor on the credit-sensitive deal will need to bear the economic cost of the credit protection program. In many bond wraps, the cost of the wrap is borne by the *investor* in the bonds—if investors demand a credit enhancement to the original issue, they pay for that credit enhancement. The issuer writes the check to the guarantor but then recovers that cost with a *lower* interest rate paid to bondholders. This is opposite to the earlier example.

Various factors can help us determine which party will bear the cost of acquiring credit protection. Some of these factors include:

- Whether the relationship between obligor and obligee is arm's-length and transactional or part of a long-running relationship; for example, a bank with a lot of business conducted with a creditor may be more inclined to absorb the cost of credit enhancement in order to keep the business than a bondholder who is doing a one-off deal.

■ Competition among and substitutes across obligors for issuing hot new products; for example, if the obligor or issuer is providing a fairly unique product and hotly demanded, the burden of credit enhancement costs may well be imposed on the obligee, whereas an obligor or issuer offering a product with lots of alternatives and substitutes available may need to bear the cost of credit enhancement.

■ Uniqueness of novel, untested product; for example, sort of the opposite of the prior variable, a designer of a new product that the market is a little suspicious about will almost certainly need to absorb the cost of credit enhancement to help make the product sell.

You can see the pattern. Ultimately, the issue of who bears the cost of acquiring credit protection is mainly a *marketing* consideration. The party with the bargaining power in the obligor/obligee relationship will probably determine who pays for the credit protection. Sometimes the obligor is in the dominant negotiating position, and the credit enhancement cost will be passed on to the obligee. But sometimes the obligee is dominant or has less to lose from not doing the deal, in which case the obligee may demand credit enhancement by the obligor that the obligor must also pay for.

DISTINCTIONS BETWEEN DIFFERENT CREDIT PROTECTION PRODUCTS

Credit (re)insurance, financial guaranties, financial surety bonds, wraps, and irrevocable letters of credit all function in much the same way and can be used for essentially the same purpose—to protect an obligee in a financial transaction from the credit risk of nonpayment by the obligor in that transaction. Despite their basic similarities, all of these products enjoy fairly widespread use in the marketplace. Yet there are a few important differences between these products that can affect the solution that is most preferred in any given financial transaction.

Traditional Credit Insurance versus Financial Guaranties

A true financial guaranty differs from a traditional insurance contract in one important way. As long as a guaranty purchaser is current on its premium payment obligations and is not attempting to defraud the guarantor, the guarantor must pay a claim against a guaranty *immediately*. Importantly, there is no adjustment process as there is with traditional insurance (see Chapter 8).

Documentation for a true guaranty, moreover, is short and to the point and contains very few covenants and restrictions. This has led many to characterize true guaranties as "pay now, sue later" credit risk transfer products. In traditional insurance, the insurer uses the adjustment process to determine how much it really owes on the claim before the payment is made, whereas with a guaranty the burden of proof is on the insurer to pay the claim in full and to sue the claimant to get the money back *later* if the insurer believes it does not have full liability on the claim.

The rapid payment and unconditional nature of guaranties make them popular for use as a credit enhancement and as a source of synthetic equity capital. The provision of a guaranty by a highly rated insurer is a signal of financial strength and, in principle, may provide a great degree of comfort to those firms engaged in commercial or financial transactions with the insurance purchaser. If the guaranty is credible, the rating agencies may upgrade the insurance purchaser to reflect the enhanced postguaranty credit quality of its assets.

Pure Financial Guaranties versus Wraps

Pure financial guaranties and wraps are virtually identical—both are types of financial guaranties and differ from traditional credit insurance in the ways mentioned in the previous section. For the most part, the distinction between pure guaranties, wraps, and financial surety bonds is a terminological one.

We discussed in the preceding section that there is a *mechanical* distinction of who writes the check for the credit protection, and this is indeed another difference—but not a very significant one.

In general, all financial guaranties are not created exactly equal, but, in principle, they are darn close.

Monoline versus Multiline Financial Guaranties

Under New York insurance law, only an insurance or reinsurance company that is specifically licensed as a financial guarantor may provide financial guaranties, including both pure guaranties and wraps.[4] The only insurers that may become licensed to provide guaranties, in turn, are *monoline* insurers (see Chapter 8) that undertake no underwriting activities apart from the provision of financial guaranties. In other words, a financial guaranty provided by a multiline insurer in New York is not likely to be a legally enforceable contract.

This may seem to be a narrow bit of global insurance law, but it has sweeping implications. Under the so-called Appleton Rule in New York insurance law, a New York-based domestic insurance or reinsurance company is prohibited from providing coverage outside of New York that is prohibited in New York.[5] Similarly, a foreign insurer or reinsurer authorized to do business in New York is bound not to undertake business activities outside the state of New York that are prohibited for New York domestic insurers unless such outside business activities are not prejudicial to New York domestic insurers.[6]

As a practical matter, the New York restrictions greatly restrict the ability of multiline insurers to provide financial guaranties to companies that are domiciled in New York or that operate under New York law. Note, however, that this does not stop multilines from providing financial guaranties in other jurisdictions. In fact, on the whole, multiline insurers are very active in the guaranty business—just not involving New York or New York-based clients.

Insurance versus Letters of Credit

Credit insurance, financial guaranties, financial surety bonds, and wraps are all very similar to one another and are all credit protection provided by insurance companies. Irrevocable letters of credit accomplish essentially the same thing as financial guaranties and are close cousins to financial surety bonds and wraps. But there are some important differences.

Capital and Debt Capacity   The obligee to which an LOC is posted has the right to draw on the LOC partially or fully anytime there is a concern about the obligor's ability or willingness to pay. The obligor would have very limited ability to stop a draw on its own credit if the obligee opts to draw on the LOC. The LOC thus essentially represents the financial capital *of the obligee* that has simply been guaranteed by a bank—that is, economically, the LOC consumes debt capacity.

Insurance and guaranties, by contrast, are financial obligations *of the guarantor* and not of the obligor. They do not represent direct capital of the obligor. As such, a bank will consider an LOC as an economic extension of credit to the firm for which the LOC is issued, thereby reducing that firm's debt capacity. This is not the case with a financial guaranty, which is an obligation entirely of the guarantor.

In some cases, a bank will require the firm obtaining the LOC to secure that LOC with collateral, and this can divert resources of the firm toward collateral that would not be required on an otherwise similar financial surety bond. Insurance and guaranties are also occasionally secured or collateralized, but this is not very common.

Adjustment LOCs can simply be drawn on by their beneficiaries—the obligee in our example. Insurance products, however, are sometimes subject to adjustment. This means that the claim may be investigated before the surety bond pays off.

As we have said, true financial guaranties are intended to avoid this problem and to put guaranties on equal footing with LOCs. But this may not be true for *all* financial guaranties (even though perhaps it should be), and is definitely not true for plain-vanilla credit insurance.

Coverage Insurance is an indemnity product and thus provides coverage to the obligee up to the amount lost. An LOC, by contrast, is often a fixed amount that may represent only a portion of the potential defaulted obligation. In this sense, the LOC may provide inferior coverage to the credit protection purchaser. At the same time, the LOC is irrevocable and often less conditional than a guaranty.

WHEN IS A GUARANTY NOT A GUARANTY?

Significant uncertainty has settled in over the financial guaranty market since 2001. This uncertainty concerns the question of whether financial guaranties are really as unconditional as they appear. In particular, several multiline insurers have relied on the New York restrictions as an excuse—perhaps legitimate, perhaps not—for not honoring a guaranty or surety obligation. We review several of the most important cases in this section to see what lessons we can draw.

Surety Bonds as Financial Guaranties

Four types of surety bonds have pushed the envelope of interpreting the New York restrictions. These four questionable types of surety bonds are:

1. *Bank depository bonds* and *excess Federal Deposit Insurance Corporation (FDIC) bonds* provide their holders with indemnity against losses above the federal insurance level arising from bank insolvency.

2. *Lease bonds* are issued to secure the ongoing performance of a lease in the event of the lessee's default on a lease payment.
3. *Advance payment supply bonds* are issued to guarantee the eventual delivery of assets that have been prepurchased through a prepaid forward or swap agreement.
4. *Retro premium payment bonds* are used to secure the debt that backs certain premium-in-arrears insurance programs, such as workers' compensation and postloss-funded finite risk (see Chapter 24).

New York law defines *fidelity and surety insurance* as:[7]

(C) Any contract bond; including a bid, payment or maintenance bond or a performance bond where the bond is guaranteeing the execution of any contract other than a contract of indebtedness or other monetary obligation;

. . .

(E) Becoming surety on, or guaranteeing the performance of, any lawful contract, not specifically provided for in this paragraph, except (i) mortgage guaranty insurance, which may only be written by an insurer authorized to write such insurance pursuant to article sixty-five of this chapter, (ii) a contract that falls within the definition of financial guaranty insurance as set forth in paragraph one of subsection (a) of section six thousand nine hundred one of this chapter, (iii) any insurance contract unless such guaranty is authorized pursuant to subsection (c) of section one thousand one hundred fourteen of this article; or (iv) service contract reimbursement insurance as specified in paragraph twenty-eight of this subsection. . . .

Now consider how New York law defines *financial guaranty insurance*:[8]

. . . a surety bond, insurance policy or, when issued by an insurer or any person doing an insurance business as defined in paragraph one of subsection (b) of section one thousand one hundred one of this chapter, an indemnity contract, and any guaranty similar to the foregoing types, under which loss is payable, upon proof of occurrence of financial loss, to an insured claimant, obligee or indemnitee as a result of any of the following events:

(A) failure of any obligor on or issuer of any debt instrument or other monetary obligation (including equity securities guar-

> *antied under a surety bond, insurance policy or indemnity con-*
> *tract) to pay when due to be paid by the obligor or scheduled at*
> *the time insured to be received by the holder of the obligation,*
> *principal, interest, premium, dividend or purchase price of or*
> *on, or other amounts due or payable with respect to, such in-*
> *strument or obligation, when such failure is the result of a finan-*
> *cial default or insolvency or, provided that such payment source*
> *is investment grade, any other failure to make payment, regard-*
> *less of whether such obligation is incurred directly or as guaran-*
> *tor by or on behalf of another obligor that has also defaulted;*
>
> . . .
>
> *(2) Notwithstanding paragraph one of this subsection, "financial*
> *guaranty insurance" shall not include:*
>
> . . .
>
> *(B) fidelity and surety insurance as defined in paragraph sixteen*
> *of subsection (a) of section one thousand one hundred thirteen*
> *of this chapter. . . .*

In other words, New York law defines a surety bond as insurance that is unrelated to the payment of a debt obligation.

In this context, we can see why the four types of surety bonds listed earlier could be troubling. A lease bond, for example, guarantees a mone-tary payment by the lessee in the event of a financial default. That would seem to be a financial guaranty, and, indeed, the New York State Insurance Department has specifically said that it considers lease bonds financial guaranties and not surety bonds.[9]

Perhaps the biggest controversy involving the enforceability of surety bonds concerns advance payment supply bonds (APSBs) and their use by Enron as credit enhancements for certain transactions undertaken with JP-Morgan Chase (JPMC). By 2001, Chase Manhattan Bank and later JPMC had arranged a total of about $3.7 billion in prepaid forward purchases of oil and gas from Enron—contracts in which JPMC made an up-front cash payment to Enron in return for a future delivery of oil or gas at a prespeci-fied price and quantity. When Enron filed for bankruptcy protection, JPMC was owed $1.6 billion in defaulted oil and gas deliveries, about $1 billion of which had been guaranteed with APSBs (Roach, 2002).

JPMC initially required Enron to obtain bank LOCs that could be drawn by JPMC in the event of a default by Enron on its future delivery obligations. Beginning in 1998, Enron asked JPMC to accept APSBs in lieu of LOCs as collateral for the future deliveries. That Enron preferred surety bonds to LOCs is hardly surprising. Recall that Enron was keen to avoid taking on new balance-sheet debt. An LOC would have counted against Enron's balance-sheet credit lines, whereas APSBs did not.

Despite their obvious appeal to Enron, JPMC was initially hesitant to accept surety bonds in place of LOCs. To assuage its concerns, the bank requested that all the sureties backing the Enron APSBs provide several forms of assurance that the APSBs "would be the functional equivalent of letters of credit, and, like letters of credit, would constitute absolute and unconditional pay-on-demand financial guarantees."[10] These assurances were apparently provided, and with JPMC's consent, APSBs began to replace LOCs as collateral. Providers of the APSBs were all multiline insurance companies, most of which were domiciled in New York, and included Liberty Mutual, Travelers Casualty & Surety, and St. Paul Fire and Marine.

On December 7, 2001—just five days after Enron filed for bankruptcy protection—JPMC filed written notice with Enron's sureties of the nearly $1 billion due under the APSBs. The sureties declined payment, arguing that the APSBs "were designed to camouflage loans by [JPMorgan] Chase to Enron, and that [JPMorgan] Chase defrauded the surety bond providers into guaranteeing what were purely financial obligations which they otherwise would not, and statutorily [under New York law] could not, have bonded."[11] In other words, the sureties claimed that the prepaids were not really commodity delivery contracts but rather were "term debt in disguise." The APSBs thus represented *financial guaranties* that cannot be offered by multiline insurers under New York insurance law, thereby ostensibly relieving the multilines of their payment obligations.

On January 2, 2003, JPMC announced that it was taking a $1.3 billion charge in the fourth quarter of 2002 largely to deal with Enron litigation matters. That charge-off reflected a settlement with insurers, reached on the same day the trial was to begin. Under the settlement, the 11 insurers agreed to pay about 60 percent of their obligations to JPMC under the APSBs, or $655 million out of the $1 billion total owed.

The reasons why the sureties claimed that the Enron-JPMC prepaid forwards and swaps were term debt and not commodity delivery contracts are discussed later in the book in Chapter 21; we have not covered enough structured or project finance just yet to get into those details here. Suffice it to say that the dispute hinged on whether the obligation that was being guaranteed was a fixed monetary amount or a delivery of commodities. If it was the latter, the sureties presumably would not have been able to challenge their obligations. If the obligation of Enron to JPMC was a fixed monetary obligation camouflaged with a commodity delivery contract, however, then the APSBs almost certainly would have been financial guaranties under New York law and hence not permissible in the first place.

"Hollywood Funding"

Starting in the mid-1990s, structured financing techniques arrived in full force in the world of film financing. Specifically, the securitization or sale of future movie revenues became a popular means by which films could be financed. Mechanically, a film production company would sell the rights to future film revenues to a special purpose entity (SPE) for a cash payment that represented the discounted net present value of the future revenues. The cash would be used by the production company to complete the film. The SPE raised this cash by issuing bonds whose P&I payments were secured by the future revenues from the film.

Although a creative application of securitization technology, the credit quality of the bonds issued by the SPE was generally well below investment grade. The film might never be completed, and, if it was, it might be a flop with audiences. Issuers of these bonds thus sought credit enhancement in the form of guaranties and wraps to enhance ratings on the structured debt.

The Hollywood Funding "Guaranties" Hollywood Funding was the name given to seven separate securitizations of private film financings.[12] The securitizations were structured by Credit Suisse First Boston (CSFB), and the cash flows on the bonds issued in the securitizations were guaranteed by HIH Casualty & General Insurance and American International Group, Inc. (AIG)'s Lexington Insurance.

A British firm called Flashpoint UK Ltd., run by an ex-Lloyd's underwriter, obtained the financing from these securitization conduits from 1996 to 1998 in order to finance the completion of several films whose revenue receivables were in turn transferred to the seven Hollywood Funding vehicles as backing for seven series of bonds. HIH and AIG guaranteed the principal and interest payments on those bonds by agreeing to meet any cash shortfall in the event that film revenues were not adequate to pay off the note holders. The existence of these guaranties was a condition of Flashpoint obtaining backing from Hollywood Funding.

Exhibit 10.8 illustrates these relations graphically and indicates that HIH guaranteed Hollywood Funding issues 1 through 3 and Lexington guaranteed bond issues 4 through 7. As before, solid lines indicate cash flows, and dashed lines indicate structures. Gray dotted lines now indicate the so-called guaranties.

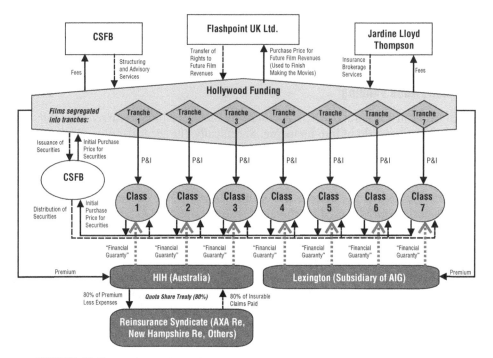

EXHIBIT 10.8 Hollywood Funding

Hollywood Funding 1 and 2 had revenues that fell short of note obligations by $31 million, and HIH paid the resulting claims. HIH then attempted to collect on the reinsurance it had secured for its guaranties. The reinsurance—an 80 percent quota share treaty (see Chapter 9)—was provided by a syndicate led by AXA Re. Other members included New Hampshire Insurance and Independent Insurance.

After HIH paid its claim to Hollywood Funding and filed its reinsurance claims, the reinsurers disputed their obligation to repay HIH on the grounds of breach of warranty—specifically, HIH should not have paid the original claim because the warranties to the policies required that six films per vehicle be made, and six films had not been made in each case. The Court of Appeals upheld the judgment by the High Court that the claims should not have been paid.

Meanwhile, AIG's Lexington subsidiary had already sued Flashpoint for failing to segregate film revenues in separate escrow accounts. Following the court decision in favor of HIH's reinsurers, Lexington refused to make payments on any claims arising on Hollywood Funding 5 and 6, citing the HIH judgment as evidence that it had no liability.

The notes issued by the Hollywood structures were rated AAA by Standard & Poor's (S&P). Following the Lexington revocation of its guaranty, notes issued by Hollywood 5 and 6 were downgraded to CCC– in February 2001. Hollywood 4, also guaranteed by Lexington, was downgraded to BB in March. Hollywood Funding 5 defaulted to its noteholders in May, and Hollywood Funding 6 defaulted in June.

The Controversy The controversy that has surrounded this disaster primarily pertains to when a guaranty is a guaranty, and who should know that. When S&P downgraded Hollywood 5 and 6, it issued the following statement:

> *After reviewing the insurance policies, Standard & Poor's believed that the policies were absolute and unconditional, that there were no conditions or warranties that needed to be satisfied in order to draw on the policies (other than the money in the escrow account being insufficient), that Lexington had waived all its defenses to payment on the policies, and that the policies met the standards of the capital market for credit enhancement of financial market instruments.*[13]

S&P further explained, "The only exclusions to payment that appear on the face of the policies . . . are exclusions relating to war, civil insurrection, invasion of foreign enemies, revolution etc., and radioactive contamination."[14]

As a matter of fact, however, AIG's Lexington had not used traditional guaranty documentation, but instead had treated the "guaranties" as ordinary property/casualty insurance, which included the usual provisions for policy nullification in the event of a breach of warranty (see Chapter 8). AIG issued the following statement in May 2001:

> *The issue here is not the refusal by an insurer to pay a claim under its policy. The real issue is whether CSFB understood what it was doing when it approached the insurance market to issue a property and casualty policy that was not drafted as the functional equivalent of a financial guarantee. Additionally, CSFB should be asked to address the standard of care and scope of liability that it undertook in organizing these transactions. . . . It may well be that the noteholders . . . expected that the policies in question were the functional equivalent of financial guarantees. But the purchaser of a note in such circumstances would rely on the efforts of others to fulfill the expectation.*[15]

The trustee of the Hollywood notes, Law Debenture Trust Corp. (Channel Islands) Ltd., has initiated legal proceedings against Lexington. One of the note holders, Asset Backed Capital (ABC), a part of Quadrant Capital, has in turn filed suit against CSFB and Jardine Lloyd Thompson (JLT), the broker of the so-called guarantees. CSFB and JLT have been accused of failing to disclose information relevant to the deal. Additionally, CSFB has been charged with failing to understand the implications of structuring the transaction. And some have claimed that CSFB also acted as a major *purchaser* of the Hollywood notes.[16]

Monoline wrappers have said privately that this episode illustrates the tendency for multiline insurers to dispute claims more often than monolines and to offer guaranty-like products that are not really guaranties. In that regard, Hollywood Funding is now regularly used as an example by those who wish to argue that financial guaranties are only as good as their *guarantors'* ability and willingness to pay. Worth noting, however, is that may well *not* be the right lesson to take from Hollywood Funding. Instead, perhaps the best lesson to learn is the need to differentiate between traditional insurance and a true financial guaranty. As providers of property/casualty insurance, AIG appears to have been well within its contractual rights to not pay based on breach of warranty, and the U.K. dispute between HIH and its reinsurers seems to confirm that. The real question—one that may well remain a mystery—is how the policies were *marketed*. If no representations were ever made that the insurance provided by Lexington was a guaranty instead of true insurance, one can hardly fault AIG and should instead probably question the interpretation of the policies as guaranties by S&P and bond investors. But if either AIG or the broker represented that the policies were guaranties and then relied on their status as traditional insurance as an excuse not to pay, that's a different story. Either way, a lot of people have generalized the Hollywood Funding case as a broad warning about the reliability of guaranties, but one should use caution in pushing this example too far.

Financial Enhancement Ratings and Multilines versus Monolines   Since May 2000, S&P has issued *two* kinds of ratings for providers of insurance. The traditional rating—the *financial strength rating* (FSR)—indicates the *ability* of an insurer to pay its claims, whereas the *financial enhancement rating* (FER) introduced in May 2000 indicates both the ability and the *willingness* of an insurer to pay its bills. Although the FER predated Hollywood Funding, it was this debacle that first made FERs popular.

FERs were originally introduced by S&P to draw attention to the distinction between monoline and multiline financial guaranty coverage. In the words of S&P:

> *Although capital markets participants are accustomed to full and timely payment in accordance with the terms of the transaction, the payment culture of multiline insurers is not necessarily focused on timeliness. Thus, the traditional practice of multiline insurers in analyzing and investigating claims may not meet the expectations of fixed-income, capital markets investors that expect prompt payment. The FER is designed, in part, to reconcile these views. Multilines carrying the FER are expected to honor claims irrespective of legal precedents and commercial disputes.*[17]

Exchange and Clearinghouse Guaranties— A Success Story So Far

Financial exchanges and clearinghouses acting as central counterparties bear the credit risk that their members will default and that such a default will impose a loss on the clearing entity in excess of any collateral, margin, and/or capital pledged. Guaranties that provide synthetic equity in the event of a loss arising from a member default can be a very cost-effective means by which clearinghouses can ensure their ongoing operations following such a default, as well as signal their integrity to the capital market.

The provision of guaranties to exchanges and clearinghouses originated in the 1990s along two separate tracks. One track was paved by Paul Palmer, then of the AAA-rated monoline Asset Guaranty Insurance Co. and now chief executive officer of Capital Credit Holdings in New York. Palmer was later joined on the brokerage side by the developer of Marsh Ltd's Exchange and Clearing House Organization (ECHO) practice, Alastair Laurie-Walker. Together, Palmer and Laurie-Walker successfully created guaranties at such notable clearinghouses as the London Stock Exchange (prior to the cessation of its clearing function to the London Clearing House in 2001), the Sydney Futures Exchange, the Stock Exchange of Singapore, and Hong Kong Securities Clearing Corporation. Under the Asset Guaranty/Marsh program, Asset Guaranty was the sole guarantor, opting to reinsure the exposures selectively and on its own account.

Quite separately, Diego Wauters of AIG began to market seemingly similar guaranties about a year after Palmer. Three successful placements by that group included the Chicago Board of Trade Clearing Corporation, OM Gruppen AB in Stockholm, and the London Clearing House. Working with Michael March, then of BankAustria, the Lexington/AIG guaranty looked and worked differently from the Asset Guaranty structure. Specifically, AIG pushed almost all of the risk out the back door to a syndicate led by BankAustria, which then spread the risk around other highly rated market participants including some of the German *Landesbänken.*

All of the Asset Guaranty policies remain in place today, although they are now provided by Asset Guaranty's successor Radian (another New York monoline). In addition, Marsh and Radian have together added several new exchanges to their list of guaranties clearinghouses, such as the New York Mercantile Exchange. Marsh has also placed programs with other guarantors, such as the guaranty of the Norwegian power exchange Nordpool by Swiss Re.

The AIG programs did not fare as well, mainly because the people providing them left AIG and BankAustria, leading to these firms terminating their provision of new coverage in this area. That left the existing customers to deal with a leaderless syndicate of banks that are essentially unfamiliar with the business of clearing and settlements. Although there has been absolutely no question about the integrity of the guaranties themselves, the problem has been more for the exchanges, which found themselves having to seek approval in advance for almost every new product offering or business decision from a group of bankers who seemed as unenthusiastic to engage in such reviews as the exchanges. All three of those policies wound down in 2002 and were either replaced with alternative facilities or with facilities brokered through the Marsh program.

Since the pioneering work by Asset Guaranty/Palmer and Marsh/Laurie-Walker and by Wauters/AIG and March/BankAustria, other capital providers have entered the market for the provision of clearinghouse guaranties as well. In September 1999, Clearnet—the clearinghouse for Paris Bourse transactions—acquired a guaranty covering €150 million in default-related losses in excess of €170 million in self-insurance capital for three years. The guaranty was placed by Société Générale, insured by Chubb, and reinsured by Swiss Re, Westdeustche Landesbank, Commerzbank, Banque Internationale a Luxembourg, and Royal Bank of Canada Insurance Co.

Similarly, in 2001 the Swiss Exchange acquired a guaranty from Zürich Financial for €30 million XS €1 million of default-related losses on its new joint venture with TradePoint called Virt-x. Listing only securities and no derivatives, the Zürich coverage of Virt-x is a substitute for implementing cash margin calls on open, unsettled positions.[18]

CHAPTER 11

Derivatives

I n this chapter, we leave the world of insurance and shift our focus on the traditional components of risk transfer to the capital market side—namely, derivatives. Our focus in this chapter will be on traditional derivatives, those derivatives intended to help firms transfer and fine-tune the market risks to which they are exposed (see Chapter 2). We discuss the function and use of derivatives in credit risk transfer in the next chapter (Chapter 12).

As we shall see in Part Three, the use of derivatives to facilitate structured financing deals has become boilerplate. The parallels between derivatives and the alternative risk transfer (ART) products discussed in Part Four of the book, moreover, are in some cases striking. Derivatives and ART forms are in some instances pure substitutes for one another. But perhaps more common is the use of derivatives by banks and (re)insurers in the financial engineering process used to *create* an ART structure. In that sense, derivatives and ART can be highly complementary products.

These two chapters are not intended to be an exhaustive introduction to derivatives. In fact, readers without a basic command of derivatives will probably not have purchased this book. Instead, we want to briefly remind ourselves of what the main derivatives building blocks are that are used by financial engineers to develop structured products. This way we won't need to undertake any disruptive segues in Parts Three and Four.

WHAT ARE DERIVATIVES?[1]

The standard definition of a derivatives transaction is a bilateral contract whose value is derived from the value of some underlying asset, reference rate, or index (Global Derivatives Study Group, 1993). This definition, however, is generally a bit too broad to be of much practical use. We have already seen, after all, that a share of common stock can be viewed as an option on the assets underlying the firm—a derivative.

We saw in Chapter 8 that the definition of "insurance" evolved through English common law into a relatively specific checklist of criteria; for example, to be an insurance contract, the buyer must have an insurable interest and be at risk of sustaining economic damage. No such institutional or legal specificity exists for derivatives, especially considering the parallel tracks of development for derivatives traded on-exchange (e.g., futures, futures options, and options on securities) and derivatives negotiated over-the-counter (e.g., forwards, swaps, and commodity and interest rate options).[2]

Economically, derivatives are transactions involving a time and place other than the here and now (Culp 2004). They invariably involve some element of futurity such as the right or obligation to buy or sell an asset at a price fixed today for delivery on a specific date in the future.

Derivatives contracts must also be based on at least one "underlying." An underlying is the asset price, reference rate, or index level from which a derivatives transaction inherits its *principal* source of value. In practice, derivatives cover a diverse spectrum of underlyings, including physical assets, exchange rates, interest rates, commodity prices, equity prices, and indexes. Practically nothing limits the assets, reference rates, or indexes that can serve as the underlying for a derivatives contract. Some derivatives, moreover, can cover more than one underlying.

Institutionally, derivatives may be negotiated either on an organized securities or futures exchange or privately between two parties, which we call over-the-counter. Table 11.1 shows the notional amounts of derivatives outstanding at year-end since 1998 by underlying and by the type of market in which the contracts were negotiated.

All derivatives either are constructed with or are one of two simple and fundamental financial building blocks: forwards and options.[3] A forward contract obligates one counterparty to buy and the other to sell an asset or its cash equivalent in the future for an agreed-upon price. In return for the payment of a premium, an option contract gives the buyer the right but not the obligation to buy or sell an asset in the future at an agreed-upon price. Smithson (1987) refers to these two building blocks as the LEGOs with which all derivatives contracts are built. Once these building blocks are defined, the cash flows on virtually any derivatives transaction can be viewed as the net cash flows on a portfolio comprised of some combination of these building blocks.

TABLE 11.1 Derivatives Outstanding, Year-End 1998–2004 (Notional Principal, $billions)

	1998	1999	2000	2001	2002	2003	2004[a]
Over-the-Counter							
Foreign Exchange	$18,011	$14,344	$15,666	$ 16,748	$ 18,448	$ 24,475	$ 26,997
Interest Rate	50,015	60,091	64,668	77,568	101,658	141,991	164,626
Equity	1,488	1,809	1,891	1,881	2,309	3,787	4,521
Commodity	408	548	662	598	923	1,406	1,270
Other	10,387	11,408	12,313	14,384	18,328	25,508	22,644
Total	$80,309	$88,202	$95,200	$111,178	$141,665	$197,167	$220,058
Exchange-Traded							
Foreign Exchange	$ 81	$ 59	$ 96	$ 93	$ 74	$ 118	$ 98
Interest rate	12,655	11,680	12,642	21,762	21,715	33,918	49,385
Equity	1,199	1,851	1,520	1,909	2,026	2,704	3,319
Total	$13,935	$13,590	$14,258	$ 23,764	$ 23,816	$ 36,740	$ 52,802

[a]As of June 2004.
Source: Bank for International Settlements.

FORWARD AND FORWARDLIKE CONTRACTS

The most basic type of derivatives contract is a forward contract. A forward contract is a bilateral contract negotiated for the delivery of a physical asset (e.g., oil or gold) or its cash equivalent at a certain time in the future for a certain price fixed at the inception of the contract. No actual transfer of ownership occurs in the underlying asset when the contract is initiated. Instead, there is simply an agreement to transfer ownership of the underlying asset at some future delivery date. Whether the cash is paid by the buyer to the seller at the inception of the contract or on the future asset delivery date distinguishes *prepaid* from *traditional* forwards.

Prepaid versus Traditional Forwards

The single most important characteristic of derivatives that distinguishes them from other financial products is the explicit time dimension of a derivatives contract. In that sense, it is perhaps more useful to think of derivatives as types of transactions rather than types of financial products.

Nobel laureate Sir John Hicks (1989, p. 42) argues that any purchase or sale of an asset (real or financial) can be divided into three parts: (1) a contract between parties including a promise to pay and a promise to deliver; (2) the actual payment of cash by the asset buyer to the seller; and (3) the actual delivery of the asset by the seller to the buyer. We generally assume that the negotiation of the contract itself in (1) is "the trade" or "the transaction"—and, by extension, that the date on which the deal is negotiated is "the trade date."[4]

With the trade date in hand, we can characterize four elemental types of transactions by simply considering variations in the timing of the second and third components of a deal vis-à-vis the trade date. When the payment of cash by the buyer and the delivery of the asset by the seller occur immediately after the trade is agreed on, we call that a *spot* transaction, or the purchase of an asset "on the spot." When the buyer agrees to remit a payment in the future for an asset that he will receive in the future, the parties have engaged in a *forward* transaction, or the purchase of an asset for future/deferred delivery. When a buyer remits immediate payment to the seller for receipt of the asset in the future, the parties have engaged in a *prepaid forward* contract. Finally, when a seller makes immediate delivery of an asset and agrees to defer payment from the buyer to the future, the counterparties have negotiated a *payment-in-arrears* forward contract. The first three types of transactions are routinely observed in financial markets. The fourth is sometimes observed in commercial or retail sales contracts (e.g., buying a magazine subscription now for payment later) but is less common in a financial market context and we thus won't spend any time here on this fourth type.

Derivatives are distinguished by some explicit element of delay in the delivery of the underlying asset or the transfer of cash. The element of futurity that is common to all derivatives is perhaps best illustrated by comparing the payoff on a spot asset purchase (i.e., purchase for immediate delivery) with the payoff on traditional and prepaid forward transactions (i.e., contracts requiring the seller to deliver an asset on a later date). The timing distinctions between these contracts are shown in Exhibit 11.1.

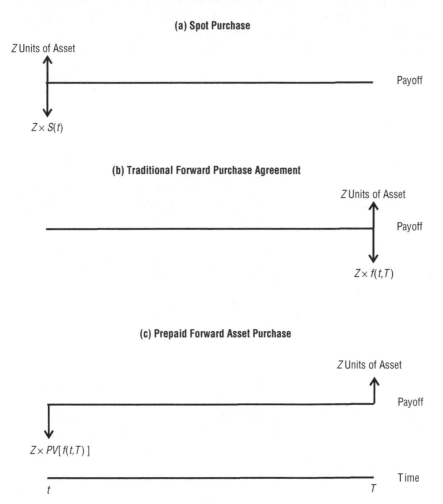

(a) Spot Purchase

Z Units of Asset

Payoff

$Z \times S(t)$

(b) Traditional Forward Purchase Agreement

Z Units of Asset

Payoff

$Z \times f(t,T)$

(c) Prepaid Forward Asset Purchase

Z Units of Asset

Payoff

$Z \times PV[f(t,T)]$

Time

t T

EXHIBIT 11.1 Transaction Types by Timing of Asset Delivery and Cash Payment

In this and subsequent similar exhibits, an up arrow indicates a cash or asset inflow, whereas a down arrow indicates a cash payment or asset delivery. All three transactions depicted in Exhibit 11.1 are shown from the perspective of the purchaser of Z units of some asset—Z barrels of oil, Z units of foreign currency, Z mortgage-backed securities, and so on.

Notice in Exhibit 11.1 that there are two differences between the transactions: the timing of the payoffs, and the amount paid by the buyer (long) to the seller (short). In the spot transaction shown in panel (a), the payment of $S(t)$ per unit simply denotes the current spot price. In panel (b), the payment by the long to the short is the price at time t for forward delivery of the asset at time T, denoted $f(t, T)$. And in panel (c), the time t payment by the long for delivery of the asset at time T is just the *present value* of the price the purchaser would have paid by deferring her payment until date T, which we denote with the present value operator $PV[\cdot]$.

The reason that the price paid by the long is comparable between the traditional and prepaid forwards but not in the spot transaction is quite simply that the two forwards give the purchaser the same thing—Z units of the asset at time T, then worth $S(T)$. In the spot transaction, by contrast, the long gets Z units of the asset now worth $S(t)$. A relationship does, of course, exist between the price of an asset bought today and the price of an asset bought for future delivery, but they are definitely not the same thing; see Culp (2004) for a more detailed discussion of what this relationship is and where it comes from.

In a typical forward purchase or sale agreement, the terms of trade—price per unit, quality, number of units, location and time of delivery, and so on—are specified when the contract is negotiated, but neither payment nor physical delivery occurs until the appointed date in the future. Forward delivery contracts are popular for facilitating the exchange of numerous underlying assets, including both physical assets like oil or gold and financial assets like bonds and foreign currency. Forward contracts may also be cash-settled, in which case the cash-equivalent value of the underlying asset is remitted by the short (i.e., the seller of the asset for future delivery) to the long (i.e., the buyer of the asset for future delivery) rather than the hard asset itself. Cash settlement is popular when the economic function played by the contract depends more on the cash flows of the contract than its physical settlement—for example, many risk management applications do not require physical delivery.

In its most basic form, a forward contract negotiated between two parties on some date t for delivery of Z units of the underlying asset by the short to the long on future date $T > t$ has a payoff to the long at maturity of

$$\pi_T^l = Z[S(T) - f(t, T)]$$

If the contract is physically settled, the long pays $Z \cdot f(t, T)$ to the short in cash, and the short delivers Z units of the asset to the long. The asset delivered has a current market price of $S(T)$ per unit and thus is worth that amount. In an otherwise-equivalent cash-settled forward, the short remits a cash payment of $Z \cdot S(T)$ to the long instead of delivering physical assets with the same value.

Like many derivatives, forward contracts are known as *zero net supply* assets—that is, for every long there is a corresponding short. To verify this, recognize that the payoff to the short in the same forward just described is

$$\pi_T^s = Z[f(t, T) - S(T)]$$

The seller in the contract—the short—thus receives $f_{t,T}$ per unit for an asset whose value at the time of sale is S_T. Clearly,

$$\pi_T^l + \pi_T^s = 0$$

As an example of a forward contract, consider an agreement that requires the long to purchase one 500-ounce bar of gold for the fixed total purchase price of $250,000. The fixed purchase price can be expressed in terms of $f(t, T) \times Z$ by noting that the size of the contract, Z, is the amount to be delivered, or 500 ounces of gold. The fixed purchase price is thus $f(t, T) = \$500/\text{oz}$. The payoff of such a forward contract is shown in Exhibit 11.2 from the perspective of the long.

Note that the *value* of the contract to the long (i.e., the gold purchaser) on delivery date T still depends on what the actual dollar price of gold is on date T. If $S(T) = \$450/\text{oz.}$, then the buyer must still remit $2,500 in return for receiving 500 ounces of gold. But the gold now has a market value at that time of only $225,000. So, the gold buyer is now paying $250,000 for a fixed amount of gold that is worth only $225,000 at time T.

Exhibit 11.3 shows an otherwise identical gold forward purchase agreement assuming that the length of the contract is one year and that the dollar interest rate is 5 percent per annum. Instead of delivering $250,000 at time T and receiving 500 ounces of gold at time T, the long now delivers the present value of $250,000 at time t—or $238,095—and receives 500

EXHIBIT 11.2   Gold Forward Purchase Contract

ounces of gold at time T. The contract is essentially the same as the traditional forward shown in Exhibit 11.2 except for the timing of the cash flow by the long.

Futures Contracts   Forward contracts are important not only because they play an important role as financial instruments in their own right but also because many other financial instruments embodying complex features can be decomposed into various combinations of long and short forward positions. Derivatives are forward-based if the contract

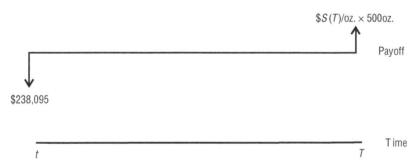

EXHIBIT 11.3   Prepaid Gold Forward Purchase Contract

can be decomposed into a forward contract or a portfolio of forward contracts.

Perhaps the most common forward-based derivatives contract is a futures contract, or a forward contract that is traded on an organized financial exchange such as the Chicago Mercantile Exchange (CME). Like forwards, futures can be based on a variety of underlyings and can be settled either physically or with cash. A popular cash-settled futures contract is the CME's Eurodollar futures contract, which has a value at expiration equal to 100 minus the then-prevailing three-month London Interbank Offered Rate (LIBOR). Eurodollar futures are currently listed with quarterly expiration dates and up to 10 years to maturity. The 10-year contract, for example, has an underlying of the three-month LIBOR prevailing 10 years hence.

Although exchange trading is the principal economic distinction between futures and forwards, that implies a lot. A necessary condition for exchange trading, for example, is at least some degree of standardization in contract terms, such as the amount of the underlying on which the contract is based. In turn, standardization facilitates offsetting, the process by which a long or short position on an organized exchange may be neutralized or reversed when a trader takes the opposite position in the same contract. Standardization and the ability to offset exchange-traded contracts usually result in relatively deeper liquidity for exchange-traded contract markets than in customized, off-exchange contracting.

Another feature typically associated with futures is the daily recognition of gains and losses. At least daily, futures exchanges mark the value of all futures accounts to current market-determined futures prices. Any gains in value from the previous mark-to-market period can be withdrawn by the winners, and those gains are financed by the losses of the losers over that period. The zero net supply feature of derivatives ensures that total gains will exactly offset total losses on any given day.

Swaps A second popular forward-based derivative is the swap contract. Swaps are privately negotiated agreements between two parties to exchange or swap cash flows or assets at specified times in the future according to some specified payment formula. Interest rate swaps and currency swaps are the most widely used, although swaps can in principle be based on any underlying asset, reference rate, or index.

The basic building blocks underlying a swap are no different from those underlying forward delivery contracts. The cash flows on a simple swap contract, in fact, can always be decomposed into the cash flows on a portfolio of forward contracts. Equivalently, a forward contract is just a one-period swap with a single settlement date.

An interest rate swap obligates the counterparties to exchange interest payments periodically for a specified period of time. In the most common form of interest rate swap, called the plain-vanilla fixed-for-floating swap, one payment is based on a floating rate of interest that resets periodically (e.g., three-month LIBOR) and the other on a rate fixed at the inception of the contract. The actual amounts exchanged are calculated based on a notional principal amount (NPA). The notional principal of interest rate swaps is not exchanged.

Exhibit 11.4 illustrates the cash flows on a typical dollar swap from the perspective of the fixed rate payer. The fixed rate K is set at the inception of the contract along with the other terms of the swap, including its notional principal amount NPA and final settlement date T. On each reset/settlement date over the life of the swap, the fixed rate payer thus pays (or receives) the net of the floating reference rate corresponding to that reset date (e.g., denoted R_{t+1} for the floating rate corresponding to the time $t + 1$ payment) less the fixed rate K adjusted by the number of interest-bearing days between reset dates and the NPA of the swap.

Currency swaps are similar to interest rate swaps in that one party makes a series of fixed or floating-rate payments to its counter party in exchange for a series of fixed or floating receipts. In a currency swap, though, the periodic fixed interest payments and receipts are in different currencies, and the principal amounts of each currency *are* exchanged at the beginning of the swap and returned at its conclusion. The principal of a currency swap is therefore *not* notional.

In addition to plain-vanilla interest rate swaps, many other types of swaps can be found, most of which are distinguished by differences in the

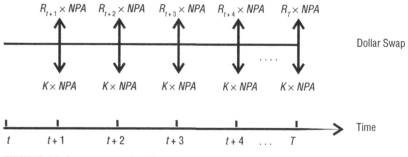

EXHIBIT 11.4 Pay Fixed Dollar Swap

key underlying economic terms of the swap. Even in fixed-for-floating interest rate swaps, numerous terms of the swap contract can be customized, including:

- The notional or reference principal amount.
- Whether the notional amount is subject to an amortization schedule, and if so what that schedule is.
- Who pays and who receives fixed-rate payments.
- The currency in which the interest and/or principal payments are to be made.
- The holiday convention governing payment schedules.
- The length of time the swap will be in effect (i.e., the swap's tenor).
- The level of the fixed rate paid by the fixed rate payer (i.e., the swap rate).
- The index to which the floating rate resets (e.g., six-month LIBOR).
- The spread (if any) to be added to the floating-rate index, reflecting considerations such as counterparty credit risk and credit enhancements to the swap.
- The frequency of cash flows.
- The day-count convention for compounding in computing payment streams.
- The frequency and timing of the floating-rate reset.
- Any special terms affecting collateral.

Derivatives based on more than one underlying are also quite common. One of the most popular multifactor derivatives is a "basis" or "diff" swap in which both legs of the interest rate swap are floating. Like an ordinary interest rate swap, the transaction will have a notional principal amount used for calculating interest payments and will have scheduled payment and settlement dates that occur periodically over the life of the swap. But unlike a plain-vanilla swap in which one party always pays a rate fixed at the inception of the transaction, both parties in a basis swap pay an amount determined by a floating reference rate.

Like forwards, swaps can also be prepaid. This is most commonly associated with commodity swaps, and we encounter these extensively in Chapter 21. Exhibit 11.5 illustrates the difference between otherwise identical prepaid and traditional commodity swaps. Panel (a) shows the traditional swap in which the long remits a periodic fixed payment of K/unit in exchange for receiving Z units of the asset worth $S(t + j)$ on any reset date $t + j$. Panel (b) shows the same swap, except that now the long makes a single large up-front payment to the short to cover all future

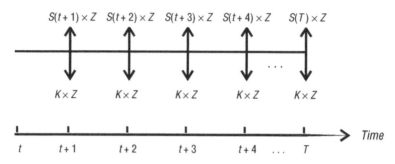

(a) Traditional Commodity Swap

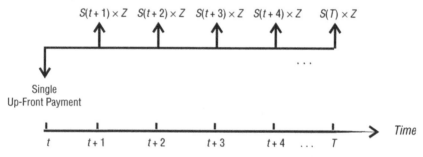

(b) Prepaid Commodity Swap

EXHIBIT 11.5   Traditional versus Prepaid Commodity Swap

deliveries. The price paid by the long should be equal to the present value of the stream of periodic fixed payments made in the traditional version of the swap.

OPTIONS

The second type of elemental building block in the world of derivatives used for market risk transfer is the option contract. Whereas forwards and forward-based derivatives create obligations to buy or sell an asset or its cash equivalent in the future, options and option-based derivatives convey on their purchasers a *right* but not an obligation to purchase or sell the underlying asset or its cash equivalent. Like forwards, options can be based on any number of underlying assets, both real and financial.

Major Types of Option Building Blocks

A *call* option gives its holder the right but not the obligation to *buy* some underlying asset or portfolio of assets at a prespecified price on or before the option's maturity date. A *put* option gives its holder the right but not the obligation to *sell* some underlying asset or portfolio of assets at a prespecified price on or before the option's maturity date.

If the right to buy or sell can be exercised at any time on or before the maturity date of the option, the option is called American-style. Options that can only be exercised *on* their maturity dates are called European-style. The preagreed price at which the buyer of the option can exercise her right to buy (in the case of a call) or sell (in the case of a put) the underlying is called the option's "strike," "striking," or "exercise" price.

The buyer of an option, called the long, pays for the rights conveyed by the contract by giving a *premium* payment to the seller of the option, called the short or the option "writer." Option buyers own limited liability assets, whereas option sellers can incur losses up to the point where the asset(s) underlying the option become worthless.

Exhibit 11.6 summarizes the payoffs at maturity for European-style calls and puts from the perspectives of both their buyers and their sellers. The options shown all have a strike price X and are based on some asset whose value at expiration of the option is denoted $A(T)$.

Panels (a) and (b) show the symmetric payoff obligations between the buyer and seller of a put option. In exchange for the limited liability right but not the obligation to sell some underlying asset at price X, the option buyer pays a premium to the option seller. (Only the payoffs are shown, not profits—the diagrams do not take into account premium paid.) If the price at time T of the underlying asset is above the put strike price X, the option is said to be out-of-the-money. The buyer would lose money if she exercised the option and thus does not do so. The seller keeps the premium and has no further obligations.

If the price at time T of the underlying asset is above the put strike price X, the option is said to be in-the-money and the buyer can exercise it for a payoff of $A(T) - X$. If the underlying price $A(T)$ exactly equals the option strike price X, the option is said to be at-the-money, but this does not guarantee the option buyer will make a profit from exercising the option. The option buyer breaks even only when the price has risen above the option strike by enough to offset the premium paid for the option.

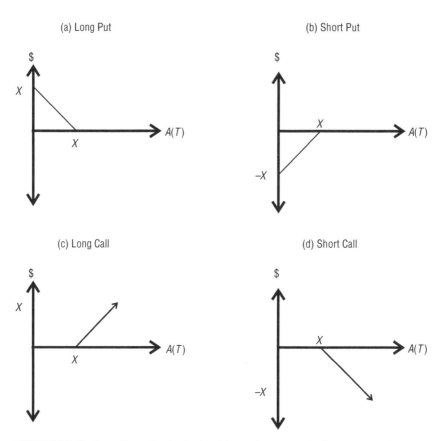

EXHIBIT 11.6   Payoffs on Basic Option Types (European-Style, at Expiration)

Because options would never be exercised at a loss by their holders, the values of purchased European-style calls and puts at maturity are usually expressed in the following way:

$$C(T) = \max[S(T) - X, 0]$$
$$P(T) = \max[X - S(T), 0]$$

The seller of these options has the opposite exposure, and terminal values of a call and put on the same underlying with strike price X are thus

$$-C(T) = -\max[S(T) - X, 0] = \min[X - S(T), 0]$$
$$-P(T) = \max[X - S(T), 0] = \min[S(T) - X, 0]$$

Note in panels (a) and (c) that the liability of the option buyer is limited to the premium paid, regardless of whether the option is a call or a put. No matter what happens to underlying prices, an additional payment is never required of the option purchaser. As panels (b) and (d) illustrate, however, the option writer, by contrast, assumes an essentially unlimited liability.[5]

Time Value versus Intrinsic Value   At expiration, any value the option has is said to be *intrinsic value*. The intrinsic value of a call at expiration thus is either zero or the difference between the expiration spot price $S(T)$ and the option's strike price. Before expiration, the market value of an option is the sum of its intrinsic value plus its *time value*.

Time value reflects the fact that no matter what the intrinsic value of the option is on any given date, that value could change again before the option matures if the underlying spot price changes. True, prices could move for or against the option holder, but because options are limited liability contracts, favorable price moves may increase the owner's final payout dollar for dollar whereas the maximum loss is zero (other than the premium paid). The longer the option has left during which time the price could move in favor of its holder, the more time value. And conversely for option sellers.

Exhibit 11.7 illustrates the concepts of time value and intrinsic value for a European-style call option with strike price X written on an underlying asset with a price on the option's maturity date of $A(T)$. The "hockey stick" payoff labeled $C(T)$ is the value of the call at maturity, which is pure intrinsic value. Twenty-five days prior to maturity, the dotted line shows the value of the call $C(T - 25)$ as a function of the underlying asset price. The different time value of the two options is revealed by the vertical distance at any given point on the graph between the valuation curve and the option's intrinsic value. At the strike price X where the only value the option has is time value, for example, $C(T - 25)$ is the time value of the 25-day option. As maturity approaches, the dashed line eventually converges to the pure intrinsic value hockey stick line.

Option Greeks   The sensitivities of an option's value to changes in different market variables often are easiest to understand from graphs such as Exhibit 11.7. Typically defined in the colorful argot called the "option Greeks" or "fraternity row," these sensitivities include terms like theta— the change in the value of an option with the passage of time. Theta can be seen on Exhibit 11.7 as the gradual drop in the valuation curves toward intrinsic value as time to maturity shortens. The shorter the time to maturity,

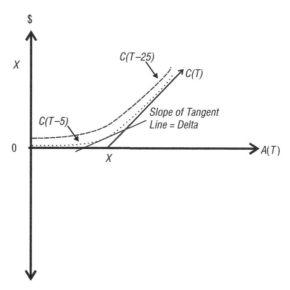

EXHIBIT 11.7   Payoff of European-Style Call
Option At and Before Maturity

the lower the valuation curve, the less the time value, and the less the total option value. This is also known as time decay; because a purchased option loses time value as time passes, it is a wasting asset.

Similarly, *delta* is the sensitivity of the change in the value of an option to a small change in the value of the underlying. This can also be seen on Exhibit 11.7 as the slope of the horizontal line tangent to the valuation curve $C(T-5)$. This slope changes depending on the underlying price at which the tangency point is being drawn. The change in delta as the underlying price changes is called *gamma*.

Finally, *vega* is the sensitivity of an option to a change in the volatility of the underlying. Because the buyer of an option has limited liability (the worst that can happen is a loss of premium for either a call or a put purchaser) the higher volatility and higher chance for a big price upswing are not accompanied by the equal risk of a major loss. Accordingly, options on more volatile assets tend to be more valuable.

Apart from these sorts of graphs, it can be equally interesting to examine how the Greeks change as a function of something other than the underlying price, such as time to maturity. Interested readers should see Hull (2003).

Put-Call Parity

The values of calls and puts are related to one another through *put-call parity*. For American-style options, put-call parity can at best be expressed as an inequality, whereas for European-style options the relationship holds *exactly* subject to the transaction costs of arbitrage. In other words, deviations from this relationship represent an exploitable arbitrage opportunity.

To keep things simple here, suppose we are working with traded options on some asset (assumed not to pay any dividends) whose time t price is $S(t)$. Let r denote the riskless interest rate, X the strike price common between a call and a put, and T the maturity date of the call and put. The basic put-call parity relationship says that at any time before T, the price of a long call and a short put are related:

$$C(t) - P(t) = S(t) - PV(X)$$

where PV indicates a present value, discounted in this case using the risk-free rate. So, buying a call and selling a put is synthetically equivalent to buying the underlying asset and borrowing X dollars at the riskless rate.

If we assume we hold a portfolio consisting of these four positions to maturity, the put-call parity relationship at maturity tells us that

$$C(T) - P(T) = S(T) - X$$

from which can immediately see that in the special case of at-the-money options, *the price of a European call and put must be equal at maturity.*

Exhibit 11.8 shows the put-call parity relationship graphically at maturity by expressing the payoff of certain claims at maturity as a function of underlying price $S(T)$. Note that these are *payoffs*, not profits and losses—that is, premium is not shown on these diagrams, just cash flows at time T. Panels (a) and (b) together are equivalent to panel (c); a short put and long call at common strike price X are economically equivalent to buying the asset for future delivery at price X. Panels (c) and (d) in turn sum to panel (e), so that a forward purchase at X plus borrowing X is equivalent to buying the asset at its current spot price.

"Exotic" Options

Apart from the plain-vanilla call and put, option products abound that represent variations on the traditional option theme. Often these are called exotic options, although some are actually deceptively simple. Any good derivatives text will provide readers with a complete survey of exotic

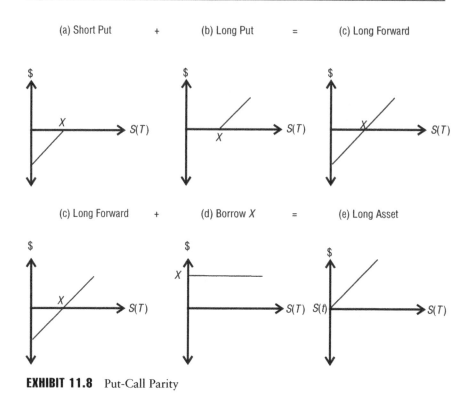

EXHIBIT 11.8   Put-Call Parity

options. In this section, we focus on summarizing the exotics that appear elsewhere in this book either as an engineered component of or as an economically substantive analogue to other structures.

Barrier Options   Barrier options involve the specification of a second kind of strike price that affects the exercisability of the option but *not* the payout of the option if exercised. A *knock-in* option is an option that is not exercisable until the price of the underlying has crossed some barrier, whereas a *knock-out* option becomes unexercisable when some barrier is reached. Usually the crossing of a barrier results in a permanent change to the option's exercisability. A *down-and-out* call, for example, is a traditional call plus the additional feature that if prices *ever* fall below some prespecified "outstrike," the option disappears forever. If the outstrike is never reached, the terminal payoff on the option is the same as if the call were a traditional European-style option. Similarly, if the "*in*strike" on a down-and-in put is X and the strike price is K, the option pays nothing for $X < S(T) < K$

but when $S(T) < X$, the put becomes exercisable with an immediate intrinsic value of $K - S(T)$.

Exhibit 11.9 illustrates the payoffs at maturity date T of European-style knock-in options based on an underlying with a time T price of $S(T)$—specifically, an up-and-in call in panel (a) and a down-and-in put in panel (b). In both cases, the strike price is X and the instrike is K. The dashed lines represent the payoffs of a traditional call and put, whereas the solid line shows the payoffs on the knock-in options. The barrier feature creates a discontinuity in the payoffs. Take the put, for example, in panel (b). The intrinsic value is positive for all $S(T) < X$, but the option is not exercisable until $S(T) < K$. When $S(T) < K$, the option is immediately exercisable at an intrinsic value of $S(T) - X$. And similarly for the call.

The inclusion of barriers into options limits the scenarios in which the option will be profitably exercised by the long, thus reducing the price vis-à-vis a traditional, unrestricted option. Barriers are often engineered into optionlike products specifically to reduce the premiums.

Binary or Digital Options A binary or digital option is an option whose payoff upon exercise does not depend on how deep in-the-money the option is. The following is an example of a binary call option with strike price X:

$$C(T) = \max(0, Z)$$

where Z is a fixed amount. The buyer gets either zero or Z, and the latter amount does not vary with the degree to which the option is in-the-money.

Two popular kinds of digital options are the *cash-or-nothing* and *asset-or-nothing* digitals. In the former, Z is a flat cash amount, whereas in the latter Z is a fixed number of units of some asset. The payoff on the

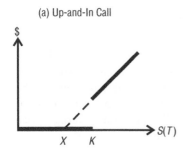

(a) Up-and-In Call

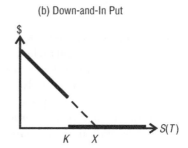

(b) Down-and-In Put

EXHIBIT 11.9 Knock-In Barrier Options

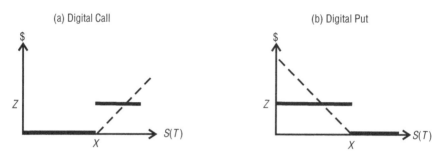

EXHIBIT 11.10   Cash-or-Nothing Binary/Digital Options

cash-or-nothing option is truly fixed in every sense. The payoff on an asset-or-nothing option does not change as the underlying price *corresponding to the option* changes, but the value of that payoff is a function of the value of the underlying asset into which the digital option exercises.

Exhibit 11.10 shows the payoffs on a digital cash-or-nothing call in panel (a) and a digital cash-or-nothing put in panel (b). The fixed payoff is Z, and the strike price in each case is X. Suppose, for example, that the options are written on crude oil and struck at $50 per barrel. If either option is in-the-money, the fixed payoff is $Z = \$100,000$. For crude prices below $50, the call expires worthless but the put pays off $100,000. For crude prices above $50, the put expires worthless and the call pays its holder $100,000. Note that this is functionally the same thing as a valued insurance contract, except, of course, that the option buyer need not have an insurable interest in the oil.

A traditional digital option is exercisable only when it is in-the-money. Alternatively, many digital options are known as *one-touch* digitals because they can be exercised for the fixed amount if the option ever goes in the money. In other words, if the underlying price ever touches a price above the strike on a call or below the strike on a put, the option is then essentially in-the-money from there out.

Average Price and Average Strike Options   "Path-dependent" options are nontraditional options whose payoffs upon exercise or at maturity depend not just on the underlying asset price at the time of exercise/maturity, but also on the *path* of underlying prices realized over some dates during the life of the option. One popular type of path-dependent option is called an *Asian* or *average price/average strike* option. For an Asian average price call option with maturity date T, the exercise value is

$$C(T) = \max[0, A(\tau1,\tau2) - X]$$

where X is the fixed strike price (as usual) and where $A(\tau1,\tau2)$ is the average price of the asset underlying the option from date $\tau1$ through date $\tau2$. The averaging period from $\tau1$ through $\tau2$ may include the trade date through the maturity date or anything in between, and the average itself may be either geometric or arithmetic. Puts work the other way around, with the terminal payoff equal to the maximum of zero or the strike less the average price.

A similar type of Asian option is an average strike option. For a call with maturity date T, the payoff at expiration on an average strike call is

$$C(T) = \max[0, S(T) - A(\tau1,\tau2)]$$

where $S(T)$ is the terminal price of the underlying and $A(\tau1,\tau2)$ is the average value of that underlying price over the period from $\tau1$ to $\tau2$.

Lookback Options   Another popular type of path-dependent option is an option on an extremum, or a *lookback* option. At maturity or upon exercise, a lookback option gives its buyer the right to choose a strike price based on *any* price the underlying has realized either over its life or over some defined interval.[6] Depending on whether the option is a call or a put, we know what a rational chooser will pick as the preferred exercise price— the realized price that maximizes the intrinsic value of the option. So, a lookback call is generally equivalent to a call whose strike price is the minimum realized price over the indicated interval, whereas a lookback put is an option with a maximum price as strike. Payoffs of lookback calls and puts at maturity are, respectively:

$$C(T) = \max[0, S(T) - S^{min}]$$
$$P(T) = \max[0, S^{max} - S(T)]$$

Ladder Options   A ladder option has a strike price that automatically changes when the underlying price moves through some predefined barrier. The buyer and seller can agree on multiple such "rungs" and a ladder of corresponding strike prices. Ladder options are popularly used to lock in some degree of in-the-moneyness of an option so that subsequent reversals before exercise or maturity do not deprive the holder of those gains.

A European ladder call option has the following payoff at maturity date T:

$$C(T) = \max[0, S(T) - X, \max[0, L_k - X]]$$

where L_k is the kth rung in the ladder of strike prices specified. The payoffs on a ladder call are shown for three different possible price paths in

Exhibit 11.11, adapted from Smithson (1998). The option strike price is
X, and the rungs in the ladder are K and L. Price Path 1 generates a payoff
equivalent to a traditional call because the terminal asset price $S(T)$ is
above both ladder rungs. For Price Path 2, the price crossed ladder rungs
K and L, but the terminal price reversed and ended up below L. The ladder payoff thus is $L - X$. And for Price Path 3, the path crosses the first
rung of the ladder K and then slides downward so that $S(T)$ is never again
above K. Because the option is a ladder, the early appreciation in the underlying price above K, however, is locked in—the final payoff for Price
Path 3 is $K - X$.

Shout Options   A *shout* option is a call or a put where the buyer can no-
tify the seller and define a ladder rung—just as in a ladder option—at
one or more times over the life of the option. Usually the buyer can
shout only once. In other words, a shout option is a ladder option where
the rung is determined over the life of the option rather than in advance.
When the buyer shouts to the seller, the intrinsic value of the option is
locked in as a minimum terminal payoff. But if only one shout is allowed, the buyer may forgo other potentially more profitable shouting
opportunities.

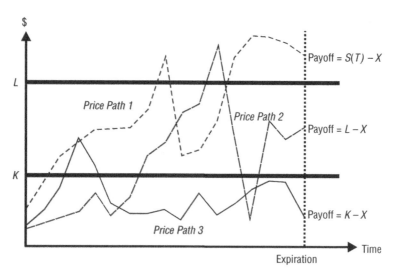

EXHIBIT 11.11   Possible Terminal Payoffs on a Ladder Option
Source: Adapted from Smithson (1998).

The payoffs of European shout calls and puts on maturity date T are defined as follows for some buyer-chosen shout level K:

$$C(T) = \max[0, S(T) - X, K - X]$$
$$P(T) = \max[0, X - S(T), X - K]$$

Compound Options A *compound* option is an option on an option. Upon exercise, the buyer receives another option rather than an actual physical asset, cash equivalent, or forward-based derivatives contract. Examples include options on caps, collars, and floors and options on a portfolio of options. Compound options can *be* calls or puts and can *be written on* calls or puts, leading to at least four combinations: a call on a call, a call on a put, a put on a call, and a put on a put.

Exchange, Rainbow, and Basket Options Another type of option where the underlying is not a simple, single asset is an exchange asset, or an option to exchange one asset for another. A European exchange option has the following value at maturity:

$$\max[S_1(T) - S_2(T), 0]$$

where $S_1(T)$ is the terminal price of asset 1 and $S_2(T)$ is the terminal price of asset 2.

Exchange options are commonly combined with a position in one of the two assets. When this is done, the net result is an option that allows the buyer to obtain the better or worse of two assets. An option that entitles its holder to obtain the better of two assets has a terminal payoff of

$$\max[S_1(T), S_2(T)] = S_1(T) - \max[S_1(T) - S_2(T), 0]$$

and an option that entitles is holder to obtain the worse of two assets has a terminal payoff of

$$\min[S_1(T), S_2(T)] = S_2(T) + \max[S_1(T) - S_2(T), 0]$$

Recall from Chapter 1 that the value of risky corporate debt is an option on the worse of two assets: riskless debt equal to the face value of the debt plus a put struck at the face value of the debt.

The exchange option is also sometimes called a *relative spread* option, a *rainbow* option, or an *outperformance* option. Rainbow options can include two or more assets, and the assets may represent a basket of other assets.

Take-or-Pay Contracts

A final product we consider is extremely popular in physically settled commodity derivatives transactions, and we will see examples of this structure later in Chapter 21. In this case, known as a *take-or-pay* contract, the long (buyer) agrees to purchase a fixed amount of the underlying commodity from the short (seller) over a period of time at a fixed price. The actual timing of deliveries, however, is determined by the long. In other words, the long commits to a fixed purchase price and total quantity but can decide when to take deliveries. If at the end of the life of the contract the buyer has not taken delivery on the entire underlying amount, the buyer still must pay for any undelivered quantity—hence, the term "take-or-pay."

Take-or-pay contracts are commonly used in the energy and metals markets. They are also popular in agricultural markets, where these products are known as *hedge to arrive* (HTA) contracts.

A take-or-pay contract seems—and in some ways *is*—more like a forward than an option. But because of the embedded quantity flexibility, take-or-pays can be more easily viewed as a combination of option positions bundled together as a single forwardlike instrument with quantity flexibility. Specifically, from the perspective of the commodity buyer, a take-or-pay is equivalent to owning an American-style call and simultaneously selling a European-style put on the underlying commodity. The two options are struck at the same price—the fixed purchase price in the contract—and have the same maturity date. The call option has an underlying quantity equal to the total amount to be purchased in the contract, and the put option has an underlying quantity at maturity equal to the unexercised portion of the American-style call.

CHAPTER 12

Credit Derivatives and Credit-Linked Notes

A s we discussed in Chapter 2, derivatives are generally distinguished from insurance by the principles of indemnity and insurable interest. Insurance is a reimbursement for actual economic damage sustained, whereas derivatives are parametric contracts whose cash flows are based on market-determined variables like interest rates and commodity prices.

In this chapter, we survey the rapidly expanding area of credit derivatives activity. Credit derivatives are bilateral derivatives contracts in which one party compensates another following an adverse triggering event on one or more reference names or assets. Virtually unused as recently as 1995, credit derivatives activity has exploded in popularity in recent years. Some estimates put the notional principal outstanding amount as high as $8.42 trillion by year-end 2004, up from $6 trillion in 2002.

Credit derivatives are the most insurance-like of all derivatives. Although they do not require an insurable interest, their payments are based on the value of one or more highly specific assets rather than just broad market indexes. Nevertheless, credit derivatives are *not* insurance; the purchaser of protection need not be susceptible to any loss, thus squarely distinguishing these contracts from indemnity contracts.

Credit derivatives come in a wide variety of flavors. We explore the mechanics of the main types of credit derivatives in the sections that follow. Where appropriate, we also examine the main differences between credit derivatives and comparable credit insurance structures we reviewed in Chapter 10. But first, let's begin with a brief overview of the market.

SCOPE OF CREDIT DERIVATIVES ACTIVITY

Fitch Ratings estimates that in 2003, the most popular credit derivatives were single-name credit default swaps (CDSs), portfolio protection

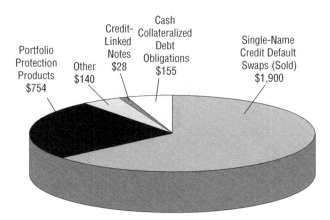

EXHIBIT 12.1   Credit Derivatives by Product, 2003 (US$billions)
Source: Fitch Ratings.

products, credit-linked notes, and collateralized debt obligations (CDOs), the latter of which we discuss in Chapters 17 and 18.[1] Exhibit 12.1 shows the relative popularity of these products in 2003.

Users of credit derivatives can be classified as *credit protection sellers* or *buyers*. In the most basic form of credit derivatives transaction, the credit protection buyer makes periodic payments (the derivatives version of credit insurance premium payments) to the credit protection seller in exchange for the right to some compensation when a default event occurs on the underlying asset or name. A name is essentially a corporate entity, and a credit derivative based on a single name may well cover a default on virtually any significant obligation of that entity. Exhibit 12.2 shows the ma-

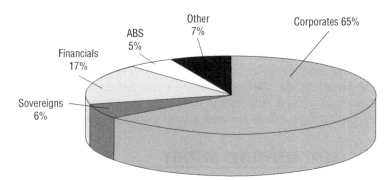

EXHIBIT 12.2   Reference Name by Type, 2003
Source: Fitch Ratings.

TABLE 12.1 Top Reference Names (Protection Sold, 2003)

1	Ford Motor Corp./Ford Motor Credit Corp.
2	General Motors/GMAC
3	France Telecom
4	DaimlerChrysler
5	Deutsche Telekom
6	General Electric/GECC
7	Altria Group
8	Telecom Italia
9	Japan
10	France
11	Italy
12	Portugal
13	Fannie Mae
14	Verizon
15	Allianz
16	Merrill Lynch
17	Volkswagen
18	AIG
19	Citigroup
20	Germany
21	Spain
22	BNP Paribas
23	Eastman Kodak
24	Time Warner
25	ABN Amro

Source: Fitch Ratings.

jor types of reference names for which credit protection was sold in 2003. Table 12.1 lists the top 25 specific names for which protection was sought that same year.

Buyers of credit protection in the global credit derivatives market include banks, broker/dealers, asset managers and hedge funds, and nonfinancial corporations. The dominant sellers of credit protection are internationally active banking institutions (including their broker/dealer affiliates). Insurance companies and financial guarantors are also active sellers of credit protection, as shown in Exhibit 12.3.

In 2003, as in prior years, the top 10 credit protection sellers represented nearly 70 percent of the total market. The top 25 protection providers for 2003 are shown in Table 12.2.

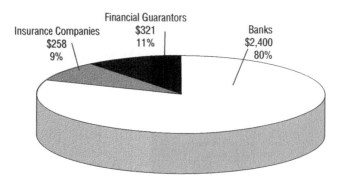

EXHIBIT 12.3   Credit Protection Sellers, 2003 (US$billions)
Source: Fitch Ratings.

TABLE 12.2   Top Credit Protection Sellers, 2003

1	JPMorgan Chase
2	Deutsche Bank
3	Goldman Sachs
4	Morgan Stanley
5	Merrill Lynch
6	Credit Suisse First Boston
7	UBS
8	Lehman Brothers
9	Citigroup
10	Bear Stearns
11	Commerzbank
12	BNP Paribas
13	Bank of America
14	Dresdner
15	ABN Amro
16	Société Générale
17	AIG
18	Barclays
19	Toronto Dominion
20	Calyon
21	HSBC
22	Ambac
23	CDC Ixis Financial Guaranty
24	KfW
25	Royal Bank of Scotland

Source: Fitch Ratings.

SINGLE-NAME CREDIT DEFAULT SWAPS

The most popular form of credit derivatives transaction is the single-name credit default swap (CDS). Although called a swap, a CDS functions much like an option—in the event of a default on an eligible obligation issued by the reference name, the contract pays off.

The single-name CDS market has grown remarkably rapidly over the past decade. Despite being an over-the-counter market (as opposed to an exchange-traded market),[2] the single-name CDS market is also now relatively liquid. Of the 1,000 or so names actively traded in 2003, about 300 were considered to be as liquid as their underlying reference bonds, if not more so (Reoch, 2003).

Single-Name CDS Mechanics

A typical single-name CDS functions almost exactly the same way as credit insurance or a financial guarantee. The credit protection purchaser makes a fixed payment (or a series of fixed payments over time) to the credit protection seller in exchange for a contingent payment upon the occurrence of an event of default by a specific obligation called the reference asset. If the triggering event of default occurs, the credit protection seller makes a cash payment to the protection buyer equal to the par/notional amount of the reference asset minus the expected recovery. The mechanics of this basic structure are shown in Exhibit 12.4.

Some of the more specific aspects and variations of CDSs are discussed in the following subsections.

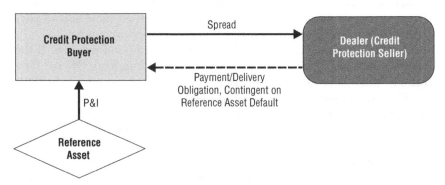

EXHIBIT 12.4   Single-Name Credit Default Swap

Contingent Obligations and Settlement Method   A CDS may be either cash-settled or physically settled. The most common type of CDS is a *cash-settled CDS* in which the credit protection seller makes a single cash payment to the credit protection buyer (upon the occurrence of an event of default) equal to the par value of the defaulted reference asset minus the current market price of the asset.[3] In such transactions, the two counterparties agree in advance to a source or method of calculating the market value of the defaulted security.

Some cash-settled CDSs—known as *digital CDSs*—specify a fixed cash payment from the protection seller to the protection buyer. Just as the traditional cash-settled CDS can be compared to indemnity insurance purchased for the reference asset, a digital CDS is comparable to a *valued* credit insurance contract. As we saw in Chapter 8, valued insurance tends to be used when the parties anticipate they will have problems reaching agreement about the true value of the underlying asset. Not surprisingly, digital CDSs thus are often associated with highly illiquid reference assets that the counterparties agree will be very difficult to price if an event of default occurs.

A *physically settled CDS* requires the credit protection buyer to deliver the defaulted reference asset to the protection seller, in return for which the protection seller pays a fixed cash amount to the buyer. The fixed cash amount is specified in advance in the contract documentation and is usually the par value of the reference security.

The distinctions among a cash-settled CDS, a digital CDS, and a physically settled CDS are evident from the diagram in Exhibit 12.5.

Payment to the Protection Seller   The payment made by the credit protection buyer to the credit protection seller in a CDS is known as the *spread* or *CDS spread*. The spread is often paid out to the protection seller in a stream of payments over time. The present value of all these spread payments is economically equivalent to a credit insurance premium.

A CDS is economically equivalent to a financed bond position. If the reference asset has a yield equivalent of the London Interbank Offered Rate (LIBOR) plus 50 basis points and can be financed using a repo at LIBOR, the 50-point net spread should be approximately equal to the CDS spread. In practice, there are some important differences between bonds and CDSs that make this relation inexact, and we will return to this later.

Reference Name   In Exhibits 12.4 and 12.5, the CDSs are based on a specific, single reference asset. Instead of assets, CDSs are most often based on a *reference name*, or the legal entity corresponding to a specific issuer or obligor.

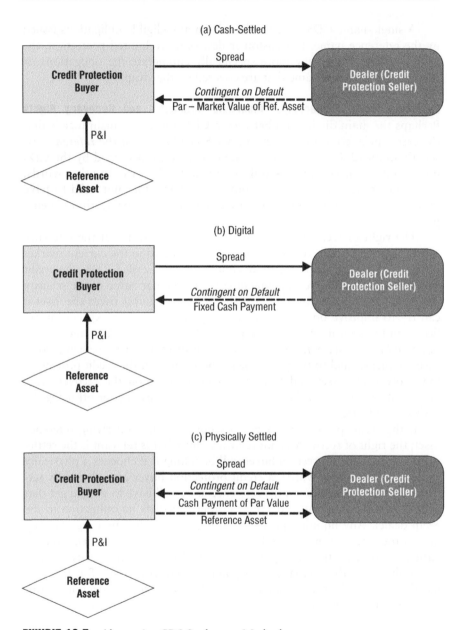

EXHIBIT 12.5   Alternative CDS Settlement Methods

A single-name CDS covers a default on any eligible obligations issued by the reference name. If a customer desires more limited protection, the CDS documentation may more specifically enumerate the obligations issued by the reference name that are covered by the swap.

Reference Asset Ownership, "Insurable Interest," and Recovery Rights

Perhaps the main distinction between a CDS and credit insurance is that the credit protection purchaser in a CDS *need not own the reference asset*. Exhibits 12.4 and 12.5 show the reference asset owned by the CDS buyer, but this need not be—and often is not—the case. In other words, unlike insurance, the protection buyer in a CDS does not need to have an insurable interest in the reference asset for which protection is being purchased.

The right of recovery generally rests with the owner of the reference asset. The expected recovery on the asset is reflected in the current market price of a security following its default. In a cash-settled CDS, the credit protection buyer receives a payment equal to the par value of the security minus the *expected* recovery, but if the protection buyer owns the asset it can try to improve on the actual recovery relative to the expectation reflected in the security price. In the physically settled CDS, by contrast, the bond *and the recovery right* are given to the swap dealer in exchange for a cash payment equal to the par value of the security. If the credit protection buyer owns the asset and believes it can improve on the recovery rate priced into the security, the protection buyer is clearly better off using the cash-settled CDS.

If the credit protection buyer does not own the underlying reference asset, the right of recovery is not relevant. But what *is* relevant is the settlement risk that the protection buyer will be taking if it chooses a physically settled CDS. In other words, a credit protection buyer in a physically settled CDS that does not own the reference asset will have to go and get that asset following an event of default in order to satisfy its obligation to the swap dealer. Any liquidity problems in the market thus may significantly impact the price the protection buyer must pay to acquire the defaulted security. To mitigate this risk, physically settled CDSs often specify deliverable obligations that actually go beyond the reference asset. But this also has the impact of turning a single-name CDS into a first-to-default portfolio CDS at the same time.

Trigger Events/Credit Events/Events of Default

Most market participants rely on the International Swaps and Derivatives Association (ISDA) credit derivatives confirm, which allows a lot of flexibility for the counterparties to define the event of default that triggers a payment on the CDS. An event of default may be as simple as a failure to make a principal or interest payment on a specified reference asset, or it could be as broad as an insolvency filing by the issuer. Other events of default that are often specified as triggers in a CDS include a downgrade of the reference asset or name, cross-default by the reference name on another asset, or repudiation of another obligation by the reference name. Events of default may also include materiality conditions, so that failures to pay are excluded if the amounts in question are immaterial.

Considerable debate has surrounded the treatment of restructuring as an event of default. Buyers of protection tend to prefer the inclusion of restructuring as an adverse credit event because restructuring usually lengthens maturity and eases payment terms on debt. Dealers tend to want it excluded for the same reason—and, dealers argue, restructuring is very difficult to define. ISDA has attempted to address these concerns with a supplement to its credit derivatives master agreement in 2001, but insurance industry participants in particular found the supplement to be unsatisfactory. For more discussion of the restructuring controversy, see Smithson (2003) and Choudhry (2004).

Fixed CDSs versus Constant Maturity CDSs

In the typical single-name CDS, the premium paid to the credit protection seller is constant even though it is paid to the protection seller gradually over the life of the contract. A new variation on this fixed CDS has emerged in recent months called the *constant maturity CDS* (CMCDS). The premium paid is variable over the life of the CMCDS contract and resets periodically to some reference fixed CDS. A CMCDS may also specify a gearing factor or participation rate that is a fraction of the reference fixed CDS premium.[4]

Bonds versus CDSs

As noted in the previous section, a CDS is basically equivalent to a financed bond position. But not quite. In fact, there are some important differences between CDSs and bonds, and these differences result in slight differences in pricing between CDSs and their bond-equivalent positions. These differences are discussed in the subsections that follow.

Deviations from Par for Cash-Settled CDSs
The payoff on a plain-vanilla cash-settled CDS is the par value of the reference asset less the market price. The market price reflects the discounted present value of expected recoveries on the reference asset.

Any given bond, however, may trade at a discount to par. In this case, the loss in the event of a default is the difference between the market price of the bond and the expected recovery reflected in the postdefault market price of the bond. This is not quite the same as the difference between the par value of the bond and its postdefault market price.

Delivery Option for Physically Settled CDSs   As noted in the prior section, a CDS may specify a whole set of deliverable obligations that are eligible for delivery by the credit protection purchaser in the event of a default. The seller will, of course, choose the cheapest bond to deliver, all else being equal. As users of futures contracts are well acquainted, this cheapest to deliver option is valuable and will, all else being equal, increase the CDS spread relative to the pure bond position.

Accrued Interest   When a default triggers payment and termination of the CDS, the credit protection seller has received spread payments up to the default date. On a bond position, there is no guarantee that the bond-holder has received or will receive accrued interest.

Liquidity   In general, the CDS market is usually less liquid than the bond market for the same reference asset. All else being equal, this tends to make the CDS spread slightly higher than the financed bond spread.

Financial Guarantees versus CDSs

The economic similarities between financial guarantees and CDSs are also obvious. But, like bonds versus CDSs, there are some important differences that should not be ignored.

Reference Asset and Trigger   Insurance tends to be more specific with respect to the reference asset or reference name that can trigger a default. As discussed, the definition of an event of default in a CDS tends to be fairly broad. This can give rise to significant differences between the triggering of a CDS and a comparable insurance product. For example, a CDS usually can be triggered only by an event of default that has been disclosed publicly. Insurance, by contrast, can be triggered by a *non*disclosed event of default.

Ongoing Coverage   When an event of default occurs on a CDS, the CDS usually terminates. Insurance remains ongoing provided the policy limit of the financial guaranty has not yet been reached. Even then, optional reinstatement provisions may allow insurance purchasers to pay an additional premium to reinstate some or all of their original policy limit even after it has been exhausted by claims.

Tax and Accounting   Financial guaranties are insurance contracts and thus subject to accounting and tax rules for insurance. A CDS, by contrast, is a derivatives contract and thus must be marked to market for accounting purposes, unlike insurance. Hedge taxation rules also apply, which may differ from insurance taxation rules. For example, premium paid on a financial guaranty is tax-deductible, whereas the CDS spread usually is not.

Early Unwinds   In the event that the credit protection seller wants to get out of an existing obligation, the options open to the seller differ based on whether the protection has been sold through a CDS or through a guaranty. In a CDS, the trade can always be unwound (i.e., terminated early in exchange for a cash payment to be agreed upon between the protection buyer and seller) as long as the credit protection buyer gives its consent. Similarly, the protection seller can assign the CDS to a new protection seller, again provided the protection buyer consents to the assignment.

Insurance is a much harder obligation from which to escape. The credit protection seller can buy reinsurance so that its risk is hedged, but that's about the only thing the protection seller can do.

PORTFOLIO CREDIT DEFAULT SWAPS

Portfolio protection products entitle their buyer to a payment following one or more defaults in a reference portfolio consisting of multiple names and/or assets. According to Fitch, portfolio credit derivatives activity grew at the rate of 49 percent in 2003 to $754 billion, about 80 percent of which originated in North America. This is a bit different from the single-name CDS market, which is more active on a global basis and has been especially popular in Europe in recent years.

Portfolio credit derivatives fall into several different categories, the most important of which are discussed in the sections that follow.

Basket CDS

A *basket CDS* is a multiname protection product. The reference obligations covered by the CDS are either all or a specifically indicated part of the obligations issued by all the reference names indicated in the swap. Theoretically, a basket CDS could be constructed to cover *all* potential defaults by *all* the reference names, thus resembling a portfolio of single-named CDSs. Because that would be extremely expensive, it is more common to see a basket CDS that covers losses arising from only a single default (or a specific group of defaults) in the portfolio of reference assets and then terminates. The question is, *which one?*

Nth to Default CDSs An nth to default CDS pays off when the nth default occurs in the reference asset portfolio. Consider, for example, a reference portfolio that consists of the public bonds issued by 100 different companies or reference names. A *first to default CDS* will pay off when the first default occurs in the reference portfolio. It does not matter what asset or company is the first to default as long as it is an obligation of one of the reference names. Following the payout on the first default, the CDS terminates.

A *second to default CDS*, by contrast, will pay off when the second default occurs in the reference portfolio. This CDS does *not* pay anything for the first default, and terminates following the payout associated with the second default.

Nth to default CDSs are popular with institutions that have a good sense of the *frequency* of defaults on an asset portfolio, but do not have a good sense of the actual names that will cause the defaults or the sequence in which they will occur. Suppose a bank makes 100 loans to different companies and expects 10 percent of the loans to default. The bank will set aside a loan loss reserve to cover those first 10 defaults. If the bank desires a bit of extra protection, it could then enter into an 11th to default CDS. The reference portfolio would be its 100 loans, and the CDS would pay off to the bank in the event of the 11th default in the loan portfolio. In this manner, the bank has protected itself against losses arising from 11 percent of its portfolio: It has reserved against the first 10 defaults, and it has obtained credit insurance on the 11th default without tying up the full amount of capital required to fund a loan loss reserve on the 11th loan.

Senior and Subordinated Basket CDSs Basket CDSs may also include more than a single asset in the default trigger and the payout by the credit protection seller to the credit protection buyer. A popular pair of CDS types of this variety is the *senior basket CDS* and *subordinated basket CDS*.

Consider, for example, a reference portfolio of 10 names with underlying credits of $1 million each. Suppose the first six defaults are associated with the subordinated piece of the reference basket, and the last four comprise the senior piece. A subordinated basket CDS would pay in the event of a default on any or all of the first six defaults, whereas a senior basket CDS would pay only for the sixth through the 10th defaults.

Limits and Attachment Points   Like its cousin in the insurance industry, a basket CDS often includes deductibles and specific attachment points. In the prior example, the portfolio we described had essentially two layers of credit risk—a subordinated $6 XS $0 layer, and a senior $4 XS $6 layer. As in a comparable insurance program, we can further carve those layers up to incorporate deductibles and limits. Many applications of basket CDSs that we explore later—in Part Three, for example—will involve deductibles equivalent to the first-loss position of a portfolio—say, the first 1 percent of defaults on a reference portfolio.

In addition, limits or sublimits are popular with nth to default and senior/sub basket CDSs. Because these contracts are triggered by the *order* in which a default occurs and not the *size* of the default, the CDSs may well limit the payout on any given default (a sublimit) or across all defaults in aggregate. In the previous example in which our reference portfolio had 10 credits of $1 million each, for example, a subordinated basket swap triggered by any of the first six losses might well still specify a maximum payout of, say, $1 million.

A senior basket swap, moreover, may be defined in terms of just its attachment point. Instead of saying that the product covers the last four defaults in a portfolio of 10 names, we might see a senior basket CDS that instead specifically covers the $4 XS $6 layer but with a deductible of $2 million. The range of possible combinations is nearly limitless, but, not surprisingly, closely corresponds to the same types of structures we observe on the insurance side of the market.

Correlation Play   Basket CDS products generally are all about default correlation risk inside the reference portfolio. If defaults are uncorrelated across names, for example, an nth to default CDS with a one-year tenor is unlikely to pay off for n at or above three. In other words, especially for portfolios of investment-grade credits, more than three uncorrelated defaults in a year would be considered highly unusual. But if instead defaults on the reference names are, say, perfectly correlated, the nth to default CDS is no different at all from the first to default CDS. Accordingly, a lot of time and attention in pricing, hedging, and using basket CDSs is dedicated to modeling and empirically analyzing the correlation risk in the underlying reference portfolio.[5]

Credit Indexes

Credit index products emerged in 2003 when JPMorgan and Morgan Stanley jointly developed the Trac-x family of CDS indexes. Not long thereafter, Deutsche Börse and seven investment banks teamed together to establish the Dow Jones iBoxx index. In April 2004, the two ventures merged and formed the Dow Jones iTraxx CDS index. A number of additional indexes have been developed since then, so that CDS indexes of various types and names are presently available in most regions of the world where CDSs are traded.

A CDS index is a portfolio product. The iTraxx Europe CDS index, for example, is constructed by the International Index Company as a static portfolio comprised of an equally weighted average of 125 CDSs based on European entities. The specific reference names included are based on a poll of active dealers together with a specific set of rules about reference name eligibility, single-name CDS trading volume, and the like. The index is tradable in five- or 10-year maturities, plus a six-month rollover period during which new series are issued and the reference portfolio is rebalanced (if required).

iTraxx CDS indexes also include a HiVol index (30 reference entities from the iTraxx Europe CDS index with the widest spreads), a number of sector indexes, a crossover index consisting of reference names with no better than a Baa3/BBB– rating (and on negative watch), and a first-to-default basket index. In addition, the Dow Jones CDX index now also provides coverage for North America and emerging markets.

Note that these CDS index products are not just published indexes—they represent tradable products whose popularity accounts in large part for the sharp rise in portfolio credit derivatives activity in 2003.

ASSET DEFAULT SWAPS

An *asset default swap* (ADS) is a single-name CDS in which the name is no longer a reference corporate entity or corporate security, but rather a securitized product. Most ADSs to date have been based on asset-backed securities, which we define and explore in Chapter 16.

To date, ADS volume has been extremely low. The primary attraction of ADSs has been their use in structures like single-tranche synthetic collateralized debt obligations, which we explore in detail in Chapter 18. Until we have that beneath our belts, further discussion of ADSs is premature.

EQUITY DEFAULT SWAPS

A relatively recent arrival to the credit derivatives scene is the *equity default swap* (EDS). As its name implies, an EDS allows a protection purchaser to obtain protection on a reference asset—this time a *stock*. Because there is no such thing as a credit event on a common stock, an EDS is really as much a market risk or price protection instrument as it is a credit instrument. This is most obvious when one considers that the trigger in an EDS is not a failure to pay, a downgrade, or the like, but rather a prespecified decline in the reference stock price—usually around 70 percent. This is called the *equity event* instead of a credit event. Clearly, then, an EDS is essentially a type of deeply out-of-the-money equity put.

In addition to defining the equity event and underlying reference equity, the documentation of an EDS—generally an ISDA master agreement so that the EDS can conform to comparable CDSs—will also specify other deal terms like term to maturity (usually around five years), notional principal amount, and the payment obligation due following the occurrence of an equity event. Some EDSs require the protection seller to make a payment to the protection buyer proportional to the underlying stock price following an equity event. An EDS of that form resembles a down-and-in put option. In other cases, the EDS protection seller must make a fixed payment following an equity event, usually in an amount equal to the notional principal amount of the EDS times $(100 - X\%)$, where X percent is a prespecified *recovery rate*. Once the equity event occurs and the payment is made, the EDS terminates. But until that event occurs, the equity protection buyer makes periodic (usually quarterly) premium payments to the protection seller. A generic example of the basic EDS structure is shown in Exhibit 12.6.

Suppose, for example, that investor Telemann and swap dealer Handel negotiate a two-year EDS in which Handel is the protection seller and Telemann the protection buyer. The reference asset is the common stock of Company Bach, which is trading at €100 per share on the EDS trade date. Suppose the equity event is defined as 75 percent of the closing stock

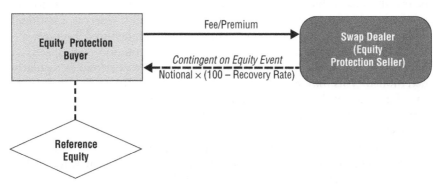

EXHIBIT 12.6 Basic Equity Default Swap

price per share on the trade date, the recovery amount is 40 percent, and the notional principal is €10 million. If at any time over the next two years the closing stock price of Company Bach trades down to or below €75 per share (i.e., 75 percent of the initial €100 per share stock price), protection seller Handel makes a fixed cash payment of €6 million—€10 million × (100% – 40%)—to protection buyer Telemann, whereupon the EDS also terminates.

As in a CDS, the protection buyer in an EDS need not have an insurable interest—the protection buyer need not actually own the stock on which protection is purchased.

TOTAL RETURN SWAPS

A third popular type of credit derivatives transaction is called a *total return swap* (TRS), or a contract in which the protection seller pays LIBOR plus a spread to the protection buyer in exchange for receiving LIBOR plus a cash amount equal to all realized interest payments on the reference asset(s) *plus* any change in the market value of the reference asset(s). Whereas a CDS compensates the credit protection buyer for only a loss resulting from an actual default, a TRS protects the buyer from the risk of defaults or declines in value associated with downgrades or other adverse credit events that do not necessarily result in any contractual nonperformance (Culp and Neves 1998a,b).

A TRS may be based on a single name or asset or multiple names and assets and may have a maturity that is the same as or shorter than the reference asset. A notional principal amount is chosen to determine the actual cash flows on the TRS, and this notional amount may or may not be the same as the face value of the reference portfolio. If the notional amount is below the face value of the reference portfolio, that is equivalent to the synthetic sale of a fraction of the underlying portfolio, whereas a notional amount above the face value of the portfolio is manufactured leverage.

When the contract begins, the TRS documentation will specify a method by which the market value of the reference portfolio is regularly determined. This may be done by one of the two parties to the swap as its calculation agent, by a contracted third party (e.g., Loan Pricing Corporation), or by reference to an index (e.g., the Citibank loan index).

Exhibit 12.7 shows the basic operation of a simple TRS. In panel (a), the contractual net cash flows are shown. The protection buyer pays all interest income on the reference portfolio plus the change in value of the portfolio, and the protection seller pays LIBOR plus a spread. Because the change in value of the portfolio may be positive or negative, the first leg of

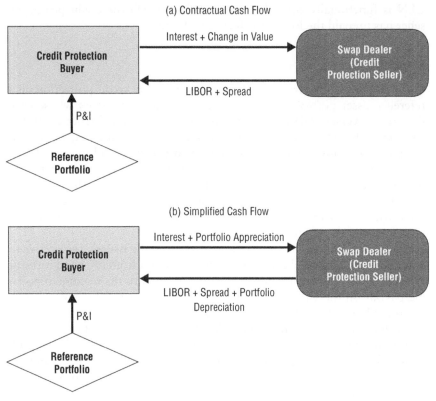

EXHIBIT 12.7 Total Return Swap

the swap depicted as such may well be a negative payment. This can be a little confusing, so we have redrawn the same transaction in panel (b) of Exhibit 12.7, this time parsing out the price change term depending on whether it is positive or negative to the appropriate swap leg.

CREDIT-LINKED NOTES (RECOURSE)

A CDS in isolation is an *unfunded* credit risk transfer instrument (see Chapter 2). Like insurance, it represents a commitment by the credit protection seller to make a payment or honor an obligation to the credit protection buyer in the event of a default. The money to cover this payment, however, has not been set aside in advance. The *funded* equivalent of a CDS is known as a *credit-linked note* (CLN). In its most basic form, a

CLN is functionally equivalent to a CDS in which the credit protection seller has prepaid the loss in the form of a bond.

Structure

In the simplest CLN structure, the entity purchasing credit protection on a reference asset portfolio issues a note or bond to investors whose cash flows are inversely related to prescribed losses on the reference portfolio. As long as the reference portfolio experiences no defined events of default, the issuer pays investors regularly scheduled principal and interest (P&I). In the event of a default on the reference portfolio, the issuer can withhold interest and, if necessary, all or part of the principal to cover the prescribed default-related loss. In return for bearing this risk, investors are compensated with an above-market interest rate prior to the realization of any default event on the reference asset.

A CLN is thus economically equivalent from the issuer's perspective to issuing a normal note plus buying credit protection from the bond investor through a CDS. The par value of the note is equal to the maximum possible payout on the CDS so that the worst-case event is fully covered with funds paid up front, but the investor has the assurance that no further calls for cash can be made by the issuer. The above-market interest earned by investors is equal to the normal interest on the bond plus the CDS spread. Despite having cash flows based on the underlying collateral assets and the CDS, the note is still a recourse instrument, as well; that is, investors bear the credit risk of the issuer.

The reference portfolio and prescribed default event(s) can include any of the structures discussed thus far. A CLN may be as straightforward as a traditional bond plus a single-name CDS or could represent a more complex basket structure. A first-to-default note, for example, is economically equivalent to a bond plus a first-to-default basket CDS. And, as with the other credit derivatives already discussed, the issuer of the CLN need not own or be the obligee on the assets in the reference portfolio.

The mechanics of this simple CLN structure are shown in Exhibit 12.8. In brief, investors make an up-front payment for the CLNs equal to their par value. Provided there are no defaults, investors receive some base interest rate (e.g., Treasury or repurchase agreement rate) plus a spread (reflecting the value of the credit protection purchased—i.e., the CDS rate). Eventually, principal is returned to the CLN investors as well, again assuming no defaults. In the event a reference asset default does occur, the par value of the reference asset minus the expected recovery rate is diverted from CLN holders to the issuer.

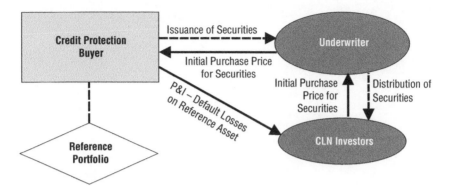

EXHIBIT 12.8 Credit-Linked Note

Benefits and Costs

The main distinction between a CDS and a CLN is whether the funds have been posted to cover the loss in advance. The unfunded CDS exposes the protection buyer to the credit risk of the protection seller, whereas the CLN does not.

At the same time, the CLN is fundamentally a *bond* and thus likely will be marketed and distributed to investors. If investors demand many of the usual features associated with a corporate bond issue—such as an external rating—this may complicate the structure quite a bit. This is a solvable problem (as we discuss explicitly when we review unfunded synthetic CDOs in Chapter 18), but it can raise the costs to the issuer of obtaining credit protection.

Structured Finance

The Structuring Process

Structured finance as we already defined it is the process by which firms raise funds in a nontraditional way, altering the firm's risk profile in the process. Or, increasingly, structured finance is the process by which firms raise funds in a manner that is independent of their fundamental creditworthiness, thus enabling them to obtain funding at a cost independent of their overall risk profile.

Structured financial products are generally designed to meet the funding and risk management needs of a single or small group of corporate borrowers, or to meet the risk/return investment appetites of a specific group of target investors. Structured financing solutions thus are more bespoke than standardized and tend to be deliberately designed to package cash flows in a way that tries to equate a highly specific supply of funds and risk transfer with an equally specific demand for those funds and risk transformation scenarios. Although certain classes of structured products have become fairly standardized, they didn't *start* that way.

This chapter is fundamental to the remainder of the book. Not only do we want to understand why the economic benefits of structuring justify this burgeoning area of financial activity, but we also need to square away some important institutional details about the process itself.

TYPES OF STRUCTURED FINANCIAL SOLUTIONS

Recall the economic balance sheet of a firm from Chapter 1, reproduced here in more generic form in Exhibit 13.1. Financial capital or corporate securities are unsecured claims on the real capital assets owned by the firm. In Exhibit 13.1, the real assets of the firm are funded by a single category of unsecured debt and a single group of common stockholders. *All* of the firm's assets in this case collectively back these two groups of

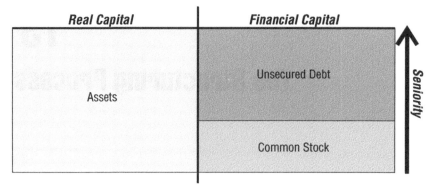

EXHIBIT 13.1 Economic Balance Sheet of a Firm, No Structured Financings

securities and their investors. In the event the firm becomes insolvent, the assets are liquidated and the proceeds used to retire each bond on a pro rata basis. The remaining funds go to equity.

Recall also from Chapter 1 that the financial capital structure of a firm is not limited to providing the firm with a source of funds. In addition, *any* and *all* retained risks arising from the firm's assets are passed from the firm as a legal entity to its owners and creditors. The retained risks of the firm's assets thus are fully transferred to its two classes of security holders in Exhibit 13.1.

Structured finance involves the financial engineering of the firm's liabilities to achieve specific financing and/or risk management objectives. In some cases, the deliberate design or redesign of financial capital claims is not enough—the firm's assets must also be repackaged. The exact nature of any structured deal depends on the precise objectives of the firm undertaking the structuring; let's refer to that firm as the *issuer* or *originator* in the structured financing deal. Using our basic economic balance sheet of the firm as an illustrative device, we turn now in the next sections to summarize the major types of structured financing deals and the typical motivations for originators to undertake them.

Securing Specific Liabilities with Specific Assets

Perhaps the simplest form of structured finance is the issuance of secured instead of unsecured debt. As shown in Exhibit 13.2, a firm can issue secured claims by setting aside specific assets as collateral to back the cash flows on the specific secured claims. This collateral is pledged to the bond or note holders to secure performance on the debt instrument, and note

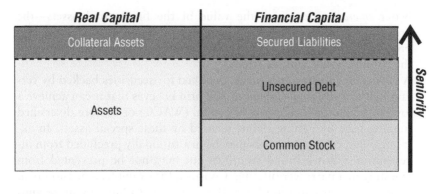

EXHIBIT 13.2   Economic Balance Sheet of a Firm with Secured Claims

holders have a perfected security interest in the collateral assets. This means that in the event the firm becomes insolvent, the collateral pledged to these secured claimants is not available to the firm's unsecured creditors and stockholders. That collateral is available exclusively to satisfy the firm's obligations on its *secured* claims.

One reason that firms engage in asset repackaging of this form is credit enhancement. By pledging specific assets as collateral to guarantee the performance of specific liabilities, the firm has removed investors in the new secured liabilities from the seniority queue in the firm's traditional capital structure. In an M&M world, this should not matter. But in a non-M&M world, securing the performance of certain assets is either beneficial to the firm, essential in order to place the liability, or both. Consider some examples, and remember that Exhibit 13.2 is the firm's *economic* balance sheet and thus includes items that would be considered off-balance-sheet in an accounting context:

- Customers or counterparties suffer from information asymmetries that prevent them from easily monitoring or verifying the firm's ability to honor long-term commitments (e.g., long-dated forward asset sales, long-dated swaps and derivatives, etc.). To satisfy customers, the firm allocates some of its assets to high-quality collateral pledged to ensure performance on the corresponding liabilities.
- Some of the firm's assets have very noisy valuations and are subject to extremely high adverse selection costs. The firm segregates these assets as collateral for issuing asset-backed securities in order to reduce noise. Sometimes this means segregating the noisy assets, and sometimes this means segregating the transparent ones. In either case, the result is a

better *overall* estimate of the value of the firm's total assets—the process of segregation itself has increased valuation transparency. This process, however, almost always also requires additional structuring of the liability, as we will see later.

■ A particular investor appetite is identified for securities backed by certain kinds of assets as collateral. The firm believes that it can achieve a lower weighted average cost of capital (WACC) or a more diversified funding base by issuing claims secured by these special assets. In extreme cases, certain investors may be institutionally precluded from investing in a firm's broad securities but may not be prevented from investing in a narrower offering. Consider, for example, a pension plan with sector concentration limits that is unable to buy any more auto company securities. If the auto company segregates out its financing activities, the new securities may be considered part of the financial sector and not the automotive sector and thus may become eligible for investment again.

Care must be taken to distinguish secured liabilities issued straight off the firm's balance sheet from securitized products, discussed next. Sometimes the two products look quite similar and often the motivations for segregating assets are the same, but there are some crucial structural differences between them.

Asset Securitization

Asset securitization is a form of structured finance in which certain real assets of the firm are sold. The payment for the acquisition of those assets by the purchasing firm is funded by the issuance of new securities whose principal and interest (P&I) obligations are backed by the newly acquired assets as collateral. Exhibit 13.3 illustrates an asset securitization using economic balance sheets.

In this example, we suppose the cash proceeds received by the original firm from the sale of part of its assets are used to retire a corresponding amount of debt, thus shrinking the firm's balance sheet. This need not be the case. We will explore a wide range of asset securitization structures in this third part of the book. In addition, we will explore what is known as a *synthetic securitization*. In such a transaction, the actual assets remain on the balance sheet of the firm but the economic risk of those assets is transferred to another firm through the use of a derivatives transaction.

Setting aside assets as collateral for securities to be issued directly by the firm is pretty similar in principle to selling those same assets for cash

(a) Before Securitization

Original Asset Owner

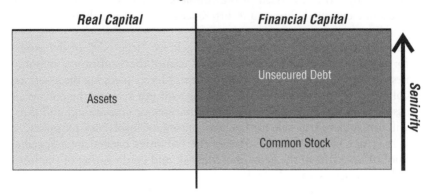

(b) After Securitization

Original Asset Owner

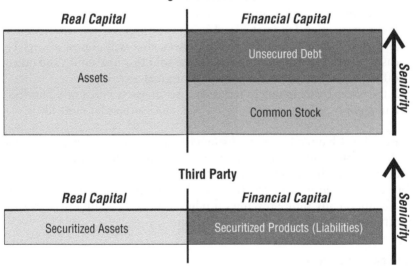

EXHIBIT 13.3 Economic Balance Sheet of a Firm with Asset Securitization

and then having the asset purchaser issue new securities collateralized by those assets. Accordingly, the economic motivations for securitization are very similar to those discussed in the simple secured asset case. But there also are some extremely important differences, some of which are:

- The original asset owner may wish to achieve "true sale" of the assets for tax and accounting purposes or to ensure the bankruptcy remoteness of the assets from the rest of the firm. Merely pledging the assets as collateral on a secured liability offering will not remove the collateral assets from the firm's balance sheet (economic or accounting) and thus will not achieve true sale for tax, accounting, or insolvency purposes.
- It may not be possible to separate the liabilities backed by a specific pool of assets from the general credit risk and credit rating of the firm unless the assets are sold first.
- Asset securitization can be used as a method of shrinking the firm's economic balance sheet, decreasing leverage, increasing debt capacity, and, if applicable, decreasing regulatory capital requirements. Merely pledging assets as collateral against a specific security issue does not necessarily accomplish any of these objectives.
- If the motivation for asset repackaging is to improve the transparency and verifiability of a given pool of assets, that will almost always be easier to accomplish when the assets are sold to a new entity and taken off the economic balance sheet of the original asset owner.
- If the issuer is attempting to reclassify a set of assets into a new business, a new entity as host for those assets will make success far more likely.

Recall in Chapter 1 that we distinguished between two types of assets that firms hold—current assets and growth opportunities. Either type of asset can be securitized. The securitization of a growth opportunity is often referred to as a *future flow securitization* because the asset being sold is really a claim on any future revenues produced by what is still just a growth opportunity at the time of the securitization.

Ring-Fencing Assets

A third type of asset repackaging involves the segregation of selected assets (possibly even a whole business inside the firm) into a separate legal entity. The entity may be a wholly owned subsidiary of the parent corporation or may be financed in whole or in part by outside investors. Either way, the objective in this kind of asset repackaging is to *ring-fence* the assets (i.e., to separate them from the rest of the firm). An example is shown in Exhibit 13.4.

(a) Before Ring-Fencing

Original Company

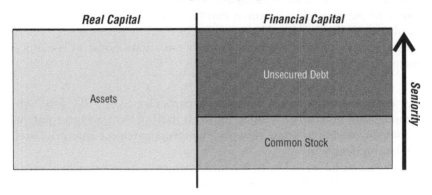

(b) After Ring-Fencing

Parent Company

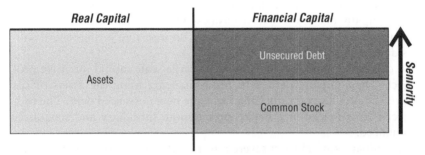

Ring-Fenced Subsidary

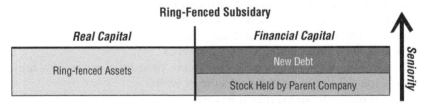

EXHIBIT 13.4 Economic Balance Sheet of a Firm with Ring-Fenced Business

Notice in this example that the subsidiary is presumed to remain consolidated on the parent company's economic balance sheet because the parent retains the (presumably substantial) equity interest. We have also allowed for the possibility, however, that the new subsidiary may issue debt backed now by the ring-fenced assets.

Ring-fencing can be beneficial in many situations. Some of the more common examples are:

- A company owns assets that pose a particular risk to the firm. Although not necessarily wishing to divest itself of the assets, the parent company wishes to house them in a bankruptcy-remote enterprise and thus ring-fences them.
- A particular business line of the firm warrants a higher degree of creditworthiness than the firm as a whole can achieve. The firm thus ring-fences the business line in a new subsidiary, overcapitalizes that subsidiary, and facilitates the subsidiary obtaining a higher credit rating than the parent. Derivative product companies or unregulated subsidiaries of investment banks are examples of this structure.
- A company decides to exit a business line or portfolio and wishes to manage the *runoff solution* separately, so it sets up a ring-fenced subsidiary to house the runoff line.
- A company is seeking financing for a large-scale capital-intensive project. The company prefers to raise financing using the assets of the project as collateral rather than to issue new unsecured debt. The project is ring-fenced in a bankruptcy-remote subsidiary and separately financed.
- A company suffers from severe adverse selection costs arising from an inability of outsiders to monitor certain assets the firm owns. The company ring-fences those assets to increase the transparency and ease of monitoring, thus hopefully reducing the adverse selection discount on its unsecured claims and lowering its WACC.
- Regulation, accounting, disclosure, or tax considerations force a firm to house certain assets in a distinct legal entity.
- A firm wishes to signal that it has engaged in preloss risk finance and cannot do so through the use of balance sheet reserves. It capitalizes a new subsidiary for this purpose, as is the case, for example, with captives (see Chapter 23).

Note from these examples that ring-fencing assets is often motivated by project financing considerations. A company believes, for example, that it can secure funding for a long-dated capital-intensive project on better terms and with better overall risk transfer by housing the project's assets in a separate legal entity. That rationale for ring-fencing assets also applies to new assets and ventures that the firm in question does not own, but plans to acquire. Consider the difference for a moment.

First imagine a below-investment-grade oil company that owns an explored but as yet undeveloped oil field with substantial proven reserves. Even with the oil field, the firm may have trouble borrowing on an unsecured basis to finance the completion of the oil field. The company could ring-fence the oil field in a bankruptcy-remote entity and then borrow against the assets of the oil field specifically as a means of financing completion of the project.

Alternatively, consider a highly rated oil company contemplating developing a large, completely unexplored oil field over the next 15 years. That firm might also choose to segregate the project for financing purposes, but for different reasons than our below-investment-grade company. In this case, the motivation for ring-fencing could well be the opposite— a desire to avoid having a *failure* of the oil field project jeopardize the financial health of the whole company. So the firm might retain some equity stake in the ring-fenced entity but then raise external funds to finance the field—funds that are backed with a claim on the field itself and not the balance sheet of the whole company.

As both examples illustrate, ring-fencing can be an attractive part of project finance for both highly rated and riskier business enterprises. Ring-fencing may be useful either when a low-quality firm cannot finance a high-quality project or when a high-quality firm does not want to run the risk of being the sole financier of a low-quality project. In both cases, the integration of risk management with financing objectives is clear.

Venture Capital Formation

We can easily extend the project finance examples in the previous section to a new venture. Suppose we consider now an undeveloped oil field that has been identified by an entrepreneur. The entrepreneur lacks the capital and the risk appetite to finance the development of the potentially expensive and long-term project out of her own pocket, and yet desires to remain a part of the project somehow.

A new venture—call it Newco—could be established specifically to house the development of the oil field. Securities would be issued as in the case of a normal corporation, and investors would be brought in to the new venture alongside the entrepreneur to share in the risks and rewards of the project.

Setting up a new firm based on a single unproven asset or project is, of course, extremely risky. As a result, Newco will probably be set up as a special purpose entity whose sole business is cultivating and developing the oil field asset. This will make it easier to secure debt and/or equity financing to complete the project, especially when liability structuring methods are also put into place.

Funded Risk Transfer or Risk Finance

Firms may deliberately structure their liabilities to help manage the market, liquidity, credit, and other risks to which they are subject. In these situations, liability structuring is virtually always a substitute for external risk transfer, as we shall see again later in this chapter.

Firms may prefer to issue structured securities as a preferred form of risk finance or risk transfer for a variety of reasons, most of which were discussed in Chapters 6 and 7. Consider, for example, a cookware manufacturer whose profits are exposed to the risk of rising copper prices. Investors in the firm's debt and equity securities want the firm to hedge, but all face prohibitively high monitoring costs. Instead of issuing *unsecured* debt and buying call options on copper, the firm could issue *structured* debt in which coupons and/or principal paid to investors in the structured products is indexed to copper prices—the higher the copper price, the more the firm's funding cost falls. This second solution, however, is much easier for investors to monitor and thus may enable the firm to escape some of the agency costs of unsecured debt.

Structured securities that are motivated mainly by risk transfer are *funded* risk management products. Credit risk or performance concerns about the counterparty could also explain the issuance of such products.

Reducing Agency Costs Among Security Holders

Structuring on the liability side can also be beneficial for firms experiencing high agency costs among and between different classes of security holders and between managers and security holders. Call, put, and conversion provisions in corporate securities, for example, often are included to mitigate such agency costs without dramatically increasing outside security holders' monitoring costs.

Meeting Specific Investor Demands

By designing securities better to meet investor demand, some companies can realize a slightly lower cost of capital or all-in funding cost. Structured securities that are designed to meet demand may also be motivated by one or more of the aforementioned economic considerations, or may be designed specifically to meet demand. In either situation, specific demands for securities can arise for several reasons:

- The combination of risk and return that a firm can offer through structuring is simply not available elsewhere in the market.
- Investors do not want to take on all the risks of the firm. They are interested only in bearing certain types of investment risk, leaving the firm either to hedge or insure the other risks or to retain those other risks. Investors in firms with multinational business, for example, may prefer not to bear the exchange rate risk that they would indeed bear if the firm did not hedge. But they may also not want the firm to hedge those risks. As a compromise, investors would seek a security that is insulated from the parts of the firm subject to exchange rate risk.
- Corporate structure and form may be dictated by legal, tax, and regulatory considerations and may not reflect the optimal risk tranching that investors seek. In this case, the firm can repackage its assets and liabilities so that its securities better reflect investor preferences than the firm's corporate structure allows.
- Some investors face external constraints on investing in certain types of securities, and structuring can be a way for those investors to access otherwise unreachable investment opportunities. Pension plans, for example, cannot invest in assets without principal protection, which may preclude participation in certain types of private equity or hedge funds. The funds can issue principal-protected indexed return notes to satisfy these investor demands.
- In some cases and depending very much on applicable laws and regulations, firms may find certain tax or regulatory advantages to issuing structured liabilities. Trust preferred stock (TruPS), for example, is attractive to many bank holding companies because the dividends paid on TruPS are treated as interest paid on debt for tax purposes (i.e.,

they are deductible). At the same time, rating agencies give issuers partial equity credit for issuing TruPS. Together, these two variables lead to a sort of tax/ratings arbitrage for which TruPS are especially well qualified. We will discuss TruPS again in Chapter 14.

STRUCTURING PROCESS

The structuring process involves different components that vary in complexity and importance based on the nature of the structuring problem. In the chapters that follow, we provide much more detail on the specifics of how any given structured financing is accomplished. Here we confine our attention to the process more generally and what may be involved in the different steps of this process.

Note that the components of the structuring process we discuss do not necessarily occur in any particular order. A firm wishing to structure solely to enhance the yield on its securities and offer investors a new investment opportunity, for example, will be far more attentive early on to investors' risk/return appetites in the design of its new securities than will a firm whose sole objective is, say, to structure as a way to ring-fence a liability.

Identification of Economic Motivation

One of the most critical aspects of the structuring process is to answer the following question: *Why structure instead of using traditional financing and/or risk transfer?* The answers to this question will vary firm by firm and situation by situation, but it is critical to ask the question and answer it *somehow*. The reasons to get the answer to this question early are twofold.

Ensure Costs Are Justified and Structuring Method Is Appropriate Different types of structured finance programs subject firms to varying types and amounts of cost. Embedding a call in an unsecured bond issued straight off the originator's balance sheet, for example, is far less costly than, say, securitizing the firm's receivables. Knowing *why* the firm will benefit from structuring is important to help that firm understand *how* it should structure. Also, if a firm pursues a structured solution on the grounds that it will somehow reduce the firm's WACC or increase the firm's expected cash

flows, the firm should be sure that the expected increase in value exceeds any costs of structuring.

The issuer or originator in a structured financing deal may know the answer to this question already, but in many cases it is often through dialogue with another party that the idea behind a structured financing is born. This third party is sometimes an advisory agent (e.g., a structuring agent or the sponsor of the structured program). Most often, the decision to structure is the result of an ongoing dialogue between the firm and one or more financial capital providers and/or one or more risk transfer counterparties.

Structuring Must be Motivated by Commercial Considerations Any good structured deal should be motivated primarily by economic and commercial fundamentals. If a deal can be put together legally in a way that also generates desirable tax, accounting, regulatory, and legal treatment, so much the better. But structured financing deals should never be defined solely to back into a desired accounting or tax result. Consequently, early identification of the primary economic or commercial motivation(s) for the structured solution is crucial.

Preliminary Cash Flow Model

Given the economic motivations of the sponsor or issuer, the structuring agent and sponsor will want to spend some time preparing an initial set of models of the *cash flow waterfalls* in the contemplated structure. The interest and principal waterfalls represent models of income on the target assets in the structure and how that income is to be applied to various expense items and to the liabilities that are planned as a part of the structured program.

At this early stage of the structuring process, the waterfalls will consist mainly of revenues on the asset side and certain expenses. For a basic portfolio of assets to be securitized, this is often a fairly trivial step that consists primarily of setting up a model of income on the asset portfolio. But for more complex project finance, whole business securitizations, future flow securitizations, and the like, modeling the waterfall even initially is by no means trivial.

The expenses in a structuring program fall into two categories: senior and subordinated. Senior expenses are expenses associated with the structuring itself—fees paid to asset trustees, custodians, project managers, and the like. Senior expenses are generally fixed and do *not* depend in any way on the performance of the structured deal. Subordinated expenses, by contrast, are often performance-related—for example, success or management fees paid to a program adviser. At early modeling stages, it is appropriate to focus on the senior expenses alone. Subordinated expenses will be allocated from the cash flow waterfall *based on what is left over later*.

The model at this stage should be set up, moreover, with at least two design features in mind. First, the model should clearly define the per-period cash flows of the structure. Otherwise, it will be of limited use later in modeling the waterfalls of the entire program and in designing the program to meet target rating agency criteria. Second, the model should also conform to the appropriate project evaluation principle of the possibilities we explored in Chapter 5. A primarily financial asset securitization being marketed to investors as a yield enhancement opportunity, for example, will probably need to be modeled in terms of return on investment (ROI), whereas a real capital development project, by contrast, will be more suited to a net present value (NPV) analysis.

Appointment of a Structuring Agent

A structured financing must be structured by someone or some firm, and the earlier that structuring agent is involved in the design process the better. The structuring agent should be a capable modeling organization with a complete understanding of the issuer's financing and risk management needs and a thorough understanding of the latest developments in credit markets, securities design principles, risk finance, and risk transfer. Structuring agents often specialize by the type of structure being contemplated (e.g., a firm that would make a wonderful structured credit product adviser might make a lousy structured runoff solution adviser).

In many situations, the structuring agent will be synonymous with the sponsor of the program or the entity that approached the issuer with the idea for the structured product offering in the first place—for example, a bank sponsor of an asset-backed commercial paper conduit (Chapter 16) or a collateral manager in an arbitrage collateralized debt obligation (Chapters 17 and 18).

In other situations, the structuring agent may be the institution that will ultimately market and distribute the structured product—namely, the investment bank or securities underwriter.

And in still other situations, the structuring agent may be some other party, such as an advisory institution or a law firm. Providers of risk transfer and risk finance to the program may also sometimes serve as effective structuring agents. An insurance or reinsurance company, for example, may be the best-suited party to provide structuring advice on a large-scale project financing initiative for which the insurer is providing multiple types of risk protection.

Identification of Investor Interest

The structuring agent and issuer in a structured financing must try its best to ensure that there will be appetite and demand for the securities it plans to issue. This almost always necessitates the early involvement of an investment bank underwriter with access to a good marketing and distribution network for placing new securities. (Most structured products are privately placed.)

As we will see shortly, the structuring process involves a lot of flexibility in terms of how the structured products are designed to allocate risk and return across prospective investors. Because structured financial programs are generally designed with one or more groups of investors in mind, knowing the needs and desires of these investors will help facilitate the process by which the new securities in the program are designed. Identification of interest from investors should occur as early as possible, and yet approaching investors too early before the economics of the deal are known will not be constructive and could expend valuable goodwill capital.

Design of the Institutional Features of the Structure

The next step in the process is the design of the institutional structure, which broadly includes all the contractual relations between the various participants who may be involved in bringing the structured product to market. Here is where some radical differences in the design of structured products can occur. Specifically, some structured financings require the creation of a new company for the specific purpose of facilitating the structured deal, called a *special purpose entity* (SPE) or *special purpose vehicle* (SPV). Not all structured deals require an SPE, whereas some deals require more than one. Sound economic, legal, tax, accounting, and regulatory counsel is essential for determining the optimal institutional structure of a deal.

Special Purpose Entities   An SPE is usually organized as either a corporation or a trust. The exact form taken depends on a wide variety of commercial, legal, tax, accounting, and regulatory considerations. Some of the most popular forms of SPEs include:

- *Special purpose corporation (SPC)*—usually a special purpose finance subsidiary of a corporation or a licensed (re)insurance company that plans to issue new securities.
- *Master trust*—can issue multiple series of securities backed by a common asset pool—very useful if the sponsor or originator wishes to "recharge" the collateral pool with new assets later.
- *Owner trusts*—formed to hold pooled nonrevolving assets.
- *Grantor trust*—passive tax vehicle that can issue a single class of securities or senior and subordinated classes of pass-through securities backed by a common asset pool, but tranching of cash flows by maturity or time is not allowed.
- *Regulated investment company*—separate company that issues securities for investment management purposes.
- *Investment trust (including real estate investment trust)*—assets may include cash, mortgage loans, debt securities (other than those issued by the owner of the trust), pass-through certificates, and certain real estate mortgage investment conduit (REMIC) and financial assets securitization investment trust (FASIT) interests.

In some structured financing deals, you see more than one SPE in a single structure. This usually means that the tax, accounting, regulatory, and disclosure rules and requirements cannot all be satisfied using a single structure. Issues that often affect the structure of the SPE—and how many are necessary to achieve the goals of the securitization—include the need to have a bankruptcy-remote entity, the need to achieve a true sale of the assets for accounting and legal purposes, the need to ring-fence specific assets or liabilities from the rest of a business, and so on.

Beware of Overstructuring If a firm is attempting to ring-fence a business, sell some of the assets in that business, and issue bankruptcy-remote claims on the remaining business, it may well be the case that *several* SPEs are required. And in that case, no one would really question the deal.

Unfortunately, many of Enron's forays into structured finance appear to have had more sinister motives, such as camouflaging the firm's true overall term indebtedness or concealing poorly performing assets—or both. And more.

In short, Enron has given a bit of a bad name to SPEs. This is not itself a reason for firms to shy away from their use. Legitimate and legal uses of SPEs predate Enron by many years, after all. Nevertheless, Enron does provide a real warning to firms about *over*structuring. If a structure begins to get too complex and to have too many SPEs and too many different strange securities and derivatives all negotiated within the same broad deal structure, it will invariably give rise to concerns about overengineering among investors, auditors, rating agencies, and regulators.

Sometimes a complex structure is genuinely required. Fine. Use it. Just be prepared to explain and disclose *clearly*—perhaps in more detail than accounting and disclosure rules require—what the structure does and why it was necessary.

In some cases, a firm will consider a complex structure to be proprietary information and will be reluctant to disclose details of the deal. If indeed the benefits of keeping the deal details confidential exceed the risks and costs, then it makes sense to do so. But firms need to be well aware of how hard that is becoming in today's political environment. Some firms thus may face a hard choice: disclose the details and purpose of a deal whose structure is proprietary and was costly to develop, or not do the deal.

Design of Securities

With the core revenue model and institutional framework in proposed preliminary form, the structuring agent and/or originator now hits the hard part: designing the liabilities of the structured financing initiative in a way that satisfies the economic motivations of the originator and that meets investor demand and interest.

The design of securities in a structured program is the result of extensive modeling efforts combined with regular surveys of interest in the market. There are several essential features of the securities to be issued in which the reconciliation of supply-side (i.e., issuer) and demand-side (i.e., investor) concerns is of paramount importance.

Maturity Structure   The maturities of different classes of securities to be issued are often dictated by the nature of the structure itself and the assets underlying that structure. The securitization of short-term receivables may involve a commercial paper or short-term note issue, for example, whereas a structured project finance loan or asset-backed security issue could well involve 25 to 30 years to maturity.

Securities with different maturities may also need to be issued. Some structures are essentially static wind-downs and thus do not require regular infusions of new funds. In this case, an original set of securities with one or perhaps two maturities generally will suffice. But other structures may be designed to service a dynamic asset portfolio that is being constantly replenished or recharged. In these situations, multiple maturities of liabilities are often required to service cash flows over different phases of the underlying structure.

Tranching and Subordination   One of the most important features in a structured finance offering is the design of the capital structure of the issuer. In a *single-class structure*, a single type of liability is issued in which all holders of the new security have a proportional pari passu claim on the assets that back the structured financing program. A *multiclass structure*, by contrast, requires the structuring agent to define two or more layers of subordination and the different cash flow tranches that relate the underlying assets to those multiple layers of subordination.

For a given capital structure, much of the structuring will involve various models of the cash flow waterfalls. Liabilities are assigned priority in the cash flow waterfall corresponding to their seniority in the issuer's capital structure, and the availability of funding to service the obligations chosen will in turn dictate the nature of interest and principal payable on the new securities.

Tranching cash flows into multiple layers of subordination is also a key consideration in how the structure transfers risk from the originator to investors. So important is this piece of the puzzle that we save our discussion of this topic until the next main section in this chapter.

Target Ratings and Enhancements

An absolutely critical component of the structuring process involves the target ratings assigned to different tranches of the structure. Rating agencies have very specific guidance about minimum requirements for a tranche in a structured program to meet a specific minimum rating, and the structuring agent will need to incorporate these constraints into the model of cash flows and the cash flow waterfalls (assuming the issue is to be rated).

With the target capital structure, target ratings, and preliminary cash flow model in hand, the structuring agent may discover that certain enhancements must be procured for the structure to satisfy the issuers, investors, and rating agencies alike. Such enhancements may include both *credit* and *liquidity* enhancements, and we will discuss these in greater detail later in this third part of the book.

Execution and Ramp-Up

The execution of deal documents in a structure usually occurs after all the various parts of the structure have been designed and set up. All participants will generally have had a chance to review draft deal documents, and all that remains is for the participants to execute those documents.

At the time of closing, the structure may not be entirely ramped up. The *ramp-up* period for any given structure is the period of time during which any asset repackaging, sales, transfers, and the like actually occur. In some structures, the ramp-up period is short and requires little more than the transfer of title of ownership from one firm to another. But in other situations we will examine later in this part of the book, funds must be obtained from investors in the new securities before assets can be purchased. And even then, asset acquisition or repackaging itself may be time-consuming. In such cases, ramping up can be a more gradual process.

TRANCHING AND SUBORDINATION

A significant amount of time and attention in the structuring process must be paid to the allocation of risk across investors in the new liabilities issued by the SPE or originator. In this section, we want to explain how the process of tranching and designing layers of subordination in a structured program is essentially equivalent to designing a *reinsurance program for the retained risks on the underlying assets.*

We saw at the end of Chapter 6 how risky debt holders can be viewed as selling synthetic asset insurance to the firm. There is no actual insurance policy, of course—hence the term *synthetic*—but it is economically equivalent. Not surprisingly, when we introduce additional layers of subordination into the firm's capital structure, we get a richer mixture of different synthetic asset insurance policies. Recall our discussion in Chapter 1 about the economic interpretation of subordination. Although we argued that *senior* debt was selling asset insurance *to the firm*, we also argued that *junior* debt was selling the equivalent of asset insurance *to senior debt*. And so on.

In this section, we begin by exploring once again how subordination and tranching decisions are tantamount to selecting attachments points in an asset reinsurance program. We then turn to explore the relation between loss distributions on the underlying assets, credit ratings, and those tranching or subordination decisions in the structuring process.

In the discussion that follows, we confine ourselves to a firm whose assets are subject primarily to a single type of risk: credit risk. This will allow us to make it much clearer how that risk can be allocated across layers and investors than if we also had to worry about a hundred other risks affecting asset performance. Nevertheless, it is important to remember that the investors in a firm's securities are subject to *all* of the risks to which the firm's assets are subject—all the *retained* risks, that is. As noted in Chapter 2, the firm may well seek to neutralize a risk or to transfer risk to external counterparties specifically to avoid passing on certain kinds or amounts of risk to investors. Whatever risks are retained by the firm—either intentionally or unintentionally—will, however, be *completely* passed on to the firm's investors, and we need to determine precisely how.

Subordination as a Credit Enhancement for More Senior Claims

As we saw in Chapters 1 and 6, the market value of financial capital—debt and equity—issued by a firm is always equal to the market value of the firm's real assets. In this sense, the financial capital can be viewed as a type of insurance sold by investors in the firm's securities to the firm itself so that losses in value on the assets are absorbed by investors, not the firm as a legal entity. The priority or seniority of financial capital claims issued by a firm, in turn, dictates the vertical layering or sequence in which different investors absorb those losses.

Perhaps the easiest way to illustrate this concept is by way of example. Suppose that a firm issues senior and junior debt, both zero-coupon and with face values of $300 million and $500 million, respectively. The firm also issues $200 million in equity. Suppose the debt all matures at the same time and the firm is wound up on that date—assets are liquidated and the firm's securities retired.

Exhibit 13.5 illustrates just how much "insurance" each category of investor is providing to the firm. Total losses (i.e., declines in asset value) are shown on the x-axis, and the gross value of the firm's remaining assets

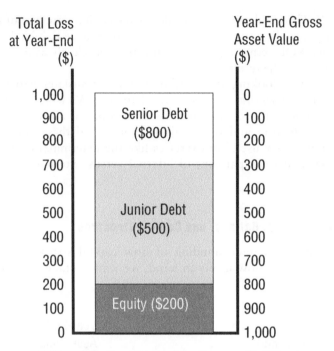

EXHIBIT 13.5 Investors as Asset Insurers ($Millions)

is shown on the y-axis. Equity absorbs the "first dollar loss" in asset value up to $200 million. For declines in asset value below $800 million, junior debt then provides up to $500 million in insurance. Finally, senior debts insure the remaining $300 million.

The outstanding securities not only insure the value of the firm's assets in aggregate, but each class of security holder essentially provides insurance or credit enhancements *to all the more senior investors in the firm's securities.* We saw this in Chapter 1 when we decomposed debt into vertical option spreads. In the current example, senior debt essentially has $700 million in credit protection provided by junior debt and equity. Until the firm's assets have declined by $700 million, senior bond holders do not experience any losses.

You probably already see how Exhibit 13.5 looks remarkably similar to an excess of loss (XOL) credit reinsurance scheme as discussed in

Chapter 9. This similarity is no accident—the capital structure of the firm is *precisely* a credit insurance program! Let's reproduce Exhibit 13.5 using reinsurance XOL vernacular to make this point as clearly as possible—see Exhibit 13.6 for the result.

This way of looking at subordination also translates naturally into the options framework discussed in Chapter 1. Viewing external risk transfer, subordination, and securities all as options allows us to apply consistent valuation and risk analysis tools to all these concepts and can be enormously useful in exercises like the determination of attachment points, cost comparisons of internal versus external risk transfer, and the like.

Loss Distributions, Ratings, and Capital Structure

With a conceptual understanding of how capital structure relates to credit risk transfer now firmly in hand, we want to take one more step

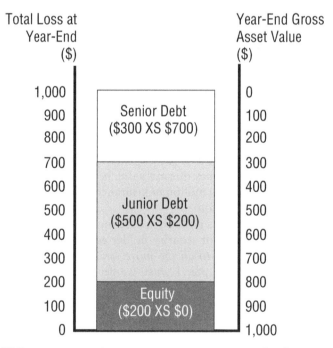

EXHIBIT 13.6 Investors as Asset Insurers (XOL Notation) ($Millions)

and see how capital structure relates explicitly to the probability of credit-related losses and, by extension, to published credit ratings. Remember, moreover, that we are looking at credit-related loss probabilities because we have assumed the only risk of our firm's assets is credit risk The framework is completely general and can be equally easily applied to situations where other risks affect the probability of incurring losses.

Our discussion will, of course, be entirely conceptual. The *actual* relation between a given portfolio of credit-sensitive assets and how that credit risk is parsed out across multiple layers of subordination in the firm's capital structure depends on a number of highly specific considerations:

- What does the loss distribution for the asset portfolio actually look like?
- What other credit enhancements or credit risk transfer structures are in place to protect the firm's security holders from asset default risk, and when exactly do those structures pay off relative to the seniority of the firm's outstanding financial capital claims?
- How do specific rating agency criteria affect the choice of different layers of subordination and risk transfer? That is, how do the particular approaches of the three major rating agencies affect the choice of attachment points that dictate the different layers of subordination chosen?

We can, however, provide an example of how the conceptual approach works. Specifically, consider a firm whose only assets consist of a portfolio of high-yield debt instruments subject to default risk. Exhibit 13.7 shows what a loss distribution might look like for such a portfolio.[1] Cumulative defaults on assets in the portfolio (expressed as a percentage of total assets) are shown on the x-axis, and the cumulative probabilities associated with those losses are shown on the y-axis. This distribution will, of course, look different for every asset portfolio, and it can be generated using a wide variety of empirical-cum-statistical methods. For now, we take the hypothetical loss distribution as a given.

By following the guidance published by rating agencies concerning asset quality, default and recovery rates, and probabilities of default, we can essentially superimpose expected credit ratings onto the loss distribution, as shown in Exhibit 13.7 (see D. Smith 2003, which suggested this exhibit). Again, the actual breakpoints across ratings *and* the exact ratings

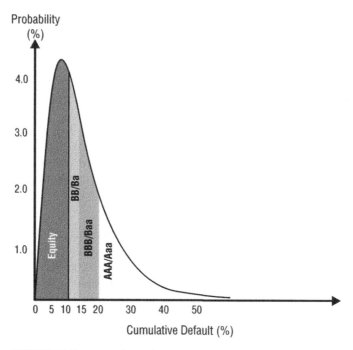

EXHIBIT 13.7 Hypothetical Loss Distribution for Portfolio of High-Yield Debt
Source: Based on D. Smith (2003).

given to the different chunks of the distribution depend on the portfolio itself as well as the way we design the securities corresponding to this portfolio. The number of tranches or layers of subordination that we choose to
issue, for example, will affect the distribution of ratings and the attachment points for each rating. So, the capital structure implied by Exhibit
13.7 is only *one possible* such capital structure, even within the confines of
this example.

We can see more clearly how the loss distribution and ratings are related to a given choice of capital structure in Exhibit 13.8. Panel (a) of the
exhibit shows the same loss distribution as in Exhibit 13.7 with its orientation changed, and panel (b) shows the capital structure corresponding to
that loss distribution.

Knowing that the risk of default will dictate the attachment points for
a given chosen number of classes of securities to issue, we can see again
how credit risk is transferred to specific classes of security holders and in

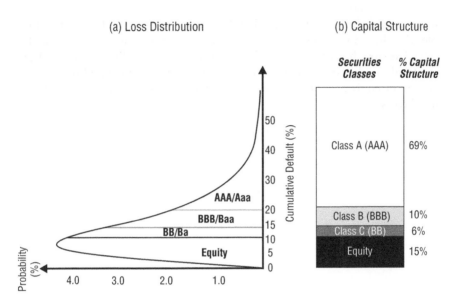

(a) Loss Distribution   (b) Capital Structure

EXHIBIT 13.8   Loss Distribution and Capital Structure
Source: Merrill Lynch.

what proportions. For this particular portfolio, the proportion of the firm's financial capital that is sufficiently insulated from default risk to receive an AAA rating is quite high: around 70 percent of the size of the asset portfolio. Similarly, the first-loss exposure (equity) is also relatively large—much larger, in fact, than will often be the case.

As we have noted, these exhibits could be generated easily in real life for a given asset portfolio and choice of subordination. The methods used by the rating agencies to assess the risk of a given tranche of securities are relatively straightforward. And now that we know this, we can use exactly these sorts of tools to determine how much of each class of security the firm needs to issue and what proportion of the total default risk affecting the portfolio is borne by each of the chosen classes of security holders.

This conceptual framework is remarkably versatile. We could also have drawn, for example, a similar diagram for a classical XOL credit insurance program to relate the attachment points to the loss distribution. We could also undertake a similar analysis for a portfolio of assets subject to some other risk than credit risk. If the loss distribution corresponds to losses arising from professional liability claims against the firm, for example, that loss distribution likely would be generated using actuarial methods. The attachment points in the program then would be determined by the total number of layers for which insurance is provided and by the target credit-equivalent quality we would like to achieve for those different loss layers.

CHAPTER 14

Hybrids, Convertibles, and Structured Notes

I n this chapter, we begin our analysis of the structured finance world with some of its most common and straightforward inhabitants—products we might collectively define as *structured corporate securities*. Unlike many other products we analyze in this part of the book, structured corporate securities remain a part of the capital structure of the originator and are liabilities on the originator's economic balance sheet. Indeed, perhaps the only major attribute that separates these products from plain-vanilla financial capital claims (see Chapter 1) is that their cash flows have been deliberately structured in an effort to match issuer financing and risk transfer objectives with perceived investor needs.

We consider here two particular types of structured corporate securities: (1) hybrids and convertibles and (2) structured notes. Hybrids are securities that are structured to combine features of both debt and equity, and convertibles are specific types of hybrids that integrate debt and equity financing by providing debt holders with the option actually to trade in their debt in exchange for equity. Regardless of their structure and reengineered cash flows, the performance of hybrids and convertibles depends *solely* on the risk of the issuing corporation. Structured notes, by contrast, are essentially prepackaged combinations of traditional debt with traditional derivatives contracts. Their performance depends directly on at least one variable or parameter that is *not* under the direct control of the issuer, such as exchange rates or commodity prices.

HYBRIDS AND CONVERTIBLES

A *hybrid security* is a security that integrates or bundles several components of a single issuer's capital structure into a single financial capital claim. A *convertible security* is a type of hybrid debt security that can be explicitly converted into preferred or common stock. Hybrids and convertibles rarely require much formal institutional structure as discussed in Chapter 13; for example, in only one structure we examine is a SPE required. All that is necessary is for the financial engineers and lawyers to agree on what the security will pay, when and how it will pay, what its depth of subordination will be, and any other salient features or covenants required to create a hybrid mixture of debt and equity.

Mezzanine Finance

Subordinated debt sometimes comes in the form of so-called mezzanine finance. Mezzanine financing is commonly used by firms to facilitate corporate actions like management buyouts or acquisitions, as well as for project finance. Mezzanine finance also may refer to junior subordinated debt that has economic attributes (e.g., price and return) more similar to equity than to senior debt.

Popularized in the 1970s and again in the 1980s, mezzanine finance is frequently used as a seed capital for growth firms, especially if the equity portion of a deal or capital structure is too low for the firm to attract more conservative and senior creditors like banks that often require a higher debt-to-equity ratio than the borrowing firm has without the mezzanine layer. Banks and insurance companies, in particular, have long viewed mezzanine finance as a hybrid or equity-like instrument for the purpose of their credit evaluations. Such perceptions arose for three somewhat different reasons. First, the interest rate on mezzanine issues is usually closer to the equity return than the rate on senior debt. Second, mezzanine debt is often accompanied with an issue of detachable warrants.[1] Finally, mezzanine finance in some cases comes in the form of preferred stock rather than a debt issue. For all of these reasons, mezzanine debt is often referred to as a hybrid.

Mezzanine debt may be subordinated to more senior claims through either blanket or springing subordination provisions. In the former case, mezzanine debt receives no principal or interest payments until more senior creditors are fully paid off. In the springing subordination case, mezzanine debt holders can receive interest payments while the more senior debt is outstanding, provided there is no event of default on the part of the issuer. If a default occurs, the subordination "springs up" and stops the payments on the mezzanine debt until senior debt has been made whole.[2]

Mandatorily Redeemable Trust Preferred Stock

Mandatorily redeemable trust preferred stock (TruPS) became a popular form of hybrid financing in 1996 when the Federal Reserve first allowed TruPS to be counted as Tier I capital in bank holding company (BHC) regulatory capital requirements. Since then, more than 800 BHCs have issued over $85 billion in TruPS.[3]

A TruPS issue consists of two distinct transactions. In the first, a special purpose trust is formed as a wholly owned subsidiary of the BHC. The trust sells beneficial and preferred interests—the TruPS—to investors. In the second transaction, the proceeds from the sale of the TruPS are used to finance the purchase of a subordinated debenture by the trust from the issuer. The debenture has identical terms to the TruPS. The TruPS is mandatorily redeemable upon payment of the junior subordinated debt. Exhibit 14.1 illustrates the basic design.

TruPS instruments were attractive primarily because the issuer could deduct interest payments to the trust on the junior debentures from its taxes. At the same time, the issuer could consolidate the trust on its balance sheet, thus allowing the debt to be treated as an intercompany loan and the TruPS to be treated as a minority interest. The net effect was that the issuer could get debt-for-tax treatment on a preferred share for which rating agencies gave partial equity credit. TruPS instruments were

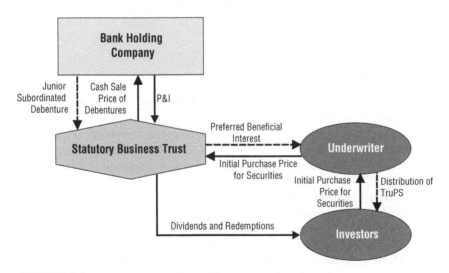

EXHIBIT 14.1 Mandatorily Redeemable Trust Preferred Stock

especially popular with banks that saw them as a tax-efficient source of Tier I capital.[4] As discussed in Appendix B, the Basel Accord defines Tier I capital to include mainly fully paid-up and issued equity, as well as certain types of "restricted core capital," such as noncumulative perpetual preferred stock and minority equity interests in consolidated subsidiaries. Restricted core capital cannot count for more than 25 percent of Tier I capital. Subordinated debt and hybrids, however, qualify only as Tier II capital. Being able to treat TruPS as a minority interest rather than subordinated debt thus was very attractive to banks.

Recent changes in accounting rules that govern special purpose entities appeared to change things substantially for TruPS. Under the new Financial Accounting Standards Board (FASB) Interpretation No. 46 (revised), *Consolidation of Variable Interest Entities* (hereinafter "FIN46R"—see Chapters 16 and 30), the issuer of the subordinated debenture to the trust that in turn issues TruPS to investors generally can no longer consolidate the trust on its balance sheet. As a result, numerous institutions have been forced to deconsolidate these trusts and show the subordinated debentures as liabilities to the subsidiary trusts.

Despite the promulgation of FIN46R, the Federal Reserve did not feel that TruPS should be excluded completely from the definition of Tier I capital. Accordingly, the Fed adopted final rules on March 1, 2005, on the capital treatment of TruPS. In general, the rules allow bank holding companies to count TruPS as part of their 25 percent restricted capital in the Tier I capital total. The rule will gradually be implemented over the next five years and appears to have saved TruPS as a popular form of hybrid finance for banks—at least for now.

Convertibles

In 1885, railroad magnate J. J. Hill believed that equity investors were systematically overestimating the risk of his railroad ventures. In need of long-term financing and a means by which to assuage investors' asymmetric information-related concerns and the predictable adverse selection costs that accompanied them, he developed the first convertible bond issue (Coxe 2000).

Convertible bonds are bonds that include an option for investors to convert their bonds into shares of the issuer's stock. Convertibles usually run from 7 to 10 years to maturity from their original issue date and have some form of call protection that limits forced early redemptions by the issuer. Hard call protection is an outright prohibition on issuer calls, whereas many convertibles contain soft call protection that limits calls only when interest rates have not moved sufficiently to cross a specified barrier. The *conversion price or ratio* specified in any convertible represents the number of shares of underlying stock that can be obtained by surrendering one bond (say, one $1,000 bond). Prior to conversion, investors in convertibles typically receive 300 to 400 basis points below the rate on comparable *non*convertible debt and 400 to 600 basis points above the dividend yield on the same firm's common stock.

Synthetically equivalent to debt plus warrants, convertible bonds are a relatively old-fashioned kind of structured debt that have proven to be an especially useful way of resolving differences between management's and investors' assessments of the firm's risk and creditworthiness. As Brennan and Schwartz (1988) have argued, convertibles are relatively insensitive to estimates of the issuer's risk because their two components—debt and an option on the firm's equity—are affected in directly opposite ways by increases in risk. An increase in (or underestimation of) the expected variance of company cash flows, while reducing the value of fixed debt claims, serves to *increase* the value of the option on the company's equity.

It is largely for this reason that the use of convertibles tends to be concentrated among smaller, high-growth companies with more volatile earnings—companies that find straight debt financing prohibitively expensive. Convertibles are ideal for such issuers because the lower interest payments reduce the risk of financial distress, an especially costly prospect for high-growth companies.

Besides being in a position to know more about the firm's prospects than investors, management also sometimes has the power to take actions that transfer value from bondholders to shareholders. This is known in the agency cost literature as the *asset substitution problem*. Management, for example, could reduce the value of outstanding bonds by entering into riskier businesses (as did savings and loans during the 1980s). Or, in another form of managerial opportunism known as *claims dilution*, they could pile lots of new debt on top of the old (as did RJR Nabisco under Kohlberg Kravis Roberts & Co.), something bondholders recognize as "event risk." Managers could also sell (or spin off, as did Marriott) assets that help support debt. And, especially when facing a heavy enough debt load, a troubled management could also fail to make necessary investments in safety, promotion, or research and development—the underinvestment problem we encountered in Part One.

Some of these actions are prevented by provisions in bond covenants. But, unless protected against these forms of managerial opportunism, bondholders can be expected to reduce the price they are willing to pay for the bonds (bonds with so-called poison puts that protect against event risk, for example, sell for lower yields than bonds without them).

This reduction in price (or increase in required yield) necessary to compensate creditors for managerial opportunism, combined with the costs of writing and enforcing covenants, are examples of the agency costs of debt that we explored.

Structured debt can reduce such costs by addressing these sources of conflict between bondholders and a management team that represents primarily the interests of shareholders. For example, puttable bonds guard against the managerial temptation to leverage or otherwise increase the risk of the company by giving bondholders the option to put the security back to the issuer. Convertibles help control this asset substitution problem, as well as the inclination of management to underinvest in tough times, by the mere fact that the convertible holders share in any gains created at the expense of the bondholders.

In addressing these agency problems and costs of asymmetric information, it's true that management could achieve the same result by using straight debt together with derivatives instead of structured debt. But one advantage of structured debt in such circumstances is that it reduces the costs incurred by creditors in monitoring the borrower's hedging activity. Structured debt reduces monitoring costs (which are a form of agency costs) by forcing the borrower to precommit itself to a hedging policy *as a condition of borrowing*.

To illustrate this point, suppose that the creditors of an exporter insist that the firm hedge its exposure to foreign exchange (FX) depreciation. To hedge, the firm could enter into agreements to sell foreign exchange forward. But that would require that the creditors continuously monitor the company's FX exposure to ensure that the exposure *remains* hedged. The debt of the exporter could instead be structured such that the principal is paid either in foreign exchange or in dollars indexed to a foreign exchange rate. This would ensure that the firm hedges its currency exposure, greatly reducing the creditors' monitoring costs and thus lowering the rate of return they would require. At the same time, the structured debt holders can (and typically do) include bond covenants that prohibit the firm from undoing its embedded hedge with transactions in the derivatives markets.

Liquid Yield Option Notes   A specific form of convertible often thought to exemplify the use of structured products to manage agency costs arising from information asymmetries is the *liquid yield option note* (LYON) introduced by Merrill Lynch in 1985. LYONs are long-dated (often 15 to 20 years), puttable, convertible, zero coupon bonds. The puts embedded in LYONs are struck at the original issue price plus accrued interest up to the put dates. In turn, the original issue price is typically at a deep discount to face value. This provides investors with downside protection up to the yield realized through any put date.

LYONs were developed in part to address the problem of asset substitution (or at least major uncertainty about risk). Indeed, holders of LYONs were doubly protected against management's increasing company risk: Either they could redeem the notes if things were turning out badly or, if the increased risk turned into the prospect of greater rewards, they could convert their claims into equity. Not surprisingly, early issuers of LYONs such as Waste Management and MCI were primarily companies in risky, or at least temporarily out-of-favor, businesses.

Convertible TruPS TruPS may also be convertible. Under the new 2005 Federal Reserve guidance on TruPS, internationally active banks are limited to holding 15 percent of their core capital in restricted core capital such as TruPS, despite the 25 percent allowance more generally for BHCs. Qualifying mandatory *convertible* preferreds, however, are exempt from this 15 percent maximum. We thus should not be surprised to find convertibility provisions in most new TruPS issues.

Preferred Equity Redemption Cumulative Stock *Preferred equity redemption cumulative stock* (PERCS)[5] has been around for just over a decade and is essentially a convertible hybrid that looks like a short put option. PERCS instruments are usually a *mandatorily* convertible security, converting into common stock after three to five years automatically. They are also callable by the issuer at a declining schedule of prices and maturity dates up to the mandatory conversion date.

PERCS instruments are designed to supplement the income of investors. They pay a cumulative preferred dividend quarterly and can generate yields for investors of 300 to 400 basis points above common stock, despite issuing at the same price (Coxe 2000). This supplementary income can be viewed as premium for writing a call option against a long stock position, thereby turning the whole structure into a short put.

Preferred Redeemable Increased Dividend Equity Securities *Preferred redeemable increased dividend equity securities* (PRIDES) are preferred shares that convert into common shares. They can be converted anytime at a premium but mandatorily convert at maturity. Beginning with the MascoTech PRIDES issue in July 1993, PRIDES now comprise nearly 15 percent of the total convertible market. They typically issue at the same price as common stock but command a 500 to 600 basis point premium over common and a 200 to 300 basis point premium over traditional preference shares in income terms (Coxe 2000).

The payoff on a PRIDES depends on the value of the issuer's common stock at maturity. Denote $S(t)$ as the price per share of the issuer's common when the PRIDES is issued, and let K be the fixed conversion price specified at that time. A PRIDES is equivalent to a short put struck at-the-money at $S(t)$ and β long calls struck at K. Mechanically, here is how this payoff is achieved:

- If $S(T) < S(t)$, PRIDES converts into one share of the issuer's common stock.
- If $S(t) \leq S(T) < K$, PRIDES converts into $S(t)/S(T)$ shares of common, or just enough to give the PRIDES holder shares with a value exactly equal to $S(t)$ per share regardless of where the closing price is relative to the initial price.
- If $S(T) \geq K$, PRIDES converts into β shares of common.

Conversion may occur prior to maturity at the option of the PRIDES investor at the conversion rate β. The issuer also may typically call a PRIDES early (after some lockout period) at a premium to the initial price plus accrued dividends. Because the written put is at-the-money and the purchased call is out-of-the-money and because one put is written for every β calls purchased, the premium collected exceeds the premium outlay. This accounts for the enhanced income of this hybrid.

Coxe (2000) offers an excellent survey of the convertible market with particular attention to the numerous variations in PRIDES available to issuers and investors (including the equally numerous acronyms that accompany these structures!).

STRUCTURED NOTES[6]

Hybrids and convertibles are structured securities that combine different elements of the same firm's capital structure or, in some cases, derivatives based on the firm's securities plus other securities. In either case, hybrids and convertibles are generally limited to combining securities and derivatives for the same firm.

Debt securities are also often linked to prices of assets *other than* those issued by the company that issues the engineered security. To distinguish these products from single-capital-structure products like hybrids and convertibles, we refer to these structures as *structured notes*.

A structured note can be synthetically replicated by, and is best understood as, a contract whose payoff features combine debt with a traditional plain-vanilla derivatives contract. A firm that issues structured debt thus can generally achieve the identical market exposure by issuing straight debt and entering into a stand-alone derivatives contract. Most structured notes are issued by corporations and government-sponsored enterprises (GSEs) like the Federal Home Loan Bank System, Fannie Mae, and Sallie Mae. The Federal Home Loan Bank System, in particular, has historically been one of the largest issuers of structured notes in the world. Structured notes issued by these entities generally are medium-term notes (MTNs) with more than a year to maturity.

As we have seen in several earlier chapters, every time a corporation issues securities, it transfers whatever risks affect its assets that have *not* been hedged or insured to investors in those securities. And as we discussed in Chapter 13, one reason that companies engage in structured financings is to match their own specific risk transfer objectives with investor demands. Embedding specific risk transfer devices into debt through a structured note issue thus is a mechanism for the firm to integrate *specific* risk transfer into a fund-raising and risk-shifting transaction.

Recall that one of the M&M assumptions is that all investors have access to the capital market on the same terms as large corporations. If this condition does not hold, the issuing firm may find itself in the position of being able to supply a differentiated product that is in special demand by investors. In their study of structured notes, Smithson and Chew (1992) argue that some complex debt instruments are designed in part to furnish investors with securities "they cannot obtain elsewhere." Commodity-linked bonds, for example, typically contain embedded long-dated forwards or options on commodity prices that are not available on organized exchanges. Investors may be willing to pay more for structured debt that allows them to take such positions, thereby reducing the issuer's weighted average cost of capital (WACC).

Another potential benefit of managing price risks with structured debt is that it avoids the corporate costs associated with the use of derivatives. Besides the costs of building expertise in derivatives markets, structured debt also allows the firm to avoid the costs of managing the counterparty credit risk associated with swaps and other over-the-counter derivatives, and the costs of managing the funding and operational risks associated with all derivatives.

In sum, the value of a structured product depends not only on its effectiveness in reducing the variability that arises from a particular risk—say, from oil price changes—but also on the net costs and benefits associated with conducting the transaction *with a particular group of investors* or, in the case of derivatives, *with a particular counterparty*. The large and growing variety of risk management products has the potential to reduce risk management costs for both managers and investors.

For ease of discussion, we distinguish between four types of structured notes: equity-linked, interest-rate-linked, currency-linked, and commodity-linked notes.

Equity-Linked Notes

The capacity to blend equity price, index, or basket exposure into corporate securities is limited only by the universe of equity derivatives, which is growing every day. Consequently, the variations on equity-indexed notes are staggering, and whole books have been written attempting to survey this area of structured notes. Here, we merely provide some of the more popular examples of such structures.

Exchangeable Debt   Perhaps the simplest equity-linked note is called *exchangeable debt*. An exchangeable bond is just like a convertible bond with one difference. Instead of allowing debt holders to convert into equity shares in the company that issued the bond, exchangeable debt allows debt holders to convert into equity shares of a company *other than the one that issued the bond*. Exchangeable debt thus is straight corporate debt plus an American-style call option on the common stock of the other firm.

In some exchangeable debt offerings, the conversion option may be cash settled in lieu of physical share delivery. In some cases, this cash-out option has additional optionality. A Cable & Wireless convertible, for example, allowed the issuer to convert into a basket of shares and cash where the ratio in the basket was subject to the issuer's discretion. And in other cases, the issuer may even convert into its own shares, provided the value of shares delivered is equal to the value of the shares of the firm underlying the exchange conversion option. News Corporation, for example, issued exchangeable debt that was convertible into shares of BSkyB, the cash equivalent of the promised BSkyB shares, or the value equivalent of the BSkyB shares if paid in News Corporation shares (Grantham 2004).

Regardless of how it is settled, exchangeable debt can be very attractive for firms with severe adverse selection problems. If investors in the firm's securities suspect the firm is being wasteful or inefficient relative to its industry peers, for example, the inclusion of a conversion option based on one or more of the firm's peers could significantly abrogate any such concerns about the investment decisions of the issuer. The issuer, however, has to pay up to send that signal by buying the option on its peer(s) that it has written to investors. In addition, the issuer now runs the risk that it could lose share capital to a competitor.

Equity Bull Notes Numerous MTNs and debt instruments have been issued in which the coupon and/or principal value of the note is indexed to an equity index or equity share price using a call option–like feature. There are so many acronyms that have been used for the vast array of these products over the years that it no longer makes sense even to track them. We shall refer to this type of structured note as an *equity bull note*. There are a few common variations worth mentioning. Interested readers should consult Kat (2002) for a much more detailed and comprehensive discussion of these and other structures.

Unprotected Bull Note A plain-vanilla unprotected bull note pays the following to investors at maturity:

$$FV[1 + \alpha R(t,\ T)] = FV\left\{1 + \alpha\left[\frac{V(T) - V(t)}{V(t)}\right]\right\}$$

where FV = face value of the bond

α = participation rate

$R(t,\ T)$ = return (% change) on the index over the life of the bond

$V(t)$ = reference equity price or index level at time t

The parameter α, called the *participation rate*, determines how much risk and reward the investor will bear in the equity price or index. With $\alpha = 1$, investors are exposed to the percentage change in the reference equity dollar for dollar. With $\alpha = 0.8$, by contrast, investors are exposed to only 80 percent of the realized percentage change in the reference equity. The unprotected bull note is economically equivalent to a zero coupon bond plus a forward contracts on the reference equity.

A bull note may also specify a *base* that enables the investor to start off in- or out-of-the-money without changing her participation rate. If the parameter β indicates the base, the payoff on the note at maturity now becomes

$$FV\left\{1 + \alpha\left[\frac{V(T) - \beta V(t)}{V(t)}\right]\right\}$$

where β is usually less than unity to start the investor off in-the-money.

Capped Bull Note   A higher base usually comes at the expense of a lower participation rate. Alternatively, a bull note with a reduced base can also have an enhanced participation rate if the payoff is capped to some maximum rate of return X:

$$FV\left(1+\min\left\{\alpha\left[\frac{V(T)-\beta V(t)}{V(t)}\right], X\right\}\right) \quad \alpha>1,\ \beta<1$$

Investors in this note have bought α forwards and sold α in-the-money call options, which is, of course, equivalent to having sold α out-of-the-money puts.

Protected Bull Note   Unprotected bull notes put the principal of the investor at risk. This can significantly limit the investors eligible to purchase these products. To increase their appeal, a principal protection feature can be added, resulting in the protected bull note.

A protected bull note that guarantees investors a minimum return of X has a payoff at maturity that can be expressed as:

$$FV\left(1+\max\left\{X,\ \alpha\left[\frac{V(T)-V(t)}{V(t)}\right]\right\}\right)$$

Instead of a zero coupon bond and a forward, the protected bull note is now equivalent to a zero and a long call option.

To take a specific example, consider the Stock Index Growth Notes (SIGNs) issued in 1991 by the Republic of Austria. Those securities were five-year MTNs whose single interest payment at maturity was linked to the S&P 500 index. The notes paid face value plus interest based on the percentage change in the S&P 500 over the preceding five years. If the stock market declined, investors received only the face value of the note. If an increase occurred, investors participated directly.

From the investors' perspective, the Republic of Austria SIGNs can be viewed as a zero coupon bond plus an embedded long at-the-money call option on the S&P 500 with a participation rate of $\alpha = 1$. If the S&P 500 declined in value over the five years, the call expired worthless and investors would receive only the face value of the bond. Any increase in the stock market, however, would translate into a higher principal repayment for investors dollar for dollar.

The SIGNs were zero coupon instruments, but this need not be the case. Consider, for example, the 1986 Salomon Brothers product called the

Standard & Poor's 500 Indexed Subordinated Note (SPIN). This was a four-year MTN with a $100 million face value and a 2 percent semiannual coupon. At maturity, the investor received the last coupon and the face value of the instrument plus 92.2 percent of any increase in the S&P 500 above 108.5 percent of the value of the S&P 500 on the date the note was issued. The participation rate thus was $\alpha = 0.922$, and the base was $\beta = 1.085$.

Equity-Linked Certificates of Deposits Similar to equity-linked notes, equity-linked certificates of deposit (CDs) were very popular from about 1993 to the very late 1990s. Equity-indexed CDs have been issued by Citicorp, Bankers Trust, Republic Bank of New York, Bank of America, and numerous other banking institutions of all sizes.

To take a specific example, consider Citicorp's Stock Index Insured Account. This five-year CD paid no coupons but at maturity returned the greater of the face value of the CD or the face value of the CD plus twice the average increase in the S&P 500 over the preceding five years. The cash flows on the Citicorp CD can be replicated by a five-year zero coupon bond and two at-the-money Asian options on the S&P 500. The investor pays for these options by forgoing the money interest that would be earned on a traditional CD. Most equity-indexed CDs are insured by the Federal Deposit Insurance Corporation, moreover, and thus can typically be issued at lower funding cost than equity-indexed notes.

Spread and Rainbow Bonds A *spread bond* or *rainbow bond* is a multifactor equity-linked note that allows investors to index their return to the relative performance of one stock versus another. Spread bonds can be based on single stocks, baskets, or indexes.

A spread bond is just the combination of a straight debt instrument (zero coupon or coupon-bearing) with a spread option, as we discussed in Chapter 11. The amount of principal repaid thus is based on the spread between two stocks relative to a strike price and can be expressed as:

$$FV\left(1 + \alpha \max\left\{\left[\frac{V_1(T) - V_1(t)}{V_1(t)}\right] - \left[\frac{V_2(T) - V_2(t)}{V_2(t)}\right]\right\} - K\right)$$

where subscripts to the stock prices or index levels indicate asset one or asset two. The participation rate is again denoted α, and the strike price K is usually zero. The option component in this special case—a two-asset spread—is also known as an *exchange option*, or the option to exchange one asset for another.

The participation rate available—as in other structures we have examined—usually depends on the cost of principal protection. Consider a one-year $1 million spread bond. If the interest rate is 4 percent, $961,538 must be invested to guarantee repayment of the $1 million principal. This leaves $88,461 to purchase the spread option. If the spread option costs $100,000, then at most a 88.46 percent participation in the spread (i.e., .8846 spread options) can be offered. Or you could offer 100 percent participation in the spread but guarantee only 93.6 percent of the principal—($1,000,000 − $100,000)(1.04)/$1,000,000.

Spread bonds can be appealing for several reasons. First, they are a funded instrument that allows portfolio managers to express a relative price view without incurring the unlimited liability associated with a comparable equity swap or equity forward spread trade. In addition, spread bonds allow retail investors to finance short stock positions.

As you might have guessed, this structure need not be limited to two assets—and, indeed, often is not. As many stocks, indexes, or baskets as an investor desires can be incorporated into the payoff. One particular flavor of this structure that has gained popularity in recent years is the *best-of-equity-and-bonds* note, which allows investors to trade some participation in an equity index for participation in a bond index or vice versa.

Interest-Rate-Indexed Notes

The second type of structured note we consider is a structured note whose principal and/or interest varies with some floating reference interest rate. These are usually coupon-bearing instruments, and most rate-indexed structured notes have their coupon payments indexed to some underlying reference rate. Some notes also involve principal indexing. The most important types of interest-rate-indexed structured notes are analyzed in this section.[7]

Floating-Rate Notes   A *floating-rate note* (FRN) is a structured note in which the borrower's interest payments are indexed or linked to a floating reference interest rate or index of interest rates. FRNs have coupon payments (usually semiannual) that are unknown when the security is first issued; the rate resets on each coupon date according to some specified formula involving the reference rate or rates. A typical FRN has coupon payments based on a spread over the London Interbank Offered Rate (LIBOR), such as six-month LIBOR plus 25 basis points (or, more simply, 6M-LIBOR+25).

The cash flows from an FRN can be replicated by a portfolio consisting of a fixed-rate coupon bond plus an interest rate swap, as shown in

Exhibit 14.2. (Recall that in these cash flow diagrams, down arrows indicate outflows and up arrows indicate inflows.) Panel (a) shows the cash flows on a level-coupon $(T - t)$-period bond from the perspective of the issuer. Face value is denoted Z, and the bond pays periodic interest at annualized coupon rate of K.

Panel (b) shows the cash flows on a $(T - t)$-period pay-floating swap,

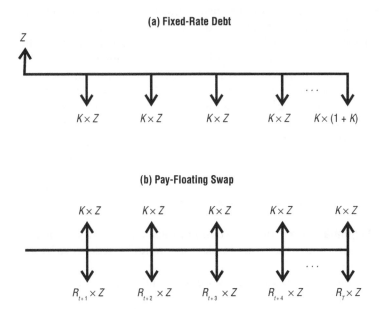

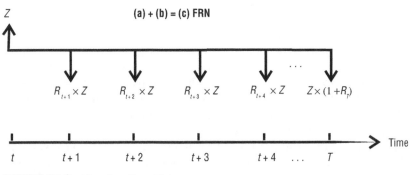

EXHIBIT 14.2 Floating-Rate Note

where each periodic floating cash flow is LIBOR plus a spread. If the bond and swap pay interest semiannually, for example, then the floating rate on each settlement date—denoted R_t for settlement date t—corresponds to six-month LIBOR set six months ago.[8] In exchange for paying this floating rate, the pay-floating firm receives a fixed interest payment each period equal to K percent of the swap's notional principal amount, denoted Z.

In Exhibit 14.2, Panels (a) and (b) clearly form a hedge portfolio for an FRN with comparable terms. The fixed payment on the bond is offset by the fixed leg of the swap, leaving the firm with only floating-rate obligations each period—obligations identical to those on the FRN.

The equivalence between issuing an FRN and issuing fixed-rate debt while entering into a pay-floating swap has important implications for the valuation and hedging of structured notes. First, arbitrage opportunities will be available if the price of the FRN is out of line with the pricing of the fixed-rate note and the swap. To achieve floating-rate financing, in other words, it may be less costly to issue fixed-rate debt and swap into floating. Second, the availability of swaps (or derivatives more generally) means that the issuer can issue the type of debt most preferred by investors, or a particular investor, and then enter into a swap to achieve the desired form of financing. Put another way, issuing an FRN and entering into a pay-fixed/receive-floating interest rate swap results in synthetic fixed-rate funding.

Inverse Floating-Rate Notes *Inverse floating-rate notes* were first issued in 1986 by Sallie Mae under the name "yield curve notes" (Ogden 1987). Inverse FRNs are also called "bull floaters" because of their appeal to investors bullish on bond prices (i.e., expecting bond prices to rise, hence interest rates to fall).[9]

The floating coupon payment at any time t on a $(T - t)$-period inverse FRN ("inverse floater") with face value Z can be expressed as:

$$C_t = Z \max(K - R_t, 0)$$

where K is a fixed percent and R_t is the floating reference rate at time t times the face value. The minimum coupon is generally zero, although structures involving a positive minimum coupon have also been offered.

The cash flows on an inverse FRN, shown in panel (d) of Exhibit 14.3, can be viewed as a combination of an FRN with face value Z, *two* pay-floating interest rate swaps (each with notional principal Z), and an interest rate cap—all maturing on date T.

In Panel (a) of Exhibit 14.3, a firm issues an FRN with face value Z and makes periodic coupon payments through date T equal to R_t. In panel (b), the firm combines the issued FRN with *two* pay-fixed interest rate

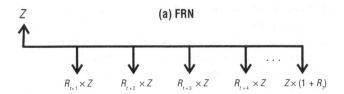

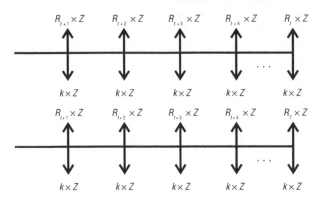

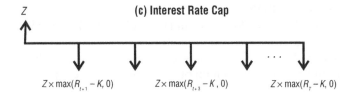

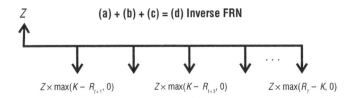

EXHIBIT 14.3 Inverse Floater

swaps, each of which has a fixed rate of k and a reference floating rate of R_t at any time t. Each period, the firm thus pays R_t on the FRN, receives $2R_t$ on the swaps, and pays $2k$ on the swaps, resulting in a net per-period cash flow of $R_t - K$, where $K = 2k$. Finally, panel (c) shows the periodic payoff on a $(T - t)$-period out-of-the-money interest rate cap with a strike rate of K that the firm has written. This last position is required to ensure that the coupon rate on the structure does not go negative.

Levered Floaters and Levered Inverse Floaters   *Levered FRNs* and *inverse FRNs* are structured so that the coupon payment changes more rapidly than the underlying interest rate changes. Bear floaters are an example of levered FRNs. A bear floater is so named because investors with a bearish sentiment about bond prices (i.e., expectation of falling bond prices, hence rising interest rates) find them appealing.

The first issuer of bear floaters is unknown, but at least one source suggests these instruments were first offered by Mellon Bank in 1986, just after the first Sallie Mae issue of an inverse floater. Mellon Bank's bear floater was a three-year floating-rate CD with a coupon formula that paid investors twice LIBOR less a fixed 9.12 percent (Smith 1988). Although a bear floater resembles a simple FRN in that the coupon payments rise with market rates, the coupon payments rise *faster* than LIBOR. In the Mellon Bank issue, for example, the leverage factor was 2, so coupon payments increased twice as rapidly as LIBOR.

In principle, a levered inverse floater is similar to a levered floater. The issuer simply chooses a leverage factor and multiplies the floating portion of the coupon payment by that factor. A levered inverse floater with a leverage factor of α and a minimum coupon of zero would pay a coupon at time t equal to

$$C_t = Z \max(K - \alpha R_t, 0)$$

where K is a fixed percent and R_t is the floating reference rate at time t. Z again denotes face value.

That levered floaters and levered inverse floaters can be decomposed into straight debt plus a bundle of derivatives contracts is evident from an example. Suppose an issuer offers an inverse floater that pays investors a coupon that declines twice as fast as LIBOR and has a minimum coupon of zero. Alternatively, the firm could issue FRNs and enter into *three* pay-fixed interest rate swaps with a fixed rate of k and a floating rate of R_t on a notional principal of Z. (Equivalently, it could enter into a single fixed-for-floating swap with notional value $3Z$.) Because the minimum coupon on the levered inverse FRN being replicated is zero, the issuer would also sell an interest rate cap struck at $3k$. The issuer's net payments from the FRN, swaps, and cap are given by

$$C_t = Z \max(3k - 2R_t, 0) = Z \max(K - 2R_t, 0)$$

where $K = 3k$. This portfolio then results in a synthetic levered inverse FRN with the same stream of coupon payments as the structured note, where $\alpha = 2$.

Range Notes A *range note* is a structured note that pays an above-market interest rate when a reference rate, such as LIBOR, falls within a specified band and pays zero otherwise. Also known as *corridor notes, accrual notes,* and *yield curve notes,* these debt instruments have been issued by the Kingdom of Sweden, Landesbank Hessen-Thuringen, Swedish Export Credit Corporation, the World Bank, and numerous commercial and merchant banks.

To take a specific example, consider a two-year accrual MTN issued by Paribas Capital Markets in 1993.[10] The Paribas MTN paid a semiannual coupon whose amount was determined not just by LIBOR, but specifically by the *number of days* in the six-month period in which LIBOR fell within a prescribed range. If LIBOR fell within the prescribed range every day during any one of the four coupon periods, the note paid a coupon of 1.35 percent over the two-year constant-maturity Treasury (CMT) rate. The coupon payments on the Paribas MTN are shown in Table 14.1.

Although the coupon payments are based on a spread over the two-year CMT rate, the level of LIBOR determines whether the note pays a coupon. Range notes are also often indexed to a CMT rate instead.

TABLE 14.1 Paribas Capital Markets Two-Year Range Note

Reference Ranges		Coupon Payment	
Coupon Period	LIBOR (%)	Time in Range (% Days)	Spread Over 2-Year CMT
1	3.25 – 4.00	100	+135 bps
2	3.50 – 4.5625	95	+108 bps
3	3.75 – 5.00	90	+80 bps
4	3.75 – 5.3125	85	+53 bps
		80	+25 bps
		75	–2 bps
		70	–30 bps

The cash flow of a range note can be replicated by a portfolio of zero coupon bonds and asset-or-nothing digital options (see Chapter 11). Investors in range notes are effectively writing the issuer digital options on the underlying reference rate, as the first coupon period in the Paribas accrual note illustrates. Supposing there are 180 days in that period, the investor has written Paribas Capital Markets 180 digital put options on LIBOR with a strike rate of 3.25 percent. If LIBOR is above 3.25 percent, the investor receives a fixed 1.35 percent over the two-year CMT rate. If LIBOR is below 3.25 percent, the investor receives nothing. The investor has also written 180 digital call options on LIBOR to Paribas with a strike rate of 4 percent, receiving payments of 1.35 percent over the two-year CMT rate only if LIBOR falls below the strike rate of the options.

Step-Up Bonds A *step-up bond* is a structured note with two types of contractually specified fixed coupon rates: a low rate during an initial period and one or more higher stepped-up rates during subsequent periods. Step-up bonds are noncallable by the issuer during the initial low-coupon period but callable during later periods.

Step-up bonds can be viewed as traditional fixed-rate bonds with embedded call options written on the reference index rate. Suppose, for example, that a step-up bond pays an initial coupon of C_1 during the noncallable period and a higher coupon C_2 during the callable step-up period. Consider an issuer who can borrow at LIBOR. An investor in this issuer's step-up bond effectively writes the issuer a European-style call option on LIBOR with a strike price of C_2 and an expiration date equal to the end of the non-call period. The investor receives C_1 during the initial period, and also receives a higher (but less than market) yield if the bond is not called. If the bond issues at par, the investor thus typically earns an above-market yield during the noncall period. This above-market yield is the de facto premium the investor collects from selling the embedded call option to the issuer.

Dual-Indexed FRNs A *dual-indexed FRN* is a structured note whose coupon payments are based on two reference interest rates. The reference rates underlying many dual-indexed notes are LIBOR and a CMT rate. An example of a dual-indexed bond is the Federal Home Loan Bank's Dual Indexed Consolidated Bonds issued in September 1993. The bonds pay investors the *difference* between the 10-year CMT rate plus a spread and six-month LIBOR. The spread increases over time according to specified schedules.

The cash flows of a dual-indexed note can be replicated by an FRN combined with a basis rate swap where the payments on the swap are indexed to two different reference rates. Consider a firm that issues FRNs with face value Z paying LIBOR periodically and that enters into a basis swap with notional principal Z to get 2×LIBOR and pay the 10-year CMT rate. The issuer has thus ensured a net semiannual coupon payment of the 10-year CMT rate *less* LIBOR. Interest rate caps and floors may also be needed to limit the minimum and maximum coupon payments.

Ladder Bonds   A *ladder bond* combines a coupon-bearing bond with a series of interest rate–based ladder options. Recall from Chapter 11 that a European ladder call option has the following payoff at maturity date T:

$$C(T) = \max[0, S(T) - X, \max(0, L_k - X)]$$

where $S(T)$ is the price of the underlying (in this case, a reference interest rate), X is the strike price or rate, and L_k is the kth rung in the ladder of strike prices specified. Readers may wish to consult Exhibit 11.11, in which the payoff of a ladder option is shown for three possible price paths.

In short, a ladder option is intended to lock in a minimum intrinsic value if and when the underlying reference rate crosses a ladder rung, L_k. Once that rate threshold has been reached, the option is always worth *at least* the ladder threshold less the strike rate. If the reference interest rate at maturity is less than the ladder threshold, the investor receives the ladder threshold rate less the strike rate. Or if the reference rate is above the ladder rate, the investor receives the normal intrinsic value payout.

Index-Amortizing Notes   One of the most popular structured notes whose principal is indexed to an interest rate is the *index-amortizing note* (IAN). IANs repay principal based on an amortization rate that is fully specified in an amortization schedule as a function of an underlying reference rate, such as LIBOR. An increase in the reference rate results in an increase in the effective maturity of the IAN. The reference rate chosen is generally correlated with prepayments on mortgage obligations or receivables of the issuer. As rates increase and the prepayments on the associated mortgages decline the IAN maturity rises.

IANs can be replicated by combining a fixed-rate coupon bond or FRN with an index-amortizing rate (IAR) swap with the same amortization schedule as the IAN. IARs, in turn, can usually be decomposed (depending on the amortization schedule) into an interest rate swap with an embedded portfolio of LIBOR straddles.

Currency-Indexed Debt

The earliest uses of swaps were primarily tied to corporate finance applications. Firms would issue debt in whatever market they perceived a comparative funding advantage and then would use swaps to redenominate their funding synthetically into their preferred currency. And, of course, corporations today generally encounter no barriers to raising funds in a foreign currency by just issuing foreign currency–denominated bonds.

Some firms, however, preferred a more customized currency risk exposure in their corporate financing activities. For this purpose, they turned to the currency-index structured note market. Two of the most popular structures are discussed next.

Dual Currency Bonds   A *dual currency bond* is a structured note that pays interest in one currency and principal in another. The coupon payments are usually denominated in the currency of the investors, and the principal is typically paid in the currency of the issuer.

One of the earliest dual currency bonds was issued by Philip Morris Credit Corporation in September 1985. The bond called for interest payments in Swiss francs of 7.25 percent on a subscription price of Sfr. 123,000,000 with a principal payment of US$57,810,000.

The straight debt component of a dual currency bond can be viewed from either the issuer's or the investors' standpoint as a fixed-rate coupon-bearing bond. From the investors' standpoint, the derivatives component of a dual currency bond is simply a forward sale of Swiss francs for U.S. dollars. From Philip Morris Credit Corporation's standpoint, the bond's derivatives component was as a portfolio of forward contracts to sell Swiss francs for U.S. dollars, with the maturity date of each forward corresponding to the coupon dates and the principal value of each forward contract equal to the Swiss franc coupon payment. The straight-debt component looked like a U.S. dollar-denominated fixed-rate bond.

Principal Exchange Rate Linked Securities (PERLS) and Reverse PERLS   *Principal exchange rate linked securities* (PERLS) are similar to dual currency bonds, but unlike dual currency bonds, both coupon and principal payments are paid in the same currency. The debt instrument in a PERLS is a coupon-bearing bond that pays interest and principal in the same currency. The principal repayment, however, is indexed to the foreign currency value of the face value of the bond at maturity. If the foreign currency appreciates relative to the currency in which coupon and interest payments are denominated, the investor receives as principal redemption more than the face value of the security. The combined position thus is equivalent to a fixed-rate bond plus a forward on the reference currency.

Consider, for example, the PERLS issued by Sallie Mae in 1987. That PERLS paid both coupons and principal in U.S. dollars, but the principal repayment was indexed to the value of the Australian dollar. The coupon payments were 12⅛ percent and the principal redemption was the U.S. dollar equivalent of A$1,452 per US$1,000 in face value. From the investors' perspective, the PERLS was equivalent to a straight bond selling at a premium because of the higher-than-market coupons plus an out-of-the-money long forward on the Australian dollar.

A *reverse PERLS* is a structured note whose principal repayment *declines* with exchange rate appreciations. Consider, for example, the reverse PERLS issued by the Ford Motor Credit Corporation in 1987. The principal redemption was indexed to the dollar/yen exchange rate. From the investors' perspective, the reverse PERLS was equivalent to a straight bond selling at a premium because of the above-market coupon plus an in-the-money short forward to sell yen for dollars and a long call option to put a floor of zero under the potential loss of principal.

The structure of a reverse PERLS is similar to an inverse floater and bear floater in that the minimum repayment (of principal) is guaranteed not to fall below zero or some other specified amount. To assure this, the forward contract embedded in the reverse PERLS is coupled with a call option on yen with a strike price of twice the spot exchange rate when the security was issued. That puts a floor of zero on the principal redemption value at maturity.

Commodity-Indexed Debt

A number of popular structured notes over the years have been simple combinations of debt plus commodity derivatives. These instruments have generally represented so-called balance sheet hedges for their issuers; that is, the commodity price risk embedded in the liability is offset by a natural commodity price exposure in the firm's assets.

Structured balance sheet hedges can be very effective for firms experiencing credit problems or debt capacity constraints. Investors may be concerned about a firm's ability to repay its unsecured debt. Such concerns might *not* exist, however, if the issuer embeds a commodity exposure into its interest and/or coupon payments, such that the issuer's debt service obligation is then positively correlated with its cash flows. The firm owes more only when its revenues or asset values are increasing, thereby providing a natural credit risk mitigant to prospective borrowers and potentially reducing the firm's WACC.

A few typical examples of these sorts of structured deals are discussed next.

Pegasus Gold-Indexed Bonds   In 1986, the Pegasus Gold Corporation issued bonds with gold warrants. Unlike most structured notes that are sold as a single product, the Pegasus bonds were actually a bundle of two distinct securities sold together. Pegasus sold fixed-rate coupon-bearing bonds that repaid a fixed principal at maturity and bundled a *detachable* gold warrant (i.e., a long-dated, cash-settled European-style call option on gold).

When the price of gold went up, Pegasus's revenues rose. Investors could exercise their gold warrants when the bonds matured and receive a higher effective principal repayment, thereby directly participating in the firm's higher revenues. In turn, Pegasus was able to offer the straight bonds to investors with a lower coupon rate.

Investors also had the alternative of *selling* their gold warrants to other investors while keeping the straight bonds. If the price of gold increased substantially, even though investors could not directly exercise the options, they could sell the detachable gold warrants and capture some of the price increase while still remaining lenders to Pegasus.

Magma Copper-Indexed Notes   In 1988, Magma Copper Company issued 10-year notes with their value linked to the price of copper. Unlike the Pegasus Gold bonds with warrants, the Magma Copper notes indexed the coupon payments (rather than the principal repayment) to the price of copper. Investors could not sell their copper options without also selling their notes.

The Magma Copper notes paid coupons to investors quarterly based on the average price of copper during the quarter of the coupon payment. The schedule of interest rates investors were paid for a given average copper price is shown in Table 14.2.

The cash flows from the Magma Copper notes can be replicated with a portfolio of a 10-year fixed-rate coupon bond and 40 embedded Asian call options on copper, each maturing on the 40 respective quarterly coupon dates.

Sonatrach Oil-Indexed Notes   In late 1989 Sonatrach, the state-owned hydrocarbon producer of Algeria, was having difficulty servicing a conventional floating-rate note issue held by a syndicate of banks. In 1990, the Chase Manhattan Bank led a restructuring in which Sonatrach's FRNs were retired with a series of inverse oil-indexed bonds. Specifically, Sonatrach issued new FRNs indexed at 100 basis points over LIBOR to a

TABLE 14.2 Coupons on the 1988 Magma Copper Bonds

Average Copper Price per Pound	Indexed Interest Rate
Above $2.00	21%
$1.80–$2.00	20%
$1.60–$1.80	19%
$1.40–$1.60	18%
$1.30–$1.40	17%
$1.20–$1.30	16%
$1.10–$1.20	15%
$1.00–$1.10	14%
$0.90–$1.00	13%
Below $0.90	12%

group of syndicate banks and wrote two-year calls on oil with a strike price of $23 to Chase. At the same time, Chase wrote seven-year calls on oil (strike $22) and wrote seven-year puts on oil (strike $16) to the syndicate banks.

In return for being granted the oil price puts and calls by Chase, the syndicate accepted a significantly lower spread over LIBOR (by some estimates, several hundred basis points lower) than what would otherwise have been Sonatrach's floating-rate cost of funds. This reduction in period-by-period interest costs in turn reduced the likelihood that Sonatrach would experience further financial trouble. The options, moreover, did not impose any additional oil price risk on Sonatrach because the oil producer was committed to additional option payments only when the price of oil rose above $23. The company's funding cost thus increased only when it could most afford the additional interest payments.

The Sonatrach notes, then, effectively managed the exposure of the company's creditors to oil price risk—in part by appealing to a group of investors (the syndicate included some of the original as well as new lenders) that showed an appetite for oil price risk. In effect, such investors were trading a reduction in their coupon rate for a play on oil price volatility. By restructuring the notes in this fashion, Chase and its investors increased the creditworthiness of Sonatrach, thereby increasing the probability of receiving their promised payoffs.

CHAPTER 15

Contingent Capital

A contingent capital facility gives a company the right to issue new debt, equity, or structured securities during a specified period of time at a predefined issue price. Most contingent capital facilities are event-contingent; some triggering event must occur before the new financial capital claims can be issued. This triggering event usually involves an unexpected and substantial loss experienced by the purchaser of the contingent capital that is highly correlated with the price of the security underlying the facility.

In this chapter,[1] we consider a number of examples of contingent capital structures and how they have been used both for preloss risk finance and for risk transfer. We pay particular attention to the distinction between the perceived benefits and drivers of contingent capital in the insurance sector vis-à-vis the noninsurance corporate world.

CONTINGENT CAPITAL FACILITIES AS OPTIONS

Contingent capital is an option to issue a corporate security. We saw in Chapter 1 how traditional corporate securities can be viewed as options. So, not surprisingly, contingent capital is essentially a *compound option*—an option on an option, where the underlying is the net value of the firm's real capital assets.

For our discussion in this chapter, however, it will suffice for us to focus only on the first layer of optionality and to treat contingent capital as essentially an option to issue a corporate security. Like any ordinary option, contingent capital then can easily be characterized by its key features: (1) the underlying asset, (2) the time period or tenor of the option, (3) the strike price, (4) the exercisability of the option, (5) the type, and (6) the option writer(s).

Underlying Asset

Contingent capital gives a firm the option to issue debt, equity, or hybrid securities, or in some cases event structured securities.[2] The type of security that can be issued under a facility is predefined at the beginning of the life of the contingent capital option, before the security is actually issued. In addition, the exact terms of the security to be issued (e.g., tenor, rate, depth of subordination, etc.) are also usually defined at the beginning of the program.

In most of the contingent capital programs that have been publicly disclosed to date, the underlying security was either deeply subordinated debt or preferred stock. Inasmuch as these are more equity-like products than not, many firms have evidently relied on contingent capital facilities as a form of contingent risk transfer. A firm that draws on a contingent debt facility following the announcement of a large loss, by contrast, is essentially exercising an in-the-money postloss risk financing option.[3]

Tenor

Regardless of the maturity of the financial capital claim that a firm may issue in a contingent capital facility, the option to issue the contingent capital has a clearly limited duration. Consider, for example, a contingent debt facility that gives a firm the right to issue five-year fixed-rate junior subordinated debt at any time over the next three months. The duration of the underlying capital claim is five years, but the duration of the contingent facility is only three months.

Strike Price and Intrinsic Value

Like any other option, a contingent capital facility includes a strike price, or the prespecified price at which new securities can be issued through the facility. The strike price is often set to reflect preloss issue terms. Accordingly, the price for the new issue is set prior to the realization of a loss arising from a specified risk and is usually tied to the price of the underlying security on the date the contingent capital program is negotiated. In other words, the facility is generally at-the-money at its inception.

The value of the contingent capital facility if drawn—the intrinsic value of the option at the time of exercise—is essentially the difference between the cost of capital accessible through the contingent capital arrangement and the cost of capital available in the open market at that time. If the firm can raise capital more cheaply in the open market than through the contingent capital program, the option will not be exercised. We thus say that the first trigger that must be "pulled" in order for the contingent capital option to be exercised is a positive intrinsic value.[4]

Exercisability

Like regular options, a contingent capital facility may be American-, European-, or Bermuda-style. Most contingent capital facilities to date have been American-style, thereby allowing their holders in principle to issue the underlying securities at almost any time over the life of the option following a brief lockup period at the front end of the deal.

Although a typical American-style option may be exercised at any time it is in-the-money, contingent capital facilities may also contain a second trigger. A second trigger is an additional condition that must be met before the option can be exercised. In this sense, contingent capital facilities are similar to barrier options (see Chapter 11). Also like barrier options, the second trigger determines only when the facility can be accessed, not the value of program when it is utilized. In other words, the second trigger affects the timing of the exercise decision but does not change the intrinsic value if an exercise occurs.

In traditional barrier options, the second trigger generally depends on the price of the asset underlying the facility. Second triggers on most contingent capital deals, by contrast, typically reference some objectively defined loss event. The experience of such a loss will, of course, likely also affect the market value of the security underlying the facility. But *both* triggers must be activated for the facility to become available. That is, the underlying security of the facility must offer the firm better terms than those available in the market, *and* the firm must experience losses arising from risks specified in the agreement.

To mitigate moral hazard, the second trigger of a contingent capital facility is sometimes tied to a variable beyond the firm's influence. A firm using contingent capital as a source of postloss finance, for example, may be specifically concerned with underinvestment problems that are correlated with negative earnings surprises. Defining the second trigger as a negative earnings surprise for that particular firm, however, would make little sense; that could exacerbate moral hazard problems rather than reduce them. An alternative might be to define the second trigger in terms of average industry earnings, thus making the facility available to the firm in the event of adverse earnings shocks correlated across firms in the industry without giving the firm any inappropriate incentives to manage its own earnings.

In other cases we will review, the second trigger is a firm-specific loss that may well be under at least partial control of the option purchaser. But in these cases, the attachment point is so far into the catastrophic layer—

and the probability of attachment is so low—that moral hazard is unlikely to be a problem.

Note that we will discuss multiple triggers in more detail again in Chapter 25 when we explore multitrigger (re)insurance contracts.

Type of Facility

Contingent capital may convey to its holder the right either to issue new financial capital (i.e., to sell a newly issued security) or to purchase a newly issued security. The former is a type of put on paid-in capital, whereas the latter represents a call.

Perhaps the most obvious example of contingent capital is a warrant. The holder of a warrant has the right but not the obligation to purchase a residual claim from the issuing firm—usually common stock—on or before a certain date at a prespecified price. Warrants can thus be viewed as contingent stock purchase agreements. Convertible debt and preferred, which contain what amount to embedded warrants, can also be viewed as forms of contingent capital, as can many executive or employee compensation options.

Because the exercise decision for warrants and convertibles rests with the investor and not with the issuing company, such securities function less as a (downside) risk management vehicle than as a cost-effective alternative for raising equity when growth opportunities emerge.[5] In this chapter, we limit our focus to contingent capital facilities in which the exercise decision is under the control of the firm (i.e., put structures).

Option Writer(s)

All contingent capital deals are essentially contingent private placements. Normally one or perhaps two firms serve as the lead option writer(s) and would-be purchaser(s) of securities that can be issued through the structures. In many cases, these firms may lead a syndicate to share in the ultimate responsibility, risk, and return of the program. By keeping participation in these structures concentrated and under the supervision of a lead, adverse selection costs arising from asymmetric information should be much lower than in a traditional securities issue for the reasons set forth in Chapter 4.

As long as the facility remains unused, the option writer(s) will collect a periodic commitment fee (i.e., premium), just like a traditional insurance contract. But unlike insurance, if the facility is exercised and the counterparty must make a payment to the owner of the facility, this is not simply cash out the door. The option writer does get a security in return for that cash payment. Accordingly, providers of contingent capital must be comfortable with the prospect of being potential long-term investors in the company that acquires contingent capital protection.

(RE)INSURANCE APPLICATIONS OF CONTINGENT CAPITAL

As noted in Appendix B, insurance companies define their regulatory capital as "surplus," comprised largely of paid-in share capital. Most primary carriers around the world are subject to regulations that specify minimums for their surplus levels or surplus-related ratios. And penalties for approaching these minimums can be quite severe, including mandatory business closure if an insurer's capital dips too low.

Contingent capital structures gained initial popularity in the insurance community in the 1990s mainly as a means of protecting capital from so-called tail events, such as extraordinarily large property losses (in excess of reinsurance) arising from catastrophic risks like tropical cyclones and earthquakes. Today, contingent capital in the insurance industry takes some of the same forms as these early surplus protection structures, and the motives still remain primarily capital preservation.

We saw in Chapter 13 how financial capital can be viewed as a type of excess of loss insurance or reinsurance. Not surprisingly, many of the uses of contingent capital in the insurance and reinsurance industries involve the use of such facilities as substitutes for outright reinsurance or retrocession. When contingent capital is functioning as a substitute for reinsurance, it is often referred to by insurance companies and rating agencies as *soft capital*. In contrast to paid-in equity capital that is "money in the bank," soft capital subjects the insurance company to the credit and performance risks of one or more third-party providers of capital. Apart from this performance risk, however, soft capital is still capital. In the language of Part One, soft capital is just risk capital by another name. Some of the structures reviewed in this section are preloss funded risk capital, whereas others are postloss funded.

Parent Guarantees as Soft Capital

Recall the example of Enterprise, Inc., in Chapter 6 in which we showed the equivalence of the transfer of credit risk to third parties (e.g., insurance companies) to the transfer of credit risk to bond or equity holders in the firm. One of the specific scenarios we explored was the provision of credit risk protection by *inside* equity holders in the form of a parent guaranty.

We saw again in Chapter 13 how different types of risk capital and risk transfer collectively define an excess of loss insurance program for the credit risky assets owned by the firm.

Given all this earlier discussion, readers won't be at all surprised to learn that parent guarantees *really are* a popular substitute for credit reinsurance, especially for monoline insurers. For several decades, explicit guarantees of insurance liabilities by the parent companies of monolines have played an important part in the total capital structure of those monoline insurance companies.

Bank Lines and Letters of Credit as Reinsurance "Soft Capital"

Paid-in capital that constitutes the surplus of an insurance company is considered by the rating agencies as "money in the bank" because securities have been issued in return for cash. A common type of contingent capital used by insurance companies for many years is known as a *soft capital* facility, which is contingent capital by another name. Unlike paid-in capital, soft capital subjects the insurance company to the credit and performance risks of one or more third-party providers of capital.

For many years, one of the most common sources of soft capital for insurance companies has been banks providing their insurance company customers with dedicated lines or letters or credit (LOCs). As we saw in Chapter 10, typical LOCs are structured to look very similar to traditional reinsurance. Specifically, when the insurance company experiences losses that exceed a certain lower attachment point, the bank provides a line or LOC to cover a certain layer of losses above that attachment point. Such soft capital facilities have historically been limited to catastrophic loss layers and scenarios (Mischel et al., 2004).

Contingent Surplus Notes

A *surplus note* is a type of debt instrument (or preferred stock) issued by an insurance company that is treated as capital for regulatory purposes. Beginning in the 1990s, several insurance companies issued *event-contingent surplus notes*. These products represent double-trigger put options on surplus notes in which the second trigger is an adverse insurance event potentially significant enough to jeopardize the regulatory minimum surplus of the insurer. Upon occurrence of such a loss, contingent surplus notes could be immediately issued to raise regulatory capital literally overnight.

Hannover Re, Nationwide, and Arkwright all issued contingent surplus notes in the 1990s.[6] In those structures, the proceeds from the sale of the contingent notes to investors were used to finance the purchase of high-quality, marketable securities such as Treasuries or repurchase agreements (repos). These securities were held in a special purpose trust. The insurance company sponsoring the contingent surplus note issue, in turn, purchased a double-trigger put option from the trust that enabled the insurer to issue surplus notes virtually immediately after the occurrence of a catastrophic underwriting loss. The premium paid by the insurer to the trust for the put option was also deposited in the collateral account.

As long as the option went unexercised, investors in the bonds earned the interest rate on the collateral assets (e.g., the Treasury rate) *plus* the commitment fee. If the triggering event occurred, the insurer could then issue surplus notes to the trust. The trust financed the purchase of those surplus notes by liquidating the collateral. From that point forward, the principal and interest (P&I) paid to investors in the structures consisted solely of the P&I payable by the insurer on the newly issued surplus notes now held in trust for investors in the program. Exhibit 15.1 illustrates the basic structure.

Although originally motivated almost solely by the need to remain compliant with regulatory capital requirements following a potentially catastrophic loss, contingent surplus notes have made a resurgence more recently. And this time, the motives for their use are quite different. Now, a primary use of contingent surplus notes is as a form of hybrid equity financing for cooperative or mutualized insurers. We will explore this issue in more detail in Chapter 23 when we discuss mutuals.

Committed Capital Facilities

Another recent variation on the old contingent surplus note theme is the *committed capital facility* (not to be confused with Swiss Re's "Committed Long-Term Capital Solutions" discussed later in this section). A committed capital facility works just like a contingent surplus note, although with less conditionality on the occurrence of specific events. Instead, a typical committed capital facility functions just like a *fully prefunded* reinsurance program.

Structurally, a SPE purchases high-quality marketable securities using the proceeds of bonds issued to investors. The SPE then writes a put option to the insurance company "beneficiary" on its own securities—usually preferred stock—that entitles the insurance company beneficiary to issue securities to the SPE at any time. When the insurance beneficiary exercises its put option, the SPE liquidates the marketable securities it holds and uses the proceeds to purchase the new securities from the insurance company under the put option agreement. Investors in the securities issued by the

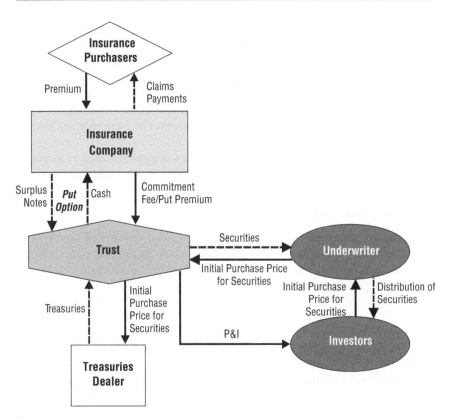

EXHIBIT 15.1 Contingent Surplus Notes

SPE receive the return on the high-quality collateral plus the put option premium until the insurance company exercises its puts. Once the puts have been exercised, investors then hold the new securities issued by the insurance company—either directly or *de facto* through their claims on the SPE that is now holding nothing else as collateral.

Consider, for example, the Anchorage Finance structure set up for the benefit of the monoline insurer Ambac Assurance Corp. in 2002. Anchorage Finance Master Trust was set up as a special purpose Delaware business trust sponsored by Merrill Lynch with four separate sub-trusts: Anchorage Finance Sub-Trusts I, II, III, and IV. Each sub-trust issued $100 million in *asset-backed capital commitment securities* (ABC securities). The proceeds of those issues were used to acquire primarily commercial paper, most of which was rated A1+ or better by S&P, which was then placed in trust with the Bank of New York.

Each sub-trust wrote a contingent equity put to Ambac allowing Ambac to issue preferred stock to the trusts. In the event the puts are exercised, the trusts liquidate the commercial paper and use the proceeds to finance the acquisition of the preferred stock. In this structure, the trusts then liquidate, and the preferred stock holdings are passed directly on to investors in the ABC securities. Prior to the put exercise, investors in ABC securities receive the CP rate plus the put premium income received by the sub-trusts.

Table 15.1 summarizes some of the other committed capital facilities put into place by monolines from late 2001 through the end of 2004.[7]

Loss Equity Puts and CatEPuts

A *loss equity put* enables a firm to issue a specified number of new equity shares at a prenegotiated fixed price if the issuer incurs a specific type of loss. In a typical loss equity put, the firm essentially pre-negotiates an equity private placement with a single counterparty (or syndicate) in the form of an agreement that allows the firm to issue and sell new stock directly to the counterparty in the event a second trigger is activated. The underlying may be preferred or common stock. If the stock is preferred, the dividend rate can be comparable to the rate paid on other preferred stock or it can be fixed.

Probably the earliest and still best-known example of a loss equity put is the *Catastrophe Equity Put* (*CatEPut*) for short. Designed by the Chicago-based insurance broker Aon working with Centre Re, CatEPuts have been issued mainly by reinsurance companies with catastrophic exposures seeking surplus protection on top of their existing reinsurance programs. The loss event that serves as the second trigger is usually highly correlated with changes in the issuer's stock price. If a property loss following an earthquake is the second trigger, for example, it makes sense for the loss level that activates the put option to be sufficiently large that a decline in the stock price can *also* be expected. This provision helps ensure that the option is providing access to equity capital on favorable terms *only* at a time when it is really needed, which reduces the premium the company must pay for the option (and the risk that is being assumed by the option writer).

The first CatEPut was placed in the fall of 1996 for RLI Corporation of Peoria, Illinois, a specialty property and casualty (P&C) insurer that sustained large losses following the Northridge earthquake in California. RLI sought additional balance sheet protection in its catastrophic excess of loss (XOL) layers for its P&C insurance lines. The second trigger in the RLI CatEPut thus was a large P&C loss that significantly exceeded its

TABLE 15.1 Committed Capital Facilities as Reinsurance

Facility Name	Insurance Company Beneficiary	Size of Facility	Initial Rating	Date of Initial Rating
Blue Water Trust I	RAM Reinsurance Co. Ltd.	$ 50mn	A+	12/16/2003
Dutch Harbor Finance I–IV	Ambac Assurance Corp.	$400mn	AA	12/4/2001
Grand Central Capital Trust I–VI	FGIC	$300mn	AA	7/15/2004
Market Street Custodial Trusts I–III	Radian Asset Assurance, Inc.	$150mn	A	9/12/2003
North Castle Custodial Trusts I–IV	MBIA Insurance Corp.	$200mn	AA	12/18/2002
North Castle Custodial Trusts V–VIII	MBIA Insurance Corp.	$200mn	AA	5/15/2003
Sutton Capital Trusts I–IV	Financial Security Assurance, Inc.	$200mn	AA	6/9/2003
Twin Reefs Pass-Through Trust	XL Financial Assurance Ltd.	$200mn	AA–	12/3/2004

existing reinsurance coverage and thus jeopardized the firm's surplus. By giving RLI the ability to issue up to $50 million in convertible preferred shares following such a loss, RLI was able to avoid running the risk of either a declining surplus or the cost of refinancing its surplus on unfavorable postloss terms.[8] RLI purchased a CatEPut again in 2000, also for $50 million.

A second CatEPut structure was placed by Aon in 1997 with Horace Mann Educators Corp. Exposed to losses from underwriting P&C, life, and retirement annuity lines, Horace Mann bought a $100 million CatEPut for similar reasons as RLI—namely, to ensure that it had secured a means by which its equity could be replenished following an extraordinarily large loss so as to avoid eroding its surplus. Horace Mann purchased a new CatEPut cover in 1999, also for $100 million.

Puttable Catastrophe Bonds

Most of the contingent capital facilities done to date have involved the combination of a put option on a traditional security with a risk-based second trigger. Now we consider a *single-trigger* deal in which the timing of the issue is not tied to a specific risk. In this example, the contingent capital facility is thus not a barrier option, but rather a plain-vanilla American put option that its issuer can exercise at its discretion (assuming it is in-the-money). Unlike the other structures considered, however, this put option was not written on a traditional security, but rather on a highly structured insurance-linked note.

In early 1998, Reliance National purchased a contingent debt option from investors entitling it to issue catastrophe (cat) bonds—that is, bonds whose interest and/or principal payments are reduced in the event of a specified disaster—at any time during the 1998–2000 period.[9] We'll discuss cat bonds in detail in Chapter 22.

The primary purpose of the Reliance III contingent capital facility was to give Reliance National access to additional reinsurance capacity for certain business lines in the event of a hardening of the reinsurance market. The strike price of the option was set slightly out-of-the-money so that, if and when they were exercised, the Reliance III cat bonds would be purchased by option holders at a slightly below-market price. The price Reliance paid to investors to secure their commitment to purchase the cat bonds was further reduced by the inclusion of a deductible in the bond underlying the option facility. In the event of a catastrophe, the issuer would thus bear the first portion of its catastrophic loss claims before any principal or interest on the bonds was diverted to cover those losses.

From 1997 through the end of 1998, Reliance National issued two early and pioneering cat bonds. The first, Reliance I, issued in early 1997 with the assistance of Sedgewick Lane Financial and INSTRAT (UK), was the first cat issue based on multiple business lines. Reliance II also involved multiple business line exposures. Not surprisingly, the cat bond underlying the Reliance III contingent debt facility imitated Reliance I and II in this regard. Specifically, 20 percent of potential note holders' principal in Reliance III would be at risk from losses on each of the following five Reliance underwriting lines: property losses in the United States above $6.5 billion, property losses in the rest of the world over $4.5 billion, Japanese or American aviation losses resulting in 250 or more fatalities, offshore marine losses over $500 million, and more than two failures from a list of 12 eligible "rocket launch" events.[10]

Committed Long-Term Capital Solutions (CLOCS)

One of the most successful forms of contingent capital products is Swiss Re's Committed Long-Term Capital Solutions (CLOCS). CLOCS can be structured as contingent debt (usually junior subordinated) or equity (usually preferred). CLOCS purchases by insurance companies have been motivated by reasons similar to CatEPuts and contingent surplus notes—namely, the protection of the insurance company's capital following an unusually large underwriting loss.

MBIA Insurance Corporation   As we discussed in Chapter 10, the main risk management concern for bond issuers and investors who purchase credit wraps from the likes of AAA/Aaa-rated U.S. monoline insurer MBIA Insurance Corporation (MBIA) is not that their insurer will become insolvent and thus be unable to stand behind the bonds in the event of a default. The major risk is instead that the insurer might lose its AAA/Aaa rating. The monoline business is essentially driven by companies that want to "rent" an AAA/Aaa rating for a bond issue and that go to the monolines to do it. Because of the importance of ratings, the monolines work closely with rating agencies before providing wraps to help ensure that the insurance they supply has a sufficiently low expected loss that it will not jeopardize the wrapper's rating.

Indeed, the monoline wrapping business is so dependent on an AAA/Aaa rating that many market observers believe that the loss of a single letter in the insurers' ratings would cause their business to dry up and force them into almost immediate insolvency. Several years ago, another large monoline insurer was rumored to be on the brink of a downgrade. The users of that firm's credit wraps expressed such concern that two of the insurer's leading investors apparently stepped in with new capital to ensure that a downgrade did not occur.

So, to guarantee access to additional capital on preloss terms after taking a major hit on its guarantee business, MBIA concluded a CLOCS transaction with Swiss Re, leading a syndicate of other (re)insurance companies, in December 2001. The Swiss Re CLOCS provides MBIA with US$150 million in coverage contingent on significant losses incurred by MBIA in its existing financial guarantee business. Upon exercise of the facility, Swiss Re purchases subordinated debt that converts to perpetual preferred stock over time. The assurance of the availability of this capital helps MBIA protect its capital base and maintain its guarantee underwriting capacity, as well as providing the insurer with a significant cushion against a rating downgrade.

Horace Mann   In September 2002, Swiss Re completed a CLOCS with Horace Mann, the insurance holding company we encountered earlier in this section as a two-time purchaser of CatEPuts. The three-year Swiss Re CLOCS deal replaced Horace Mann's CatEPut program and enabled the insurer to issue up to $75 million in cumulative convertible preferred shares following the occurrence of catastrophic insurance losses above a predefined trigger level. In lieu of issuing stock, the deal gave Horace Mann the right instead to enter into a 10 percent one-year quota share treaty (QST) with Swiss Re—a form of contingent cover, as we discuss in Chapter 26.

CORPORATE APPLICATIONS OF CONTINGENT CAPITAL

As we have now seen, most insurance users of contingent capital sought these solutions as a form of capital preservation, both to avoid any risk of a regulatory shortfall in their surpluses and to preserve underwriting capacity following a catastrophic loss. Corporate users of contingent capital—banks and non-financials alike—have also found contingent capital structures of significant interest. Capital preservation may well be a motivator in at least *some* of the deals done to date, but definitely is not the primary driver of all of them.

Committed Lines of Credit

Probably the oldest and most frequently used form of contingent capital is a *committed line of credit*.[11] In such an arrangement, a bank agrees to extend up to some maximum amount of credit to a corporate borrower for a specific period of time. The corporation can draw on the line at any time, provided the firm meets any predefined criteria specified by the lender as a condition for the credit line.[12] If and when the corporation makes a partial or full draw on the line, the draw becomes an actual loan that must be repaid at a predetermined interest rate. A committed credit line typically cannot be canceled or revoked by the bank.

The borrower may draw on its credit line partially or fully or some combination thereof (e.g., a partial draw followed by a repayment followed by another draw). Although a committed line usually does not include an explicit second trigger, a firm will typically draw on a line after the firm has experienced a significant depletion to its liquidity, often as a result of a major financial loss. As long as this event does not cause a material degradation in the financial condition of the borrower, however, the committed line will serve as an excellent source of liquidity. In return for this option to incur debt, the borrower owes a commitment fee to the bank on any undrawn balances.

Committed credit lines thus can easily be viewed as contingent risk finance. The earlier deals we explored were either contingent equity deals or contingent junior subordinated debt—in either case, closer to risk transfer than risk finance. Committed credit lines, however, serve almost no risk transfer purpose and are used entirely as a form of contingent *financing*. We have examined in detail the potential benefits of such a product in Chapters 3, 4, and 7 (e.g., mitigating liquidity related underinvestment problems, reducing adverse selection costs of postloss financing, controlling agency costs, etc.).

CLOCS Revisited

We encountered CLOCS in the previous section when we discussed insurance company uses of contingent capital. As with many of Swiss Re's innovative capital management products, the CLOCS product has also enjoyed success in the *non*insurance world. Two particularly noteworthy such deals are summarized next.

Royal Bank of Canada   In October 2000, Swiss Re negotiated a committed capital facility with the Royal Bank of Canada (RBC) in which Swiss Re would provide C$200 million (US$133 million) to RBC in exchange for preferred stock in RBC at the financing spread prevailing on October 27, 2000, the date on which the CLOCS deal was negotiated.[13]

Like most banks, RBC maintains a practice of holding excess reserves (relative to the minimum capital requirements prescribed by Basel) to avoid having to replenish reserves on unfavorable, postloss financing terms. Banks tend to fund their excess reserves when earnings and cash flows are unusually strong. One unfortunate side effect of this practice is that retained earnings are diverted into dedicated loan-loss reserves rather than being available to finance, say, future investment spending. So, although excess reserves can be prudent in light of the Basel requirements, they can be particularly costly for banks given the potential underinvestment problems that may result from having so much internal funding capacity dedicated to surplus reserves.

RBC used CLOCS as a way of both funding its excess reserves and maintaining a buffer of funds between its loan-loss reserves and its minimum capital requirement. Using CLOCS enabled RBC to avoid issuing new securities just to finance what was already an excess reserve requirement. At the same time, because the CLOCS facility is activated when the bank incurs exceptional credit losses (i.e., losses well beyond the first dollar and other losses in "lower layers" of reserves), the facility still gave the bank the comfort of having adequate reserves in the event of a major credit loss.[14]

The committed capital facility appears to have helped RBC in several ways. First, it gave RBC a lower-cost method of prefunding its loan-loss reserves. As RBC executive David McKay explained, "It costs the same to fund your reserves whether they're geared for the first amount of credit loss or the last amount of loss. . . . What is different is the probability of using the first loss amounts versus the last loss amounts. Keeping [paid-in] capital on the balance sheet for a last loss amount is not very efficient."[15]

The CLOCS structure also helped RBC improve its financial ratios. Swapping balance sheet reserves for contingent capital increases RBC's return on equity, for example. Although the facility, if drawn, would convert into Tier I regulatory capital under the Basel Accord, the contingent nature of the facility greatly reduced the cost to RBC of maintaining a surplus of capital over its reserves.

From Swiss Re's perspective, the risk of the deal includes the possibility that a shock to the Canadian economy could sharply increase losses on RBC's loans. Swiss Re undertook a due diligence and risk modeling effort to satisfy itself that the pricing was commensurate with the risk. Swiss Re did not syndicate or reinsure any of the RBC deal.

Compagnie Financière Michelin   Together with Société Générale (SocGen), Swiss Re also placed a CLOCS facility with Switzerland's Compagnie Financière Michelin, the financial and holding company for French tire maker Michelin. The deal has been heralded as one of the most innovative and successful corporate financing transactions of the past decade.

The Michelin deal is actually part bank debt and part CLOCS. In the bank portion of the deal, Michelin was given the right for up to five years (that is, from the inception of the deal in late 2000 through the end of 2005) to draw on a bank credit facility from SocGen. In return for this right, Michelin paid a commitment fee of 35 basis points per annum. Essentially a committed line of credit on long-term debt, the SocGen part of the deal did not involve a second trigger.

For the CLOCS piece of the deal, Swiss Re granted Michelin a five-year put option on subordinated debt maturing in 2012.[16] The CLOCS option contains a second trigger: The put can be exercised only when the combined average growth rate of gross domestic product (GDP) in the European and U.S. markets in which Michelin is active falls below 1.5 percent (from 2001 to 2003) or below 2 percent (from 2004 to 2005). This tying of the second trigger to an external macroeconomic variable works to limit any potential moral hazard problem. At the same time, the fact that Michelin's earnings are highly correlated with gross domestic product (GDP) growth in these markets helps to limit the company's basis risk. Largely because of the inclusion of the second trigger, the commitment fee Michelin paid Swiss Re was five basis points per annum below the commitment fee paid on the bank piece to SocGen.

Unlike the RBC deal, Swiss Re syndicated the Michelin deal by bringing its deal both to insurance markets like Credit Suisse's Winterthur and to major European banking markets. This increased the supply of capital available to Michelin by so much that the overall cost of the deal to the company became highly attractive. In fact, the deal probably would never have been placed in either the traditional bank syndication or Eurobond markets, in part because the longest maturity of most corporate debt is 10 years from the issue date as compared to the (possibly) 12-year tenor of the securities issued following an exercise of the facility by Michelin.

The Michelin CLOCS deal is a good illustration of how companies can use contingent capital as a source of financial "slack," or liquid capital held in reserve, to fund value-enhancing investment opportunities that might arise. If Michelin faces an expansion or acquisition opportunity during good times, it can likely afford to finance the expansion out of internal funds or by issuing new securities on favorable terms. But after a period of poor earnings performance, Michelin might lack the funds to carry out its strategic investment program. In this sense, CLOCS provide Michelin with a relatively efficient kind of insurance against this underinvestment problem—an insurance policy that is likely to be considerably less expensive than holding more capital on the balance sheet.

Trombone Convertibles and M&A-Contingent Financing

A *trombone convertible bond* is a type of contingent equity structure that evolved specifically in response to a need for contingent financing related to mergers and acquisitions (M&A) activity. In a trombone convertible, conversion is mandatory at one of two possible call dates and at two different prices. The second call date is contingent on the occurrence of some M&A-related event and is designed to give existing shareholders a discount on a successful acquisition bid, but *only* on a successful bid.

Trombones were originally associated with rights offerings in U.K. M&As. A classic problem faced by firms wishing to finance an acquisition with a rights issue is that the acquisition may be contingent on some specific event whose outcome is unknown at the time of the rights issue; approvals by U.S. and U.K. antitrust authorities are common such events, for example. If the condition is not ultimately satisfied and the acquisition falls through, the firm is left with far too much cash.

A trombone addresses this problem with its two call dates. The first call occurs at the time of the rights offering. The second call is contingent on the reference event occurring. If the condition is satisfied and the acquisition is a go, the second call gives investors full participation in the rights issue. If the event does not occur, the investors do not have to make a second payment but also receive fewer shares upon eventual conversion.

U.K. food and beverage firm Allied-Lyons planned a £739 million acquisition of Spanish drinks producer Pedro Domecq Group in 1994. Agreements for the acquisition were signed on March 24 of that year, and the rights issue circular was posted the next day. The closing date for the acceptance of the rights offering was April 15, but the EC (European Community) Commission had until April 28 to approve the merger.

Under the Allied-Lyons trombone, shareholders were offered a 2-for-13 rights issue of stock units convertible automatically into new shares in the merged firm. Investors had two payment obligations totaling £4.90 per share. The first installment was payable when the rights issue closed on April 15, 1994, but the second installment was contingent on approval by the EC Commission of the merger. If the approval occurred, all fully paid stock units under the rights agreement would convert to new shares the day after the approval. If the approval did not occur, no second payment was required and the partly paid rights were converted 2-for-1 into existing shares.[17]

The trombone convertible gave Allied-Lyons access to equity, but only if the firm truly needed to raise that equity as part of its planned acquisition. In addition, the structure of the trombone made it possible for existing shareholders to participate in the M&A at a discount. So successful was the Allied-Lyons trombone that these structures began showing up fairly often in M&A activity. Other firms that have used trombones for M&A-contingent equity include Tomkins, Grand Metropolitan Tiphook, Thorn, Dixon's, and British Aerospace.

Reverse Convertibles

A *reverse convertible* is a type of hybrid security that essentially builds a contingent equity facility into a bond. Extremely popular in Germany and Switzerland, reverse convertibles are equivalent to coupon-bearing corporate bonds plus a put option on the issuer's common stock. Unlike traditional convertibles, however, reverse convertibles typically involve European-style put options held by the issuer. That is, the issuer cannot convert the debt into equity shares prior to the bond's maturity. But at maturity, if the share price of the issuer's common stock is below the strike price specified in the option (usually set at-the-money when the bond is first issued), the bonds are redeemed with the issuer's shares rather than a fixed cash payment of the bond's stated principal.[18]

Coupons on reverse convertibles issued to date have been quite high to compensate investors for bearing significant downside equity risk. Some reverse convertibles pay a lower coupon by including a second trigger that limits risk for the investor. Unlike other contingent capital facilities explored thus far, the second trigger of most reverse convertibles is, like the first trigger, based on the stock price of the issuer, thus making the embedded equity put equivalent to a knock-in barrier put option.[19]

Consider, for example, a down-and-in reverse convertible issued by Company Beethoven with a face value of $10, an exercise price of $10 per share, and an instrike of $8 per share. If Beethoven's stock price is worth, say, $6, then investors receive shares worth $4 less than the par value of the bond. If Beethoven's stock price is, say, $9 at maturity, investors in the bond receive the par value of $10. But had Beethoven instead issued a normal reverse convertible, a $9 stock price would trigger a below-par redemption in shares worth $1 less than par. Because the down-and-in reverse convertible allows for redemption at par below the at-the-money strike, the coupon paid on the down-and-in reverse is lower.

Note that reverse convertibles are contingent capital in the sense that they enable a firm to alter its capital *structure*. But, unlike the other kinds of contingent capital discussed so far, reverse convertibles do not involve a specific risk trigger (other than the stock price), nor do they enable firms to raise *new* capital. In that sense, reverse convertibles are similar to any securities with embedded options for the issuer to exchange one type of capital for another. Other examples include capped common stock such as preferred equity redemption cumulative stock (PERCS) and dividend enhance convertible stock (DECS), convertible TruPS, and other convertible structures reviewed in Chapter 14.

SYNTHETIC CONTINGENT CAPITAL

In many cases, plain-vanilla equity derivatives can be constructed to function as synthetic contingent capital structures. That virtually all contingent capital deals we have examined can be viewed as types of option contracts is clear confirmation that derivatives themselves can be used as a source of contingent capital *in principle*. Actual examples of firms using plain-vanilla derivatives for the explicit purpose of synthesizing risk finance, however, are more limited. One recent example will show how the process can work.

Biotechnology firm Cephalon, Inc., adopted a do-it-yourself contingent capital program in the spring of 1997. The contingent capital facility involved the purchase by Cephalon of European-style call options on its own stock with a capped upside. The company's motive was to create a *cash* insurance policy that would generate a major cash inflow in the event that the Food and Drug Administration (FDA) approved Cephalon's flagship new drug, Myotrophin.[20]

In August 1992, Cephalon raised $38.7 million from Cephalon Clinical Partners LP (CCP), a research and development limited partnership, to fund the development of Myotrophin. CCP owned the exclusive license for the drug but granted Cephalon an interim license for about two years. For this interim sales and distribution right, Cephalon agreed to make a $16 million cash payment to CCP when and if the FDA approved the drug.

In addition, FDA approval of the drug would give Cephalon the right to buy back the drug from CCP for a cash purchase price of $40 million plus the $16 million fixed approval payment. Cephalon would also owe royalties to CCP for 11 years after the two-year interim licensing period. Alternatively, Cephalon was entitled to tendering for CCP shares either in cash or in Cephalon stock. The company estimated that would cost about $125 million, plus another $20 million or so to develop the drug.

Mainly for accounting reasons, Cephalon preferred the idea of the share tender. Management was confident that it could raise $80 million to $100 million externally but that it needed another mechanism of cash generation for the rest. The option program was the solution.

Working with SBC Warburg, Cephalon thus designed a program in which it would purchase call options on 2.5 million shares of Cephalon stock from SBC Warburg for a price of 490,000 Cephalon shares. The options were European-style and Asian, settling to the average price of Cephalon stock observed on the 20 trading days prior to the October 31, 1997, option maturity. If in-the-money, the options enabled Cephalon to settle the options in cash or as a cash-for-stock purchase. The calls were struck at $21.50 per share and capped at $39.50 per share.

So, if the FDA approved Myotrophin, Cephalon—assuming a major stock price rally—expected to cash out on its option position to the tune of about $45 million. In management's eyes, this would cover the anticipated funding shortfall and provide Cephalon with enough cash to buy back the drug from CCP and develop it.

One can see various economic motives for this deal from Part One interlaced into this transaction. Concern that access to external funds would be limited was clearly predicated on some notion of deadweight costs of external finance, such as adverse selection or other asymmetric information costs. Similarly, the underlying fear of management was an underinvestment-type problem in which the firm might have to forgo buying back and/or developing a new drug because of short-term cash funding constraints. In this sense, the contingent capital solution with SBC Warburg was indeed a creative source of postloss financing.

As it turned out, the FDA did not approve Myotrophin, and the options purchased by the firm expired worthless. Nevertheless, the program had all the hallmarks of a well-designed value-adding contingent capital deal on an *ex ante* basis.

More of these sorts of synthetic contingent capital structures are likely to be in the pipeline. Stay tuned.

CHAPTER 16

Securitization

In Chapters 14 and 15, we looked at structured forms of corporate securities that were specifically tailored forms of integrated financing and risk management. The risks that such structures can be and have been used to transfer include both financial and insurance risks.

In this and the next several chapters, we turn to consider more specifically the use of structured finance for the integration of corporate finance and the disposition of *credit* risk. The products we consider in Chapters 16 to 18 (and, depending on whom you ask, in Chapter 19 as well) define what is known as the *global structured credit market*. Although all the structuring methods used to manage credit risk explored in these chapters also work with other forms of risk, we focus on situations in which the only assets of the issuing firm are credit-sensitive assets (e.g., a bond portfolio).

We saw in Chapter 13 that a firm's corporate securities can be viewed as a type of asset insurance program. If the firm's only major risk exposure on its assets is credit risk, the securities issued by the firm represent a layered *credit* insurance program. We now take a step further and suppose the firm does not issue financial capital claims based on its assets directly, but rather simply sells the assets. (Remember that one way to transfer the credit risk of a credit-sensitive asset to another party is to transfer the asset itself to another party.) The purchaser of those assets acts as the single credit insurer for the firm. That asset purchaser then essentially *reinsures* the credit-sensitive assets by issuing securities of its own.

The process by which a firm sells credit-sensitive assets to a third party that in turn issues securities whose cash flows are backed by the original assets as collateral is known as the *securitization* of credit-sensitive assets. Securitization thus has both a *financing* and a *risk transfer* impact on the original firm: The sale of the asset for cash usually results in a net cash inflow, while at the same time transferring the credit risk of the asset from its original owner to the purchaser (which then transfers the risk again to the holders of the new securities collateralized by the asset). We generally refer to a security issued in a securitization as a *securitized product* or an *asset-backed security* (ABS).

This chapter also represents a departure from the previous two chapters in an institutional sense. Whereas structured corporate securities and contingent capital required minimal structuring apart from the design of the securities, the structuring process itself becomes much more important when we consider securitization and securitization-like structures. This chapter thus also serves as an important illustration of the mechanics of the structuring process applied to an asset divestiture. Many of the institutional issues we consider in this chapter—including the roles of various institutions and questions about accounting and legal consolidation—will also be relevant in later discussions of noncredit structured financing arrangements. Despite the importance of these institutional considerations, however, we remind readers that this is not a how-to handbook on securitization. Those exist, and readers interested in that level of detail about securitization should refer to those other sources—for example, Davidson et al. (2003).

Following our discussion of the securitization process, we turn to describe several specific early securitized products that define the structured credit market. We save our discussion of the most recent generation of credit-sensitive securitized products—collateralized debt obligations—for Chapters 17, 18, and 19.

SECURITIZATION PROCESS

Securitization is the process by which an asset (or asset pool) is sold for cash, which in turn is raised by the sale of securities whose cash flows are collateralized by the principal and interest (P&I) income on the original asset pool. As noted, we consider in this section only securitization that is motivated primarily by the institutional desire to combine a financing method with credit risk management.

Participants in a Securitization

A securitization often involves numerous parties working together to make various parts of the deal fit together as a whole. Not all types of participants are involved in every securitization; the exact nature of the involved institutions depends on the specific deal. We nevertheless review all the major participants in a securitization in the following sections. Exhibit 16.1

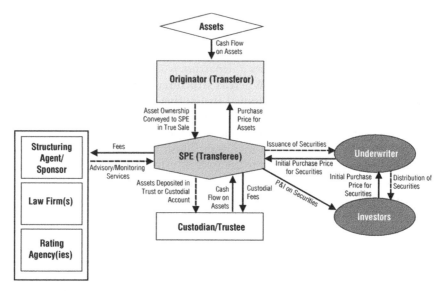

EXHIBIT 16.1   Basic Securitization Structure

provides a graphical illustration of the securitization process with all possible parties involved.

Sponsor   The *sponsor* of a securitization program is the institution that initiates the securitization process. The sponsor is the institution that basically first suggests the idea of securitization and then begins to set the wheels in motion.

When a bank is the originator and is seeking to securitize all or part of a loan portfolio, the bank is also usually the sponsor. But when a nonfinancial corporation is the originator and considers securitizing assets like trade receivables, we often find that a financial institution advising the firm (e.g., its primary relationship banker) actually initiates the securitization process.

A sponsor of a securitization may or may not be the owner of the assets to be sold in the securitization. When a sponsor is separate and distinct from the asset owner, the sponsor rarely takes any kind of ownership role in the securitization process. The sponsor generally acts in that case solely as an adviser.

Originator/Transferor   The original asset owner is known as the *originator* or *transferor* in a securitization. This is the institution that desires to convert credit-sensitive assets into cash, thereby monetizing an asset (i.e., converting an asset into an immediate cash flow) and transferring the credit risk of that asset to other capital market participants. We saw in Chapter 10, for example, that a corporation can manage the credit risk of its trade receivables either by buying trade credit insurance or by factoring the problematic receivables. Now we consider a third possibility: the securitization of trade credit receivables, in which the originator is the corporation that will sell its receivables for cash and insulate itself from defaults by trade creditors.

Asset Purchaser/Transferee/Securitized Product Issuer   In the case of a bilateral asset sale or divestiture by the originator, the *asset purchaser* or *transferee* is the counterparty to the bilateral asset sale. Factoring, for example, is the bilateral sale of a problem trade receivable by the original corporate trade obligee to the factor, resulting in a transfer of cash from the factor to the original trade credit obligee and an assumption of all the risks and rewards of the trade credit receivable by the factor. The original obligee is the originator, and the factor is the transferee.

What sets apart a securitization from a bilateral asset sale is the issuance of securitized products by the transferee to finance the asset purchase and to further pass along some or all of the risks of the assets being acquired. In almost all securitizations, this requires the insertion of a company or trust in between the originator and the end purchasers of the securitized products whose purpose is to facilitate the securitization.

In some securitizations, an existing firm may serve as the intermediary. Probably the best examples are Fannie Mae and Freddie Mac in the mortgage market; these institutions buy mortgages from originating banks and then issue mortgage-backed securities whose cash flows are backed by original mortgage pools. Given the focus of this book on corporations, however, we have virtually no occasion to look at mortgage securitization markets.

In most securitizations, a brand-new entity is usually set up for the sole business purpose of intermediating the securitization process. We refer to this intermediary as a *special purpose entity* (SPE) or *special purpose vehicle* (SPV). You may recall that we already encountered an SPE in the Hollywood Funding example of Chapter 11.

The mechanics of the issuance of securitized products differ a bit depending on whether the SPE is set up as a trust or as a corporation. Exhibits 16.2 and 16.3 compare the two different situations. If the SPE is a corporation (Exhibit 16.2), the originator sells the assets to the SPE for cash and the SPE issues the securitized products as claims on the SPE itself (i.e., on the assets of the SPE).

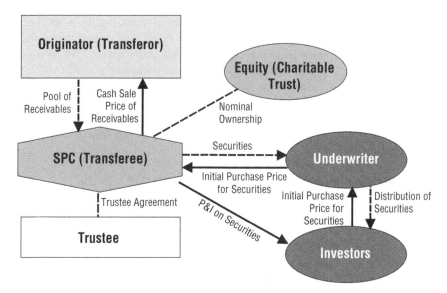

EXHIBIT 16.2   Securitization Structure with Corporate SPE

In the past, the equity of a corporate SPE was often defined to be a relatively small portion of the SPE's assets. In some cases, the equity was defined to have a fixed value so that the equity holders did not really bear any of the traditional residual risks. In this situation, the equity was often retained by the originator and then donated to a charitable trust. The purpose was to ensure the independence of the SPE from the originator for purposes of achieving "true sale" treatment for the assets and avoiding the need to consolidate the SPE on the accounting statements of the originator. This has changed with the advent of FIN46R, which is discussed briefly later in this chapter and in detail by Forrester and Neuhausen in Chapter 30.

The mechanics of the asset conveyance and securities issue work a little differently when the SPE is a trust, and the mechanics can vary depending on the type of trust used, the type of originator, and the reasons for the securitization. An example is shown in Exhibit 16.3. In the example, the structure contains two distinct SPEs. SPE 1 is organized as a *master trust* or special purpose company (SPC) and purchases the assets or receivables from the originator, financing this cash purchase with the issuance of securitized products. The original assets do not, however, serve as collateral for the newly issued securitized products, as in the case with the SPC that we saw in Exhibit 16.2. In this example, SPE 1 deposits the assets it purchased

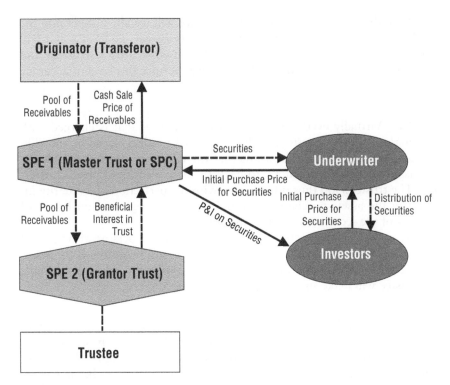

EXHIBIT 16.3 Securitization Structure with Trust SPE

into SPE 2, organized in this example as a *grantor trust*. In return for this deposit, the SPE 1 receives a *beneficial interest* in the grantor trust—a certificate that represents a claim on the grantor trust's assets. Because the assets of SPE 2 are those assets conveyed by the originator, the beneficial interest is equivalent to an undivided proportional claim on the original assets. These beneficial interests then serve as collateral to back the issuance of the securitized products issued by SPE 1. Alternatively, SPE 1 may simply sell the beneficial interests directly to investors for cash.

This could have been accomplished with a single SPE. The originator would have conveyed the assets to a trust in exchange for a beneficial interest in the trust and then sold those beneficial interests for cash. But that would have left the originator "in the loop." To ensure that the original assets can be accounted for as sold, remain bankruptcy-remote from the originator, and achieve the most favorable available tax status, the two SPEs are used instead.

Note that in future diagrams of deals, we will usually not get into the level of detail required to differentiate between trusts and SPCs and will generally use a diagram like Exhibit 16.2 even when a trust structure and multiple SPEs actually underlie the deal. We sacrifice this level of accuracy for clarity.

Trustee   Virtually every securitization has a *trustee* that is charged with looking out for the investors in the securitized product issued by the SPE. In most securitizations, this means that the trustee is also responsible for the assets pledged as collateral to back the new securitized product offering. The trustee's job thus often begins with the perfection of a security interest in the assets purchased by a SPE from the originator on behalf of holders of the securities issued by the SPE.

As a part of its function, the trustee also often acts as an impartial third party to monitor the assets underlying the securitization. If the assets must conform to certain minimum credit quality standards, for example, the trustee will make sure this is indeed the case.

Custodian and/or Servicer   For some assets, it is efficient to allow the cash flows on the underlying assets to be collected and disbursed by a *custodian*. Custodians were originally used mainly for the safekeeping of physical securities. In the past few decades, custodians have evolved to become more of a cash flow intermediary for owners of securities—for example, collecting dividends and interest payments on stocks and bonds when they are due and then redistributing those proceeds to the owner of those stocks and bonds. Custodians also often have very high quality information about the assets of which they have custody, thus making them natural providers of data and analytical software tools.

In many cases, the trustee and custodian are one and the same, but this need not be the case.

Like custodians, *servicers* are often included in a securitization deal if there was a role for them prior to the deal. A servicer is responsible for collections on receivables on behalf of an asset owner, and servicing rights are often considered to be a valuable asset in terms of both customer relationship management and financial profitability (e.g., earning interest on the float). Especially if the originator or an affiliate of the originator is the servicer, it is often the case that the servicing agreements will continue as before after the originator conveys the assets. Instead of distributing the funds to the originator, the servicer will now distribute them to the trustee or custodian connected to the SPE.

Structuring Agent   A *structuring agent* functions as a sort of general contractor for the securitization process. The agent is engaged to provide advisory services on how the assets acquired by the transferee from the originator are repackaged into new securities. The design of the securitized products (including terms like maturity, depth of subordination, target credit rating, etc.) are mainly the responsibility of the structuring agent. These design considerations are determined based largely on perceived investor demand (i.e., who will want to buy the securities, what will be the desired credit rating, what is the right size, etc.).

The structuring agent is also responsible for modeling the interest and principal cash flow waterfalls of the deal and determining what, if any, risk management activities need to be undertaken as a part of the structure. The amount and types of credit enhancements required for certain tranches of securities, for example, would be determined by the structuring agent.

The structuring agent generally works closely with the sponsor of the program, and the two are often one and the same.

Underwriter   At least one *underwriter* is responsible for marketing and distributing the securities that have been issued by the transferee. As in any underwriting, the underwriter of a structured product offering may use a best efforts contract or a fixed commitment contract to place the newly issued securitized products.

Rating Agencies   Many structured products are rated by one or more of the major rating agencies—Standard & Poor's (S&P), Moody's, and Fitch. In addition, several other more stylized rating agency boutiques may also be engaged to render their external assessments of the credit quality of the securities issued by the transferee.

Rating agencies typically offer both *issue* and *issuer* credit ratings. Many structured financial transactions involve issue ratings, at least on the senior classes of securities issued by the SPE. In certain markets, ratings are gospel; without a good one, an issue may well be doomed to fail. Certain types of insurance products also may rely heavily on external ratings. A monoline insurer, for example, is unlikely to provide a financial guarantee to an unrated entity.

Several rating agencies offer what some people call *shadow ratings* or *nonpublished ratings*. Mechanically, a rating agency is engaged on a consulting basis to indicate what the customer needs to do in order to obtain an official published rating. These nonpublished ratings are often sufficient if the objective is to satisfy an insider or an insurance company. But if the demand for a securitized product is deemed to be based on a true rating, then a published issue rating of the securitized product will almost certainly be required.

Law Firms Do not underestimate the importance of good legal counsel in the structuring process. A good outside counsel should exhibit several characteristics to be useful in the structuring process:

- Experienced in securitization and structuring.
- Well-versed in any specific international jurisdictions that the structure might involve.
- Credible as a securitization expert to other involved parties (especially rating agencies and regulators).
- Proactively willing to help customers avoid certain pitfalls of structuring, especially with regard to inappropriate accounting, disclosure, and regulatory compliance policies.

The sound opinion of outside counsel is essential to ensure that a securitization structure is properly constructed—for example, that the assets conveyed are bankruptcy remote from the originator, that the tax treatment of the SPE's income is clear, that the proper legal form and jurisdiction/domicile for the SPE are chosen, that no parties involved in the structure have an unresolved or undisclosed conflict of interest, that the documentation is watertight, and that the structure makes economic sense.

In addition, as the last point indicates, a good securitization law firm should not be bashful in warning clients about what it considers to be inappropriate structures (e.g., structures reverse engineered to get a specific accounting result, structures designed entirely for tax purposes with no other commercial purpose, etc.).

Because of the number of high-level professionals involved in a securitization, total fees paid to advisers and professionals can escalate rapidly, and looking for areas to cut costs is tempting and, in many cases, prudent. *But do not skimp on your legal counsel.* Especially in today's market, getting the best legal advice that money can buy is the right way to approach the legal end of a securitization.

Regulatory Agencies Some types of securitization structure may attract the attention of local, state, national, or international regulators either directly or indirectly. If a regulated institution (e.g., a bank or an insurance company) is the originator, for example, regulators may take an active role in the securitization to ensure that the securitization is compliant with extant laws and regulations.

Regulatory agency involvement may also arise through the securitized product issuance. In the United States, securities underwriting is regulated by the Securities and Exchange Commission (SEC). Because most securitized products are securities, the SEC may have some involvement. The exact nature of the SEC's role depends on the exact type of security issued, whether it is a so-called exempt security, and the like.

External Risk Transfer and Risk Finance Counterparties Securitization structures not only involve the reapportionment of the credit risk of the underlying assets into tranches that back new securities, but securitization may itself create new risks. To the extent the structuring agent and/or sponsor decides that external risk finance and/or risk transfer is required as a part of the securitization structure, firms that act as counterparties to external risk transfer and risk finance will play a role in the securitization.

The issue of risk management in a securitization structure is sufficiently important that we discuss it separately in several subsections later in this chapter.

Consolidation

One of the biggest challenges in structuring a securitization is ensuring that the originator avoids having to consolidate the assets it has sold back up onto its balance sheet, thus negating the fundamental purpose of the transaction as asset divestiture for the dual purposes of raising funds and transferring credit risk. In Chapter 30, Forrester and Neuhausen survey the state of current accounting and disclosure as concerns the issue of consolidation.

Methods of Consolidation In order to realize the benefits of securitization, the assets being used to collateralize the issuance of ABSs must *truly be sold*; this is known as "true sale" for legal purposes. In addition, a securitization usually needs to satisfy *accounting for true sale* treatment, which is also associated with the need for the SPE transferee to be a nonconsolidated independent entity relative to the sponsor and/or originator.

Consolidation principles are relevant when one firm has some voting ownership interest and possibly control of another legally separate entity. The issue is how to reflect the financial performance and condition of the affiliate on the investor's financial statements. *Full consolidation* applies when the investor has more than 50 percent voting interest in a subsidiary. In this case, all components of the subsidiary's assets, liabilities, revenues, expenses, and cash flows are combined onto the investor's financial statements in full detail.

Line-by-line consolidation, by contrast, applies when the investor has "significant interest" in an affiliate (20 to 50 percent voting interests) but not "control." In this case, the *equity method* is used. The investor's share of earnings from the investment in the affiliate is reported as a single amount in the investor's income statement. The original investment is recorded as a cost and is adjusted periodically to reflect the share of the affiliate's earnings. Components of the affiliate's financial statements are not reflected on the financial statements of the investor.

Early Consolidation Guidelines   Traditional generally accepted accounting principles (GAAP) guidance holds that the owner of a controlling interest in a SPE should consolidate the SPE on its financials. About 15 years ago, the Emerging Issues Task Force (EITF) of the Financial Accounting Standards Board (FASB) decided that some more specific guidance was required for SPEs whose business purposes were limited. In particular, special guidance was deemed necessary for relationships between lessees and lessors when the SPE is the lessor. The EITF guidance suggested that a lessee should consolidate a SPE lessor *unless*:

- The SPE lessor was owned by an entity other than the SPE, where "ownership" in this context meant a "substantial" residual equity investment at risk. Substantial residual risk and reward and substantial equity investment were widely interpreted to mean residual equity of at least 3 percent of the SPE's assets.
- The SPE lessor had significant transactions with parties other than the lessee.
- The substantive residual risks and rewards of the SPE's assets rested with an entity other than the SPE lessee.

Application of the EITF criteria for leases was criticized, however, when applied to all securitizations. First, 3 percent was deemed too small as a third-party investment. Second, it was too easy to structure around consolidation. Finally, the EITF guidance did not make it clear how transactions between the sponsor and the SPE affected the consolidation outcome, even when those transactions altered the risks to the sponsor.

To clarify some of the ambiguities under the EITF leasing guidance, the FASB adopted new guidance in 2000 in FAS140, *Accounting for Transfers and Servicing of Financial Assets and Extinguishments of Liabilities*. The FAS140 criteria set forth four guiding principles for when an asset conveyance could receive accounting for true sale treatment and when the SPE did not have to be consolidated on the originator's balance sheet:

1. The SPE is bankruptcy remote and the assets in the SPE are sufficiently isolated from the originator to survive Chapter 7 or 11 bankruptcy.
2. Permissible activities of the SPE must be significantly limited, must be specified at deal inception/incorporation of the vehicle, and can be changed only with approval of a majority of interest holders other than the originator or its affiliates or agents.
3. The originator must surrender "effective control" over the assets.
4. The SPE must have the right to pledge/resell/exchange the assets acquired from the originator—the purchaser of the assets must have a "perfected interest" in the acquired assets.

FAS140 also defined what is known as a *qualified SPE* (QSPE) that need not be consolidated by the originator. In order to receive QSPE status, the following conditions had to hold:

- The SPE must be "demonstrably distinct" from the originator and any affiliates of the originator.
- The SPE may hold only passive financial assets and passive derivatives used for hedging.
- Sale or disposition of assets by the QSPE must be prescribed in deal documents and may never be discretionary.

The FAS140 criteria added a lot of clarity to the consolidation debate, but they by no means eliminated all ambiguities. A number of gray areas remained—for example, regarding the question of what constituted "effective control" over the assets by the originator. Consider some examples of agreements that pushed this criterion in FAS140 to the limits of interpretation: agreements for the originator to repurchase the assets; agreements giving the originator the ability to cause the return of the assets; agreements by the originator to compensate the new asset owner for any losses and to participate completely in any upside (i.e., to retain a substantive economic interest in the assets in question).

Enron's FAS140 Transactions Of the many transactions in which Enron engaged that have created controversy in the world of structured finance, a whole group of deals specifically fell into the aforementioned gray areas of FAS140—so much so that FASB has since adopted additional guidance on consolidation following the collapse of Enron.

In a typical FAS140 transaction, Enron's basic objective was to camouflage term debt as payment received for the sale of an asset in a securitization. Enron accounted for these cash flows in operating cash flows as gains on sale rather than as debt. Yet, closer scrutiny of the structures reveals that many of them appeared to fail the FAS140 criteria: Enron never really relinquished full control and its economic interest in the assets being "sold."

Consider, for example, the securitization depicted in Exhibit 16.4, known collectively as the McGarret A transaction. In this deal, Enron Energy Services (EES), a wholly owned subsidiary of Enron, had shares and warrants in a firm called The New Power Company (TNPC). Although in-the-money, these shares and warrants were restricted and could not be cashed in with the issuer for some time. So, Enron engaged in a so-called securitization to try to monetize these warrants—that is, to convert their current intrinsic value to realized cash.

Specifically, EES sold a part of its TNPC warrant position to a limited liability company (LLC) called McGarret I in return for $20 million in cash and a Class A interest in McGarret I. The Class A interest had full voting

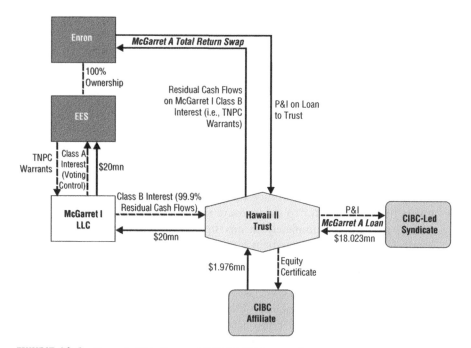

EXHIBIT 16.4 Enron's "McGarret A" FAS140 Transaction

control over the LLC but was entitled to only 0.1 percent of the residual cash flows of the entity. McGarret I raised the $20 million it needed to finance the purchase of TNPC warrants by issuing a Class B interest to an SPE called Hawaii II Trust for $20 million. The Class B interest had no voting rights but received a distribution of 99.9 percent of the residual cash flows on the assets held by McGarret I—namely, the TNPC warrants. The Hawaii II Trust in turn raised the $20 million through a $18.023 million loan from a banking syndicate led by the Canadian Imperial Bank of Commerce (CIBC) and by the sale of an equity certificate to a CIBC affiliate for $1.976 million.

To complete the structure, Enron entered into a total return swap (TRS) with Hawaii II Trust. On the TRS, Enron paid the P&I due to the banking syndicate and CIBC on the loans to the Hawaii II Trust. In return, the Hawaii II Trust paid to Enron the residual cash flows on the McGarret I Class B interest.

The court-appointed examiner of Enron's bankruptcy, Neal Batson, concluded that, like other FAS140 transactions, this particular deal was inappropriately accounted for and disclosed. First, Batson was led to believe that CIBC's equity certificate was more debt than equity and was not actually equity at risk, thus failing the 3 percent test. Second, the TRS between Enron and Hawaii II Trust transformed the credit risk of the trust creditors into "pure Enron" credit risk; the performance of the TNPC warrants did not matter. Third, through the TRS, Enron retained a substantive economic stake in the assets being securitized. For all these reasons, Batson concluded that Hawaii II should have been consolidated on Enron's financials. This meant that the TNPC warrants were not really sold and that the $20 million booked as operating cash flow should have been accounted for as term debt.

FIN46R—The Anti-Enron Rule   Primarily as a result of Enron's alleged malfeasance in structured financing activities, much of which concerned SPEs that were never disclosed or consolidated but should have been, the FASB promulgated a new rule governing the consolidation of SPEs in January 2003 and revised the rule in December 2003. Known as FIN46R, the new rule is discussed in detail in Chapter 30 by Forrester and Neuhausen.

In brief, FIN46R defines certain types of SPEs as *variable interest entities* (VIEs) if the SPE is nonpassive and requires subordinated financial support for its activities above and beyond the equity issued by the entity. A *variable interest* (VI) in a VIE is defined as any contract that changes in value when the net asset value of the VIE changes and may include equity, subordinated debt, subordinated interests and compensation, credit protection and credit support instruments, derivatives, and the like. The holder of the VI that is exposed to the largest expected loss or gain is the *primary beneficiary* (PB) of the VIE and must consolidate the VIE on its financials. Again, Forrester and Neuhausen explore the role in much greater detail in their excellent Chapter 30.

Credit, Liquidity, and Interest Rate Risk Management

We noted earlier in this section that risk transfer counterparties are important participants in a securitization structure to help address credit, liquidity, and interest rate risks. All of these risks could, of course, be passed directly to investors in the ABSs issued by the SPE, just as we saw in Chapter 13. Unlike traditional corporate security issues, however, securitized products are often designed to investor demand. A large part of this is achieving a desired credit rating on the debt instruments issued by the SPE.

The management of risk is a sufficiently important part of the securitization and credit risk transfer process that we devote the next three main sections of this chapter to how these risks are typically managed in a securitization: credit enhancement, liquidity support, and interest rate and currency risk.

CREDIT ENHANCEMENT

An important part of the structuring process involves the management and distribution of credit risk on the underlying asset pool to end investors in the securitized products issued by the SPE. We already saw in Chapter 13 how subordination can be used to allocate credit risk across different layers of subordination, and this is as true for securities issued by a SPE as it is for securities issued by any other corporation. But sometimes this is not enough. Other credit enhancements in lieu of or in addition to subordination may be desired to ensure that the securities issued by the SPE satisfy investor demands, rating agency requirements, regulatory requirements, and the like. These credit enhancements may either be *internal* or *external*.

The particular mixture of internal credit enhancements chosen for a given securitization is essentially up to the structuring agent. A wide range of variables may affect the choice and amount of different types of credit enhancements used, including the cost of different credit enhancements, credit exposure limits to credit support providers, reputation and clientele effects with credit support providers, and the like. Let's examine the spectrum of possibilities that the structuring agent has.

Internal Credit Enhancement (C/E)

Internal credit enhancements are credit enhancements that are provided by a participant inside the structure, such as the original asset owner and transferor or the investors in the securities issued by the SPE. Choosing multiple levels of subordination, as discussed, is an internal credit enhancement; that is, it redistributes the total credit risk of the underlying asset pool across investors in securitized products, but does not change the total amount of credit risk borne by investors in the securitized products in aggregate.

Apart from subordination, the most common form of internal C/E is known as *overcollateralization* (O/C). A structure is overcollateralized when the assets exceed the fixed liabilities or debt. Overcollateralization thus is a way of increasing the value of equity in the structure. In the context of Chapter 13, we know that additional equity is a credit enhancement for all the more senior liabilities issued by the SPE.

Direct Equity Issue Upon first thought, an obvious way to create O/C in a structure is for the SPE to issue debt with a smaller notional or par amount than the amount of collateral acquired to back those securities. That would, of course, create funding problems for the SPE. If the SPE has $100 in assets and issues only $80 in debt, the surplus $20 would indeed constitute O/C. But from where did the $20 come? If the assets are *worth* $100, they must have *cost* $100.

One possible answer is to issue $20 in equity to an investor. This would work, of course, but it is impractical in many structured financing situations. In a lot of structured finance and securitization deals, the appetite for the equity tranche is fairly limited.

Another possibility is to issue the equity to an insider; we saw this in Chapter 13 when we looked at the parental guaranty. In the context of this chapter, the analogue would be to issue equity to the originator. The problem this creates is that it might violate the need for independence between the originator/transferor and the transferee. In the example, the originator would have 20 percent of the equity and be at risk for the first $20 in defaults on the asset pool. This would probably not qualify as a true sale for accounting and disclosure purposes, and the originator might well end up consolidating the assets it was attempting to sell right back up on its balance sheet.

Thankfully, issuing equity to the originator is not the only way to get O/C funded by the originator.

Holdback A very easy way to create O/C that is funded by the originator without creating consolidation, accounting, tax, and control problems is through a mechanism called *holdback*. Holdback is the difference between the price actually paid by the SPE to acquire assets from the originator and the true value of those assets. If the SPE pays a fair price to the originator, there is no holdback. But by deliberately purchasing the assets at a discount, O/C is created. In the earlier numerical example, the SPE might issue $80 of debt and $1 of equity and then spend the $81 on assets that have a true value of $100. This would create a $19 O/C as a credit enhancement for the debt tranche. But how did we arrive at the $19 amount we need as C/E?

Holdback in most structures is defined as a multiple of historical losses on the underlying collateral pool. The credit quality and rating on the collateral relative to the rating the structuring agent and sponsor want to see on the ABSs also are important considerations.

Cash Collateral Account   Another easy way to get O/C funded by the originator is for the originator to deposit cash money in a *cash collateral account* (CCA). A CCA serves as a cash reserve against losses and provides a credit enhancement to all the securities issued by the SPE.

It may be very tempting for the originator to try to make the CCA contingent on the actual loss experience of the assets conveyed to the SPE. If the assets are sold to the SPE and never experience any defaults, the originator would ideally like its cash back rather than see the cash revert to the owners of the equity in the SPE. Unfortunately, this may not be possible. A CCA that depends on actual asset performance may create a dependence between the originator and the SPE that makes it impossible for the originator to avoid consolidation of the SPE. See Chapter 24, and check with your firm's accounting experts for a final answer on this one.

Note that holdback and an originator-funded CCA are essentially substitutes for one another. Both are a way of obtaining funds from the originator. True, a CCA might be funded by, say, equity investors—a sort of risk capital as discussed at the end of Chapter 13 and in Appendix C. But this is relatively uncommon. Generally, if a structure needs internal credit enhancement from investors, it will come through some mixture of the subordination design of the securitized product issue and what we call the excess spread, to which we now turn.

Excess Spread   The *gross excess spread* internal to a structure is the difference between interest earned on the collateral assets and interest paid on the debt liabilities of the SPE. The *net excess spread* is the gross excess spread minus senior fees and expenses.[1]

The excess spread is the cash flow equivalent of retained earnings for the structure. In a normal corporation, some or all of this might be paid out to equity holders as a dividend. In a securitization, the excess spread can be diverted to service interest (and possibly principal) payments on the debt in the event that the cash flows on the assets prove inadequate to service the debt.

Mechanically, excess spread can be diverted on a preloss or postloss basis (see Chapter 7). When being used for preloss finance, the excess spread is not paid out to equity holders until after it has reached some threshold amount. The excess spread in the early life of the structure, for example, may be diverted into a CCA until the CCA reaches some target level—say, 20 percent of total assets. Once the CCA has been funded to that target, equity holders may begin to receive a periodic distribution, unless the CCA falls below the 20 percent level, at which point the spread is diverted again. Or, if the structure is designed to be especially conservative, the excess spread will be diverted into a CCA throughout the life of the structure and released to equity holders only after the debt issued by the SPE matures.

Alternatively, the excess spread can be paid out as an equity dividend unless and until the underlying assets begin to default. At that time, the spread may be diverted to cover the losses. The only real difference is who earns the investment income on the invested spread. If it is paid out to equity holders and only diverted to debt when losses occur, equity holders enjoy the investment income on the early distributions. If the excess spread is diverted to fund a CCA in the early life of the structure, the investment income accrues to the structure and provides additional O/C.

The excess spread may also be used to fund *liquidity reserves*; we discuss those in the next section.

Example of Internal Credit Enhancement   Let's put all the pieces together and see how this works in practice. Suppose the originator is a bank wishing to securitize a $100 million loan portfolio with an interest rate of the London Interbank Offered Rate (LIBOR) plus 100 basis points per annum. Suppose the senior expenses of the SPE amount to 10 basis points per annum, and that the SPE issues two classes of securities—senior debt with a face value of $80 million and subordinated debt with a face value of $20 million. There is no equity, but the subordinated debt functions as equity. The coupon rate on the senior debt is LIBOR plus 50 basis points. The subordinated debt gets an interest rate equal to the realized excess spread.

In this structure, let's suppose there is no holdback but that the originator makes a one-time irrevocable contribution of cash to the SPE in the amount of $5 million. The proceeds are used by the trustee of the SPE to fund a cash collateral account—the $5 million is invested in marketable securities.

Internal credit enhancement is also obtained from subordinated debt holders through the excess spread. Without any interest payment defaults on the assets, the net excess spread (in millions of dollars) is

$$\$100(L + 100) - \$100(10) - \$80(L + 50) = 20(L + 250)$$

where L denotes LIBOR. If we ignore the LIBOR component, the total credit enhancement of the senior tranche of securities expressed as a percentage of the original collateral amount is then 27.5 percent: 20 percent from subordination (\$20mn/\$100mn), 5 percent from the CCA (\$5mn/\$100mn), and 2.5 percent from the excess spread (\$2.5mn/\$100mn).

External Credit Enhancement

External credit enhancements in a structure represent credit risk transfer from the SPE to another firm. We have essentially explored the possibilities already in Chapters 10 and 12. We review the possibilities here; it is worth a little repetition to see how the concepts from these chapters function inside a structured financing arrangement.

So that we don't need to get too bogged down with differences between principal and interest, let's work with a modified version of the previous numerical example, now assuming that the SPE issues zero coupon debt, \$80 million of which is senior and \$20 million of which is subordinated.

Insurance, Wraps, and Guaranties　The SPE could buy a financial guaranty for the collateral assets it holds or a wrap for the tranche(s) of securities issued against that collateral as discussed in Chapter 10. Either way, in the event that the principal and interest (P&I) on the collateral assets is insufficient to service the P&I on the asset-backed securities issued by the SPE, the guarantor would make up the difference.

Consider a wrap first, and suppose the full P&I of the \$80 million in senior debt is wrapped. In the event that the underlying assets have a market value of below \$80 million, the wrapper will assume the responsibility of making up the difference so that senior bondholders are fully repaid.

A financial guaranty could accomplish the same thing. The SPE would simply buy a guaranty of the underlying \$100 million in collateral assets with a deductible of \$20 million and a policy limit of \$100 million.

In either case, the senior debt should receive the credit rating of the financial guarantor, regardless of the other credit enhancements in the structure undertaken by the SPE and its structuring agent.

Letter of Credit As we saw in Chapter 10, an alternative to credit insurance products is a letter of credit (LOC). The SPE would simply obtain a $80 million LOC from a bank, where the bank is writing the LOC as it would a financial guaranty. The LOC can be drawn in the event that defaults on the assets owned by the SPE exceed $20 million and will ensure adequate funds to fully repay senior bondholders.

Credit Default Swap The SPE could, of course, also enter into a senior/sub basket credit default swap (CDS) with the $100 million in collateral assets serving as the reference portfolio and a $20 million deductible. The CDS would then provide complete credit insurance to the SPE for losses above $20 million. This first $20 million in losses would be absorbed by the subordinated debt tranche or perhaps the internal credit enhancements in the structure. In any event, the CDS would guarantee that at least $80 million in the underlying assets is insured against credit losses, thus fully protecting the $80 million in senior debt.

The senior debt in this case would be rated based on the credit quality of the credit support seller in the CDS and/or any collateral pledged to back the CDS by the credit support provider.

Put Option on Assets A final external form of credit support is a traditional put option based on the assets held by the SPE as collateral against the ABS issue. A put enables the SPE to sell the collateral assets to the put counterparty for a fixed price. In the event that the underlying collateral defaults and reduces the market value of the collateral assets, the put can be exercised and the collateral sold for a fixed cash amount. If the put is originally struck at-the-money, the exercise generates a cash flow equal to the original par value of the assets. Alternatively, the put can be struck out-of-the-money and combined with other forms of credit support.

LIQUIDITY SUPPORT

Liquidity risk is a major risk endemic to many securitization structures. Liquidity risk is the risk that the underlying portfolio of assets acting as collateral for an ABS issue may not generate enough cash to service the P&I obligations of the ABSs issued by the transferee SPE. Liquidity risk can arise from delinquencies in the underlying assets, or can be structural in nature.

As an example of the former, suppose the assets that have been conveyed to the SPE are trade receivables. If some or all of the obligors are late with their required payments, we don't necessarily call that a credit default—just a late payment. But a late payment may well deprive the SPE of cash that it needs to honor its interest and/or principal obligations on the securities it has issued.

Structural liquidity mismatches are also common in SPEs. Continuing the prior example, suppose that a portfolio of trade receivables is securitized to back a series of interest-bearing bonds. Trade receivables, however, are *non*-interest-bearing assets. Even if all obligors pay their bills on time, the SPE may still have inadequate cash to fund its securities, especially early in the life of the SPE. Or consider instead a portfolio of corporate bonds that all pay semiannual coupons in June and December that serves as collateral for senior and subordinated bonds that pay interest quarterly on a LIBOR basis. The cash inflows on the collateral are badly mismatched to the cash outflows. (This example also illustrates how interest rate risk can creep into many securitizations. We deal with that in the next main section.)

Liquidity Support and Credit Ratings

The key to understanding liquidity is understanding the *cash flow waterfall* of a structured deal. Securitization structures generally involve an *interest waterfall* and a *principal waterfall* that separately dictate the priority and order in which cash inflows on the underlying assets are applied to service cash outflows on the ABS liabilities of the SPE. Liquidity risk management in a structure is the process by which internal and external liquidity support facilities are used to ensure that the enhanced cash flow waterfall is capable of supporting the target or desired credit ratings and payment obligations on the structure's outstanding liabilities.

Rating agency criteria are often the drivers of the design of liquidity enhancements and liquidity support facilities. A structuring agent, together with the sponsor of a securitization, will define target credit ratings on the securities to be issued. Liquidity support is then all about satisfying the specific criteria set forth by the different agencies.

In most structures, liquidity support criteria require at least 100 percent of the value of the collateral in the structure to be backed with liquidity support from a source that has a rating at least as high as the desired rating on the securitized product. In addition, rating agencies generally apply several types of tests to structures on an ongoing basis to determine liquidity support adequacy. The *interest coverage* (I/C) test is applied to the interest cash flow waterfall and is designed to ensure a minimum amount of cash on hand to service upcoming scheduled interest payments.

An O/C test looks at *overcollateralization* in the structure (as discussed in the previous section) as a measure of liquidity support for the ongoing interest and principal waterfalls. O/C tests may be defined in terms of market values of assets versus liabilities or cash flows. The former is usually a measure of credit enhancement, whereas cash flow O/C tests tend to be measures of liquidity adequacy. The *debt service coverage ratio* (DSCR) of a waterfall indicates the adequacy of liquidity support in terms of a cash O/C test. The DSCR is expressed as a multiple and indicates the percentage O/C that should back a structure on a cash (as opposed to market value) basis.

Minimum I/C and O/C thresholds vary based on the target rating of the security being serviced and the type of structure (i.e., the underlying collateral). Some structures also involve additional tests, such as *tail* or *lockup* tests that look at cash flow adequacy over very long periods of time under stress scenarios.

Internal Liquidity Support

As in the case of credit enhancement, some liquidity support can be obtained through attention to structuring. Two forms of internal liquidity support can go a long way toward ensuring that the cash flow waterfall is adequate to support the target credit ratings of the structured securities issued by the SPE.

Liability Design and Maturity Structure We saw in Chapter 13 that structuring different layers of subordination in the liabilities of a structure is a means by which credit risk can be allocated to different investors in a structure. Similarly, we now see here that structuring liabilities can accomplish the same thing for liquidity risk management. But instead of structuring subordination, managing liquidity risk usually involves the deliberate structuring of *maturity*.

Maturity structuring to manage liquidity risk would be as simple as matching maturities of assets and liabilities if the cash inflows on the underlying collateral pool were entirely known. In other words, if liquidity risk is created by a *structural* mismatch between the timing of cash inflows on the collateral pool and outflows on the planned securities, we can easily restructure the maturities of the securities we plan to issue to "define the problem away." In an earlier example, we indicated that a structural cash flow mismatch would arise if we held a portfolio of bonds with semiannual coupons and then issued securities with quarterly interest payments. We could easily address that problem by just issuing securities with semiannual coupons instead. The problem is that we often don't want to do that; we chose in the first place to issue securities with quarterly interest payments because that, presumably, is what we determined that our investors demand. In addition, we still have to worry about unexpected liquidity shocks to the waterfalls arising from late interest and principal payments on the collateral pool.

Market participants have developed several structural solutions to liquidity risk management that are not quite as overly simplistic as the simple example just offered—and, hence, are much more robust. One such example is for the SPE to issue a new type of security that goes under various names, such as *liquidity enhancement notes, secured liquidity notes, extendable notes,* or *callable notes.* We will call them *extendable notes* (ENs).

A typical EN has a stated final maturity *and* an interim maturity date. When the interim maturity date arrives, the note is redeemed if and only if the interest and principal cash flow waterfalls on senior securities are more than adequate to meet their various liquidity support tests. If the cash flow waterfall is not adequate to service the securities senior to the ENs, the notes have their maturities automatically extended to the stated final maturity date. This is not considered an adverse credit or liquidity event by rating agencies because the interim maturity date was more of a call date than a stated maturity. Once the interim date has passed, however, the structure has to worry about repaying the ENs as well as the rest of the liabilities.

The period of time between the interim and final maturity date on an EN is known as the *amortization period*. During this time, the collateral manager must begin selling assets in the underlying collateral pool to generate adequate cash flows to service the principal waterfall inclusive of the ENs. External liquidity support facilities are also often paired with ENs to ensure that the final repayment on the ENs is not in question.

A good illustration of the use of ENs appears later in this chapter in the discussion of asset-backed commercial paper (ABCP) conduits.

Reserves   Internal liquidity support also comes in the form of funded liquidity reserves. Liquidity reserves are essentially cash accounts set aside to ensure that the interest and principal waterfalls always have adequate cash on hand to satisfy the rating agency tests. Although these reserves may be funded with an initial contribution from the sponsor or originator, it is more common to fund the reserve from the cash flow waterfall of the structure itself—specifically by diverting the excess spread into the liquidity reserve.

Liquidity reserves usually correspond to the liquidity tests that the structure must satisfy. A typical structure thus might include an I/C reserve, a cash O/C reserve, and perhaps a tail reserve.

External Liquidity Support

True liquidity support is distinguished carefully from credit support. External liquidity support providers are often not willing to provide guarantees or other forms of credit protection, partly for accounting reasons.[2] Consequently, external liquidity support facilities are carefully structured to provide liquidity without providing too much true credit risk transfer. In the language of Part One, *external liquidity support thus is pure risk finance, not risk transfer.*

Letters of Credit with Recourse For many years, the most popular liquidity support facility for a securitization structure was an irrevocable letter of credit in which the bank extending the LOC has recourse for draws to be repaid. Under the original Basel Accord, moreover, banks did not have to hold capital against LOCs with less than 365 days to maturity, so 364-day LOCs were commonly observed. When used for liquidity support instead of credit support, the bank providing the LOC generally enjoys full recourse to the originator or sponsor of the program.

Exhibit 16.5 illustrates the mechanics of an LOC with recourse. In the event of a delinquent payment or adverse liquidity shock to the underlying collateral pool, the SPE (or the trustee or collateral manager) can draw on the LOC up to its limit to provide short-term liquidity. Unlike an LOC used as a financial guarantee, however, this is no longer considered a credit instrument of the drawing institution, but rather of the institution to which

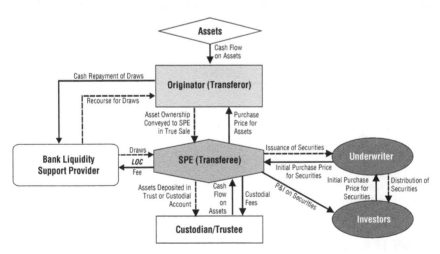

EXHIBIT 16.5 Liquidity Support with a Letter of Credit

the bank has recourse in the LOC—as said, usually the originator. In other words, once the LOC has been drawn by the LOC, the bank essentially has a loan obligation from the originator to repay the debt. Repayment also acts to recharge the facility so that the LOC may be drawn again for liquidity risk management, if required.

Over time, several developments have made the use of LOCs less popular for liquidity support provision. The first is the coming advent of Basel II that changes bank capital adequacy guidelines and will now require banks to allocate capital to short-term LOCs. (See Appendix B and Chapter 26.) The second are new accounting rules under which the independence of the SPE from the originator may be jeopardized if the recourse for the LOC comes from the originator or sponsor. For these and other reasons, LOCs are waning as the preferred form of liquidity support in securitization programs.

Asset Swaps

Exhibit 16.6 shows the cash flows on a derivatives contract known as an *asset swap*. In the transaction, the fixed cash flows on a fixed-rate reference asset or portfolio are periodically paid to a swap dealer in exchange for a LIBOR-based floating-rate payment. Asset swaps are commonly used to convert fixed coupon payments on bonds into floating LIBOR equivalents. In addition to swapping a fixed for floating exposure, the asset swap may also be used to alter the timing of the cash flows for the original asset owner—for example, swapping a fixed *semiannual* income stream for a floating *quarterly* income stream. The spread X in Exhibit 16.6 is the *asset swap rate*.

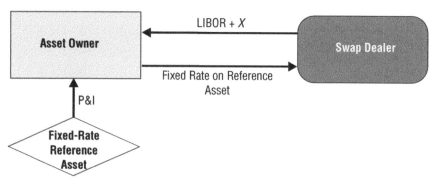

EXHIBIT 16.6 Asset Swap

Asset swaps are often used for liquidity support purposes to convert the cash inflows on the underlying collateral in a securitization structure into a cash flow stream that matches the cash outflows on the ABS liabilities of the structure. Exhibit 16.7 illustrates how this works. The SPE essentially pays interest to the swap dealer on the underlying collateral pool *as it is received*, in return for which the SPE receives a floating payment stream that matches the timing of the floating-rate liabilities of the SPE.

Asset swaps originated as cash market instruments in which investors could transform a bond-equivalent coupon income stream into a money market–equivalent income stream. Over time, asset swaps have developed a close correspondence to credit derivatives and are now even considered to be credit derivatives by many. This is not surprising, given that a credit default swap can be viewed in terms of an asset swap for valuation purposes.

In order to use asset swaps for *just* liquidity support, there are usually provisions that any defaulted collateral is subtracted from the notional principal amount of the asset swap. Otherwise, the swap dealer would also become a credit support provider and the product would be a total return swap, not an asset swap. By subtracting defaulted obligations from the notional, the swap dealer is only receiving interest and paying back a LIBOR equivalent on *live* bonds.

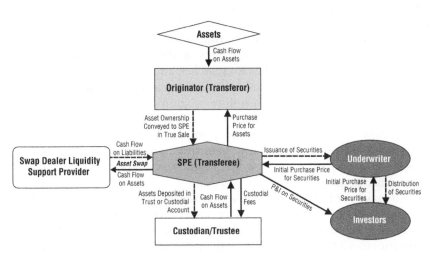

EXHIBIT 16.7 Liquidity Support with an Asset Swap

INTEREST RATE AND CURRENCY RISK

A third type of risk that often affects a securitization program is interest rate and currency risk. Interest rate risk may arise when the assets and liabilities of the structure have a fixed-rate/floating-rate basis mismatch; for example, assets pay fixed-rate coupons and liabilities pay floating-rate interest. Interest rate risk also arises from asset/liability maturity mismatches. When assets and liabilities are not equivalent maturities, interest rate changes can erode the net spread in a structure.

Another reason why asset swaps have become a popular replacement for LOCs for liquidity risk management is that such swaps also generally solve the related interest rate risk management program within a structure. But if not, the structure can still easily be hedged against interest rate risk through other interest rate derivatives like forward rate agreements (FRAs), plain-vanilla rate swaps, Eurodollar futures, and the like.

Similarly, multicurrency asset swaps or single-currency asset swaps together with other currency derivatives provide an effective solution to problems arising from any structural currency mismatch between the assets and liabilities of the structure.

SECURITIZATION AS CREDIT RISK REINSURANCE

As we noted at the beginning of this chapter, the sale of credit-sensitive assets by the originator to the SPE has virtually the same risk management impact on the originator as if the originator had purchased credit insurance or a guaranty on its asset portfolio. And as we saw in Chapter 13, the issuance of securities that represent claims on debt can be viewed as excess of loss credit insurance. Put the two together, and the issuance of securities by the SPE backed by the credit-sensitive assets acquired from the originator acts like an XOL credit *reinsurance* program. The precise allocation of losses across layers depends entirely on the cash flow waterfall and, in particular, how various credit enhancements fit into the waterfall. And, of course, the various types, amounts, maturities, and levels of subordination of ABSs also affect how we view the program as a type of synthetic credit reinsurance program.

To make our basic point clear, let's consider a simple example. Suppose an originator sells $100 million in credit-sensitive assets to an SPE. Through some mixture of holdback and depositing into a CCA, the originator provides $10 million in C/E to the structure. In addition, the originator retains the $1 million equity tranche of the structure. Suppose the SPE issues subordinated debt with a face value of $79 million and senior debt with a face value of $20 million. Let's assume the debt is zero coupon for simplicity. Finally, assume the $10 million C/E is applied to the cash flow waterfall between the equity and subordinated debt layers. That means that $11 million of underlying asset defaults must occur before subordinated debt begins to experience any losses.[3]

Exhibit 16.8 shows the resulting program from an XOL credit reinsurance perspective, with each shade of gray representing a different category of investors. The first $11 million defaults on the underlying collateral are borne by the originator through the equity and C/E. The next $79 million are borne by subordinated debt holders. Finally, the senior debt holders have $10 million of the outstanding $20 million at risk, but only for underlying collateral defaults in the $10 XS $90 layer.

Note that the top half of the senior debt portion of the graph—the $10 XS $100 layer—is white to indicate that it is not at risk. With only $100 million in underlying assets and $10 million in C/E, the worst-case scenario for senior debt holders is a loss of *half* their principal. So, we have designed a structure that has 90 percent C/E for senior debt—80 percent from subordination ($79 million in sub debt plus $1 million in equity) and 10 percent from internal C/E.

The $11 million at risk from the originator can be interpreted as the deductible of the original credit insurance sold by the SPE to the originator.

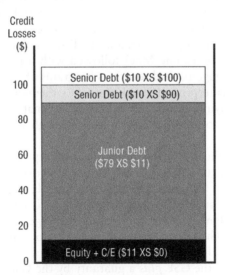

EXHIBIT 16.8 Securitization as a
Synthetic Credit Reinsurance Program

Although the originator has sold the credit-sensitive assets, it still retains this first $11 million loss exposure, which is, of course, exactly the definition of a deductible or a planned retention.

FROM ABS AND ABCP TO CDO

In reality, there is a wide range of securitization structures that can accommodate various types of credit-sensitive assets. These programs may be distinguished based on the type of securities issued as ABSs, the maturity of those securities, the levels of subordination, the mix of C/Es, the type and nature of liquidity support, and so on. An almost endless number of permutations is possible.

We focus in the next chapter on ABSs that are part of the structured credit market—namely, collateralized debt obligations (CDOs) and CDO-like structures. But CDOs are a comparatively recent arrival on the ABS scene, and a brief digression on some of the predecessors to CDOs will prove useful.

Mortgage-Backed Securities

The first major class of ABS was the mortgage-backed security (MBS), first issued in 1970 by the Government National Mortgage Association (GNMA) in the form of a pass-through MBS. The Federal Home Loan Mortgage Corporation (FHLMC or Freddie Mac) issued mortgage pass-through securities just a year later, and the Federal National Mortgage Association (FNMA or Fannie Mae) followed with a pass-through issue in 1981. In the mortgage-backed securities programs of three of these government-sponsored enterprises (GSEs), the GSEs themselves play the role of the transferee, buying mortgage loans from originators and then pooling them as collateral to fund P&I on the pass-through securities they issue to investors.

Exhibit 16.9 illustrates the mechanics of a typical pass-through MBS securitization structure. A loan is made by a bank originator to a borrower for the purchase of a home, and the home is pledged as collateral for the loan. The P&I on such loans, moreover, may be insured through either a private label mortgage insurer or a government agency (e.g., the Veterans Administration). The originator exchanges the loan for a MBS (often a trust certificate) with a GSE. The MBS may be the same loan that the originator conveyed to the GSE *plus* a guaranty by the GSE on the P&I of the MBS, or the MBS may represent fractional interests in a portfolio of loans. The originator then sells the MBS to investors for cash.

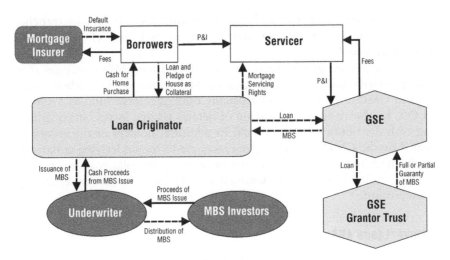

EXHIBIT 16.9 Pass-Through Mortgage-Backed Security

Most GSEs provide some form of P&I guaranty to holders of their pass-through MBSs. The GSE thus acts as the primary credit enhancer, and, as a result of the AAA ratings of the GSEs, the investor in the MBS bears minimal credit risk. In fact, MBSs are generally not considered "credit market" products; MBSs enjoy a separate classification as a securitized product unto themselves and apart from other ABSs. MBS investors do, however, bear *other* risks of the underlying mortgage loan(s), including prepayment and interest rate risk.

A pass-through is a single-class ABS; all holders of the same class of MBS have the same priority and enjoy pro rata distributions of the underlying cash flows. Multiclass MBSs are also a big part of the MBS market, the most popular of which are known as a *collateralized mortgage obligation* (CMO) and a *real estate mortgage investment conduit* (REMIC). REMICs involve the issuance of several classes of securities backed by a pool of pass-through MBSs, whole mortgage loans and loan participations, or both, and are issued both by certain GSEs and by several private-label mortgage structuring agents. CMO classes are structured to allocate *prepayment risk* (not default risk) across different classes of security. In a traditional sequential-pay CMO, for example, tranches are assigned priority corresponding to the seniority of the class of security associated with each tranche. Principal payments in the cash flow waterfall then are made sequentially in that order of priority. In this manner, the bonds issued through a CMO structure have interest rate risk, prepayment risk, and effective maturities that vary by tranche, thus allowing investors a greater ability to pick and choose among risk/return profiles.

Credit enhancements are generally not used for CMO structures that rely primarily on agency mortgage-backed securities. For whole-loan-backed CMOs, the CMO issuer usually holds a reserve fund as a source of O/C to absorb some proportion of default-related losses before affecting cash distributions to investors. In addition, holders of the securities issued by the CMO are often given recourse to the underlying collateral. In the event the issuer of the securities defaults, the collateral thus reverts to the bondholders, thereby making the credit quality of the issuer largely unimportant.

Nonmortgage ABSs

In addition to being collateralized by mortgage loans, ABSs may also be collateralized by nonmortgage assets. The first such securitized product was issued in 1985 by First Boston and was collateralized by computer leases originated by Sperry.

In a typical ABS structure, the obligor in a credit-sensitive transaction conveys a specific pool or pools of receivables to a SPE that in turn issues securities—usually multiple classes—based on the original asset pool(s). When the pool of assets either defaults or is fully repaid, the securities issued by the SPE are then fully paid off and the SPE winds down. In other words, most ABS structures are self-terminating and have a finite life that depends on the life of the original assets conveyed. Most ABSs have maturities that run from two to five years.

The structure underlying a given ABS issue depends a great deal on the nature of the collateral. Different types of assets and receivables create specific problems that must be addressed in a securitization. There are far too many bells, whistles, and structuring issues in the ABS market to discuss here, especially since this is not primarily a book on traditional ABSs. Fortunately, there is a good selection of reference texts to which interested readers may turn for all you want to know and are afraid to ask about the ABS market and various asset-specific structuring considerations.

For now, we content ourselves with a typical example, the 2001 issue of auto loan–backed securities by Toyota Motor Credit Corp. (TMCC). The structure is shown in Exhibit 16.10. The original assets are $1.5 billion in fixed-rate auto loan obligations to TMCC, which are conveyed to the SPE (Toyota Auto Receivables 2001-B Owner Trust) for cash. In addition, TMCC funds a CCA with an initial cash deposit. The SPE in turn issues $418 million in senior fixed-rate debt and $1.082 billion in

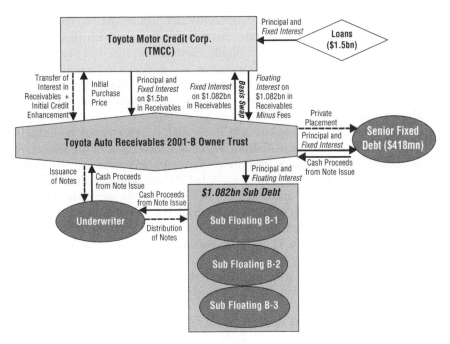

EXHIBIT 16.10 Auto Loan–Backed Security

subordinated debt. The floating-rate debt is split into three classes and pays a *floating* interest rate.

To manage interest rate and liquidity risk inside the structure arising from a mismatch between fixed-rate assets and floating-rate debt on $1.082 billion of the deal, the SPE enters into a plain-vanilla interest rate swap with TMCC with a notional amount of $1.082 billion. The SPE pays a fixed rate to TMCC in exchange for receiving a floating rate that then services the floating-rate subordinated debt.

Asset-Backed Commercial Paper Programs

A particularly important credit-sensitive ABS—in fact, predating the Sperry ABS issue by a year—is the asset-backed commercial paper (ABCP) program. In the early 1980s, banks became increasingly unable to offer competitive financing to their corporate customers and were losing them to the emerging commercial paper (CP) market. Thanks to the Basel Accord, banks had to allocate capital to balance sheet loans and thus could not compete with the CP market by simply increasing loan underwriting volume.

As a solution, the banking community developed ABCPs. These programs were conduits for corporate clients of banks to convert their receivables into short-term financing at highly competitive rates, but because the actual issuance of securities was through a SPE designed to be independent of the bank, banks could assist and participate in their corporate customers' capital formation process without inflating their balance sheets with new loans.

The structure of a typical ABCP conduit is represented in Exhibit 16.11. The ABCP shown in Exhibit 16.11 is known as a *multiseller conduit* because the receivables from more than one originator are combined in the same collateral pool to back a single CP issue. Many traditional ABS issues, by contrast, are *single-seller* programs; for example, in Exhibit 16.10, the only originator of collateral to back the securitization is TMCC.

Some other important differences between ABS and ABCP structures can be seen in Exhibit 16.11. First, the securities issued in an ABCP program by the SPE are short-term CP. Unlike ABSs, ABCP issues neither trade in an active secondary market nor have long maturities. Instead, the paper is typically held to maturity by end investors for holding periods of often only a few months.

Second, ABS conduits usually involve a one-time conveyance of assets

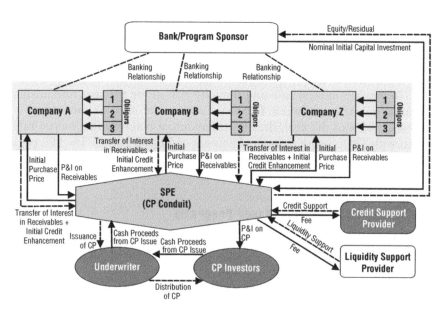

EXHIBIT 16.11 Multiseller Asset-Backed Commercial Paper Conduit
Source: Kavanagh, Bohemio, and Edwards (1992).

to the SPE, and the SPE then winds down after the receivables are repaid and the securities fully paid off. In a typical ABCP program, by contrast, the SPE continually purchases *new* assets or receivables and rolls over outstanding commercial paper issues. In other words, a typical ABCP conduit is a "continuous conveyance" vehicle that is regularly purchasing new receivables with new CP issues.

Third, ABS issues generally are senior-sub, multiclass structures. The ABCP shown issues only a single type of security, and all holders of the CP issued by the SPE have equal seniority in the SPE's capital structure.

Receivables securitized in ABCPs are often trade credit receivables, such as credit card, auto loan, and capital lease receivables. Credit enhancement comes in part from each originator, usually through holdback against the initial purchase price. External credit support also is usually provided through a LOC, wrap, or CDS.

Liquidity support is generally critically important for an ABCP given the nature of the assets and liabilities. Typical receivables conveyed to ABCPs often have no fixed maturity date, are prone to unscheduled principal payments, and either do not bear interest or bear interest on a fixed-rate basis. The CP liabilities issued by the SPE, by contrast, generally are short-term and floating-rate.

The continuous conveyance of receivables also exacerbates liquidity and interest rate risks. Not only must new receivable purchases be financed with the issuance of new CP, but the retiring CP also must be financed on a rolling basis. Because of the significant of liquidity risk in an ABCP, rating agency requirements for liquidity support are particularly stringent for these structures.

Liquidity support has commonly been provided through LOCs with recourse either back to the originators and/or to the sponsoring bank. In addition, the use of extendable or callable notes by ABCPs has become increasingly common.

When ABCPs first began, the sponsoring bank usually would try to play as many roles as possible. Typically, the sponsoring bank will play the role of *either* credit *or* liquidity support provider, but not both. In addition, the sponsor often retained the equity or residual tranche in the SPE. In response to bank regulators' concerns about excessive involvement (i.e., the risk that regulators would force banks to consolidate the SPE on its balance sheet was high), many banks opted to define the value of that equity investment as a small, fixed number and then to gift that equity to a charitable trust.

The advent of consolidation rule FIN46R (discussed in Chapter 30) has posed particular challenges for ABCPs. Under this new rule, bank sponsors will find it very hard to avoid consolidation of ABCP programs on their balance sheets without severely restricting their own participation in these structures. But recall the whole purpose of ABCPs initially was for banks to provide their corporate customers with an alternative source of borrowing and credit risk management that was off-balance-sheet for the bank but that still allowed banks to participate somehow. The less banks can participate, the less incentive they have to sponsor these programs.

One recent solution has been for ABCPs to offer *expected loss notes*. These are debt securities that are subordinated to the CP issued by an ABCP, as well as to any extendable or callable notes issued for liquidity enhancement to the facility. Defaults in the underlying collateral are allocated to these expected loss notes first, thus making these notes behave like equity. Selling these notes to third parties like hedge funds then usually allows the bank sponsor to avoid consolidation of the program under FIN46R.

CHAPTER 17

Cash Collateralized
Debt Obligations

One of the most important innovations in the structured credit market in the past several decades was the *collateralized debt obligation* (CDO). A CDO is an asset-backed security structure—traditionally multiclass—in which the securitized products issued have principal and interest (P&I) backed by the cash flows on a pool of debt instrument collateral. CDOs exist in numerous different forms for a range of economic purposes. Perhaps more interestingly, the growth in CDO activity together with the application of securitization technology (i.e., the securitization process as outlined in Chapter 16) creates a very useful conceptual framework for evaluating all structured financing activities in general and credit risk transfer in particular.

A few short chapters cannot possibly do justice to the intricacies of the CDO market. Fortunately, those wanting a more in-depth look at CDO activity will find no shortage of books—for example, Choudhry (2004), Deacon (2004), Goodman and Fabozzi (2002), Smithson (2003), and Tavakoli (2003). This chapter and the next are intended to provide an overview of CDO activity, as well as a discussion of how CDO activity fits into the broader themes of structured finance, structured insurance, risk, and capital on which this book is primarily focused. In this chapter, we focus on introducing the general concepts of the CDO universe, and we explore the mechanics of *cash CDOs*, CDOs in which securitization is employed to convey credit-sensitive assets to a special purpose entity (SPE) that in turn issues securities backed by those credit-sensitive assets. In the next chapter, we explore *synthetic CDOs*, or structures in which an SPE engages in a synthetic securitization (instead of an actual asset acquisition) by selling credit protection using credit derivatives.

TYPES OF CDOs

Moody's Investors Service estimates that the rated volume of CDOs was just over $90 billion in 2004, representing more than 200 deals.[1] Before attempting to dissect the structures underlying this explosive and constantly innovating market, we need to begin with some basic idea of how to separate structures inside the CDO market into categories. There are several different dimensions that distinguish CDOs today, and we review these in the sections that follow.

Type of Collateral

CDOs are often distinguished based on the type of collateral that backs the P&I on the securitized products issued in the CDO structure. We generally can separate CDO collateral based on whether the underlying debt consists of loans, bonds, or both. CDOs backed entirely with loans as collateral are called *collateralized loan obligations* (CLOs), whereas bond-backed CDOs are called *collateralized bond obligations* (CBOs).

The first CDO rated by Moody's was Drexel Burnham Lambert's Long Run Bond deal executed in 1988 and developed by none other than Michael Milken.[2] The transactions that followed in the 1980s and early 1990s were almost all CLOs based on leveraged commercial and industrial loans, often associated with highly leveraged transactions like leveraged buyouts (LBOs).

In 1997, CDOs also began to include structured debt and asset-backed securities (ABSs) in their collateral portfolios. Known today as *structured finance CDOs* or more generally as *resecuritizations*, the structured securities that now serve as collateral for CDOs may include ABSs, notes (and perhaps equity) issued by other CDOs, commercial and residential mortgage-backed securities (CMBSs and RMBSs, respectively), trust preferred stock (TruPS), and the like.

Exhibit 17.1 shows the relative distribution of collateral types in the CDO market in 2004.

Economic Motivations of Issuers

CDOs are also distinguished based on their economic purpose. In this context, a CDO may be a *balance sheet CDO* or an *arbitrage CDO*. A balance sheet CDO is undertaken specifically because the owner of an asset portfolio seeks to divest itself of some or all of those assets. Reasons for wanting to sell the assets include credit risk management, fund-

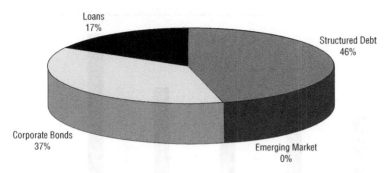

EXHIBIT 17.1   CDOs by Collateral Type, 2004
Source: Moody's Investors Service; Mayer Brown Rowe & Maw.
Note: Balance sheet synthetic collateralized debt obligation (SCDO) collateral is assumed to be loans, whereas arbitrage SCDO collateral is assumed to be bonds.

raising, balance sheet management, preservation of debt capacity, and more. An arbitrage CDO, by contrast, is undertaken primarily as an investment management tool. In other words, the corporate financing objectives of the owner of the original asset are not a driving consideration. Instead, arbitrage CDOs represent the efforts of collateral managers and structuring agents to combine the tools of asset management with financial engineering to try to offer investors a new and superior investment product.

The relative amounts issued of each type from 2000 to April 22, 2005, are shown in Exhibit 17.2.[3] A more detailed discussion of the two economic motivations to undertake a CDO appears in the following sections.

BALANCE SHEET CDOs

A balance sheet CDO is characterized by the feature that the originator of the assets is usually the institution from which the CDO acquires the debt collateral. Accordingly, balance sheet CDOs are economically motivated by the originator first and foremost. The precise objectives for issuers to enter into balance sheet CDOs are the classical themes of this book—the need to reduce credit risk combined with the need to monetize current assets into cash, thus freeing up debt capacity, reducing balance sheet leverage, decreasing expected costs of financial distress, and so on.

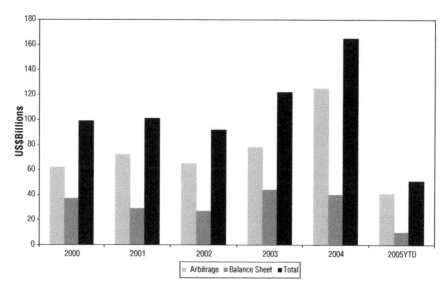

EXHIBIT 17.2   CDOs by Economic Purpose, 2000–2005YTD
Source: JPMorgan; Mayer Brown Rowe and Maw.

Structure

Balance sheet CDOs generally do not have independent collateral managers. The assets conveyed to the CDO are usually selected by the originator, perhaps in consultation with a sponsor and/or structuring agent (see Chapters 13 and 16). The originator in a balance sheet CDO, moreover, is usually a bank. As such, balance sheet CDOs are usually comprised of loan assets (i.e., they are CLOs).

In a typical balance sheet CDO, the bank selects a portfolio of 100+ loans or loan participations to be sold—usually with a total size of $1 billion and up—and then conveys those loans in a true sale to an SPE. In addition to subordination, the credit enhancement (C/E) in a typical balance sheet CDO usually includes a cash collateral account (CCA) funded by the originator and the diversion of excess spread, which generally runs about 50 basis points per annum. The originator usually also retains the residual interest in a balance sheet CDO.

One of the earliest traditional balance sheet CDOs is the Rose Funding transaction done in 1996 by National Westminster Bank PLC. Rose Funding was a $5 billion structure based on 200 loans comprising 15 percent to 20 percent of NatWest's loan portfolio. The classes of notes issued by Rose Funding included a senior revolver and senior fixed note with investors in

17 countries. Rose Funding provides a model for the typical structure of a balance sheet CLO and is shown (in simplified form) in Exhibit 17.3.[4]

Motivations and Benefits

A balance sheet CDO represents the securitization of credit-sensitive assets into multiple tranches of financial capital claims. In short, a CDO is a form of asset divestiture. Whether motivated primarily by the desire to raise funds or to reduce credit risk, the sale of assets also deprives the originator of any future benefits of asset ownership. What are the reasons for banks to undertake such a strategy?

Customized Credit Risk Transfer As discussed in Chapter 16, a senior-sub securitization functions like synthetic credit reinsurance, and the balance sheet CDO is the prototypical example of this—at least from a risk perspective. The residual tranche functions like the deductible, and other more senior securities sold to third-party investors provide the different excess of loss (XOL) layers of credit reinsurance for the underlying assets.[5] CDOs thus allow a firm to sell a single portfolio of assets to

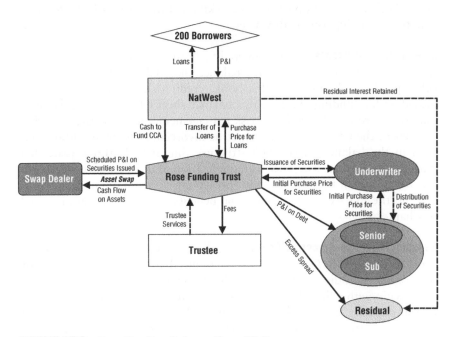

EXHIBIT 17.3 Rose Funding Balance Sheet CDO

different groups of investors who may have specific risk appetites for particular loss exposures within the portfolio.

Although credit reinsurance facilitates the same kind of repackaging of risk into loss layers, it limits the credit protection purchaser to reinsurance companies. CDOs allow corporate credit protection buyers to diversify their sources of credit protection by exploiting noninsurance investor demand. From the investor standpoint, CDOs allow investors to hold highly specific risks associated with firms, thus enabling them to diversify away firm-specific risks and better diversify across loss layers and trigger points. This is something for which investors are willing to pay, which makes the pricing of CDOs fairly competitive.

Note that the retention of the residual tranche by the originator can pose consolidation problems for the originator, especially in a FIN46R world. The residual retention, however, is a crucial component of the structure because of the incentive effects it creates. As with other insurance, the synthetic credit insurance created when the originator sells its loans to the SPE is an indemnity form of protection that is subject to moral hazard and adverse selection (see Chapter 2). Forcing the issuer to retain a deductible-like equity stake is a key part of mitigating moral hazard. Without it, investors in the CDO securities may worry that the bank has "reverse cherry-picked" its loan portfolio (i.e., skimmed the cream off the top and sold the remaining low-quality assets).

Monetization of Assets   Although credit risk management is a clear consequence and important motive for balance sheet CDO activity, like many other products discussed in this book, credit risk management is integrated with a funding objective in a balance sheet CDO. Because the original assets *are sold for cash*, the risk management and corporate financing impacts of the CDO structure cannot be divorced. Equally important motives in the balance sheet CDO structure thus include those associated with the actual asset sale, such as monetization of those assets for cash, reducing the size of the balance sheet, preserving or maintaining debt capacity, and the like—essentially the same benefits of securitization discussed in Chapter 16.

Reducing Adverse Selection Costs   Recall that another benefit of securitization mentioned in Chapter 14 can be reduced adverse selection costs for the originator leading to a lower weighted average cost of capital (WACC). If we begin with a firm that has all its assets thrown into "the firm," a lack of transparency combined with the usual lemons and adverse selection problem can sometimes make it difficult for firms to achieve their true cost of funding in traditional public securities markets.

CDOs are relatively transparent and thus can provide a mechanism by which firms can divorce their complex, nontraditional credit-sensitive assets from their other assets. In the process, the assets that were originally hard to assess have now been placed into a self-contained structure, credit and liquidity enhanced, and put on display for investors. This can reduce the adverse selection discount those securities might otherwise command, which will, of course, be reflected in the sale price of those assets to the SPE.

In addition, separating out complex credits from the firm as a whole can reduce the capacity for the firm to mismanage those assets and deploy them in negative net present value (NPV) endeavors. Selling the assets through a CDO thus may also lead to a slight reduction in WACC by reducing agency costs.

Funded Credit Protection   The up-front cash flow associated with the securitization of assets in a balance sheet CDO not only has a financing impact on the originator, but it also affects the credit risk of the originator with respect to the credit risk transfer counterparties (as opposed to the credit risk of the underlying collateral assets). Traditional balance sheet CDOs represent a *fully funded* credit risk transfer solution, as distinct from classical insurance and plain-vanilla credit derivatives (excluding credit-linked notes). Insurance and derivatives expose their users to the credit risk of default, nonperformance, and disputed claims because the money is not paid until the loss event occurs. In a balance sheet CDO, like a credit-linked note (CLN), the credit risky assets have been sold for cash up front, and there is little chance that a subsequent default can result in nonpayment.

Regulatory Capital Arbitrage   Optimizing the regulatory capital charge facing the originator is another powerful motivation underlying a lot of bank balance sheet CDO activity to date. Smithson (2003) notes, for example, that the Rose Funding structure described in Exhibit 17.3 reportedly freed up about $400 million in regulatory capital for NatWest. How does this work exactly?

Under the original version of the Basel Accord (see Chapter 29 by Kavanagh and Appendix B), banks must allocate financial capital to traditional commercial and industrial (C&I) loans in an amount equal to 8 percent of the face value of those loans. Consider, for example, a $500 million loan portfolio that earns an effective average rate of the London Interbank Offered Rate (LIBOR) plus 135 basis points with a funding cost of LIBOR + 35. The net interest income on the loans thus is 100 basis points, or $5 million, and the capital charge is $40 million. The return on equity (ROE) of the portfolio thus is 12.5 percent.

The Basel-required regulatory capital on securitized loan assets is equal to the lesser of the capital charge on the unlevered investment or 100 percent of the retained liability resulting from the securitization (i.e., the equity). If the bank retains 2 percent of the residual in the CDO, for example, the capital charge is $10 million (*not* 8 percent of $10 million!). If the senior expenses of the SPE are 35 basis points, the excess spread (which accrues to the bank unless needed to cover defaults) is now 65 basis points. So the ROE is now 32.5 percent (= $3.25mn/$10 mn).

Even with a lower net interest income and a higher percentage capital charge, the ROE for the bank is lower post-CDO because the equity at risk in the CDO is substantially below the equity at risk in the loan portfolio.

Basel II will change things a bit, but the basic idea of using securitization as an integrated mechanism for credit risk transfer, financing, and regulatory capital relief is likely to remain a driving force behind balance sheet CDO activity for some time to come.

Rating Considerations

Structured finance products are usually rated by one or more of the three main rating agencies.[6] Agencies typically begin with a careful look at the underlying assets in the collateral pool and then continue to evaluate the risks endemic to the structure itself.

Collateral Requirements and Asset Quality Tests The composition of the collateral portfolio or reference asset portfolio underlying the CDO is perhaps the primary focus of the rating agencies. The variables that the agencies may examine in their analysis of the collateral pool include:

- Specific credit information about the population of underlying assets, including ratings, recovery rates, credit enhancements, and the like.
- Concentration and diversity of assets.
- Industry diversity.
- Proportion of the pool in high-risk assets.
- Weighted average rating factor (WARF).

Both S&P and Fitch tend to focus on running specific obligors through their own proprietary models, whereas Moody's relies more heavily on models resting on industry diversity scoring. Detailed discussions of the rating agency methodologies can be obtained from the agencies themselves.

Coverage Tests Rating agencies generally require at least two types of coverage tests to protect note holders in the CDO on an ongoing basis. An *overcollateralization (O/C) test* requires that the *O/C ratio* for a specific tranche is always above some minimum. For a given tranche in a CDO, the O/C ratio is the sum of the principal value of the collateral portfolio plus any allocated C/E divided by the sum of the face value of securities issued in that tranche plus the face values of all more senior tranches. A CDO that issues Class A, B, and C notes, for example, would compute the O/C ratio for Class B as the par value of the portfolio divided by the principal on the Class A and B notes.

Similarly, an *interest coverage (I/C) test* requires the *I/C ratio* for a given tranche to exceed a defined threshold at all times. The I/C ratio is defined as the ratio of the sum of scheduled interest on the collateral assets and any allocated credit enhancement to the sum of scheduled interest on the tranche in question plus all tranches senior to that one.

Both the O/C and I/C tests are extremely sensitive to the allocation of credit enhancements. Although the subordination of the CDO's liabilities is usually the main determinant of internal O/C and I/C, the priority of different credit enhancements in the interest and principal waterfalls can make a big difference. A good structuring agent is generally the best way to ensure that a CDO is designed to meet these rating agency tests on an ongoing basis.

ARBITRAGE CDOs

As distinct from balance sheet CDOs, so-called arbitrage CDOs involve firms designated as collateral managers that select and acquire specific debt assets as collateral. These assets are often acquired on the open market rather than from the assets' originators, and frequently are bonds rather than loans (making many arbitrage CDOs into CBOs). The objective of an arbitrage CDO is to try to generate trading profits from perceived arbitrage opportunities—usually so-called ratings arbitrage—and trading opportunities designed to achieve an all-in refinancing cost on issuing securities that is below the cost of purchasing them.

Structure

The structure of a cash arbitrage CDO (see Exhibit 17.4) looks quite similar to the structure of a balance sheet CDO with a few exceptions. Unlike a balance sheet CDO in which a structuring agent and/or sponsor together with an originator determine the assets to be conveyed to the CDO, an arbitrage CDO has a *collateral manager* that is appointed to select and possibly manage the underlying pool of assets to back the CDO. These assets

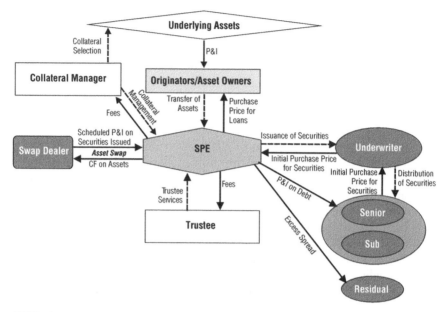

EXHIBIT 17.4   Arbitrage CDO

are sold to the SPE for cash, and the assets are then deposited in trust for the investors in the securities issued by the SPE. The new securitized products issued are backed by the P&I on the collateral portfolio, plus the usual credit and perhaps liquidity supports.

The assets underlying an arbitrage CDO may be loans or bonds and may come from one or more asset owners. These asset owners may be originators of the assets or may have themselves acquired the assets on the secondary market.

Notice also in Exhibit 17.4 that the residual tranche is not necessarily retained by any participant internal to the structure. If an asset underlying the CDO is obtained from an originator, moral hazard and adverse selection problems are mitigated through other forms of C/E, such as holdback or a mandatory deposit to fund a CCA. Retention of the residual, however, is *not* usually used for this purpose here. In the typical arbitrage CDO, the residual either is sold as a separate security or is retained by the collateral manager in its trading portfolio. (See the related discussion in Chapter 18 on single-tranche CDOs.)

Cash Flow versus Market Value CDOs   Almost all new arbitrage CDO issues are known as *cash flow CDOs*,[7] but this was not always the case. Arbitrage CDOs also may be *market value CDOs*. The difference concerns the sources of funds to feed the interest and principal waterfalls and the associated coverage triggers.

In a cash flow CDO, the interest and principal waterfalls are funded by normal scheduled P&I on the collateral portfolio. In a market value CDO, by contrast, the waterfalls may be funded instead by liquidation of the asset collateral. Because market value CDOs are rapidly disappearing, we don't need to spend any real time on them.

Static versus Managed Portfolios Many CDOs involve the selection of a pool of collateral assets during the design and structuring phase, after which the CDO simply runs its course and winds down. Such is the case with many balance sheet CDOs. Arbitrage CDOs, however, may involve some degree of ongoing management of the collateral portfolio. Asset management comes in essentially two forms: light management and active management.

A *lightly managed* portfolio generally involves discretionary trading decisions made by the collateral manager concerning the resolution of problematic positions. The manager of a lightly managed portfolio can sell a bond before an event of default occurs, for example, whereas a concerned collateral manager in a static CDO must sit by and watch. *Active management*, by contrast, generally involves much more discretion for active trading by the collateral manager. Actively managed arbitrage CDO portfolios are often periodically recharged or replenished as a part of the manager's strategy to achieve superior returns.

All CDOs have what is known as a *ramp-up period*, or the time during which the original assets are acquired. The larger and more complex the portfolio, the longer the ramp-up period. And the more counterparties or originators involved in the acquisition, the longer the ramp-up period.

Actively managed CDOs then enter a *reinvestment period*, during which time principal on existing collateral is used to finance the acquisition of new collateral rather than to pay down existing note holders in the structure. This generally requires choosing maturities of securities to be issued by the CDO with a year or so beyond the reinvestment period.

Most CDOs involves loans or bonds that call for principal repayment in one lump sum on a specific date—usually at the end of the life of the loan/bond. Known as a "bullet repayment," this means that the only interim cash flows are the interest payments on the debt. But this also means that most structures also include an *amortization period* following the reinvestment period for each tranche of securities, during which time income on the collateral is diverted into a cash reserve account that will finance the eventual bullet repayment of the principal.

By issuing multiple maturities, the CDO can lengthen the effective reinvestment horizon. If half of the securities issued mature in three years and half in five years, for example, only half of the portfolio needs to be shifted from reinvestment to amortization mode in year two to finance the year three bullet repayments. The other half can remain in reinvestment mode until year four. External liquidity support may also prove helpful to facilitate active management of this kind.

The degree of active management and collateral manager discretion may impact the structure and operation of the CDO in several ways. One avenue by which management can affect a CDO is in the areas of accounting and disclosure. A qualified special purpose entity (QSPE), for example, is exempt from FIN46R, and a QSPE is distinguished from a regular SPE or variable interest entity (VIE) largely based on its degree of passivity. In addition, static and lightly managed portfolios usually involve minimal fees paid to the collateral manager. In an actively managed portfolio, by contrast, the collateral manager usually receives some performance-based compensation. Performance fees may be subordinated in the capital structure of the issuer, and in some cases may simply represent retention of some piece of the equity tranche.

Motivations and Benefits

The collateral manager that selects the assets in an arbitrage CDO is often a professional fund manager, such as an investment bank, asset management firm, or insurance company (on the asset side, not the underwriting side). Arbitrage CDOs may be asset-backed or structured finance CDOs. Typical asset holdings usually include 50+ securities with a total size of $100 million and up. Arbitrage CDO collateral managers and the CDOs they run usually specialize by the type of collateral held (e.g., high-yield debt, Brady bond, emerging market debt, sovereign debt, etc.).

Arbitrage CDOs account for the vast bulk of CDO activity, as we saw in Exhibit 17.2. Because arbitrage CDOs are essentially yield-enhancement investment structures, collateral managers are forever chasing yields. Of particular concern to an arbitrage CDO manager is the so-called CDO *funding gap*, or the difference between the yield on the asset portfolio and the yield on the CDO liabilities (plus CDO structure senior fees and costs). The higher the funding gap, the higher the interest rate can be for the CDO's highly subordinated debt and the higher the expected return on equity.

Table 17.1 summarizes the funding gap for the most popular European CDO structures as of November 2004. Those CDOs for which year-end 2003 statistics are reported had virtually no 2004 activity.

TABLE 17.1 European CDO Funding Gap

	CBO BBB	CBO BB	CLO BB/B		ABS BBB		CDS A
	Dec-03	Dec-03	Dec-03	Nov-04	Dec-03	Nov-04	Dec-03
Asset Yield Weighted Average	4.54	6.22	5.29	5.21	3.95	3.34	0.67
Costs and Expenses							
Interest Expense	2.78	3.07	2.90	2.55	2.83	2.51	0.35
Net Hedging Costs	1.78	1.61	0.00	0.00	0.00	0.00	
Administrative Costs	0.31	0.56	0.56	0.56	0.31	0.31	0.18
Amortized Debt Issue Costs	0.39	0.44	0.42	0.42	0.38	0.38	0.20
Subtotal, Costs and Expenses	5.27	5.68	3.88	3.53	3.52	3.20	0.73
Funding Gap	-0.73	0.54	1.41	1.68	0.43	0.15	-0.06
Equity Return (No Default)	-14.56	3.83	14.12	16.78	10.72	3.69	-1.56
Equity % of Capital Structure	5	14	10	10	4	4	4
Spread over EURIBOR Weighted Average	0.75	1.23	0.97	0.61	0.77	0.43	0.18

Source: Merrill Lynch.

The funding gap, of course, also affects the economics of balance sheet CDOs. An originator would, after all, not eschew credit insurance and credit derivatives in favor of a balance sheet CDO at a negative spread. The funding gap must be large enough, moreover, to pay a competitive interest rate on the debt securities issued. But because the originator retains the equity tranche, a high expected return on equity is *not* a requirement of a balance sheet CDO.

Exhibit 17.5 summarizes the 2004 CDO market by issuer motivation and collateral type. Of the deals summarized, 92 percent are arbitrage transactions. Of those, the majority are backed by loans, structured notes, or ABSs. A small proportion (9 percent) represents CDOs backed by trust preferred stock issues (TruPS). Only a fractional 3 percent of the CDO universe in 2004 consisted of pure CBOs.

Figures such as Exhibit 17.5 can change a lot from year to year depending on where the perceived yields are and on what is happening with the funding gap.

Rating Considerations

Rating agencies are attentive to basically the same issues regarding collateral quality in both balance sheet and arbitrage CDOs. Similarly, coverage tests are fundamentally similar on balance sheet and cash flow arbitrage CDOs.

Market value arbitrage CDOs, however, have different coverage tests and thus are evaluated differently from cash flow CDOs. The main distinction is the definition, calculation, and enforcement of I/C and O/C tests. In a market value CDO, I/C and O/C tests are based on the ability of the col-

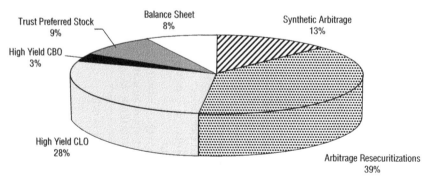

EXHIBIT 17.5 CDO Collateral in 2004 (Proportion of Total Transactions)
Source: Moody's Investors Service; Mayer Brown Rowe and Maw.

lateral manager to liquidate assets quickly and at fair market prices. Advance rates and/or haircuts are applied to collateral to reflect market and market liquidity risks. In other words, the nominal value of a given collateral asset may receive less than 100% credit when plugged into an I/C or O/C test. Instead, a *discounted* market value is used to reflect the price at which the collateral can presumably be safely liquidated to finance the structure's waterfall.

CASH CDOs AS WHOLE CAPITAL STRUCTURE PRODUCTS

Cash CDOs are often referred to as *whole capital structure* products. The reason should be fairly obvious. Because the SPE issuer has sold securities to fund the acquisition of the entire underlying portfolio of assets, the whole capital structure of the CDO's SPE is sold to third-party investors (with the exception of any subordinated or equity tranche retention in the first-loss layer by the originator in a balance sheet program). As we saw back in Chapter 1, the SPE has created financial capital that represents an exhaustive set of claims on the capital assets on the left-hand side of the SPE's economic balance sheet.

CHAPTER 18

Synthetic Collateralized Debt Obligations

Cash CDOs like those explored in Chapter 17 involve the conveyance or true sale of assets to a transferee in exchange for cash. A *synthetic collateralized debt obligation* (SCDO), by contrast, does *not* involve the actual sale of assets. Instead, the originator acquires credit protection using credit derivatives.

Although SCDOs did not really emerge until the late 1990s, they now account for a large portion of the overall CDO market. Despite their relatively short time in the market, moreover, SCDOs have already undergone a remarkably rapid evolution in form and structure. The SCDO market today is almost totally different from the market in the late 1990s.

In this chapter, we will embark on a whirlwind tour of the fascinating world of SCDOs. Much detail must necessarily be omitted in the interest of brevity, but, as noted in Chapter 17, interested readers will have no difficulty pursing SCDOs in more detail on their own. One can spend hours on end reading about SCDOs without ever leaving the web sites of the three rating agencies.

We begin with a discussion of what we call "first-generation" SCDO structures. These were the original SCDOs that gave birth to the synthetic CDO market in the late 1990s. We will examine not only the structures, but also the reasons for the huge popularity of these products. We then turn to summarize the "second-generation" SCDOs that have more recently developed and taken the market by storm. (Virtually all new SCDOs in 2004 were second-generation products.)

FIRST-GENERATION SCDO STRUCTURES

As we have discussed at various points in the book thus far, risk transfer can be fully or partially funded or unfunded. Nowhere is this distinction better illustrated than in the original SCDO market, in which fully funded and partially funded structures that were otherwise similar in purpose nevertheless still boasted some pretty remarkable differences in structure and design. We begin with a review of the early fully funded structures in the market before turning to partially funded structures. The section concludes with a discussion of regulatory capital issues associated with fully and partially funded balance sheet SCDOs.

Fully Funded SCDOs

Full funding means that securities have been issued and funds collected from investors in an amount adequate to cover any potential default-related loss on the underlying asset portfolio. In cash CDOs, full funding of credit risk transfer occurred because the credit-risky assets were bought with cash from the originator (balance sheet) or owner (arbitrage).

In synthetic CDOs, assets do not change ownership; the economic exposure to the asset is acquired synthetically through the sale of credit protection. Full funding here thus means that cash has been raised from investors in an amount adequate to cover the maximum possible payout on any credit protection sold, which, in turn, is enough to cover a 100 percent default rate on the asset portfolio. Fully funded synthetic CDOs thus are whole capital structure CDOs.

Like their cash market relatives discussed in Chapter 17, fully funded SCDOs can be motivated by either balance sheet or arbitrage considerations, and motive does to some extent affect the structure and design of the vehicles. We will in the next two subsections describe the basic structural distinctions between fully funded balance sheet and arbitrage CDOs, but this is not a dichotomy to which we will adhere in the rest of the chapter. Once the basic distinctions between arbitrage and balance sheet structures are understood, we can assume those distinctions will apply to whatever product we may at the time be discussing.

Fully Funded Balance Sheet SCDOs   In a *fully funded balance sheet SCDO*, a reference portfolio is defined by the originator, and notes are issued by a special purpose entity (SPE) in the same amount as the size of the reference portfolio. The proceeds from the note issue are invested with a trustee in high-quality marketable securities such as government bonds or term repurchase agreements (repos). These securities are then pledged as collateral to the originator as a performance guarantee on the credit protection sold by the SPE to the originator through a credit default swap (CDS). The originator, in turn, remits premium payments on the CDS, which are added to the low-risk collateral portfolio over time.

Any required payments on the CDS have priority in the cash flow waterfall. Default payments on the CDS thus are first covered by premium collected to date from the originator, then by investment income on the collateral portfolio, and then, as necessary, by liquidation of the securities in the collateral portfolio. Holders of notes issued by the SPE receive whatever is left over from the principal and interest (P&I) on the low-risk collateral portfolio after any required payments on the CDS. Exhibit 18.1 shows the basic structure of a fully funded balance sheet SCDO.

Notice in Exhibit 18.1 that the assets held by the trustee are still held in trust for the note holders, but now receive secondary priority in the cash flow waterfall. Accordingly, the trustee's obligation to the note holders is superseded by application of cash flows on the collateral to the originator

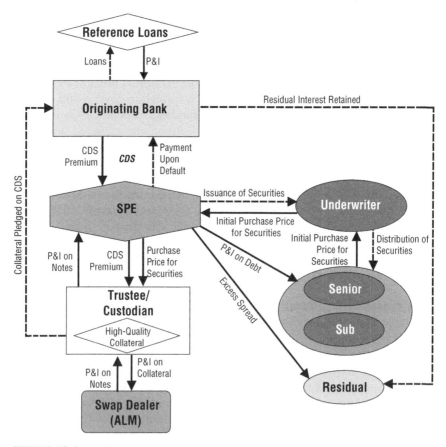

EXHIBIT 18.1   Fully Funded Arbitrage SCDO

for any required payments on the CDS. In other words, the collateral assets held by the trustee now serve as de facto (if not also de jure) collateral on the SPE's sale of credit protection through the CDS.

Note also that, as in the case of a traditional CDO, a swap dealer typically performs the usual asset-liability management (ALM) risk management and liquidity smoothing function through an asset swap of the interest on the high-quality collateral for the scheduled P&I on the note obligations of the SPE.

Fully Funded Arbitrage SCDOs A *fully funded arbitrage SCDO* is similar to its fully funded balance sheet SCDO cousin, with the same basic differences between balance sheet and arbitrage structures as we encountered in Chapter 17. Namely, the SPE issuer now works with a collateral manager to construct a reference portfolio whose retranched cash flows are believed to be of some interest to investors purely as a yield enhancement opportunity. The reference portfolio is synthetically securitized when the SPE sells credit protection using CDSs. The counterparties to these CDSs need not be the originators of the assets. They may have purchased the assets on the secondary market, or may simply be dealers or end users of credit default swaps. The composition of the reference portfolio, moreover, may change over time depending on whether the structure is passive/static, lightly managed, or actively managed.

Exhibit 18.2 shows the typical structure of an arbitrage SCDO.

Note also in this case that the residual or equity tranche is now available for sale or retained by the collateral manager. There is no need for the credit protection buyers to retain an equity exposure in this structure because they may not be the originators of the asset. As derivatives rather than insurance, moreover, CDSs are not typically considered to suffer from moral hazard problems that would necessitate a variable-interest deductible like the equity tranche of the structure.

Fully Funded Credit-Linked Notes Both the balance sheet and arbitrage examples we just reviewed were multiclass structures. If we issue a single class of securities that fully funds the sale of credit protection on a reference portfolio, we refer to that as a *credit-linked note* (CLN). Recall we discussed CLNs in Chapter 12. The only difference between those CLNs and the CLNs discussed here is the identity of the issuer. The Chapter 12 CLNs were direct obligations of the originator, whereas now we consider CLNs that are the sole class of fixed obligation issued by the SPE that has acquired its asset exposure synthetically.

For a given asset portfolio, suppose we generate an empirical loss distribution relating cumulative losses on the portfolio (as a percentage of

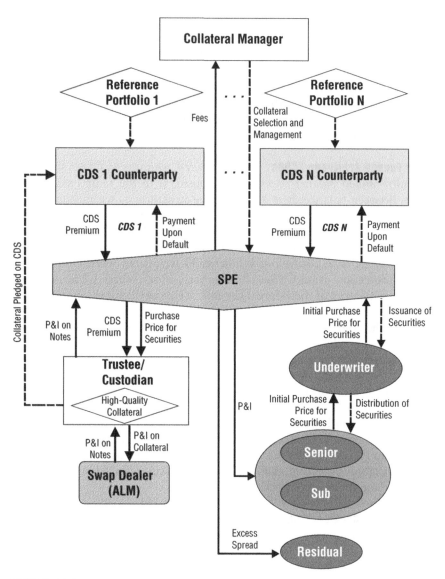

EXHIBIT 18.2 Fully Funded Arbitrage SCDO

portfolio size) to the probability of those losses being realized. In Exhibit 18.3 we relate that loss distribution to the capital structure of the SPE in the same manner we have done in earlier chapters. Because the CLN is fully funded, the size of the CLN issue corresponds to the size of the asset portfolio so that the solution is fully funded.[1] But because there is only a single layer of subordination, all losses are borne equally pro rata by holders of the CLN. The program thus represents a full credit insurance policy on the asset portfolio with *horizontal* layering instead of the usually vertical or blended layering—see Chapter 9.

Partially Funded SCDO

Few synthetic CDOs are now or ever were fully funded. Selling the entire capital structure of the issuer and synthetically securitizing the whole portfolio often was just too hard; it was (and is) time-consuming, expensive, and structuring-intensive, and required numerous different investors with varying appetites for risk. As spreads and the yield gap have steadily narrowed, moreover, the available income on a given reference asset portfolio has become too low to support an attractive expected return on the equity

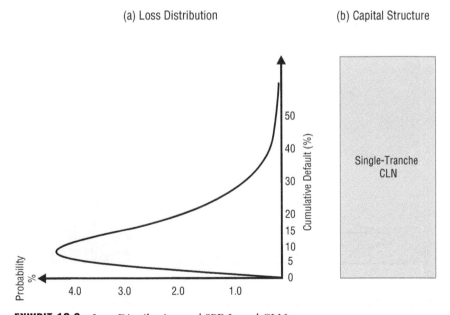

EXHIBIT 18.3   Loss Distribution and SPE-Issued CLN

tranche and even some of the subordinated debt tranches. Selling the whole capital structure of the CDO issuer in a low funding gap environment put too much pressure on issuers.

So, firms began to engage in funded credit risk transfer to investors for only a *part* of their asset portfolios. In such partially funded CDOs, the remaining portion of the portfolio either is retained or becomes the reference portfolio for an *unfunded* credit risk transfer product.

Partially funded SCDOs were popularized with the advent of JPMorgan's Broad Index Secured Trust Offering (BISTRO) in 1997. In a partially funded SCDO, securities are issued and funds set aside to cover only a portion of the defaults on the reference portfolio. Specifically, the funded part of the structure is designed so that the senior class of securities issued against the funded piece of the underlying reference portfolio will qualify as an AAA risk. The unfunded piece of the structure corresponding to the more senior part of the portfolio is called the *super-senior* piece. Exhibit 18.4 illustrates a BISTRO-like capital structure as related to a hypothetical loss distribution on the underlying reference portfolio.

From a structuring standpoint, the funded part of the deal looks just like a fully funded SCDO. Different classes of notes are issued to investors that transfer the default risk on this part of the reference portfolio in ex-

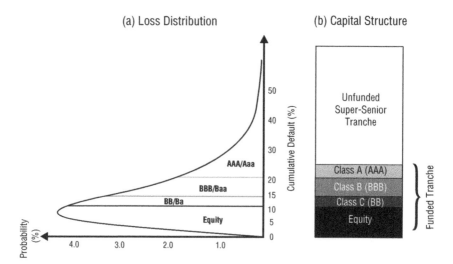

EXHIBIT 18.4 Loss Distribution and Capital Structure of SPE in a Partially Funded SCDO
Source: Merrill Lynch.

change for an above-market rate if defaults are less than expected. This rate is financed out of the base rate earned on high-quality collateral that the trustee acquires for the SPE using the proceeds of the bond issue *plus* a credit risk premium financed by the sale of a CDS by the SPE on the junior tranche of the portfolio. The funded piece thus corresponds to our usual excess of loss (XOL) credit reinsurance program.

The structure of the deal is shown in Exhibit 18.5 for a hypothetical reference portfolio of $100 million, the first $15 million of which is the funded piece. The unfunded super-senior piece thus is the remaining $85 XS $15 layer. In the structure shown, the originator has purchased protection for the super-senior piece on an *unfunded* basis using a super-senior CDS. This is common in partially funded balance sheet SCDOs.

A typical partially funded multiclass SCDO will be based on a reference portfolio of 100 or so credits, all or most of which are investment grade.[2] At least one class of notes issued in this structure against the funded portion of the reference portfolio is AAA-rated.[3] If the underlying collateral is comprised of investment-grade assets, the AAA slice of the loss distribution usually attaches at the 15 to 20 percent cumulative loss point on the actual loss distribution corresponding to the example shown in Exhibit 18.3. This leaves 80 to 85 percent of the portfolio in the super-senior tranche.

Because the funded tranche is designed so that the most senior securities issued against that tranche of the underlying synthetic asset portfolio are AAA, the super-senior tranche is incredibly low-risk. With even just 10 percent of the portfolio funded, the super-senior tranche will experience default-related losses only after 10 percent of the portfolio has defaulted first. The probability of this is extremely low, and so is the price of credit risk transfer at this level. The default rate on investment-grade bonds is around 25 to 30 basis points. Because the super-senior piece is superior to that, the price of credit risk transfer for the super-senior piece will generally command a premium below 15 basis points. The additional unfunded protection for the super-senior piece afforded by the super-senior CDS thus is relatively cheap.

To take a concrete example, consider the Amadeus Funding deal of December 1998. As BankAustria and Creditanstalt were finalizing their merger late that year, both had substantial asset-backed security (ABS) portfolios and both had decided to securitize some big part of them. Both, moreover, had already decided to work with Citibank. So, even before the merger was finalized, BankAustria securitized $1.2 billion of its ABSs in a partially funded SCDO.[4]

BankAustria's $1.2 billion was split into three tranches: a junior first-loss tranche of $24 million (which BankAustria retained), an AA senior

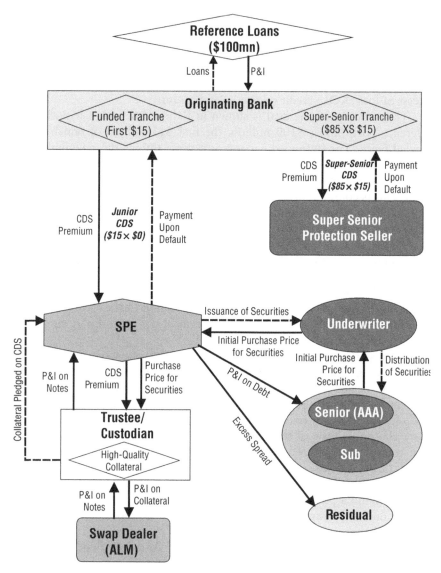

EXHIBIT 18.5 Partially Funded SCDO with Super-Senior CDS

tranche corresponding to the $48mn XS $24mn layer, and a super-senior $1.128bn XS $72mn tranche. Amadeus Funding issued the AA bonds at 3M-LIBOR+87.5 with five years to maturity. The $1.128 billion super-senior piece was then hedged with a CDS negotiated with Citibank. The cost of the CDS was well below the coupon rate on a $1.128 billion AAA-rated senior debenture, which would have been the alternative funding cost had BankAustria opted for a fully funded CBO. On net, BankAustria secured $1.2 billion in protection with a 2 percent deductible for under 100 basis points (Hay 1999).

Regulatory Capital Considerations in Balance Sheet SCDOs

We saw in Chapter 17 how cash CDOs can help banks improve the return on equity (ROE) of their loan portfolios and optimize their allocation of regulatory capital. So, too, can SCDOs prove beneficial to bank originators. All balance sheet SCDOs thus will be designed to exploit these benefits. Whether or not an arbitrage SCDO is constructed to minimize regulatory capital charges depends on whether the collateral manager is selling protection to a bank originator subject to the Basel Accord.

Fully Funded Structures   The regulatory capital charge to the synthetic asset seller (i.e., credit protection purchaser) in an SCDO is 100 percent of the retained residual tranche plus a capital charge for the swap. The capital the bank must allocate to the CDS is based on the quality of the assets backing the CDS. If the CDS is collateralized with Treasuries, for example, the risk weight is 0 percent. But this also means the investment income on the collateral that is used to pay interest to noteholders is fairly low.

As an alternative, the bank could enter into a CDS with an institution whose general balance-sheet asset quality is enough to merit a low risk weight. Obligations of Organization for Economic Cooperation and Development (OECD) banks, for example, carry a 20 percent risk weight. Although not as good as the zero weight on Treasuries, doing a CDS with an OECD bank would enable the trustee to hold slightly higher yielding assets than if those assets collateralizing the swap had to be left in Treasuries for regulatory capital reasons.

Consider, for example, a bank with a $500 million loan portfolio that synthetically securitizes those assets by buying credit protection from an SPE using a CDS. The bank retains the equity tranche issued by the SPE, which is 1 percent of the deal. If the CDS is collateralized with Treasuries, the bank's capital requirement is $5 million, representing the $5 million charge for the retained equity interest. The zero-weighted Treasuries add nothing to the bank's capital requirement. If the CDS is collateralized with AAA-rated securities (which have a 100 percent risk weight), the capital requirement is 9 percent of the deal, or $45 million—$5 million for the equity and another $40 million for AAA securities backing the CDS. In both cases, the CDS is presumed to be *fully* collateralized up to the maximum possible payout.

Now suppose the bank enters into a CDS with an OECD bank. The OECD bank itself has credits that are risk-weighted at 20 percent, so the capital requirement for the bank is now the $5 million charge on the retained equity plus $8 million (8 percent of $500 million at a 20 percent risk weight) or $13 million total. The OECD bank, of course, is not the issuer of the securitized products. That responsibility remains the SPE's. Mechanically, the OECD thus is interspersed between the SPE and the originating bank as what we call a *fronting credit protection provider*. Specifically, the OECD bank writes credit protection to the originator in a CDS backed only by its balance sheet as a performance guarantee. The bank in turn buys equivalent credit protection in an identical CDS in which the SPE is the credit protection seller. The SPE still invests the proceeds of its securities issue in collateral, but now pledges that collateral to the OECD bank.

The CDS fully collateralized with Treasuries gave the originator a lower capital charge, but also gave investors in the CDO tranches a lower base rate. Although the fronting protection structure is not quite as good as the Treasury structure from a capital charge perspective, the collateral held by the SPE is now pledged to the OECD bank and not to the originator. The collateral thus plays no role in the capital charge. Provided the OECD bank will agree from a credit risk management standpoint, the SPE thus is free now to hold, say, AAA assets as collateral, thereby getting a higher base rate for investors.

Because the collateral held by the trustee for the SPE is pledged to the CDS written by the SPE and has priority over the liabilities of the SPE in the SPE's cash flow waterfall, there is minimal chance that the collateral will be inadequate to cover the maximum payment on the CDS in the event that *all* of the reference assets underlying the CDS default. Depending on the assets held by the trustee as collateral against the CDS, investors may bear some market risk that the value of the collateral might decline in value. With an OECD bank selling fronting protection, however, the bank buying the CDS from the SPE to hedge the credit protection it sells to the originator will provide some external discipline on the asset selection for the collateral. The bank can be expected to adhere to its own collateral policies and thus also may require the SPE to discount the collateral it holds to reflect potential market risk losses that might occur prior to liquidation of the collateral. If the SPE wants to hold AAA assets, for example, it may get only 80 to 90 percent credit for each dollar of collateral held to reflect the market risk of AAA securities. In this case, the SPE would need to come up with the difference through some other credit enhancement (C/E) to the structure, such as a cash contribution from the originator.

The greater risk is liquidity risk, which in the SCDO structure with the OECD bank can take two forms. The first is the usual form of liquidity risk discussed in Chapters 13 and 16: the risk that cash income on the collateral held by the trustee is mismatched to the interest payments due on the SPE's liabilities. The usual asset swap with a swap dealer can be used to address this problem.

Managing liquidity risk is doubly important if the face value of the collateral on a risk-adjusted basis (i.e., after any haircut applied by the OECD bank) is less than the full value of the reference asset portfolio. In this case, the income in the cash flow waterfall will build up additional credit and liquidity enhancement over time *for later defaults*, but the structure remains highly exposed to the liquidity risk of large default-related losses early in the life of the program. If the asset swap counterparty is unprepared to cover this liquidity risk, the structure may require additional liquidity enhancement.

Partially Funded Structures In a partially funded SCDO in which the issuer acquires credit exposure synthetically directly from a bank originator, regulatory capital charges can be held to a minimum on the funded piece in the same way that we just discussed for the fully funded structure—through an OECD bank fronting protection seller. That leaves only the question of the capital on the super-senior piece.

The capital treatment for the super-senior piece depends on what the originator does with it. Left on the balance sheet unfunded, the assets receive their normal risk weight. Alternatively, the originator may choose to acquire protection for the super-senior piece (for reasons already discussed). This can be done through a collateralized CDS or a CDS with an OECD bank—either the same one fronting for the mezzanine CDS or a different one. Exhibit 18.6 illustrates.

Exhibit 18.6 can also be used to visualize what the fully funded structure would look like with a fronting protection provider. Just ignore the super-senior piece and assume that the funded piece in Exhibit 18.6 is 100 percent of the reference portfolio. In the BankAustria Amadeus Funding structure examined earlier, for example, one estimate suggests that BankAustria cut its regulatory capital requirement from around $120 million to around $26 million on its $1.2 billion ABS portfolio for a total all-in cost of below 100 basis points over three-month LIBOR.[5]

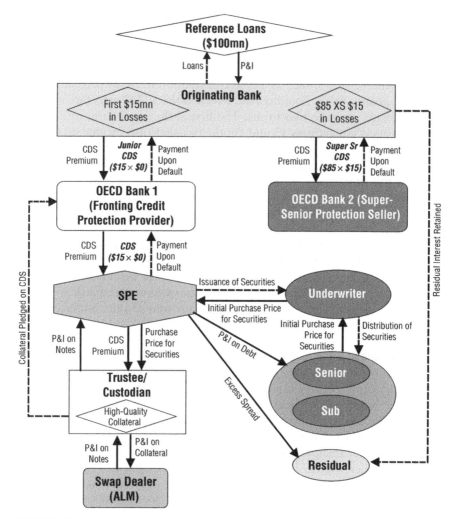

EXHIBIT 18.6 Partially Funded Balance Sheet SCDO with Fronting Protection
Provider and Super-Senior Protection

APPEAL OF SYNTHETIC STRUCTURES

SCDOs originated in the late 1990s primarily as an alternative to traditional balance sheet CDOs for bank credit risk management. Fueled by the growth in the credit derivatives market, SCDOs became increasingly popular for their original purpose of credit portfolio management, as well as for use in arbitrage CDOs. They have tremendous appeal among issuers/originators and investors alike.

Operational Benefits

An oft-cited benefit of SCDOs vis-à-vis traditional CDOs is the purely operational advantage of SCDOs in avoiding restrictions against and covenants concerning loan sales. Especially in the syndicated bank loan arena, restrictions on the resale of loans and loan participations can greatly complicate a traditional securitization. Similarly, portfolios with loans in multiple legal jurisdictions often are hard to securitize because of differences in local tax, accounting, and regulation, as well as differences in the criteria for achieving a true sale. The same economic result as a securitization can be obtained using SCDOs without these and other operational hassles associated with actual asset divestiture.

Flexibility in Design

Constructing a customized synthetic reference portfolio is generally far easier than divesting a true portfolio of assets. CDS documentation is much easier to finalize than loan documentation, and CDS structures rarely require time-consuming activities like obtaining the consent of individual obligors for an actual asset transfer. Also, CDSs provide tremendous flexibility to banks for combining different loans and risk exposures in a single credit protection structure.

The CDS market at the root of SCDO activity, moreover, has rapidly grown into a liquid and robust market for the purchase and sale of credit protection. As the market has both broadened and deepened, the range of structures—only some of which were surveyed in Chapter 12—has significantly increased the capacity of banks to tailor their exact risk management needs to actual transactions. Structural design features like Nth to default, senior-sub basket protection, deductibles, tailored loss layering, and the like all make SCDOs an effective and efficient form of credit risk transfer.

Ease of Documentation

As the credit derivatives market has grown steadily, the pro forma documentation underlying credit derivatives has become more and more robust. The numerous disruptive credit events during the 2000–2002 period (see Harris and Kramer, Chapter 31) seemed only to heighten attention to documentation issues and to make the market even more attentive to the need for standardization.

Loan documentation and the deal documents underlying a typical securitization or asset sale, by contrast, remain highly cumbersome and complex and a long, long way from standardized. Some would argue that this alone is a sufficient reason to eschew traditional CDOs in favor of their synthetic cousins.

Selective Risk Transfer and Asymmetric Information

Investors often prefer synthetic CDO structures because they separate out the pure credit component of credit-sensitive assets from the other risks inherent to the asset, such as sovereign or political risk and currency risk. Originators may actually share this desire.

Recall that one reason the plain-vanilla interest rate swap market was so successful in its early days was that swaps provided banks and other financial institutions a way to separate out the interest rate risk of a loan from the credit risk of a loan. Similarly, credit derivatives now allow banks to peel away that layer, as well. Some originators may perceive some comparative advantage in bearing noncredit risks of their loans, such as currency risk. Whole asset securitization deprives firms of the ability to engage in selective risk transfer, whereas SCDOs do not.

Cost of Capital

In a traditional CDO, the most senior tranche is the senior note in the capital structure of the SPE to which the asset portfolio has been conveyed. The best case is that senior tranche is rated AAA, which will probably price around 35 to 75 basis points.

The weighted average cost of capital (WACC) of the originator will usually be lower using a partially funded SCDO because that structure—through the super-senior piece—essentially enables the bank to access better-than-AAA financing on at least part of its assets.

In effect, this is exploiting a weakness in current credit market pricing conventions, so heavily driven by external ratings that obviously lack a category above AAA that the market is prepared to price. The price of that

"AAAA" tranche is the price of the super-senior protection in an SCDO, and the SCDO structure is by far the most efficient means by which banks and other originators can at present access this rate and this correspondingly lower WACC.

SECOND-GENERATION SCDO STRUCTURES

As the SCDO market burgeoned and funding gaps tightened, investors seeking synthetic CDO exposure began to search for new structures and designs. At the same time, the deepening and broadening of the CDS market made it increasingly popular for banks and investors alike to fine-tune their credit risk transfer of single-name and portfolio exposures alike. Together, this led to an evolution in the SCDO market and SCDO product design. The following sections discuss the major new structures in this second wave of SCDO innovation.

Single-Tranche SCDOs

In 2004, *single-tranche SCDOs* (STSCDOs) accounted for virtually all new SCDO issuance. An STSCDO—sometimes called a *bespoke CDO*—is an investor-driven or reverse enquiry transaction in which an investor approaches an issuer, collateral manager, or structuring agent and requests a specific bundle of cash flows and risk exposure in the form of a security. The exposure requested is generally some mezzanine tranche of a reference asset portfolio that the issuer can construct at its discretion using a series of single-name CDSs.

After being contacted by an investor the issuer selects a reference portfolio, enters into one or more credit derivatives to synthesize a SCDO-like exposure to that reference portfolio, and then issues a single class of securities backed by the piece of the reference portfolio that investors demand. The reference portfolio typically includes 50 to 100 investment-grade credits with a high diversity across industries.[6]

Unlike the multiclass partially funded SCDOs examined in the previous section, the issuer of an STSCDO generally retains the other tranches of exposure to the reference portfolio, dynamically hedging them using credit derivatives, repos, and the like instead of attempting to place some or all of these securities as additional classes of securities.[7] The issuer may *later* decide to sell securities backed by other tranches in the deal, but does not wait to find buyers for those tranches before closing the STSCDO deal. This is a primary attraction of STSCDOs because it means that the time from first inquiry by investors to deal closing and execution can be very short. When the issuer has to place multiple classes of securities, the documentation becomes much more complicated, the underwriting and distribution process can get lengthy, and the time to completion for the whole deal can get quite long. Not so with a STSCDO.

Exhibit 18.7 shows a hypothetical loss distribution on some reference portfolio, where investors have indicated an isolated interest in a specific mezzanine tranche of that reference portfolio. You can see from the diagram that this leaves the first-loss position and the more senior piece unfunded at the time the securities corresponding to the single mezzanine tranche are issued.

Because a single class of security is now being issued against the mezzanine tranche of the portfolio and the issuer retains the unfunded first-loss and senior pieces (at least initially), the note issued is essentially a CLN. And as noted earlier in this chapter and in Chapter 12, CLNs need not be issued by an SPE. They may be, but they may also just as easily be issued directly by the originating bank that receives the reverse inquiry from investors.

Resecuritizations and CDO²

A *synthetic resecuritization* is a CDO that repackages pieces of other CDOs into new securities. In some cases, all of the collateral in these struc-

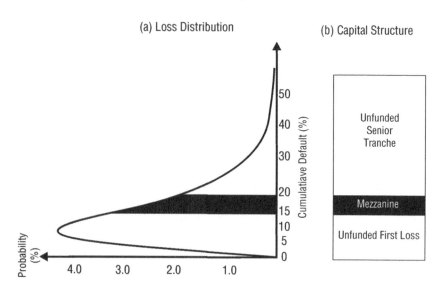

EXHIBIT 18.7 Loss Distribution and Securities Issued in a Single-Tranche SCDO
Source: Merrill Lynch.

tures is in the form of securities, but these securities are themselves CLN issues from SCDOs. Industry and rating agency standards still consider these structures synthetic because the CLNs are synthetic products.

A CDO^2 transaction—also known as a *CDO of CDOs* or *CDO squared*—is essentially just a synthetic form of resecuritization. Not all resecuritizations are CDO^2 transactions. Resecuritizations can be done using traditional ABSs, as well as commercial mortgage-backed securities (CMBSs), residential mortgage-backed securities (RMBSs), real estate investment trusts (REITs), and CLNs. Even before the CDO^2 market began in earnest with the 1998 ZAIS Group-sponsored ZING transactions, CDO managers had already been including tranches from other CDOs in the structured finance basket of their collateral pools. Mezzanine tranches of CDOs were especially popular as collateral for other CDOs because of their high spreads and near or just below investment-grade ratings.[8]

The mechanics of a CDO^2 deal are no different from those of the funded and partially funded multiclass SCDOs we have already examined in this chapter. The difference is entirely in the collateral held against the securities issued. As such, the same economic motives for engaging in first-generation SCDOs (e.g., capital relief, targeting specific investor demands, ratings arbitrage, etc.) can also motivate CDO^2 deals.

In addition, CDO^2 transactions are a popular means by which the bits and pieces of other CDOs can be sold. Specifically, many collateral managers in arbitrage SCDOs find that the residual tranche is quite hard to place in the market. Sometimes the subordinated tranches of the mezzanine layer also prove challenging to sell. As a result, the collateral manager ends up with chunks of mostly junior exposures left in its own trading book. A CDO^2 deal provides a good opportunity for the cash flows on those otherwise-undesirable tranches to be repackaged and sold through a resecuritization.

ST-CDO²

In Europe, CDO^2s are populated almost entirely with STSCDO securities. The CDO manager actually buys the securities issued in 100 or so STSCDO transactions and then holds those securities as collateral for the liabilities that it issues. Exhibit 18.8 shows the conceptual basics of such a structure.

In many cases, the CDO^2 is also a single-tranche structure, in which case it is called a *ST-CDO²*, as shown in Exhibit 18.9.

ST-CDO²s provide a huge amount of flexibility to tailor attachment points in multiple reference portfolios to end investor needs, but they also

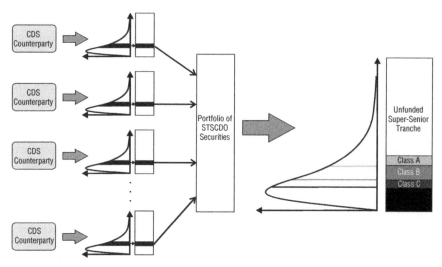

EXHIBIT 18.8   CDO² of STSCDOs
Source: Merrill Lynch.

can be very complex and hard to analyze. The effective level of subordination achieved by the investors in the single-tranche security issued by an ST-CDO² depends on the attachment point and rating of the underlying STSCDOs in the ST-CDO² collateral pool. Although the correlation between the CDSs that underlie the combined credit pool and the likely overlap in reference names across those constituent CDSs also play a role, let's

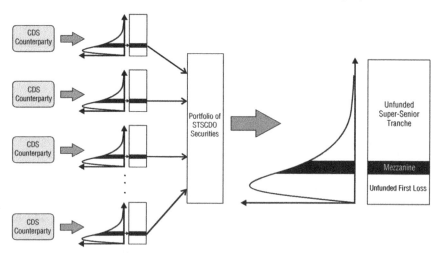

EXHIBIT 18.9   ST-CDO² of STSCDOs
Source: Merrill Lynch.

hold those constant for the moment so that we can focus on the rating and attachment point. In short, a low attachment point and rating on the underlying STSCDOs can be combined with a high attachment point on the ST-CDO^2 to yield the same rating and risk level as a high attachment point and rating on the underlying together with a low attachment point in the ST-CDO^2 (Batchvarov, Davletova, and Davies 2004). This kind of trade-off is what makes the ST-CDO^2 structure versatile for meeting virtually any investor demand, but it also necessitates a careful analysis of risk by prospective holders of the end security.

Master CDO

A *master CDO* is a CDO backed with a pool of ABSs *and* a basket of STSCDO issues. The master CDO structure is also sometimes called a *repackaging*.

Master CDOs emerged mainly in Europe, where the bulk of CDO activity involves structures backed by ABSs or structured debt collateral. Because of very tight spreads in the past two years in mezzanine ABS issues, the funding gap on a pure European ABS CDO has become tight—see Table 17.1. Sponsors have found it harder and harder to place all the tranches in a traditional CDO, and have encountered particular difficulties selling equity tranches; with a funding gap that is too low, the expected return on equity is not high enough to justify the risk of the position.

To increase the funding gap and make the CDO more attractive, banks began to include a basket of STSCDOs along with the portfolio of ABSs or structured debt, either in a cash/synthetic hybrid or purely synthetically. In fact, one reason for the explosion in demand for STSCDOs has been the specific desire to include them in master CDO deals. Sponsors of ABS CDOs simply contact one or more banks and request STSCDOs to complement their ABS CDOs in a master CDO structure. As already discussed, the bank can easily construct an STSCDO using a single-name CDS or portfolio CDS in very little time. Not surprisingly, the combination of higher-yielding customized STSCDO tranches with a portfolio of ABSs can easily be structured to produce a more attractive funding gap and a more customized security offering.

FLIRTING WITH INSURANCE?[9]

We established many chapters ago that credit derivatives are not insurance. The purchaser of credit protection need not have an insurable interest in the reference asset or portfolio. An event of default that triggers a payment on a CDS, moreover, may not give rise to an economic loss on the corresponding asset or portfolio at the same time that the CDS is triggered. If the credit protection purchaser does not own the reference asset, no loss will occur for which the CDS payment might be construed as a reimbursement. Even if the original obligee is the credit protection purchaser, the CDS may pay well before the economic loss on the underlying asset is realized given the definitions of events of default in standardized CDS documentation. Either way, there has never been much question that credit derivatives are not insurance, provided they are properly documented and structured.

Cash CDOs appear to be equally safe, even if the cash CDO is a resecuritization. Because assets are being sold for an up-front cash payment, there is no contingent future payment that would resemble an insurance transaction.

Even synthetic CDOs would seem to be a fair distance from the gray line separating insurance and derivatives. Because credit exposure is acquired synthetically using mainly CDSs, the CDO should be safe as long as the underlying CDSs are safe.

Synthetic resecuritizations, however, may push the line separating insurance and derivatives to its near breaking point. As we have now seen, synthetic resecuritizations involve the acquisition of credit exposure on securitized products using credit derivatives. As we saw in Chapter 13, however, securitized products are almost always issued by SPEs that are bankruptcy remote from originators. The underlying bankruptcy or default of an originator thus may not lead to a corresponding default on the securitized products.

Forrester (2003) notes that in the absence of a set of uncontroversial events of default to include in CDS master agreements based on structured products, market participants have tended to define their own events of default for CDSs based on structured products as follows: The reference asset is irrevocably written down; the reference asset is downgraded; or the securitized product is restructured somehow. Forrester (2003) then observes: "As can readily be seen, such credit events move significantly closer to 'loss'—since in these events it is more likely that there will be in fact a recognized loss by the holder of the referenced [securitized product]."

Caution and prudence together with continuous marketwide efforts at establishing standard definitions of events of default for ABSs will eventually eliminate the uncertainties associated with this problem. Yet the lesson here is a clear one. Despite the increasing convergence of insurance and capital markets products, regulation has not kept pace. Users of these products must navigate carefully through potentially dangerous minefields to achieve the full economic benefits of convergence that regulation does not yet embrace.

CHAPTER 19

Structured Synthetic Hybrids

In this chapter we consider a new but rapidly emerging structured product that we might call *structured synthetic hybrids*. These products use synthetic collateralized debt obligation (CDO) technology to synthesize securities that represent blended claims on synthetic credit and equity. They are quite literally the CDO analogues to hybrid securities (see Chapter 14).

The appeal of these structures rests largely on the successful evolution (albeit still in its nascent phase) of the equity default swap (EDS) market. Recall from Chapter 12 that an EDS is essentially a deeply out-of-the-money long-dated equity put option—usually a digital. But the EDS is constructed to be virtually the same as a credit default swap (CDS), thus allowing investors the chance to use the two products together to get a synthetic combination of debt and equity.

Because most EDSs define an equity event to be a substantial decline in the stock price of the reference name, the probability that an EDS will move into the money before a comparable CDS is extremely high. Conversely, because all debt obligations are senior in capital structure to equity, it is hard to imagine a default on debt that triggers a CDS payment that does not *also* result in the triggering of an EDS on the same name. This creates some volatility in the EDS-CDS spread or basis, which has been used in some of the structures discussed in this chapter as a source of yield enhancement to entice investors.

Few structured synthetic hybrid deals have been done to date, so this chapter is relatively brief. But the more the EDS market develops, the more we should anticipate additional innovation of these already novel products.

EQUITY DEFAULT OBLIGATIONS

An *equity default obligation* (EDO) is a synthetic collateralized debt obligation (SCDO) that includes one or more EDSs as part of the synthetic collateral. (See Chapter 12 for our discussion of EDSs.) Structurally, they are essentially the same as SCDOs. The only real difference is the loss distribution of the assets that serve as synthetic collateral for the CDO's liabilities. A typical EDO is comprised of a relatively broad range of credits—corporate, sovereign, and so on. The equity exposure to these credits is acquired through either multiple single-name EDSs or a portfolio EDS, possibly in combination with other types of collateral.

One of the most straightforward EDO deals done to date was the Zest transaction arranged by Daiwa Securities that closed in March 2004.[1] In that deal, the reference portfolio consisted of 30 blue-chip Japanese firms. The special purpose entity (SPE) acquired exposure to these firms in a portfolio EDS negotiated with a single counterparty. The equity event for each reference name was a 70 percent stock price decline, and the payoff was a percentage of the stock price. The reference portfolio had a notional value of ¥31.5 billion. The SPE in turn issued ¥31.5 billion of securities in five layers of subordination. The three most senior tranches were rated A3, Baa2, and Ba2, respectively, by Moody's. The basic structure of the deal is shown in Exhibit 19.1.

Not all the equity exposures in EDOs are long. Structures with long-short hedge-fund-like exposures are also being observed. Consider, for example, CEDO I Plc, closed in May 2005 and sponsored by Credit Suisse First Boston. In this structure, multiple tranches of notes are issued against a portfolio comprised of 60 *long* EDSs referencing corporate entities (called the "Risk Portfolio") and 60 *short* EDSs also referencing corporate entities, possibly (likely) different from the reference entities underlying the long EDSs (called the "Insurance Portfolio").[2]

HYBRID CDO

When EDSs and CDSs are combined as collateral, the resulting EDO is sometimes called a *hybrid CDO*. In fact, the first major EDO was itself a hybrid—the Odysseus deal arranged by JPMorgan in December 2003.[3] The reference portfolio consisted of 100 blue-chip firms with a weighted average rating (WAR) by Moody's of Baa2. The notional amount of the reference portfolio was €1.2 billion, 90 percent of which was acquired through CDSs and the other 10 percent of which through EDSs. The EDSs defined an equity event as a 70 percent decline in the stock price of each reference name, and the recovery rate was 50 percent of the notional amount. The deal was a single-tranche SCDO (STSCDO), with the single €30 million mezzanine tranche receiving an Aa2 rating. The structure is shown in Exhibit 19.2.

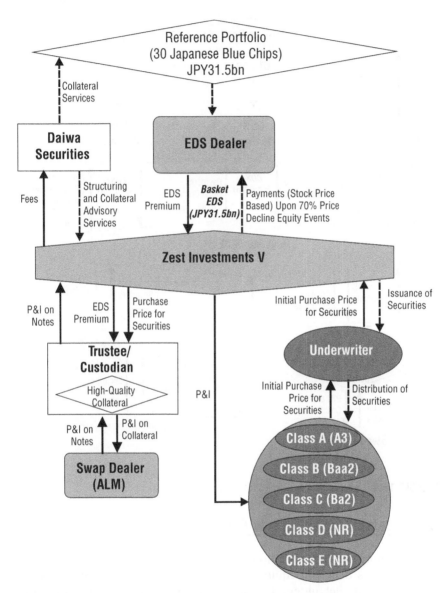

EXHIBIT 19.1   Zest Equity Default Obligation (EDO) (March 2004)
Source: Moody's Investors Service, Zest V Pre-Sale Report (March 18, 2004).

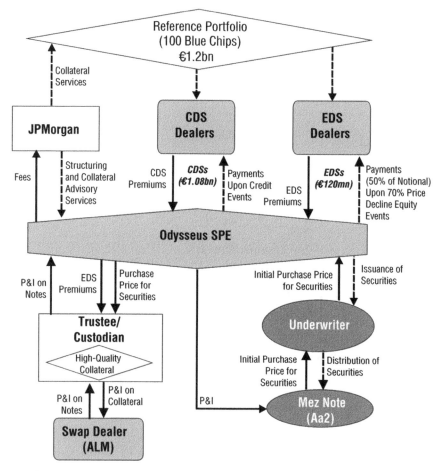

EXHIBIT 19.2   Odysseus Hybrid EDO (December 2003)

Nth to Default Basket Hybrid CDO

A much more complex variation of the Odysseus hybrid CDO is a CDO that combines debt and equity exposure based on the sequential occurrence of a credit default event *or* an equity event. This type of transaction is typified by the September 2004 Chrome Funding ACEO deal, sponsored by CDC IXIS Capital Markets.[4]

The Chrome deal defined 30 baskets, each of which contained exposures based on four reference names, none of which overlapped across baskets. Inside each basket were four transactions: three single-name CDSs and one single-name EDS. The 90 total CDSs had an average Moody's rating of A2, whereas the 30 EDSs had a WAR of A1 from Moody's. All the EDSs defined an equity event as a 70 percent price decline and specified a 50 percent notional recovery rate.

With each basket defined, the SPE sold credit protection in the form of 30 *second*-to-default (2tD) basket swaps. In most cases, an equity event will occur before a credit event, thus implying that much of this structure's economic exposure will be derived from the first CDS default in each basket.

The capital structure of the SPE involved four levels of subordinated debt: 3% XS 1.7%, 3% XS 3.35%, 4% XS 5.4%, and 3% XS 6.2%. The 1.7 percent first-loss tranche, 90.8 percent senior tranche, and all the gaps between the four specified subordination levels were retained and delta-hedged by the issuer.[5] The notes were rated A1, Aa2, Aaa, and Aaa, respectively.[6] The structure of this deal is shown in Exhibit 19.3.

Davletova, Batchvarov, and Davies (2004) provide an interesting and thoughtful analysis of this structure. They argue that the EDSs in each basket can be viewed as CDSs but with a much higher default probability, given that an EDS will nearly always be triggered before a CDS on the same reference name. The 2tD basket then can be viewed as a type of STSCDO, suggesting that the structure as a whole is analogous to a CDO[2] of STSCDOs. Exhibit 19.4 illustrates with a set of hypothetical loss distributions mapped to the final capital structure of the Chrome deal.

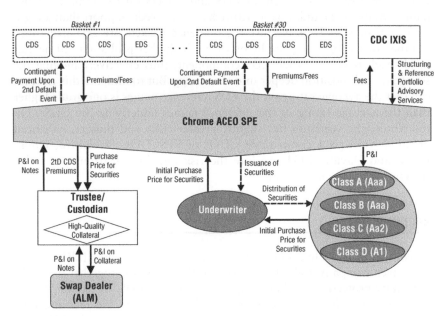

EXHIBIT 19.3 Chrome Funding ACEO (December 2003)

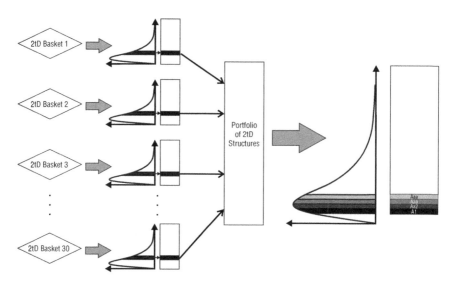

EXHIBIT 19.4   Loss Distributions and Cap Structure of Chrome ACEO

The main rationale for including an EDS in the credit baskets is the relatively large spread between an EDS and a CDS on the same reference name. On the one hand, this structure has more credit support than a regular CDO^2 of STSCDOs because the reference baskets are 2tD structures. On the other hand, this may be offset by the higher probability of default inside each basket on each EDS component, thus effectively moving the second default position deeper into the money. But to mitigate this risk, recall that the average rating on the EDS reference names is one grade higher than the average rating of the reference names underlying the CDSs. On the whole, the structure has slightly greater risks and thus an enhanced premium vis-à-vis a comparable CDO^2 of STSCDOs. Davletova, Batchvarov, and Davies (2004) explore the risk and loss distribution of this structure in much more detail.

REBOUND NOTES

A *rebound note* is a hybrid that combines a floating-rate note (FRN) issued by a given company and a CDS based on that company together with selling equity protection on that company through an EDS.[7] If neither the equity event nor the credit event occurs, the investor in the rebound note receives the yield on the FRN plus the difference between the EDS premium collected and the CDS premium paid. If the equity event occurs but not the credit event, the investor may be completely wiped out in the note. But if an equity event occurs followed by a credit event, the principal rebounds back to the investor.

Recall from Chapter 12 that typical credit events giving rise to payment by the protection seller in a CDS include bankruptcy, failure to pay on an obligation, and the like. An EDS, however, is essentially a deeply out-of-the-money put on the stock of the reference entity. The equity event that triggers a payment on a EDS is usually a 70 percent decline in the stock price. The equity event thus will almost always occur prior to the credit event, thus leading to the positive EDS-CDS spread.[8] The structure of a rebound note issue is shown in Exhibit 19.5.

The appeal of rebound notes to investors is primarily to facilitate capital structure arbitrage. To see why, just recall our discussion in Chapter 1.

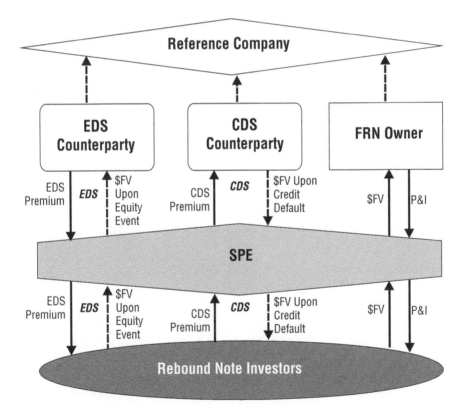

EXHIBIT 19.5 Rebound Notes

Debt can be viewed as a loan plus a short put on the firm's net assets, and equity can be viewed as a long call on the firm's net assets. In a Modigliani and Miller (M&M) world, the EDS-CDS premium thus just reflects the difference in these option premiums for the asset value scenarios corresponding to the definition of the equity and credit events. In reality, the two may differ.

In this sense, although the rebound note is not a corporate financing instrument per se (because it relies on either products that already have been issued or derivatives on existing products), the availability of rebound notes in the market clearly increases the *efficiency* of the reference issuer's corporate financing decisions by helping to ensure a tight linkage between the option-equivalent values of debt and equity.

CHAPTER 20

Securitizing Private Equity and Hedge Funds

This chapter summarizes the part of the global structured finance market dedicated to the securitization of private equity (PE) and hedge funds. Because the process of creating these securitized managed funds is essentially similar to the collateralized debt obligation (CDO) creation process, these structures are known collectively as *collateralized fund obligations* (CFOs).

To date, only a few dozen CFOs have been executed and brought to market successfully. These deals have all occurred since 1999 and have been generally well-received by investors. The market continues to demonstrate some appetite for the deals that are brought, but the low volume of deal flow suggests that this may be a niche appetite. In the past year, however, CFOs backed by private equity have started to show signs of heightened investor interest. Only time will tell whether the CFO market will ever experience even near-comparable growth to the CDO market, but the products to date are sufficiently interesting and have been sufficiently successful to justify their inclusion here.

We begin this chapter by reviewing the unique nature of the collateral assets that back CFOs. We then turn to review two basically different types of CFO structures: fully funded single-tranche CFOs, and multiclass CFOs. We provide examples of noteworthy deals throughout the discussion.

HEDGE FUNDS AND PRIVATE EQUITY FUNDS AS COLLATERAL

Before examining the structures that now define the CFO universe, it makes sense to spend a little time discussing the underlying collateral that backs these structured product offerings. Unlike CDOs and EDOs that are based on straight corporate debt or equity exposures, CFOs are usually based on actively managed *funds*—a fund of private equity investments, a hedge fund, a portfolio or fund of funds, or an index of funds. This gives rise to certain structuring challenges, as well as opportunities.

Because hedge and PE funds are both primarily investment vehicles, it seems odd at first glance that there would be much benefit to repackaging and restructuring these investment pools into new securities that are also marketed and sold mainly as investment opportunities. Yet, it is precisely the limitations on the capital structures of hedge funds and PE funds that can constrain their access to capital. For one thing, most investments in hedge funds and PE funds take the form of restricted equity, such as limited or general partnership interests. This kind of structure impedes the fund from relying on structuring its liabilities as a means of engaging in selective risk transfer. Instead, all investors in these funds are forced to bear a proportional share of *all* the risks of the underlying investments.

The difficulties faced by hedge and PE funds in structuring their liabilities can have three distinct negative consequences. First, potential investors in a fund that might be interested in a specific part of the fund's risk profile without wanting to bear all the risk pari passu with other investors and partners may be excluded in traditional structures. Second, the partnership structure can make it difficult for funds to attract smaller retail investors, thus limiting investors to high net worth individuals, family offices, and other asset managers. And, finally, the lack of diversity in liabilities can make it difficult for certain investors to participate in hedge and PE funds because of institutional constraints (e.g., maximum leverage positions, prohibitions on investing in securities without principal protection, rating agency constraints or targets, etc.).

Although CFOs include both hedge funds and PE as collateral, these two investment management vehicles are very different creatures. We summarize the salient features of each in the next two subsections.

Hedge Funds

A hedge fund is an investment vehicle that is typically associated with higher-risk, higher-expected-return strategies than a traditional mutual fund, for which investors pay extra performance incentive fees. Hedge funds derived their name originally from the concept of "market neutral" investing—that is, a fund that promises a high alpha but a near-zero beta through a mix of long and short positions. Today, hedge funds come in many different types; some of the most popular ones are:[1]

- *Equity market neutral*—equity funds that attempt to remain market neutral through offsetting positions.

- *Event-driven*—funds that are focused mainly on profit opportunities arising from specific events; some funds are driven by single events (e.g., convertible arbitrage and distressed funds), and others are multistrategy.
- *Long/short*—driven by pairs investing of individual long positions versus short sales.
- *Tactical trading*—quantitative model-driven funds often focused on market timing plays.
- *Global macro*—often model-driven investment strategies across numerous asset classes and global markets—high alpha and low beta attained through "whole market" mispricings.

Hedge fund participation usually occurs through a master partnership structure in which the fund's adviser(s) and/or key sponsor(s) are the general partners (GPs). External investment generally comes in the form of limited partner (LP) interests. Exiting a fund often requires an LP to provide the GP with notice well in advance of the planned redemption date. Exits may be further constrained by long minimum initial holding periods or lockout periods.

A major constraint facing many prospective hedge fund investors has always been the risk of a loss of principal. Pension plans and certain other institutional investors, for example, are rarely authorized to engage in investments for which a loss of principal is a real possibility. Until the advent of hedge fund-linked structured securities, participating in hedge fund returns without the full risks of hedge fund partnership investments was essentially impossible.

Private Equity Funds

Private equity is an important source of corporate financing and risk transfer, especially for firms that have difficulty accessing the traditional public securities markets. Private equity includes both venture and nonventure investments. Venture PE is typically associated with firms—often small or medium-sized—in early capitalization stages, whereas nonventure PE includes funding for buyouts, restructurings, distress workouts, and the like.

Private equity is frequently placed through PE funds. A typical PE fund is organized as a partnership, with a general partner (GP) actively managing the specific investments of the fund. Limited partners (LPs) are investors in the fund that agree to fund a certain amount of capital calls, usually over the first 5 to 10 years of the fund.

PE funds have been securitized through a CDO-like process on several occasions. The tranched capital structure of CDOs is a natural fit to private equity collateral. The structuring process greatly increases the range of risk/return opportunities in the fund available for private equity fund investors. In addition, increased liquidity, decreased volatility, increased transparency, and heightened competitiveness (through better benchmarking) are natural consequences for the underlying private equity market as private equity–backed CDOs increase in popularity.

Private equity does, of course, pose some considerable challenges to the structuring process. Some of these challenges are purely structural and legal. LP interests is a fund, for example, are generally transferable only with permission of the GP and even then may be subject to additional restrictions. Other challenges in securitizing PE fund interests arise more from the nature and risks of the PE business itself.

Private equity funds typically have a net cash flow profile over time that resembles the pattern shown in Exhibit 20.1, known as the *J-curve*. High up-front costs, the ramp-up period, capital calls, and high debt service obligations on what can be substantial amounts of senior debt all lead to substantial cash outflows early in the life of a typical fund. At the same time, distributions on the fund's investments often do not begin in earnest

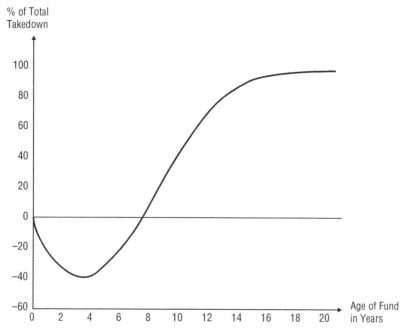

EXHIBIT 20.1 The J-Curve for a Typical Private Equity Fund

until well into the life of a fund. The result is a substantial dip in net cash flows early in the life of a fund, followed by a recovery. But from a structuring standpoint, this kind of net cash flow profile suggests that significant attention will have to be paid to liquidity support.

A major appeal of applying the CDO technology to private equity collateral is the ability to bring structured financing solutions to bear on the J-curve problem. With careful attention by the structuring agent, the cash flow waterfall of the structure can be reengineered to distribute the net cash flows over time much more evenly than in the underlying fund. Internal liquidity support can be provided through careful tranching of the liabilities of the private equity–backed CFO—tranching in terms of both depth of subordination and maturity. In addition, external liquidity support through banking products, derivatives, and structured insurance can provide an important source of liquidity enhancement.

Rating agency considerations cannot, of course, be ignored. In addition to careful evaluations of the quality of the underlying private equity as the sole source of collateral in a CFO (e.g., credit quality, diversity scoring, recovery rates, etc.), the agencies will also take their usual conservative approach to liquidity and credit risk management internal to the structure.

Notably, virtually all CFOs to date have been market value CDOs. This means that the usual rating agency tests are assessed on mark-to-market values of the collateral assets rather than the cash flow waterfall. As discussed in Chapters 17 and 18, market value CDOs have not met with much success in the broad CDO market, although this appears to make sense structurally for CDOs backed by managed funds as collateral. It may well be that CFOs are the only viable niche in which market value CDOs will continue to survive.

SINGLE-TRANCHE CAPITAL-PROTECTED NOTES

The first group of products we examine are notes that provide a single class of investors with participation in a managed hedge or PE fund and yet also offer downside protection against a loss of principal. These products are much more analogous to credit-linked notes (CLNs) and structured notes (see Chapters 12 and 14) than to true CDO structures (see Chapters 17 through 19). In particular, these products are single-tranche but *not* in the sense of the single-tranche synthetic collateralized debt obligations (STSCDOs) we explored in Chapter 18. Importantly, the single-tranche products discussed here are *fully funded* whole capital structure liabilities that can be issued by a special purpose entity (SPE) without significant amounts of structuring. These simple early structures are often referred to as fund-indexed *capital-protected notes* (CPNs).

A number of different variations on the basic CPN theme have been observed in the market. We differentiate between the products to date by examining two different structuring issues: the method by which the exposure to the reference fund(s) is incorporated into the payoff of the CPN, and the method by which downside/principal protection is integrated into the structured CPN.

Referencing the Fund Exposure

A major distinction between the structures that we have seen over time in the CFO area concerns the means by which the structured product allows investors to participate in the performance of the underlying hedge fund(s) or private equity fund(s). In short, this exposure can be acquired through direct investment in the fund(s) or synthetically using derivatives.

Direct Investment   In the earliest structured CPNs, principal protection was obtained by issuing the security at par and then investing the *present value* (PV) of the principal in zero coupon stripped Treasuries. Whatever was left was then invested in hedge fund shares. Suppose, for example, we consider a three-year CPN with a face value of $1 million issued at a time when the three-year stripped Treasury rate is 5 percent. The CPN is issued for $1 million, and that amount is guaranteed by investing $863,800 in a three-year zero with a face value of $1 million. When the CPN comes due in three years, the Treasuries will be redeemable at par for $1 million, thereby guaranteeing the principal on the CPN.

The remaining $136,200 left over from the initial issue price after the Treasury purchase was then available for investing in hedge fund shares. Like many of the equity-linked structures we examined in Chapter 14, investors could choose a *participation rate* (or *gearing*) that dictated the note holders' proportional participation in the hedge fund's return, as well as a *base* that dictated exactly what percentage of principal was fully protected. A higher participation rate generally implied a lower base, and conversely.

Structurally, the sponsor of the note issue would set up an SPE that in turn would issue the notes to investors. The cash collected would be allocated between Treasuries and the hedge fund partnership interests. Generally there was no additional liquidity enhancement required; the notes paid interest only when the hedge fund made positive distributions to investors (including the SPE) over the life of the note. The mechanics of the structure are shown in Exhibit 20.2.

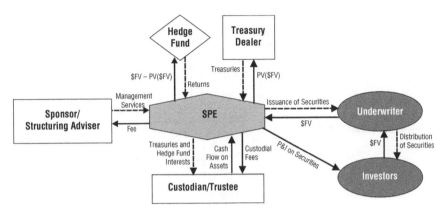

EXHIBIT 20.2 Capital-Protected Hedge Fund-Linked Note, Direct Investment in Hedge Fund
FV—face value; PV—present value.

In these early structures, the gearing on structures with 100 percent principal protection was relatively low, leaving limited upside potential for investors and allowing absolutely no leverage. So much of the initial investment was required on the Treasuries that the remaining unleveraged investment in the reference fund was often considered too small to be interesting to investors.

Synthetic Investment Using Options Derivatives dealers and reinsurance companies began to indicate a willingness to write options based on specific hedge and PE funds in the late 1990s, thus leading to another type of principal-protected fund-indexed note. Mechanically and structurally, second-generation CPNs were fairly similar to their first-generation predecessors. An SPE would issue the CPN at par and then invest the present value of the principal in zero coupon stripped Treasuries as before. But in the new products, the remaining funds could be used to purchase options on the fund rather than actual shares in the hedge fund. Exhibit 20.3 shows the basic structural design.

By buying options on fund shares, investors achieve greater gearing through the embedded leverage inherent to an option contract than in the earlier deals. Investors also were no longer limited to at-the-money investments in the hedge fund, as was the case with first-generation issues. In these second-generation CPNs, the options could be purchased out-of-the-money or in-the-money. This would, of course, imply a higher or lower

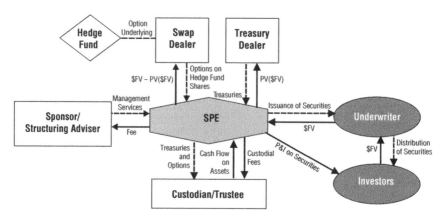

EXHIBIT 20.3   Capital-Protected Hedge Fund-Linked Note Investment in Options on Hedge Fund Shares
FV—face value; PV—present value.

participation rate (i.e., number of options available for purchase). Investors also sometimes increased their participation rate by opting for Asian-style options—of course, this was a higher participation rate in a different kind of product!

The biggest constraint to the development of these second-generation CPNs has been the limited depth of the hedge fund options market and the virtual nonexistence of options on private equity vehicles. Without a market for hedge fund options, the swap dealer writing the option to the SPE is forced to hedge its exposure some other way. Because hedge fund "shares" are usually restricted partnership interests, delta hedging is not very effective or realistic. Instead, dealers would have to use the paucity of hedge fund index products, or some other more general index derivatives contract. Either way, without the ability to buy the same option being written to the SPE, the swap dealer is forced to take on significant basis risk.

Principal Protection

Many institutional investors are precluded from heavily investing (or investing at all) in securities with embedded unfunded leverage positions or investing in securities that do not provide principal protection. The structuring challenge in designing these products thus has always been derived from the difficulty of pursuing two seemingly incompatible objectives: principal protection on the one hand, and an attractive balance between the investor's participation rate and base share price on the other hand. Recall from Chapter 14 that the appreciation rate dictates the extent to which a CPN investor participates in hedge fund returns, and the base is when that participation begins relative to the price of hedge fund shares when the note is purchased.

There have been at least three different types of structures that provide investors with principal protection. We discuss the differences in these structures next.

Fully Funded Cash Collateral Account We have already explored in the prior section the first possible way to guarantee principal in a structured note. Namely, the proceeds from the initial offering of securities can be used to fund fully a cash collateral account (CCA) of zero coupon Treasuries that will grow in value over time to exactly the required principal repayment amount. But we have also seen that this is not the most efficient structure in the world. Among other things, it forces investors to surrender significant upside in order to get a floor on their invested capital.

Constant Proportional Portfolio Insurance If the shares of a hedge or PE fund can be traded, a second means by which a sponsor of a fully funded single-tranche CFO can include principal protection is through the use of *synthetic options*—that is, delta hedging with bonds and shares of the fund to replicate synthetically a floor on the principal of the security. The most popular means of accomplishing this in structures to date has been through the use of constant proportional portfolio insurance (CPPI), originally popularized in equity markets in the mid-1980s.

Structurally, the SPE issuer of the CPNs invests the proceeds from the CPN issue in shares of the reference PE or hedge fund and in zero coupon Treasuries. But instead of purchasing full protection of principal as discussed in the previous section, the amount of protection purchased is now allowed to vary with the value of the hedge fund shares.

The sponsor of the CPN issue will define the *floor* in a typical structure as the amount that would need to be invested in Treasuries at any time t to guarantee the full repayment of principal at maturity date T. If the principal amount of the issue is $\$X$, the floor has a value on any date $t + j$ of

$$F(t + j, T) = PV_{t+j,T}(X)$$

where $PV_{t+j,T}(\cdot)$ denotes the risk-free present value of a time T dollar as of time $t + j$. Note this is not necessarily the *actual* amount invested in Treasuries, just the amount that would be required to fully fund a CCA as in the previous section.

To determine the actual amount invested in Treasuries, the structure then defines a *cushion* on any date $t + j$ as

$$C(t + j) = \lambda[V(t + j) - F(t + j, T)]$$

where $V(t + j)$ is the value of the combined portfolio of Treasuries and hedge or PE fund shares on date $t + j$. The multiplier λ is a leverage factor. The cushion is then invested in the hedge fund, with the balance of the remaining funds invested in the Treasury protection component. Note that on date t at initial issue,

$$C(t) = \lambda[X - F(t, T)]$$

Periodically, the portfolio is rebalanced so that greater protection is secured when the value of the hedge fund investment is declining.

An example may help illustrate. Suppose we consider as earlier a three-year CPN with a face value of $1 million issued at a time when the three-year stripped Treasury rate is 5 percent. The CPN issues for $1 million. The floor is $863,800 on the issue date, which is the amount that would need to be *fully invested* in Treasuries to *guarantee* a return of principal three years hence. If the multiplier is unity, we have essentially the same structure as we discussed in the first part of this section—$136,200 is invested in hedge fund shares, and $863,800 in Treasuries. But if the multiplier is instead, say, 1.2, then the cushion is

$$C(t) = 1.2(\$1,000,000 - \$863,800) = \$163,400$$

which means that $163,400 is invested in hedge fund shares and the remaining $836,600 is invested in Treasuries.

Now suppose after a year that the value of the portfolio has declined to $950,000. At the same time, the value of the floor has risen to $907,000. The cushion is then $51,600. So, the SPE rebalances the portfolio to $51,600 in fund shares and $898,400 in Treasuries.

Alternatively, what if a year into the deal the value of the portfolio has risen to $1,050,000? With a floor of $907,000 the cushion is then $171,600. So the SPE increases its allocation of funds in hedge fund shares. Note in this case that the Treasury allocation has also risen in *absolute terms* to $878,400. The *percentage* allocation in hedge fund shares, however, is the same as before.

In reality, such a structure would likely be rebalanced significantly more often than annually, but the example shows how the basic concept of CPPI works. Declines in the value of the hedge fund portfolio result in a relative shift away from hedge fund shares toward Treasuries, and conversely for a significant increase in value.

Naturally, CPPI provides a greater upside for investors still seeking some semblance of principal protection. The problem, of course, is that the amount of principal protection depends on the actual size of the Treasury portfolio. Ramping up the Treasury portfolio (or, more specifically, getting out of hedge fund shares) during a volatile market decline could prove exceedingly difficult and costly, especially for the relatively illiquid hedge fund market. So, the greater upside in such structures must be carefully weighed against the risks.

Let's consider a specific example of a hedge fund-linked CPN that relied on CPPI to synthesize its downside protection. This particular instrument was an indexed Eurobond issued by Société Générale Acceptance NV and guaranteed by Société Générale.[2] The note was listed on the Luxembourg Stock Exchange and settled through Clearstream, like many Eurobonds.

The bond was issued on July 17, 2001, with an original maturity of five years. The total issue was $20 million with each bond having a face value of $10,000, and the bonds were issued at par. The bonds guaranteed 100 percent of principal as capital protection and also provided 100 percent participation in the reference fund, which was the SCS Alternative Fund (SCSAF). The SCSAF was managed by Lyxor Asset Management (a wholly owned SocGen subsidiary) and utilized Strategic Capital Services Alliance as its investment adviser.

Ten business days prior to the final maturity of the bond, SCSAF would settle redemptions at a defined net asset value (NAV) that we can denote $V(T)$ per unit of the fund. The redemption value of the SCSAF-index Eurobond then was defined to be

$$\max\left[\$10,000, \$10,000 + \left(\frac{V(T)-100}{100}\right)\right]$$

On an ongoing basis, the issuer of the note defined a *reference level* corresponding to what we have called the floor and a *trading level* corresponding to what we have called the cushion with a multiplier of 4. The reference level begins at $75 and increases linearly each day to reach a value of $100 at maturity; this is an approximate present value curve that dictates the amount required to fully guarantee principal repayment.

At inception, the net asset value of the fund was at 100 per share. With a floor of $75 and a multiplier of 4, that means the initial cushion or trading level was 4($100 − $75) = $100 so that the issuer of the Eurobond was 100 percent invested in hedge fund shares from the beginning.

Suppose that six months into the life of the bond the NAV of the SCSAF had risen to $110. The reference level or floor would have risen a bit, but only to $77.50. In that case, the trading level was 130 percent of current NAV, which meant that the issuer would actually borrow and lever up to buy more hedge fund shares.

But now imagine that a year into the life of the bond, the NAV of SCSAF has fallen to $78 per share. Meanwhile, the floor has grown to $80. This implies a trading level of –8 percent, so the issuer must invest 20 percent of its assets in Treasuries and the remainder in the hedge fund.

Financial Guarantees Apart from funding a Treasury reserve account or engaging in dynamic rebalancing to synthesize a floor, principal protection can also be obtained through external credit risk transfer. Two early private equity deals illustrate how nicely this solution can work.

The first major private equity CFO was completed in June 1999. The SPE issuer was Princess Private Equity Holding Ltd., a Guernsey SPE jointly owned by Swiss Re (19.9 percent) and Partners Group (81.1 percent), an asset management group based in Zug, Switzerland. The collateral manager and lead investment adviser was Princess Management and Insurance Ltd., also jointly owned by Swiss Re and Partners Group—49.9 percent and 50.1 percent, respectively.

The assets of the SPE consisted of investments in 17 specific private equity partnerships, diversified across sectors. Investments were authorized in chunks of $9 million to $15 million per fund. All distributions on these funds were used to finance new private equity investments over the life of the structure.

On the liability side, the SPE issued a single tranche of securities (listed in both Luxembourg and Frankfurt) payable in 2010. The initial issue called for $525 million and a possible additional $475 million to fund an overcollateralization (O/C) account and help manage the liquidity risk of the structure. Each bond had a face value of $1,000.

In addition to the embedded O/C, liquidity risk was addressed by making the single class of liabilities zero coupon and convertible. In other words, the bonds paid no interim interest at all. They were convertible at $100 per share into Princess Private Equity Holding shares from April 2007. The conversion price rose by $0.375 per share each quarter through the stated maturity date on the bonds.

Credit risk in the structure was addressed externally through a wrap provided by Princess Management and Insurance that was in turn partially reinsured with Swiss Re. Fitch rated the deal AAA, thanks to the Swiss Re protections. The structure of the deal is shown in Exhibit 20.4.

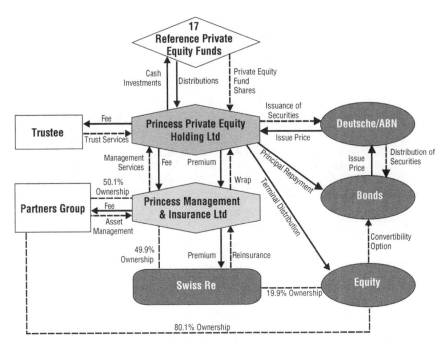

EXHIBIT 20.4 Princess Private Equity (June 1999)

The Princess deal was lauded as a great success for several reasons. First, the small size of the notes made the bonds accessible even to retail investors, allowing a totally new group of investors to participate in private equity who otherwise would have been precluded by the high fund minimums. Second, by "turning equity into debt" the securitization was able to attract institutional investors whose *equity* participation in funds was significantly more restricted than their *debt* participation. Third, whereas most private equity funds have an extended ramp-up period, Princess began fully funded. Fourth, the O/C embedded in the overissuance of securities effectively combated any J-curve problems.

Instrumental to the structure was that the bonds were wrapped to AAA (see Chapter 10). That insurance cost about 300 to 500 basis points per year and was financed out of the cash flow waterfall of the structure. Recall that in the hedge fund CPNs we examined, *guaranteed* principal protection had to be acquired either by sacrificing a tremendous amount of upside or by buying potentially illiquid, exotic, and expensive options. Princess eliminated that problem by acquiring principal protection from

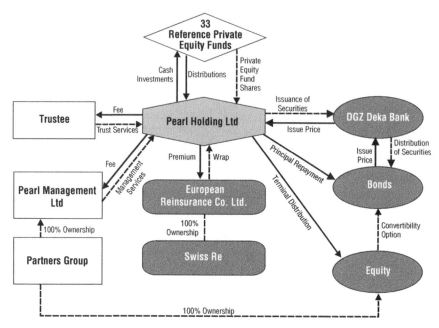

EXHIBIT 20.5 Pearl Private Equity (September 2000)

Swiss Re, arguably at a much lower cost and without sacrificing nearly as much upside.

A close cousin to Princess, Pearl was completed in September 2000. The SPE issuer was Pearl Holding Ltd., a Guernsey SPE owned by Partners Group. The collateral manager and lead investment adviser was Pearl Management Ltd., also a subsidiary of Partners Group.

The collateral assets of Pearl consisted of investments in 33 private equity partnerships, diversified across styles. On the liability side, Pearl issued a single tranche of securities (listed in Luxembourg) payable in 2010. The initial issue of €660 million was convertible into Pearl Holding shares from 2008 at a conversion premium that rose by 1.5 percent per quarter. Unlike the Princess bonds, the single class of Pearl bonds was coupon-bearing at 2 percent per annum. The coupon was kept deliberately low to help manage the J-curve risk.

Credit risk in the structure was addressed by a wrap of all principal and interest (P&I) payments provided by European International Reinsurance Co. Ltd., a wholly owned subsidiary of Swiss Re, at a cost of 180 basis points per annum. The issue was rated AA+. The structure of the deal is shown in Exhibit 20.5.

Partners Group continued its structured financial product development in August 2002 with the closing of Premier I and Premier II. Working with Merrill Lynch as the arranger and SocGen as the P&I guarantor, Premier involved a total issue of €137 million in single-tranche notes backed by an actively managed fund of hedge funds.

MULTICLASS CFOs

True CDO technology arrived on the CFO scene in 2001 when the first multiclass structured fund-based products were observed. Apart from offering multiple classes of liabilities, these structures also represented departures from the single-tranche deals discussed in the previous section in terms of liquidity and credit enhancement methods used. And perhaps most importantly, the more robust CDO structuring technology greatly enhanced the flexibility of issuers to design liabilities to specific investors' demands. Some of the design considerations with which issuers have struggled are:[3]

- What should be the capital structure of the vehicle, and what should be the debt/equity split?
- Should the structure be funded or revolving?
- Should debt coupons be fixed or floating?
- Should the securities be discounted or contingent?
- Should the debt be convertible, exchangeable, or neither?

Just to give readers a flavor of the kinds of deals we have seen to date and how the market has evolved (and is evolving), we discuss several of the noteworthy and/or pioneering multiclass CFO deals to date. Our discussion is by no means exhaustive—rather more of a "selected greatest hits."

Prime Edge Private Equity CFO

The Prime Edge Capital PLC private equity CDO in June 2001 involved the issue of €150 million in three classes of notes and thus represented the first multiclass CFO. The proceeds from the issue were invested in a diversified pool of private equity funds of funds. The lead manager was the Swiss boutique Capital Dynamics, which, along with Rainer Marc Frey (RMF) and Hamilton Lane Advisors, managed the collateral selection, investment management process, and risk management of the structure.

Deutsche Bank arranged the structure and placed the securities, which included a €72 million senior tranche paying Europe Interbank Offered

Rate (EURIBOR) plus 100 basis points semiannually, a €33 million junior tranche, and a €45 million equity tranche. The senior and subordinated securities were originally rated A and BBB, respectively, and Allianz Risk Transfer wrapped both issues to AA. The cost was €8.4 million for the senior wrap and €38.5 million for the junior wrap. In addition, the structure included an internal credit enhancement (C/E) through a 160 percent O/C (in the form of overcommitment).

The liquidity support for the facility was provided by staggering the ramp-up period over the first five years. In addition, Allianz Risk Transfer provided €40 million in committed liquidity support. That together with the 160 percent O/C helped manage the J-curve risk of the structure.

Diversified Strategies Hedge Fund CFO

The first multiclass CFO collateralized with hedge fund investments was the Diversified Strategies deal brought to market in May 2002 by Credit Suisse First Boston (CSFB). The offering raised $250 million for its sponsor Investcorp, which Investcorp invested in its Diversified Strategies Fund II—a fund of hedge funds diversified across strategies.

The liabilities of the structure included $125 million of senior AAA notes priced at 6M-LIBOR+60, an A-rated $32.5 million tranche priced at 6M-LIBOR+160, and two BBB-rated mezzanine tranches with face values of $10 million (priced at 6M-LIBOR+280) and €16.2 million (priced at 6M-EURIBOR+270). The structure also included a $67.5 million equity tranche that was partially retained by Investcorp.

MAST Hedge Fund CFO

Around the same time that Diversified Strategies was brought to market by CSFB, JPMorgan was busy bringing Man Glenwood Alternative Strategies I (MAST 1) to market. Very similar in structure and spirit to Diversified Strategies, MAST had collateral assets consisting of interests in about 35 hedge funds designed to mimic the Man Glenwood multistrategy fund run by Man Investment Products. Man was also the manager of the $550 million CFO issue.

The liabilities of the MAST structure included four rated tranches: a $242 million AAA senior tranche priced at LIBOR+70, an AA layer split into a $13 million floating-rate tranche (LIBOR+95) and a $20 million fixed-rate tranche (6.17% fixed, or LIBOR+95 equivalent), and an A-rated layer also split into floating and fixed tranches. The A-rated floater had a face value of $37.25 million (LIBOR+185), and the A-rated fixed-rate bond had a level coupon of 6.98 percent (LIBOR+185 equivalent) against a $4 million principal. The liabilities also included a BBB-rated $57.75 million mezzanine layer (LIBOR+300), an unrated $11 million subordinated tranche retained by Man, and $165 million in unrated equity.

The MAST offering was reportedly very successful. JPMorgan and Man Group brought a second $500 million follow-up deal to the market in MAST 2 about a year later. The basic idea of MAST 2 was similar to MAST 1, but the structure was a much more complex master trust structure.

Pine Street and Silver Leaf PE CFOs

Following the Prime Edge offering, several additional structures were brought to market in which firms sought to securitize their existing PE holdings. In December 2003, American International Group, Inc. (AIG) sponsored the $1 billion Pine Street deal, a securitization of some of its own PE portfolio. Pine Street was a return to the old single-tranche structure—a single AAA-rated bond was issued, with AIG retaining a residual tranche.

Silver Leaf closed in May 2003 and also represented a securitization of some of one firm's existing PE balance sheet holdings—this time Deutsche Bank's. The €468 million equivalent in assets included about 65 LP interests in various PE funds, especially concentrating on the industrial, business products, and consumer services sectors with vintages (year of fund inception) staggered from 1993 to 1997. Deutsche retained a $187 million equity tranche and provided a 40 percent liquidity support facility that was wrapped by XL Capital. Although the deal was static and did involve a reinvestment phase, an additional 30 percent liquidity reserve was funded by the internal cash flow waterfall to cover J-curve risks.

The liabilities of Silver Leaf included 11 different tranches of securities, all with a stated legal maturity of May 2013. The liabilities included three senior tranches rated AAA, AA, and A that were broken into fixed- and floating-rate bonds denominated in both dollars and euros, as well as a mezzanine tranche with a similar split across currencies and coupon types. The Silver Leaf deal was not wrapped or enhanced in any way and thus was one of the first structures to stand alone in its ratings.

SVG Diamond Private Equity CFO

The SVG Diamond deal closed in August 2004 and represents one of the more recent mature and sophisticated versions of a PE securitization that truly utilizes the full-blown CDO methodology and process. The structure is a good illustration of the evolution in the market away from the early and relatively plain-vanilla single-tranche capital-protected notes toward a more earnest CDO model applied to private equity. In addition, SVG Diamond was also the first managed arbitrage CFO supporting primarily *new* PE investments.

The SVG Diamond structure is essentially a double-securitization structure. SVG Diamond Holdings PLC, a Channel Islands SPE, is the investor in the actual PE funds. These funds and certain other assets (discussed later) serve as collateral for an issue of Private Equity Investment Notes (PEI Notes) that are issued exclusively to SVG Diamond Private Equity PLC, an Ireland SPE. SVG Diamond Private Equity, in turn, issues notes to end investors that are fully collateralized with the PEI Notes. Both SPEs are bankruptcy-remote variable interest entities (VIEs) under FIN46R, and all voting equity shares in both SPEs are held by a charitable trust (see Chapter 16). The basic structure of the SVG Diamond issue is shown in Exhibit 20.6.

Assets/Collateral   SVG Diamond Holdings, working with SVG Advisers Ltd., actively manages the PE collateral pool that ultimately backs the structured product issue. Although the portfolio is actively managed, the

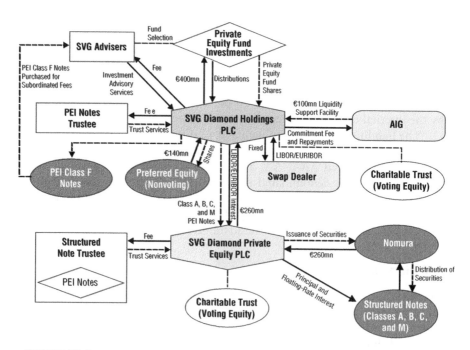

EXHIBIT 20.6   SVG Diamond (August 2004)

investment guidelines limit permissible investments to ensure adequate collateral diversity and credit quality. Table 20.1 summarizes the investment guidelines of SVG Diamond Holdings' fund investments, which are generally focused on U.S. and European buyout funds. The collateral assets underlying the fully ramped-up deal consisted of LP interests in about 40 PE funds representing about 500 underlying companies. Diversification across vintages was a major goal, where the vintage of a fund is essentially the year of its inception.

Although the program has liabilities with stated maturities of 2026, the *expected* maturities of the liabilities are 2013 to 2015. The life cycle of the deal is similar to the life cycle of most cash CDOs as discussed in Chapter 17. During the initial ramp-up phase, SVG Diamond Holdings will invest mainly in secondaries (i.e., funds that already exist at the time of SVG

TABLE 20.1 Investment Guidelines for SVG Diamond Holdings PE Portfolio

Criterion	Maximum Permitted Commitment (MPC)
Type of Private Equity Fund Investment	
Buyout	Min 70% Total Commitments
	Max 100% MPC
Venture	Max 10% MPC
Mezzanine	Max 15% MPC
Maximum Single Fund Commitment	
No Greater than the Higher of €20 Million or 4% MPC	
Manager Commitment Concentration	
Same Manager	Max 20% MPC
Minimum Number of Managers	10 Managers at €250mn commitment
	20 Managers at €500mn commitment
Currency/Geographical Concentration	
Europe/€	Min 40%/Max 60% MPC
U.S./$	Min 40%/Max 60% MPC
Other	Max 7.5% OECD MPC
Vintage Commitment Concentration	
Any Single Vintage	Max 20% MPC
Fund Commitment Concentration	
Minimum Number of Funds	20 funds at €250mn commitment
	40 funds at €500mn commitment

Diamond's investment). The primaries (i.e., new funds) will be ramped up as rapidly as practicable over the first three years. The reinvestment will span the first seven years of the deal, during which all distributions on PE investments will be used to finance new PE fund investments. In year seven the structure enters the amortization period. At its height, the program is expected to ramp up to a projected €540 million invested.

Liabilities The structured products issued by SVG Diamond Private Equity consist of three classes of senior debt and one mezzanine issue, all of which is floating-rate. Table 20.2 summarizes the presale details of the liability structure of the SVG Diamond Private Equity SPE.[4]

The P&I cash flow waterfalls to service obligations on the liabilities are sequential-pay structures based on seniority. Interest payments on Class A thus have priority over interest payments to Class B note holders, and so on. Similarly, no principal on a class of securities may be distributed until the principal on all more senior classes is paid down. As with most arbitrage CDOs, certain performance-based fees to managers are treated as subordinated expenses in the waterfall, whereas other nonperformance expenses are senior. Mezzanine interest, moreover, may be withheld and deferred to maturity if required for credit or liquidity support purposes.

The senior and mezzanine notes are the only liabilities of the SVG Diamond PE SPE. These notes are fully collateralized with PEI Notes (floating-rate) issued by SVG Diamond Holdings. Those PEI Notes are also issued in A, B, C, and M classes and have identical terms to the structured issues of SVG Diamond PE. SVG Diamond PE thus has an economic balance sheet as shown in Exhibit 20.7.

The PEI issuer, SVG Diamond Holdings, acquires the PE fund LP interests to back the PEI Notes that it issues to SVG Diamond PE. In addition, SVG Diamond Holding also issues fixed-rate Class F notes and preferred

TABLE 20.2 SVG Diamond Liabilities (€400 Million Total Issue)

Class	Presale Credit Ratings[a]	Amount[b]	% of Total Offering	Stated Maturity	Expected Maturity	C/E (%)[c]
A	AAA/Aaa/AAA	€85mn	21.25%	Aug 2026	Nov 2013	78.75%
B	AA/Aa2/AA	€80mn	20	Aug 2026	May 2014	58.75
C	A/A2/A	€15mn	3.75	Aug 2026	Nov 2014	55
M	NR/Baa2/BBB	€80mn	20	Aug 2026	May 2015	35

[a]S&P/Moody's/Fitch.
[b]Some of each issue may be floated in dollars at the issuer's discretion.
[c]Percent of capital structure junior to obligation.

Assets	Liabilities and Equity	
Class A PEI Notes (€85mn)	Class A Notes (€85mn)	
Class B PEI Notes (€80mn)	Class B Notes (€80mn)	Seniority/Priority
Class C PEI Notes (€15mn)	Class C Notes (€15mn)	
Class M PEI Notes (€80mn)	Class M Notes (€80mn)	

EXHIBIT 20.7   Balance Sheet of SVG Diamond Private Equity

stock. The investment adviser purchases all the Class F notes and about one-third of the preferred stock.

The €140 million in preferred equity is undrawn when issued. It may be funded anytime cash is required by SVG Diamond Holding to pay non-deferrable obligations (including senior fees and expenses) or to meet capital calls in the PE investment portfolio. The funding obligation for the preferred shares rises in favor of SVG Diamond Holdings by 6M-LIBOR until the equity is called. Holders of the preference shares can optionally fully fund those shares at any time and avoid the price increase. The preferred stock thus functions a bit like contingent capital, as discussed in Chapter 15. To mitigate the credit risk borne by the issuer on any undrawn preferred stock, SVG Diamond Holdings requires the preferred stock purchasers to have a minimum credit rating of A-1/AA– (S&P), Prime-1/Aa3 (Moody's), or F-1/A+ (Fitch) or to obtain a financial guaranty from a guarantor with at least those credit ratings.

Liquidity Support, Credit Enhancement, and Performance Tests   The first level of liquidity support for the structure is the contingent preferred stock issued by SVG Diamond Holdings. In the event all the preferred stock has been drawn and the SPE still lacks cash to honor capital calls or to pay senior expenses, the structure also includes a €100 million liquidity support facility provided by AIG. Repayment of any draws on the liquidity facility has priority in the cash flow waterfall to any debt servicing on the PEI Notes issued.

In addition, a reserve account is funded by the cash flow waterfall. Cash begins to accrue in the reserve account when the reinvestment period of the structure ends and the amortization period begins. No principal shall be repaid on the PEI Notes until the reserve account has been fully funded. Once funded, the reserve account must at all times exceed a minimum balance that represents a percentage of all unfunded senior expenses and obligations, including the debt service coverage ratio (DSCR) on the outstanding PEI Notes. The reserve account is also intended to facilitate timely defeasance of the liquidity support facility, which shall be withdrawn when the reserve account is equal to six months of senior expenses plus 78 percent of all unfunded payment obligations.

All of the C/E in the structure comes from subordination. There is no excess spread available apart from the diversion of funds into the reserve account.

The structure also maintains a set of rigid ongoing performance requirements and test conditions that the structure must satisfy on a continuing basis. The balance sheet of SVG Diamond Holdings is shown in Exhibit 20.8, and the notation in that balance sheet will help serve as a

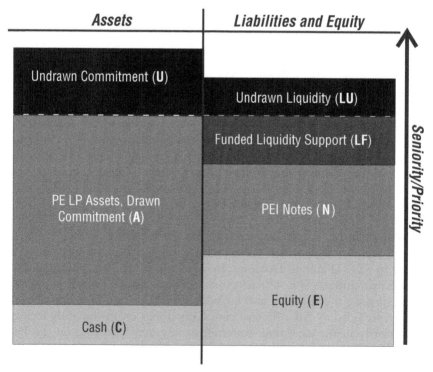

EXHIBIT 20.8   Balance Sheet of SVG Diamond Holdings

TABLE 20.3 Structural Liquidity and Performance Tests

Test	Definition	Remedy/Description
Liquidity Tests		
Cash	$C \geq €10\text{mn}$	Reinvestment halted when liquidity is too low.
Commitment Capacity	$^U/_{C+LU} \leq 140\%$	Ensure adequate resources to service undrawn commitments—similar to standard DSCR requirement.
Performance Tests		
Gearing (Assets)	$^E/_{A+C} \geq 22.25\%$	Reinvestment halted if subordinated erodes too much.
Gearing (Commitments)	$^E/_{U+A} \geq 25\%$	Commitments restricted when LP returns are poor and equity is eroded.
Total Commitment	$^{E+N}/_{U+A} \geq 75\%$	Restrict total exposure in relation to balance sheet size.
Asset Erosion	$E \leq €70\text{mn}$ $C \leq \max(€75\text{mn} - A^*, 0)$	If Class A PEI Notes outstanding, protects those notes from underperformance. A^* is the original face value of Class A notes less current remaining notional principal on Class A.
Equity	$E \geq €0$	During amortization phase, mezzanine cash flows diverted to repay senior notes' principal.

guide to interpreting the ongoing performance tests for the structure that are summarized in Table 20.3.

Interest Rate and Currency Risk Management A standard asset swap is used at the level of the PEI issuer (SVG Diamond Holdings) to swap fixed-rate distribution income on the PE funds into a floating LIBOR-based cash flow.

Notably, there is no derivatives transaction or insurance/guarantee structure to deal with currency risk. Because the PE target funds are denominated in multiple currencies, however, there is potentially substantial currency risk in the structure. To mitigate the impact of currency fluctuations, the structured product issuer, SVG Diamond Private Equity, plans to issue its Class A, B, C, and M notes in two series: a dollar-denominated series and a euro-denominated series. There is still some risk of a currency mismatch because the portfolio will not be ramped up when the maturity structure of the liabilities must be chosen for actual issuance. To respond to the remaining risk, the structuring agent has incorporated residual currency volatility into its reserve management model and cash flow waterfall stress tests.

CHAPTER 21

Project and Principal Finance

We can define *project finance* as the extension of credit to finance an economic unit where the future cash flows from that economic unit and/or the market values of the assets dedicated to that unit serve as collateral for the loan. Project finance is generally applicable to long-term capital-intensive projects, often involving considerable outlays well in advance of revenue generation.

Project finance is historically associated with development and infrastructure projects. The structured financing of large-scale capital-intensive projects collateralized by the assets or future flows of that project is often referred to as *principal finance* when the project is unrelated to development or infrastructure projects. Although the operating divisions in a firm that handle project and principal finance may differ, the structures and credit instruments generally do not, and we will draw minimal distinctions between project and principal finance in this chapter.

Typical examples of projects amenable to project or principal financing include:

- Infrastructure development projects (e.g., roads, rail lines, networks).
- Energy projects (e.g., large-scale generation plants, transmission and distribution systems, oil and gas exploration, drilling, and refining).
- Environmental projects (e.g., water supply and treatment, waste spillage and cleanup, hazardous materials disposal and cleanup, natural resource management).
- Latent assets (e.g., research and development (R&D), intellectual property, pharmaceutical patents).
- Illiquid or unusual venture start-ups or mergers and acquisitions (M&A) activity.

This chapter begins with a brief review of the project financing process itself—the participants, phases, and risks, as well as the benefits of bringing structured financing solutions to bear on project financing problems. We then analyze four different types of project financing structures:

1. Securitization structures and project finance collateralized debt obligations (CDOs) that serve as synthetic credit reinsurance and/or synthetic refinancing vehicles for original project lenders.
2. Future flow securitizations of exports and other receivables for development and infrastructure financing.
3. Future flow securitizations related to principal finance rather than development finance (including whole business securitizations and intellectual property securitizations).
4. Synthetic project finance and securitizations of synthetic project finance using prepaid commodity forwards and swaps.

PROJECT AND PRINCIPAL FINANCE

In this section we want to spend a little time reviewing project finance generally. We have already defined what project finance is and mentioned some examples of projects for which project financing methods may be used. So, we begin here with a review of the main participants in a project financing, followed by a discussion of the phases of a typical project, the major risks associated with each phase, and some specific financing considerations of which to be aware in a project financing context.

Participants in a Project

The various institutions participating in a capital-intensive project can be small in number and tailored to the project or large in number and much more diverse. We review in this section the roles of some of the potential participants in a project, noting well that not all projects will have a role defined for each participant discussed.

The number and type of participants in a project are of more than merely passing academic interest. Frequently, participants in a project bear some of the risks and returns of the project. The allocation of risk in a project thus is no longer just a function of the capital structure of the project financier. A typical project financing structure is shown in Exhibit 21.1.

Sponsor   Each project has a sponsor, and that is the firm or firms that initiate(s) the project. Quite frequently, the sponsor retains a substantial equity stake in the project and thus is also the project's "owner." In many cases, the sponsor would be happy to own and finance the project on its

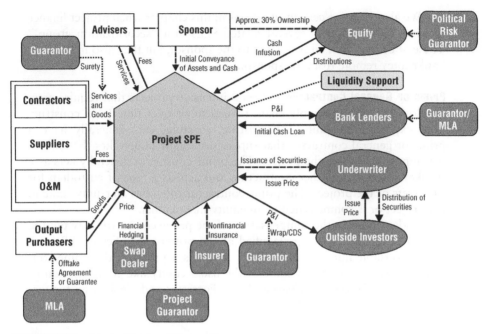

EXHIBIT 21.1 Typical Project Finance Structure

balance sheet—if it could. But for various reasons (see Chapter 13), it may not be desirable or even possible to finance the project on an unsecured basis with full recourse to the sponsor.

Project SPE/Securitization Group Many projects that are financed using structured financing techniques require ring-fencing from the sponsor, as we discussed in Chapter 13. The legal entity chosen to house the project—including its current assets and liabilities, future claims on cash flows, and the like—may be any kind of special purpose entity (SPE). As in prior chapters, the SPE is usually either a corporation or a trust, but in the case of certain projects may also be a more specifically tailored organizational form such as a joint venture, a cogeneration project, and so forth.

The SPE must be bankruptcy remote. Unlike certain securitizations, however, the SPE need not necessarily be independent of the sponsor on a consolidation basis. It may well be that the sponsor is perfectly willing to carry the SPE on its accounting balance sheet. And investors may be equally happy to invest in securities issued by the SPE on that basis. What matters is that the securities are *nonrecourse*, which requires bankruptcy remoteness but not sponsor independence.

We also examine certain situations in this chapter when project finance requires the creation of several related SPEs in a "securitization group." These SPEs may well all be related to the sponsor, but they also must *all* be bankruptcy remote from the sponsor.

Prime or General Contractor   Capital-intensive projects that require asset development and/or supply chain management over time (e.g., construction, exploration, planting, harvesting, roasting, etc.) generally have a prime or general contractor that supervises and/or undertakes the bulk of development work in the project. The prime contractor generally acts as a turnkey in engaging other contractors and acts as a type of custodian for the assets of the project. The prime contractor often has an equity stake in the project or is compensated in an equity-like manner.

Under FIN46R, the compensation of the prime contractor may put the contractor at risk of being classified as the primary beneficiary (PB) of a project variable interest entity (VIE). If this is a problem, the prime contractor may have to forgo some of the usual equity-like compensation to avoid consolidation. See Chapter 30 by Forrester and Neuhausen for further discussion of this problem.

Operator   If the project involves physical asset operations, the operator is the firm that manages the assets on an ongoing basis. Operators generally work as contractors to the project, but may also be employees of the sponsor.

A business model commonly applied to project management is called the *build-operate-transfer* (BOT) model. In this model, a single firm is responsible for building a project and then operating it for a while. After getting the project up and running successfully, the project is then transferred back to its original sponsor. Large-scale information technology (IT) projects, for example, are frequently developed using a BOT model. In this model, the operator and prime contractor are likely to be one and the same.

Contractors   A project may involve a large number of potential service providers, broadly known as contractors. Especially for projects that have a significant amount of construction or physical asset development and maintenance, contractors generally provide most or all of those types of services. Contractors are generally engaged by and responsible to the prime contractor. They are usually compensated at a fixed price and participate in neither the residual risks nor the rewards of the project itself. On the contrary, contractors are often a significant *source* of project risk arising from potential nonperformance.

Input Suppliers and Output Purchasers   Many projects are situated in the middle of a supply chain and thus must purchase inputs and/or sell outputs in order to generate a cash flow stream. Consider some examples:

- Large-scale agricultural projects require the purchase of seed and fertilizer and involve the eventual sale of the crop.
- Energy generation projects may require the purchase of a commodity or some other input (e.g., coal or natural gas) in order to engage in the generation of electricity, which is then sold on the output market.
- Infrastructure development projects involve construction and asset maintenance input purchases on an ongoing basis; the output sold depends on the project (e.g., tolls collected on a toll road, government payments on a public infrastructure project, etc.).
- Large-scale IT projects require hardware and software purchases; output is sold to the user of the IT system through a transfer pricing or explicit pricing scheme or on the open market.

In these and other cases, the input suppliers and output purchasers are part of the project. Like contractors and laborers, these participants are generally not investors in the project nor do they participate in the project's residual income. On the contrary, input supplies and output sales tend to be a significant source of risk in a project (e.g., a tightening spread between output sale price and input purchase price, trade credit risk, nonperformance risk, etc.).

Lenders/Investors   External providers of debt financing are an essential part of project finance, especially given the long-term nature of most projects and the unpredictable pattern of their cash flows. Investors and lenders provide these funds externally *and* bear proportional risks in the project. The risks borne by different classes of investors depend on the structuring of the project's liabilities, risk-sharing arrangements with other project participants, and the usual internal and/or external credit enhancement (C/E) of the structure.

(Re)Insurance Companies   Finding a major project without the involvement of one or more (re)insurance companies is a real rarity. Projects are generally rife with both nonfinancial and financial risks, and procuring adequate investment in the project without some external risk transfer is often quite simply impossible. In fact, (re)insurers play such a large role in some projects that they become de facto or de jure co-sponsors of the project and may well participate in some way through the project's equity. At a minimum, expect to see them in one or more places as guarantors and sureties for contractors, input purchases, output sales, and offtake agreements; as guarantors of other forms of intermediate trade credit; and often as liquidity support providers to the working capital layer of a project.

Derivatives Counterparties   For projects involving substantial amounts of financial risk, hedging is often a prerequisite to fund-raising. Especially if the financial risk is not a core component of the revenues of the project, investors likely will not want to bear noncore financial risks as a result of their extension of credit to the project venture. A U.S. sportswear company that sets up a factory in Thailand, for example, may need to raise some of its project funds in dollars to finance a project whose revenues and costs are mostly denominated in the Thai bhat. Investors in the project may be perfectly happy to invest in the project defined as a sportswear factory but may be less enthusiastic to take on substantial dollar/bhat risk. In that and similar cases, derivatives will likely be the preferred form of risk transfer.

Local Government and Multilateral Agencies   Development finance projects are often quasi-public projects and generally involve the participation of one or more local government entities. In some cases, a government agency may be the sponsor of the project and/or the sole purchaser of the project's output; for example, a harbor tunnel is built as a public service and thus is "purchased" for the residents of the area by a local government agency.

Multilateral agencies and export credit agencies may also play a role in project finance. This role may vary depending on the type and nature of the project but can include the provision of financial guarantees to investors, input purchase or output sale subsidies or commitments, direct lenders, asset guarantors, and so on. Examples of multilateral agencies often associated with project financing include the World Bank and International Finance Corporation (IFC), the International Monetary Fund, various national export credit agencies and export-import banks, and various regional development banks (e.g., Inter-American Development Bank, Asian Development Bank). Some countries have other specialized entities dedicated to international project finance support, as well. The U.S. Overseas Private Investment Corporation (OPIC), for example, essentially provides political risk insurance to U.S. corporations making foreign direct investments in politically unstable regimes.

Project Advisers and Structuring Agent   As in any structured finance deal (see Chapter 13), a project is also likely to involve a number of advisory participants providing professional services such as legal counsel, tax and accounting advisory services, and trust/custody services to facilitate perfection and maintenance of various security interests in assets. Most projects financed using structured financing techniques will involve a structuring agent, as well, to assist with the design of the purely financial side of the project.

Typical Phases of a Project

Most capital-intensive projects can be divided into five distinct phases:

1. Preproject design.
2. Development.
3. Construction/asset development.
4. Testing.
5. Operation and maintenance.

The risks associated with a project, in particular, depend strongly on the phase the project is in, and this will also impact the availability and access to different sources of project finance. As with the participants in projects discussed in the prior section, not all projects have all of these phases.

Preproject Design   During the preproject design phase, the sponsor of the project evaluates the economic viability of the project using the appropriate method out of those presented in Chapter 5 and then determines how the project will proceed—specifically, whether it can be done as an internal project by the sponsor alone or whether it needs to be ring-fenced and developed using project management and project financing techniques. The only participants in this phase of the project are likely to be the sponsor and its advisory service providers.

Development   A project in the development stage is subject to rigorous analysis very early on. A revenue and cash flow model is developed, and any required third-party feasibility studies that are needed to support the project are undertaken.

A project management team is generally appointed to take ownership of the project as the sponsor. The first major task of that team is to tender for and engage a prime contractor. Most of the time in the development phase is then spent with the prime contractor tendering for and selecting contractors and subcontractors, identifying sources of required inputs and input providers, and the like.

Fund-raising is generally completed by the end of the development phase of a project because such funds will rapidly become necessary to cover the large costs awaiting in the next phase.

Construction/Asset Development Usually the longest and most costly phase in a large-scale project is the construction and/or asset development phase. Depending on the project, this is the phase during which the project is sited, prepared, and built or developed. An industrial project, for example, would require the selection and procurement of a site for the production facility, fabrication and construction of machines and materials, and procurement of production inputs and processes. An agricultural project, to take another example, also involves site selection and procurement, input identification and procurement, planting, sewing, seeding, and so on depending on the project.

Testing The testing phase of a project includes alpha and beta tests (with and without live customers) and is the part of the project in which it makes the transition from assets under development to assets in use. The testing phase may also include commissioning, licensing, regulatory approvals, tax filings, and the like. Finally, the testing phase ends with the project's start-up.

Operation and Maintenance The operation and maintenance (O&M) phase of a project is when the project goes live. This is usually the first time in the life of a project that any revenues are generated. Costs incurred include variable operating costs, but also asset and project maintenance. A significant part of the O&M phase of a project is the process by which the assets that have been developed are used and maintained.

Project Risks

A ring-fenced project is subject to all kinds of risk, financial and nonfinancial alike. The nature of the risks to which the project is subject depends in large part on the phase in which the project is currently located. The risks affecting a project during the O&M phase, in particular, tend to be very different from the risks to which a project is subject in all the earlier phases. Following Forrester (2005), we can distinguish between the risks of the first four phases in a project—*project completion risk*—and the last O&M phase of a project, in terms of both what the risks are and how they can be managed.

Project Completion Risk Consider the kinds of risks to which a project may be subject during the first four design-and-development phases:

- Liabilities (e.g., workers' compensation, labor or contractor-related, environmental, etc.).

- Cost overruns.
- Delays.
- Liquidated damages or penalties.
- Asset destruction (e.g., catastrophe, terrorism, vandalism, weather, etc.).

In general, Forrester (2005) defines project completion risk as the risks that a project will be:

- *Not finished at all*—a catastrophic outcome in which no revenues ever materialize.
- *Not finished on time*—an outcome in which revenues are in the best case delayed and in the worst case later and lower than expected, and accompanied by various contractual and/or regulatory penalties for nonperformance on schedule.
- *Not in compliance*—the risk that a finished project is not compliant with local and international regulations and standards, thus resulting in potentially lower-than-expected output, fines and penalties, and higher-than-expected costs of production.
- *Not within budget*—the risk that initial estimates of required funds were too low and the sponsor has to go back to the market to finance a substantial cost overrun.

Forrester (2005) outlines several prudent alternatives for a project management team to explore as sound risk management for project completion risk. Paraphrasing his discussion, these project completion risk management principles include:

- Rely as much as possible on proven and established technologies.
- Execute strong, robust, and well-vetted contracts, especially with construction contracts.
- Obtain surety or performance guarantees from contractors on construction and asset development.
- Utilize qualified experts and experienced, creditworthy construction contractors.
- Obtain performance and/or financial guarantees from the sponsor as required and as available.
- Maintain reserves and/or stand-by liquidity support to finance cost overruns on a preloss risk financing basis.
- Rely as much as possible on contingent input purchase contracts, such as take-or-pay contracts, that permit flexibility in the timing of input purchases to match the actual timing of the project.

Operation and Maintenance Risks In addition to project completion risks, any given project is also subject to a whole range of financial and nonfinancial risks during the O&M phase. Some of these risks may be:

- Loss of revenue from unexpected declines in demand or increases in aggregate supply.
- Unexpected increases in operating costs.
- Asset impairment, degregation, or destruction.
- Loss of revenue from business interruption or lack of business continuity.
- Insecure property rights (e.g., unenforceable patents, political risk, capital controls, expropriation).
- Labor disputes and local labor management problems.
- Liability (e.g., workers' comp, product, environmental, etc.).
- Erosion of profits from noncore financial risks (e.g., interest rate risk, exchange rate risk, etc.).

Forrester (2005) suggests that the methods of managing O&M risk are not so different from the means by which project completion risks can be managed:

- Rely as much as possible on proven and established technologies.
- Execute strong, robust, and well-vetted contracts, especially in maintenance contracts and operator agreements.
- Obtain surety or performance guarantees from operators, contractors, and suppliers.
- Utilize experienced, creditworthy O&M contractors.
- Maintain reserves and/or stand-by liquidity support to finance O&M costs on a preloss risk financing basis.
- Utilize incentive-compatible fees and compensation arrangements with O&M providers.
- Procure external guarantees when practical and economically feasible.

Potential Benefits of Structured Project Finance

In this section, we review some of the reasons that structured finance can make project finance easier, more practical, and, in some cases, less costly. Interested readers should also consult Finnerty (1996) for an excellent in-depth analysis of project finance as compared to direct finance. Finnerty also adopts a corporate finance perspective to project finance and thus justifies project financing decisions using reasons that readers of the current book will find familiar.

Capacity Relief for Banks   Banks are primary providers of project financing, but bank finance comes with a few costs. Most importantly, banks rely very heavily on short-term financial capital to finance their own operations. Given the extremely long-term nature of many projects, banks will be forced to tolerate potentially huge asset/liability mismatches in order to match-fund projects unless some form of refinancing mechanism is available to them. If not, bank financing can become quite expensive; banks will have to allocate economic capital to their asset/liability mismatch, and that can be very expensive for such a long-dated mismatch.

Structured financing solutions can provide banks with a means of synthetically refinancing these loans, thus allowing banks to treat them as shorter-term than they actually are for asset/liability management purposes. This in turn significantly increases the capacity of banks to participate in project lending without having to charge extortionate premiums for the capital they would have to hold against unfunded long-dated loans.

Diversification of Funding Sources   Structured financing also helps diversify funding sources on a project away from banks, thereby reducing credit concentration inside a given structure. This is good for the project sponsor because it reduces the credit exposure of the structure to the banking sector and diversifies that exposure across multiple sectors of the economy.

Diversification of funding can also help encourage bank participation in a project syndicate or arrangement. A bank, for example, may be at an internal credit limit with other banks providing capital, credit support, or liquidity support to the project. That limit could preclude the bank from participating significantly in the project, not because of project credit concerns but because of the role played by other banks inside the structure.

Covenants, Approvals, and Agency Costs   Especially in project finance, banks and private placement counterparties both tend to insist on numerous covenants and various approval rights concerning the project itself. This can become cumbersome for the project management team. Apart from creating delays and concerns about micromanagement, two other significant problems can arise from such heavy reliance on covenants and approvals.

One problem—well described and documented by Rajan (1992) and discussed in Culp and Miller (1995)—is the tendency of banks to be hypersensitive to small changes in the conditional expected net present value (NPV) of projects. Because of the long-term nature of projects and the generally extensive reliance of all projects on bank debt, banks don't require much negative information to get spooked about a project. More often than not, a bank's tendency is to pull the plug on a project too soon. This is the primary reason why it is rarely considered optimal for any firm to have 100 percent of its debt in the form of bank loans, and what is true in general is even more true in the case of long-dated, capital-intensive project finance.

Overreliance on covenants and approvals also creates agency costs. Potentially serious interdebt agency costs can arise as different project lenders begin to argue about the differences in covenants across different categories of project debt. Even if the debt is carefully structured to minimize such concerns, the need to tread carefully through the agency cost minefield can substantially increase the cost of structuring. Including non-bank debt that is more reliant on observable risk indicators like credit ratings is a good way to reduce the dependency of the whole program on covenant-intensive borrowings.

Sponsor Equity and Agency Costs   A real problem in project finance is that the sponsor of the project usually considers its role in the project to be special. Sometimes it is; perhaps the sponsor has legitimately vested interests in the project, such as an investment of technology or a large proportion of the input supply. Sometimes it isn't; perhaps the sponsor had the idea for the project but has little or no comparative value added beyond that and has limited capital to invest. In either case, the feeling that the sponsor's role is special can give rise to severe agency costs.

Financially, a sponsor's participation in a project is reflected by its equity retention. A typical project sponsor will often feel entitled to all or most of the equity but will not be able to retain more than 30 percent or so because of the need for external funds. This can leave the sponsor feeling that its 30 percent stake is really more important than just a 30 percent share of common stock in a company. This can create pernicious interequity agency conflicts and severe corporate governance problems, often leading to litigation and dispute resolution that can badly bog down a project.

Perhaps more importantly, the *appearance* of this sort of a problem will give rise to significant adverse selection costs on the firm's project debt. In other words, creditors concerned about a sponsor that seems all too willing to expropriate its other equity holders will certainly suspect that they, too, could be expropriated and will demand a potentially significant discount on their securities accordingly. Even if expropriation is not a concern, debt holders may still demand a heavy adverse selection discount to penalize a sponsor that has overestimated its management skills.

Structured solutions can help address this problem at least to some extent by creating a more granular set of financial capital claims on the project. Sponsors, for example, may retain their 30 percent equity piece but 100 percent of the common, with the remaining equity coming from preference shares—possibly convertible into common to further align interests. Such an arrangement would allow the sponsor's role to be genuinely unique but would *not* precipitate disputes between members of the same level of subordination. Or, conversely, in some structures it makes more sense to give the sponsor the preferred layer and to issue the common. That way sponsors can still be rewarded but no longer can exert undue governance influence on the program.

Although structuring can help address this problem, it won't eliminate it. Sound corporate governance together with a healthy degree of expectations management is the best antidote to renegade inside equity.

Credit Enhancement and Guarantees   Ring-fenced projects may be easier to credit enhance than the same project left commingled on the sponsor's economic balance sheet. As we have seen already at various points in this Part Three, the CDO technology is especially useful for apportioning credit risk across different tranches of securities. That process of distributing credit risk often includes procuring internal and/or external credit enhancement, and the CDO form naturally facilitates this process.

As we saw in our description of risks and risk management in project finance, projects often require multiple types of guarantees (both financial and performance). Repackaging the credit risk of a project financing through a CDO-like conduit can make these guarantees easier to obtain, to customize, and to package.

Mitigating Underinvestment and Increasing Debt Capacity   Recall from Chapter 3 that too much risky debt can cause a debt overhang that results in equity holders quashing positive NPV projects because the benefits are disproportionately borne by debt and the costs by equity. Separating out a project and financing it outside the sponsor more closely connects debt and equity, better aligns the interests of the two, and reduces the likelihood of project rejection based on aggregate indebtedness (John and John 1991; Finnerty 1996).

For similar reasons, separately financing a project using structured finance methods can increase the total debt capacity of the sponsor. With the assets left on the sponsor's balance sheet, the firm may be sufficiently leveraged that additional debt capacity is lacking. If the reason for this leverage is related to informational asymmetries (as in the underinvestment model), then separately financing different packages of assets with specific debt offerings may allow the firm to achieve a greater total indebtedness than if the assets remain commingled at the sponsor level.

If a primary motivation for project financing is to free up debt capacity at the sponsor level, deconsolidation of the project will be required. Unlike certain other cases in which the project SPE need only be bankruptcy remote from the sponsor, in this situation the project likely will have to achieve true sale treatment to a project SPE for which the project sponsor is *not* the primary beneficiary under FIN46R.

Project Finance versus Principal Finance

Project and principal finance are really the same thing, but you wouldn't know it to look at the way deal flow is handled. Especially in the investment banking world, project finance is generally regarded as development, municipal, or emerging market financing of infrastructure projects, whereas principal finance is a corporate financing function in the high-yield privately placed debt arena. In fact, the economic principles of the two areas are the same: borrowing against the asset values or future cash flows associated with a long-term business unit or asset portfolio.

There are, however, some important practical differences between principal and project finance. Principal finance is often associated with lending related to ventures, M&A activity, R&D, and other latent assets. As a result, the projects underlying principal finance frequently do not have the phases that development and infrastructure projects have, as discussed earlier. These sorts of distinctions will become more obvious when we encounter them in examples later in this chapter. The important thing to recognize is that these distinctions are mostly terminological and institutional and do not really change the economics of the debt structures we will be examining.

PROJECT LOAN SECURITIZATIONS

The first type of structured project financing that we consider here is the securitization of project loans, which typically occurs for one of three main reasons. The first is when a single lender—usually a multilateral agency or export credit agency—is acting as the de facto or de jure guarantor for a large project loan but does not wish to keep the full loan exposure on its books. That institution may then securitize all or part of a loan or loan participation to refinance it, thereby both managing its own risk exposure and freeing up debt capacity for additional lending.

Second, as noted earlier, some project lenders rely on securitization as a means of refinancing very long-dated exposures with a shorter-term funding cost basis. In this case, securitizing the loans in a traditional securitization or CDO can solve the problem. In fact, securitization may be the *only* solution to this problem for some projects. Synthetic refinancings are naturally amenable to the CDO technology for several reasons. The first is the CDO structuring process in which the risks of the refinancing can be distributed across specific tranches and marketed to investors accordingly. But perhaps more importantly, bundling project loans for securitization through a CDO allows individual loans to be refinanced *on a portfolio basis*, which can facilitate more robust risk management and can significantly reduce the costs of synthetic refinancing.

Finally, banks may pursue financing and/or risk transfer objectives using *synthetic* securitization, as we saw in Chapter 18. The motivations are essentially the same as actual securitization, but the mechanics are different and can allow for greater fine-tuning of the synthetic reinsurance aspects of the program. We have also seen how partially funded synthetic securitizations can lower an originator's weighted average cost of capital (WACC) by exploiting the super-senior tranche of the underlying collateral reference pool.

For a detailed and very informative additional discussion of project finance securitizations, see also Forrester's Chapter 32 in Part Five.

Single-Loan Securitization

The securitization of a single project loan usually arises when a single lender or syndicate is providing credit to a project borrower on a fronting basis only. This could occur because the credit is subsidized, part of an allocated credit program, or bundled with a guaranty, in which cases the single lender is usually a multilateral agency or export credit agency. Just because the single lender or syndicate is willing to front 100 percent of the loan, however, does not mean the lender wishes to retain the exposure, and securitization is an easy means of refinancing participations in the original loan.

To take an example, Apasco S.A. de C.V. was Mexico's largest cement producer in 1995. It had the unfortunate timing of needing to complete a $154 million expansion of its production facilities right after the peso crisis in the mid-1990s. Because of the precipitous peso devaluation, Mexico's sovereign credit risk was perceived as quite high, which in turn trickled down to restrict the supply and raise the price of corporate credit as well.

To raise funds for the expansion project, the IFC extended Apasco a $100 million loan. But of that amount, the IFC was willing to retain only $15 million of the exposure. So, the IFC set up a Delaware trust and sold an $85 million participation in the Apasco loan to the trust in exchange for cash. The trust financed the acquisition of the loan participation by issuing a single tranche of BBB+-rated notes. The notes had a fixed coupon of 9 percent, equivalent to LIBOR+275. Four insurance companies—Prudential Insurance, John Hancock Mutual Life, Northwestern Mutual, and Sun America—bought up the entire issue. Exhibit 21.2 shows the basic structure.

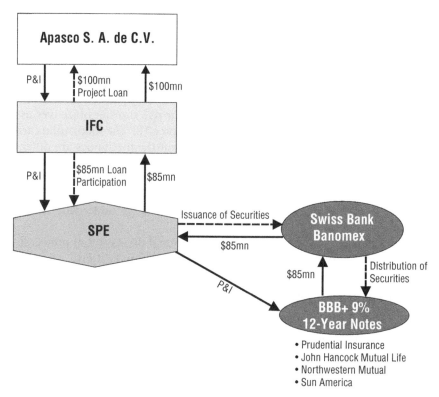

EXHIBIT 21.2 Apasco S.A. de C.V.

Portfolio Securitization

The Eiffel 1 structure is another interesting example of a traditional project finance securitization (a fully funded single-tranche CDO deal) in which a bundle of project finance loans are securitized.[1] The objective was to allow construction companies participating in a large-scale infrastructure project to monetize a portion of their expected construction receivables over time, thereby funding the working capital layer for these construction companies. The Eiffel structure was also a noteworthy deal in its own right because it represented the first project finance CDO in which bonds were issued backed by revenues *from a specific phase of a project* rather than against the project as a whole. The structure and its liabilities ended up with a higher rating than any of the sponsors without the notes being totally delinked from the credit risk of the sponsors.

In the 1990s, Portugal began a large road construction initiative backed with public/private partnerships in which the government entered into concession agreements with private parties. Most loans to date have been project loans to the concessionaires based on their ability to repay the loan over 30 years with revenues derived from the whole project. Eiffel 1 FTC, however, was backed solely *by the construction phase* of several toll road projects—traffic, O&M, and other phases are not included (either risk or return).

The major construction firms for these toll road projects—all of which are below investment grade—are Mota Engil SGPS, S.A.; Bento Pedroso Construcções, S.A.; and Obras Públicas e Cimento Armado, S.A. These construction firms form consortiums called *agrupamentos complementares de empresas* (ACEs) to serve the toll road contracts. Eiffel 1 finances four toll road concessions (concessionaires): Beira Litoral e Alta (Lusitânia), Costa da Prata (Vianor), Grande Porto (Portuscale), and Auto Estrada do Norte (Norace). Specifically, the concessionaires draw advances under facility agreements to honor a schedule of expected construction payments to the ACEs and later repay the loans out of toll road revenues.

The securitization in this case, which closed in October 2004, involved the conveyance by the ACEs to an SPE of credits that represented their rights to all cash payments due from the concessionaires. The SPE was set up as a fund, with its sole liability being a single class of five-year 3.36 percent coupon-bearing fund participation units with a pari passu claim on the cash flows into the SPE. The units were rated BBB– by S&P at presale and were issued at par for a total amount of €256.6 million. The structure is depicted in Exhibit 21.3.

The primary C/E internal to the deal is overcollateralization (O/C). Total expected construction payments to the ACEs under the toll road concession agreements were €1,292,993,896, representing an almost 500 percent O/C embedded into the structure. In addition, the structure had additional C/E and liquidity support from two internal reserve accounts funded by diversion of the excess spread between construction credit payments and the fixed coupon rate on the fund participation units into two reserve accounts. First, a debt service account was established to cover the next six months of interest due at any time. Second, a lockup and tail-end reserve account was established to cover debt service for the last nine months of the deal. Excess spread was diverted to fund these accounts as long as the relevant debt service coverage ratios (DSCRs) were below 3× in the accounts. When the DSCR of the structure went over 3×, any excess spread from the cash flow waterfall was returned to the ACEs in the form of a deferred payment for the credits.

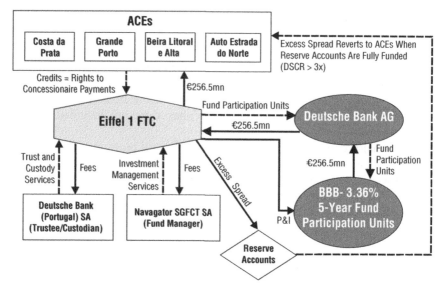

EXHIBIT 21.3 Eiffel 1 FTC

Stress scenarios together with the base scenario suggested that the structure had an overall DSCR of 3.33×.

Synthetic Project Loan Securitization

The Essential Public Infrastructure Capital PLC (EPIC) deal closed in late 2004 and is an excellent example of the use of a synthetic collateralized debt obligation (SCDO) structure to provide synthetic refinancing to the original creditor on a portfolio of large-scale project loans.[2] This particular structure provided the originating bank with access to partially funded credit protection on its project portfolio, thereby freeing up internal credit lines to the infrastructure project finance sector on a very favorable funding cost basis. Without the credit protection afforded by this structure, the originating bank may well have been unable to exploit additional credit-sensitive lending in the project finance arena.

The reference collateral portfolio in EPIC was a portfolio of 25 public infrastructure loans originated by Depfa Bank PLC in Ireland worth approximately £394 million. All loans were part of either the U.K.'s Private Finance Initiative (PFI) or its Public Private Partnership (PPP) pro-

TABLE 21.1 EPIC PLC Liabilities at Presale (October 2004)

Class	Preliminary Rating	Preliminary Size	C/E	Scenario Loss Rate	Legal Maturity
A+	AAA	£0.25mn	9.00%	3.57%	June 2038
A	AAA	£17.72mn	4.50	3.57	June 2038
B	AA	£3.94mn	3.50	2.77	June 2038
C	A	£2.95mn	2.75	2.37	June 2038
D	BBB	£2.95mn	2.00	1.79	June 2038
E	BB	£3.94mn	1.00	0.90	June 2038

Source: Standard & Poor's.

gram. Any individual PFI or PPP project is a public infrastructure or works project housed in a separate SPE and financed by private sector funds under a special government-granted concession arrangement with the SPE.

The EPIC deal—arranged and structured by Merrill Lynch—involved the issuance of £31.75 million in six classes of floating-rate notes (FRNs) by the SPE Essential Public Infrastructure Capital PLC. The details on the liabilities at presale are shown in Table 21.1 based on information provided in the S&P presale report. To collateralize those securities, the SPE purchased £31.75 million in *Schuldscheine*—essentially a type of credit-linked note (CLN)—from KfW Bankengruppe. The reference portfolio to which the CLNs were indexed was the £394 million Depfa project loan portfolio.

KfW invested the proceeds from the CLN issue in marketable securities and then sold credit protection to Depfa on the first £31.75 million of losses in its reference loan portfolio. With no events of default, the CLN paid interest to the SPE equal to the interest earned on the low-risk collateral plus the credit default swap (CDS) premium collected by KfW. In the event of a default, principal and interest (P&I) on the *Schuldscheine* could be withheld to fund CDS payments up to the face value of the FRNs issued by the SPE and *Schuldscheine* issued by KfW. The *Schuldscheine* were issued in six classes that were exactly matched in size and subordination to the six classes of FRNs issued by the SPE.

In addition, KfW also sold protection to Depfa on the £358.02 million XS £35.69 million super-senior piece of its reference loan portfolio. KfW hedged that super-senior swap by entering into a mirroring CDS as the credit protection purchaser with another swap dealer counterparty. The structure of the deal is shown in Exhibit 21.4.

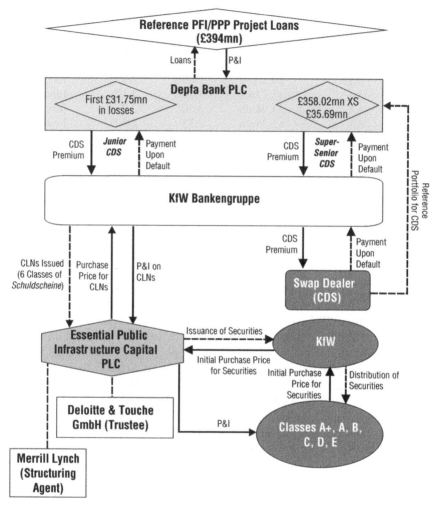

EXHIBIT 21.4   Essential Public Infrastructure Capital (EPIC)

FUTURE FLOW SECURITIZATIONS: DEVELOPMENT AND INFRASTRUCTURE

A *future flow securitization* is a type of structured project financing in which the future revenues from a project are securitized and monetized to raise cash immediately. In many cases, that cash is used to finance the same project that will later generate the future flows on which the securitization is based. In other cases, the future flows on one project are securitized to finance a new but similar or related project.

Future flow securitizations in the classical project finance area are often associated with the securitization of export receivables. In recent years, securitizing financial receivables has also begun to occur in development-related project finance. Apart from development-related project finance, future flow securitizations are also associated with principal finance, or the financing of nondevelopment projects that range from M&A activity to the monetization of latent assets like patents and other intellectual property (IP). We save our discussion of those nondevelopment securitizations for the next major section of this chapter, focusing in this section on development-related future flow securitizations.

In development finance, future flow securitizations have been mainly emerging market financing tools. Mexico and Brazil have accounted for over half of all development finance future flow securitizations through 2003. Historically, these have primarily been securitizations of export receivables. But more recently, a wider range of future flows have been the subject of securitizations. Another recent trend in development-related future flow securitization has been the move toward monoline wraps as a form of C/E. From 1996 to 1999, only 14 percent of the transactions were wrapped by a monoline. This number rose to 43 percent in the 2000–2003 period. Recent years have also seen a rise in financial receivables securitizations compared to the more traditional commodity-based future flow securitizations (Heberle 2003).

Secured Export Notes

Development-based future flow securitizations began very simplistically, more as structured notes (see Chapter 14) than CDO-like structures. Specifically, a *secured export note* (SEN) is a bond whose P&I are secured by a future flow of export receivables. Popular from the mid-1980s until the late 1990s, SENs were issued as direct obligations of the originator—not through a SPE. Although lenders could collateralize their credit exposures with the future exports by the borrower, they were still exposed to the general credit risk of the issuer and had recourse to the sponsor.

Mechanically, the receivables on a future flow of exports are pledged to a reserve account—often housed in a different country than the sponsor/issuer—that is funded over time as payments for the exports are received by the sponsor. If the exports are sold through prepaid or traditional forward contracts, they are fixed-price sales and thus not subject to the risk of declining export prices. But if the exports are sold at spot or close-to-spot prices, the issuer will need to use some kind of traditional derivatives

464STRUCTURED FINANCE

structure to eliminate the spot price risk on the collateral. The possibly hedged funds in the reserve account then serve as collateral to secure the SENs issued by the sponsor.

Example: Met-Mex Penoles S.A. de C.V. An example of a very typical standard-issue SEN is shown in Exhibit 21.5. The actual deal shown was the December 1993 issue of SENs by Met-Mex Penoles S.A. de C.V. Met-Mex was at the time the largest refined silver mining operation in the world and a wholly owned subsidiary of Industrias Penoles S.A. de C.V., the Mexican mining, metallurgy, and chemicals conglomerate.

The $100 issue was motivated by a need for Met-Mex to expand its local smelting operations. Bank loans were available but very expensive on a full-recourse unsecured basis. So Met-Mex issued a single class of bonds with a five-year stated maturity backed by a future flow of silver sales by Met-Mex to Sumitomo. The referenced sales were accomplished through a combination of a take-or-pay contract and a series of at-the-money silver put options written by Sumitomo to Met-Mex. Under the put options, Sumitomo was required to buy as much silver from Met-Mex *at prevailing market prices* as was needed to ensure that Met-Mex could meet its debt service obligation on the SENs. The remainder of the silver was purchased by Sumitomo through the take-or-pay, as defined in Chapter 11.

The SEN enabled Met-Mex to borrow at a much lower cost of funds than was available to the firm on an unsecured basis. The Sumitomo agreement pledged the silver sales to the bondholders in a way that both eliminated the market price risk of silver price fluctuations and allowed Sumitomo's own AA credit rating at the time to filter down to bondholders.

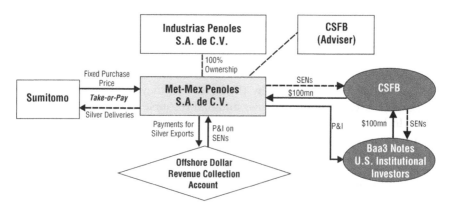

EXHIBIT 21.5   Met-Mex Penoles S.A. de C.V. Secured Export Note

Example: Corpoven Accrogas In July 1993, Corpoven SA—the liquefied natural gas (LNG) subsidiary of Venezuelan oil company Petroleos de Venezuela (PDVSA)—issued $275 million in two classes of SENs to raise money toward the development of the Accrogas LNG Production Complex. The note issue was supplemented with a $70 million infusion from the sponsor PDVSA and $195 million in export credit loans from three export credit agencies (Coface in France, SACE in Italy, and the U.S. Export-Import or EXIM Bank).

Corpoven secured its note issue with receivables from LNG sales, in this case primarily to Dow Hydrocarbons and Enron Liquids. In the Met-Mex deal, the market risk of silver sales was mitigated using a take-or-pay contract plus a series of put options. In the Corpoven structure, market risk was eliminated by using prepaid forwards to sell the LNG to Dow and Enron. As the prepayments on LNG sales came in over time, those funds were deposited in a special reserve account that backed the Corpoven note issuance.

Unlike the Met-Mex deal, the Corpoven transaction involved two different classes of securities, both of which were direct obligations of Corpoven and thus gave note holders partial recourse to Corpoven and PDVSA. One class of notes was a $125 million issue of 6.5-year notes paying periodic interest of 250 basis points over the CMT rate. These notes were distributed through Cigna to an insurance syndicate and carried a BBB rating. The other class of note was a $150 million issue of six-year BBB notes paying 225 over LIBOR issued by Banque Paribas to a bank syndicate. Exhibit 21.6 summarizes the structure.

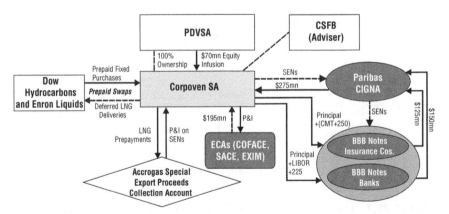

EXHIBIT 21.6 Corpoven Accrogas Secured Export Notes

Development Finance Futures Flow Securitizations

Toward the mid to late 1990s, SENs declined in popularity, mainly because investors remained worried about their credit exposures to the whole balance sheets of the project sponsors. To remedy this problem, a more classical securitization approach was adopted in which the receivables on a future flow of exports were conveyed to a bankruptcy-remote SPE that in turn issued nonrecourse export receivables-backed notes.

Export Receivables Securitizations   The June 2000 securitization of current and future liquefied natural gas (LNG) sales receivables by the Qatar General Petroleum Corp. (QGPC) is a good example of the basic structure of an export receivables securitization. This particular deal was motivated by a need by QGPC to raise $1.2 billion for a planned expansion of production facilities. The first $800 million for the expansion was raised through two syndicated bank loans, and QGPC went to the capital market for the remaining $400 million.

In this securitization structure (shown in Exhibit 21.7), LNG sales to customers generated receivables that were conveyed to an SPE called QGPC Finance for the price of $400 million. Payments on the receivables were subsequently passed on to an account in the SPE's name. Those receivables and the payments into that collection account acted as collateral for a single class of certificates issued to investors by the SPE for the sub-

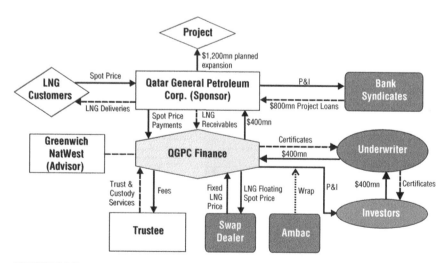

EXHIBIT 21.7   Qatar General Petroleum Corp. Liquid Natural Gas Export Receivables Securitization

scription price of $400 million. Ambac provided a monoline wrap of the certificates to AAA.

The receivables in this case were largely LNG sales to customers at spot prices. This meant that the P&I on the certificates were subject to the market risk of declining LNG prices. To hedge that risk, the SPE entered into a pay-floating commodity swap with a swap dealer, allowing the SPE to convert a stream of spot price-based receivables into a stream of fixed-price payments. This eliminated market risk from the collateral backing the certificates.

The QGPC export securitization program discussed here is a simplified abstraction from the real program, which was a bit more complex. Qatar-Gas II—the $12.8 billion program that closed in February 2005—was even more complex. We have left the program general here so that it can give us an idea of the *basic* form that almost all export receivables securitizations have taken. But when it comes to bells and whistles added to these programs, there is no limit.

Other Development Finance Future Flow Securitizations   In addition to commodity export receivables securitizations, development-linked project finance has also included service-related export receivables securitizations. Airline ticket receivables, for example, have been securitized previously by airlines including LAN Chile, Avianca Airlines, and Korean Air.[3] Securitizations have also included *financial* future flows, such as electronic remittances either grouped by type (e.g., credit card remittances) or consolidated into bundles called diversified payment rights (DPRs). Toll road revenues and uncollected taxes are still other types of future flows that have been securitized as a part of project or development finance. Table 21.2 provides a summary of the top issuers of development-related future flow securitizations from 1996 through November 2003 as compiled by Heberle (2003).

FUTURE FLOW SECURITIZATIONS: PRINCIPAL FINANCE

Securitizing a future flow, as we have seen, can be useful both in transferring asset risk to investors in the securitized products and in monetizing a stream of future cash flows into a single current cash inflow. This application of securitization technology to future flows *outside* the area of development finance has also been very popular, especially in the similar field of principal finance. We examine here three of the more creative examples of these sorts of deals in this section.

TABLE 21.2 Top Issuers of Future Flow Securitizations for Development Finance, 1996–2003

Issuer	Country	Number of Deals	Issuance ($mns)	Collateral
United Mexican States	Mexico	1	$6,000	Oil
Petroleos Mexicanos (PEMEX)	Mexico	18	5,000	Oil
Petroleos de Venezuela (PDVSA)	Venezuela	11	3,515	Oil
Banamex	Mexico	8	2,080	Electronic Remittances
Akbank	Turkey	7	1,775	Credit Card Remittances
Petrobras	Brazil	6	1,500	Fuel
Banco do Brasil	Brazil	6	1,330	Electronic Remittances
Aracruz	Brazil	3	900	Export Receivables
YFP SA	Argentina	4	778	Oil
Grupo Minero Mexico	Mexico	3	720	Minerals
Bancomer	Mexico	3	650	Credit Card Remittances
Unibanco	Brazil	3	625	Diversified Payment Rights
Vakifbank	Turkey	4	605	Trade Payments
Banco Itau	Brazil	4	600	Diversified Payment Rights
Companhia Vale do Rio Doce (CVRD)	Brazil	4	550	Iron Ore
Visanet	Brazil	2	500	Credit Card Remittances
China Ocean Shipping Co.	China	1	500	Export Receivables
Empresa Colombiana de Petroleos	Colombia	2	466	Oil
Province of Buenos Aires	Argentina	1	462	Tax Revenues
Autopista del Maipo SC	Chile	1	421	Toll Road Receivables

Source: Heberle (2003).

Turning Beer into Cash

The English public house or pub is a permanent fixture in the landscape of English culture. Over 60,000 public houses or pubs exist in the United Kingdom. In 1989, the U.K. Beer Orders Act forced U.K. brewers to sell off half the pubs they owned in excess of 2,000 in order to prevent breweries from exploiting market dominance at more than one point on the supply chain by selling beer to pubs and then reselling it to people.

Large pub companies called PubCos sprung up to buy the pubs that the breweries had to sell. But it many cases, these PubCos did not have adequate financing to front the purchase of the pubs. The securitization of future pub revenues was an obvious source of collateral for obtaining those funds on a secured basis. At the same time, integrated breweries also began relying on the securitization of pub revenues to finance O&M on existing properties, to refinance earlier loans, and to finance selected carve-ups of their pub estates and portfolios.

The collateral in a typical pub securitization is income from tenanted leases granted by the pub owners. A typical tenanted lease generates three types of revenues: rental income, margins on tied-in beer sales, and a share of income on gaming machines. In May 2005, the breakdown of revenues for pub owner/operator Punch Taverns, for example, was 43 percent rental income and 47 percent beer.[4]

The general structure of a typical pub securitization is shown in Exhibit 21.8.[5] In addition to raising funds, a typical pub securitization also involves the ring-fencing of assets from the rest of the sponsor's operations to shield the securitization group from all external liabilities unrelated to the pub financing. The securitization group consists of an SPE structured products issuer, an SPE borrower, and an operating company. The latter two are often one and the same.

The SPE issuer raises funds by issuing future flow-backed notes. These funds are lent to the SPE borrower, and the borrower can then invest these funds in the operating company, use them to refinance a prior transaction,

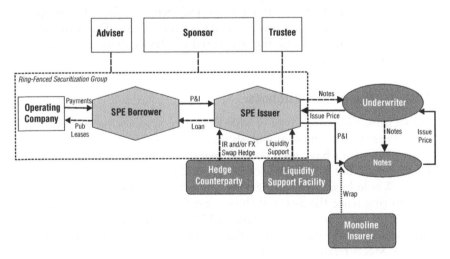

EXHIBIT 21.8   General Pub Securitization

apply them to pay down previous principal- or project-related bridge loans, or use them in any other activity *provided* that activity is tied to pub revenues. The SPE issuer has a perfected security interest in the pub assets as collateral for its loan, and the P&I stream on that loan then backs the P&I on the structured product offering.

The structure generally involves significant credit and liquidity enhancements. Internal C/E and liquidity enhancement are created through embedded O/C, subordination and tranching of liabilities, and strict DSCR requirements on free cash flows and/or earnings before interest, taxes, depreciation, and amortization (EBITDA). An interest rate swap is generally negotiated with the SPE issuer to manage the risk of reduced cash flows that often accompanies high interest rate scenarios. The SPE issuer also generally obtains external liquidity support for one to two years of debt service. Finally, most of these securitizations to date have involved a monoline wrap on at least some tranches of securities.

To take a specific example, the Punch Taverns Finance PLC offering closed on November 3, 2003. This £1.825 million issue was essentially a refinancing of several earlier transactions that had since been tapped and merged. The notes in the issue comprised four classes in total. The two senior classes involved both fixed- and floating-rate offerings. Maturities ranged from six years on one of the senior offerings to 27 years on the most subordinated debenture. The collateral backing these liabilities was a loan by Punch Taverns Finance PLC to Punch Taverns Ltd. (PTL) secured by the future cash flows from 4,183 pubs. PTL also managed and operated those pubs. The Royal Bank of Scotland provided the interest rate swap hedge, Barclays and Lloyds TSB provided liquidity support, and Ambac wrapped a portion of the notes issued. The structure is shown in Exhibit 21.9, and the structured product liabilities are summarized in Table 21.3.

Whole Business Securitizations

Pub securitizations are a type of what the rating agencies like to call *corporate securitizations*, more popularly known as *whole business securitizations*. These deals have been popular mainly in Europe and have included not just pubs but also water companies and health care industry participants. Whole business securitizations are often motivated by a perceived need to ring-fence the assets of the business in question from the broader business of the sponsor to facilitate an M&A or a business-wide financing arrangement. They are also a popular means for facilitating the refinancing of prior M&A-related bridge loans.

Consider, for example, the £366 million issue in July 2004 by South

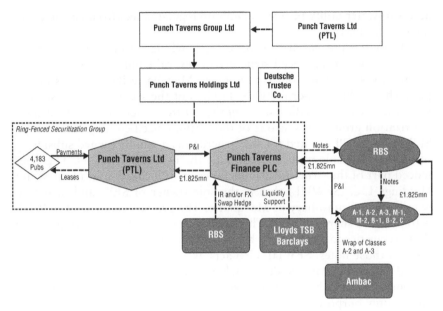

EXHIBIT 21.9 Punch Taverns Finance PLC (November 2003)
Source: Standard & Poor's.

East Water (Finance) Ltd. (SEWFL). The issue was motivated mainly by a desire on the part of Macquarie Bank to refinance an original loan it incurred to finance its acquisition of South East Water (SEW) in October 2004.[6] SEW is the second-largest water company in England and Wales, serving just over half a million customers in the South and East of the United Kingdom. It holds a license to operate, thus creating unique market

TABLE 21.3 Liabilities of Punch Taverns Finance PLC

Class	Rating (S&P)	Principal	Interest	Maturity
A-1	A	£270mn	7.27%	April 15, 2022
A-2	AAA[a]	£300mn	6.82%	July 15, 2020
A-3	AAA[a]	£150mn	3M-LIBOR+32	April 15, 2009
M-1	A	£200mn	5.88%	October 15, 2026
M-2	A	£400mn	3M-LIBOR+115	October 15, 2026
B-1	BBB	£140mn	7.57%	April 15, 2026
B-2	BBB	£150mn	8.37%	July 15, 2029
C	BBB	£215mn	6.47%	April 15, 2033

[a]Wrapped to AAA by Ambac.
Source: Standard & Poor's.

access to water utility payments and rate-regulated fees from customers in the regions it serves.

As in the pub securitization case, a whole business securitization also relies on a ring-fenced structure of several companies whose assets are totally separated from the sponsor (Macquarie Bank in this example). The credit risk borne by the holders of the secured notes issued in the structure is the credit risk of *all* the entities inside the ring-fenced securitization group. SEW is one of those ring-fenced entities. In addition, SEWFL is an SPE created for the structure as a wholly owned subsidiary of SEW whose sole purpose is to issue the notes to investors. The ring-fenced part of the structure also includes an SPE called South East Water Holdings Ltd. (SEWHL) that is the sole owner of SEW and in turn a wholly owned subsidiary of Macquarie. The primary purpose of SEWHL is to hold the shares in SEW. This facilitates the legal process of pledging those securities to a trustee on behalf of note holders as collateral for the P&I on those notes. SEWHL also acts as a conduit to get the funds obtained from the note holders back to Macquarie without necessarily causing concerns about the independence of the ring-fenced entities for bankruptcy purposes.

The liabilities of SEWFL included two tranches totaling £366 million—£166 million in 25-year traditional bonds and £200 million in 15-year index-linked bonds. The latter were issued as nominal bonds and then transformed into structured notes (see Chapter 14) by swapping the income on the nominal bonds for a retail price index (RPI)-linked cash flow to create synthetic RPI-indexed real bonds.[7]

Of the £366 million raised by SEWFL, £3.6 million was used to fund a senior interest reserve, £25 million was used to finance a new capital expenditure program, and the remainder was used to refinance the acquisition funding raised by Macquarie to acquire SEW the year before. The deal was liquidity enhanced externally with a bank line and internally with reserves to be funded by the cash flow waterfall of the structure and subsequent debt issues. The bonds were wrapped to AAA by Ambac.

Intellectual Property Securitizations

Beginning with the famed "Bowie Bond" issued in 1997, the interest in securitizing latent assets like intellectual property (IP) exploded. The basic idea behind an IP securitization is the same as in any other future flow securitization: to convert future revenues accruing to an asset or project into a current cash amount that can be paid to the owner. With IP, the asset is the licensed IP and the future flow is the stream of licensing revenues. The owner is the licensee.

Recall from Chapter 10 our discussion of the Hollywood Funding controversy. Although we discussed that example in the context of how things did *not* work out, the more general concept has nevertheless been very popular—namely, securitizing future film royalties. In many cases, the securitization is targeted at a film that is over budget during the production phase. The monetization of future royalties generates an up-front cash payment to film owners that is then used to finance the completion of the film. Although these structures have had a checkered history from the standpoint of performance and maintaining their ratings, they have been extremely useful to film producers.

Another application of intellectual property securitization is pharmaceutical patents—often discussed, but rarely attempted.

Each IP securitization done to date has looked a bit different from the others, and we have already seen a fairly good example of one in Hollywood Funding. Despite the problems that ensued concerning the guarantees of the Hollywood Funding bonds, the structure depicted in Exhibit 10.8 is broadly representative of what these kinds of deals look like.

Nevertheless, let's have a look at one more IP securitization structure. We'll look at the original—the Bowie bond of 1997, which involved the securitization by David Bowie of the publishing and recording rights on up to 300 of his *previously recorded* songs. The sale of the license to use these songs raised $55 million for Bowie and also eliminated the risk of a decline in the popularity of his earlier works.[8] The Bowie bonds were 15-year notes with a weighted-average life of 10 years and a fixed coupon of 7.9 percent.

In addition to the usual features of a securitization, the SPE generally also owns a put on the IP struck at-the-money on the deal date. The SPE can at any time put the title of ownership to the IP and license fees to a guarantor in return for a fixed sale price. This ensures that a decline in the value of the IP asset (e.g., decline in popularity of previously recorded Bowie songs) will not jeopardize note P&I payments.[9] The SPE then assigns the put to the trustee as further collateral for the notes.

SYNTHETIC COMMODITY-BASED PROJECT FINANCING

Commodity-based businesses may also engage in project or principal finance *synthetically* by using derivatives. As explained and documented in Culp (2004), the use of prepaid commodity derivatives (see Chapter 11) as a synthetic form of project or trade finance dates back to the Assyrians. Just imagine a farmer who has a viable wheat field but is considered too much of a credit risk to borrow on an unsecured basis without incurring significant deadweight costs of external finance. Yet without borrowing the farmer cannot pay his workers to tend the field and bring the crop to harvest. Instead of searching for a money lender, the farmer may instead sell his crop using a prepaid forward, generating cash income *now* that can be used to pay workers to bring the crop to term. That the crop whose harvest is being financed is also the underlying in the forward contract does not matter.

Buying a commodity for future delivery at a fixed price set in advance (i.e., going long a forward) is economically equivalent to buying the commodity for immediate delivery and storing it over time. The total purchasing cost is equal to the interest cost of financing the purchase plus the physical cost of storage less any benefit to be had from actually having the asset on hand (Culp 2004). In a traditional forward contract, the long pays for its purchase on the same future date that it receives the asset from the short. In a prepaid forward contract, the long pays for its future delivery at the beginning of the life of the transaction instead and thus is essentially combining a traditional forward with a money loan to the asset seller. This is project or principal finance by any other name! Of course, the means by which this sort of project finance is executed in practice is a bit more complicated.

Synthetic Project Financing Structures and Sources of Funds

Using a prepaid as the basis for synthetic project financing may involve as many as five different pieces that together form a single structure. These pieces are:

1. *Prepaid Leg.* An asset purchaser—often an SPE—makes an up-front cash payment to the asset seller (i.e., project borrower) in return for a commitment to a future delivery or deliveries of the asset. The prepaid is documented as a derivatives contract and receives accounting and tax treatment as a derivatives transaction. If the prepaid purchase is associated with a single future delivery, the transaction is a prepaid forward. Most of the time, however, a single prepayment is made for a series of future deliveries (e.g., deliveries once a month for a year beginning five years hence). In the latter case, the derivatives contract is a prepaid swap.

2. *C/E Leg.* The prepaid asset purchaser is bearing significant credit risk by paying for an asset now that the seller commits to deliver later. In the event of a default by the obligor, the asset may not be fully developed. The buyer, moreover, does not have a first-interest lien perfected

in the underlying asset when buying the asset forward. So, the buyer will demand some form of significant C/E from the seller to secure the delivery obligation. Popular types of C/E posted in synthetic project financing deals include letters of credit (LOCs), advance payment supply bonds (i.e., nonfinancial sureties—see Chapter 10), and funded trade credit insurance. We review some of the issues surrounding the choice of C/E later in this chapter.

3. *Offtake Leg.* The buyer of the asset is rarely an end user of the asset, especially when the buyer is an SPE established solely to facilitate a synthetic commodity financing structure. A typical synthetic financing structure thus also includes an offtake agreement, or an agreement through which the asset purchaser (SPE) sells the asset when it is delivered by the seller/borrower. The offtake agreement may be a take-or-pay contract, a forward or swap, an option, or simply a future transaction on a spot or futures market.

4. *Hedge Leg.* Depending on whether the offtake agreement is a fixed-price sale agreement, the SPE buyer of the asset may be exposed to the risk of price declines in the asset over the life of the prepaid. A fixed-price offtake agreement will hedge that risk, but a variable-price offtake or a future spot market sale will require the SPE to hedge this market risk with a traditional forward or swap.

5. *Financing Leg.* The SPE purchasing the asset generally borrows these funds from one or more lenders. The future delivery obligations plus the C/E are posted as collateral for the loan. The financing for the structure can be provided by a bank or an insurance company, by a syndicate, or through a securitization of the hedged, credit-enhanced future flow.

Exhibits 21.10, 21.11, and 21.12 show three common variations of these legs. In Exhibit 21.10, the SPE takes physical delivery of the asset over time, sells the asset on the spot market, and hedges that spot price risk with a traditional (not prepaid) pay-floating commodity swap or forward.

In Exhibit 21.11, the offtake agreement is itself a fixed-price forward sale. This means that the SPE asset purchaser need not hedge any longer. But notice this just pushes the hedging problem one level down—the counterparty to the offtake agreement is now bearing that market risk, and *it* likely will now enter into a commodity price hedge.

And in Exhibit 21.12, the lender assumes both the offtake and hedging responsibilities. Instead of extending a money loan to the SPE secured with the future deliveries on the SPE's prepaid asset purchase, now the bank simply enters into a mirroring prepaid with the SPE. The lender is then left to dispose of the asset and hedge the market risk of that future asset sale.

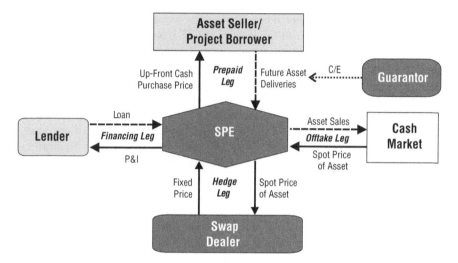

EXHIBIT 21.10 Synthetic Project Finance Using Prepaids, General

In any of the three structures, a single bank or bank syndicate—or perhaps (re)insurance companies—can serve as the synthetic project financier. But the synthetic structure also naturally lends itself to fund-raising through a future flow securitization, where the future flow is the hedged revenue stream associated with the future commodity deliveries.

An excellent example of this kind of program is Enron's Volumetric

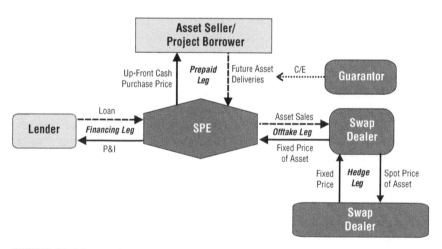

EXHIBIT 21.11 Synthetic Project Finance Using Prepaids, Offtake, and Hedge Combined

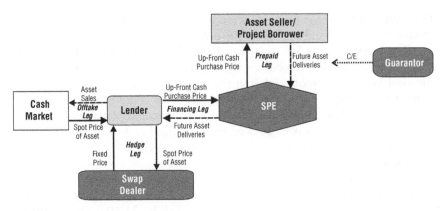

EXHIBIT 21.12 Synthetic Project Finance Using Prepaids; Bank Lender Assumes Offtake and Hedging Responsibilities

Production Payments (VPP) program. A highly successful program in the 1980s and 1990s, the VPP program was targeted at fledging or struggling natural gas companies and played an integral role in deepening and making more liquid the deregulated natural gas trading market. Most of the customers of Enron in the VPP program were of questionable financial health overall. They were poor candidates for obtaining full-recourse unsecured credit on favorable terms, and they were not active in natural gas trading markets. Nevertheless, each VPP customer did have at least one gas field. Often these fields were undeveloped but had substantial proven reserves. The essence of the VPP program was to provide the owners of these fields with cash adequate to bring the fields into production and then to use the proceeds from the producing fields to repay the cash loans.

Because of concerns about the overall credit quality of the firms participating in the VPP program, Enron required each sponsor firm to ring-fence the natural gas production assets for which they were seeking financing in a single bankruptcy-remote project SPE or a single securitization group. Enron then prepurchased some of the production from each of the ring-fenced SPEs using prepaid swaps.

Enron itself, of course, was never flush with funds. On the contrary, one of Enron's problems that led to some of its most suspicious activities derived from the firm's blend of relatively weak financial strength (the firm never saw north of BBB+) and stretched liquidity combined with an insatiable appetite for new debt.[10] A perfect solution for Enron to obtain the funds it needed to finance the prepaids without incurring new bank debt in the process thus was to securitize the future flows from the prepaids. In one specific example, Enron established the Cactus Funds SPE to which the future flows on the prepaids were sold in a true conveyance. The cash from the sale was used to finance the prepaids.

The Cactus Funds SPE then acted just like the SPE in Exhibit 21.10. Over time as deliveries occurred from Enron to Cactus, Cactus sold the physical asset in the spot market at the current market price. To hedge the market risk of those sales, Cactus used pay-fixed commodity swaps. And to raise the funds to finance the prepaid, Cactus issued two classes of securities whose cash flows were backed by the hedged cash proceeds from the future gas deliveries. The Class A interest was purchased mainly by banks, and the Class B interest by GE Capital.

The structure of this deal is shown in Exhibit 21.13. Notice that the portion of the graph from Enron and below (including the Cactus SPE, the spot market sale, and the hedge) is similar to Exhibit 21.10 with one difference. In Exhibit 21.10, the SPE buys future commodity deliveries with a prepaid forward or swap, whereas in Exhibit 21.13 the Cactus SPE is buying the actual receivables on the future flow generated by the prepaid forwards. The transaction in Exhibit 21.13 is a *true sale* of the receivables, whereas the transaction in Exhibit 21.10 is just a derivatives contract. The structures thus would have potentially different accounting, tax, regula-

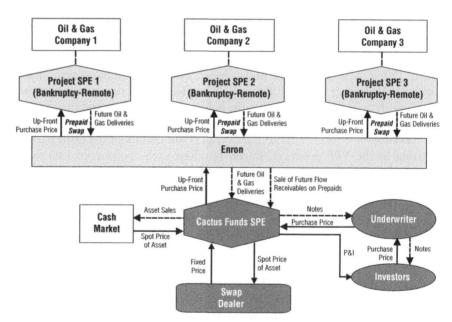

EXHIBIT 21.13 Securitized Synthetic Project Financing: Enron's Volumetric Production Payments Program

tory, and reporting requirements. Yet it is absolutely clear how the two transactions are playing an identical role *economically*, thus confirming our earlier claim that prepaid forwards and swaps are just synthetic project finance securitizations documented as derivatives.

Credit Enhancement in the Prepaids

One practical difference between a true sale of receivables pursuant to a series of prepaids and the prepaid itself is the credit risk. In the securitization, a first-interest lien is perfected against the commodity delivery receivables, whereas in the derivatives contract this is not the case. All that the derivatives contract guarantees in the event of default is that the contract will be terminated early, marked to market, and bilaterally netted. The derivatives counterparty does *not* have a perfected interest in the underlying commodity. And that's not enough. So the prepaid forward purchaser will demand additional C/E, which may come in the form of the usual credit enhancements discussed in Part Two.

Although Enron's VPP program is one of the textbook examples of how prepaids can be used properly to facilitate project finance, Enron also offers us a series of controversies on how prepaids can be abused and can malfunction badly. When Enron failed in December 2002, it had about $15 billion in cash prepayments from JPMorgan Chase and Citigroup booked against future oil and gas deliveries. Over time, Enron had entered into similar deals with other banks, including Credit Suisse. Enron appears to have accounted for the cash inflows on these prepaids as cash flows from operations offset with price risk management liabilities. Critics contend, however, that Enron's prepaids were not really prepaids, but rather "bank debt in disguise." Accordingly, critics maintain that not accounting for these deals as term debt allowed Enron to understate its leverage by about $15 billion, enough to materially mislead outsiders about the firm's true financial condition.

This is hardly the place to try to resolve this argument. Although the topic may be relevant, the facts are certainly not all yet known. And it may be some time before all the facts are in. Until the various legal proceedings have moved forward, speculating about the facts underlying this debate is hardly productive. Nevertheless, there are issues here that we do need to consider: namely, what the Enron controversy has taught us *about the credit enhancements that can be used with prepaids.*

To facilitate our analysis of this specific problem amidst a highly complex set of transactions with various facts still unknown, we must content ourselves to examine a *representative* transaction structure. This is similar to the later deals conducted between JPMorgan Chase (JPMC), Enron, and an SPE called Mahonia Limited, but not exactly the same. This is instead a simplified transaction structure for presentation and analysis purposes, and is not intended to represent accurately a specific deal between Enron and any particular bank. Nevertheless, this stylized example is more than sufficient to facilitate an analysis of the controversy surrounding the credit enhancements on Enron's prepaids. We will consider two controversies in that regard.

Advance Payment Supply Bonds and Mahonia   Our representative deal is illustrated in Exhibit 21.14. The bank lender is JPMorgan Chase. The SPE, called Mahonia Limited, was a Channel Islands SPE set up at the behest of Chase in December 1992 by Mourant du Feu & Jeune, acting on behalf of the Eastmoss Trust. Mahonia was not specifically established to conduct transactions with Enron. At the time, Chase was questioning whether a national bank had statutory authority to accept physical delivery of commodities, and Mahonia was originally established as a vehicle by which such deliveries from Chase customers could be made without posing regulatory problems for Chase. The transactions originally contemplated did not proceed, but the Mahonia entity had already been set up. Enron first approached Chase to do a prepaid in June 1993, and Mahonia was identified as a suitable vehicle for conducting that transaction. Between 1993 and 2001 when Enron failed, JPMC, Mahonia, and Enron had negotiated at least 12 prepaid deals. The representative deal shown in Exhibit 21.14 is similar to the later deals (roughly from 1999 onwards).

In many of Mahonia's earlier deals, in particular, two things were different from the representative late deal shown in Exhibit 21.14. First, in

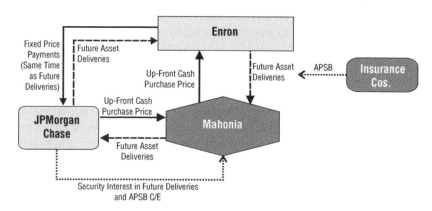

EXHIBIT 21.14   Generic "Late Mahonia" Enron Deal

the early Mahonia deals Mahonia sold its physical deliveries on the spot market or the New York Mercantile Exchange (NYMEX) futures market and hedged those sales on the NYMEX or with a swap dealer. The hedged revenues obtained from the physical product sales acted as collateral for a loan from JPMC that financed the original prepayment of oil and gas from Enron. In the Exhibit 21.14 late deal, by contrast, Mahonia has instead executed a mirroring prepaid with JPMC, leaving the bank to deal with the offtake and hedge legs of the deal—just as in Exhibit 21.12. But unlike Exhibit 21.12 where the bank sells product to the market and hedges with a commodity swap, JPMC now simultaneously disposes of the physical product and hedges the market risk of that sale by doing a commodity swap (traditional, not prepaid) *with Enron*. In other words, the asset purchased by Mahonia from Enron is now eventually making its way *back to Enron* via Mahonia and JPMC.

A second important distinction between the late deal depicted in Exhibit 21.14 and the earlier Mahonia deals is the reliance on insurance companies to provide C/E for Enron's obligations on the prepaid in the form of advance payment supply bonds (APSBs). Recall from Chapter 10, APSBs are commercial sureties that guarantee the delivery of a physical commodity. In the earlier Mahonia deals, by contrast, JPMC had required Enron to obtain bank LOCs that could be drawn in the event of default on the prepaid delivery obligation to Mahonia. JPMC then had a perfected security interest in the prepaid deliveries and the LOC to cover any potential defaults.

Beginning in 1998, Enron asked JPMC to let Mahonia accept APSBs in lieu of LOCs as C/E for the Enron-Mahonia prepaids. JPMC was initially hesitant to accept surety bonds in place of LOCs. To assuage its concerns, the bank requested that all the sureties backing the Enron APSBs provide several forms of assurance that the APSBs "would be the functional equivalent of letters of credit, and, like letters of credit, would constitute absolute and unconditional pay-on-demand financial guarantees."[11] These assurances were apparently provided, and with JPMC's consent, APSBs began to replace LOCs as collateral pledged to Mahonia. Providers of the APSBs were all multiline insurance companies, most of which were domiciled in New York, and included Liberty Mutual, Travelers Casualty & Surety, and St. Paul Fire and Marine.

On December 7, 2001—five days after Enron filed for bankruptcy protection—JPMC filed written notice with Enron's sureties of the nearly $1 billion due to Mahonia and JPMC under the APSBs. The sureties declined payment, arguing that the APSBs "were designed to camouflage loans by [JPMorgan] Chase to Enron, and that [JPMorgan] Chase defrauded the surety bond providers into guaranteeing what were purely financial obligations which they otherwise would not, and statutorily [under New York law] could not, have bonded."[12] In other words, the sureties claimed that because the prepaids were "bank debt in disguise," the APSBs represented *financial guarantees* that cannot be offered by multiline insurers under New York insurance law.

Consulting Exhibit 21.14, one can see what the multilines were attempting to assert. In short, they argued that the movement of oil and gas from Enron to Mahonia to JPMC and back to Enron was circular, primarily because they contended that Mahonia was really just an unconsolidated subsidiary of JPMC disguised as a separate company. As a result, the natural gas legs of the deals canceled out, leaving only fixed cash flows—an up-front payment from JPMC to Mahonia that funds Mahonia's up-front payment to Enron (which the insurers contend was really just a payment from JPMC to Enron), and a later fixed payment from Enron directly back to JPMC. If true, the combined structure would in fact represent a *financial* transaction, and not a *commodity* transaction. And therein lies the essential distinction between legitimate APSBs and financial guarantees. The sureties claimed they thought they were underwriting legitimate sureties to bond physical commodity deliveries, which should be legal under New York law. But in retrospect, they claimed the structure was a financial deal and hence illegal for multilines under New York law, thus relieving them of their payment obligations.

On January 2, 2003, JPMC announced that it was taking a $1.3 billion charge in the fourth quarter of 2002 largely to deal with Enron litigation matters. That charge-off reflected a settlement with insurers, reached on the same day the trial was to begin. As suggested by the 7.5 percent increase in JPMC's stock price the day word leaked out about the settlement, the settlement was a bigger victory for JPMC than expected. Under the settlement, the 11 insurers agreed to pay about 51 percent of their obligations to JPMC under the APSBs, or $655 million out of the $1 billion total owed.

West Landesbank and Mahonia XII   One might be tempted to conclude from the prior section that LOCs are always superior to APSBs and insurance products as a C/E to structures like prepaids. That's wrong, too, as another Enron episode illustrates.

The last of the 12 deals between JPMC, Mahonia, and Enron was a $350 million prepaid deal that closed in September 2001 just weeks before Enron filed for bankruptcy protection. Unlike every prior deal, Mahonia XII, as it was called, consisted of three *entirely cash-settled swap transactions*. Whether or not product actually flowed in the earlier deals remains to be seen, but in this deal it was not even intended to do so. The first swap was a prepaid swap between Mahonia and Enron in which Mahonia paid $350 million in return for a promised future cash payment tied to the future market price of natural gas. The second swap was a mirroring prepaid swap between JPMC and Mahonia in which JPMC paid $350 million to Mahonia up front in return for the right to receive a floating cash payment later tied to the future natural gas price. Finally, the third swap was a traditional (not prepaid) swap between JPMC and Enron in which JPMC made floating payments tied to future natural gas prices in exchange for a fixed $356 million cash payment from Enron.

The C/E for this deal consisted of two LOCs, one for $165 million posted by West Landesbank (WestLB) and the other for $150 million posted by JPMC. The structure is shown in Exhibit 21.15.

When Mahonia demanded a draw on the WestLB LOC on December 5, 2001, WestLB disputed its obligation to pay. The situation is similar to the dispute in New York between JPMC and the multiline insurers, except, importantly, the legality of APSBs is not relevant here and was not a part of WestLB's arguments in support of its nonpayment. Instead, WestLB claimed simply that it was a victim of fraud—that JPMC and Mahonia had conspired to hide the true nature of the three swaps together as a bank loan in disguise, that these transactions had not been properly accounted for under U.S. generally accepted accounting principles (GAAP), and that WestLB had been fraudulently induced to provide the LOC under circumstances of which it was not made adequately aware.

On August 3, 2004, in the U.K. High Court of Justice, Judge Cook ruled against WestLB and instructed the bank to honor the draw on its

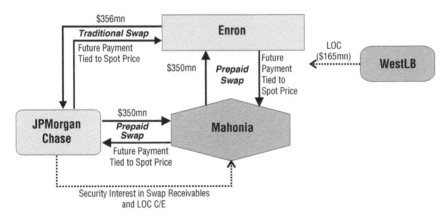

EXHIBIT 21.15 Mahonia XII (September 2001)

LOC. His dismissal of WestLB's claims was based primarily on his opinion that Mahonia was an independent corporation and not an unconsolidated subsidiary of JPMC and that the three swaps were independent transactions. The fact that they netted down to a fixed-for-fixed payment *ex post* did not itself invalidate their independence as three stand-alone agreements *ex ante*.

What Lessons? No matter how the facts underlying the Mahonia prepaid ultimately work out, an important lesson to take away from the two disputes we have just discussed is the need to take seriously legal and regulatory issues about the use of credit protection products and solutions. No matter how much the market for risk finance, risk transfer, and pure financing has converged at the level of the corporate users, the same cannot be said for regulation, case law, accounting, and tax. Users of these products must remain vigilant and clearly aware that they may well be standing on a slippery legal slope.

There is no single "this product is better than that one" takeaway from the Enron/Mahonia controversy. The lesson—one we have emphasized throughout this book—is simply to expect the unexpected, pay up for good outside legal advice, and, when in doubt, don't do it—whatever "it" may be.

Structured Insurance and Alternative Risk Transfer

Risk Securitizations and Insurance-Linked Notes

In Part Three, we discussed actual and synthetic securitizations of quite a broad spectrum of assets, ranging from loans and bonds to future flows and whole businesses. A natural way to make the transition into Part Four of this book on structured insurance and alternative risk transfer (ART) is to consider a product very much at the intersection of these two areas—*insurance-linked notes* (ILNs). ILNs are structured products issued in a process that we might call a *risk securitization*. In a typical risk securitization, securities are issued to fully fund a risk transfer agreement between the securities issuer and a sponsor/originator.[1] The goal is not raising funds for the sponsor, but rather managing risk.

In this terminology, synthetic collateralized debt obligations (SCDOs; see Chapter 18) are credit risk securitizations. The sponsor/originator buys credit default protection from a special purpose entity (SPE) that funds that protection through the issuance of bonds whose principal and interest (P&I) may be diverted to cover any required default-related payments. This does not generate a cash inflow for the originator, but it does result in full risk transfer (assuming the true independence of the SPE—see Chapter 16).

Although SCDOs are credit risk securitizations, they are not generally regarded as ILNs. The reason is that credit protection in a SCDO is sold by the SPE (on behalf of bondholders) to the originator using *derivatives*, not insurance. The structures we examine in this chapter, by contrast, rely on true insurance, reinsurance, or retrocession agreements sold by an SPE on behalf of its investors to an insurance purchaser. Motivations for insurance companies and nonfinancial corporations to procure protection through this mechanism rather than traditional insurance include capacity constraints in (re)insurance markets, better pricing from the capital markets (a very recent development), and the usual reasons for structured finance that we have now discussed at length (e.g., lower agency costs).

ILNs have also enjoyed tremendous appeal *with investors*. In many cases, securitized products and derivatives-based structured financing vehicles represent the first and/or most practical way for institutional investors to access alternative asset classes, like catastrophic insurance risk. The appeal of such instruments from a portfolio management perspective has indeed been well documented.[2]

We begin this chapter with an overview of the basic mechanics of a risk securitization and the creation of one or more classes of ILNs. This same basic structure will serve as a template for basically all the deals we then examine in later sections. Following this overview, we then briefly explore the "insurance cat bond" market—ILN programs sponsored by insurance companies to procure catastrophic property coverage and, more recently, other types of coverage. We then turn to explore *corporate* issuances of ILNs, or direct insurance purchases by corporations from the capital market. We conclude with a discussion of certain derivatives structures that can be used for similar risk transfer purposes to those discussed in the rest of the chapter.

GENERAL STRUCTURE

Any given ILN may have its own unique features, but most have the same basic structure and design. Most ILN structures, moreover, look just like a fully funded SCDO (see, for example, Exhibit 18.1). This similarity is not accidental. What is a SCDO, after all, but an issuance of securities to fund the sale of credit protection to a firm?

Exhibit 22.1 shows the basic setup behind a typical ILN. An SPE is established at the behest of the sponsor or originator, which may be a (re)insurance company or a corporation. The SPE is bankruptcy remote from the sponsor, unconsolidated with and independent of the sponsor, and licensed as either a primary insurance company or a reinsurer in its domicile. The capital structure of the SPE represents the ILN. As we saw with CDOs, they may be single-class or multiclass and may cover various layers of subordination. The proceeds of the ILN issue by the SPE are surrendered to a trustee, which invests the assets in low-risk marketable securities (e.g., repos, Treasuries, AAA corporates).

The risk transfer in the structure occurs through a (re)insurance contract between the sponsor and the SPE. This contract can be pretty much any kind of (re)insurance contract imaginable; if it can be underwritten directly, it can be underwritten with an SPE counterparty as part of an ILN issue. The contract may also contain the usual features of (re)insurance, including a deductible, policy limit, co-pay provision, and the like. In ex-

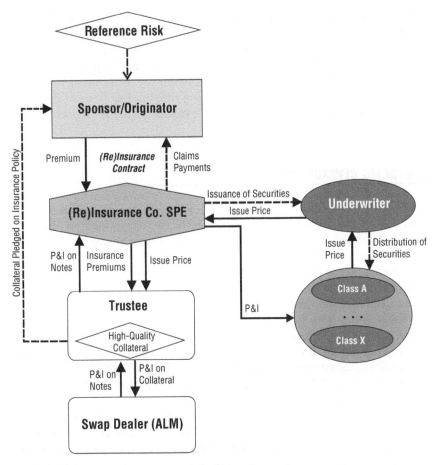

EXHIBIT 22.1 Typical Insurance-Linked Note Structure

change for this coverage, the sponsor pays premium periodically to the SPE (re)insurer (usually quarterly or annually). That premium is then ceded to the trustee and added to the low-risk collateral in trust.

The securities held in trust by the trustee are pledged first to cover payments on the (re)insurance contract, with all remaining amounts available for distribution to the note holders in the structure. Any claims on the (re)insurance policy are financed first out of the investment income and premium in the collateral portfolio and then by the liquidation of collateral assets. There is often some overcollateralization (O/C) embedded into these structures thanks to the investment income, so that the total market value of the collateral pool should virtually never be less than the policy limit on the (re)insurance contract.

The structure is liquidity enhanced with an asset swap; that is, actual income earned on high-quality collateral is periodically paid to a swap dealer in exchange for floating payments based on the London Interbank Offered Rate (LIBOR) to match the floating-rate funding basis of the SPE's ILN liabilities. Additional internal and external liquidity and credit enhancements also may be used.

SYNTHETIC REINSURANCE

The vast majority of ILNs that have been issued to date have been used to fund reinsurance or retrocession coverage in the reinsurance market and have been linked to catastrophic (re)insurance losses arising from natural disasters such as earthquakes, hailstorms, tropical cyclones, windstorms, tornadoes, and the like. In other words, most ILNs to date have been sponsored by insurance or reinsurance companies as a new source of reinsurance or retrocession capacity.

ILNs sponsored by insurance or reinsurance companies are often called *cat bonds*. This term derives from the historical use of these products in creating additional reinsurance or retrocession capacity for firms underwriting catastrophic layers in property lines or property subject to catastrophic risks. Often regarded as the most triumphant and archetypical ART form, the cat bond industry is still relatively small compared to other structured products and compared to outright catastrophic reinsurance coverage. Nevertheless, cat bonds were among the earliest "convergence" products in between capital markets and insurance and would be worthy of study on that basis alone.

As Lane and Beckwith explain in their excellent survey of cat bond and ILN activity for 2004 (Chapter 33), however, the market for cat bonds has started to enter a period of really significant growth in the past year or two. Especially noteworthy has been a significant decline in spreads that now make cat bonds a much more cost-effective source of reinsurance or retrocession. In the past, cat bonds had been a *pure* capacity play—a source of additional catastrophic coverage when coverage was not available any other way. Now cat bonds are starting to give the primary insurance, reinsurance, and retrocession markets a real run for their money.

Because of the volume of material available on cat bonds, this section will be kept reasonably brief and limited to a discussion of the basic form and prevalent structures in the cat bond world. Readers should review Lane and Beckwith's Chapter 33 for more deal-specific information. Substantial additional information on cat bond activity can also be found at the web site for Lane Financial LLC, www.lanefinancialllc.com.

Basic Mechanics of Cat Bonds

A cat bond is the insurance analogue of an SCDO (see Chapter 18); instead of the security issuer selling protection to the originator using derivatives, the issuer sells *reinsurance* or *retrocession* to the originator that is fully funded with the issue of one or more classes of securities.

The sponsor of a cat bond issue is generally the insurance or reinsurance company that would like to purchase reinsurance or retrocession from investors in the capital market. An SPE is set up that is bankruptcy remote from and unconsolidated with the sponsor, and the SPE is the issuer of the ILNs or cat bonds. The proceeds from the ILN issue are given to a trustee along with the premiums paid by the ceding (re)insurer. The investment income on the liquid assets acquired by the trustee is swapped for a LIBOR-based cash flow. Exhibit 22.2 shows the basic structure if the sponsor is a reinsurer seeking retrocession from the SPE.

As in a typical SCDO, the trustee serves the dual purpose of monitoring the performance of the whole structure on behalf of ILN investors and ensuring that the collateral assets are applied to the cash flow waterfall of the structure with the appropriate priorities. The funds on deposit with the trust are first used to finance any claims made by the ceding (re)insurer on the reinsuring SPE, and any remaining funds belong to investors in the notes.

So far so good—by now this is certainly familiar territory to us. But the basic structure is where the similarity to SCDOs ends. Because of the nature of catastrophic insurance, cat bond structures do look different from traditional SCDOs in a few important ways that we summarize in the next few subsections.

Maturity of Liabilities We saw in Chapters 13, 16, 17, and 18 how the maturity structure of the liabilities in a securitization can help manage the liquidity risk inherent to the structure. In the case of cat bonds, things are a little more complicated.

In a basic cat bond structure, claims on the reinsurance or retrocession policy written by the SPE are financed out of the premiums collected and investment income on the trust collateral. If that is inadequate, collateral assets in the trust can be liquidated, resulting in reductions of principal returned to holders of securities issued by the SPE. If multiple classes of securities are issued, the principal reductions are applied to the securities in reverse order of their priority in the SPE's capital structure.

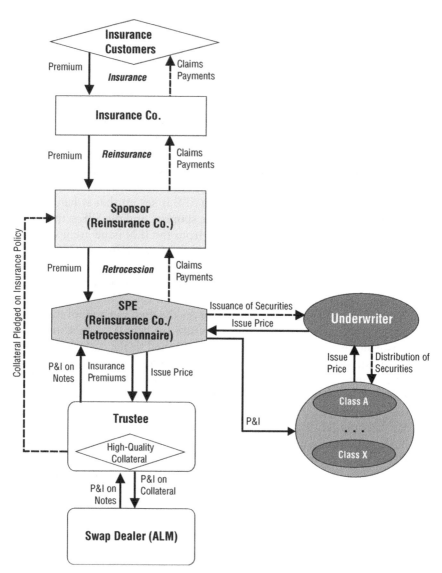

EXHIBIT 22.2 Typical Cat Bond Structure

Alternatively, a claim by the ceding (re)insurer may result in a *delay* in principal repayment rather than a permanent forfeiture. Through the use of defeasance provisions, some proportion of the principal would be returned on schedule. The rest would be returned later and may be funded by the purchase of zero coupon securities using the proceeds from the guaranteed portion of the original issue, much like the capital-protected notes (CPNs) we examined in Chapter 20.

The effective and actual maturities of cat bonds often differ, however, for reasons other than defeasance. In particular, property claims arising from natural catastrophes are often reported gradually over a long period of time after the triggering event occurs, remaining classified as incurred but not reported (IBNR) losses for longer than most other kinds of property claims. When a peril gives rise to a covered loss toward the end of the life of the bonds, the SPE can often optionally extend the maturity of the bonds to include the full loss development period.

Ratings Most early cat bond issues that were regarded as successful involved at least two tranches of securities, the senior of which was rated investment grade. Credit enhancement (C/E) was provided through a buildup of O/C financed by a diversion of any excess spread and/or a monoline wrap. Then for a long time, the trend in cat bond issues was toward lower-rated securities or offerings that were entirely unrated. Most cat bond offerings are once again rated these days, but even in the recent multitranche issues the senior bonds may not be rated investment grade.

As the rating of cat bonds has evolved, so has the participation in cat bond issues. Early issues were bought largely by money managers, mutual funds, and pension plans. But the more recent lower-rated or unrated issues have been placed mainly with hedge funds and insurance companies. Funds of cat bonds have also arisen as intermediary vehicles that are themselves eligible to buy cat bonds and which then sell shares in their funds to institutions that may not be eligible to buy the bonds outright.

Events, Triggers, and Losses The triggering event for cat bonds may either be single-peril (e.g., a single tropical cyclone damaging a specific firm) or multiperil (e.g., multiple earthquakes, such as one on the East Coast and one on the West). If the specified events occur during the risk period specified in a cat bond structure—which may or may not encompass the entire life of the bond—the event trigger is activated.

Some cat bonds have a trigger and payout that are *full indemnity*. In such cases, the reinsurance contract is based on actual claims paid by the

SPE to the reinsurance company, and those claims payments in turn determine the P&I left over for cat bond investors. Indemnity structures, however, are not very transparent, are hard to price, and give rise to concerns about moral hazard. Even with the usual protections like deductibles and co-payment provisions, investors have been skeptical that cat bond programs designed by a reinsurer for the purpose of providing that reinsurer with new capacity will be neutral to the investor. As a result, three other types of cat bond triggers and payouts have also enjoyed widespread use.

In *indexed* cat bond products, the trigger and/or claims payment is based on the realized value of some index, not the actual portfolio of claims underwritten by the insurance purchaser. Index-based loss claims are based on the loss development in one or more specific catastrophic loss indexes (e.g., a Property Claim Services or PCS regional index). Index products are popular when there is a concern about moral hazard or adverse selection at the ceding (re)insurer, but the cost of using an index is the introduction of basis risk. Indemnity-based deals that are based on actual damages sustained by specific businesses result in coverage that matches a cedant's loss experience. Introducing an index of damages eliminates the cedant's ability to manipulate losses, but at the same time increases the likelihood that the coverage will poorly track the actual damages sustained.

A third alternative is a *parametric* trigger and payout. In these deals, the trigger enabling a reinsurer to file a claim is a catastrophic loss event defined in terms of some objective parameters usually involving the location and size of the disaster (e.g., epicenter and Richter scale magnitude of an earthquake, landfall point for the eye of a tropical cycle with a size based on the Safir-Simpson scale, etc.). Cat bonds with parametric triggers often also have claims payouts defined in terms of those triggers, so that an increasing proportion of principal is withheld from investors and paid as claims to the reinsurer for larger and closer catastrophic events.

Finally, some cat bonds are *modeled loss* bonds. In these cases, the trigger and claims payment are based on one or more parameters that are fed into a model of how a catastrophe will affect the insurance purchaser directly. Claims are thus based on *expected* losses, not actual losses. These sorts of deals are increasingly popular and seem to represent a good middle ground between too much moral hazard in indemnity structures and too much basis risk in indexed structures.

Examples

Given the diversity of cat bonds issued to date, perhaps the best way to get a feel for the wide degree of variance across these structures is to present a few examples. These examples are neither exhaustive nor perfectly representative. They are shown simply to demonstrate the range of what has been done.

Swiss Re/SR Earthquake Fund Ltd. In 1997, the SR Earthquake Fund Ltd. SPE issued $137 million in four classes of notes whose repayment schedule was linked to the SPE's payment of claims to Swiss Re on a $111.9 million catastrophic retrocession cover. The triggering event was a California earthquake, and the SPE's contingent liability to Swiss Re was based on the largest insured loss from a single earthquake over a two-year period of time as determined by PCS. The SR Earthquake bonds thus were single-peril, indexed cat bonds.

The SR Earthquake retrocession was a value contract, not a true indemnity contract. Depending on the size of the loss, the principal of the bonds is reduced by a fixed amount depending on their priority. The first two classes of SR Earthquake bonds were the first cat bonds to be rated investment grade—Baa3 by Moody's and BBB– by Fitch. A maximum of 60 percent of the principal was at risk, with the remaining amount self-collateralized by the SPE's acquisition of Treasuries. Class A-1 paid a fixed rate of 8.645 percent, and Class A-2 paid 255 basis points over 3M-LIBOR.

The third class had up to 100 percent principal at risk and paid 10.493 percent. Class B was rated Ba1/BB and had a principal risk tied to the PCS index losses arising from a California earthquake. The most subordinated issue, Class C, paid 11.952 percent and had no rating. Unlike the other three classes, principal losses were not based on the indemnity payments by the SPE. Instead, Class C bondholders forfeited 100 percent of their principal in the event that the largest California quake led to PCS-reported insured losses exceeding $12 billion.

From a financial engineering standpoint, each class of bond in the SR Earthquake structure can be viewed as a coupon bond plus one or more binary options. Class C, for example, either returns full principal in the event of no quake resulting in over $12 billion in PCS index losses or returns nothing. From the SPE's perspective, this is equivalent to a coupon bond plus a digital call on PCS index losses (i.e., put on PCS index-implied property values) struck at $12 billion with a fixed payout of $14.7 million, the total size of the Class C note issue.

The Class A and B bonds are synthetically equivalent to coupon bonds plus long vertical spreads consisting of digital options. In the Class B note case, for example, the SPV withholds no principal for losses under $18.5 billion, $12.4 million for losses above $18.5 billion, $24.8 million for losses above $21 billion, and $37.2 million for losses above $24 billion.

The first piece of the binary vertical spread is a long call on PCS losses struck at $18.5 billion with a fixed payment of $12.4 million. The second component is a long digital call struck at $21 billion with a fixed payout of $24.8 million. But without an additional leg, *both* options would be in-the-money at loss levels above $21 billion. To limit the *total* holdback to $24.8 million, the spread thus also must include a *short* digital call on PCS losses struck at $21 billion with a fixed payout of $12.4 million. For loss levels above $21 billion, all three options are in-the-money, and the net is +$12.4 million on the long call struck at $18.5 billion, +$24.8 million on the long call struck at $21 billion, and −$12.4 million on the short call struck at $21 billion. And so on for the rest of the loss trigger levels, as well as for the Class A notes.

The SR Earthquake bonds included a one-year loss development period. A natural tension concerned scheduled principal repayments over loss development periods. Reinsurers prefer longer loss development periods, because reported losses only grow with time. The longer the period included in the retrocession agreement, the more Swiss Re would recover from bondholders. On the other side, investors clearly prefer a return of principal as quickly as possible. As a compromise, the SR Earthquake bonds required regular comparisons during the loss development period of estimated losses with a growing loss benchmark. If loss development is steadily growing, the trustee keeps the principal on reserve as a source of potential future claims by Swiss Re for up to a year. But when loss development stabilizes below a predefined trigger relative to the benchmark, principal is released for amortization.

Tokio Marine & Fire/Parametric Re   The Cayman Islands SPE Parametric Re issued bonds in 1997 and simultaneously entered into a reinsurance agreement with Tokio Marine & Fire. Unlike the SR Earthquake bonds where the trigger was index-based, the Parametric Re issue involved a parametric trigger based on the physical attributes of the event.

The insured event was an earthquake in or around Tokyo. The structure defined an "inner" and "outer" grid with Tokyo roughly at the geographic center. Upon the occurrence of an earthquake, the quake epicenter would serve as the basis for whether the event was deemed to have occurred in the inner or outer grid. The location and magnitude of the quake then determined the required payment from Parametric Re to Tokio Marine on the reinsurance. A quake that registered 7.4 on the Japan Meteorological Association (JMA) scale, for example, would involve a holdback by the SPE trustee of 44 percent of principal on the outstanding notes if the event occurred in the outer grid or a hold-back of 70 percent for quakes with inner grid epicenters. These amounts held back from note holders then would be used to pay Tokio Marine in the reinsurance agreement between Tokio and Parametric Re.

The Parametric Re issue involved two classes of securities. Notes with a face value of $80 million were fully exposed to quake risk, whereas "units" were not. Units with a total issue value of $20 million included $10 million in defeasance certificates with no quake exposure and another $10 million in notes fully exposed to quake risk. The defeasance certificates were structured in a manner similar to the CPNs discussed for hedge funds and private equity funds in Chapter 20.

One advantage of a parametric trigger like the one Parametric Re employed is the speed of payment. No loss development period is required, and claims can be funded by the trustee's investments of the proceeds from the original issue plus the premium received and any investment income generated on those investments. In addition, some find parametric trigger structures easier to hedge or reinsure. All that is required to virtually eliminate basis risk is another instrument that can be indexed to the same trigger.

USAA/Residential Re   One of the best-known cat bond issues was undertaken in 1997 by the United States Automobile Association (USAA) based on a single peril: hurricanes in the eastern United States. Two classes of bonds were issued from which $477 million was raised, nearly four times the planned subscription amount. Class A securities in the amount of $87 million were issued with a coupon of LIBOR plus 273 basis points. Class B bonds totaled about $313 million and had an interest rate of LIBOR plus 576 basis points. The interest on both bonds was at risk. The Class B securities also had principal at risk, whereas $77 million of the $477 million in funds collected from the issue were used to guarantee principal repayment on the Class A bonds. The A and B bonds were rated AAA and BB by Fitch, respectively.

Unlike the two prior structures, Residential Re's reinsurance contract of USAA was a true indemnity contract. In the event of a single hurricane hitting one or more of the 20 eastern states, the policy provided excess of loss (XOL) coverage to USAA with a co-pay—specifically, 80 percent of $500 million XS $1 billion of actual USAA losses were covered by the policy.

St. Paul Companies/Georgetown Re   St. Paul Companies undertook a $68.5 million securitization in 1996 to create additional retrocessional capacity for its reinsurance subsidiary St. Paul Re so that it could take advantage of a then-strong demand for catastrophic XOL reinsurance in North America.

Georgetown Re was capitalized by the issue of both notes ($44.5 million) and preferred stock ($23.2 million) with expirations in 2007 and 2000, respectively. The notes guaranteed a principal return through the investment of note issue proceeds by the SPE in zero coupon marketable securities (see Chapter 20), thus leading to an AAA rating for the notes. The unrated preferred stock had no principal protection.

The Georgetown Re structure did not involve any specific definition of triggering events. Instead, St. Paul Re ceded part of its catastrophic XOL policy line to Georgetown Re in a classical proportional treaty lasting 10 years. The interest payments on the notes and shares and the principal repayment on the shares were then determined based on the overall performance of the ceded business lines. By including both the underwriting and investment sides of its catastrophic XOL business, St. Paul Re ensured that the resulting cession was well diversified and thus proved very attractive to investors at the time.

Winterthur Hail Bonds   Eschewing securitization through an SPE structure, the Swiss primary insurance carrier Winterthur went directly to the capital market in 1997 by issuing insurance-based structured notes (i.e., straight bonds plus embedded insurance derivatives). The bonds were three-year subordinated convertible debt instruments with face value CHF400 million.

In addition to a conversion provision, the bonds included what Winterthur called "WinCat coupons," or coupons indexed to a catastrophic triggering event. During the reference period, Winterthur would count the number of motor vehicle claims on which it had to pay out as a direct result of hail or storm damage. If the number was 6,000 or more, the Win-Cat Coupons were reset to zero. Otherwise, the WinCat coupon was set at a rate one-third higher than the interest rate on Winterthur's traditional convertibles. The conversion premium was 7 percent. Although the risk transfer provided to Winterthur is estimated only to have been around CHF9 million, the issue is widely regarded as having been a success.[3]

From a financial engineering perspective, the subordinated WinCat convertibles can be viewed as subordinated convertible debt plus a portfolio of knock-out options attached to the normal coupons of the bond. The trigger on the knock-out options was the number of motor vehicle claims in the corresponding reference period. If the option was not knocked out, bondholders would receive their promised coupon rate. So, the knock-out options were also binary.

Not Just Cat Risk Anymore

What began as a source of additional capacity for catastrophic property coverage quickly migrated to other insurance lines as reinsurers realized that cat bond structures could be used for essentially *any* kind of insurance risk. The only limitation on what insurance risks can provide the foundation for an ILN issue is cost. In most cases, ILNs are a more expensive way for a (re)insurer to acquire reinsurance or retrocession; the direct underwriting market is almost always cheaper. For many years, the only risks for which insurance companies turned to the capital market were those risks that were already saturated inside the insurance industry, like cat risk. As times have changed and cat bond spreads have fallen, ILNs have become a more cost-effective alternative to traditional reinsurance and retrocession, and, not surprisingly, the types of risks being securitized have expanded accordingly.

Somewhat misleadingly, these structures, some of which are discussed next (and see also Lane and Beckwith's Chapter 33), are often still called "cat bonds."

Trade Credit Retrocession The 1999 issue of Synthetic European Credit Tracking Securities (SECTRS) provides a good illustration of how securitized products can be used as a method of creating bulk capacity in the noncat reinsurance area. Specifically, SECTRS were used to construct a synthetic retrocession for Gerling Credit Insurance Group's reinsurance of certain European trade credits.

SECTRS 1999-1 Ltd was established as a Cayman Islands SPE and licensed reinsurer to provide €455 million in retrocession cover to Namur Re SA based on a portfolio of 92,000 businesses selected at random in the trade insurance market. Namur Re SA was a subsidiary of Gerling-Konzern Speziale Kreditverischerungs AG, in turn a subsidiary of Gerling Credit Insurance Group (GCIG) and Gerling-Konzern Globale Rückversicherungs AG. Namur Re provided trade credit *re*insurance mainly to credit insurer GCIG.

Three classes of securities were issued for maturity three years after the issue date. Interest on the securities was payable quarterly in arrears and equal to LIBOR plus a spread: 45, 85, and 170 basis points over 3M-EURIBOR for Classes A, B, and C, respectively. As shown in Exhibit 22.3, Chase acts as the trustee and is given both the proceeds of the security issue and the premium paid by Namur to the SPE. This is invested in marketable securities, and interest on the securities is swapped with Goldman Sachs Mitsui Marine Derivative Products LP for a EURIBOR-based stable income stream that is used to pay interest on the notes.

The SPE provides reinsurance to Namur Re on an XOL basis for three separate reference portfolios into which the 92,000 reference businesses are divided. To determine the retrocession payment structure, an annual count is made of the number of businesses in the reference portfolio that have experienced a trade credit default event in the prior annual

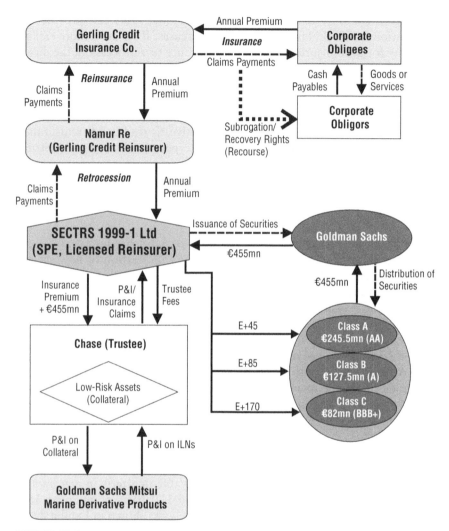

EXHIBIT 22.3   Gerling Trade Credit ILNs (SECTRS)

period. In addition, a cumulative count is maintained for years 2 and 3 of the structure. The retrocession trigger is activated either when the annual count exceeds the annual attachment point for any of the three policies or when the cumulative count exceeds the cumulative attachment point. The payment due from the SPE to the ceding reinsurer is then determined by multiplying the excess of the annual or cumulative count above the lower attachment point by a predefined recovery rate. Each policy also includes an upper limit.

The end result is a series of three securities whose principal repayments are reduced based on the claims the SPE receives as retrocessionaire for Namur Re on the reference portfolio of trade credits. The ceding reinsurer, in turn, has successfully accessed significant bulk capacity *directly from the capital market.*

Life Acquisition Costs, Mortality and Expense Fees, and Surplus Securitizations

Very little in this book has addressed life insurance, but it remains one of the largest parts of the global (re)insurance industry. And unlike almost all of the other risks discussed here, life insurance is fundamentally different because it *will* eventually pay off. Excluding the odd disqualification of suicide or a lazy beneficiary, life insurance will inevitably result in a claim. The main risks of a life insurance program thus are twofold: how to finance a costly life insurance business, and how to manage the mortality risk regarding people's live expectancies. Morbid though it seems, life insurance is really an asset/liability management problem. Life insurance claims can be funded with ease if the timing of the claims is known. To the extent that timing is unknown, the asset-liability management (ALM) gap management is the tricky part.

One problem faced by life insurers is the cash strain they bear shortly after underwriting a life insurance policy on policy acquisition costs. Every variable annuity or life policy sold generates a brokerage and/or distribution cost that the insurer must pay immediately, despite only earning the cash flow back over the first three to five years of the policy life. This can create a drag on a life insurer's balance sheet.[4]

Three of the early and notable life insurance–related securitizations were aimed at securitizing these life policy acquisition costs.[5] In 1996 and 1997, American Skandia Life Assurance Corp. conducted a series of four transactions in which it conveyed to its parent 80 percent to 100 percent of its rights to receive future mortality and expense (M&E) charges and contingent deferred sales charges on a portion of its life program. The parent paid the insurance company an amount essentially equal to the present value of those expected future claims, much as in a loss portfolio transfer. The parent, in turn, securitized the future fees through an SPE backed with those receivables.

A second life securitization was undertaken by U.K. mutual insurer National Provident Institution (NPI). In a simpler structure, NPI securitized the future profits on a large block of its life policies. NPI established the SPV Mutual Securitisation PLC to issue two classes of limited recourse bonds, both of which received interest and principal based on the emerging surplus on NPI's block of life policies. The two classes of securities were separated by the dates of their principal repayments to amortize the expected surplus development over time. Class A repaid principal from 1998 to 2012, and Class B from 2012 to 2022. By securitizing its surplus, NPI was able to generate cash in 1998 for a surplus that would emerge only over many years. In many ways, the NPI securitization thus can be viewed more as a synthetic finite risk transaction (see Chapter 24) than a classical risk transfer.

A third life transaction was conducted by Germany's reinsurance giant Hannover Re in conjunction with Rabobank. To finance the expansion of its life lines across Europe, Hannover and Rabobank set up a Dublin-based SPE called Interpolis Re, owned by Rabobank. Hannover retroceded 75 percent of its defined reinsurance treaties to Interpolis in a quota share treaty. In return, Rabobank made a 100 million deutschemark loan to Interpolis, on which Hannover could draw for liquidity. Take out the SPE and the transaction is essentially just an asset swap. But with the SPE in the middle, Hannover received liquidity from Rabobank. Interpolis absorbed the reinsurance risk, but Rabobank in turn receives 75 percent of the profits on the future business.

Life insurance companies have also been engaging for several years in securitizations of the embedded value of life insurance programs. U.K. life insurer Woolwich, working in late 2003 with Barclays Capital, transferred £400 million to investors. The structure did not transfer mortality risk (see the next subsection for that), but essentially monetized an expected surplus. Actual losses in the surplus relative to its embedded expected value then were borne by investors in the securities.

Variable-Rate Mortality Notes   In December 2003, Swiss Re once again (note how many of these ILNs have the Swiss Re moniker on them) moved the market in a new direction with the first securitization of excess mortality risk in a life policy line. Vita Capital Ltd., a Cayman Islands SPE, issued $250 million of notes with principal at risk to deteriorations in a European mortality index. The three-and-a-half-year bonds were rated A+ and had a coupon of 135 basis points over LIBOR.

Mechanically, the ILNs worked just like the other ones we have examined. The notes were issued and the proceeds deposited in a trust account, along with premium paid by Swiss Re to the SPE. If mortality rates exceed 130 percent of an index amount, collateral is liquidated to honor mortality loss claims failed by Swiss Re. Principal on the ILNs is forgone according to a sliding scale, where 100 percent of principal is withheld by the SPE to pay claims from Swiss Re when mortality rates hit 150 percent of the index amount.

See Chapter 33 by Lane and Beckwith for additional discussion of this deal, as well as several other innovative new structures in the life insurance area.

Casualty Insurance   The first securitization of casualty risk occurred in late summer of 2005 when Oil Casualty Insurance Ltd. (OCIL) procured $405 million in casualty reinsurance over three years from the SPE Avalon Re. Three tranches of notes were issued—each with a face value of $135 million—that provide $135 XS $300, $135 XS $450, and $135 XS $600 in cover to the insurance company.

CORPORATE RISK SECURITIZATIONS

The concept of a cat bond first migrated into corporate risk management in the mid-1990s for a purpose very similar to the cat bond programs sponsored by insurers. The first corporate cat bond was sponsored by Oriental Land Co., the owner/operator of Tokyo Disneyland. Oriental Land had previously bought no catastrophic insurance for Tokyo Disneyland, thus surprising the market that its first acquisition of such insurance would be through a cat bond and not direct underwriting. Nevertheless, availability and pricing on Japanese catastrophic property coverage in the mid to late 1990s was considered tight and hard. The success of the initiative demonstrated the sensibility of the capital market alternative.

Since then, corporations have increasingly looked to the capital markets for insurance coverage. The risks that have been securitized have expanded well past just traditional catastrophic property coverage, and the pricing of the deals continues over time to become more and more favorable. This section reviews some of the most important and interesting cat bond structures to date, and we can be sure that the list will be dated by the time this book appears in print. This is a fast-moving and exciting area where structured finance meets structured insurance, and it is its early days.

Earthquakes and Theme Parks

At least two deals to date have been designed to enable the owner of a major theme park to buy insurance triggered by the occurrence of an earthquake near the theme park. The deals are a bit different, and we will discuss them separately.

Oriental Land/Tokyo Disneyland   Oriental Land Co., the owner/operator of Tokyo Disneyland, procured insurance against damage to the theme park from earthquakes with an April 1999 structure. The structure was unusual and creative in several ways. In particular, both the trigger and the payout were parametric, resulting in a payment to Oriental Land of a prespecified amount upon occurrence of the triggering event. The insurance thus was a *valued* contract and not an indemnity contract. Because claims payments on the policy did not depend on the actual damage sustained and yet would only pay in the event some real damage had occurred, Oriental Land had the flexibility to use the proceeds from the policy to cover any losses that it wanted arising from the quake—such as property damage or, say, business interruption (BI)-related losses. A traditional insurance contract would have been much more limiting.

In addition, Oriental Land was unique because it contained two distinct components, one of which was risk transfer and the other of which instead served as a source of postloss risk financing.

The risk transfer piece of the deal was a $100 million issue by the Cayman Islands SPE Concentric Ltd. In usual risk securitization form, the proceeds from the issue were invested by the bond trustee in highly rated securities whose coupons were swapped into LIBOR. Oriental Land then purchased insurance from Concentric with a trigger and payout tied to the location and size of a quake.[6] The insurance premium was added to the funds held by the trustee.

The $100 million Concentric issue was a single class of notes rated BB+/Ba1 and paying LIBOR plus 310 basis points through a final maturity date of May 2004. Principal repayment on the securities was based on a sliding scale linked to the same parameters governing the claims on the insurance policy by Oriental Land on Concentric. These parameters are illustrated on Exhibit 22.4 and depend on the size and location of the quake relative to the location of the theme park in Maihama. The policy is triggered for quakes of 6.5 and up on the JMA scale within 10 kilometers of Maihama, for quakes of 7.1 and up on the JMA scale within 50 kilometers of Maihama, and for quakes of 7.6 and up on the JMA scale within 75 kilometers of Maihama. The Oriental Land policy pays (and, hence, bondholders sacrifice) $25 million for the minimum-magnitude quake in each location band. The policy payout then rises in steps as the severity of the quake increases up to a maximum payout of $100 million at 7.5, 7.7, and 7.9 for the three bands, respectively. A quake measuring 7.5 on the JMA scale within 10 kilometers of the theme park thus results in a maximum payout on the policy and a total loss of principal by the note holders. Similarly, the full $100 million is paid on a 7.9 quake if it is within 75 kilometers of Maihama.

The second piece of the Oriental Land structure was a contingent debt offering (see Chapter 15) by Oriental Land to the SPE Circle Maihama Ltd. Specifically, Circle Maihama issued $100 million in A-rated extendable notes to investors at the rate of LIBOR plus 75 basis points. Proceeds

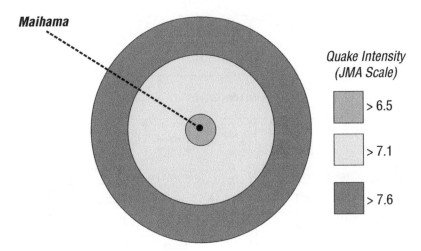

EXHIBIT 22.4   Parametric Trigger and Payout for Oriental Land/Tokyo Disneyland (May 1999)

were invested in a trust comprised of AAA-rated assets along with the option premium paid by Oriental Land to Circle Maihama Ltd. and swapped into LIBOR+75. The second trigger in the contingent debt facility is the occurrence of a quake that triggers the Concentric insurance policy. Should that occur in the first three years of the deal, the swap counterparty would liquidate the low-risk investments in the trust and purchase a $100 million five-year bond from Oriental Land. Investors would henceforth be paid interest on the Oriental Land bond. If the quake occurred in years 4 or 5, the new collateral backing the extendable notes would be a four-year Oriental Land bond and a three-year Oriental Land bond, respectively.

Mechanically, the Circle Maihama part of the deal is structured using an asset swap between the swap counterparty and the trust acting on behalf of the bondholders. As long as the Concentric trigger is not pulled, the trust pays AAA-rated returns to the swap dealer in exchange for LIBOR+75. But if the Concentric trigger is pulled, the swap dealer must buy the Oriental bond and begin to pay interest on *that* asset to note holders. Until the option is exercised by Oriental to issue the new bond, the swap dealer—not Oriental—is responsible for paying the LIBOR+75 interest to note holders. A sketch of the entire Oriental structure is shown in Exhibit 22.5.

This contingent debt component of the Oriental Land deal was pure risk financing for Oriental Land. Although the issuance of the debt was conditional on a quake, the payoffs on the extendable bonds were not. True, the quake might cause damage that would affect Oriental's ability to

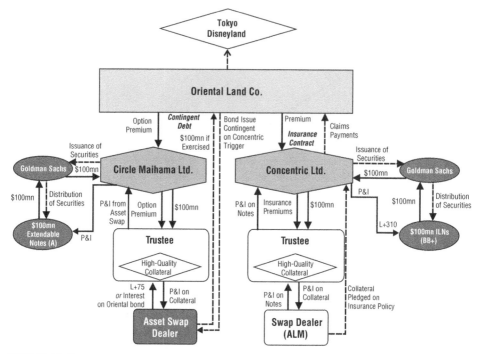

EXHIBIT 22.5 Oriental Land/Tokyo Disneyland

pay, but that credit risk would affect investors in this contingent capital facility the same way that it would affect investors in the unsecured debt of Oriental Land.

Vivendi Universal/Universal Studios, California In December 2002, Vivendi Universal SA sought protection from the capital markets for damage to its California-based Universal Studies properties.[7] The securities were issued by a Cayman Islands SPE called Studio Re and included two tranches: a $150 million bond tranche (BB+/Ba3) placed by Goldman Sachs due July 2006, and a $25 million preferred share issue (BB/B1) arranged by Swiss Re Capital Markets redeemable July 2006.

The Vivendi–Universal Studios structure involved a modeled loss trigger and payout, where losses included Universal Studios' losses arising from a California earthquake as a result of a weighted mix of property damage, workers' compensation claims, and business interruption (BI).

The structure itself was like a two-tranche CDO deal, with the preferred shares taking the first loss. The bonds and shares issued with interest rates of 517 and 811 basis points over LIBOR, respectively.

Residual Value Protection (Toyota Motor Credit Corporation)

Like other automotive firms, the Toyota Motor Credit Corporation (TMCC) faces a risk that the *residual value* of a car that has been leased could fall below the market value of the automobile. Most leases contain a provision allowing the lessee to purchase the vehicle at the end of a lease period. If the market price is below the residual value of the car, the lessee will likely exercise her option to buy the car. This means that most cars returned to TMCC result in an immediate loss equal to the difference between the residual value of the car and its resale value.

One way for firms facing residual value risk to address that risk is through straight-out insurance or residual value guaranties. This is the tack that three participants in the airline financing arena have taken. TMCC opted instead to buy insurance from the capital market directly.

Grammercy Place Insurance Ltd. was an SPE and Cayman Islands–registered insurance company whose single purpose was to provide direct residual value insurance to TMCC. The underlying pool of assets was a predetermined pool of about 260,000 auto and light-duty truck leases originated by Toyota and Lexus dealers that were assigned to and serviced by TMCC.

Under the terms of the insurance contract between Grammercy and TMCC, TMCC paid a quarterly premium to Grammercy for the residual value insurance. In turn, Grammercy provided annual coverage to TMCC for three years for the risk of residual value losses. The multiyear coverage was structured as three separate insurance policies, each of which included a 10 percent co-payment provision so that TMCC retained 10 percent of each year's annual residual value loss. In addition, each year's coverage involved a deductible equal to approximately 9 percent of the aggregate initial residual value of all the leases covered by the underlying policy.

Grammercy issued three classes of securities, all of which were FRNs paying interest quarterly equal to 3M-LIBOR plus a spread. The original issue amount called for about $60 million of senior Class A notes, $283 million of mezzanine Class B securities, and $222 million of highly subordinated Class C bonds. The total issue was planned for just over $566 million.

The proceeds from this security issue were placed in a trust collateral account managed by Chase. The cash subscription issue was used by Chase to acquire marketable and liquid high-quality securities. The interest on these securities was paid to Goldman Sachs Mitsui Marine Derivative Products LP through an asset swap in exchange for a more stable quarterly LIBOR-based cash flow that Grammercy used to fund periodic interest payments to note holders.

Because the insurance policy was annual with an October maturity, each October TMCC would submit to Grammercy its residual value claims—losses in excess of the deductible for that year minus the 10 percent co-insurance requirement. If the investment income and premium paid to date were inadequate to finance the claim, a portion of the collateral in the trust account would be liquidated (and the corresponding part of the asset swap notional principal reduced). Proceeds from the collateral liquidation would be used to pay any TMCC claims, with the remainder being used to make a scheduled principal repayment on the notes, according to Table 22.1.

Principal repayments are made to each class of Grammercy note holder based on priority. If the value of the liquidated collateral less claims paid to TMCC is not enough to cover the scheduled principal repayments on all three classes for that year, the note holders bear the loss. In the event there is a surplus in years 1 or 2, it can be applied to a subsequent year's deficit.[8]

The Class A, B, and C notes had maturities of one, two, and three years, respectively. Principal on each class of note was at risk if sales prices on the reference portfolio fell by more than 23 percent, 15 percent, and 9 percent (respectively) below expectations. The notes were priced at 23, 45, and 325 basis points over three-month LIBOR, respectively, and were rated AA, A, and BB. Exhibit 22.6 shows the simplified structure.

Credit Default Insurance (Freddie Mac)

Morgan Stanley's Mortgage Default Recourse Notes (MODERNs) are notes issued by a Channel Islands SPE called G3 Mortgage Reinsurance

TABLE 22.1 Principal Repayment Schedule on Grammercy TMCC Notes

Class	First Policy (October 1999)	Second Policy (October 2000)	Third Policy (October 2001)
Class A	$ 22,650,000	$ 23,230,000	$ 14,800,000
Class B	105,690,000	108,390,000	69,050,000
Class C	83,040,000	85,170,000	54,260,000
Total	$211,380,000	$216,790,000	$138,110,000

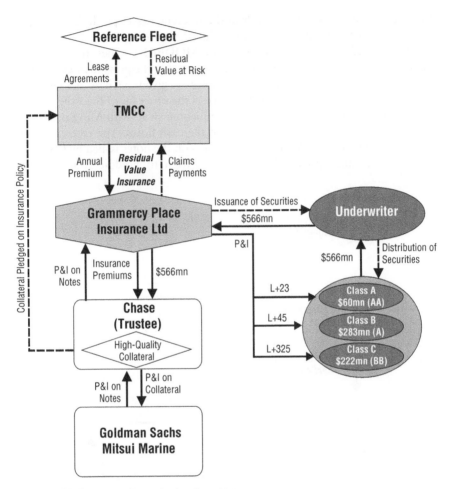

EXHIBIT 22.6 TMCC Residual Value ILNs

Ltd. that allow the Federal Home Loan Mortgage Corporation (Freddie Mac) to obtain default insurance coverage through a securitization conduit rather than directly from a (re)insurer. MODERNs include five classes of securities with 10 years to maturity that pay principal and interest based on the default record of an underlying $15 billion pool of fixed-rate, single-family 30-year mortgages originated in 1996.

MODERNs holders receive LIBOR plus a spread based on the outstanding principal amount. The principal is recalculated each period to include only the *nondefaulted* principal on the underlying mortgage assets.

In the event of a mortgage default in the reference asset pool, the principal repayment to MODERNs holders is reduced accordingly.

Exhibit 22.7 shows the structure of MODERNs. They function very much like the TMCC Grammercy notes explored in the previous section. Proceeds from the sale of the five classes of notes are given to Chase, acting as the collateral manager and trustee. Chase invests the proceeds of the issue in marketable securities and then enters into an income swap with Morgan Stanley Capital Services to smooth the timing of the cash flows. The receivables on the swap are used to make interest payments on the notes issued by G3.

The insurance policy that G3 has written to Freddie Mac requires

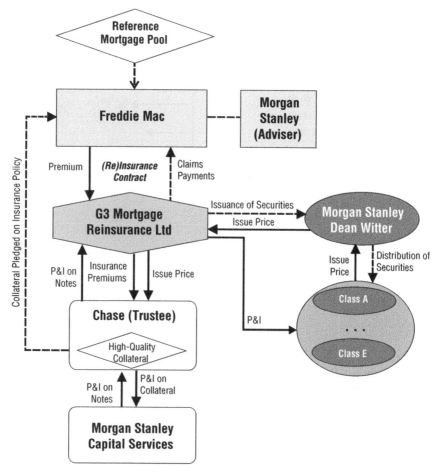

EXHIBIT 22.7   Mortgage Default Recourse Notes (MODERNs)

monthly premium payments by Freddie Mac that are added to the collateral account. In turn, the collateral account—including premium, the value of securities held, and income generated by those securities—is used to finance claims from Freddie Mac arising from defaults on its mortgage portfolio. The remaining value of the assets in the collateral account is used to make scheduled principal repayments to the note holders based on the priority of their class.

Transmission and Distribution Asset Insurance (Electricité de France)

Property damage arising from windstorms has been significant in continental Europe since the mid-1990s. Particularly catastrophic were the December 1999 European windstorms Lothar and Martin that wreaked havoc on the French and Swiss property sectors and insurance industries. Many asserted that one result of the damage caused by these storms was a dramatic increase in certain kinds of insurance of property deemed to be especially at risk to such weather phenomena (in terms of both the size of the potential losses and the likelihood of those losses).

One of the major affected parties was Electricité de France (EDF), the French national power company and one of the largest electric utilities in the world. In particular, EDF sustained significant damage from Lothar and Martin to its transmission and distribution (T&D) assets, including lines and wires, transformers, pylons, and other ground-level components of the French electric grid vulnerable to severe surface weather events like windstorms. Following the storms, EDF was apparently unable to find insurance in the amounts it sought and at a price it considered fair. The utility decided to check to see whether the capital market might offer better capacity and pricing, and it did.

The EDF Pylon structure was a €190 million offering in January 2004 by the Pylon Ltd. SPE, arranged and placed by CDC IXIS Capital Markets and Swiss Re. The offering included two classes of five-year securities: a subordinated tranche of €120 million (rated BB+/Ba1) and a €70 million (BBB+/A2) senior tranche. These two tranches of securities provided up to €190 million in cover to EDF for T&D losses arising from one or more severe windstorms. The structure is shown in Exhibit 22.8.

The trigger for the Pylon bonds was parametric, based on actual wind speeds run through a model and calibrated to expected T&D damage that EDF would sustain from the simulated winds (heavily weighted toward damage in the southwestern part of France). The first storm in five years would cause the subordinated tranche to lose P&I on a sliding scale based on the estimated severity of damage. Investors in the senior tranche would

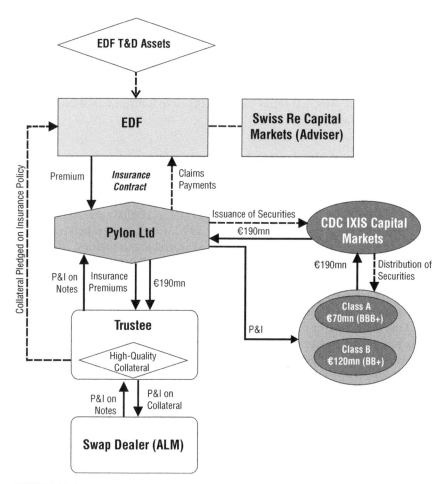

EXHIBIT 22.8 Electricité de France/Pylon

be at risk of losing P&I on a similar sliding scale based on the occurrence of a *second* storm within five years, and then only after the complete exhaustion of the more junior layer.

The EDF Pylon issue was interesting in part because it involved insurance of a core business risk. The other corporate ILNs we have examined were all designed to procure insurance for their sponsors that was real enough, but nevertheless *not* the primary business risks of the enterprises. EDF, however, is very much in the T&D business.

Insurance companies get very nervous when asked to insure core risks. Not only are moral hazard and adverse selection significant concerns, but the insurer also may perceive itself to be at a permanent informational disadvantage—for example, if the insurer knows as much about power lines as EDF, why isn't the insurer a power company?

Traditional insurance could, in principle, have been structured to address these concerns, but the ILN issue was much more amenable. Especially important was the trigger and payout being based on a modeled parametric loss, which is actually a more common feature of ILNs than classic insurance. Also, the extensive modeling efforts required to disclose the risks of the deal to investors arguably surpassed the basic due diligence that traditional insurance would have required, thus reducing the adverse selection costs of the ILN issue vis-à-vis a more traditional alternative.

Business Interruption Insurance (FIFA Event Cancellation)

October 2003 saw another novel corporate risk securitization with the closing of a $260 million issue by the international football association, Federation Internationale de Football Association (FIFA) designed to secure BI or event cancellation insurance protection for the World Cup.

FIFA guaranties about CHF2 billion to sponsors, marketing agencies, and television stations for World Cup coverage. About CHF1.5 million of that amount comes from contractually guaranteed receipts to television, leaving CHF500 million at risk in francs, euros, and dollars. In the event of a cancellation, that remaining amount would likely be lost unless the commitments can be insured.

Cancellation of the World Cup had become a major concern in some quarters following the tragic terrorist attacks on the United States in 2001. Subsequent to those events, FIFA found capacity tight and pricing high for event cancellation insurance. AXA Re pulled out of a FIFA terrorism cancellation policy early, and a Berkshire Hathaway replacement program proved to be extremely expensive. So, FIFA went to the market.

Golden Goal Finance Ltd. is an SPE that sells BI insurance to FIFA. The policy is triggered if initial and subsequent events lead to cancellation or relocation of the July 2006 scheduled World Cup. Specifically, payout occurs if no winner can be determined before August 31, 2007. Of the 64 matches, 32 is enough to determine a winner. The trigger excludes an outbreak of a world war and player/team strike but includes other BI risks, such as terrorism.

Working with Credit Suisse First Boston (CSFB) and Swiss Re Capital Markets, the $260 million-equivalent Golden Goal issue included a single class of security in four issues: $210 million of A-1 bonds paying 3M-LIBOR+150 basis points, CHF30 million of A-2 bonds paying 2.851 percent fixed, €16 million of A-3 bonds paying 3M-EURIBOR+150, and

$10 million of A-4 bonds paying 3.895 percent fixed. All four issues were rated AAA/A3. Twenty-five percent of principal on all issues is repaid in December 2005 and not at risk. The remaining principal is repaid across all four issues ratably based on the remaining collateral (held in Guaranteed Investment Certificates or GICs) left over after claims are paid on the FIFA policy. The structure is shown in Exhibit 22.9.

Although details of the structure have been hard to identify, it seems likely that the structure included the usual ALM swap. The structure does

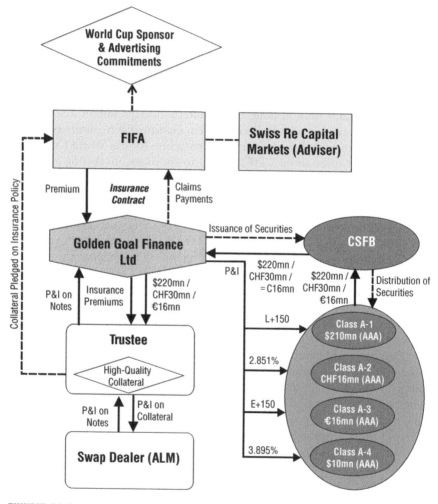

EXHIBIT 22.9   FIFA/Golden Goal Finance

not, however, seem to have included a currency swap. Instead, the securities were offered in three currencies and apparently left in those currencies when deposited into the trust. Premium payments *and* claims payments were seemingly also in three currencies. In principle, the structure thus was naturally hedged against currency risk through currency-matched assets and liabilities.

DERIVATIVES STRUCTURES

As we saw throughout Part Three, much of what can be done with insurance can also be done with derivatives if one is attentive to the legal and institutional distinctions between the products. We have looked at the relative pros and cons of each elsewhere. In this section, we note a few of the derivatives structures that resemble some of the risk securitizations discussed.

Cat Swaps

A cat swap is a floating-for-floating swap contract in which one reinsurer makes insurance-linked cash payments to another reinsurer following a triggering event in exchange for receiving LIBOR plus a spread. Consider, for example, the 1998 cat swap between Swiss Re and Mitsui Marine. That transaction was almost identical to the Tokio Marine/Parametric Re structure, except that Mitsui Marine accomplished a risk transfer similar to Tokio Marine directly using a swap rather than a securitization. The trigger parameters underlying the swap were the same as those used in the Parametric Re bond deal.

Specifically, Mitsui agreed to periodically pay Swiss Re (i.e., the swap counterparty) LIBOR plus 375 basis points for three years.[9] In return, Swiss Re agreed to make up to $30 million in contingent payments to Mitsui Marine in the event of an earthquake with an epicenter near Tokyo and a JMA rating of at least 7.1.

Cat Basis Swaps or Risk Swaps

Swiss Re and Tokio Marine completed a one-year $450 million swap agreement in 2001 that allows the reinsurers to literally swap catastrophic exposures with one another. The transaction involves three separate tranches, each of which is based on $150 million. The three tranches involve an exchange of Swiss Re's California earthquake exposures for Tokio Marine's Japanese earthquake exposures, Swiss Re's Florida hurricane risks for Tokio Marine's Japanese typhoon losses, and Swiss Re's French storm liabilities for Tokio Marine's Japanese cyclone liabilities. The transaction was bundled under a single master swap agreement and has been referred to as a *risk swap* or *cat basis swap*.

Exchange-Traded Catastrophic Derivatives[10]

The Chicago Board of Trade (CBOT) introduced in 1992 exchange-traded derivatives contracts whose underlyings are based on catastrophic insurance losses.[11] In 2000, the contracts were delisted for trading. Although still a favorite subject for theoreticians to discuss, exchange-traded cat products have never passed the market test.

ISO Futures and Futures Options In December 1992, the CBOT introduced catastrophe insurance futures contracts (Cats). Separate contracts were listed for insured catastrophic losses by region. In addition to a national loss contract, the CBOT listed contracts covering catastrophic property losses in the Eastern, Midwestern, and Western sections of the United States. These regional contracts were intended to track broadly insured losses arising from hurricanes, tornadoes, and earthquakes, respectively.

Because no underlying asset was readily identifiable for such contracts, the CBOT created an index that imparts values to the futures contracts by the contracts' reference to the index level at settlement. The index was based on losses reported quarterly to the independent Insurance Services Office (ISO), which collects information from about 100 insurance companies. The specific settlement value of the futures was based on a sample of companies selected by the ISO. The CBOT futures had a notional amount of $25,000.

A central concept for understanding Cat futures is the notion of an "event quarter." The event quarter is the quarter in which insured losses on which the futures are based *occur*. The CBOT listed four futures contracts for any particular year: March, June, September, and December. The listed contract months corresponded to the month in which the event quarter underlying the contract ended (e.g., March for the first quarter). Contracts were listed for trading four quarters before the beginning of event quarters.

To take a specific example, suppose the current time period is denoted as time t, and any increments to t are quarters. If time t denotes January, $t + 1$ is March, $t + 2$ is June, and so on. For a futures contract maturing at time $t + 2$, the CBOT defined the settlement value of the contract for the long:

$$F_{t+2,t+2} = \$25,000 \min\left(2, \frac{L_{t,t+1}}{P_{t,t+1}}\right) \qquad (22.1)$$

where $F_{t+2,t+2}$ denotes the time $t + 2$ price of a contract maturing at time $t + 2$, $L_{t,t+1}$ denotes the reported losses incurred (based on the ISO index) from time t to $t + 1$, and $P_{t,t+1}$ denotes the value of the premiums collected by the companies in the ISO index for losses incurred between t and $t + 1$. The underlying of the contract was not the *level* of losses, but rather the *loss ratio*, which was subject to a capped loss ratio of 2. If the ratio of losses to premiums collected exceeded 2, the long could still receive only \$50,000 per contract.

Variables used to calculate the settlement value of the contract, losses and premiums collected, were based on aggregate figures reported to and estimated by the ISO. The value of the contract thus was based on a loss ratio *for the pool of companies in the ISO index.* The ISO announced that pool of companies when the futures contract was listed. At that time, the ISO also announced the estimated value of the premium pool collected by those companies for the relevant event quarter. Premium was thus constant and known for the life of a futures contract, theoretically making its value a function of expected loss liabilities only.

Although the contract described in equation (22.1) settles at time $t + 2$, losses and premiums alike are indexed by a t, $t + 1$ subscript. Both losses and premiums on which the contract's settlement value was calculated were based on the event quarter starting at time t and ending at time $t + 1$. The quarter between time $t + 1$ to $t + 2$ was called the *runoff quarter* and was included to allow for a lag in the reporting of losses to the ISO. Although $L_{t,t+1}$ is an estimate of losses *occurring* between t and $t + 1$, losses continued to be *reported* on that quarter through settlement date $t + 2$. The settlement value of the contract thus was based on catastrophic losses *incurred* between t and $t + 1$ and *reported* between t and $t + 2$.

Cummins and Geman (1995) provide a simple illustrative example of how an insurer might have used the Cat futures contract to hedge catastrophic risk *as an alternative to reinsurance.* To recap their example, suppose the insurer expects to collect premiums of \$5 million and pay loss claims of \$600,000 on catastrophic events that occur in the eastern United States between January and March. The loss ratio thus is expected to be 0.12, so the insurer is concerned about losses *in excess* of this ratio.

As an alternative to reinsurance, the insurer might go long at time t a number of Eastern Cat futures determined as:

$$\Delta_{t,t+2} = \frac{P^*_{t,t+1}}{\$25,000}\left(\frac{\delta}{\rho_{t,t+2}}\right) \tag{22.2}$$

where $\Delta_{t,t+2}$ is the number of contracts held long at time t maturing at time $t+2$, $P^*_{t,t+1}$ is the premium collected *by the insurer*, δ is the proportion of the expected loss the insurer wants to hedge, and $\rho_{t,t+2}$ is the proportion of total losses expected to be reported *to the ISO* between t and $t+2$.

Suppose the hedger expects 80 percent of all losses reported to both itself and the ISO to be reported by June, when the March contract settles, so that $\rho_{t,t+2} = 0.80$. If the insurer wants to hedge *all* its underwriting risk, $\delta = 1.0$. Substituting the values of $\rho_{t,t+2}$, δ, and $P^*_{t,t+1} = \$5,000,000$ into (22.2), the insurer evidently goes long 250 futures contracts at time t: ($5 mn./$25,000) × (1/0.8) = 250.

When the contract matures at time $t+2$, suppose the *actual* losses on which the insurer must pay claims are $630,000, or 5 percent higher than expected. The actual loss ratio thus would be 0.126. As a percentage of premium collected, the insurer has unexpectedly lost 5 percent, or $250,000.

Assume for this example that the losses reflected in the ISO index are perfectly correlated with the losses the insurer actually experienced. In that case, the futures price will have increased by 5 percent relative to whatever its initial price was.[12] For *each contract* the insurer is long, the company will *gain* $1,000 on its futures transaction: ($25,000/contract) × 0.05 × 0.80 = $1,000. For $\Delta_{t,t+2} = 250$, the insurer thus makes $250,000 on its futures hedge, *exactly* offsetting the unexpected loss (as a proportion of premium collected) due to the unanticipated higher loss liability.

In mid-1993, the CBOT augmented the Cat futures by listing options on Cat futures. At maturity, the holder of a Cat call thus had the option of entering into a long Cat futures contract at the strike price. For a Cat put, the option purchaser had the option at maturity of entering into a *short* futures contract at the strike price.

At the time they were introduced, Cat futures and options on futures seemed to many like a good idea. Most market participants never agreed, though. The National CAT options volume in November 1993, six months after the options first were listed, was 3,650 contracts traded for the month. By comparison, the CBOT's successful futures contract on long-term U.S. Treasury bonds had a *daily* volume on November 1, 1993, of 407,202 contracts. By June 1994, the product's one-year anniversary, volume had fallen to 98 contracts traded for the month. And in June 1995, *no* such contracts were traded. From their original listing in June 1993 through October 1995, the *total* volume of National Cat options traded was only 5,668 contracts. Total cumulative volumes for the Eastern, Midwestern, and Western Cats from their introduction through October 1995 were 12,742 contracts, 60 contracts, and 44 contracts, respectively. So, the number of bond futures traded in one day was an order of magnitude greater than the volume of the most successful of the Cat contracts over the entire life of the contract. Cat futures and options died a slow, quiet death.

PCS Options   Rather than try to salvage catastrophic futures, the CBOT decided in 1995 that *options* had the most promising prospects as insurance derivatives. The CBOT dispensed with the Cat contracts altogether and introduced options based on PCS indexes. Unlike the Cat options, the PCS options were cash-settled options with an underlying cash value determined by a new index. PCS options did *not* call for delivery of a futures contract; the CBOT did not even list PCS futures for trading.

PCS provides estimates of nine catastrophic loss indexes on a daily basis. These indexes are geographical and track PCS-estimated insured catastrophe losses nationally, by region (Eastern, Northeastern, Southeastern, Midwestern, Western), and by state (Florida, Texas, and California).

Unlike the ISO index, the PCS index measures a *loss*, not a loss ratio. The PCS index value for any region is PCS's loss estimate divided by $100 million. To arrive at those catastrophic loss index values, PCS surveys at least 70 percent of companies, agents, and adjusters involved with catastrophic insurance. PCS's industry loss estimates are based on this survey, adjusted for nonsurveyed market share, and adjusted again to take into account PCS's "National Insurance Risk Profile."

For each of the nine PCS indexes, the CBOT listed PCS options, available in both large-cap and small-cap forms. Large-cap PCS options track estimated catastrophic losses ranging from $20 billion to $50 billion, whereas small-cap PCS options track only losses of less than $20 billion.

As with the earlier Cat options, PCS options had settlement values based on an event period plus a runoff period. All but the Western and California PCS options had quarterly event periods, and options thus were listed corresponding to the ends of those four event quarters: March, June, September, and December. For the Western and California indexes, the event period was *annual*.

Many felt that the one-quarter runoff period for Cat futures had been inadequate for a large enough proportion of losses to be reported, so PCS options purchasers had a choice between two loss development periods: 6 or 12 months. The options traded until the last day of the development period.

The settlement value for PCS options was based on the settlement value for the relevant PCS index, or the PCS loss estimate divided by $100 million. For convenience, the index value is rounded to the nearest first decimal. An estimated loss of $53 million, for example, has a true index value of 0.53. Rounded to 0.50, it implies an "industry loss equivalent" of $50 million.

PCS options were defined so that each index point was worth $200. A PCS loss index value of 0.50, for example, had a cash-equivalent option value of $100: 0.50 × $200 = $100. Strike prices for PCS options were listed in integer multiples of 5 index points. For large-cap options, strikes of 200 to 495 were available, and for small-cap options, strikes from 5 to 195 were listed.

On the settlement date, the exercise value of a small-cap PCS call option with an event period from t to $t + 1$ (e.g., first quarter) and a six-month development period (e.g., second and third quarters) was

$$C_{t+3}^{sc} = \$200 \; \max[\min(I_{t,t+1}, 200) - K, 0] \qquad (22.3)$$

where C_{t+3} denotes the settlement value of the call at the end of the development period, $I_{t,t+1}$ is the value of the underlying PCS index based on losses *incurred* from t to $t + 1$ and *reported* from t to $t + 3$, and K is the strike price. The minimand reflects the definition of the option as a small-cap option—that is, gains on the option are capped at an index level of 200, or an industry loss equivalent of $20 billion. The maximand reflects the option's financial trigger—that is, the exercise value of the option cannot be negative.

For an otherwise identical large-cap call, the exercise value of the option was

$$C_{t+3}^{sc} = \$200 \; \max\{\max[\min(I_{t,t+1}, 500), 200] - K, 0\} \qquad (22.4)$$

The minimand reflects a cap on the index level at 500. Unlike equation (22.3), equation (22.4) contains *two* maximands. The first reflects the definition of the contract as a large-cap option, on which the index value is always at least 200. This extra maximand was not present in equation (22.3) only because the lower bound of losses covered by the small-cap options was $0. The outermost maximand, as before, reflects the limited liability of calls.

One of the reasons that supporters of the PCS products expected them to succeed was the synthetic equivalence between a vertical spread and XOL reinsurance. A long vertical spread with strikes of 100 and 120, for example, locks in a vertical layer of protection between index levels of 100 and 120 and thus is synthetically equivalent to catastrophic XOL coverage at those levels.

The products also created an opportunity for reinsurers to design new, tailored types of structures. Lane (1998a) suggests how to use PCS options to construct synthetic *accelerated quota shares*, for example, in which the share of losses that the option user is hedging increases as the penetration of the loss layer gets larger.

Failure or Bad Timing?   Despite all efforts to construct a superior cata-strophic insurance derivatives contract, the PCS options ultimately befell the same fate as their ISO predecessors. Why?

One problem clearly was the absence of natural hedgers on both sides of the market. The appeal of buying a vertical spread makes sense only if there is a party willing to write it. Although reinsurance and retrocession are both common enough practices that one might have ex-pected a two-sided market to emerge, it never did. Perhaps one reason was simply the concern of competition from the relatively concentrated reinsurance sector.

Another possible explanation for the failures of the two contracts con-cerns the *sequencing* of the evolution of substitutes and complements in de-rivatives activity. Exchange-traded derivatives are typically part of a process called "commodization" in which customized transactions negoti-ated in opaque, bilateral settings evolve toward more standardized transac-tions negotiated on formal markets.

Culp (2001) summarizes the process by which cash-market and for-ward transactions have been commodized into exchange-traded derivatives such as futures. Like securitized products, however, exchange-traded deriv-atives did not *replace* privately negotiated cash and derivatives transac-tions. Instead, exchange-traded products evolved *alongside* their off-exchange and cash market cousins.

A strategic planning issue faced by every futures exchange concerns the sequencing of listing a standardized product that is in the midst of the com-modization process. Specifically, it is possible to list an exchange-traded product too early in the commodization cycle for the product to be de-manded. Mortgage-backed securities, for example, likely would have been very unpopular had the Federal National Mortgage Association (FNMA) not first begun issuing pass-through securities.

A possible hindrance to the evolution of exchange-traded cata-strophic loss derivatives was simply the lack of well-developed privately negotiated derivatives and securitization activity in the underlying catastrophic insurance pools. Standardized contracts thus may not have been demanded—not until more customized off-exchange transactions evolve from the primary and reinsurance contracts responsible for the pool of capital at risk.

If true, then the prospects for the success of exchange-traded catastrophic derivatives *someday* might still be very real. Just not yet.

CHAPTER 23

Captives, Protected Cells, and Mutuals

We saw in Chapter 2 that a firm can choose to retain, neutralize, or transfer the risks to which it is subject. We further saw in Part Three that a firm that retains a risk is really still buying insurance for those risks, but it is buying insurance from its own stock and from bondholders. Sometimes a retention is a deliberate decision (e.g., to retain a core risk that is a necessary component of the firm's profits, to reduce moral hazard, to mitigate adverse selection costs, etc.). Other times a retention is driven solely by cost alone—a firm would transfer the risk if it made economic sense, but the weighted average cost of capital (WACC) of the firm is so far below the cost of external risk transfer that it simply does not make sense to insure externally. Regardless of the reason for the retention, firms that do retain some of their risks often wish to finance those retentions explicitly. This desire may be motivated by a need to insulate the firm from wild fluctuations in net asset values (NAVs), periodic cash flows, and/or earnings.

These days, *pure* risk financing products are relatively rare. Most prefunded retentions are blended somehow with external risk transfer as firms seek to achieve their optimal bundle of internal and external financing and insurance. Nevertheless, certain kinds of structured insurance transactions are still motivated primarily by a desire to engage in risk finance. We explore some of those solutions in this chapter,[1] beginning with the clearest form of risk finance there is: self-insurance. We then turn to more organized forms of self-insurance—namely, captives, rent-a-captives, and protected cell companies (PCCs). We conclude with a discussion of mutuals or self-insurance syndicates that combine the self-insurance activities of participants with access to peer group risk transfer, usually at attachment points well in excess of working capital layers.

BALANCE SHEET SELF-INSURANCE

Alternative risk transfer (ART)—now more commonly known as structured insurance—first gained widespread acceptance as an industry term in the 1970s to describe organized self-insurance programs. As insurance markets hardened and produced rising premiums and declining capacity, corporations wanted to emphasize to insurers that they could often seek the protection they needed through *alternative* means, the most obvious of which was self-insurance.

Self-insurance is essentially any organized form of prefunded retention that involves an insurance-like transfer pricing structure but does not require the firm to set up or rely upon a separate organization to accomplish this. Self-insurance undertaken through a wholly owned subsidiary with an insurance license involves the use of captives, and for now we discuss only *non*captive methods of self-insurance.

Self-Insurance: The Recognition Problem

Self-insurance is the prefunding of risk internally using insurance-like internal contracting and transfer pricing methods. This makes the most sense when a firm has enough homogeneous risk exposures and loss opportunities that its aggregate expected losses are reasonably stable and predictable, thus allowing the firm to fund the self-insurance equivalent of unearned premium and loss reserves.[2] When it is difficult to estimate such expected losses with any degree of precision, however, it is also difficult to prefund any retention of those expected losses.

Numerous mechanisms exist for a firm to self-insure. The most obvious is just through financial slack: maintaining adequate financial flexibility and current cash balances to fund any reasonable-sized loss. But that is *post*loss finance. If a firm truly wishes to *pre*fund a potential loss, its alternatives become much more limited.

One way of prefunding a loss is through the use of economic loss reserves. The challenge lies in the administration of the reserve and getting outsiders to recognize the funds in the reserve as having been *credibly committed* to funding the identified risk. But investors tend to be suspicious of reserves. For one thing, they can be too easily reversed, and often for reasons having little to do with the original risk ostensibly being reserved against. Late in 2004, for example, a major U.S. manufacturing firm reversed a product liability reserve with no explanation, and the firm's share price plummeted for the rest of the day following that announcement.

The lack of credibility associated with loss reserves is often called a "cookie jar" problem. Some might feel this is an issue only for firms explicitly concerned with managing the risk of unexpected changes in earnings, but, in fact, a noncredible reserve can be just as much a problem for firms whose risk management focus is on net asset value or cash flows, as well. Especially for firms already suffering from high costs of information asymmetries, adverse selection concerns will only exacerbate investor fears that managers may be tempted to reverse a loss reserve. And there are good reasons for worrying about this—remember the potential underinvestment problem. So, the cookie jar problem is not just a credibility and recognition problem. The risk that a firm will be tempted to reverse a reserve to get its hands on the earmarked cash *is a real risk*, not just an accounting concern.

For risks whose impact on the firm can be measured with some degree of confidence, the firm can at least take an accounting reserve for self-insurance. In some cases, however, accounting rules do not even allow a reserve to be taken (e.g., if a loss is probable but impossible to quantify). In such cases, the firm may actually have set aside funds, but will be unable to deduct those funds from current earnings to reflect the future loss being self-insured.

There are a few ways, however, that firms can self-insure credibly and reliably. One is through the judicious management of deductibles in existing insurance programs. As already noted in Chapters 8 and 9, a deductible on a primary insurance policy or on a reinsurance treaty or facultative cession creates a retention for the ceding firm. Although the main purpose of including a deductible is to protect the (re)insurer from possible moral hazard problems, the deductible can also be voluntarily increased by the ceding firm if the firm wishes to increase its retention deliberately.

Pseudo-self-insurance acquired through voluntary increases in a deductible are obviously specific to the risk(s) underlying the (re)insurance policy in question. Consider, for example, a U.S. firm that has over $1 million in losses per year on a workers' compensation program. If most or all of the firm's workers are concentrated in a single state, such a firm may be qualified to establish a self-insurance program for its workers comp liabilities that must be registered with the state. In lieu of creating a formal, state-registered self-insurance program, many companies in this situation choose instead to self-insure through substantially increasing the deductible on their primary workers comp insurance coverage. An insurer with this kind of deductible program need not register it with the state as a formal self-insurance program. In practice, however, an insurer offering firms this kind of self-insurance option will often require the ceding firm to establish technical reserves backed with marketable securities against this self-insurance deductible.[3]

Another self-insurance mechanism that does not suffer the recognition and credibility problems of loss reserves is a self-insurance pool. Despite its name, a self-insurance pool is not a vehicle in which companies can pool and self-insure their risks. Instead, self-insurance pools are means by which risk can be *financed* more effectively when firms pool their self-insurance *funds*.

As noted earlier, one characteristic of self-insurance is a reasonably large base of losses from which expected losses can be predicted in a relatively stable manner. Self-insurance becomes difficult to fund when losses are large and arrive sporadically. In this situation, a larger pool of funds exposed to different *time patterns of losses* can be beneficial—hence the rationale for a self-insurance pool.

Self-insurance pools are similar to mutual insurance companies that we will discuss later in this chapter, although they are not chartered as insurance companies per se. Participating entities contribute funds to the polled entity and then agree to "insure one another." As a practical consequence, this does not mean that the risks of each firm are transferred to the pool, but rather that the risk in the *unfavorable timing in the arrival rate* of claims or losses is transferred to the pool. If the loss exposures of the participants in the pool are diverse enough, then the pool provides a way for the collective participants to smooth the timing of those losses so that expected losses over time are easier to predict and prefund than if all the loss exposures were left in constituent firms.

Benefits and Costs of Self-Insurance

Self-insurance can offer several potential benefits over traditional insurance purchased on the market, one of which is frequently preferable pricing. A self-insurance structure not only avoids the load associated with traditional insurance, but also is immune from any of the costs of asymmetric information typically associated with traditional insurance. In other words, the self-insuring firm can observe both its own risk management actions and its own risks and thus can avoid the adverse pricing or contract features included by traditional insurers to mitigate adverse selection and moral hazard.

Pure self-insurance and risk reserves also allow the self-insurer to retain the interest earnings on the premium, which is now retained within the company through a transfer pricing structure. Funds are also available in these two structures immediately to cover losses. Note that a self-insurance pool may not allow the same freedom of premium investment and the same speed of funds delivery as reserves or pure self-insurance, however, because a separate organization representing the interests of multiple firms is now in the picture.

CAPTIVES AND OTHER RISK FINANCING VEHICLES

If a company wants to engage in a credible form of preloss finance, the use of a captive or captivelike structure is often the best solution. A *captive* insurance or reinsurance company is a type of organized self-insurance program in which a firm actually sets up its own insurance company to fund and manage its retained risks. Captives became immensely popular in the late 1970s, but softening insurance and reinsurance premiums led to a decline in their usage through the 1980s. As the desire for firms to realize the benefits of captives especially regarding *enterprise-wide risk management* increased substantially in the 1990s, however, captives have once again become very popular tools for both financing retained risks and engaging in selective risk transfers—that is, for fine-tuning a firm's preloss risk financing strategy together with its risk transfer program.

Numerous types of captives exist in the world today. Some of the major variations for each type are discussed in the following subsections, with the caveat that in this section we limit our discussion to those captive and captivelike structures whose purpose is *pure risk finance*. We discuss structures that are more of a risk finance/risk transfer blend in the subsequent section.

Single-Parent Captives

A single-parent captive is the simplest captive structure in which a firm sets up a captive in order to manage its retained risks—and, in some cases, to manage the risks of the firm more generally as a dedicated enterprise-wide risk management structure.[4] Single-parent captives primarily serve the purpose of insuring the retained risks of the firm sponsoring the captive, although some firms have increasingly been extending the insurance coverage provided by captives to their products, customers, and suppliers.[5]

Single-Parent Captive Insurers A single-parent captive insurance company, depicted in Exhibit 23.1, is a wholly owned subsidiary of the sponsoring corporation, or the entity that is seeking to fund its retained risks.[6] To accomplish this, the sponsor capitalizes the captive by using either internal funds or the proceeds of externally issued financial claims to purchase the equity of the captive. The amount of equity required in the captive depends on the type of captive structure and is discussed in a later section. The captive invests the proceeds of its equity sale to the sponsor in low-risk, marketable securities that function as risk reserves for the captive on behalf of the sponsoring corporation.

In addition to the equity infusion required to capitalize the captive

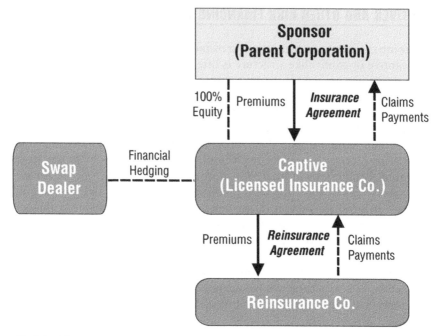

EXHIBIT 23.1 Single-Parent Captive
Source: Wöhrmann (1998).

initially, the sponsoring program then pays premiums to the captive for insurance against risks that the firm wishes to retain and self-insure. The captive, in turn, is licensed as an actual insurance company and thus uses the premiums to fund unearned premium and loss reserves that, together with its equity, back the contingent payment obligations it accepts to the parent in return for receiving premium.

A captive can be managed by the sponsoring corporation, independent managers appointed by the sponsor to the captive itself, or, for a fee, a captive management firm. Companies active in captive management include large (re)insurers like Zürich Financial and large insurance brokers like Aon and Marsh.

Prefunded retentions are commonly associated with high-frequency, low-severity loss events. Captives thus usually retain these types of risks. To the extent the sponsoring corporation may wish to seek insurance to manage its other low-frequency, high-severity exposures, the captive *also* assumes responsibility for managing such risks, including possibly transferring them to other participants. As Exhibit 23.1 shows, for example, the captive may utilize reinsurance to off-load the risks to which the sponsoring firm is subject that it has elected *not* to retain. Note that this is *re*insurance because the captive itself is an insurer that has provided the sponsoring firm with primary coverage.

Similarly, swaps and other derivatives can be negotiated with the swap dealer for the same purpose. In either case, the sponsor prefunds not the expected loss but rather the cost of the risk transfer, and then enters into some kind of contingency agreement with the captive that mimics the captive's risk transfer transactions.

Consider a specific example of sponsoring firm BigChip, a silicon chip manufacturer and distributor. Suppose BigChip is exposed to three risks: the risk of damage to chips in shipments BigChip has guaranteed, the risk of an earthquake causing significant damage to its California headquarters and main production facility, and the risk of fluctuations in the yen/dollar exchange rate arising from the fact that most of BigChip's chip sales are to Japan.

Firm BigChip may set up a captive insurer called BigChip Insurance Co., capitalized by BigChip through a purchase of 100 percent of BigChip Insurance Co.'s common stock. BigChip might then decide that the first risk—damage to chip shipments—constitutes a core business risk *and* is characterized by a high frequency of small losses. The earthquake and foreign exchange risk, however, are risks BigChip decides to transfer rather than retain and finance.

Accordingly, BigChip enters into three transactions with BigChip Insurance. The first is a per-occurrence insurance contract with no deductible and no co-insurance that compensates BigChip for annual losses per occurrence on damaged chips in transit, in exchange for which BigChip pays an annual premium to BigChip Insurance. BigChip Insurance then retains 100 percent of this risk and finances any losses out of its equity (which must be at least as high as the expected losses on chip shipments) plus its allocation of premium into unearned premium and loss reserves (with corresponding investments in short-term interest-bearing assets to fund those liabilities).

In a second transaction, BigChip pays a premium to BigChip Insurance for a catastrophic excess of loss (XOL) policy triggered by a California earthquake—say, with an attachment point of $100 million, no deductible, and no co-pay provision. Because this is a risk that BigChip does *not* wish to retain, BigChip then reinsurers the entire catastrophic loss layer with one or more reinsurers. If the reinsurer(s) request(s) a deductible and/or co-insurance provision, BigChip Insurance will have a *forced retention* of that portion of its catastrophic risks on behalf of BigChip. The insurance policy between BigChip and BigChip Insurance will likely not reflect this deductible and co-pay so that BigChip Insurance is the sole retention agent in the structure.

Finally, BigChip and BigChip Insurance execute a series of foreign exchange forwards, swaps, options, and/or cross-currency swaps on the dollar/yen rate to hedge the sponsor's currency risk. These derivatives will be mirroring transactions for whatever derivatives BigChip Insurance executes with one or more swap dealers.

A major attraction of the captive structure is the retention of underwriting profits and investment income on assets held to back unearned premium and loss reserves. If the actual losses underwritten by the captive are lower than expected, the sponsor can repatriate those underwriting profits—plus any investment income—in the form of dividends paid by the captive to its sole equity holder, the sponsor.

Another oft-cited benefit of captives is the ability of corporates to acquire insurance products directly from *re*insurance companies—something that is hard for the corporate as a noninsurer to do without a captive. Reinsurance companies tend to be relatively less regulated, more sophisticated, and more amenable to designing custom programs than insurance companies. Access to the reinsurance market thus is in itself a major appeal of captives to some firms.

Single-Parent Captive Reinsurers   A major issue for a sponsoring company to determine in setting up a captive structure is the domicile for the captive. Variables that can affect a firm's captive domicile choice:[7]

- Restrictions on captive investments.
- Reinsurance restrictions.
- Financial reporting requirements.
- Minimum capital requirements.
- Premium and other taxes.
- Underwriting restrictions.
- Reserve requirements.
- Tax relationship of domicile with home country of sponsoring corporation.
- Domicile currency stability.
- Privacy protections.
- Local infrastructure and stability.

Accordingly, firms often incorporate and charter their captives in jurisdictions other than the primary jurisdiction in which the sponsoring firm is incorporated.

When local laws, regulations, or tax requirements require sponsoring firms to obtain *local* insurance coverage, firms may opt for a captive structure in which the captive is incorporated and chartered as a *re*insurance company rather than an insurance company, as discussed in the prior section. The sponsoring corporation then gets a local insurer, called a *fronting insurer*, to pass through its premium and coverage to the captive reinsurer. The structure of a single-parent captive reinsurer with a fronting insurer is shown on Exhibit 23.2.

Licensing the captive as a reinsurer has certain costs. The fronting insurer will demand some arrangement fees; Kloman (1998) estimates that the costs of a fronting insurer range from 5 to 30 percent of total premiums. But generally the benefits of fronting outweigh the costs, especially when regulation essentially necessitates this structure.

At the same time, setting up a captive as a reinsurance company also has some distinct benefits. Reinsurance companies tend to be subject to

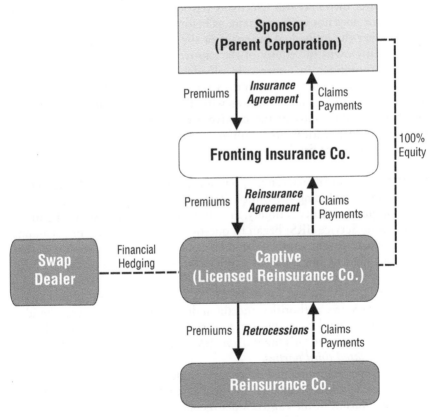

EXHIBIT 23.2 Single-Parent Captive with Fronting Insurer
Source: Wöhrmann (1998, 2001).

significantly lower-cost regulation than primary carriers. In fact, the vast majority of single-parent captives today are in fact *re*insurance companies.

Single-Parent Multibranch Captive Reinsurers   Some multinational conglomerates prefer to manage their risks on a local subsidiary basis rather than an enterprise-wide basis. Even if a firm prefers instead to centralize its risk management decision-making, transactions executed for risk transfer or risk financing purposes may still require local insurers for multiple local jurisdictions. In this case, a firm can set up a single-parent multibranch captive reinsurance company.

Shown in Exhibit 23.3, a multibranch structure involves the separate payment of premium and insurance on risk by each branch (or, at least, by each branch in jurisdictions for which a fronting insurer is required) to a separate fronting company, all of which then cede to the captive reinsurer. The reinsurer then may still selectively retrocede or hedge certain risks that the sponsor does not wish to retain, as before.

Whether the individual branches or the sponsoring corporation holding company owns the equity of the captive is essentially up to the sponsoring corporation. In either case, dividends arising from underwriting profits and investment income in the captive are paid back to the sponsoring company at some level. Here as with all captives, it is important to remember that the funds in the captive are still part of the funds of the sponsoring corporation—the captive is merely a device to credibly self-insure, not alter the firm's capital structure.

Taxation   In general insurance, premium payments are tax deductible in most regimes, including the United States. Funding a self-insurance reserve does not qualify for deductibility, and, to make things consistent, the Internal Revenue Service (IRS) began to question the deductibility of premiums paid to single-parent captives by their sponsors. The IRS view was that premiums paid to single-parent captives were just a form of capital infusion, and claims payments were really just dividends.

In 1992, a litmus test for deductibility first began to get serious attention from U.S. tax authorities and the judicial system, leading to the idea that premiums paid by a sponsor to a single-parent captive could be deducted from the sponsor's taxes *if the captive writes 30 percent of its business to unrelated third parties.*

The 30 percent unrelated third-party underwriting rule also affects the taxation of investment income in the United States. With no unrelated third-party business, the captive's net income is subject to corporate taxation at the sponsor level. If the 30 percent rule applies, investment income may be exempt from sponsor taxation—or, at least, the taxes paid on the

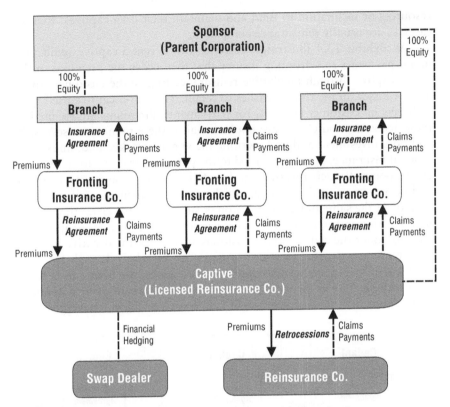

EXHIBIT 23.3 Multibranch Single-Parent Captive with Fronting Insurers
Source: Wöhrmann (1999, 2001).

captive's net income in its home domicile will be deductible against any net income tax at the sponsor level.

Rent-a-Captives and Protected Cell Companies

In the late 1990s, the offering by (re)insurance firms and insurance brokers of rent-a-captives became another important ART solution for firms wishing to retain a large portion of their risks while seeking preloss financing for losses arising from those risks. A rent-a-captive structure is a multiparticipant structure in which the participants do not actually own any part of the rent-a-captive's equity.

As shown in Exhibit 23.4, rent-a-captives are set up, maintained/managed, and owned by market participants like (re)insurance companies or insurance brokers for the benefit and use of corporations that lack the resources or inclination to fund and maintain their own captives. Rent-a-captives are usually reinsurance companies.

As Exhibit 23.4 illustrates, customers of a rent-a-captive remit premium payments to a fronting insurer that then cedes the premium to the rent-a-captive through facultative reinsurance to give the customer coverage for losses on the risks it wishes to retain. The rent-a-captive itself typically sets up customer accounts for participants. Premiums are credited to these accounts, and claims are booked against these premium reserves. In addition, investment and underwriting income are tracked and, unlike traditional insurance, may be returned to the participants in the form of a low claims bonus. Participants thus can benefit in much the same way as if they had been owners of the captive, but the equity investment itself is not required. At the same time, if the customer submits a large claim that results in a negative customer balance, the general funds of the rent-a-captive are used to honor the claim and the customer owes back the negative balance.

Premium payments to rent-a-captives can be relatively high for firms with questionable financial strength. In these cases, the premium is really doing double duty as the usual premium *plus* collateral to cover potentially large claims that the customer might later have a problem repaying.

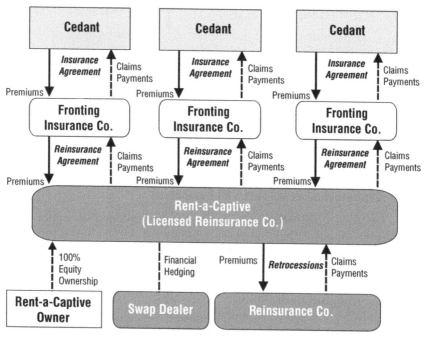

EXHIBIT 23.4   Rent-a-Captive

The main purpose of having more than one firm in the same structure is reducing overhead and costs. There is no *intended* risk transfer between participants. In their purest form, rent-a-captives are intended to provide only risk finance services. The accounts maintained for customers are theoretically segregated so that each customer's premium is equal to that customer's average loss. And in some rent-a-captives, claims by any given customer were strictly limited to funds in the account, which meant that a lot of collateral had to be deposited into an account to cover any large claims.

In the event of insolvency, however, some began to worry about *ex post* mutualization. For example, if a customer submits a claim that exceeds the resources in its account, the rent-a-captive may honor the claim. A subsequent failure of the participant to rectify its negative balance, however, could eventually precipitate insolvency at the rent-a-captive, thus forcing other customers to have their funds applied to the original customer's claim without ever getting fully repaid for that. The main reason for this concern about *ex post* mutualization is the legal structure of the rent-a-captive. Fundamentally, it is just a reinsurance company. Customer accounts are a useful management tool, but were not viewed as providing any real legal separateness to different customers' assets.

To mitigate these concerns without abandoning the idea behind a rent-a-captive, captive management organizations began to offer *protected cell companies* (PCCs) around 1997 as a rent-a-captive alternative.[8] A PCC is set up essentially like a rent-a-captive except that customer accounts are legally ring-fenced to achieve true segregation, segregation that would remain in place following an insolvency. In some cases, the PCC itself may even be set up as a master trust with each account representing a separate affiliated trust. The mechanics of a typical PCC structure are shown in Exhibit 23.5.

The legal concerns about rent-a-captives were never really tested in a live insolvency proceeding. Market participants' fears about rent-a-captives have been largely assuaged by PCCs, but it should be noted that PCCs have also yet to be tested under insolvency laws.

Benefits of Captives

Captive structures are not for every firm. As noted in the case of self-insurance earlier in the chapter, the benefits of a captive or captivelike structure are most likely to be realized when a firm has a good historical claim or loss experience so that expected losses can be estimated with reasonable precision and so that the ratio between claims incurred and premium paid is reasonably low. In addition, firms seeking to utilize a captive structure need adequate financial resources and cash flows to fund an

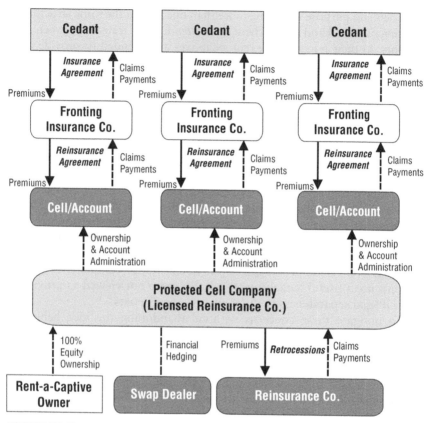

EXHIBIT 23.5   Protected Cell Company

annual premium payment large enough to justify the expenses of a captive. Minimum premium written in order for a single-parent captive to make sense is usually around $700,000, although using a rent-a-captive or PCC structure can reduce this amount to as little as $100,000 per annum.[9]

If a captive structure *does* make economic sense for a sponsoring (captive) or participating (PCC) firm, the potential benefits relative to traditional insurance can be substantial. Some of these benefits also apply to hedging programs run out of a captive rather than the sponsoring firm's treasury or risk management function.

Adverse Selection Costs   We already noted in this chapter and Chapter 7 that self-insurance is sometimes cheaper than risk transfer because it allows the firm to avoid adverse selection costs. Remember, though, to compare the two different kinds of adverse selection costs we have encountered. One source of adverse selection is the lemons problem in insurance markets. Here, self-insurance will unquestionably win out over traditional insurance because there is no lemons problem in pricing insurance you buy from yourself. When the market truly overestimates your risk profile, adverse selection costs in insurance may drive a firm to self-insure. At the same time, self-insurance must be funded, and this often occurs through the issuance of new financial claims. Here, the firm has to pay the adverse selection costs arising from the fact that securities markets are also markets for lemons. If self-insurance reserves and premiums can be funded internally, retention may well represent a cost savings vis-à-vis external risk transfer. If not, the relative magnitudes of the two kinds of adverse selection costs need to be carefully compared.

Operational Cost Savings Quite apart from the benefits of avoiding post-loss external financing costs with self-insurance, the captive route specifically can also generate a cost savings for sponsors and participants for several reasons. First, as we noted earlier, reinsurance obtained through a captive can be both cheaper and more flexible than primary insurance. Setting up a captive with a fronting insurer does require sometimes significant outlays to the fronting insurer, but these outlays can at times be significantly smaller than the cost savings associated with reinsurance. Similarly, any risks the sponsor or participant does not wish to retain can be retroceded by the captive, again at rates often preferable to those that could be obtained by direct insurance.

A major reason that reinsurance companies are willing to quote favorable rates to captives is that captive relationships with their reinsurers tend to be reasonably long-term. A reinsurer dealing with a captive thus knows that there likely will be long-term relationship gains, as well as potential advisory and servicing fees, and thus may be more willing to aggressively price the reinsurance itself.

A second potential source of cost savings in a captive structure comes in the form of potentially reduced retrocession rates. If the captive can market the risks the sponsor does not wish to retain to several reinsurers, then reinsurers will more easily be able to assume specific risk layers with which they are most comfortable. Optimal layering through facultative or treaty XOL coverage can often be cheaper than direct insurance or reinsurance in which the whole layer is forced onto a single retrocessionaire or reinsurer.

A third cost savings is the potential for lower reinsurance rates arising from diminished moral hazard problems. Because much of the risk is being retained by the sponsor, any insurers or reinsurers need not worry too much about hidden actions that might increase their exposure; the sponsor will usually be on the hook for the early losses.

Signaling   Some argue that captives can be used as a signaling mechanism. Scordis and Porat (1998), for example, argue that captives are a "status symbol" for the managers that set them up and can be used to signal management's commitment to taking risk management seriously.

Similarly, Eva Air used its formation of a Singapore-domiciled captive as a competitive signaling tool against its primary competitor, Taiwan-based China Airlines. Eva claimed that its captive, Martinair Insurance, was proof of Eva's financial commitment to airline safety because it was literally putting its own money behind the risk.[10] Indeed, this is not an implausible interpretation of at least some captives.

Cash Flow Volatility Reduction   Retained risks are essentially insured internally, and internal insurance premiums can be paid using transfer pricing. Classical insurance, by contrast, usually required prepayment of premiums annually. The ability for a firm that self-insures to choose the timing of its premium payments can create a valuable cash flow smoothing tool. Even within a captive structure, the sponsor usually can plan premium payments to occur at a time most advantageous to the sponsor.

Investment Income and Reserve Management   Users of self-insurance or captives retain the investment income generated by assets held to offset premium and loss reserves. By retaining this investment income, the cost of insurance capital is reduced, possibly creating a significant capital structure advantage for users of prefunded retention and captive programs.

Tax Considerations   Tax considerations alone should not drive the establishment of captives and mutuals, but nor should the savings that tax deductions can generate in a captive structure be ignored. These tax savings depend strongly on both the domicile of the captive and the location of the sponsoring firm. But as long as the captive is set up as a legitimate insurance company in a recognized domicile, several home jurisdictions still allow at least some deductions for captive payments and expenses such as certain realized losses and reported or incurred but not reported (IBNR) loss reserves. Many captive domiciles have tax laws designed to accord favorable treatment to captives in this manner. If the sponsor retains its risks internally without using a captive, not all of these tax savings can be realized.

Reduced Agency Costs of Overinvestment—No Cookie Jars   Captives and mutuals can also help firms reduce the agency costs of overinvestment and the recognition risk discussed earlier in the chapter with regard to reserves. By forcing the sponsor to disgorge internal funds to the captive in the form of premium payments, the management of the captive then becomes responsible for applying those funds to their specified purpose of controlling retained risks and associated losses.

Agency cost reductions associated with the formation of a captive are likely to be higher for single-parent captives run either by their own management or by a third-party captive management firm than for mutuals. Although adding an additional layer of separation between the security holders of the sponsor and the management of the captive might seem to increase agency costs, the captive *itself* is such a transparent special-purpose company that monitoring its management is relatively easy. Relying on management whose incentives are limited *just* to managing the captive thus makes it more likely that overinvestment decisions could be observed and dealt with appropriately. This transparency is also further rationale for vesting enterprise-wide risk management responsibilities in the captive, as well.

Enhanced Funding Risk Management   One criticism of captives, in particular, is that they tie up the firm's internal funds. Although potentially mitigating overinvestment problems, this can lead to *under*investment problems by depleting the cash available for a firm to make its investment decisions.

One way around this problem is to opt for pure self-insurance or earmarked risk capital reserves instead of a captive. In this situation, the funds could be withdrawn from the reserve to fund investments if absolutely required, whereas the funds tied up in a captive are difficult to repatriate quickly. But in this case, the funds earmarked as a risk reserve are no longer really playing that role. Either the funds have been set aside to cover retained risks or they have not! It's a cookie jar or it isn't a cookie jar; there is no middle ground, at least where investor perceptions are concerned.

Some captive domiciles recognize this problem and address it by allowing captives and mutuals to make loans to their sponsoring corporation(s). Vermont and Hawaii, for example, allow captive lending to their parents on a largely unrestricted basis, whereas otherwise-popular Bermuda heavily restricts such loans.[11] In this case, the firm can essentially engage in *internal borrowing* to finance investment decisions that might otherwise have to be forgone for purely cash flow reasons (see Chapters 3 and 4). Because the loan from the captive to the parent is an internal loan, the terms likely will be favorable and the cash transfer rapid. But in domiciles where such lending is restricted, potential underinvestment problems arising from depleted internal cash must be weighed against the benefits of allocating cash to prefunded retentions.

Managing the Working Capital Layer of the Corporation   To view captives in isolation is to recognize their essential role as organized self-insurance risk finance programs. But in reality, captives are generally the *first* step in corporate risk management, *not* the last. We have already seen, for example, that captives often still rely on reinsurers to acquire external protection for certain risks—or, more likely, for risks above certain attachment points.

For corporations that approach financial and nonfinancial risk management in a truly integrated way, captives are good organizational forms of fine-tuning their retentions and often their working capital layer. All risk is shifted into the captive for consolidated and integrated management, but the captive does not stop there. Excess protection may still be acquired above the firm's working capital layer—perhaps at higher attachment points for some risks than others. We can see examples of this in Chapter 25.

Importantly, captives are often the first step in a broader integrated risk management program that combines multiple structured insurance solutions. Specifically, captives often participate in *mutuals* for the purpose of transferring the risk above the firm's working capital layer. Mutuals are a hybrid form of risk finance and risk transfer—more the latter than the former, but with some financing element playing a role, as well. Corporations that opt to join a mutual often do so through their captive.

MUTUALS OR "SELF-INSURANCE SYNDICATES"

As we mentioned in Chapter 8, a *mutual insurance company* is any insurance company in which the owners and the policyholders are one and the same. In many cases, we immediately think of large conglomerated mutuals like Liberty Mutual or Massachusetts Mutual that have thousands of customers with highly diffuse ownership stakes. These types of mutuals, moreover, generally offer a fairly commodized product line.

In this section, we want to focus on a different kind of mutual insurance company. The shareholders are still the policyholders, but these mutuals tend to have less than a thousand shareholder members—often less than a hundred, and sometimes as few as 5 to 10—and tend to offer more specialized product coverage. Quite often the products offered by these types of mutuals are deliberately intended to complement existing qualified self-insurance programs like captives and thus offer protection at high attachment points for very specific risks.

It's a bit unfortunate that the industry uses the term *mutual* to describe both of these very different types of insurance companies. Perhaps a more accurate description of the mutuals we review in this chapter would be *self-insurance syndicates*. A traditional insurance syndicate is a group of (re)insurance companies that share the risks, costs, and profits of underwriting a single policy or policy line. A self-insurance syndicate, by extension, is a group of firms (mostly corporations and their captives) that share the risks, costs, and profits of underwriting policies that only syndicate members can buy.

Benefits of Mutualization

The basic distinction between self-insurance and insurance rests on the lack of commingled exposures in the former. Insurance companies, by contrast, thrive on and require commingling of exposures to achieve efficiencies in risk management and control. Because mutuals are essentially insurance companies whose customers are also the owners, it makes sense to review briefly the potential benefits of mutualization before turning to the more specific structural and design issues affecting the self-insurance syndicate type of mutual today.

First, the concept of portfolio diversification is one of the most fundamental and important ideas in finance. Provided the risks of losses at multiple firms are not perfectly correlated, the sum of the component risks will always exceed the portfolio of combined risks.

A second reason that aggregating or mutualizing loss exposures can lead to risk reduction is driven by the informational benefits often associated with aggregation. Specifically, probabilistic inference is often more reliable when performed at the portfolio level. Hardy (1999) explains:

> *A single event defies prediction, but the mass remains always practically the same or varies in ways in which we can predict. It is obvious that any device by which we can base our business decisions on the average which we can predict, instead of on the single event, which is uncertain, means the elimination of risk. The larger the number of cases observed the less is the deviation of results from those which a priori were most probable.* (pp. 21–22)

In statistics, the *central limit theorem* tells us that the distribution of the *average risk* from a large group of i.i.d. random variables is approximately normal, regardless of the shapes and properties of the individual risk distributions.[12] Whereas any individual distribution may be difficult to use for statistical inference, the normal distribution certainly is not. So, combination of risk greatly enhances our capacity to draw reliable inferences about the nature of the underlying group of risks.

Note carefully that this is the volatility of the *average* loss in a portfolio. Any given individual liability thus may be arbitrarily large. We thus have not necessarily reduced our *maximum* loss on any given component risk. But in reducing the volatility of our average loss, we have significantly increased our ability to manage the consolidated exposure by improving our ability to *measure* that risk and thus to predict our losses.

In principle, risk combination of the form just described can be used to turn many individual risks into a more manageable agglomeration. And, perhaps more important, the premium charged by an insurer should be equal to the *expected loss*, and the expected loss on a portfolio can be estimated with greater precision than the expected loss on any component risk. This means that mutualization can reduce the costs of reserve management and decrease the frequency of claims whose average levels exceed premium collected.

Design Considerations for Self-Insurance Syndicates

If a firm decides that it wants to participate in a self-insurance syndicate in lieu of pure self-insurance or in lieu of procuring a policy from an existing shareholder-owned insurance company, the basic structure resembles a multiparent captive—essentially the same as a single-parent multibranch captive (see Exhibit 23.3) except that each branch is now a *separate firm* that is both a purchaser of insurance from the mutual *and* a shareholder. A typical multiparent captive a.k.a. mutual insurer a.k.a. self-insurance syndicate is shown in Exhibit 23.6. Note that the presence of fronting insurers is not required and will be driven by the same domicile considerations as in the single-parent case.

Self-insurance syndicates often come in the form of *group* or *association* captives. A group captive is a captive insurance or reinsurance company that collects premium from multiple sponsors and in turn agrees to underwrite certain risks of those sponsors. Group captives are often set up by industry trade associations on behalf of their members.

At its height, the International Air Transport Association's captive Airline Mutual Insurance (AMI), for example, had 44 active participants and offered full liability and damage policies for 110 airlines.[13] Similarly, Energy Insurance and Mutual Limited is the group captive representing numerous U.S. electricity and gas utilities. When each member is too small to justify the expenses of having its own captive, this structure can make sense. Alternatively, situations in which self-insurance pools make sense can also explain group or association captives; the benefits of pooling premiums and risks allow the group captive to achieve a smoother time profile of loss payouts than would be possible in any individual participant's situation. Similarly, *risk retention groups* are specific types of multiparent captives formed under U.S. liability law specifically for the purpose of insuring certain liability risks.

When a mutual is not offered by a trade association, questions quickly arise concerning the membership of a mutual: What is the right number of firms? How related should the firms be? And so on. Again, there is no simple set of rules, but there are some important guidelines.

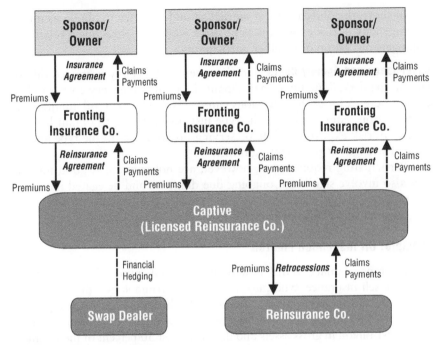

EXHIBIT 23.6 Multiparent Captive or Mutual

Risk Exposures and Financial Condition A well-designed mutual should have members whose underlying risk exposures lead to losses with low correlation in order to maximize the benefits of diversification. At the same time, the exposures should be similar enough that a huge cross-subsidy across risk types does not occur. Two firms whose loss profiles are uncorrelated would not make good mutual members if the reason for the low correlation is that one firm never experiences losses and the other experiences losses all the time. Yes, combining the exposures would diversify the loss profile, but at the pure expense of the stronger party.

In general, firms participating in a mutual should not be completely different in terms of size and financial strength. If one participant is a below-investment-grade firm with under $1 billion in assets, it may be tough to attract a $100 billion AAA firm as the second member. Some dispersion in size and financial strength makes sense, but not too much.

Similarly, it often makes sense for mutuals to be industry or sector specific. This depends to some extent, however, on the nature of the liability the mutual is insuring. Product liability risk in the pharmaceutical industry, for example, is not likely to be correlated across firms that are otherwise fairly similar. This could make a good foundation for a mutual.

In short, the objective for a mutual should be to try to obtain as much heterogeneity in risk exposures as possible while still attracting a relatively homogeneous group of member participants.

Governance and Agency Costs   To the extent there is any perceived difference in the overall quality of participants in a mutual, agency costs can become severe. A lot of these tensions can be resolved by careful attention to participation requirements of the type just noted: trying to obtain heterogeneity in risk exposures while preserving homogeneity in the type and financial strength of participating firms.

Participating requirements, however, are not enough. A good mutual will also involve significant ongoing due diligence and delegated monitoring of participants. Participation requirements combat adverse selection, but ongoing surveillance is required to mitigate moral hazard.

Example: Oil Insurance Limited

Oil Insurance Limited (OIL) is a Bermuda-based mutual insurance company—a self-insurance syndicate in our new terminology—that has been serving the energy industry since it was established in 1972. Originally comprised of 16 members, OIL now has about 84 members. Members must have at least $1 billion in gross assets and derive at least 50 percent of their annual revenues from energy market operations. Firms must also have a minimum credit rating of BBB–/Baa3 to be eligible for membership. Some members of OIL participate directly in OIL, whereas others participate via their captive and use OIL for *re*insurance of certain exposures retained in the captive.

OIL insurance policies are designed to help members cover the risk of property damage, "well control" risks (e.g., restoration and redrilling), and third-party environmental liability risk. OIL policies are limited to $250 million per occurrence. In addition, to control correlated risks within the industry, an aggregation limit puts a $1 billion cap on OIL's exposure to claims from multiple shareholders arising from any single occurrence.

Shareholders may choose their own deductibles and attachment points. Deductibles are in $5 million increments with a minimum per occurrence deductible of $5 million. Electric utilities, however, have a minimum required retention of $20 million per occurrence. Layers that attach at $750 million and above are eligible for deductible discounts.

Risk pooling in OIL is based on two distinct risk categories. Of OIL's 84 members, 20 had a lower attachment point of $5 million at the time of this writing. OIL considers itself more of a catastrophic insurance provider, however, and thus dislikes insuring working capital layers. This has led to some controversy about the $5mn XS $5mn layer in particular. For some OIL members, this is pure working capital, but for others it is not. Among other issues, this creates a concern that the premiums assessed for firms with higher attachment points would create too much of a cross-subsidy for those seeking protection in the $5mn XS $5mn layer.

To address this issue, OIL treats the $5mn XS $5mn layer as a separate risk pool from the policies that attach at $10 million and up. This enables OIL to assess premiums on the $5mn XS $5mn layer rather than self-fund that specific risk pool without any cross-subsidy from those with higher attachment points.

In 2004, OIL reported a net operating loss of $548 million. Net premiums earned were $443 million with $238 million in investment income. Underwriting losses of $777 million were reported on 12 loss events that resulted in 20 claims. OIL is currently rated A+/A1 and had total assets and shareholders' equity at year-end 2004 of $4.4 billion and $994 million, respectively.

CAPTIVES AND MUTUALS AS USERS OF OTHER STRUCTURED SOLUTIONS

The structures we reviewed in this chapter are rarely "end solutions" for their users. Very little risk is put into a captive and then just left there to run its course. Much more common is that captives are the first step in a corporation's risk management process.

We have seen in this chapter that captives are an organized structure in which to manage risk and to manage a retention with preloss finance. But we also noted at the time that captives are themselves often users of reinsurance, swaps, and other ART forms. In fact, captives are quite frequently customers for other structured insurance products. True, the primary goal of the captive is to manage a retention, but not all risk transferred to the captive need be retained to accomplish this objective. Captives thus are frequently buyers of reinsurance (sometimes as participants in reinsurance mutuals) as well as users of finite risk, contingent capital, and multiline, multitrigger structures that we will discuss in upcoming chapters.

Mutuals also are not end repositories of risk. Like captives and like any other corporation, mutuals can also engage in risk securitizations, reinsurance, finite risk, and so on. Mutuals can also be big users of derivatives.

Consider, for example, that one of the biggest concerns in a mutual structure is the failure of a participant. One solution to that problem would be for the mutual to utilize any of the numerous structured credit solutions discussed in Part Three, such as buying credit protection on a risky participant using a credit default swap (CDS), an equity default swap (EDS), or perhaps even a collateralized debt obligation (CDO).

Finite Risk

Defined very crudely, *finite risk* includes a range of risk management solutions in which the (re)insurance company's downside is limited and the insured participates in its own positive claims experience. To achieve both ends, the total premium in a finite program is typically a significant proportion of the maximum possible claim. Finite risk solutions essentially represent a hybrid of risk finance and risk transfer.

At the time of this writing, to say that finite risk is under fire would be roughly like calling World War II a small skirmish. Finite risk in 2005 has become what derivatives were 10 years ago: a hot button for controversy and a potential invitation to a long period of unpleasant investigations, litigation, and perhaps—Heaven forbid—new regulations. The company that has borne the brunt of that assault is American International Group (AIG). AIG's troubles began with an investigation by the Securities and Exchange Commission (SEC) into a relatively small finite risk deal and culminated with the resignation of its longtime chairman, Hank Greenberg; a potentially significant restatement of the company's own accounts; and a host of threatened and pending litigation and investigative proceedings. Other firms associated with potential finite abuses include companies like Brightpoint and the now-defunct HIH Insurance in Australia.

Despite the recent controversy, this chapter very deliberately avoids discussion of any of those firm-specific alleged abuses of finite. Too little is factually known in the public domain to make a complete analysis possible at the time of this writing, and speculation without adequate facts is irresponsible folly. If anything, perhaps a little *less* commentary on finite in the press and by public prosecutors is a more responsible course of action. Let the

---

This chapter is based on joint work with J. B. Heaton, who is nevertheless blameless from any remaining errors, omissions, or specific viewpoints expressed.

firms that have been accused of wrongdoing have their day in court, and until then, let's wait for the facts before rushing to judgment.

Recent controversy has demonstrated, however, the potential for the abuse of finite risk solutions. In the case of finite, there are numerous legitimate uses of the product. To the extent there have been abuses, these relate much more to how firms have accounted for and disclosed finite programs—not to the programs themselves. And on this issue— areas where finite may be abused by inappropriate accounting and/or disclosure—we *will* comment. We just won't name any firm names when we do so.

Finite is hard to define, so the chapter begins uncharacteristically with a simple example to illustrate what kind of risk management problems may lead a firm to consider finite, why, and what benefits can be achieved from properly using finite. We then turn to consider what finite *is*, which we do in several different sections. First we consider the main features that distinguish finite risk from traditional insurance. Next we review the nature of the liabilities that finite can be used to manage, followed by a review of the distinction between funded and unfunded finite programs. Finally, we consider several specific named products that are popular specific forms of finite. We then summarize some positive experiences that firms have had using finite structures to date, choosing, as explained, to eschew the negative stories about finite in favor of some of the many *good* case studies.

One last note before we begin the chapter. Finite risk products have applications for both corporate end users and as a form of reinsurance or retrocession for insurance companies. For consistency, we shall use the term *finite risk* (or *finite*) to refer to corporate applications of this product type, and use the term *financial reinsurance* to refer to applications within the (re)insurance industry. Because the focus of this book is on *corporate* risk management, we spend very little time discussing financial reinsurance. It should be noted, however, that almost all the alleged abuses of finite to date have been abuses of financial reinsurance, *not* finite deals done by corporations.

A SIMPLE EXAMPLE

Finite risk products were originally developed and offered by Centre Re, later to become Centre Solutions.[1] Proponents of finite risk solutions typically eschew the description of these alternative risk transfer (ART) forms as "products," preferring instead to think of finite risk as a "structuring methodology" more than a one-off risk transfer solution technique. This is entirely correct. Finite risk is *not* a single, stand-alone risk management product. It is a *group* of products that are often used in conjunction with other forms of structured insurance, and it is generally very misleading to try to view these deals in complete isolation. Unfortunately, this also makes it hard for us to define our own subject matter.

Because finite is so difficult to define, let's take the admittedly unscientific approach of defining a finite risk structured insurance transaction by example. First, let's set up the nature of the problems that finite risk is well suited to help corporations address. Then, let's characterize what the solution looks like. After that, we can get deeper into the details of the complex area of structured insurance activity.

So, suppose we have a railcar manufacturer whose primary business has also given rise to an asbestos liability risk. The company is willing to take its lumps for this and sets aside $500 million to cover the present value of claims as they steadily flow in over the next five years. This is a start, but the railcar company faces three ongoing potential problems.

First, claims may not show up *steadily* over five years. If they all arrive tomorrow, for example, the $500 million may not have grown to a large enough amount to cover the losses. Being right about the present value is not enough. Claimants want their cash *now*.

Second, what happens if $500 million is not enough? Many corporate users of finite face exotic risks that, like asbestos liability, are awfully hard to quantify and thus need additional insurance coverage on top of the $500 million already set aside to finance the risk. The $500 million estimate itself, after all, presumably came from some probabilistic estimation. Perhaps it was the expected or 50th percentile loss. That still leaves a lot of room for the *actual* loss to come in well above $500 million.

Finally and perhaps most importantly, what does the firm *do* with the $500 million it wants to set aside? If all it does is take a charge against earnings to set up a reserve, investors are likely to be suspicious. We explained why investors don't much like balance sheet reserves in Chapters 3, 7, and 23. In short, nothing really keeps a firm from using those funds for other purposes, or from arbitrarily deciding to add them back to earnings in the future when revised estimates of the loss might help the company make an earnings target. Reaching into a $500 million cookie jar is awfully tempting, after all. And if the firm *does* reach into the cookie jar and reverses a reserve, that can send an extremely negative signal to the capital markets. Ironically, finite risk transactions are often thought to lead to earnings smoothing, but the alternative of a balance sheet reserve can actually be far worse!

Accounting rules, moreover, may not even allow the firm to expense reserves against current earnings *at all* if the risk being reserved against is possible but not sufficiently predictable. In that case, the firm may actually end up making no changes to earnings when it sets aside a reserve. Investors then won't even know about the reserve, and none of the benefits of preloss finance will make their way into the firm's earnings. Arguably, in this case, the firm may well have *over*stated its earnings. At a minimum, the *quality* of the firm's earnings is significantly degraded by reserving for a loss that accounting policy refuses to recognize, and this is unfortunately very often the case with exotic tail-end event risks like environmental liability, mergers and acquisitions (M&A) liability, asbestos or silicosis risk, product liability, and the like.

Finite could be a good solution—perhaps the *only* good solution—for the company in this example. A typical finite structure would require the company to pay a $500 million premium to a highly rated reinsurance company for, say, $600 million in asbestos liability insurance over a three-year term. The $500 million would be expensed against earnings as the premium is paid, probably quarterly over the life of the program. This would reduce earnings, just as you would want to be the case to signal the loss for which the functional equivalent of a reserve is being taken.

If the claims materialize, the company is covered up to $600 million in losses, even if they occur more rapidly than anticipated. If claims are lower than expected, the company gets a low claims bonus (a partial refund of its premium). The company has converted a potentially huge risk into a currently known expense and has done so *credibly*.

Properly motivated, implemented, and disclosed, finite risk transactions like this one can help a firm purchase prudent protection against hard-to-predict catastrophic risks, enhance the quality of its earnings, and achieve credibility with investors for a strong risk management program. Finite risk products thus can help firms finance liabilities whose outcomes are unknown while simultaneously transferring the risk that the firm may have underestimated the true retention associated with those risks. In short, finite risk products provide an appealing means by which a firm can combine a *credible* preloss financing structure together with a classical risk transfer component.

What if the firm doesn't actually have $500 million in cash sitting around to pay the insurer up front (or to fully fund the reserve)? In that case, the insurer may enter into a different kind of finite structure that essentially allows the railcar manufacturer to get $100 million in insurance and to borrow the $500 million retention when and if the asbestos claims arrive. The railcar company then repays the $500 million at a more convenient time. This is a classic form of risk finance and, properly disclosed, can be very helpful in situations where there simply is no capacity for insurance below the $500 million attachment point.

Noninsurance corporations typically find finite risk products useful for managing exotic tail risks that are not core to their primary business activities, ring-fencing assets or business risks in M&A transactions or in conjunction with product financing, for managing runoff solutions, and for funding retentions when outright insurance is not available in the loss layers the firm would prefer to insure outright but cannot.

TYPICAL FINITE RISK STRUCTURES

Now that we have introduced and motivated the concept of finite by way of an example, let us turn to the more practical and specific aspects of finite risk coverage. As noted, finite risk is more of a structuring methodology than a financial or reinsurance product. It is the process by which risk finance and risk transfer are blended or integrated into a single hybrid risk management program so that a customer can prefund a retention, manage the timing risks of that retention, and obtain excess of loss (XOL) risk transfer for losses above the retention, all in one single blended program. A huge number of products and solutions potentially fall under this umbrella.

In this section, we try to provide some more specificity to the meaning of finite risk solutions. To do so, we consider three specific topics:

1. Characteristics that typically distinguish finite risk structures from traditional (re)insurance.
2. The nature of the liabilities typically covered by finite risk programs.
3. The degree to which the program is fully, partially, or not funded.

We then turn to review a few of the specific finite risk products in the structured finite arena.

Characteristics of Finite Risk Structures

The distinctions between classical reinsurance and finite risk products are subtle but critically important in helping firms determine which risk transformation solution is the right one. The main features that distinguish most finite risk products from traditional insurance are discussed in the next few subsections. Not every finite contract will have all of these features, and the characteristics shown cannot be considered a definitive list of necessary and sufficient conditions for a structure to be considered a finite risk deal. But for the most part, this set of characteristics seems as good as any for describing a typical finite transaction.

Material Risk Transfer In order to qualify as a legitimate form of (re)insurance, a finite risk transfer must involve a material amount of risk transfer. Recall from Chapters 8 and 9 that insurance contracts generally involve at least four types of risk:

1. *Underwriting risk*—the risk that premiums collected are insufficient to cover realized losses.
2. *Credit risk*—the risk that a (re)insurer will not fully honor all of its contingent obligations to its cedant customers.
3. *Investment risk*—the risk that the income generated by an insurer when premium collected is invested in assets is below the expected income reflected in the reinsurer's premium pricing.
4. *Timing risk*—the risk that actual loss claims occur at a faster rate than expected and that invested reserves are too low to fund those claims when they occur.

A true finite risk contract must involve material risk transfer of all four of these risks. This was not always the case, however, and some of the early versions of finite risk (and perhaps a few of the recent more controversial ones?) focused purely on the transfer of timing risk to the exclusion of underwriting risk.

In an early Lloyd's of London structure called *time and distance* policies, for example, these historical predecessors to modern finite risk contracts involved the payment of a large premium by the cedant to a reinsurer and then specified a *fixed schedule* by which premiums were returned to the cedant. This schedule, however, did not have anything to do with the actual timing of claims made by the ceding insurer and essentially represented more of a cash deposit than a risk transfer device. Accordingly, the only material risk transferred in a time and distance policy was timing risk, and the main purpose of these transactions seems to have been pure income stabilization (i.e., cash flow and/or earnings smoothing). Such a policy would not, however, be considered a legitimate finite risk transaction today.

Determining "how much risk transfer is enough" depends, of course, on why the determination is being made. The optimal amount of risk transfer in a finite structure from the standpoint of the customer is really derivative of its optimal capital structure and may or may not correspond to extant tax, disclosure, accounting, and other regulations. Regulations, of course, must be respected, but even in that context regulatory definitions of "adequate risk transfer" have been ambiguous to date. Clearly, a traditional insurance contract represents "full risk transfer" in the sense that the cedant has paid a premium equal to its *expected* loss to prevent bearing its *actual* loss, and the reinsurer in turn bears the risk completely that unexpected losses may exceed the expected loss reflected in the premium. And clearly, a time and distance policy represents no risk transfer inasmuch as the only payment obligation of the reinsurer is to honor a fixed schedule of payments unrelated to actual loss development experience. "Partial risk transfer" is, alas, everything in between.

Until very recently, a rule of thumb practiced by most accountants was to deem a transaction as involving material risk transfer if there was at least a 10 percent probability that the reinsurer would incur an underwriting loss on an amount equal to at least 10 percent of the policy limit. A program with a $1.05 million policy limit and a $1 million premium would fail that so-called 10/10 test or 10/10 rule. The maximum loss to the insurer would be only $50,000 under such a policy. Even if that loss was 95 percent likely to occur, $50,000 is only 5 percent of the policy limit. Similarly, a $100,000 XS $1,000,000 program would also fail the test if the risk of a loss in excess of $1 million is under 10 percent.

Unfortunately, this rule of thumb was only just that: a rule of thumb, not a statutory or regulatory requirement. It was also subject to modeling interpretation when it came to assessing the probability of exceedance.

Following some of the recent widely publicized controversies about finite, many accountants now prefer a 15/15 or even 20/20 rule. In some cases, an accounting firm may wish to see as much as 25/25—for example, at least a 25 percent chance of incurring a loss above $1 million in a $1.25 XS $1 program.

Cedant Participates in Positive Claims Experience   A longstanding marketing problem faced by (re)insurers has been the perception that (re)insurance does not add value if claims are rarely made. We know that looking at whether or not a *loss* occurred, however, is far from the same thing as looking at a *risk*. A loss is just an adverse outcome of a risk, but risk does not always lead to losses. The right time to determine whether (re)insurance increases the value of the firm is *ex ante*, of course, using the principles we developed in Part One.

Nevertheless, reinsurers also recognize that their rates reflect certain assumptions about adverse selection and moral hazard—assumptions that tend to raise prices because of the lemons problem explored in Chapter 4. Over time, if the claims experience of a customer helps the reinsurer realize that it has *not* insured a lemon, then it can make sense to allow the customer to participate in its positive claims and loss development experience through a partial rebate of premium. Indeed, a partial premium rebate can make sense even without a lemons problem purely for marketing purposes—depending, of course, on the level of the initial premium.

Finite risk premiums often are quite high, but looking only at premiums on these ART contracts can be misleading for the aforementioned reason. Regardless of the quoted premium, the *total cost* to the cedant of a finite risk program is usually a function of the actual claims or loss experience. Investment income also may be included in the overall assessment of a cedant's experience with the policy.

The mechanics by which profit and loss sharing is accomplished in a finite risk transaction depend on the nature of the transaction and the particular counterparties to that transaction. In general, this sharing is accomplished through the use of an *experience account* that tracks the paper profits and losses on the actual underlying deal. Premium paid by the cedant to the (re)insurer is credited to the account, as is interest on invested premium reserves. Losses and various charges incurred by the (re)insurer are debited to the account. At the end of the term of the finite risk structure, the (re)insurer and cedant essentially split the balance in the experience account, whether a net gain or a net loss.

Limited Liability for the Reinsurer Notwithstanding the requirement that a finite transaction involve material transfer of all risk types, a distinguishing feature of a finite risk contract is generally that it exposes the (re)insurer to a limited or finite amount of underwriting risk. The limitations of liability provisions in finite risk contracts are hardly so distinguishing on their own as to reveal the difference between finite risk and traditional reinsurance. Virtually all traditional insurance and reinsurance contracts involve some kind of policy limit.

What is special about finite risk contracts is usually the mechanisms by which the underwriting risk of the (re)insurer is limited. The policy limit, of course, is important, but perhaps more important in a typical finite risk structure is the level of the premium relative to the policy limit.

Recall from Part Two that premium is equal to the actuarially fair price of insurance plus premium loading and perhaps a small markup. If a customer opts voluntarily to cede more than that amount to the carrier as premium, the amount in excess of the actuarial premium plus load is essentially a form of risk finance. As we saw in Chapter 7, a primary motivation for risk finance is prefunding a loss so that the *cash flow risk* of a retention does not lead to problems like underinvestment. We will return later in this section to a discussion of the benefits of finite risk contracts, but the high premium relative to the policy limit is often a significant part of that benefit.

Multiyear Like many other ART and structured insurance products and unlike most traditional (re)insurance, finite risk contracts generally have a tenor of more than a year.

Risk in the Risk Transfer Component

Finite risk structures can be either *prospective* or *retrospective* with regard to the risks the structures are intended to cover. Recall from Chapter 8 that a bilateral contract between two parties that references the specific occurrence of a risk event (e.g., fire, flood, liability loss, crime, etc.) can be prospective, retrospective, or retroactive depending on the effective dates on the contract vis-à-vis the risk coverage period. For ease of reference, Exhibit 8.1 is reproduced more generically here as Exhibit 24.1,

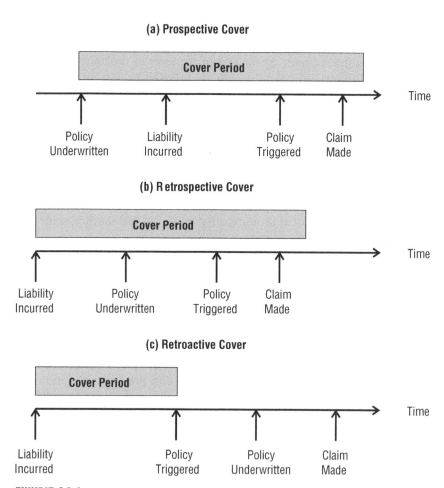

EXHIBIT 24.1   Retrospective versus Prospective versus Retroactive Cover

which compares four different dates in the life of a would-be insurance policy:

1. *Policy underwritten.* A policy is bound that allows the insurance purchaser to pay a premium in exchange for the right to make a claim of loss and to receive all or partial reimbursement of that loss upon the occurrence of a specific triggering event during a specified risk coverage period.
2. *Liability incurred.* The event that exposes the insurance purchaser to a risk of loss occurs.
3. *Policy triggered.* The risk of loss actually becomes a known loss, thereby triggering the insurance contract.
4. *Claim made.* The insurance purchaser files a claim for reimbursement of actual damage sustained.

A lot of confusion arises as to the distinction between the date on which a liability is incurred and the date a policy is triggered. The distinction is the same distinction that separates a risk from a loss. Liability under an insurance policy that is eligible for potential reimbursement is the time that a firm *assumes a risk*, whereas the policy trigger date is the date on which that risk no longer represents a potential loss but in fact has become an *actual* loss.

As long as the policy has not been triggered before the policy underwriting date and the risk cover period are over, that means that the outcome of the policy is not known. The insurance purchaser is *at risk*, which means that the risk might still translate into a loss—or possibly not. But once the policy trigger has been pulled or the risk coverage period has ended without the trigger being pulled, the outcome is *known with certainty*. This situation is what we call here a *retroactive* cover—a cover that is intended to pay off based on an event whose outcome is known at the time the policy is signed. This is *not* insurance, and this does *not* represent risk transfer.

If the possibility for a loss exists when the policy is signed, however, the policy can in principle involve material risk transfer even if the liability or risk exposure was incurred before the policy was underwritten. We call that a *retrospective* policy. Consider some examples:

- A crime occurred but has not yet been detected.
- A product was released for which its producer faces product liability as a result of a defect, but the defect is not yet known.

- A chemical thought to be safe is dumped in a residential stream but is later found to cause cancer.
- A typhoon destabilizes the foundation underlying shoreline property, but the instability is undetected initially.

All of the above examples of retrospective risk can be the legitimate source of insurance or finite risk deals provided the policies are bound before the uncertainty about the loss exposure is revealed. That the event leading to the loss exposure happened in the past is not really material.

The third possibility is that the policy is underwritten before the liability is even incurred, which means by definition that the policy trigger has not been pulled. On such *prospective* programs, there is little doubt that the contract is insurance.

Preloss versus Postloss Financing

Yet another important distinction between different finite risk solutions is the degree to which the structure is preloss funded either in whole or in part—or not at all. We know from Chapter 7 that the funding of a risk management structure can be questioned for *any* risk management product, and we have seen ample examples of viable, legitimate products that are both fully funded, such as commodity debt obligations (CDOs) and credit-linked notes (CLNs), and that are completely unfunded (e.g., traditional derivatives and insurance). Whether a deal is or is not funded does not change its inherent legitimacy, but it can affect the rationale for firms to use the different forms of products—and, as we shall see later in this chapter, it can dramatically affect how firms should *account for and disclose* their finite solutions.

Let's again use a simple example to help us differentiate between funded and unfunded finite structures. Consider a corporation facing potential environmental cleanup cost liabilities of $400 million over the next, say, three years. The first $350 million has about a 50 percent chance of being realized, and the next $50 million has about a 15 percent chance of being realized. Exhibit 24.2 compares preloss funded and postloss funded finite risk solutions to help manage this risk. For simplicity, we're going to ignore transaction costs, including arrangement fees.

In panel (a) of Exhibit 24.2, we first consider a *preloss funded* finite program. The corporation essentially sets aside the first $350 million in cash but is concerned that a balance sheet reserve will not be as credible with investors as a finite program. So, the company enters into a finite program for three years in which it cedes the initial $350 million to a reinsurer at the inception of the program. If the liability turns into a realized loss over the life of the program, the reinsurer uses the premium to cover the first

(a) Preloss Funded

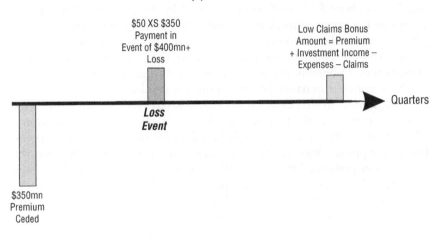

$50 XS $350
Payment in
Event of $400mn+
Loss

Low Claims Bonus
Amount = Premium
+ Investment Income −
Expenses − Claims

Quarters

*Loss
Event*

$350mn
Premium
Ceded

(b) Postloss Funded

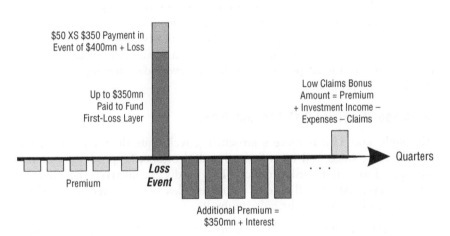

$50 XS $350 Payment in
Event of $400mn + Loss

Up to $350mn
Paid to Fund
First-Loss Layer

Low Claims Bonus
Amount = Premium
+ Investment Income −
Expenses − Claims

Quarters

Premium

*Loss
Event*

Additional Premium =
$350mn + Interest

EXHIBIT 24.2 Funded versus Unfunded Finite

$350 million in losses and provides an additional $50 XS $350 in coverage. Losses above $400 million are retained by the company. But if losses are below the expected level, at the end of the program the company is eligible for a low claims bonus out of any program surplus, where the program surplus is equal to the premium collected plus investment income earned on that premium minus claims payments and expenses.

Now consider in panel (b) a program that is substantially the same but *postloss funded*. In that case, the corporation pays only a commitment fee or small premium to the reinsurer in advance of any loss. If no loss occurs, a low claims bonus is again possible based on the surplus after three years. But now suppose a loss occurs. In this case and unlike the previous one, the firm has not prefunded the first $350 million layer, *but it has still retained that layer*. In effect, the reinsurer makes a $350 million payment to the company to cover the first layer of losses. The reinsurer also provides excess coverage of $50 XS $350. But in this case, the company's subsequent premiums on the program now rise so that the present value of those future premiums is equal to $350 million as of the date of the loss.

The additional premium required on the unfunded program is often called *retrospectively rated premium* or *contingent premium*. In effect, the additional premium in the program is economically equivalent (at least in this example) to the principal and interest on a $350 million loan made by the reinsurer to the corporation on the loss event date through the end of the life of the program.

Some Specific Finite Risk Product Types

Although finite risk is more a structuring technique than a product, the market has named and identified a handful of specific products that are considered to be finite risk products. This hardly encompasses the whole finite universe, but it will give us a clearer idea of the range of solutions available to firms under the finite umbrella.

Loss Portfolio Transfers   A *loss portfolio transfer* (LPT) is the cession by a firm of all remaining unclaimed losses associated with a previously incurred liability. In addition to paying an arrangement fee, the cedant also typically pays a premium equal to the net present value (NPV) of reserves it has set aside for the transferred liability *plus* a premium to compensate the (re)insurer for the underwriting and other risks assumed. An LPT thus enables a firm to exchange an uncertain liability in the form of a stream of unrealized losses over time for a certain liability whose present value is equal to the expected NPV of the unrealized losses plus a risk premium and a fee. An LPT is generally a preloss funded finite risk structure intended to deal with retrospective liability.

The principal risk that the cedant transfers to the (re)insurer through an LPT is the risk that losses or claims arrive at a much faster rate than expected. In that case, the investment income on the reserves—and perhaps the reserves themselves—may be inadequate to fund the losses. A time series of losses that occurs more slowly than expected, by contrast, will represent an opportunity for a net gain that the (re)insurer would typically share with the cedant. LPTs thus are risk-financing mechanisms through which firms can address the timing risk of a liability.

LPTs can be attractive for various reasons. For insurers, LPTs provide a low-cost means of synthetically exiting or ring-fencing a business very quickly. LPTs can help corporations with captives, for example, wind up certain self-insurance lines if the firm alters its retention decision for certain risks. LPTs are also useful to nonfinancial corporations in securing financing for runoff solutions, especially in the area of environmental claims and cleanup cost allocation.

The principal benefit of an LPT, as already discussed, is that it enhances a firm's quality of earnings by enabling it to take a credible reserve. If the firm cannot cede its reserves to a reinsurer through a mechanism like an LPT, the firm is left with an escrow account. Even if the firm can account for the reserves in earnings, all the problems of reserves discussed in previous chapters still apply: They can appear to be cookie jars, they can be seen to cause *either* agency costs of free cash flow *or* underinvestment problems, and they can send very clear signals to investors when they are reversed. An LPT suffers from none of those problems.

Adverse Development Covers An *adverse development cover* (ADC)—sometimes also called a *retrospective excess of loss* (RXL) cover—is a finite risk ART form in which a (re)insurer agrees to provide XOL coverage for losses incurred on a retrospective liability that exceeds the cedant's current reserves or planned retention. ADCs are commonly used by firms to manage their incurred but not reported (IBNR) liabilities.

ADCs do not involve the cession either of a liability/loss portfolio or of reserves by the cedant to the (re)insurer. As a result, ADCs do not really provide firms with the opportunity to combine any preloss financing with their XOL protection. Instead, the (re)insurer simply agrees to compensate the cedant for any losses above an attachment point set equal to a defined retention level. The retention may or may not be funded by the purchaser of the ADC, but if it has been funded, those funds are left with the protection purchaser and are *not* ceded to the reinsurer as they would be in an LPT. ADCs may also involve a policy limit, but a cedant is free to layer ADCs in the same manner that traditional XOL reinsurance can be layered to address concerns over catastrophic loss development layers.

ADCs can be useful for firms in a variety of situations. ADCs are commonly used to cap old liabilities that are of concern in a merger or an acquisition. When the acquiring firm or merger partner is concerned that a liability could be much greater than the target firm has planned for in its reserve holdings, the cession of XOL risk through an ADC can provide the target firm with a good remedy for such concerns on the part of its suitor.

In addition, ADCs are widely regarded as important devices for combating adverse selection problems associated with "black hole" risks that investors consider impossible to estimate reliably and reserve against. A firm that enters a charge-off against its earnings for a liability that has not been fully realized, for example, may be suspected of possessing superior information about the liability that leads to underreporting. Or a firm that first announces a tail-end risk event such as environment liability will almost certainly be suspected of underestimating the total liability its first time around. A firm wishing to counter such fears by investors can take out an ADC to lock in its liability at the charge-off amount and thus signal its confidence that the charge-off was indeed correct.[2]

Finally, ADCs can improve the ability of cedants to find favorable pricing for catastrophic XOL layers with lower attachment points above the policy limit on the ADC itself. Especially if there is limited or no capacity for insurance in primary or excess layers, an ADC may be the only way a firm can obtain coverage.

Retrospective Aggregate Loss Covers A *retrospective aggregate loss* (RAL) cover involves a cession of reserves to a reinsurer that represents only a *partial* prefunding of expected losses. In a typical RAL, the cedant can finance existing and IBNR losses by paying a premium to a (re)insurer equal to the current value of those reserves but less than the present value of *all* expected liabilities. In our earlier example where the firm expected $350 million in environmental claims, $150 million of those claims might be IBNR or existing claims and might correspond to a funded reserve. Just like an LPT, the RAL purchaser cedes both the $150 million *and* the associated liability to the (re)insurer. But unlike an LPT, an RAL also usually includes a provision that requires the cedant to pay for any losses over the ceded amount or above a defined loss ratio *when those losses are actually incurred by the cedant* in the form of retrospectively rated premiums.

In the LPT, the risk of a very large claim arriving unexpectedly early in the loss development cycle was borne solely by the (re)insurer, perhaps subject only to an aggregate or per risk policy limit. But the RAL specifically forces the cedant to retain some of this timing risk. The RAL thus involves less timing risk for the (re)insurer than an LPT.

At the same time, the RAL is less cash-intensive and tends to allow the firm to prefinance losses in its working capital layer. For firms less concerned about preloss finance *outside* the working capital layer, an RAL can make sense. Firms using RALs must be particularly attentive to disclosure issues, as we shall see again later. At face value, an RAL can be used to increase the balance sheet equity of the cedant by replacing the technical reserves allocated to an unknown liability with a fixed premium payment whose value is less than the current technical reserves. But precisely because the value of the premium is below the expected loss, the retrospectively rated premiums in the program give rise to a contingent liability that can be significant.

Finite Quota Share Treaties   A *finite quota share treaty* is a form of financial reinsurance used primarily by insurance companies to manage *pro*spective liabilities on a partially funded basis. Corporate applications are limited. Nevertheless, as one of the named forms of finite it is worth mentioning.

Recall from Chapter 9 that a quota share treaty (QST) is a form of proportional reinsurance in which the reinsurer agrees to pay a fixed proportion of claims and loss adjustment expenses on a line of policies in return for receiving a proportion of the premium. In a traditional quota share agreement, the potential liability of the reinsurer is limited only by the policy limits on the original policies ceded. If there are no policy limits, the liability of the reinsurer is potentially unlimited.

The only real difference between a *finite* QST and a *traditional* QST is the explicit limitation of liability for the reinsurer in the former. Whether or not the ceded policies underlying the treaty have policy limits, the finite quota share imposes a contractual maximum obligation on the reinsurer.

Finite QSTs are used mainly to increase the accounting surplus of the cedant and thus can be potentially abused if inadequate attention is paid to disclosure. In a finite QST, the primary insurer cedes part of its unearned premium to the reinsurer along with the concomitant liabilities. In return for this, the cedant receives a so-called ceding commission. In this manner, the unearned premium is converted into *current income*. The finite quota share treaty thus is a pure risk financing product, converting an as yet unrealized stream of expected profits into a current income item that inflates the surplus of the cedant.

The ceding commission together with the investment income on the unearned premium reserves are expected to more than cover actual claims arising on the new policy line. In the event that unexpected losses occur, the assuming reinsurer is often given the right to recover those losses from the ceding insurer over the term of the agreement (Monti and Barile 1995).

Just as the reinsurer wants to limit its loss exposure, the primary cedant also wants to retain the majority of profits on the underlying business line. To facilitate this, the ceding commission is often tied to a sliding scale that varies with the loss ratio; say, a 1 percent increase in commission paid for every 1 percent reduction in the actual loss ratio up to a maximum of 100 percent (Carter, Lucas, and Ralph 2000). Alternatively, an experience fund can be established with a preagreed sharing rule for redistributing the profits between the cedant and reinsurer at the end of the life of the contract.

If the primary goal of a finite QST is to raise the accounting surplus or shareholders' equity of an insurance company, isn't that misleading almost by definition? Not necessarily. As noted, it depends on how the program is disclosed. An insurance company may have a real economic incentive to monetize unearned premium reserves into shareholders' equity. This could, for example, free up debt capacity, increase underwriting capacity, or reduce the expected costs of financial distress for the firm. It can also help a firm mitigate underinvestment problems to the extent that capital is tied up in an unearned premium reserve. At the same time, of course, a finite QST could also serve inappropriately as a vehicle for delaying the recognition of losses or inflating the equity portion of the balance sheet. It all depends on why the program was done *and* how well it is explained to investors.

Spread Loss Treaties   A second form of financial reinsurance product is called a *spread loss treaty* (SLT) and, like finite QSTs, represents a form of risk financing popular mainly for insurance companies. SLTs apply to prospective liabilities and generally are unfunded. In an SLT, the cedant pays an annual premium into an experience account over the multiyear term of the contract. Investment income on reserves is credited to the experience account, and actual losses plus the reinsurer's arrangement fees are debited. If the fund goes into deficit, the primary insurer must pay increased premiums to restore the fund to balance—including perhaps a final payment to ensure that the fund is in balance when the SLT expires. But if the fund is in surplus, the net investment income of the fund is distributed to the cedant. A surplus at the end of the life of the SLT results in a sharing of profits and thus a partial premium refund to the cedant.

The reinsurer's obligation is to make payments for claims as they occur, even if such claims create a deficit in the experience account. Any such losses are cumulated and then redistributed over the remaining term of the agreement, which can be quite long. The net effect of this from the perspective of the cedant is that the reinsurer is essentially prefunding losses and allowing the cedant to spread those losses out over a much longer period of time rather than incur them as they arise. The reinsurer does bear some underwriting risk in that structure, but usually subject to either annual or an aggregate policy limit.

The SLT structure allows cedants to smooth the volatility of their claims payments and hence their earnings. This can, of course, be either used or abused. For example, SLTs are particularly popular for single-parent captives as a means of helping reduce the earnings volatility of the captive's parent/sponsor.[3] Arguably this is not misleading because the entire amount of capital invested in the captive has *already been recognized as a risk retention*. The problems come when SLTs are used to camouflage retained risks and losses with the appearance of real insurance.

LEGITIMATE TRANSACTIONS VERSUS OPPORTUNITIES FOR ABUSE

Now that we have examined five popular types of finite risk deals, let's turn now to consider some of the features of these programs that create opportunities for abuse. We will also be attentive along the way to arguing that there are also plenty of opportunities for *legitimate* uses of these products. Nevertheless, what are some of the hot buttons and red flags to bulls?

The common denominator of abuse usually concerns the degree to which the transaction is accounted for, disclosed, and represented to investors as achieving "significant risk transfer" when in fact it achieves little or no risk transfer. The fact that a finite program contains a risk financing component will never in and of itself be a problem. The desire of a company to manage the timing risk of an as yet unknown liability is a legitimate economic motivation to engage in cash flow risk management, as we saw in Chapters 3 and 7. We have seen numerous examples of this throughout Part Three; for instance, every time a special purpose entity (SPE) in a structured credit deal swaps coupon income on a collateral portfolio for a quarterly LIBOR-based income stream, the SPE is managing the timing risk that its assets may not generate cash fast enough to service the liabilities of the structure. *There is nothing wrong with this.*

Yet a program that transfers only timing risk will not qualify as insurance. If the only risk is timing risk, the transaction is a deposit or a loan, not an insurance contract, and must be accounted for as such.

But conversely, *just because a program has a component intended to address timing risk does not automatically mean the structure as a whole is suspect.*

So where, then, are the problems? Let's explore several specific areas of potential abuse.

Retroactive Cover

Finite risk structures are common for prospective and retrospective liabilities. When dealing with retro*active* liabilities, however, the contract is no longer insurance. There is no risk transfer, after all, if there is *no risk*.

To put it bluntly, trying to execute retroactive insurance is equivalent to insuring against a *known outcome*. As long as there is still risk and uncertainty about the outcome of a liability—Will it damage the firm or not? If so, how much?—then finite or any other insurance contract can be underwritten. But the moment the damage is known with certainty, any contract predicated on that particular backward-looking trigger is no longer managing risk; it is just shifting funds.

Firms can still *do* this, of course. They just cannot account for and disclose what they are doing as insurance. Under U.S. generally accepted accounting principles (GAAP), a firm is allowed to net the benefit of an insurance program against the associated loss as long as the recovery is considered "probable." At the same time, the premium paid can be expensed over the life of the policy. If the recovery is "possible" but not "probable," the insurance cannot be used to reduce the size of the loss. And if the recovery is "known with certainty," then the recovery can be netted against the loss, but in that case the *entire premium* must be expensed in the same quarter that the loss and recovery are recognized and netted.

So, for example, suppose a firm buys $1.1 million of insurance at a cost of $1 million to cover the risk of the destruction of a machine over the next five years. If the machine is teetering on the brink so that a recovery is probable, the firm can charge off the loss on the machine *and* net the $1.1 million recovery now against that expected loss. The $1 million in premium is expensed gradually over five years. This $1 million, of course, represents the retained portion of the loss that the firm wishes to pay but cannot credibly reserve against. So far so good.

Now suppose the machine was already destroyed last year and the policy is written to cover any destruction of the machine from last year through the end of five years from now. What the firm *should* do is take the $1.1 million charge-off now for the loss of the machine, net the $1.1 million recoverable on the contract against it now, *and* expense the entire $1 million in premium *now*. There is no risk, after all, so there is no risk transfer and there is no justification for amortizing the premium over the life of a redundant policy.

But let's suppose the firm has already told investors it had a great quarter with no charge-offs. If it wants to play accounting games, the firm could try to inappropriately treat this finite deal as insurance, using the

$1.1 million expected recovery to offset the $1.1 million charge-off and avoiding any hit to earnings today. Instead, the firm would gradually take the hit to earnings over the next five years. This is *not* okay—it is earnings smoothing, plain and simple.

Note well, however, that the problem here is *not* with the contract structure itself. The problem is entirely a failure of the firm to account for a retroactive contract as a depository instrument. If there is no risk transfer, there can be no accounting for and disclosure of the structure as risk transfer.

Undisclosed Debt in Postloss Funded Programs

Postloss funded finite programs can be very useful. When markets are hard and coverage is not available for firms in the primary or excess layers, unfunded finite may be literally the only way to get some kind of coverage. And most would heartily agree that risk finance for the forced retention is better than wandering into the risk event completely unprotected. Another way to say this in the language of Part One is that risk transfer helps protect the firm's equity holders. When that is not available, risk financing can be a way to secure new debt on preloss terms, thus protecting *debt* holders from the costs of distress debt financing or the deepening insolvency problem. For a cash-strapped firm in particular, better risk finance than nothing at all.

At the same time, insurance is insurance—and debt is debt. Many unfunded finite programs are essentially a blend of contingent debt and excess of loss insurance coverage. And as we saw in Chapter 15, *there is nothing inherently wrong with contingent debt*. The question that many have asked about unfunded programs is whether they have been properly accounted for and disclosed. If a firm has a $50 XS $350 unfunded ADC, that means a loss event of $400 million will involve a pure insurance payment of $50 million by the reinsurer and a loan to the cedant of $350 million to cover the retained first layer. That $350 million is then usually paid back through contingent premium or restrospectively rated premium—premium that is really principal and interest on the debt.

Although debt and insurance are accounted for differently, the difference is not that significant. Both items are on the balance sheet. But investors may care *where* on the balance sheet. As Enron has taught us, for example, the amount of term debt carried by a firm can be a very important variable, affecting debt covenants, credit lines, credit enhancements and collateral requirements, and the like. Concealing term debt inside an insurance program thus is arguably fraudulent accounting.

The bigger problem is arguably with *disclosure*. If you have disclosed that you have $400 million "in insurance" on the aforementioned program, investors and other firms are likely to deduce that you have $400 million *in risk transfer*. That's quite a different picture than telling investors you have borrowed another $350 million contingent on the loss event and then have $50 million of insurance.

There is an easy solution to this problem. If a firm wants to do an unfunded program, perhaps in lieu of unfunded finite, the better way is to combine a true Committed Long-Term Capital Solutions (CLOCS)-like contingent debt structure with a $50 XS $350 insurance cover. If the excess insurance is multiyear and multiline as discussed in the next chapter, you can probably still get all the same benefits of a low claims bonus, option reinstatement, and the like. You really sacrifice only the appearance that the first layer is insurance—which it isn't. So, the answer is—go ahead and do the structure in which you borrow the $350 million retention and insure the excess; just do that using contingent debt and insurance rather than finite. This will result in the appropriate accounting and tax treatment and, importantly, a proper disclosure.

Note that we're not saying *all* postloss funded finite programs are disclosed improperly, are irresponsible, or are debt in disguise. That's plainly not true. Remember our goal in this section is to highlight opportunities for abuse and easy ways to assuage concerned investors about those. We're not trying to indict the whole class of unfunded finite products.

Other Potentially Troublesome Features

Finite structures may contain various other provisions designed to affect the timing of cash flows under the program and the degree of true risk transfer. Properly disclosed, explained, and accounted for, these additional features can help users of the products achieve a significant degree of customization in their risk management programs. But they can also present opportunities for concealing the true nature of the finite program, especially with respect to the true amount of risk finance vis-à-vis risk transfer in the structure.

Consider some examples of additional features often found in finite deals that can cause trouble for firms that are anything other than transparent about these terms.

Loss Corridors and Blending
The term *blended finite* has several different meanings in a finite risk context. To some, it merely reinforces that finite itself blends risk finance and risk transfer. To others, blended finite programs refer to finite programs combined or integrated with other ART

forms. It is not uncommon, for example, to see a captive or a mutual seek protection that includes a finite program integrated with a multiline cover (see Chapter 25). Such a program might well be called blended finite by some.

Blending can also refer to the manner in which the risk transfer component of the structure is integrated into the deal at various attachment points. In the example we used earlier, we had a $400 million program that consisted of a $350 million preloss financing layer and a $50 million pure insurance component. The latter encompassed the $50 XS $350 layer. But suppose instead that the program was structured so that a $1 million insurance layer attached after every $7 million in retention up to $400 million. In other words, insurance would cover $1 XS $7, $1 XS $15, $1 XS $23, ..., $1 XS $391, and $1 XS $399. The total coverage would still be $400, with a total retention of $350 million and total insurance of $50 million. The only difference is the layering.

It's possible that this kind of layering is intended to match some corporate retention need, but not likely. More likely is that the blending scheme is intended to distribute the insurance part of the program into lower loss layers so as to increase the probability that the risk transfer component will be used. This can make sense, as it may lead to greater risk transfer than if all $50 million is in the excess of $350 layer. At the same time, this sort of program is awfully confusing and hard to describe, much less to rationalize. Beware.

Mandatory Reinstatement Provisions   A *reinstatement* in a (re)insurance program occurs if a policy limit can be refreshed after a loss has reached its limit. Optional reinstatement provisions are common features of ART forms like multiline programs, as we will see in Chapters 25 and 26. With an optional reinstatement provision, the insurer has the right to pay additional premium to reinstate a policy limit after it is exhausted. This is a type of *contingent cover* or *contingent insurance* that we will discuss in Chapter 26.

Mandatory reinstatement means that the protection purchaser in a finite program is automatically assessed an additional premium to reinstate a limit following a loss. On the one hand, this would seem to increase the risk transfer component of the structure. On the other hand, the mandatory reinstatement creates a source of additional known premium payments for the insurer. On a probability-adjusted basis, the net impact can be *reduced* risk transfer overall. If the aggregate limit of cover is reached in the final six months of a three-year structure, for example, the probability that the entire aggregate limit would be exhausted again over the next six months is remote at best. A mandatory reinstatement of the full limit in that case would be largely redundant from a capacity perspective, but it could increase the total premium outlay by enough to significantly reduce the risk borne by the reinsurer.

Abuse of the Low Claims Bonus Feature   One of the essential features of most finite deals is the low claims bonus. If premium plus investment income less expenses and claims results in a surplus, at least some of that surplus is likely to revert to the insurance purchaser.[4] Provided the policy runs its natural course, this feature of a program does not in any way reduce the *ex ante* risk transfer. It merely takes any favorable result *ex post* and divides the gain between the reinsurer and the cedant.

The real problem lies in programs where a low claims bonus is combined with *retroactive cover*. Recall that retroactive cover applies when there is no real risk or uncertainty about the outcome of the insurable event. It either did happen or it didn't. Now imagine that Company Scully enters into a finite structure with Reinsurer Mulder. Suppose the premium is $50 million, the policy limit is $75 million, and the cover is retroactive. If the event *did* occur and caused $50 million of damage, Scully has essentially used the finite transaction to make a $50 million *deposit* with Mulder. If the event did *not* occur, Scully is still assured of getting $50 million back (plus interest and less expenses). Again, Scully has made a deposit.

Early Termination and Tear-Up Agreements   Some finite risk deals include early termination provisions. In and of itself, this does not necessarily reduce the risk transfer component of a structure. It depends entirely on how the program is structured. If a program allows for early termination in such a way that the premium reverts back to the cedant, a tear-up clause can function much like an abused low claims bonus—as a means by which a premium *deposit* is returned to a cedant without any real risk transfer occurring in the process.

EXAMPLES OF LEGITIMATE USES OF FINITE

Despite the opportunities for finite risk structures to be abused, the real economic benefits they can provide for firms cannot be forgotten. Importantly, there have been numerous instances where abuses do *not* appear to have occurred—where, in fact, finite risk turned out to be a creative and effective corporate risk management solution. Let's examine a few of those cases here.

Ring-Fencing an Environmental Liability with Finite

The Iron Mountain Copper Mine is a Superfund site in Redding, California, owned by the Stauffer Management Co. of Wilmington, Delaware.[5] Stauffer Management is the sole potentially responsible party (PRP) under Superfund, which generally holds any PRP to a Superfund site jointly and severally liable for the entire cleanup costs of that site. Stauffer Management became the PRP to Iron Mountain because it manages the assets and liabilities of the former Stauffer Chemical Company, which acquired Mountain Copper Ltd. in the 1960s. It was Mountain Copper's mining operations above and below ground that fractured Iron Mountain, creating the Superfund liability by exposing the mountain's mineral deposits to oxygen, water, and bacteria and thereby generating substantial acidic runoff.

Mining operations ceased at Iron Mountain in 1963, at which time the federal government developed the Spring Creek Debris Dam to control the release of acidic water runoff from the mine. The Environmental Protection Agency (EPA) listed Iron Mountain as a Superfund site in 1983 with Stauffer as the sole PRP responsible for its cleanup. Eleven years later, the State of California and the EPA concluded the dam was not enough and ordered Stauffer to begin removing all the contaminants from the water.

Stauffer Management settled its Superfund claim in 2000 with the EPA and several other federal and California agencies for approximately $160 million.[6] Of that amount, $7.1 million was a settlement with the EPA, $10 million represented a mandatory contribution to other federal and California agencies for future regional environmental improvement projects, and $139.4 million was the premium Stauffer paid for a finite risk LPT obtained from American International Specialty Lines Insurance Co., a subsidiary of AIG. The structure of the LPT is shown in Exhibit 24.3.

Under the LPT agreement, the parties have agreed to contract IT Corp. for the actual cleanup of the Iron Mountain site. The parties estimated the cost of cleanup to be about $4.1 million per annum over the next three decades for an inflation-adjusted total of about $201 million. Under the finite risk policy, Stauffer cedes all of its past, current, and future liabilities on the Iron Mountain site to AIG along with the finite risk premium. The premium payment of $139.4 million was funded by Stauffer out of its current cleanup reserves for the site, plus some insurance coverage under prior policies.

The LPT agreement then obliges AIG to reimburse IT Corp. for 90 percent of the actual cleanup costs incurred each year on the Iron Mountain site up to a maximum of $4.1 million per year. IT Corp. bears the risk of higher annual clean-up costs subject to two other protections. First, if inflation causes an increase in costs by up to $900,000 in a single year, IT

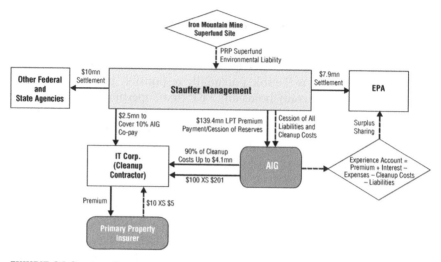

EXHIBIT 24.3   Stauffer Management Loss Portfolio Transfer for Iron Mountain Copper Superfund Site

Corp. can carry forward that additional cost into a subsequent year in which costs are below $4.1 million. Second, AIG also provides IT Corp. with $100 million in aggregate XOL coverage for cost overruns specifically triggered by catastrophic perils such as excessive rainfall or earthquakes, subject to a $5 million limit per peril.

IT Corp. must finance the remaining 10 percent of its actual annual cleanup costs as a co-payment on the finite risk policy, although Stauffer agreed to prepay in a lump sum approximately $2.5 million to IT Corp. that it can use toward its 10 percent residual co-pay requirement. IT Corp. bears all of the timing risk on how that additional 10 percent in costs is accrued, as well as the timing risks on the cleanup costs themselves. In return, the finite risk policy includes a type of experience account in which IT Corp. retains some of the surplus if aggregate cleanup costs fall below $201 million over the next 30 years. The EPA receives another portion of that surplus, if it exists.

Covering the Excess Layer for Asbestos Liability with Finite

Turner & Newall, a United Kingdom motor components manufacturer, utilized an ADC to combat a concern among investors and analysts that it had inadequately reserved against a major liability.[7] The liability for

Turner & Newall was a series of asbestos claims associated with some of its discontinued operations.

Turner & Newall self-insured its asbestos claims by establishing a captive and then reinsured some of that underwriting risk with an ADC for $815mn XS $1,125mn. The ADC had a 15-year tenor and, like other finite risk products, contained an agreement for a partial premium rebate if actual loss developments were favorable relative to its reserve holdings after the 15 years.

Ring-Fencing the Liabilities of a Discontinued Business with Finite

In a more general case, the multinational firm Hanson PLC was concerned when it acquired building materials company Beazer PLC that Beazer's discontinued U.S. operations would create an impediment to growth for the new conglomerate. Hanson self-insured the liabilities of Beazer's U.S. operations through a captive, and the captive, in turn, acquired $80mn XS $100mn in an ADC in perpetuity.[8] Specifically, Hanson ring-fenced the liabilities of Beazer's discontinued U.S. operations using an ADC.

Exiting a Business Line (Runoff Solution) Using Finite

Frontier Insurance Company was a specialized property/casualty insurer that ran into financial problems in 2000.[9] It had $70 million in debt and had suffered significant losses on its physicians malpractice insurance line. Frontier's losses were due both to inadequate reserves to cover total losses *and* to the unexpectedly rapid development of losses on the portfolio. Frontier had to replenish reserves several times to cover the time path of claims.

In the second quarter of 2000, Frontier entered into an option on a bundled finite risk agreement with Berkshire Hathaway's National Indemnity. If exercised, the option delivered $800 million in coverage to Frontier, of which $514 million was an ADC that created XOL reinsurance for any aggregate losses in excess of Frontier's then-current reserves. The remaining $286 million in cover involved a cession of its current reserves to National Indemnity through an LPT, thus protecting Frontier from further unexpected accelerations in the timing of its claims submissions. National Indemnity thus allowed Frontier to transfer the underwriting risks and finance the timing risks of its existing physicians malpractice line. In other words, National Indemnity allowed Frontier to finance its timing risks by replacing its reserves with synthetic debt and enabled the insurer to transfer its excess underwriting risks and replace those risks with synthetic equity.

Frontier exercised its option to obtain the $800 million in coverage in late 2000. After ring-fencing its liabilities in this manner, Frontier was able to cleanly exit this line of business and withdraw from the market in 2001.

Partially Funding a High Retention

A large energy firm found that its mandated retentions had escalated to $5 million for property, boiler and machinery, mechanical breakdown, and transmission and distribution (T&D) coverage, but the firm was only comfortable that it could prefund $2.5 million of those retentions. Its reinsurer—Zürich Corporate Solutions—helped the client convert the $2.5 XS $2.5 layer of its retention into a more fungible layer of debt capital through an unfunded finite program that blended a $2.5 XS $2.5 postloss risk finance layer with a $5 XS $5 layer of pure risk transfer (using an integrated multiline program, as will be discussed in Chapter 25).

This example illustrates that unfunded programs need not be problematic just because they are unfunded. Like many unfunded programs, the unfunded risk finance layer is unfunded because the firm is not comfortable retaining that layer of risk but simply cannot obtain risk transfer coverage at that layer. Rather than leave the risk unaddressed (and hence borne by equity holders), the firm essentially enters into a contingent debt facility to fund the part of its retention between the lower attachment point that it *can* fund and the lower attachment point of the true risk transfer layer.

Replacing a Nonrenewed Integrated Multiline, Multiyear Program[10]

A professional services firm had been relying on a multiline, multiyear integrated program (see Chapter 25 for a discussion of such programs) for its financial lines coverage. When that program did not renew, the services firm also found that replacing certain of the coverage lines in the traditional single-year, single-line market was prohibitively expensive *and* that coverage was available only at extremely high attachment points. Not only was the company unable to secure the coverage it wanted on fiduciary liability and on a blanket bond, but the services firm had contracts with customers that *required* errors and omissions (E&O) coverage at specified limits that the firm could no longer obtain. Apart from facing extraordinarily high rates at undesirably high attachment points, the firm literally found its core business at risk from its seeming inability to insure noncore E&O risks.

AIG Risk Finance proposed a blended E&O, fiduciary liability, and blanket bond finite program. The program involved a combination of retentions, co-insurance, high aggregate limits, premium installment payments, retrospectively rated premiums, and more, but ultimately delivered a solution that secured the desired coverage.

This program again illustrates that unfunded or partially funded finite solutions are not always problematic. It also illustrates, however, the need to be careful in representing a program accurately. If the customers of this firm simply require E&O exposure indemnification, an unfunded finite program like the one described will work fine. But the company would want to be careful in its representations to be clear that some portion of this exposure has been *financed*. In the end, AIG has indeed covered the risk, but it has done so by financing a part of the risk. The customer in this or a similar case probably would *not* want to claim that the insurance program was 100 percent *risk transfer* or equivalent to classical indemnity insurance. But provided it is disclosed properly and conforms to the requirements set forth by the firm's customers, the program is quite sensible on its face.

SOUND PRINCIPLES FOR FINITE

In today's environment, like it or not, some users of finite should be losing sleep—and will lose more as regulatory scrutiny increases and litigation builds. Yet, properly used and disclosed, finite is a valuable risk management tool. Indeed, some firms *not* using finite may be avoiding it at the expense of their shareholders, risking sleepless nights in their future for not managing risks that finite can help mitigate.

Like junk bonds in the 1980s and derivatives in the 1990s, finite risk invites scrutiny mainly because it is not well understood and has been associated with a few high-profile abuses. One thing we know about financial innovation: accounting, disclosure, and regulation have a hard time keeping up. What's a responsible firm to do?

Finite with Principles

With the recent attacks on finite, the best prophylactic for current and potential users is to hunker down and determine whether finite is appropriate for them, and most importantly, that it is being accounted for and disclosed properly. After the so-called derivatives losses of the mid-1990s, many firms undertook "derivatives risk audits." Then as now, sound advice to firms thinking of what finite means to them is to implement a similar "insurance risk and disclosure audit."

Those seeking a simple checklist of things to do to make finite acceptable to them won't fund it. As with *all* structured finance and structured insurance, there are too many variations on deal terms and themes to draw sweeping generalizations—a fact that some regulators may have forgotten, as well. There simply is no list of magic conditions that are both necessary and sufficient to make finite or any other structured program okay.

We can, however, get halfway there and identify a few conditions that are necessary for responsible transacting, even if not always sufficient. The principles presented below were developed by the head of an ART practice at a major reinsurer and are adapted to the text here with permission.

Economic Purpose   A structured transaction should be undertaken because it is consistent with firm value maximization and because it fits into the integrated risk and capital management strategy of the firm that we explored in Part One. If an economically motivated deal can also be structured to achieve desirable accounting, tax, and regulatory treatment, *great*! But the underlying motivation for the deal should not be to reverse engineer a specifically desired tax or accounting target.

Transparency   Here's an easy litmus test: If the only way that a structured finance or insurance deal makes sense is that *no one finds out you did it*, then *don't do it*. As obvious as this seems, don't forget that a lot of the structuring business does involve proprietary modeling and product design. There is a natural tension between the desire to disclose details of a deal to assuage any concerns or misunderstandings about their economic purpose and the desire to keep costly proprietary information internal. But in this market, the scale is tipped toward the former. Without adequate transparency and disclosure, it is likely that the deal will get misunderstood or questioned. So, the real question is whether, if the deal is worth doing, it is worth disclosing—in detail.

At a minimum, disclosure about the economic purpose and basic design of structured programs should be included in the management disclosure and analysis section of 10-Ks. Better still is actually to provide descriptive information about the deal publicly—on the firm's web site, through interviews with key financial reporters, and the like.

Adverse Selection and Cookie Jars   Beware of cookie jars. Fear of cookie jars is one reason that security markets are markets for lemons in the first place, as we explored in Chapter 4. Structured insurance and finite can often be *remedies* to cookie jar problems, but, of course, they can also themselves create cookie jars; for example, trying to classify a retroactive cover (i.e., deposit) as insurance is just moving earnings around in time and is a classic cookie jar problem.

Attention should be paid to making structures *credible*, and part of this means making them *intelligible*. Overengineered deals in a post-Enron world immediately raise suspicions that there is a cookie jar lurking somewhere inside those hundreds of SPEs and finite deals.

One way to avoid the cookie jar syndrome in the finite area is to utilize finite mainly for *noncore business risks*. When finite is used on a core risk that is directly under management's control, moral hazard comes into play and there is too much temptation to use the program specifically to achieve a desired earnings result. When finite is applied to noncore risks, management cannot affect the outcome of the risk, and the firm's earnings do not depend so critically on the result. So there is less temptation to trade dollars around.

Quality of Earnings   As we explained in Chapters 5 and 6, earnings will never be a good substitute for cash flows, and yet we must tolerate and live with earnings—and with the fact that a lot of others also pay attention to earnings. In using structured finance and insurance products, the best way to evaluate earnings is the quality of information earnings convey, not the number itself.

We have already explained in this chapter how finite can be used to enhance the quality of earnings. When a firm cannot take an accounting reserve for a loss that is hard to estimate (i.e., the recovery is possible but not probable), traditional insurance is a good alternative. But when risk transfer is either not desired at lower retentions or not available, using finite as a credible alternative to a loss reserve makes the firm's earnings *more informative* than just setting aside cash that investors cannot see and that does not impact the firm's earnings.

This sword cuts both ways, of course. Most finite programs increase shareholder equity or, for insurance companies, the surplus by replacing an unknown stream of liabilities with a known premium outlay. That can be an accurate representation of the economics of the deal if the finite structure contains adequate risk transfer. But if not, finite can be used to conceal leverage and overstate the value of equity, thus diminishing the informativeness of financial statements and earnings.

Users of finite should regularly ask themselves the following question: Does this transaction make my financial statements more closely represent the true cash flows and risks of the business? If not, then consider disclosing the purpose and impact of the deal in excruciating detail, or just not doing the deal. Alternatively, consider asking: Does this deal make my firm look financially stronger than it really is? If yes, then don't do it.

Financial Flexibility   Structured insurance is generally intended to help firms optimize their risk and capital and their debt/equity mix. Programs that lock firms into inflexible solutions often are at odds with the corporate finance drivers that led firms to consider those solutions in the first place.

As we have noted, too much flexibility in a finite deal can limit the true risk transfer that occurs, and users must be attentive of this. At the same time, some flexibility is what makes these structures more desirable than more rigid alternatives like captives or traditional insurance.

A Cautionary Policy Note

At the policy level, we urge deliberateness. Ambiguous accounting and disclosure rules added to a post-Enron siege mentality have led to a guilty-before-proven-innocent attitude toward finite and its users. Yet, each case should be carefully evaluated on its own with awareness that finite can be used properly as well as abused. Rushing to judgment about finite is tempting, but dangerous. Consider how much insurance industry capital has already been burned up by the regulatory bulls in the china shop to date. Yes, abusers of finite must be held accountable. At the same time, a firm is innocent until proven guilty, even in highly complex insurance matters. Let these firms have their day in court before drawing conclusions.

CHAPTER 25

Multiline and Multitrigger Insurance Structures

Enterprise-wide risk management (EWRM) *as a business process* allows firms to exploit risk management and corporate financing efficiencies through more comprehensive risk identification, measurement, and control.[1] In response to the increasingly widespread recognition of the importance of EWRM as a management tool, many of the major players in the reinsurance world began to offer *integrated risk management* (IRM) products designed to provide enterprise-wide risk transfer solutions. The simultaneous coverage of multiple risks and the ability of firms seeking IRM solutions to participate with the capital provider in any *ex post* profits have made them even more attractive, albeit to a select group of users to date.

Some of the IRM products reviewed here have been remarkably successful at helping firms manage their overall cost of capital and optimize their balance sheets, whereas other such IRM products have been dismal failures, culminating in the widely publicized dismantling of several IRM programs by such notable firms as Honeywell and Mobil Oil. In this chapter, we explore the mechanics, benefits, and costs of the two primary types of IRM products—multi*line* comprehensive risk transfer products, and multi*trigger* alternative risk transfer (ART) forms. In particular, we will attempt to distinguish between IRM ART forms that have come and gone as a passing fad versus those that seem to be here to stay and that can genuinely help firms revolutionize the way they finance themselves and manage their risks. Our discussions of the mechanics, benefits, and issues surrounding each of the two types of programs will each be followed with some successful examples and cases of the two program types.

MULTILINE INTEGRATED RISK TRANSFER

The relation between the sequencing of cumulative losses borne by risk transfer counterparties and the types of risk giving rise to those losses is often different for traditional and structured insurance products. Recall from Chapter 8 that traditional insurance and reinsurance programs are usually characterized by blended layering, or the allocation of risks into silos and the transfer of those risks in layers—either horizontal (i.e., each dollar loss is shared by different insurers); vertical (i.e., cumulative dollar losses are insured by different insurers based on the order in which the losses occur); or both. In several notable alternative risk transfer products, by contrast, risk and loss are now being combined into single integrated packages.

Blended versus Integrated Cover

The main distinction between a traditional blended insurance program that covers multiple risks and a truly integrated multiline program is the means by which capital is allocated to risk. A traditional multirisk blended layer insurance program covers multiple risks in name only. Each risk still has its own deductible, its own limits and attachment points, and its own capital. In a truly integrated multiline program, by contrast, a single block of capital is used to back multiple risks at the same time with a common deductible and a common limit. This distinction is probably best understood by way of an example.

Traditional Blended-Layer Silo-by-Silo Insurance   Consider, for example, a traditional program for, say, a multinationally active petrochemical firm. Suppose the firm manages the following risk through insurance and/or financial hedging on a traditional blended cover basis with the following attachment points per risk silo:

- *Property damage:* $7 XS $3 (primary).
- *Noncertified terrorism-related property damage:* $100 XS $100 (catastrophic).
- *Professional indemnity (PI):* $2 XS $1 (primary), $7 XS $3 (excess).
- *Directors and officers (D&O) (Side B):* $5 XS $1 (primary), $4 XS $6 (excess).
- *Product liability:* $90 XS $10 (excess).
- *Business interruption (BI):* $5 XS $5 (primary), $40 XS $10 (excess).
- *Foreign exchange (FX) risk:* $10 XS $0 (primary).
- *Oil price risk:* $50 XS $50 (excess).

The associated layer-cake diagram of coverage is shown on Exhibit 25.1. The program as a whole (excluding Side A D&O) gives the firm a total of $320 million in coverage relative to a $170 million retention.

Note that we excluded Side A D&O coverage from our total. The reason is that Side A D&O coverage is the part of a structured D&O program that is paid for by the company but for which directors and officers are the beneficiaries. This kind of coverage is essential to getting high-quality directors and officers, and it rarely involves a deductible. Although the company bears the expense of incurring the Side A coverage, the insurance is not an asset for the company. Side B D&O coverage, by contrast, is written in the name of the company and *is* a contingent asset of the firm. Side B coverage—which often *does* include a deductible—may be used to cover expenses incurred by the firm itself. Under the new Sarbanes-Oxley prohibitions on extensions of credit by firms to their directors and officers, however, it is the Side A coverage that really counts.

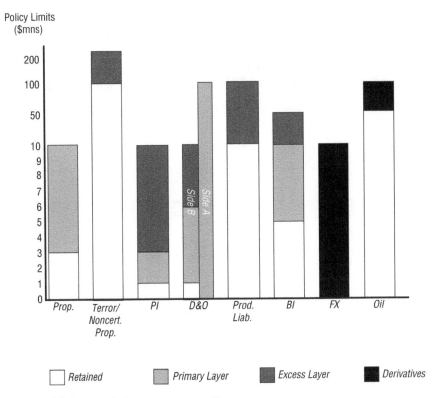

EXHIBIT 25.1 Blended Layer Insurance Program

Four types of coverage are shown on Exhibit 25.1. The first are the unshaded areas that represent retentions. The light gray areas represent primary insurance coverage. These coverage levels cover the firm's working capital layer and perhaps a bit more but do not constitute catastrophic coverage. The dark gray areas represent excess layers. Assume that all primary coverage is provided by a single carrier, and all excess coverage by a second insurance company. Finally, the black areas represent financial risks covered with derivatives.

Most of this program is vertically layered. Horizontal layering is evident in only the Side A D&O program. The Side A part of a D&O program is the D&O insurance that the company buys with its directors and officers as direct beneficiaries; this pays the directors and officers directly and is not an asset for the company. The other part of the D&O program reimburses the company before the directors and does represent a contingent asset of the company.

Integrated Multiline Coverage Now consider an integrated multiline version of a similar program for the same firm. For comparability, suppose the program is a one-year program that provides coverage for the same risks as the traditional blended layer program (except Side A D&O, which we treat separately for reasons noted earlier). Now, however, the multiline program—shown in Exhibit 25.2—defines a single aggregate

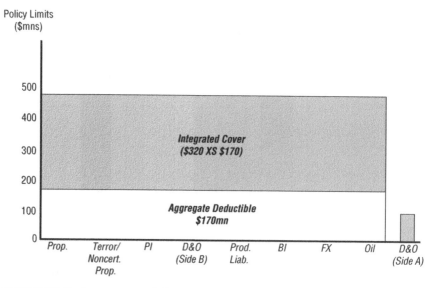

EXHIBIT 25.2 Integrated Multiline Program

annual deductible of $170 million and a single aggregate annual policy limit of $490 million, thus providing $320 XS $170 in _integrated_ cover. _Any_ recorded loss arising from _any_ risk counts toward the deductible and the policy limit. A single property damage claim of $500 million will satisfy the entire deductible and exhaust the entire program. Five $100 million claims for property damage, product liability, PI, BI, and D&O Side B will exhaust the program just as quickly.

In this example, the total retention and coverage provided are identical in the traditional and integrated programs, and we have not taken into account a number of specific features that multiline programs usually have. Our objective thus far is just to be clear about what the basic difference is in the traditional and integrated structures, but now we turn to look at the features of multiline programs with a more realistic perspective.

Features of Multiline Programs

As a practical matter, multiline policies may be created using either the "attachment method" or the "single text method."[2] If the attachment method is used, several individual policies are grouped together or "attached" using a single master agreement that creates the integrated risk policy. The single text method, by contrast, involves the drafting of a new agreement that encompasses the terms of all the component agreements. The former is generally cheaper, but requires significant attention to conflicts and overlaps in definitions and policy terms.

Unlike the simplified example in the prior section, most multiline programs are _multiyear_—that is, they involve a single premium, deductible, and limit that applies for the life of the program, which is often three to five years. The premium may be paid periodically over the life of the program, but it is not reset annually as in traditional structures. Some IRM products also combine risk- or occurrence-specific limits with aggregate limits to help firms further customize their exposures.

Because of their multiyear nature, integrated multiline programs usually have optional reinstatement provisions. This is essentially an option to reinstate an exhausted limit for an additional premium. Reinstatement of a limit can be expensive, but this option can also be very valuable, especially early in the life of the program. Imagine that six months into a three-year program, a one-time $400 million Side B D&O claim is filed. The deductible is hit and the program reimburses the firm for $310 million of losses. But without a reinstatement provision, the firm is then in the awkward position of essentially being _uninsured on all the risks in the policy for the next two and a half years._ At a time like that, the cost of reinstatement may not seem as bad as the alternative of remaining uncovered.

Multiline programs may also have optional catastrophic drop-downs or attachments to specific risks to allow the firm to supplement the limit on a single risk. Imagine, for example, that our chemical firm wanted $100 XS $400 in noncertified property coverage. The firm could arrange to have this "snapped on" to the integrated program in Exhibit 24.2.

Finally, some multiline programs include a low claims bonus rebate feature that enables the insured to participate in their own positive loss development experience (and perhaps investment income) alongside the insurer in certain circumstances.

Potential Benefits and Rationale

Integrated risk management products arose in the 1990s as a response to the perceived need for enterprise-wide risk management *products* that matched EWRM *processes* that corporations were beginning to put in place, as we discussed in Chapter 2. In particular, many believed that the well-known efficiencies associated with identifying, measuring, and monitoring risk from an EWRM perspective (Culp 2001) could be repeated at the transactional level as well. IRM products thus arose as an explicit effort to reduce some of the inefficiencies known to be associated with classical silo-by-silo risk transfer products.

Let's explore some of these apparent benefits of integrated multiline coverage in the following subsections.

Capital Efficiency   One major inefficiency often associated with a traditional blended layer (re)insurance program is the overcommitment of capital such programs can engender. Consider again the layered program in Exhibit 25.1 in which at least one separate policy cover is taken out for each risk. Such a structure achieves a full risk transfer for each risk *and* over time. But if the occurrence of large losses *across risks* is not perfectly correlated, the firm will never actually need all of this insurance capacity *at the same time*. If foreign exchange losses and property damage do not occur at the same time, for example, allocating capacity to the expected or worst-case loss on a risk-specific basis *badly overinsures the firm*. On a correlation-adjusted portfolio basis, the *total* loss exposure of the firm is lower than the sum of the two individual risk silos.

IRM products can, in principle, help address this problem in two ways. First, firms can allocate less capital to their risks at a lower total cost when correlations across both time and risk types are factored into the premium charged for the policy. Second, firms can achieve a more customized, tailor-made blanket of coverage that includes only those risks with which the firm is truly concerned about transferring to another party.

One-Stop Shopping Most multiline policies are provided by a single carrier, thus creating potentially significant "one-stop shopping" benefits for the corporate customer. At a basic level, the transaction costs, premium loading, and total arrangement fees may be significantly lower on the program (subject to a caveat we'll discuss a bit later). IRM products also usually have simplified renewal and/or reinstatement features.

Dealing with a single primary risk transfer counterparty can also benefit the customer and (re)insurer in terms of relationship management issues. The more comprehensive the program, the more the reinsurance provider of the IRM program will need to understand the business and risks of the client. This can lead to better overall customer relationship management than when each insurance policy is separately brokered and placed. The higher quality of information the (re)insurer acquires about the customer may also reduce adverse selection costs and lower the costs of information asymmetries.

From the company's perspective, one-stop shopping is a double-edged sword with regard to credit risk. On the one hand, the company does not need to engage in credit risk analysis and limits administration for a large number of carriers if a single provider is chosen through a multiline program. On the other hand, the company's credit risk is now completely undiversified—all its eggs are in the basket that assumes the (re)insurer will be both able and willing to pay its required claims on the policy. Not surprisingly, large-scale IRM programs have been offered only by the very top echelon and best-rated reinsurance companies globally.

"Mind the Gap" Many readers of this treatise have at some point in their lives probably ridden the London Underground or Heathrow Express. Part and parcel of the experience is the loud proclamation by the lady who tells us to "mind the gap" as we enter and exit the trains. Unfortunately, many corporations with complicated multirisk insurance programs have at some point or another stumbled into a gap—one carrier claims that a specific claim is covered by another carrier's policy and vice versa, two carriers dispute a definition that defines the nature of the claim, a single carrier disputes a claim altogether on the basis of incomplete representations and warranties, and so on. With these examples firmly in mind, IRM programs that rely on single-text drafting methods can be an extremely effective way of "minding the gap."[3]

One of the benefits of IRM programs most frequently cited by users of these products is the benefit of integrated documentation associated with IRM programs using the single text method. Because the single text method is a top-down, holistic approach to covering *all* risks, significant benefits can be realized through consistency in definitions and terminology, consistency across risk lines in representations and warranties, minimal overlaps, and reduced potential for ambiguities and coverage gaps. Do *not* underestimate the value of achieving consistency across insurance documentation!

Comprehensive Risk Identification That an IRM program (single text method) is a top-down holistic risk transfer structure also has the benefit of forcing the corporation to take a serious look at its total risk profile. As noted in Chapter 2, one of the key ingredients to a sound risk management process is the process by which a firm systematically *identifies* the risks to which it is subject. Many corporations resist the administrative burden and cost of having a separate risk identification exercise that is undertaken periodically, but that process suddenly serves double duty when it is already required for the construction of a multiline IRM program.

Users that have enjoyed successful experiences with IRM products regularly claim that one benefit is that it forces them to revisit the issue of enterprise-wide risk identification periodically. Again, this may seem minor, but it's not; this has been a real, pronounced benefit for firms that have properly used and implemented IRM programs together with their (re)insurance provider.

Obtaining Better Risk Layering for Problematic Exposures On a silo-by-silo basis, some (re)insurers are nervous about providing certain types of insurance coverage at low attachment points. Terrorism-related risk, certain product liability risks, many environmental risks, and the like often are difficult for corporations to transfer in lower-loss layers. But when these risks are combined in an integrated program, the *effective* attachment point suddenly becomes much closer to what the firm could not ever achieve on a stand-alone basis.

A good example of this concerns terrorism-related insurance—specifically, terrorism-related property, liability, or BI insurance claims. The federal Terrorism Risk Insurance Act of 2002 (TRIA) provides federally subsidized reinsurance for the coverage of certain terrorism-related risks underwritten by primary carriers through the end of December 2005. In its current form, the program provides up to 90 percent reinsurance for all eligible claims in excess of deductibles up to a program cap of $100 billion per year. Eligibility requires, among other things, that the claims being reinsured are a direct result of a *certified* act of terrorism. Certification is required by the secretary of the Treasury in concurrence with the attorney general and secretary of state and applies only to an event that causes in excess of $5 million in damage and is

> *a violent act or an act that is dangerous to human life, property or infrastructure and is committed by an individual or individuals acting on behalf of any foreign person or foreign interest, as part of an effort to coerce the civilian population of the United States or to influence the policy or affect the conduct of the United States Government by coercion.*

Many insurers and reinsurers are still reluctant to provide coverage for terrorism-related losses, except as mandated. Exclusions in coverage can arise from policy exclusions on which the (re)insurer insists or coverage gaps under TRIA. In either case, a corporation may seek cover that simply does not attach until losses are already significant. In the example in Exhibit 25.1, the firm has sought protection for *noncertified* terrorism-related property damage but was able to obtain this coverage only in the $100 XS $100 layer.

When this is combined into an IRM program, the total deductible is $170 million, but because this now covers *all* risks, the *effective* portion of the deductible to noncertified terrorism-related property damage is much lower than before. In principle, the aggregate deductible level should be set in an IRM to cover the firm's desired retention *on a portfolio basis*, recognizing that all risks will not result in simultaneous losses. When the cross-line correlations are taken into account, the deductible in an IRM program may well be much lower than the sum of the first-loss retentions in the traditional program. Especially in this case, the coverage and access a firm can achieve to exotic risk coverage like terrorism may be much more comprehensive in an IRM program than on a stand-alone basis.

Beware the Illusion of Cost Savings

Some multiline policies have been very successful, whereas others have been dismal failures. In some cases, products marketed by large and reputable reinsurance firms were never bought and subsequently taken off the market entirely, whereas in other cases the failures involved actually dismantling of multiline programs by their buyers. These failures have led many to question the viability of multiline policies.

Practitioners, commentators, and even providers of multiline products have given several reasons for the failure of multiline products to take off.[4] A major reason frequently cited is that some of the providers of early solutions emphasized the nature of multiline products as off-the-shelf products rather than tailor-made risk transfer solutions.[5] Similarly, many IRM products have met with little success because they tried to emphasize cost savings rather than optimal risk transfer or capital efficiency—and these are *not* the same thing. In particular, aggressive multiline policies can create significant costs for the insurance provider that are difficult to recover if the main selling point of the product is a lower premium.

Especially when the program includes financial risks, the (re)insurer will rarely wish to retain 100 percent of the risk exposures in all categories. Consequently, the (re)insurer is still faced with hedging, reinsuring, or retroceding the risks it is not prepared to retain. Integrating risks in the same policy allows the firm to charge a lower premium *in principle* because imperfect correlations across underwriting and timing risks allow better diversification. But unless the (re)insurer can hedge or reinsure the risks it does not wish to retain *using a similarly integrated product*, the cost to the (re)insurer will essentially be the sum of the premiums of the risk transfer solutions for each risk managed separately.

In other words, many IRM products allow a (re)insurer to offer an integrated solution but in turn merely push the unbundling problem back one level. Because a (re)insurer will not offer policies at a loss, the *load* added to the original deal thus must ultimately still reflect the cost of risk transfer undertaken on a risk-by-risk basis.

A highly publicized illustration of this problem was the placement of an IRM solution with Honeywell that covered traditional insurance risks plus the foreign exchange risk facing the company. When Honeywell merged with AlliedSignal, an assessment of the IRM program revealed that had Honeywell purchased separate insurance policies and engaged in classical hedging solutions to address its foreign exchange risk, it would have ended up with a cheaper risk transfer solution. Accordingly, the program was terminated and dismantled.

Mobil Oil also dismantled an IRM product—Swiss Re's BETA—in 1999 for the same reasons. And Utah-based petrochemical company Huntsman claims this was the reason it opted not to buy the Risk Solutions product offered by XL Capital and Cigna in the first place, claiming that its coverage with 30 different insurers was simply cheaper than the proposed combined policy.[6]

Most of the negative experiences associated with IRM programs to date seem to be primarily—albeit not entirely—related to the *financial* risk component, where reinsurers simply have no cost advantage in offering protection vis-à-vis using stand-alone derivatives. For this reason, some major providers of IRM solutions simply will no longer include financial risks in IRM multiline programs.

Risk Integration: From Two to Many

The risks covered by these programs range from two to many. Let's consider first an example of a simple two-risk IRM program and then turn to consider the more comprehensive programs.

Two-Risk Example: The Cigna-XL Property/Casualty Twinpack

At the more focused end of the IRM spectrum are products now sometimes known as "Twinpacks" that only bundle two related risks. A very popular such product was the joint offering by Cigna and XL Capital (an insurance provider that, along with the (re)insurance group Ace Ltd gained prominence for being only catastrophic capital providers in their early days). The Cigna/XL Twinpack covers high-layer property and casualty losses. Customers usually retain aggregate losses below about $2 million per annum, and then either seek traditional insurance for $6 million to $10 million in excess of that $2 million lower attachment point.[7]

Exhibits 25.3 through 25.5 illustrate the distinction between the traditional separate-silo approach to property and casualty insurance and the ART multiline approach of Twinpacks. In Exhibit 25.3, a traditional two-silo approach is shown in which a firm buys two separate and independent policies for property and casualty coverage. Each policy has a $2 million annual deductible or lower attachment point, and each provides coverage of $6 million. In Exhibit 25.4, the integrated multiline version of the same policy is shown, where the aggregate deductible is now $4 million and the aggregate policy limit is $16 million. Both programs thus provide up to $12 million in coverage and a $4 million retention. The difference is entirely in how that $12 million capital and $4 million deductible are allocated to the two risks.

Exhibit 25.5 highlights the differences in coverage provided by the multiline policy. The white and black regions of the figure are common to both programs—the white being the common retention, and the black the common area of coverage. The two gray areas highlight the trade-off between the two programs. In short, moving from the two-policy program to the integrated Twinpack forces the firm to give up the coverage areas in light gray as new retentions but in turn creates new coverage areas shaded in dark gray.

The major distinction between the programs can be seen if we focus on either a catastrophic property or casualty claim year. Suppose, for example, that property losses are negligible but casualty claims approach the $16 million limit in a year. The Twinpack provides better coverage by reimbursing $12 million of damages. In the two-policy program, by contrast, $6 million is reimbursed and the other $8 million in capital sits idly by unused on the property policy.

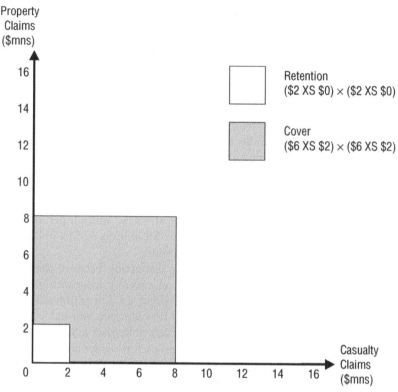

EXHIBIT 25.3 Traditional Property/Casualty Two-Silo Cover

This beneficial aspect of the Twinpack, however, is also its biggest cost. Now suppose that the firm incurs a single-occurrence $16 million casualty loss in the first week of a one-year program. The firm is still fully reimbursed by nonretained cover of $12 million, but the firm is now completely uninsured for the rest of the year. And if the program happens to be multiyear, the uncovered period may be much longer!

This really encapsulates the simultaneous blessing-and-curse nature of IRM programs very nicely. In a traditional program, capital is allocated risk by risk. This can be extremely inefficient if losses arising from those risks have a low or negative correlation. But if large losses across risks are highly correlated, the integrated program can actually create more problems than it solves. This is ultimately an empirical problem.

Also worth noting is that all of our examples have tried to keep apples-to-apples comparisons in which the total retention and the total cover

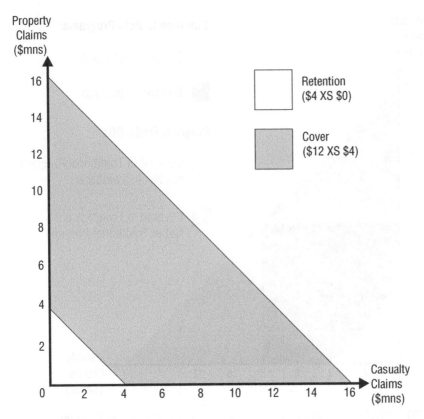

EXHIBIT 25.4 Property/Casualty Twinpack

in the traditional and IRM programs are the same. Of course this won't be the case most of the time! The real benefits from these programs can best be extracted when the corporate client works closely with the structuring agent to optimize the attachment points to the actual empirical correlations across risks. When risks are strongly negatively correlated across time, the IRM program can facilitate a lower total attachment point and/or a higher combined limit than the stand-alone programs *if* those correlations are properly analyzed and factored into the attachment points.

This highlights again the importance of the "relationship benefit" of IRM programs. Having a single risk capital provider/(re)insurer that is willing to spend time and effort to help a client really get the most out of a program like this is the key to its success. (Re)insurers that try to offer this

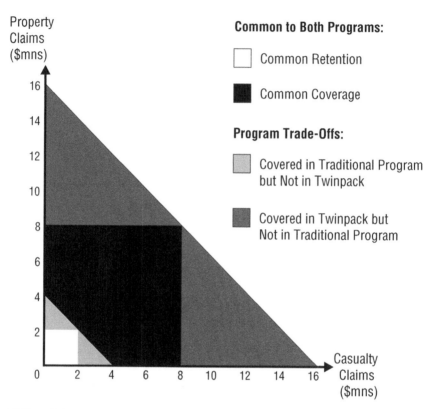

EXHIBIT 25.5 Comparison of Twinpack to Traditional Two-Silo Program

sort of product on a commodized or turnkey basis, by contrast, are unlikely to meet with the same degree of success.

As also noted, however, structuring a program like this to optimize the client's risk capital allocation across risks is costly. Although intuition says that two negatively correlated risks bundled into a Twinpack should lead to a cheaper policy, don't think of it that way. It will likely lead to *better coverage* and *better utilization of capital*, but the costs required to identify that optimal coverage bundle may more than offset the risk diversification benefit. The program still may be worth doing, however, even if it is more expensive. It all depends on the deadweight costs of suboptimally allocated risk capital and how the optimized-coverage program affects the client's weighted average cost of capital (WACC) and expected cash flows.

Comprehensive Firmwide Risk Programs   Many of the large reinsurance players have IRM product offerings. Some of the providers of these products include Centre Solutions (part of Zürich Financial), XL Capital, AIG, Munich-American Risk Partners, and Cigna. Some of these have been of the highly focused variety we saw in Twinpacks, but most—especially most of the early, initial product offerings—were far more ambitious. Again attempting to exploit the EWRM phenomenon, many early offerings were extremely comprehensive and stopped one step short of trying to provide earnings per share (EPS) insurance.

Swiss Re's Multi-line Aggregated and Combined Risk Optimization (MACRO), for example, was a multiline product aimed at nonfinancial corporations to help them bundle and tailor their exposure profiles and retention decisions. MACRO was a multiline, multiyear structure that had a single annual aggregate deductible, a single aggregate exposure limit, and occurrence-specific catastrophic excess of loss (XOL) supplements per risk silo at the customer's option. The program also allowed automatic or optional reinstatement if the customer wished to simplify rollover decisions.

In the case of AIG's Commodity-Embedded Insurance (COIN), the objective was to provide a product that delivered very close to EPS insurance. By including essentially all the major risk exposures that a firm might face, a multiline policy essentially functions as a synthetic equity infusion for the firm that can be accessed any time total annual losses exceed the deductible. AIG's Snow, Temperature, or Rain Management (STORM) program is a similar EPS insurance structure with a bias toward helping firms manage adverse weather-related events.

EXAMPLES OF MULTILINE STRUCTURES

Although integrated IRM multiline policies are not for all firms, those that identify the right counterparty, are attentive to structuring issues, are aware of the impact of customized and integrated risk management on total premium outlays, and are able to identify a correlation structure across risks that argues for integration can potentially reap significant benefits from IRM programs. Union Carbide renewed a major multiline IRM product in 2000,[8] and both Mead Corp. and Sun Microsystems claim to have saved over 20 percent by consolidating their numerous risk transfer policies into a single structure.[9]

We next consider several specific examples of successful IRM multiline programs. Let's pay particular attention to what it is that made these programs successful in the eyes of their users. Note that some of the firms and deal terms are not disclosed, but this should not be interpreted to mean they are not real. All examples discussed are real deals that closed to the best of my knowledge.

Large National Nursing Home[10]

A large national nursing home with several substantial product liability claims over the past decade sought coverage in excess of a $20 million retention. Unfortunately, losses in the firm's $40 XS $20 layer had been especially erratic. In some policy years, that layer experienced no losses, whereas in other years the full limit of coverage was used. Exacerbated by a rapidly hardening market, the result was that a traditional single-year, single-line program was extremely expensive and not particularly well matched to the firm's *overall* risk tolerance and loss experience.

Working with AIG Risk Finance, the nursing home acquired a $40mn XS $20mn (per annum) integrated multiline, multiyear policy with a $110 million aggregate limit over the five years spanned by the program. Aggregating across risks and years stabilized the loss estimate and permitted much more favorable pricing.

Despite being comfortable with the $20 million retention layer, the program also included several added protections. First, optional drop-down coverage was available in the event that a high frequency of losses in the retention layer occurred in any given year whose *total* exceeds $40 million. Second, the program also included an optional "limit acceleration" feature that allowed it to accelerate annual limits for an additional premium, thereby enabling the nursing home to cover any extraordinarily large claims in a given year by borrowing capital from a future policy year. The optional drop-down and limit acceleration features represent *contingent cover* and are discussed again in Chapter 26.

This is an excellent example of precisely what multiline, multiyear programs are intended to accomplish. The firm was able to obtain customized coverage that was both capital-efficient and relatively much more favorably priced than if the firm had sought coverage on a single-year, monoline basis.

Large Telecom

Zurich Corporate Solutions (ZCS), a division of Zurich American Insurance Company, implemented a successful IRM program with a large telecom provider. Working with Marsh, ZCS was able to help the firm identify an integrated multiline program that achieved its two primary objectives: improve the cost-efficiency of its risk management program while simultaneously assuring stable multiyear capacity, and reduced the

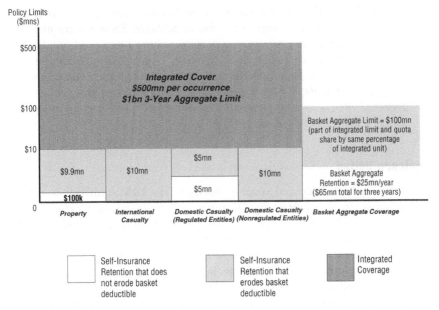

EXHIBIT 25.6 Zurich Corporate Solutions Multiline Program for a Large Telecom
Source: Zurich Corporate Solutions, a division of Zurich American Insurance Company.
Note: Y-axis is not to scale.

inefficiencies and administrative burdens of the more traditional silo-by-silo approach.

The program itself bundled property and casualty into a single integrated three-year structure. Limits were $500 million per occurrence and $1 billion for the term aggregate. ZCS was the lead arranger, but other reinsurers also participated in the program underwriting. Exhibit 25.6 illustrates the program in more detail.

The director of the telecom's risk management unit claims that the program was a huge success and helped the firm achieve both of its risk management objectives (cost-efficient access to stable multiyear capacity and reduced administrative burden). He explains:

> *In designing our global program, we wanted to make certain that we partnered with world-class markets and that capacity would be available over the term of the project. We have certainly achieved*

this goal. In addition, our integrated global program has insulated us from the drastic swings in market conditions. Since we are not starting from square one in negotiating pricing terms and conditions, we are much closer to a "routine" anniversary discussion than many of our peers who are attempting to negotiate complete program renewals. We look back and say that implementing an integrated program was a great idea back then—and it is an even better idea in today's market.[11]

Agricore United

One of the often-discussed success stories in the IRM multiline world is the program first adopted by Winnipeg, Canada–based United Grain Growers (UGG) and later renewed by Agricore United, created in 2001 by the merger of UGG and Agricore. Agricore United is Canada's leading farmer-directed agribusiness. It is the top seller of crop nutrition and crop protection products in Canada, one of Canada's leading grain handling and marketing businesses, and a major provider to farmers and end users of a complete line of products and services to help its customers market agricultural products domestically and internationally.

The Agricore United program is explored and analyzed in thoughtful detail in Chapter 34 by Harrington, Niehaus, and Risko. To review the program here would be entirely redundant. Their analysis is complete, and readers are directed there to learn more about it.

In brief, Agricore entered into a multiline program that pays off for below-expected revenues on grain sales. The program specifically covers grain handling volume, property damage, BI, and casualty risk. The primary attraction of the program to Agricore was that it helps Agricore optimize its overall coverage—that is, manage its capital more efficiently. The program also helped Agricore consolidate its coverage, thus reducing gaps, inconsistencies, and administrative burden. All around, Agricore and Swiss Re alike have deemed the program a huge success.

Fortune 500 Consumer Products Company[12]

An undisclosed Fortune 500 consumer products company had already implemented an integrated multiline program successfully and initially approached ZCS for additional capacity. Ultimately, the whole program was renegotiated with ZCS as the lead underwriter. The program bound in January 2002 and is shown in layer-cake form in Exhibit 25.7.

Again, a major attraction of this program to its buyer seems to have been customization. When the client first approached ZCS, it was already happy with its initial multiline cover and the providers of that cover. The client specifically indicated that it did not want to sacrifice the benefits of long-term relationships with the original program sponsor.

Yet, by their very nature, all IRM programs tend to be relationship-oriented. The addition of ZCS to the picture did *not* require the client to relinquish either its other program or its other relationships. On the contrary, it allowed the program to become bigger and more customized by adding features offered by ZCS that were not available in the original program.

This program also illustrates a truism for a lot of ART products. Like many of the structured finance solutions we examined in Part Three, structured insurance solutions are also very often provided by *many* reinsurance firms. There is usually a single lead arranger and structuring agent, but the risk sharing often occurs in these programs cooperatively across several firms—if not up front, then on the back end through the reinsurance and retrocession markets.

Global Financial Services Company[13]

A global financial services company with more than 100 operating subsidiaries around the world was concerned about the combined risk of high-frequency losses across financial lines insurance and the risk of a single catastrophic "shock loss." The firm was also having difficulty transfer pricing its financial lines insurance across its affiliates. Its 18 financial lines included unauthorized or rogue trading, computer crime, and a number of other exotic risks.

AIG Risk Finance structured a $200 million integrated program that was specifically intended to help the firm close its coverage gaps and tightly integrate its multiple risk exposures. In the program, AIG essentially provided multiline, multiyear coverage that "surrounded the client's existing coverages and filled key coverage gaps."[14]

Managing Supplier Credit Risk: An OEM Supplier[15]

A company manufactures consumer products on behalf of an original equipment manufacturer (OEM), and the OEM sells the products under its own name. The OEM supplier indemnifies the OEM for product liability

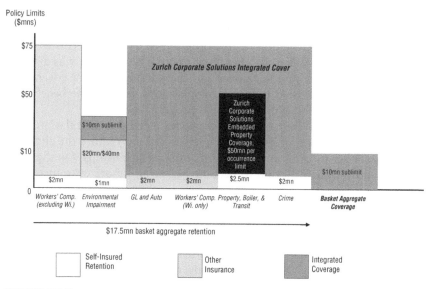

EXHIBIT 25.7 Consumer Products Company Multiline Program with Zurich Corporate Solutions
Source: Zurich Corporate Solutions, a division of Zurich American Insurance Company.
Note: Y-axis is not to scale.

risk that was historically secured with an excess of loss (XOL) product liability insurance policy.

In the 1990s as insurance markets hardened, the OEM supplier's retention on its product liability policy rose from several hundred thousand dollars per occurrence to several million per occurrence. The OEM supplier set up a captive and financed its retention in that manner, still relying on external XOL coverage for the high-loss layers.

For several years, the captive was an acceptable solution to the OEM. But because the captive was essentially *self*-insurance, the OEM started to build up a significant credit exposure to the OEM supplier (both in trade credit terms and on the product liability program). When this credit exposure reached a maximum tolerable level, the OEM demanded that the OEM supplier either prefund a defined limit of coverage with cash or replace some of the captive-insured retention layer with external coverage. The requested cash collateral amount was equal to the OEM's estimate of expected product liability losses plus a catastrophic layer. The OEM supplier maintained that this expected loss plus cat layer were collectively very unlikely to be reached and that fully funding that amount of its retention with cash was excessively and unnecessarily costly.

AIG Risk Finance structured a multiyear program that replaced the captive retention layer in the OEM supplier's product liability program. AIG worked with the OEM supplier to define the program's per-occurrence, annual, and aggregate limits based on historical losses that were much more in line with the OEM supplier's own reserve calculations than the collateral threshold demanded by the OEM. The OEM supplier also believed that continued improvements in its own processes would reduce those claims even further. The program thus included an experience account that provided a low claims bonus rebate in the event that premium plus investment income minus actual losses is returned to the OEM supplier at the end of the life of the program. Alternatively, the program contained a commutation option to terminate the AIG program early and assume all pending and future claims in exchange for a cash payment from AIG equal to the current value of the experience account.

This solution provides an excellent anecdotal illustration of how structuring can be an effective way of resolving the adverse consequences of asymmetric information. Clearly, the OEM demanded a much higher level of collateralization than did AIG because the two firms had radically different estimates of the potential product liability losses that could occur. The OEM, of course, had a strong incentive to be conservative, whereas with careful due diligence AIG was able to become comfortable with a much lower number collateralizing the same potential loss. The AIG cover was, of course, perfectly acceptable to the OEM, and the OEM supplier was able to secure protection at a cost much more in line with its own information and expectations.

MULTITRIGGER IRM PRODUCTS

All of the discussion in the prior section involved IRM products with a single trigger. As long as aggregate losses on the different risk silos covered by a multiline policy exceed the deductible, the policy is triggered and an indemnity payment can be sought for economic losses sustained. The single trigger is the condition that losses exceed the retention or deductible.

IRM products may also contain second triggers. Recall that we introduced second triggers in Chapter 15 when we discussed contingent capital.

In fact, most of the second-trigger products we reviewed were provided by (re)insurance companies, so it is not surprising to realize that many other ART forms apart from contingent capital also contain such second triggers. When we discussed second triggers in Chapter 15, we did so only in the context of contingent capital and, even for those products, our discussion was fairly preliminary. We return to this concept now and discuss second triggers in more detail: how they can be structured, why they can make sense, and some examples of firms that have benefited from their inclusion in an ART program.

Mechanics of Multitrigger Structures

In an indemnity contract, at least one trigger is always that the insured party sustains economic losses arising from an insurable interest. Many traditional insurance products also include a second trigger tied to the occurrence of a discrete event, such as the realization of a hazard (e.g., a flood occurs). In insurance parlance, the occurrence of the flood *and* the loss resulting from the flood are viewed *together* as a single trigger: It is a *flood-related loss* above the lower attachment point that triggers the policy.

In keeping with insurance jargon, we thus consider "discrete" triggers like the occurrence of an accident to be part of the terms of a policy and the definition of an insurable interest—in other words, part of the *first* trigger. When we consider multiple triggers here, we thus will always be considering triggers specifically intended to go beyond the traditional policy condition of an event-related loss.

Triggers and Moral Hazard   Doherty (2000) classifies triggers as either "internal" or "external," where the former is based on some variable specific to the cedant or corporate insurance purchaser (e.g., bad earnings) and where the latter is outside the immediate control of the firm—for example, the gross domestic product (GDP) trigger on the Michelin deal we examined in Chapter 15.

Although risk transfer solutions based only on internal triggers do exist, they are not very common. And we should not be terribly surprised by this. The first trigger in a (re)insurance program is that the cedant incurs a specific loss and thus is already under the control of the insurance purchaser and hence subject to moral hazard. The addition of a second trigger that is also under the control of the insurer would expose the (re)insurance provider to significant moral hazard. Even if payment on the contract is valued and not indemnity, basing a trigger solely on variables under the firm's control can mitigate the firm's incentive to manage its risks effectively and can even create perverse incentives for fraud or deliberate under-performance. Accordingly, double trigger ART forms usually involve at least one external trigger.

As noted earlier, reinsurers are very reluctant to include financial risks in multiline programs. And for good reason—as said before, the reinsurer has no comparative advantage in bearing and underwriting that risk and would likely just hedge the risk through with derivatives, passing on the costs of the hedge to the customer and suggesting the customer would have been better off going to a derivatives dealer on its own. An unwillingness of the reinsurer to *underwrite* financial risk, however, does not mean the reinsurer is unwilling to allow financial risk-based *policy triggers*. On the contrary, conditioning a program on a second external trigger that is financial can be attractive for both the reinsurer and the customer. Financial variables are highly transparent and hard to manipulate, thus keeping moral hazard and adverse selection costs to a minimum. And this may be a good way for the corporation to get some protection against financial risk without asking the reinsurer to underwrite that risk in a classical risk transfer arrangement.

Fixed versus Variable versus Switching Triggers A *fixed* trigger is a Boolean or binary operator that is either "on" or "off" based entirely on whether some condition is satisfied. A flood either has or has not occurred and caused damage. An adverse stock price change of 10 percent or more either has or has not occurred. A decline in the insurance purchaser's earnings before interest, taxes, depreciation, and amortization (EBITDA) either is or is not greater than a decline in an EBITDA index. And so on. In a program with a fixed second trigger, the payout is almost always independent of the second trigger. In other words, just like a barrier option, the second trigger determines *when* the contract pays but does not affect *how much*.

A *variable* trigger is a functional relationship between the risk being underwritten and some other variable risk parameter. When the variable trigger is a second trigger on insurance of only a single risk, the variable trigger can usually be expressed as an index to which the deductible of the program is tied.

Finally, a *switching* trigger is a trigger in a multiline policy that varies based on some weighting scheme of the multiple risks covered by the policy.[16]

Let's look at the differences in these three types of triggers with an example. First, we will discuss a monoline insurance program. Consider, for example, an A-rated oil company with relatively high leverage. The firm is concerned about business interruption and financial distress costs that will arise if it sustains too many losses on its distribution assets (e.g., pipelines).

All else being equal, the oil company considers this a core business risk and prefers to retain as much of that risk exposure as possible, but its credit rating and leverage do not permit this for catastrophic levels. So, the company buys catastrophic property insurance for its distribution assets. The question is how much and at what attachment point—that is, how much can the company afford to retain.

First, suppose that the oil company and its reinsurer work together to run the required simulations, stress tests, and correlation analyses and agree that losses to distribution assets above $500 million can be retained provided that oil prices remain above $35 per barrel. The oil company, moreover, is unable on its own to influence the market price of oil. A double-trigger program thus is constructed that reimburses the oil company for up to $750 million in actual losses to distribution assets in excess of $500 million, but *only* when oil prices are below $35 per barrel.

The amount of total coverage available on the policy has not changed—the policy still pays a maximum of $750 million. What is different is *when* the policy pays. By conditioning the program on the price of oil, the company and reinsurer have reduced the scenarios in which the policy pays out. All else being equal, this should reduce the premium on the cover by eliminating situations in which asset damage between the prescribed attachment points occurs but when the company does not need the reimbursement for that loss.

Now suppose that the oil company and reinsurer can actually go further than determining a discrete threshold at which BI and distress costs will begin to occur and a specific oil price level will be required to fund a retention. Instead, the reinsurer and oil company define a more general functional relationship between oil prices and damage to distribution assets. The higher the oil price, the more funds the oil company has to fund a retention and the higher the deductible on the insurance program for distribution assets can be. Conversely, lower oil prices facilitate a higher retention. In essence, a variable second trigger has *indexed the first-trigger deductible* to the price of oil.

The impact of a variable second trigger on cost depends on our point of comparison. Relative to a traditional program, premium should be lower because we have added restrictions on when the policy can be exercised. Whether the variable second-trigger program is cheaper than the fixed second-trigger program, however, depends on the exact nature of the variable relationship.

The third type of trigger is associated with multiline programs and is also a functional specification of a relationship between the two risks.

Technically, a switching trigger program is not double-trigger; the definition of the switching trigger includes all the information we need. The switching trigger is usually intended to reduce the total coverage in a program at all times except when the multiple risk exposures are *all* generating high claims.

Let's return to our earlier example of the property/casualty Twinpack. Exhibit 25.8 now illustrates the coverage area of the Twinpack with a switching trigger. Instead of a constant aggregate deductible at $4 million, the deductible now depends on the performance of the two underwriting portfolios. When property losses are extremely low, the casualty deductible rises up to $10 million. And when casualty losses are very low, the property deductible rises gradually to $10 million as well. Only

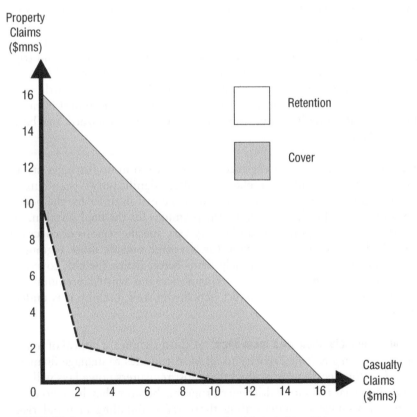

EXHIBIT 25.8 Property/Casualty Twinpack with Switching Trigger

when the losses are equally distributed is the deductible at its original level of $4 million.

Benefits of Multiple Triggers

Taking a traditional program or a multiline program and adding an addition trigger can be very simple, and yet remarkably beneficial. In fact, both customers *and* reinsurance companies seem to like dual-trigger programs. Let's consider some of the reasons for the appeal of these programs.

Simple Device for Mitigating Moral Hazard   As we saw in Chapter 15, one principal benefit of second triggers is the mitigation of moral hazard problems. By making a indemnity policy conditional on a trigger or event whose outcome the risk transfer purchaser cannot influence, the (re)insurer can be comfortable that losses have not been deliberately caused or loss mitigation mechanisms underutilized. Importantly, as noted earlier, second triggers of this sort affect the ability of the insured party to make a claim but do *not* generally affect the amount of the claim itself. So, second triggers facilitate convergence between the best of the insurance world (i.e., reimbursement for actual damage sustained) and the derivatives world (i.e., simplicity and lack of contract terms required to mitigate moral hazard). They help ART suppliers and users alike reduce moral hazard and basis risk *together.*

Cost   A second reason for the recent proliferation in multitrigger structures is that they tend to be cheaper—often significantly—than single-trigger solutions. The more conditions must be met in order for the policy to be drawn on, the cheaper will be the premium for the final solution. To the extent that a corporation can identify very specific regions of coverage with which it is concerned, paying for coverage outside those regions is pure waste. Second triggers can help firms better define the risk coverage they really need, thus reducing overinsurance and wasted premium expenses. The supplier of the product benefits as well, because it is underwriting less risk.

Managing Financial Risk with Insurance   A third significant appeal of multitrigger programs is their capacity to allow corporates to manage financial risk *indirectly*. Recall we explained that most reinsurers nowadays will not include financial risks in multitrigger programs because they have no comparative advantage in underwriting those risks. Bundling financial risks into a multiline program just forces the reinsurer to hedge out that portion of the underwriting exposure separately using derivatives, thus erasing any potential cost savings from portfolio effects. Incorporating financial risk into a program *through a trigger*, however, is an entirely different story. That is something a reinsurer *can* do without dramatically raising costs for customers. Not surprisingly, financial second triggers thus are very popular in multiline programs. It is perhaps the only way for a corporate customer to get the benefits of bundling financial risk into an insurance program— through the trigger, not the payout.

EXAMPLES OF MULTITRIGGER STRUCTURES

In this section, we review some examples of successful multitrigger programs that have been implemented to date. In most cases, the specific identity of the customer has not been publicly identified, but that does not mean the examples are hypothetical. On the contrary, all of these examples represent actual deals that have been done in the market to date.

Swiss Re's Telecom Business Interruption Protection Program

A good example of a creative double-trigger program can be found in Swiss Re's BI protection, a package specifically tailored to and aimed at the BI concerns of telecommunications firms.[17] The BI protection structure uses a fixed first trigger and a variable second trigger, and has a payment to the policyholder that is determined by the same variables underlying the second trigger.

The basic premise of the Swiss Re BI policy is that BI losses are most damaging to firms when they occur at the same time that a firm is experiencing worse-than-normal cash flows. The first trigger is a traditional fixed trigger that ensures the policy can be activated only if economic losses arise as a direct result of operational risks leading to business interruption. The hazards and risks included in the policy include large property damage, natural disasters, information technology (IT) systems failures, billing problems, malicious computer sabotage, and the like. The second variable trigger is based on the cash flows of the firm relative to the cash flows of an industry peer group. Specifically, the firm's EBITDA is compared to the EBITDA of its peers. When the firm's EBITDA growth rate falls to, say, more than three percentage points below the growth rate of an index of other telecom firms, the second trigger is activated. The value of the policy to the holder is then based on this EBITDA shortfall.

The value of this particular transaction in the context of the issues we explored in Part One is almost immediately obvious. First, the BI protection with an underperformance EBITDA second trigger creates access to preloss finance for the firm on preloss financing terms. Second, the product reduces cash flow volatility and will help its users mitigate underinvestment problems. Third, managerial risk aversion or asset substitutions problems that could lead managers to pursue projects with excessively low volatility will be less likely with a BI protection cover triggered at times of cash and earnings shortfalls. Finally, the cover will allow the firm to reduce paid-in capital reserves during normal business periods, thereby increasing debt capacity for users.

Power Market Protection

Late June 1998 was a stressful period for the deregulated U.S. power market. Following a series of defaults by several independent power producers (namely, Federal Energy and Power Corporation of America), a number of utilities were left without power purchase contracts on which they were relying to receive power that they had already resold to other customers. When the defaults occurred, utilities had to cover their now-defaulted power purchases either with their own generation or by purchasing power on the spot market. In the Midwest, spot prices at one point rose to nearly $7,500 per megawatt hour (compared to a normal average price at that time of year of $35 to $50/MWh). One utility reported incurring losses at the rate of almost $100 million *an hour* as the utility struggled to honor its power sales in the face of widespread defaults on prearranged power purchase agreements. Huge financial losses were incurred by several utilities, and some cities ended up in the dark for a few hours anyway.

FirstEnergy   At least two double-trigger insurance programs emerged in direct response to the catastrophic events in the power market of summer 1998. One program was instituted by one of the hardest-hit utilities in June 1998, Ohio-based FirstEnergy. FirstEnergy was the victim of extremely bad luck in the summer of 1998. Three events occurred within days of each other in late June 1998 that created serious problems for FirstEnergy:

1. A transformer failed at a coal-fired plant outside of Cleveland, causing a loss of 600 megawatts of generating capacity.
2. A tornado knocked out the power lines to a Toledo-based FirstEnergy nuclear power generator, causing another 600-megawatt loss in generating capacity.

3. The daisy chain of defaults set in motion by the failures of Federal Energy and Power Corporation of America caused several of FirstEnergy's power purchase contracts to default.

Thanks to this triple header from hell, FirstEnergy's 1998 earnings were down by about $100 million owing to the costs it incurred buying power on the spot market in an effort to keep the lights on for its customers.

The FirstEnergy double-trigger program was executed with ACE USA Power Products, Inc., and provides up to $100 million in cover in the event that FirstEnergy loses 600 megawatts or more of generating capacity at a time when the spot market price of power is $74/MWh or higher. The program has a deductible of $25 million and a 10 percent copay provision.[18]

Just one year later in the summer of 1999, both triggers were pulled yet again. But unlike the prior summer, the problems in 1999 did *not* include widespread counterparty defaults, so FirstEnergy was able to cover many of its power sale commitments using derivatives. Total losses thus did not exceed the $25 million deductible, and no claims were made on the policy. Nevertheless, given the catastrophic events of the year before, there is little doubt that FirstEnergy's management, shareholders, and customers all rested easier in 1999 knowing that the ACE policy was in place.

Great Bay Power Corp.   Great Bay Power Corp. (GBPC), based in Portsmouth, New Hampshire, adopted a similar double-trigger program in response to the 1998 power market crisis. The program combined BI cover for an unplanned power plant shutdown with a trigger based on the market price of power at the time of the shutdown. The program pays off in the event that a plant shutdown occurs at the same time the spot market price of power is above a predefined strike price (which has not been disclosed).

Hospital Coverage of Insurance and Investment Portfolio Risks[19]

Like many large health care organizations and hospitals operating in the United States, this particular firm—let's just call it The Hospital because the customer identity has not been disclosed—was heavily dependent on its investment portfolio for operating income. The Hospital's investment portfolio consisted mainly of a $1 billion trust invested largely in equities. In the first half of the 1990s, the value of The Hospital's endowment had nearly doubled given the performance of global equity markets.

Especially given the value of its investment portfolio, The Hospital was comfortable with a substantial retention on its insurance risks, but was concerned that a large insurance loss might occur at the same time as a substantial reversal in equity markets. So, working with Zurich Corporate Solutions, The Hospital implemented a double-trigger multiline IRM program that covered up to $200 million in insurance-related losses over three years (subject to a $100 million per occurrence limit) on risks such as professional indemnity, property, casualty, crime, and employment practices. The program also included aggregate stop-loss coverage that would erode based on the adverse performance of several equity indexes, including the S&P 500 and Russell 2000. The program is illustrated in Exhibit 25.9.

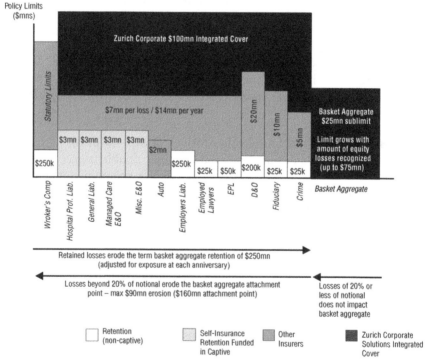

EXHIBIT 25.9 Zurich Corporate Solutions Hospital Insurance and Equity Protection Multiline Double-Trigger Program
Source: Zurich Corporate Solutions, a division of Zurich American Insurance Company.
Note: Y-axis is not to scale.

Industry Loss Warranties

Industry loss warranties (ILWs) originated in London in the late 1980s. They were mainly used on an isolated and ad hoc basis in response to a lack of retrocession capacity and an almost complete absence of retro-on-retro cover (McDonnell 2002). But the period from 1989 to 1992 saw the occurrence of three spectacularly large insurance loss events: Hurricane Hugo in 1989 ($5.990 billion in insured losses), Typhoon Mireille in Japan in 1991 ($7.338 billion in insured losses), and Hurricane Andrew in 1992 ($20.185 billion in insured losses). Those events in turn persuaded insurers and reinsurers that protection for property underwriting at attachment points of $5 billion to $10 billion was no longer a ridiculous idea.

The use of ILWs as an alternative form of reinsurance and retrocession was one of the results of that period of concentrated losses. Clearly, no reinsurance company is keen to purchase any more protection than is absolutely essential at those kinds of catastrophe levels. Given that one catastrophic loss was likely to occur along with others, the attraction of a double-triggered product as a cheaper alternative to reinsurance and retro capacity began to mount.

An ILW is a double-trigger reinsurance contract in which the first trigger is the insured's own property losses and the second trigger is the aggregate loss to the insurance industry. Aggregate losses in ILWs are generally defined based on the performance of a reputable industry loss index, such as the Property Claim Services (PCS) or Sigma index.

ILWs are typically structured in two forms. *Occurrence ILWs* are intended to provide protection against severe losses, whereas *aggregate ILWs* are targeted at reinsurers concerned primarily with the frequency of large claims. Most ILWs have a binary payoff structure. Once the warranty limits are triggered, the policy pays the entire policy limit. Some ILWs, however, have prorated payoffs in which the holder of the ILW receives a prorated portion of the industry loss if the two triggers are activated. In both types of ILWs, the indexed industry loss usually dominates the first trigger and dictates when the program pays off. As a result, these products, while useful, can be subject to significant index-related basis risks.

DUAL-TRIGGER INSURANCE VERSUS DERIVATIVES AND FAS 133

As noted earlier in the book and again in this chapter, one of the principal benefits of multitrigger structures is their capacity to blend the best of the insurance and capital market worlds. A product can retain the indemnity payoff features of insurance but through the addition of a derivatives-like financial second trigger can mitigate moral hazard. Properly designed, the result should be a contract with minimal moral hazard *and* minimal basis risk.

Occasionally, however, dual-trigger structures have walked right up to the line distinguishing insurance and derivatives and challenged that line. In the late 1990s, concerns began to be voiced that the derivatives-like features common to second triggers could themselves be considered "embedded derivatives," in which case FAS133 on the accounting treatment for derivatives might apply. And in a few cases, even greater concerns began to surface that the *whole product* might be deemed a derivatives contract.

In April 2001, the Financial Accounting Standards Board (FASB) reaffirmed that property and casualty contracts with second triggers could be accounted for exclusively as insurance as long as the structure satisfies three conditions:[20]

1. The purchaser of the structure receives a benefit payment only if an insurable event occurs.
2. The benefit amount paid to the purchaser of the product cannot exceed the actual economic damage sustained.
3. The benefit amount paid to the purchaser is triggered by the outcome of an insurance event that either is unknown or cannot at the time of the underwriting be deemed "highly probable." In other words, the contract must facilitate true risk transfer.

This interpretation was fairly aggressive in defending the ART world as "insurance turf." Some dual-trigger structures are much more derivatives-like than others. Yet FASB seeks to take the position that as long as the contract has an indemnity payoff and is not virtually guaranteed to pay off, the structure will continue to be deemed an insurance contract for accounting purposes.[21]

CHAPTER 26

Contingent Cover

The form of structured insurance called *contingent insurance or contingent cover* is essentially an option to enter into a (re)insurance contract at a prenegotiated premium and on predefined terms. Most popular forms of contingent cover are options embedded into specific products, and some forms of contingent cover are created through the structuring process. In fact, we have already seen how some products themselves function as stand-alone contingent insurance by their nature—for example, surety bonds and monoline wraps, explored in Chapter 10.

In this chapter, we explore some of the types of contingent cover that have been used in the market to date. Some are more prevalent than others, but the demand for contingent insurance has been rising slowly but steadily over the past decade as the demand for structured insurance has risen more generally. Further innovations of this building block can be expected. But for now, our discussion here will be brief.

PREMIUM PROTECTION OPTIONS

One source of optionality in the insurance market is the family of products and solutions that provide premium or price protection to corporate insurance purchasers. Before we explore some of these structured insurance solutions, it makes sense to begin with a brief review of what rates change over time and give rise to the demand for price protection.

Time Variation in Premium and the Underwriting Cycle

The pricing of insurance, reinsurance, and retrocession was discussed briefly in Chapters 8 and 9. Insurance rate making is often considered to be heavily influenced by *cyclical* factors that lead to what we call "soft" and "hard" markets. What *causes* this cyclicality is constantly debated, and the lack of agreement on this issue is one reason why premium insurance is not very common even in the structured insurance world. No matter how contentious the explanation(s), however, insurance premiums and rates do exhibit fairly significant time variation that can give rise to a demand for price protection. There are at least two reasons insurance premiums exhibit significant variation over time.

Underwriting Cycle   Property, casualty, and liability insurance have historically exhibited pronounced time series variations in profits and rates around a stable long-run average. Peak to peak, this *underwriting cycle* in the United States is about six years in duration. The underwriting cycle is often blamed for hard and soft markets.

One explanation for the underwriting cycle is cyclicality in the cost of capital arising from systematic risk. For example, if world stock returns are a source of systematic risk that affect all companies' costs of capital, some cyclicality in insurance rates could be due to nothing more than cyclicality in cost of capital arising from the normal ups and downs of equity markets.

Another explanation often given to the underwriting cycle—related to the first—is the heavy allocation that most insurance companies make of their reserve assets into equities. Equities, in turn, exhibit considerable time variation. During and after periods of slow growth or negative returns on equities, some argue that insurers must raise prices to stabilize their reserves.

Yet another anecdotal explanation of the underwriting cycle is the so-called business risk premium. The idea is just that corporate insurance rates rise as business risks become structurally more risky to underwrite. This might occur, for example, because of an economic downturn in the business cycle. Cyclicality in the business cycle could in turn impart cyclicality into insurance rates. But this is again just a restatement that systematic risk can affect prices in a cyclical manner.

Recent Loss Experiences   As a matter of pure theory, the rate on a (re)insurance contract should equal the expected loss on the contract plus premium loading and perhaps a small markup for profit margin. Except to the extent that some cost data may be available only after some lag, all the variables that define insurance rates are *forward-looking*. The *expected loss*, in particular, is not set to make up for past losses in excess of premium, but rather is intended to coverage average *future* losses.

Although hard to dispute as a theoretical matter, the idea that recent significant claims-related losses would not put upward pressure on rates is no less than heretical to most practitioners. How could one imagine that premiums on directors and officers (D&O) insurance programs should not rise following an Enron? Or that earthquake insurance premiums would not rise following a 9.0 California temblor? Or that property insurance for certified acts of terrorism would be immune to the events of 9/11?

We have to be a little bit careful here, though. In *these* examples, rates might very well rise in direct response to recent events. There is a big difference, however, between rates that rise because expected future losses rise and rates that go up because (re)insurers want a new customer or a renewal to pay for the (re)insurer's underpricing of a prior policy line. D&O rates that rise following an Enron and certain property rates that rise following a major act of terrorism could be explained by an increase in market participants' probabilistic estimates of the likelihood of default.

Rates could also rise because of an event so large that it affects *aggregate* industry capital. Total underwriting capacity, after all, is a function of total industry capitalization. At any given firm, underwriting capacity is a function of both the firm's supply and its cost of capital. In the event of either a sharp increase in the cost of capital or a sharp reduction in the supply of capital, an insurance company can either decrease its coverage offered or increase rates.

Large losses that can lead to "rational" increases in premium are those losses that are correlated with *aggregate capital shocks*. Typically this means that the loss is not just large but is correlated across insurers. In order for this rationale to make sense, it must essentially affect *all* insurance providers or the *aggregate* supply of insurance, as well as *re*insurance and retrocession.

Structured Price Protection

Corporations that believe they are in a soft market moving into a hard one or that expect a secular rate increase as a result of an event like 9/11 will often seek protection against premium hikes. As discussed in various earlier parts in this book, some firms may simply substitute away from risk transfer toward funded retentions and risk financing solutions. But if risk transfer is deemed truly *essential*, then firms have no choice but either to pay higher prices or to try to lock in future prices at current rates.

Multiyear Protection   Although multiyear coverage might not at first sound like an option on insurance, of course it is. The basic idea is no different from locking in a multiperiod interest rate by issuing long-dated debt rather than remaining at the mercy of the yield curve and issuing short-dated debt. The big difference between debt and insurance maturities, however, is that the maturity choice of debt can always be easily changed at low cost through the use of derivatives; for example, a firm with six-month floating-rate debt can trivially swap that into five-year fixed-rate debt by entering a pay-fixed swap. In large part because of the limited use of multiyear plain-vanilla products, however, no such market exists for swapping insurance maturities. The multiyear deals to date have typically also been structured insurance deals, moreover, making it difficult to construct any kind of representative and transparent forward curve of insurance rates.

If a company does want multiyear coverage, the absence of other instruments to facilitate this means that the company likely will have to negotiate an existing (re)insurance product or alternative risk transfer (ART) form with a multiyear term. And with a lack of transparent forward curves, this further implies that some disagreement about the pricing of multiyear coverage is likely to result. A corporation that wants to lock in a current low rate in a soft market, for example, may well find a (re)insurance counterparty that is reluctant to quote the current low rate for a multiyear term.

Nevertheless, many (re)insurers claim surprise that corporations do not at least explore multiyear coverage more often than they do. Clients instead tend to assume they will get a multiyear quote on unfavorable terms. And perhaps they will. The value of locking in a single rate for multiyear coverage will differ from company to company based on the various economic factors discussed in Part One. But precisely for this reason, it may be worth exploring this alternative more frequently than is currently done.

Price Caps   In the 1999–2002 soft market period, several insurance companies offered their clients stand-alone price protection products. Instead of being bundled into existing policies as a multiyear premium, these separate products were essentially price protection options that referenced the terms of some other policy. Despite their obvious appeal, few risk managers apparently took advantage of these products (Erhart 2002).

Reinsurance price caps are also available from some reinsurers, but have enjoyed almost no use whatsoever.

CONTINGENT COVER EMBEDDED IN EXISTING PROGRAMS

The virtue of a multiline program is its integration of capital across multiple risk types. Most such programs, as we saw in Chapter 25, have a single per-occurrence deductible and a limit. Multiline programs, moreover, are generally also multiyear covers, thus usually also leading to an aggregate coverage limit over the lifetime of the program.

Although the integrated nature of these programs is what makes them appealing, they can also create certain limitations for users. Most of these limitations can easily be addressed by structuring—specifically, by embedding certain types of contingent cover optionality into the broad multiline program. Some specific examples are discussed next. In some cases, the embedded options discussed are also available for embedding into more traditional monoline structures.

Readers will note the similarity between some of these features of optionality found in multiline programs with the different types of reinsurance treaties discussed in Chapter 9. This similarity is no accident. The options discussed are ways of incorporating features of different kinds of reinsurance cover into a single multiline program, which is the whole point of an *integrated* program.

Optional Reinstatement

Optional reinstatement allows the insurance purchaser to pay a premium for the right to reset a policy limit after it has been exhausted. This is economically equivalent to an option to repurchase an identical insurance package after the first one has been fully used. Optional reinstatement is especially common on multiyear and multiline programs where the consequences of remaining uninsured after a huge loss on a single risk early in the life of the program might be severe.

Aggregate Retention Protection Provisions

Aggregate retention protection is designed to help purchasers of multiline coverage address a series of high-frequency low-severity losses. Because the aggregate deductible of multiline programs tends to be relatively high, it can sometimes be the case that a purchaser experiences a series of losses under the per-occurrence deductible layer, all of which, however, may add up to a relatively significant total loss.

Aggregate retention protection allows the multiline purchaser to remit additional premium for the right to optionally supplement a series of small retained losses with new excess of loss (XOL) coverage. Suppose, for example, that a multiline program provides \$200 XS \$100 in cover per occurrence for three years with an aggregate three-year policy limit of \$400 million. Now suppose that one of the risks covered in the program—say, crime and fidelity—generates a series of 10 \$50 million claims in the first two years of the program, seven of which occur in the first year. None of these claims would satisfy the per-occurrence deductible of the program, and yet the total loss in the first year alone would be $350 million, rising to $500 million by the end of year 2.

If the program includes aggregate retention protection, the corporate purchaser can remit additional premium to provide drop-down XOL coverage on crime and fidelity risk. The new coverage supplements the multiline program rather than replaces it, and yet functions as a stand-alone crime and fidelity program once it is put into place. The program will specify an aggregate deductible and limit and will relieve the firm of the pressure to retain such an extensive number of losses that would otherwise fall into the retention layer of the multiline program.

We saw an example of aggregate retention protection in Chapter 25 when we considered the case of the large U.S. nursing home seeking protection in case a series of claims below its $20 million lower attachment point collectively exceeded $40 million.

Optional Limit Acceleration

We also encountered another embedded form of contingent cover in the nursing home case in Chapter 25 that we called optional limit acceleration. That does not actually give its holder the right to acquire new cover altogether, but rather allows the firm to borrow capital over time inside a multiyear program. In the example in which we introduced this idea last chapter, the nursing home had $40 XS $20 covered each year for five years. In the event of, say, a $80 million claim in one year, the annual limit that year could be increased to $60 XS $20 and the limit reduced to $20 XS $20 in a later year. When the later year arrives, the coverage would be lower, but could also itself be raised through optional reinstatement.

Nth Aggregate Limit Cover

An Nth *aggregate limit cover* is intended to provide additional coverage to firms that have exceeded their *aggregate* limit in a multiline program. Our earlier example was a $200 XS $100 multiline program with an aggregate limit of $400 million over the three policy years. Two catastrophic losses of $300 million each or four of $200 million each would exhaust the program's aggregate limit, despite each loss remaining below the per-occurrence limit.

For additional premium, a multiline insurance purchaser can create additional catastrophic coverage after the Nth catastrophic loss during the life of the policy. The value of N depends on the per-occurrence limit and deductible relative to the potential size of a catastrophic loss, but N is usually equal to three or four.

Suppose, for example, we have the aforementioned program in place and pay additional premium for a third aggregate limit cover of an additional $300 million. If we sustain two $300 million losses, we get reimbursed $200 million on each but then immediately reach our aggregate limit. Because of our third aggregate limit cover, however, the second claim triggers an immediate drop-down of another $300 million in cover. In most programs, access to the new $300 million would still require exceeding the per-occurrence program deductible of $100 million, and any given claim might also still be subject to the per-occurrence limit. But no additional aggregate deductible would apply.

CONTINGENT INSURANCE-LINKED NOTES

In Chapter 15, we explored the Reliance III puttable catastrophic insurance-linked note (ILN). Recall that structure provided Reliance with the ability to issue a new ILN at its discretion. We called that a contingent capital deal. Reliance III was *also* a form of contingent cover, inasmuch as the principal and interest (P&I) on the newly issued bonds in the deal could be diverted to fund catastrophic property claims losses incurred by Reliance.

The reason that the Reliance III puttable cat bond was contingent *capital* as well as contingent cover is that the bond was issued directly by Reliance and represented new debt financing. The ILNs, moreover, were recourse notes that exposed investors to Reliance credit risk.

A similar structure (shown in Exhibit 26.1) was developed by Allianz that allowed the German insurance giant to procure contingent *cover* without simultaneously raising debt capital on its own balance sheet. The motivations were similar to those underlying the Reliance III structure. Concerned that a major catastrophic loss would lead to a hardening in the regular reinsurance market and a lack of retrocession capacity, Allianz sought to place a cap on its future reinsurance costs by using the option on an ILN issue.

The option was sold to investors in 1999 by special purpose entity (SPE) Gemini Re and gave Allianz three years during which that option could be exercised. If the option is exercised, the writers of the option to Allianz agreed to purchase three-year ILNs whose principal and interest payments were linked to losses on European windstorms and hailstorms. Called *subscription agreements*, the options knock in when wind and hail losses reach a specified triggering amount. In exchange for preagreeing to

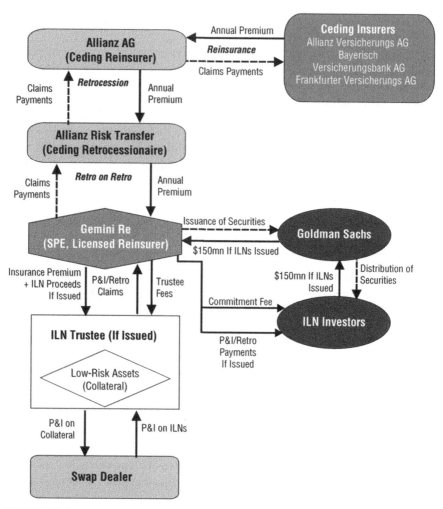

EXHIBIT 26.1   Allianz Risk Transfer Option to Issue Cat Bonds

purchase the notes at a specified price, the option writers receive an annual commitment fee.

The notes underlying the option were for an original principal of $150 million. If the options are exercised by Allianz and trigger a purchase of the notes, the structure functions much like the ILNs we explored in Chapter 22. The note proceeds are placed in a collateral account in Gemini Re and are invested in reserve assets to fund insurance claims. As usual, Gemini Re engages in a swap to smooth the actual investment income on the investment portfolio into a London Interbank Offered Rate (LIBOR)-based cash flow stream suitable for servicing the notes.

Gemini Re in turn entered into a retrocession agreement with Allianz Risk Transfer, itself a retrocessionaire for Allianz AG. The holders of the notes issued by Gemini Re receive a basic interest payment of a spread over LIBOR unless the retrocession agreement between Gemini Re and Allianz Risk Transfer results in claims payments. In that case, both the interest and principal of the notes may not be completely paid off.

Case and Issue Studies

The Emerging Role of
Patent Law in Risk Finance

J. B. Heaton

To the Founding Fathers borrowing from English patent law, extending patent protection to financial innovations would have seemed quite strange. As one leading scholar has noted:

> [I]t would have been seen as absurd for an entrepreneur to file a patent on a new finance technique such as publicly traded corporate shares, techniques for obtaining private financing for a bridge to compete with an existing bridge, or a security interest in uncut timber. These were the earmarks of commerce, of enterprise; laudable surely, but something altogether distinct from the realm of "invention" and the "useful arts."[1]

Nevertheless, two hundred years later few can doubt that new finance techniques are patentable subject matter.

This article explores the potential implications of patent law for risk finance. As Christopher L. Culp notes in his risk management text,[2] "perhaps nowhere are the opportunities for structured risk management solutions more interesting . . . than in the [alternative risk transfer] area of insurance—an area that has quite rapidly come to include total risk and integrated insurance, securitized products, and derivatives." While few can question the important role that continuing financial innovation will have

---

This article is reprinted by permission from the *Journal of Risk Finance* (Winter 2001). J. B. Heaton, J.D., Ph.D., is an attorney at Bartlit Beck Herman Palenchar & Scott in Chicago.

on traditional financial and insurance products, little concern has been focused on the possible effects of intellectual property law—especially patent law—on the alternative risk transfer field. Trends in patent law and litigation, combined with increased patenting activity in insurance, securitized products, and derivatives, suggest that alternative risk transfer professionals should take seriously the changing legal landscape.

It is difficult to overestimate the potential effects of a valid patent on any field of commercial endeavor. Patents are enormously powerful legal devices. The owner of a United States patent has the legal right to exclude others from making, using, offering to sell, or selling the patented invention for a term of 20 years. The patent owner may license these rights to others, granting them the right (on an exclusive or nonexclusive basis) to make, use, or sell the patented invention. In addition—and perhaps more visibly—patent owners can enforce their patent rights in a federal civil lawsuit. If victorious in a patent infringement lawsuit, patent owners can recover damages and/or permanent injunctions forbidding the acts that infringe the patent. For companies whose existence rests on patentable technologies, patent litigation can be all-out legal warfare. For that company's customers, patent litigation can determine whether products or services it has purchased in the past will be available in the future, and at what price and quality. More ominously, customers themselves can face liability for infringement.

The arcane world of patents and patent law is emerging as an important business concern to risk professionals. *Risk* magazine recently reported on widespread criticism of a patent awarded to Columbia University for a quasi–Monte Carlo method (U.S. Patent No. 5,940,810: "Estimation Method and System for Complex Securities Using Low-Discrepancy Deterministic Sequences"). A recent *Wall Street Journal* article reports on an emerging legal battle between the American Stock Exchange and two inventors over a patented process related to exchange-traded funds (U.S. Patent No. 5,806,048: "Open End Mutual Fund Securitization Process"). In August 2000, Amex filed a complaint in U.S. District Court (patent cases must be brought in federal court, not state court), seeking a declaration that the patent is invalid, while the patent's owner, Mopex, Inc., filed its own patent infringement lawsuit against Amex only days later. The litigation is pending as of this writing.

Applications for new financial and insurance patents are now surely but secretly in process at the United States Patent and Trademark Office (patent applications are now held secret by the Patent and Trademark Office for the first 18 months after filing). The increase in financial patenting activity is mainly attributable to changes in the legal landscape. In particular, both the federal courts and Congress have signaled that financial inventions, once previously thought to be outside the scope of strong patent protection, will be treated by the patent laws as on par with inventions in more traditional fields like bioengineering and manufacturing machines. The changing legal landscape may have a significant effect on future development and sale of cutting-edge financial and insurance products.

Already, it is clear that financial patents are proliferating. Lerner (2000b) estimates that hundreds of financial and insurance patent applications are in process at the United States Patent and Trademark Office. The main effect of recent legal developments has been to increase confidence that these patents—if granted by the Patent and Trademark Office—will be upheld by the federal courts in later litigation. It is also clear that some owners of these patents will aggressively assert them against alleged infringers. Visible examples of patent lawsuits—such as Amazon.com, Inc.'s successful effort to enjoin BarnesandNoble.com, Inc. from using "one-click" technology (*Amazon.com, Inc. v. Barnesandnoble.com, Inc.*, 53 U.S.P.Q. 2d 1115 [W.D. Wash. 1999])—are likely to embolden financial patent holders in their discussions with potential infringers. Bottom line: the proliferation of financial patenting and the aggressive assertion of patent rights against alleged infringers may lead to high-stakes litigation over intellectual property rights in the alternative risk transfer field.

BASICS OF PATENTABILITY

The essence of patent protection is the right to exclude others from making, using, and selling the claimed invention. The Congressional authority to enact patent legislation derives from Article I, Section 8, Clause 8 of the United States Constitution, granting the power "To promote the progress of science and useful arts, by securing for limited times to authors and inventors the exclusive right to their respective writings and discoveries." Pursuant to this authority, Congress has enacted several patent laws through the years. While even a basic introduction to patent law is beyond the scope of this article, the conditions for patentability are important to an understanding of the emerging role of patent law in risk finance.

In general, an inventor wishing to obtain a patent must comply with four legal requirements for patentability. A patentable invention is (1) of patentable subject matter; (2) useful; (3) new; and (4) nonobvious.

Not everything is patentable. Some inventions are outside the scope of patent law, no matter how useful, new, or nonobvious they might be. For example, a printed book is not patentable subject matter (but may be protectable under copyright law) despite the fact that its teachings might be useful, new, and not at all obvious to any reader. Typically, patentable subject matter was thought to include machines and manufactures, with later acceptance of processes, chemical compositions, and bioengineered products. Outside of the patentable subject matter category were laws of nature, natural phenomena, and abstract ideas.

Only "useful" products or processes are patentable: the patented product or process must "work" to produce some result of some benefit. It need not work well, however, and (at least on its own) the usefulness requirement does not require that the patented product or process work better than anything preceding it does. A patent application on a "time machine" claiming the invention of allowing travel back to a prespecified date would likely be rejected as impossible, and thus not useful. Further, a chemical compound with no known use to humanity would also likely be rejected on these grounds. However, a chocolate-powered automobile that traveled at speeds up to 2 miles per hour might very well pass the usefulness test.

A patentable invention must be "new." The patent laws test the novelty of an invention by reference to the relevant "prior art" in the field of the patent's invention. In general terms, fleshed out by particular statutes and case law, an invention is not new if the elements of the claim are contained in a single piece of relevant prior art. For example, suppose a relevant published journal article contained each element—either expressly or inherently—of a patent "claim." (Patent claims are statutorily required [35 U.S.C. §112] statements "particularly pointing out and distinctly claiming the subject matter which the applicant regards as his invention.") That claim would be "anticipated" by the prior art. Put simply, an anticipated invention is not new, and is not patentable.

Finally, an invention is not patentable if it is "obvious." Obviousness differs from anticipation in the sense that no single piece of relevant prior art must contain (either expressly or inherently) all the teachings of a particular claim. Instead, the test is whether the invention would have been obvious to a person of ordinary skill in the art. The "person of ordinary skill in the art" is a legal construct, a hypothetical individual assumed to be aware of all of the pertinent prior art, but not necessarily a genius in the field.

While the conditions of patentability must be satisfied first at the patent application stage, each of these matters can be (and usually is) revisited in litigation. That is, although an issued patent enjoys a legal presumption of validity (35 U.S.C. §282), the alleged infringer during the course of litigation may rebut that presumption. Because of the unique challenges of overcoming this presumption, and because of the typically high stakes involved, patent litigation is typically highly complex and costly civil litigation that requires the skills of top trial teams and technical experts.

ILLUSTRATION: METHOD OF EXERCISING A CAT (U.S. PAT. NO. 5,443,036)

In litigation, financial patent holders will face intense scrutiny of, among many other things, their satisfaction of the legal requirements for patentability described above and summarized in Exhibit 27.1. To fix ideas about the four requirements described above it is useful to examine a short, easily understood patent. Exhibit 27.2 provides excerpts from U.S. Patent No. 5,443,036, "Method of Exercising a Cat." Despite the topic of this article, the "cat" exercised in the method of the patent is an animal, and not a financial instrument related to catastrophic risk. Putting aside the pun, the patent reveals some of the issues that might arise in risk finance patent litigation, without delving into the complex factual matters likely to arise in real finance patents.

Consider first the patent's "abstract" appearing on the front page of the patent as a matter of course. The abstract provides a summary of the patent:

> *A method for inducing cats to exercise consists of directing a beam of invisible light produced by a handheld laser apparatus onto the floor or wall or other opaque surface in the vicinity of the cat, then moving the laser so as to cause the bright pattern of light to move in an irregular way fascinating to cats, and to any other animal with a chase instinct.*

EXHIBIT 27.1   The Legal Requirements of Patentability Under U.S. Law

Requirement	Explanation
Patentable Subject Matter	The invention must fall into a category eligible for patent protection; not everything can be patented.
Useful	The invention must have some utility, though it need not work well and need not be superior to preexisting products or processes.
New	The invention must not have been described in a relevant piece of prior art (e.g., in a prior patent or published article).
Nonobvious	The invention must not have been obvious to a hypothetical person of ordinary skill in the art, assumed to be knowledgeable of all the relevant prior art.

EXHIBIT 27.2   U.S. Patent No. 5,443,036, Method of Exercising a Cat

Title	**Method of Exercising a Cat**
Number	5,443,036
Inventors	Kevin T. Amiss; Martin H. Abbott
Issued/ Filed Dates	August 22, 1995/November 2, 1993
Abstract	A method for inducing cats to exercise consists of directing a beam of invisible light produced by a handheld laser apparatus onto the floor or wall or other opaque surface in the vicinity of the cat, then moving the laser so as to cause the bright pattern of light to move in an irregular way fascinating to cats, and to any other animal with a chase instinct.
Background of the Invention	1. Technical Field The present invention relates to recreational and amusement devices for domestic animals and, more particularly, to a method for exercising and entertaining cats. 2. Discussion of the Prior Art Cats are not characteristically disposed toward voluntary aerobic exercise. It becomes the burden of the cat owner to create situations of sufficient interest to the feline to induce even short-lived and modest exertion for the health and well-being of the pet. Cats are, however, fascinated by light and enthralled by unpredictable jumpy movements, as, for instance, by the bobbing end of a piece of handheld string or yarn, or a ball rolling and bouncing across a floor. Intense sunlight reflected from a mirror or focused through a prism, if the room is sufficiently dark, will, when moved irregularly, cause even the more sedentary of cats to scamper after the lighted image in an amusing and therapeutic game of "cat and mouse." The disruption of having to darken a room to stage a cat workout and the uncertainty of collecting a convenient sunbeam in a lens or mirror render these approaches to establishing a regular life-enhancing cat exercise routine inconvenient at best.
Summary of the Invention	Accordingly, it is an object of the present invention to provide an improved method of exercising a cat in normal day and night lighting environments. It is a further object of the present invention to provide a method of providing amusing, entertaining and healthy exercise for a cat.

EXHIBIT 27.2 *(Continued)*

Title	Method of Exercising a Cat
	It is yet another object of the present invention to teach a method of exercising a cat effortlessly at any time. In accordance with the present invention, a light amplification by stimulated emission of radiation (laser) device in a small handheld configuration is used to project and move a bright pattern of light around a room to amuse and exercise a cat. The method is effective, simple, convenient, and inexpensive to practice and provides healthy exercise for the cat and amusement and entertainment for both the cat and the owner. These and other objects, features, and advantages of the present invention will become apparent from the following description and accompanying drawings of one specific embodiment thereof.
Claims	What is claimed is: 1. A method of inducing aerobic exercise in an unrestrained cat comprising the steps of: (a) directing an intense coherent beam of invisible light produced by a handheld laser apparatus to produce a bright, highly focused pattern of light at the intersection of the beam and an opaque surface, said pattern being of visual interest to a cat; and (b) selectively redirecting said beam out of the cat's immediate reach to induce said cat to run and chase said beam and pattern of light around an exercise area. 2. The method of claim 1 wherein said bright pattern of light is small in area relative to a paw of the cat. 3. The method of claim 1 wherein said beam remains invisible between said laser and said opaque surface until impinging on said opaque surface. 4. The method of claim 1 wherein step (b) includes sweeping said beam at an angular speed to cause said pattern to move along said opaque surface at a speed in the range of five to twenty-five feet per second.

In other words, the patent concerns a method for causing a cat to exercise by using a laser pointer to create a point of light that will evoke the chase instinct of the cat.

The '036 patent (practitioners typically refer to a patent by its last three numbers) has four claims:

What is claimed is:

1. A method of inducing aerobic exercise in an unrestrained cat comprising the steps of:

(a) directing an intense coherent beam of invisible light produced by a handheld laser apparatus to produce a bright, highly focused pattern of light at the intersection of the beam and an opaque surface, said pattern being of visual interest to a cat; and

(b) selectively redirecting said beam out of the cat's immediate reach to induce said cat to run and chase said beam and pattern of light around an exercise area.

2. The method of claim 1 wherein said bright pattern of light is small in area relative to a paw of the cat.

3. The method of claim 1 wherein said beam remains invisible between said laser and said opaque surface until impinging on said opaque surface.

4. The method of claim 1 wherein step (b) includes sweeping said beam at an angular speed to cause said pattern to move along said opaque surface at a speed in the range of five to twenty-five feet per second.

The '036 patent may appear ridiculous to some observers, and indeed the patent is a favorite of critics of the patent system and the review applied by the United States Patent and Trademark Office. Nevertheless, it is important to examine the issues raised by the '036 patent in legal terms. Doing so shows just how difficult can be the problem of dealing with an asserted U.S. patent.

Suppose, for example, that one wanted to challenge the validity of the '036 patent on the basis of the four requirements of patentability discussed above. Consider first the requirement of patentable subject matter. To pass this requirement, the method of exercising a cat covered by the '036 claims must fall within the types of subject matter covered by patent law. A method for exercising a cat may very well do so. A "process" can be patented (35 U.S.C. §101): "Whoever invents or discovers any new and useful process, machine, manufacture, or composition of matter, or any new and useful improvement thereof, may obtain a patent therefor, subject to the conditions and requirements of this title." The patent statute (35 U.S.C. §100(b)) further defines the term "process" to include a "method": "The term 'process' means process, art or method, and includes a new use of a known process, machine, manufacture, composition of matter, or material."

But there are some interesting issues for litigation here. For example, what would be the effect of the necessity for human participation in the method? As a general rule, the requirement of human mental participation renders a process unpatentable. See, for example, *Johnson v. Duquesne Light Co.*, 29 F.2d 784 (W.D. Pa. 1928), aff'd, 34 F.2d 1020 (3d Cir. 1929). As claim 1 states, the method requires that the individual engages in the action of "selectively redirecting said beam out of the cat's immediate reach[.]" That sounds like a requirement for substantial human mental participation, and may render the claim invalid.

Next, consider the requirement that the invention be "useful." Here, matters seem easy, as they often are in utility inquiries. The author of this article will attest that the method works. Using a laser pointed to create a pinpoint of light can induce the cat to chase the pinpoint, providing the intended exercise.

Whether or not the invention is new—that is, whether elements of the claim are contained in a single piece of relevant prior art—would require substantial research. The lawyer (or his/her expert) would scour publications in the field and past patents to determine if anyone had ever disclosed the method of exercising a cat using a laser pointer. Note that here it matters not whether anyone (including the author) had employed the method in secret prior to the application date (November 2, 1993). What matters is whether all the elements of the claimed invention appeared in a reference that could be available to a potential inventor. Suppose, counterfactually, that there was a published article in *Cat Fancy* magazine, titled "Exercise Your Cat with a Laser Pointer," dated January 1993, and disclosing the exact method taught by the '036 patent. In that case, the patent would be invalid because the invention would not be "new." Obviously, the search for prior art is an important part of any patent litigation effort.

Also important is the obviousness inquiry. To many, it is here where the '036 patent might have its most serious problem. The patent itself—in the section titled "Background of the Invention"—discloses the well-known fact that "Intense sunlight reflected from a mirror or focused through a prism, if the room is sufficiently dark, will, when moved irregularly, cause even the more sedentary of cats to scamper after the lighted image in an amusing and therapeutic game of 'cat and mouse.'" (The author of this article was once fond of "exercising" his own cat by reflecting light off the back of a CD and onto the walls of his apartment.) Is the use of a laser pointer obvious to anyone who has employed these methods? If so, the patent could be invalid on these obviousness grounds alone, even if the method was never written down in a relevant piece of prior art.

In litigation, all these questions of patentability (and many other questions as well) are up for grabs, and juries will decide questions like anticipation. In many cases, expert analysis may help, but the task is not an easy one. Consider the use of expert analysis to show that certain financial patents were "obvious" in light of prior art. There must be some motivation to combine the prior art references or practices in ways that render the invention obvious. That motivation can come from the prior art references themselves, the knowledge of one of ordinary skill in the art, or even from the nature of the problem to be solved, but the showing must be clear.

The road for an alleged infringer is not an easy one for another reason as well. Patent cases are typically tried to juries. Juries are prone to form a strong hypothesis that a patent issued by the Patent and Trademark Office is valid, not knowing that most inventions are never tested by examiners, that patent examiners are often overworked and sometimes underqualified, and that patent applications are secret and not subjected to any meaningful adversary process unless litigated.

But alleged infringers are not the only ones with problems. The problem of detecting infringement is substantial for patent holders, especially for methods that can be practiced in relative secrecy. Consider again the '036 patent. How could the inventors know whether or not the author of this article had ever given up the CD method for the (admittedly superior) laser pointer method? If the infringer cannot be identified, the right to exclusive use is worth little. A similar problem may face some current and future financial patent holders.

A FEW EXAMPLES OF RISK FINANCE PATENTS

Moving beyond arguably silly patents, it is instructive to look at some real risk finance patents. These are patents that on their face purport to claim rights to inventions that have undoubted application to risk finance applications. Exhibit 27.3 presents brief descriptions of three such patents (see Heaton [2000] for detailed examples of several other financial patents).

The first patent (U.S. Pat. No. 5,940,810) is the controversial one issued to Columbia University for quasi–Monte Carlo methods. Rather than covering a risk finance product per se, the Columbia University patent cov-

EXHIBIT 27.3 Examples of Risk Finance Patents

Title	Estimation Method and System for Complex Securities Using Low-Discrepancy Deterministic Sequences	System and Method of Risk Transfer and Risk Diversification Including Means to Assure with Assurance of Timely Payment and Segregation of the Interests of Capital	System and Method for Replacing a Liability with Insurance and for Analyzing Data and Generating Documents Pertaining to a Premium Financing Mechanism Paying for Such Insurance
U.S. Patent No.	5,940,810	5,704,045	6,026,364
Issued/Filed Dates	August 17, 1999/ July 30, 1997	December 30, 1997/ January 9, 1995	February 15, 2000/ July 28, 1997
Inventors	Joseph F. Traub, Spassimir Paskov, Irwin F. Vanderhoof	Douglas L. King, Alasdair G. Barclay, Rockie C. Wellman	Brian L. Whitworth
Assignee	The Trustees of Columbia University in the City of New York	Investors Guaranty Fund, Ltd.	
Subject Matter	Quasi–Monte Carlo derivatives pricing	Risk transfer	Premium financing mechanism

ers a tool for pricing a financial instrument. Its subject matter is most easily grasped by reference to its abstract. The abstract reads:

> *In securities trading, in setting the initial offering price of a financial instrument, or in later revaluation as financial parameters such as interest rates may change, an estimate of the value of the instrument may be represented as a multi-dimensional integral. For evaluation of the integral, numerical integration is preferred with the integrand being sampled at deterministic points having a low-discrepancy property. The technique produces approximate values at significant computational savings and with greater reliability as compared with the Monte Carlo technique.*

To a lawyer, the real meat of a patent is its "claims." Claim 1 of the '810 patent provides a more technical description of the invention, using language meant to convey as precisely as possible what exactly the inventor intends to claim:

> 1. *A method for one of buying, holding and selling a complex security, comprising:*
> *(i) deriving a multivariate integrand which, when integrated over a domain of integration having at least 50 dimensions, represents an estimated value of the security;*
> *(ii) calculating, by computer, integrand values at points in the domain of integration which are obtained from a low-discrepancy deterministic sequence;*
> *(iii) combining the integrand values, by computer, to approximate the estimated value; and*
> *(iv) effecting, based on the estimated value, one of buying, holding and selling the security.*

The '810 patent contains 21 additional claims, many of which relate to (or, in patent parlance, are "dependent" on) the claim recited above. In simple terms, the '810 patent claims the exclusive right to use any method that contains all the elements of any of its claims. In this case, those claims relate to the use of what are more commonly known as "quasi–Monte Carlo" methods. To fall under claim 1, for example, use of the method must be "by computer" since that is a recited limitation in element (ii). If, for example, it were possible to solve in one's head the integration problem presented in element (i), then that use would not infringe the '810 patent. The limitations of such a "design around" are obvious to all but the most gifted mental calculators.

The second patent described in Exhibit 27.3—U.S. Pat. No. 5,704,045— purports to cover a "System and Method of Risk Transfer and Risk Diversification Including Means to Assure with Assurance of Timely Payment and Segregation of the Interests of Capital." Again, the abstract provides a snapshot of the patent's intended coverage:

> *A system and method of accepting risk through contractual obligations transfers a portion of the risk to investors and includes means for absolute assurance of timely payment to contract holders, and segregation, of the interests of particular investors to specifically identified risks in a risk to capital matching system. The system creates separate ledgers and segregated reserves to tailor particular products for specific needs including transferring*

difficult-to-place risks. The system creates agreements which promise payments, based on loss from risks including investment risks. Data processing provides legally segregated relationship management links, supervising and balancing the interests of professionals in a risk transfer and diversification system.

The '045 patent has 74 claims. Claim 1 is as follows:

1. *A method employing operatively interconnected, input, output and data processing means for facilitating through an entity, the transfer and acceptance of specifically defined risks through the entity from risk transferors to capital providers accepting the risk transferred, the method comprising:*
 creating an entity for facilitating the transfer of risk from one or more risk transferors through the entity to capital providers accepting the risk through the entity;
 creating and maintaining a communications system for communications between risk transferors and capital providers through the entity;
 creating within the entity a capital reserve system;
 exchanging information between and among one or more risk transferors, one or more capital providers and the entity relating to the nature and character of the risk for the purpose of one or more willing risk transferors entering into a policy/contract with one or more willing capital providers having defined obligations including the maximum monetary exposure on the risk and the duration thereof; and
 causing the capital provider(s) to transfer sufficient capital to the capital reserve system prior to the effective date of such contract which capital when combined with risk compensation and other income is sufficient to meet any and all such defined obligations during such contract period.

The '045 patent appears to be assigned to Investors Guaranty Fund, Ltd., as part of the intellectual property underlying an "insurance securitization" system.[3] Investors Guaranty Fund, Ltd. was involved in litigation with Morgan Stanley over some elements of a system for converting specific insurance risks into capital market securities. See *Investors Guaranty Fund, Ltd. v. Morgan Stanley & Co.*, 50 U.S.P.Q.2d 1523 (S.D.N.Y. 1998). That litigation, however, does not appear to have involved the '045 patent, which issued after the events at issue there.

The third patent in Exhibit 27.3—U.S. Pat. No. 6,026,364—covers a

"System and Method for Replacing a Liability with Insurance and for Analyzing Data and Generating Documents Pertaining to a Premium Financing Mechanism Paying for Such Insurance," and is the invention of Brian L. Whitworth, an individual entrepreneur from Malibu, California, with a background in insurance and financial product development.

The abstract of the '364 patent is as follows:

> *A system and method for replacing a self insurance with insurance, employing a premium financing mechanism with a payout pattern determined in consideration of an estimated payout of the self insurance to pay for the insurance, identifying employers for whom leaving self insurance may be desirable, and, in one preferred embodiment, analyzing data and generating documents and/or computer-readable data files pertaining to such a premium financing mechanism.*

The '364 patent has 63 claims, starting with claim 1:

> *1. A system for analyzing data and generating documents pertaining to a premium financing mechanism, the system comprising:*
> *a computer executable program or programs adapted to:*
> *access estimate data of a cost of self insurance, a cost of insurance, and savings realized by replacing self insurance with insurance;*
> *access risk data pertaining to a transaction wherein a bond is employed to pay for said insurance to replace said self insurance;*
> *process said estimate data to provide data usable by a printer to generate a document pertaining to a bond proposed to pay for said insurance; and*
> *process said risk data to provide data usable by a printer to generate documents pertaining to an issuance of said bond.*

The '364 patent's inventor makes clear on his web site that he is monitoring financial activity for possible infringement of his patents (emphasis in original):

> *Finally, if you are an investment banker, actuary, insurance carrier, insurance broker, self insured company or municipality, and you will be involved in a departure from self insurance which uses sophisticated analysis or long term financing, please contact us regarding our patents. We are happy to consult on these transac-*

tions. We also will be happy to spend a small amount of time (at no charge) verifying whether your transaction or analysis is likely to infringe any of the patents' claims. *The patents have over 130 claims relating to these types of transactions, so the coverage is quite broad. We will do our best to prevent accidental infringement and prevent unnecessary worries regarding analysis or transactions which will not infringe.*[4]

EVOLUTION OF FINANCIAL PATENTS: A THUMBNAIL SKETCH

The United States Supreme Court has noted that Congress intended that patent protection might extend to "anything under the sun that is made by man."[5] Still, most readers will note that patents have played no significant role in the surge of financial innovation over past decades (see Lerner [2000]).

Simplicity certainly cannot explain the paucity of financial patents. To the contrary, financial engineering is a highly technical and complex field, whose "inventions" are often beyond the grasp of those without strong training in mathematics, computer science, and modern financial economics. At a technical level, critical financial innovations may be every bit as "complex" as more traditional fields of patent law protection like biotechnology and electrical engineering.

Nor can the failure to employ patent law protection be ascribed to any obvious superiority of other forms of intellectual property protection. Consider the two alternative mechanisms traditionally employed by financial innovators to "protect" the fruits of financial invention: secrecy and first-mover advantages. Secrecy probably has been the predominant means of protection for financial inventions like the computer code and financial mathematics underlying cutting-edge derivatives pricing models. Secrecy can facilitate significant nonpatent legal protection, including contractual nondisclosure agreements and state trade secrets law. First-mover advantages—getting to market first and exploiting the gains from doing so—have been more important for protecting the financial innovation embodied in new security designs (see Tufano [1989]). Although few doubt the ability of competing investment banks to reverse-engineer widely offered products, first-movers appear to gain something from being first out the door with an innovative new offering.

However, both secrecy and first-mover advantages possess inherent weaknesses. Secrecy is vulnerable to the constant risk of disclosure, and (with an important recent exception noted below) secret inventions are not protectable against subsequent patents on the same inventions. First-mover advantages are less susceptible to this problem since the invention is disclosed in the first use or sale, limiting its later patentability and enforcement against the first inventor.[6] But the first-mover advantage may leave significant value on the table for competitors. Tufano (1989), for example, found that rivals imitated 35 of 58 studied financial innovations within one year of introduction. In addition, the incrementalism so prevalent in financial engineering—where one financial innovation builds in small ways on an earlier one—means that an early patent might allow even greater returns from an important financial innovation than otherwise available from the first-mover's nonlegal advantages alone.

Finally, the paucity of patent protection in the financial field cannot be explained by any general discomfort with legal and regulatory rules. Indeed, many observers link many important financial innovations directly *to* legal and regulatory rules, especially tax rules (see Miller 1986]; Gergen and Schmitz [1997]).

The best explanation for the past rarity of financial patents is instead that few financial "inventors" believed that their financial innovations were patentable subject matter. Or, more accurately, the risks that a court would find that a given financial invention was not patentable subject matter was high enough that the value of the patent was low. What has been important in the evolution of financial patents is the development of greater certainty over the patentability of computing methods and mathematical algorithms. Financial patents tend to implicate both areas.

Even a summary of the long and twisting legal history of the patentability of computing methods and mathematical algorithms is beyond the scope of this article. Suffice to say, however, that legal standards eventually began to embrace the patentability of computer-implemented inventions and then to dismiss with the need for a computer implementation per se, so long as the mathematical algorithm was not simply a mathematical formula in the abstract.

In a series of important decisions, the Supreme Court first presented seemingly high hurdles to patentability, suggesting that computer programs might be simply unpatentable mathematical algorithms. The Court then appeared to soften this position for computer programs performing useful functions. The lower courts further developed tests to determine whether computer programs were patentable subject matter, and the role that the presence of a "mathematical algorithm" might play in that determination.

An important application of this development occurred in a relatively early and important patent case surrounding a financial patent. In 1983, the U.S. District Court of Delaware held that a patent related to Merrill Lynch's Cash Management Account (CMA) claimed patentable subject matter because the claims covered the use of a computer to effectuate a business activity. Linking the computer to the business method of the CMA proved the key to Merrill Lynch's litigation success, and Dean Witter Reynolds eventually paid Merrill Lynch a license fee to offer its own CMA product.

By any measure, however, the concern with financial patents is related to a recent and highly influential opinion of the Court of Appeals for the Federal Circuit. The Federal Circuit has responsibility for patent law appeals in the United States. In 1998, it decided the case of *State Street Bank v. Signature Financial*, 47 U.S.P.Q.2d (BNA) 1596 (Fed. Cir. 1998). In that case, the district court (the lower court where the initial complaint was filed) ruled that subject matter claimed in the patent was not patentable subject matter. On appeal, the Federal Circuit reversed, holding that Signature Financial's software system for managing a "Hub and Spoke" mutual fund pooling system was patentable subject matter.

Against the background of earlier case law, the *State Street* decision was influential because it laid to rest any continuing doubt as to the patentability of "business methods," made clear that computer programs were patentable subject matter, and eliminated substantial doubt over the patentability of mathematically derived inventions. In perhaps its most important holding for financial patenting, the court stated:

> *Today, we hold that the transformation of data, representing discrete dollar amounts, by a machine through a series of mathematical calculations into a final share price, constitutes a practical application of a mathematical algorithm, formula, or calculation, because it produces a useful, concrete and tangible result—a final share price momentarily fixed for recording and reporting purposes and even accepted and relied upon by regulatory authorities and in subsequent trades.*

In the later case of *AT&T Corp. v. Excel Communications, Inc.*, 50 U.S.P.Q.2d (BNA) 1447 (Fed. Cir. 1999), the Federal Circuit made clear that the presence of a "machine" was unimportant: the patentability of claims containing mathematical algorithms is the same regardless of the form, machine, or process in which a particular claim is drafted.

The general viability of the Federal Circuit's interpretation was confirmed when, on November 29, 1999, Congress amended 35 U.S.C. §273 to provide that an alleged infringer of a business method patent can assert as a defense that it reduced the subject matter to practice at least one year prior to the effective filing date of the patent, and commercially used the subject matter before the effective filing date of the patent. The amendment was intended to protect users of business methods who had not patented their earlier inventions, but now were being sued by those who had. The implicit acceptance by Congress of the business method patent suggests that the Federal Circuit is unlikely to change its position in the future.

Thus, the important legal changes leading to greater financial patenting concern clarification of subject matter requirement. Decisions like *State Street* and *AT&T v. Excel* make clear that the subject matter requirement is no longer going to prevent most interesting financial inventions from being patented. This means that other requirements of patentability—usefulness, novelty, and nonobviousness—will become the key focus, as is the case in patent litigation in more well-established fields. Since inventions that are not useful are typically of little financial value, this means that the real focus will be on novelty and nonobviousness.

CONCLUSION

This article has explored the emerging role that patent law will play in financial and insurance innovation. Given recent legal shifts, it seems likely that patent law will become increasingly important in controlling the sale and use of newly designed financial products and widely used pricing and risk management software (as opposed to proprietary models). The evolution of legal views of patentable subject matter, and an increasing willingness of small companies to leverage intellectual property rights, suggests that intellectual property law—the laws pertaining to patents, copyrights, trademarks, and trade secrets—will play an increasingly important role in the process of financial innovation.

It is also important, however, to keep patent law in its proper perspective. Many financial firms will continue to rely on first mover advantages and trade secret law to protect their intellectual property investment. This may be particularly true in financial engineering. Trade secret law, in particular, offers substantial advantages in that it enables a company to keep its proprietary information secret. Considering that the technological life of pricing models and the like may be obsolete by the time a patent issues, secrecy will continue to be an important source of protection for inventions in the financial engineering field. Nevertheless, the message to alternative risk transfer professionals is that as innovation in the field continues, the once ignored possibility of patent protection must be taken seriously from both offensive and defensive standpoints.

CHAPTER 28

Critical Distinctions between Weather Derivatives and Insurance

Andrea S. Kramer

Weather risks[1] are carefully considered and evaluated by a wide range of businesses. Temperature variations, climate fluctuations, and weather fronts mean money. Lots of money. For example, electric utilities and distributors do not sell as much electricity during a cool summer as they do in a hot one. And gas utilities and heating oil distributors do not sell as much fuel for heating in a mild winter as they do in a cold one.

It is estimated that 20 percent of the U.S. economy is sensitive to weather conditions.[2] Weather derivatives and weather insurance products have developed to help weather-sensitive businesses protect themselves against weather-related risks. Prior to entering into a weather-related derivative or insurance contract, a company with a weather risk must evaluate the appropriateness of the product for its particular needs, the comfort level of its board of directors or senior management, its regulatory environment, and its tax situation.

Weather products, irrespective of whether structured as derivatives or as insurance contracts, rely on weather-related factors, such as heating degree days (HDDs), cooling degree days (CDDs), perceived temperature or chill indexes, snowfall and snow depth indexes, precipitation and rainfall, humidity indexes, water flow, and sunshine indexes. Weather products can protect against reduced demand or sales for the company's products or

Ms. Kramer is a partner of McDermott Will & Emery and heads the firm's Financial Products, Trading, and Derivatives Group. © 2005 Andrea S. Kramer.

services (often referred to as "volume risk"). Weather products can also protect against increased supply or sales costs (often referred to as "price risk"). And they can protect against volatility in a company's revenues or net income.

Weather derivatives and weather insurance have a number of similarities. Indeed, weather derivatives often function, in many circumstances, as the financial equivalent of indemnity contracts and financial guarantees. But functional equivalence is one thing and legal equivalence is quite another. If weather derivatives are incorrectly deemed to be insurance, the consequences under state insurance law would be highly adverse for this vibrant and valuable financial market. As a result, it is critically important to distinguish between insurance (as state-regulated service contracts) and derivatives (as financial market transactions).

If a derivatives contract were found to be an insurance policy, the derivative could be sold only by a licensed insurance broker. Thus, a derivatives counterparty that is not so licensed—if ultimately found to have been selling insurance—would be acting unlawfully. In California, this would be a misdemeanor.[3] In Connecticut, fines, imprisonment, or both can be imposed for acting as an "insurance producer" without a license.[4] Under Delaware law, a Delaware corporation can lose its "charter" to do business[5] if it acts "as an insurer" without a "certificate of authority"[6] to conduct an insurance business.[7] In New York, insurance law violations are misdemeanors,[8] with fines increasing for subsequent violations.[9] And in Illinois, no one can "sell, solicit, or negotiate insurance" unless properly licensed under the insurance laws.[10]

In this chapter, I first look at weather derivatives, describing what they are and how they are regulated. Second, I look at weather insurance contracts, focusing on the legal distinctions between insurance and derivatives. Third, I highlight some key differences in the way derivatives and insurance contracts are documented. And fourth, I discuss some key tax differences between weather derivatives and insurance contracts.

WHAT ARE WEATHER DERIVATIVES?

Weather derivatives are financial contracts between two parties, with contract values based on changes in specified weather conditions. They can be traded on exchanges (as futures contracts or options on futures),[11] or they can be entered into as bilateral contracts between two parties, which is referred to as having been entered into in the over-the-counter (OTC) market.

Popular OTC derivatives include options, caps, floors, collars, swaps, and cash-settled forward contracts. As a general rule, one party to a weather derivative is paid if the specified weather-related payment event results. And, with a derivatives contract, neither party needs to prove that it has incurred a financial loss in order to collect the specified payment.

Upon entering into a derivatives contract, the two parties agree to the specific payment calculations reflected in the trade confirmation. For example, payout terms can be tied to a specified dollar amount multiplied by the HDD (or CDD) level specified in the contract and the actual HDD (or CDD) level reported in the specified location during the specified time period.[12] The payment calculation is made and payment is due, without regard to whether one party can show proof of a loss or that it has an insurable risk. And, neither party to a derivatives contract needs to be regulated as an insurance company.

Businesses with active trading operations (for physical commodities and derivatives) may find weather derivatives less intimidating than those businesses without similar experiences. As a result, experienced market participants may be more willing to enter into derivatives than companies without such experiences. In addition, those market participants without weather risk exposure can nevertheless enter into derivatives, without a need to demonstrate an insurable risk or to prove a loss due to weather risk.

Who Has Jurisdiction over Weather Derivatives?

"Weather" is included in the definition of a "commodity" in the Commodity Exchange Act (CEA).[13] This means that weather derivatives are subject to the federal commodities laws unless a transaction qualifies for an exemption or exclusion from the CEA.

For weather derivatives, an important exemption from federal regulation applies if the derivatives contract falls within the category of "excluded swap transactions" in CEA §2(g).[14] Under this exclusion, the CEA does not apply to "any agreement, contract, or transaction in a commodity other than an agricultural commodity" if the agreement, contract, or transaction meets three requirements.

First, the contract must be entered into by parties that meet the definition of "eligible contract participant" at the time they enter into the transaction. For these purposes, the definition of "eligible contract participant" tracks the former definition of "eligible swap participant" at Rule 35.1(b)(2) of the Commodity Futures Trading Commission (CFTC).[15]

Second, the contract must be subject to individual negotiation by the parties. Bilateral derivatives contracts negotiated between two parties are generally viewed as contracts subject to individual negotiation, and they, therefore, meet this requirement.

And third, the contract cannot be executed or traded on a trading facility, such as an established commodities exchange or a centralized electronic market.

The exemption for "excluded swap transactions" is not the only place to look because another CEA exclusion or exemption might apply to a particular transaction. In addition to the "excluded swap transactions" exemption, another exclusion or exemption from the CEA might apply to a particular transaction. Even if a derivative product or its parties fail to meet all of the requirements to qualify as an "excluded swap transaction," another exemption (such as the exemption for so-called trade options) might be available to a particular transaction.

WHAT IS INSURANCE?

Insurance contracts are defined, and individually regulated, by each of the 50 states in the United States (as well as the District of Columbia). In addition, each state has it own requirements that must be met by insurers, insurance agents, and others who solicit insurance customers in that state. A leading insurance treatise defines insurance under U.S. law as:

> *A contract by which one party (the insurer), for a consideration that is usually paid in money . . . promises to make a certain payment, usually of money, upon the destruction or injury of something in which the other party (the insured) has an interest. [cite omitted] In other words, the purpose of insurance is to transfer risk from the insured to the insurer. Insurance companies act as financial intermediaries by providing a financial risk transfer service that is funded by the payment of insurance premiums that they receive from policyholders.*[16]

Given the broad range of insurance contracts now available to protect against a wide range of business and financial risks, a single definition of insurance cannot be applied to all contracts that are regulated as insurance. As a result, the analysis of what qualifies as insurance becomes difficult. For example, defining an insurance contract as a contract that "transfers and distributes risk" in and of itself is simply too broad. This definition improperly sweeps into "insurance" many financial market transactions (including derivatives) that are not thought of, regulated, documented, or taxed as insurance. Yet, certain other contracts are viewed as insurance contracts even though they do not "transfer" risk but rather "finance" or mitigate specified business or financial risks.

In evaluating whether a particular contract should be treated as insurance, five characteristics are typically applied to the contract:

1. First, the insured must have an "insurable risk" (such as the risk of a financial loss on the occurrence of a disaster, theft, or weather event) with respect to a "fortuitous event" that is capable of a financial estimate.[17]

2. Second, the insured must "transfer" its "risk of loss" to an insurance company (referred to as "risk shifting" or "underwriting"), under a contract that provides the insured with an "indemnity" against the loss (with the indemnity limited to the insured's actual loss).

3. Third, the insured must pay a "premium" to the insurance company for the insurance company to assume the insured's insurable risk.

4. Fourth, the insurance company typically assumes the risks covered in the insurance contract as part of a larger program for managing loss by holding a large pool of contracts covering similar risks. This pool is often large enough that actual losses are expected to fall within expected statistical benchmarks (referred to as "risk distribution" or "risk spreading").[18]

5. Fifth, before the insured can collect under the contract, it must demonstrate that its injury was from an "insurable risk" as the result of an "insured event." In other words, the insured must prove that it actually suffered a loss that was covered by the contract.

Bottom line: An insurance contract must cover the risk that an insured will suffer an insured loss; payment is due under the contract only if there is proof of an insured loss; and payment is limited to an amount equal to the lesser of the insured's actual loss or the maximum amount of loss covered by the contract. In addition, the insured can collect under the insurance contract only after it has provided proof of its loss, and it can collect for its loss only up to the amount provided in the contract.

DISTINCTIONS BETWEEN INSURANCE AND DERIVATIVES

Case law wrestles with the definition of insurance,[19] because insurance can often be broadly defined. Additional requirements are imposed so that the word *insurance* is not found in every contract where one party indemnifies the other party against a specified economic risk. But even if insurance is defined quite broadly in the case law, insurance regulators do not define it as broadly for insurance regulatory purposes. Even though the demarcation between insurance products and other risk-shifting contracts has blurred in recent years, bright-line distinctions between insurance contracts and derivatives remain critically important.

Let's look at New York State insurance law as an illustration of how an important U.S. jurisdiction determines whether a contract is subject to insurance regulation. New York is a key insurance regulator, with jurisdiction over most of the largest insurance companies in the United States. As a consequence, New York's view of when a contract constitutes insurance is often highly persuasive to other state insurance regulators. Under New York law, insurance is an agreement where one party (the insurance company) is obligated to confer a benefit of pecuniary value to another party (the insured or beneficiary), depending on a fortuitous event (beyond the control of either party) in which the insured or beneficiary has, or is expected to have, a material interest that will be adversely affected if the fortuitous event occurs.[20] In determining whether a risk-shifting contract is insurance, New York's basic approach is entirely consistent with the earlier discussion in the section "What Is Insurance?"

The New York Insurance Department (NYID) consistently finds that derivatives contracts are not insurance contracts as long as the payments due under the contracts are not dependent on proving an actual loss. For example, in considering catastrophe options (cat options) that provide for payment in the event of a specified natural disaster (such as a hurricane or major storm), the NYID stated in a June 25, 1998, opinion letter (the Cat Options Opinion) that cat options were not insurance contracts.[21] The Cat Options Opinion addressed options that provided that a specified amount (unrelated to losses actually incurred by the purchaser) would be payable to the purchaser if a specified catastrophic event (such as a hurricane or major storm) occurred. The purchaser did not need to be injured by the catastrophic event specified in the contract in order to collect the specified contract amount. Rather, the issuer was obligated to pay the purchaser without regard to whether the purchaser actually suffered a loss because of the catastrophic event specified in the contract. Because the purchaser did not need to prove that it had suffered a loss, the NYID concluded that the cat options were not insurance contracts.

If the cat options had, instead, been structured to provide for a payment to the purchaser *only* if the purchaser had suffered a loss with respect to an insurable interest, the NYID would have treated the cat options as insurance contracts, requiring both licensure and compliance with New York insurance requirements.

In the Cat Options Opinion, the NYID essentially made the following distinction: A "derivative product" transfers risk *without regard* to whether its purchaser has actually suffered a loss. An "insurance contract," on the other hand, transfers the risk of the purchaser's own and actual fortuitous—but insurable—loss to the issuer of the contract.

On February 15, 2000, the NYID applied the Cat Option Opinion analysis to weather derivatives (Weather Derivatives Opinion).[22] In the Weather Derivatives Opinion, the NYID concluded that weather derivatives are not insurance contracts under New York insurance law because payment to the purchaser does not depend on the purchaser having suffered a loss. In fact, neither the amount of the payment nor the triggering event of a derivative bears a relationship to the purchaser's loss.[23] And most recently, the NYID concluded that a credit default swap is not an insurance contract[24] because the "seller" must pay the "buyer" upon the occurrence of a "negative credit event" without regard to whether the buyer has "suffered a loss." It appears clear, therefore, at least under New York law, that a weather derivatives contract that does not tie payment to the actual loss experience of the protection buyer is not insurance.

For payment under an insurance contract, many other states (in addition to New York) require an insured to incur a loss and to prove that the insured actually incurred the loss. The statutory and judicial requirements for finding insurance in many states also include the key elements of an insurable risk and protection against a proven loss.[25]

ANALYSIS OF WEATHER DERIVATIVES AS INSURANCE DISCREDITED

A careful look at the differences between derivatives and insurance is especially important in light of recent developments at the National Association of Insurance Commissioners (NAIC). In 2003 the NAIC's Crop Insurance Working Group circulated an ill-advised and unpersuasive draft paper entitled "Weather Financial Instruments (Temperature): Insurance or Capital Markets Products?"[26] The NAIC draft paper glossed over the structural differences between derivatives and insurance, reaching the erroneous conclusion that weather derivatives were really insurance contracts. Because the NAIC is made up of insurance regulators from each of the 50 states, the District of Columbia, and the four U.S. territories, NAIC pronouncements—as well as its draft papers—require careful attention, no matter how unfounded the positions advanced in its draft papers may ultimately be.

The NAIC draft paper (in asserting that weather derivatives were really "disguised" insurance products) called into question well-established distinctions between insurance and derivatives. Given the NAIC's mission to assist state insurance regulators,[27] the NAIC draft paper was an inappropriate attempt at a jurisdictional grab.

At the NAIC's 2004 winter meeting, the Insurance Securitization Working Group (ISWG) was assigned the NAIC draft paper for its consideration. After discussions and comments, ISWG rejected the NAIC draft paper in February 2004. Immediately following, at the NAIC's Spring National Meeting in March, the NAIC draft paper was also rejected by the NAIC's Property and Casualty Committee, which tabled the draft and ended future discussions for the time being. Bottom line: The NAIC draft paper did not receive any serious support from the larger NAIC membership.

The ill-advised NAIC draft paper emphasizes the importance of understanding the distinctions between derivatives and insurance products. In this section, I dismiss a few of the points incorrectly raised in the NAIC draft paper to support its position.

In attempting to build the case that weather derivatives were actually products "disguised as 'non-insurance' products to avoid being classified and regulated as insurance products,"[28] the NAIC draft paper ignored well-established legal distinctions between derivatives and insurance. Without focusing on—or even acknowledging—these critical legal distinctions, the NAIC draft paper asserted that if weather derivatives had been classified as insurance, (1) insurance regulatory scrutiny would minimize the likelihood of price manipulation in the natural gas market,[29] (2) consumer protections would inure to the "benefit of the buying public,"[30] and (3) states would increase "needed revenues" through the imposition of a premium tax on these newly designated insurance contracts.[31] These assertions are all unfounded and not based on established law. First, the NAIC draft paper did not seem to understand the issues in the natural gas market that lead to allegations of price manipulation. Second, there have never been any problems with weather derivatives that in any way suggest a need for consumer protections. And third, although the states would benefit from additional revenues, states cannot impose tax on derivatives contracts simply by calling them insurance (i.e., impose a tax that applies only to insurance contracts).

Because the NAIC draft paper has been tabled, I will not take the time to demonstrate in any detail why the premises and assertions set out in it are unfounded.[32] But the fact the paper was drafted and circulated in the first place clearly demonstrates the importance of understanding the distinctions between weather derivatives and insurance products.

DOCUMENTATION CONSIDERATIONS

Given the possible overlap between weather-related derivatives and insurance contracts, the way in which a contract is documented is often important in determining whether the contract is a derivative or an insurance contract.

Derivatives Documentation

Derivatives transactions are typically documented under standard so-called master agreements issued by the International Swaps and Derivatives Association (ISDA).[33] The parties negotiate a customized schedule, which becomes part of the ISDA master agreement. The schedule and the standard form ISDA master agreement establish general legal terms that apply to all derivatives transactions between the parties (such as which party has the right to make the calculations under the contract, what the payment terms are for early terminations, and applicable governing law). The parties negotiate the terms of any credit support and the requirements for posting collateral, if appropriate, which become part of the ISDA master agreement. Individual transactions are reflected on separate trade confirmations, setting out the economic terms of each individual transaction, while also becoming part of the ISDA master agreement.[34]

Important protections are available to parties to derivatives transactions if their contracts are documented under a "Master Swap Agreement" (which often includes an ISDA master agreement, schedule, and individual trade confirmations). First, a Master Swap Agreement typically provides for netting of payments to be made or received on multiple derivatives transactions between the parties on the same day and in the same currency. Second, if one of the parties to the Master Swap Agreement becomes insolvent (or files a bankruptcy petition), the other party has special rights under the U.S. bankruptcy laws to terminate the Master Swap Agreement and to offset (or net out) any termination values or payments.[35] And third, certain other types of derivatives contracts are excluded from the "automatic stay" provisions of the U.S. bankruptcy laws, allowing certain setoffs for those transactions.[36] These protections can be enormously valuable to the solvent derivatives party.

Insurance Contracts

Insurance contracts are typically documented under a packet of documents that consist (as completed by the insured) of the actual insurance policy (as offered to all prospective purchasers); declarations (specifying the contractual terms applicable to the insured), the insurance application (as completed by the insured), and any schedules, exhibits, or endorsements that are attached to or accompany the actual insurance policy.

A Derivatives Contract or an Insurance Contract?

A contract offered by a licensed insurance company to transfer a purchaser's weather risk to the insurance company is likely to be viewed as insurance if the purchaser must prove it has suffered a loss before receiving a payment under the contract.

A contract is likely to be viewed as a derivative, on the other hand, if the weather risk is documented under a bilateral agreement between two parties (typically, under an ISDA master agreement), where payment is based on a calculation specified in the contract without regard to whether the party entitled to receive the payment has incurred a loss.

To further refine this general rule, a derivatives contract could (but need not) include a disclaimer that the contract is not intended to be insurance, the contract is not suitable as a substitute for insurance, and the contract is not guaranteed by any "Property and Casualty Guaranty Fund or Association" under applicable state law. One final point: Any marketing materials with respect to a weather derivatives transaction should not focus on the similarities between the contract and insurance.

TAX DISTINCTIONS

Businesses managing their weather-related risks must evaluate the tax treatment of the risk management products (derivatives and insurance contracts) available to them.

Taxation of Weather Derivatives

Weather derivatives are difficult to categorize under established tax rules that generally apply to derivative products because weather derivatives do not usually relate to an identifiable asset or property owned by the business that enters into the derivative. This causes tax uncertainty because U.S. tax laws attempt to distinguish between capital gains and losses and ordinary gains and losses on the basis of the nature of an underlying asset or property in the taxpayer's hands.

Derivatives can be categorized in different ways for U.S. tax purposes. For example, weather derivatives might be characterized as notional principal contracts (NPCs) under Treas. Reg. §1.446-3, as options subject to section 1234 of the Internal Revenue Code (IRC), or as contracts governed by IRC §1234A.[37]

Although a detailed discussion of the tax treatment of various types of derivative products is beyond the scope of this paper, I would like to make the point that, while there may be legitimate policy reasons for taxing weather derivatives in the same manner as other derivatives, existing tax code and regulatory provisions provide little assurance as to the tax treatment of weather derivatives. As a result, if weather derivatives do not qualify as tax hedging transactions within the meaning of IRC §§1221(a)(7) and 1221(b)(2) and Treas. Reg. §1.1221-2, tax character and timing of gains and losses is unclear.

Tax Hedge Qualifications

Once a company identifies a weather derivative that it believes can protect it from a weather-related risk, a key tax question is whether the transaction meets the tax definition of a *hedge*. Gains and losses on derivatives transactions that meet the tax hedge definition receive ordinary income and loss treatment. If the transaction is not a tax hedge, losses are treated as capital losses, even if the transaction protects the company from a business risk. Under general tax rules, capital losses can be deducted only to the extent the company has capital gains from other sources. If a company does not generate capital gains, capital losses are worthless. To obtain favorable tax hedge treatment for a transaction that meets the tax hedge definition, the company must be sure it meets the tax identification requirements set out in the Treasury regulations.

Tax Hedge Defined   A tax hedge is defined as a transaction entered into in the normal course of a company's trade or business *primarily* to manage its interest rate, price, or currency risks with respect to ordinary property, borrowings, or ordinary obligations. Certain anticipated risks can be hedged for tax purposes.

Under current tax law, the risk being hedged must be with respect to ordinary property, borrowings, or ordinary obligations (the risk being hedged is referred to as the "hedged item"). For tax purposes, ordinary property includes property that, if sold by the company, could not produce capital gain or loss. A dealer's inventory, such as natural gas or heating oil, is ordinary property that the dealer can hedge. Similarly, electricity sold by a utility or power marketer is ordinary property that can be hedged.

Transactions that protect overall business profitability (such as volume or revenue risk), in contrast, are not directly related to ordinary property, borrowings, or ordinary obligations. Many weather derivatives transactions manage weather-related volume or revenue risks resulting in reduced demand for, or sales of, a company's products or services. As a result, transactions that protect a company's revenue stream or its net income against volume or revenue risk are not tax hedges under current tax law.

Treasury Authority to Expand Tax Hedging Categories The tax law requirement that a company must hedge ordinary property, borrowings, or obligations means that favorable tax hedging treatment is not available for many legitimate risk management activities. To modernize the tax rules with respect to hedging, Congress in December 2000 specifically authorized the Treasury Department to issue regulations extending the hedging definition to the management of other risks that the Treasury prescribes in regulations.[38] At the date of this writing, the Treasury has not issued regulations extending the benefits of tax hedging to weather-related volume and revenue risks that are not tied to ordinary property, borrowings, or ordinary obligations.

I see no policy reasons for the U.S. tax laws to prohibit tax hedging in situations where a company—in the normal course of its business—seeks to manage its risks against reduced volume or revenue simply because those business risks cannot be attributed to ordinary property, ordinary obligations, or borrowings.[39]

Identification Requirements If a transaction qualifies as a tax hedge, the company must identify the hedge in accordance with the regulations. Ordinary loss treatment is not automatically available to a hedger. Rather, the transaction must be properly identified as a hedge on the day on which the company enters into the hedge, and the hedged item must be identified on a "substantially contemporaneously" basis.

Whipsaw Rules Under tax whipsaw rules, if a company does not properly identify a tax hedge, gains from the transaction are ordinary while losses are capital. A similar whipsaw rule applies to transactions improperly identified as hedges.

Hedge Timing Treasury regulations require a company to account for any gains and losses on its hedges under a tax accounting method that clearly reflects the company's income. According to Treas. Reg. §1.446-4(b), a company has some flexibility to choose its tax accounting method if the tax accounting method clearly reflects its income.

Taxation of Insurance Contracts

As discussed earlier, a weather insurance policy provides a company with insurance coverage if the weather conditions specified in the contracts result in an insurable loss that the company can prove it suffered.

For tax purposes, premiums paid to buy an insurance policy to protect against weather-related losses are deductible against the company's income, when paid as ordinary and necessary business expenses.[40] In addition, the insurance proceeds received from certain types of insurance are generally not taxed, unless the proceeds exceed the company's tax basis of the property lost or if the proceeds represent lost business profits.

If a U.S. company purchases casualty or accident insurance (with respect to hazards, risks, losses, or liabilities incurred in the United States) from a foreign insurance company, the party that pays the premium has the obligation to pay an excise tax to the Treasury. This excise tax is imposed on premiums paid by the U.S. company to the foreign insurance company.[41]

Special tax rules apply to those companies that issue insurance contracts. One special rule is that insurance companies are taxed as corporations under U.S. tax laws. Another special rule is that insurance companies receive certain exemptions from current taxation. Whether a contract is treated as insurance for U.S. tax purposes depends on whether the contract (1) is designated as insurance, (2) reflects terms generally associated with insurance, and (3) is treated as insurance by relevant state insurance regulators.[42]

With respect to a weather-related risk, assume a company pays a premium to an insurance company that, in turn, agrees to pay the company's losses or expenses from the triggering of the weather-related event specified in the contract. Let's also assume that the contract is written as an insurance policy, it relates to a fortuitous weather event, and it provides that the company paying the premium receives an indemnity against specified losses.

For tax purposes, such a contract should qualify as insurance *if* the insurance company pools the risks that it assumes from similar contracts. If the insurance company does not pool these risks, the contract is not insurance for tax purposes. In fact, because of this pooling requirement for tax purposes, courts have found certain contracts that are treated as insurance and regulated by state insurance regulators to be not treated as insurance for tax purposes.[43]

CONCLUSION

Companies interested in protecting themselves against weather-related risks must carefully consider the advantages and disadvantages of entering into weather derivatives or insurance contracts. Although there are no definitive rules as to which terms qualify a contract as either a derivative or an insurance contract, this chapter provides the framework to evaluate these important issues.

CHAPTER 29

Is Insurance a Substitute for Capital under the Revised Basel Accord?

Barbara T. Kavanagh

A n issue central to this book is that insurance can be viewed as a substitute—either partial or complete—for capital itself. Although economics may argue in favor of that perspective, regulatory authorities often approach the question with a differing set of concerns. Inevitably, their views are significantly affected by witnessing "tail events," the extreme failures and losses that make news headlines and reinforce their raison d'être. The commercial banking sector fits neatly into this paradigm; it is generally a heavily regulated industry because of banks' central role in any economy. Most or all banking regulatory authorities view capital as their core mantra. In the United States, for example, the capital of a bank is all that stands between it and the federal safety net: Once its capital is exhausted or near-exhausted, the Federal Deposit Insurance Corporation (FDIC) must step in to ensure an orderly liquidation or transfer of ownership while maintaining economic stability. Consistent with their overseas analogues, U.S. banking regulators carefully design regulations defining capital itself, and what constitutes sufficient capital in relation to the risk profile of an insured financial institution.

Ms. Kavanagh is an independent risk management consultant based in northern Virginia specializing in structured transactions and securitization. She began her professional career with 14 years inside the Federal Reserve and worked subsequently as a consultant with KPMG Peat Marwick and as senior credit officer in the U.S. investment banking arm of a large foreign bank.

The commercial and investment banking businesses have become increasingly global during the past quarter of a century. As national boundaries were crossed, competitive inequities inevitably arose as each national regulatory authority defined "adequate capital" differently for those under its jurisdiction. Recognizing the dilemma associated with this, as well as the fact that systemic risks were also crossing national boundaries as banks globalized, the Bank for International Settlements (BIS) and its regulatory subcommittees were born. Based in Basel, Switzerland, it promulgated the first set of internationally subscribed capital standards in the 1980s. In the mid-1980s, participating national regulatory authorities (generally those from the G-7 countries) crafted a common capital adequacy framework that was adopted in final form in 1988 as the Basel Accord. The participating agencies then returned to their respective jurisdictions and promulgated implementing regulations within their countries consistent with the Basel framework of standards. Now known as Basel I, it was fairly simplistic but an important landmark. National banking authorities had generally agreed that banks in their respective jurisdictions would be asked to hold $8 in capital against each $100 of loans they booked.

In June 2004, the BIS released Basel II, a lengthy and much more complex new capital adequacy framework intended for wide application throughout the financial services sector globally. It was more than five years in the making. All of the national regulatory agencies participating in that forum are now in the nascent stages of promulgating regulations in their respective jurisdictions that implement that framework. The question inevitably arises as to whether insurance can serve as either a partial or complete capital substitute *in that framework*—and if so, subject to what constraints?

At the time of writing of this chapter, U.S. financial services regulators have subscribed broadly to the Basel II principles, but are only in the earliest stages of defining rules for implementation in the United States. Late 2006 is likely to be the very earliest implementation date for Basel II, and a gradual phase-in of rules and regulations over a time frame beginning in 2006 and continuing thereafter is most likely. Despite that seemingly distant date, though, the majority of large institutions long ago began weighing the implications of Basel II for their capital adequacy. As a result, discussion of the implications of risk transfer mechanisms and insurance products in a regulatory capital context is already under way.

Basel II is a substantially more complex risk-based capital framework than its precursor, Basel I. Basel I dates back to 1988 and focused predominantly on credit risk, although it did undergo a significant amendment in the mid-1990s in an attempt to explicitly capture market risk, particularly in trading books. In contrast, Basel II contains sections on several different risk dimensions—credit risk, market risk, and operational risk, as well as a separate, complex chapter on securitization and securitized products. In short, the pendulum has swung dramatically from the oversimplicity often attributed to Basel I to Basel II's attempt to capture most risk dimensions and assign analytically founded capital charges to each.

The following narrative briefly discusses aspects of the Basel II framework relating to operational risk and the use of insurance products or risk transfer mechanisms in the context of capital that must be allocated to operational risks. Those capital charges for operational risk are anything but trivial. A few major institutions have already estimated that operating risk capital allocations may well equal or exceed their capital allocations against market risk. To the extent those capital charges may be reduced by qualifying insurance products, interest in such products or structures is likely to be high. A brief summary of the operational risk aspects of the Basel II capital framework follows.

DEFINITION OF OPERATIONAL RISK AND RELATED RISK TYPES

In its final form, the text of the Basel II documents has defined operational risk as the "risk of loss resulting from inadequate or failed internal processes, people and systems or from external events." It explicitly excludes strategic and reputational risk dimensions, but includes legal risk in all its forms—for example, private sector litigation and the cost of related settlements to regulatory supervisory actions and any associated fines or penalties.[1]

From an insurer's perspective, this definition is sweepingly broad. If one looks, however, at any of several working papers or BIS publications in this area during the years leading up to release of the final framework, a better understanding of risk types captured under the operational risk heading, and insurance products covering at least portions of these risks, is gained. Work by BIS subgroups generally identifies the following seven subcategories or risk types under the category of operational risk, to which existing insurance-based products can be more easily mapped:[2]

1. *Internal Fraud.* This category is intended to cover acts of fraud or misappropriation of property where at least one participant in the scheme is an employee. Examples given include theft, extortion, embezzlement,

robbery, insider trading or intentional mismarking of trading positions, forgery or check kiting, or deliberate tax evasion.

2. *External Fraud.* This category covers the same types of acts as internal fraud but when conducted exclusively by a third party.

3. *Employment Practices and Workplace Safety.* This category is intended to include losses stemming from diversity/discrimination events, personal injury claims, workers' compensation cases, or, more generally, losses from acts inconsistent with health, safety, or employment laws and policies.

4. *Clients, Products, and Business Practices.* This category captures suitability and fiduciary issues, as well as inappropriate business or market practices, product defects (including model errors), and disputes regarding advisory businesses. Examples given include lender liability, suitability/disclosure issues such as "Know your customer," antitrust or money laundering matters, market manipulation, and improper trading on a firm's account.

5. *Damage to Physical Assets.* This category is intended to cover both losses stemming from effects of natural disasters on physical assets as well as such other events as terrorism or vandalism.

6. *Business Disruption and System Failures.* Relatively self-explanatory, this category captures utility outages or disruptions, or failures in hardware, software, or telecommunications equipment.

7. *Execution, Delivery and Process Management.* This final category covers a broad spectrum of residual operational risks. It includes vendor/supplier disputes and outsourcing issues; counterparty disputes or misperformance; matters pertaining to customer account management, including client permissions and incomplete or missing related legal documents; and such reporting matters as inaccurate external releases. This category is also intended to include transaction capture, execution, and maintenance (e.g., incorrect data entry, accounting error, or delivery failure).

This list makes evident that a number of existing insurance products cover pieces of the operational risk dimension—blanket bond insurance (is that a bank product or an insurance product?), business interruption policies, and the newer "rogue trader" coverage that became the subject of interest after a string of sensational losses in trading rooms at several large banks globally. In addition, some newer basket policies have supposedly bundled pieces of the seven categories for coverage under one contract. Reviewing the list also makes clear, though, that a number of operational risks are not typically covered by conventional insurance products. The list also makes transparent the dilemma faced by regulators—the metrics of calculating partial capital relief when pieces of operational risk are transferred to third parties for finite periods of time.

RISK MEASUREMENT, CAPITAL ALLOCATION, AND RELIEF FOR INSURANCE

Basel II allows for three different risk measurement techniques in the world of operational risk: (1) the Basic Indicator Approach, (BIA), (2) the Standardized Approach (SA), and (3) the Advanced Measurement Approach (AMA). Unfortunately, Basel II does not provide for any regulatory capital relief through use of insurance products when either the Basic Indicator Approach or the Standardized Approach is used for operational risk. As such, we set those approaches aside and simply note that they are much more simplistic approaches to measurement than the Advanced Measurement Approach: Under the SA, Basel assigns different capital percentages to different business lines, where those formulas relate required capital levels to revenues generated by each of those major business lines; in the BIA case, a single percentage of overall gross income is assigned to operating risk.

In the United States, institutions with either $250 billion in total assets or $10 billion in foreign exposure will be subject to Basel II; smaller companies may opt for Basel II as opposed to remaining under the capital constraints of the original Basel Accord. Unfortunately, in the United States, all institutions subject to Basel II capital constraints may use *only* the AMA approach for measuring capital allocations against operating risk. Under the AMA or Advanced Measurement Approach, a bank's own internal models and measurement techniques are the basis for calculating regulatory capital requirements. Relying on one's own models and data, however, is conditional on approval by local regulatory bodies. While Basel II describes a very general standard of qualitative and quantitative criteria that institutions must meet to qualify for application of AMA, the ultimate determination and approval authority is vested in local regulatory authorities.

Notably, Basel provisions relating to AMA in the context of operating risk require use of five years' worth of historical data. That data can consist of both an institution's own data representing its own history, as well as industry-wide data (e.g., for projecting likelihood of tail or catastrophic events, where an institution lacks such data for its own time series it may draw on industry-wide data). Although January 2008 seems likely at this point as the first date of compulsory compliance in the United States, many institutions are now accumulating their own data for purposes of meeting the five-year data requirement.

INSURANCE AS A RISK MITIGANT

As currently written, Basel II limits the maximum amount of capital relief available through insurance-based products to 20 percent of the total operational risk capital charge calculated under the AMA. In order to qualify for any capital reduction, the following de minimis criteria are laid out in Basel II:[3]

> *The insurance policy must have an initial term of at least one year. Haircuts will be applied to policies with less than one year to maturity, with hair cuts increasing to the 100 percent level for those structures or products with 90 days or less to expiry.*

> - *The policy must provide for a minimum notice for cancellation of at least 90 days.*
> - *The insuring party must have a claims-paying rating of at least A or its equivalent.*
> - *Insurance must be through a third party. That is, in the event an affiliate or captive writes the policy initially, the resulting exposure must be transferred to a third party in order to be eligible for capital relief at the consolidated organization level.*
> - *The insurance policy must contain no exclusions or limitations associated with supervisory actions. Further, receivership or insolvency cannot render null or void policy coverage and claims relating to past acts prior to failure of the institution but discovered at the time of failure or shortly thereafter by the liquidating agent.*
> - *Last, consistent with Basel II's emphasis on market discipline and transparency, the financial institution must disclose its use of insurance for purposes of capital relief and risk mitigation.*

Note that these criteria are those of the Basel II documents pertaining to operational risk. Each regulator, in implementing capital adequacy regulations and laws locally, is free to expand those de minimis criteria as is deemed appropriate. One should expect that to be the case if local market convention contains idiosyncratic practices or law requiring address.

DATA DILEMMA AND 20 PERCENT CAPITAL RELIEF LIMITATION

A number of quantitative studies were undertaken by regulatory bodies in the five years or more leading up to adoption of Basel II. This was particularly the case in the area of operational risk and related capital requirements for several reasons, including:

- Historical time series of data on operational risk losses have not customarily been maintained by financial institutions.
- In the few cases where time series data were being accumulated, sample size with respect to tail events has been universally problematic. That is, institutions often had data points for high-frequency, low-severity loss events, but little or no personal history with respect to low-frequency, high-loss data points.
- Incentives for industry pooling of such data, or commercial availability of such data, did not exist on a wide scale prior to BIS' indication of intent to allocate capital explicitly against this risk dimension. Since that time, commercial data sources have become available, and pooling of historical data among market participants has been taking place. Nonetheless, a number of data hurdles remain (e.g., addressing inherent data biases, appropriateness of applying external data to individual institutions, and entry into new business lines where no historical data exists).

BIS working papers make available the results of its data surveys in the operational risk arena. In that context, they make transparent where proposed capital charges for simpler capital allocation approaches stem from—that is, which business lines and risk subtypes noted earlier—and where historic losses have been to date. Nonetheless, a number of data issues continue to be discussed (including sufficient sample size in tail events and potential data biases). Regulatory studies and academic research continue in this area.

At first pass, many are disappointed with the 20 percent cap on capital relief expressed in Basel II. But conversations with regulators make two very important points clear in this area. First, the 20 percent cap was set as a "first approximation" and only after surveys reportedly showed no market participant came close to that level of insurance coverage at this juncture. Second, and perhaps more importantly, the BIS and national regulatory authorities explicitly note their receptiveness to modifying this number. Officials fully expect product innovation in the marketplace that will lead to increased operational capital relief. They further express receptiveness to modifying this cap so long as contracts are readily enforceable, insurers demonstrate willingness to pay promptly, and the amount of capital relief afforded can be analytically justified.

PRECURSORS TO FURTHER REGULATORY CAPITAL RELIEF

Regulatory authorities emphasize that at least at this juncture, the 20 percent relief provision does not seem to be a binding constraint. At least in the United States, no structured transactions have been proposed by industry participants representing attempts to transfer operating risk to a third party. This is likely a function of two facts: (1) related regulations have not yet been proposed by authorities to implement Basel II locally, and (2) industry participants are still refining calculations and measurements of operational risk. Those calculations and time series are requisite to determining potential capital allocations in this area.

Conversations with authorities on this subject, however, make clear that the following important list of four precursors must be addressed by industry participants before such structure-specific conversations can be had:

1. Institutions must map existing insurance coverage to each of the operating risk subtypes noted in the earlier section of this chapter.
2. While authorities are allowing institutions to use industry data in combination with their own historical data, an institution will need to cogently rationalize the applicability/relevancy of that industry data to its own case.
3. In designing its operating risk model and modeling approach, an institution will have to assign a probability of payment by the insurer in the event of a claim. Assigned probabilities will have to be substantiated. In both the United States and major European markets, willingness to pay and timeliness of insurance payments under a claim are issues of concern to regulatory authorities.
4. Any insurance or risk transfer structure proposed in the context of operational risk will have to address the willingness to pay and timeliness of payment issue in order to gain regulatory capital relief.

CONCLUSION

The market for operational risk transfer products is likely to grow dramatically over the next several years. The text of Basel II documents makes clear that regulatory authorities are willing to consider insurance as a capital substitute, albeit it will initially be subject to some constraints. Although no "operational risk specific" structures have been seen to date in the U.S. marketplace, they are likely to be forthcoming. In the absence of clear local definition of that capital charge, however, they will only appear in the context of institutions interested in efficient economic capital usage. Based only on Basel II information, however, regulatory capital charges for this risk dimension are very material and provide an incentive for institutions to determine the cost of obtaining such insurance versus their own cost of capital. To the extent those same risk inputs also feed into institutions' internal risk-adjusted capital allocation methodologies and/or affect executive compensation, interest in operational risk transfer products will also grow from an economic capital perspective.

While the 20 percent limitation on relief may, prima facie, seem small, there is latitude for revision of that number upward if substantiated. Many or most institutions have room for significantly increased levels of insurance before broaching this cap; further, the cap itself is viewed by regulatory authorities as flexible. There is also a distinct possibility that the dollar equivalent of the cap will change over time as time series of data become increasingly robust and more populated on an institution-by-institution basis.

Constraints on the extent of expansion in this market will likely stem from the following: insurers demonstrating a capacity to pay, but hesitant or unwilling to do so absent litigation; a failure to find mutually acceptable language making insurance contracts multiyear in term (and thus more like capital from a regulatory perspective), yet still containing protective provisions that allow insurers to fail to renew in the case of material adverse year-to-year changes; and the regulatory interpretive process. Basel II crosses multiple regulatory jurisdictions, and may, in some countries such as the United States, require several regulatory agencies to reach a consensus on approving hybrid or novel products before offering operational capital relief. At this point, however, the prospects seem bright.

CHAPTER 30

Is My SPE a VIE under FIN46R, and, If So, So What?

J. Paul Forrester and Benjamin S. Neuhausen

Special purpose entities (SPEs) are widely used in a variety of project and other structured financings as they generally facilitate the isolation of risk and the assignment of responsibility therefor under definitive transaction agreements and other documents and instruments. In addition, if the SPE is not consolidated with a transaction sponsor, this may allow the sponsor to participate in more transactions than it could if the SPE had to be consolidated in the sponsor's financial statements.

Recently, under substantial political and other pressure to act following the alleged abuses of SPEs by Enron[1] and others, the U.S. Financial Accounting Standards Board (FASB) issued new guidance on consolidation—FASB Interpretation No. 46 (revised December 2003) (FIN46R), *Consolidation of Variable Interest Entities*, an interpretation of Accounting Research Bulletin (ARB) 51. In sharp contrast to the slow progress on its major consolidation project,[2] FASB adopted an expedited schedule for the

A prior version of this article was published in the *Journal of Structured and Project Finance* (Fall 2003).

J. Paul Forrester is a partner of Mayer Brown Rowe & Maw LLP, an international law firm, and is based in its Chicago office. He can be reached at (312) 701-7366 and jforrester@mayerbrownrowe.com.

Benjamin S. Neuhausen is the National Director of Accounting of BDO Seidman, LLP, a national professional services firm, and is based in its Chicago office. He can be reached at (312) 616-4661 and bneuhausen@bdo.com.

release of FIN46R that considerably truncated the usually deliberative and protracted FASB standard-setting process. After 11 months of public meetings and extensive consultation and deliberations, in January 2003 FASB released FIN46 and over the next 12 months released eight interpretive FASB Staff Positions (FSPs),[3] in which FASB elaborated and refined its FIN46 guidance. Finally, in December 2003, FASB released a comprehensive revision of FIN46 (FIN46R). Since the recent release of FIN46R, questions regarding its application and interpretation have already resulted in the release of a further proposed FSP regarding FIN46R.[4] In addition, the FASB's Emerging Issues Task Force (EITF) in Issue 04-7, *Determining Whether an Interest Is a Variable Interest in a Potential Variable Interest Entity*, is struggling with the fundamental concept of variable interest under FIN46R.[5]

Readers of this article expecting a definitive answer to the question posed by its title will probably be disappointed. However, many existing SPEs that were not consolidated under prior guidance may be consolidated by their sponsors under FIN46R, unless they are substantially restructured. Similarly, sponsors entering new structured financing transactions likely will need to structure them differently than in the past to avoid consolidation. FIN46R will present opportunities for entities that are willing to record additional assets and liabilities; they will be able to collect fees for assuming risks that cause them to consolidate SPEs that other entities don't wish to consolidate.

FIN46R represents a significant departure from prior U.S. generally accepted accounting principles (GAAP) and was described by FASB as "principles-based" guidance rather than the traditional "rules-based" FASB guidance. Traditional GAAP guidance on consolidation requires that the owner of a controlling financial interest (usually achieved through ownership of a majority of the voting equity) in an entity should consolidate that entity. However, about 15 years ago, accountants realized that this traditional guidance didn't work very well for SPEs whose activities and business decisions are limited. The EITF developed a different consolidation model[6] for leasing SPEs that in practice was applied by analogy to other kinds of SPEs. In EITF Issue 90-15, the EITF concluded that a lessee should consolidate an SPE lessor unless one of the following three conditions was satisfied:

1. The legal owner of the SPE was an entity (or entities) other than the lessee and had a substantive residual equity investment at risk. (In practice, residual equity equal to 3 percent of assets was often considered sufficiently substantive.)
2. The SPE had significant transactions with other parties.

3. The substantive residual risks and residual rewards of the SPE's assets rested with someone other than the lessee.

This EITF guidance was criticized for making it too easy to avoid consolidation. Residual equity equal to 3 percent of assets was criticized as too little third-party investment at risk. In addition, although it was clear that the legal owners needed to have risk of loss, it was unclear to what extent the SPE could enter into transactions with the sponsor, such as guarantees or derivatives that reduced the risks borne by the SPE "owners." In FIN46R, FASB concluded, like the EITF beforehand, that consolidation guidance based on residual risks and rewards, rather than voting control, was necessary for a class of entities. However, FASB defined the class of entity more broadly and established different criteria.

In fact, FASB had apparent difficulty defining SPEs and in FIN46R adopts a new concept of variable interest entity (VIE). Essentially, a VIE is an entity that is thinly capitalized or whose equity owners do not have the usual risks and rights of equity owners, and that is not otherwise excluded from the scope of FIN46R, as more fully discussed later. Thus, VIEs can include a wide variety of entities, including potentially SPEs used for structured and project finance transactions. As discussed in more detail later, the role of the SPE and the nature of the transaction for which it was formed will be important in applying FIN46R and in determining whether the SPE is a VIE thereunder. This article will examine FIN46R in the context of SPEs used in structured credit transactions—for example, collateralized debt obligation (CDO) transactions—and project finance transactions to illustrate such differences.

The requirements of FIN46R are deceptively brief and take only 41 (only 29 in FIN46) paragraphs and, excluding the accompanying Appendixes, 29 (only 13 in FIN46) pages to state. However, a recent "summary" of FIN46 comprises 77 pages and concludes that the broad scope of this new and complex standard is often ambiguous, and professional judgment will be needed to apply many of its provisions.[7] Following the release of FIN46R, several of the major accounting firms have published extensive interpretive guides to FIN46R.[8]

SCOPE EXCEPTIONS

Certain enterprises are excluded from the scope of FIN46R, although some of these exclusions are unlikely to apply to structured or project finance transactions. By its terms, there are two main exclusions from FIN46R's broad scope:[9] (1) a transferor of financial assets and its affiliates shall not consolidate a qualified special purpose entity (QSPE) as described in paragraph 35 of FAS140 or a former QSPE as described in paragraph 25 of FAS140; and (2) an enterprise that holds variable interests (VIs) in a QSPE or such former QSPE shall not consolidate that entity unless that enterprise has the unilateral ability to cause the entity to liquidate or to change that entity so that it no longer meets the conditions of paragraph 25 or 35 of FAS140. The effect of this scope exclusion will be to exempt most (if not all) static CDOs since these can be structured as QSPEs. Although the requirements for QSPEs under FAS140 are beyond the scope of this article, generally FAS140 requires that the QSPE hold only financial assets and related hedges that have been legally isolated from the transferor and that the QSPE be effectively "brain dead" (that is, the QSPE's activities, including buying and selling such assets, are prescribed by the transaction documents and the QSPE does not make discretionary decisions).[10] As a practical matter, project SPEs generally hold nonfinancial assets and are not QSPEs.

VARIABLE INTERESTS

Under FIN46R, variable interests (VIs) are contractual, ownership, or other pecuniary interests in an entity that change with changes in the entity's net asset value and include the following seven types:

1. Equity investments to the extent that they are at risk, as well as subordinated beneficial interests and subordinated debt instruments.
2. Guarantees, put options, and similar obligations.
3. Forward contracts.
4. Derivative interests and compound instruments.
5. Service contracts.
6. Leases.
7. VIs of one VIE in another VIE.

Clearly, for project SPEs all project contracts will have to be carefully analyzed to determine whether they have the requisite characteristics of VIs. This will likely require professional judgment, since (apart from the earlier examples and some related discussion in Appendix B to FIN46R) FIN46R states that each interest is different and must be analyzed based on the facts and circumstances of each situation. Given the wide variety of project-related agreements in practice and the significant variation therein for transaction-specific requirements, such analysis will often be complex and time-consuming, and consistency of determination in substantially similar situations and among differing accounting firms will be a constant challenge.

For structured finance transactions, there also likely will be a wide variety of potential VIs, especially with respect to derivatives that, under FIN46R, are to be examined for their "option-like, forward-like or other variable characteristics." Obviously, professional judgment will be required in this regard, although over time some accounting consensus or application conventions may appear.

Some VIs are interests in specified assets of a VIE. For example, a residual value guarantee would be a VI in the specified asset, and nonrecourse debt would be a VI in the assets to which the lender has a claim. If the specified assets represent more than 50 percent of the VIE's assets, the VIs are considered VIs in the VIE, and the accounting is the same as if the interests did not relate to specified assets. If the specified assets represent 50 percent or less of the VIE's assets, then the VIs are considered VIs in the specified assets only, but not VIs in the overall VIE. However, if the specified assets are financed exclusively with nonrecourse debt and specifically identified equity, the specified assets may constitute a silo that would be treated as if it were a separate VIE.

Suppose a project VIE is created to own and operate three similar facilities (for example, pipelines) of similar values for three different users. Because each pipeline represents about 33 percent of the VIE's total assets, holders of VIs in specific pipelines are considered to hold only interests in pipelines, not interests in the overall VIE. As a result, no entity that holds only VIs in one pipeline would be a primary beneficiary (PB) of the VIE as a whole. Further, the potential variability in the returns to the VIs in the individual pipelines would be excluded in computing the potential variability in the returns to the VIs in the overall VIE. However, if the financing for each pipeline (both debt and equity) is entirely "walled off" from the financing for the other pipelines, then each pipeline would be treated as if it were a separate VIE.

EXPECTED LOSSES AND EXPECTED RESIDUAL RETURNS

Expected losses (ELs) represent the potential unfavorable variability in the profits of a VIE. Expected residual returns (ERRs) represent the potential favorable variability in the profits of a VIE. The term *expected losses* is somewhat a misnomer, because it does not refer to actual or expected GAAP losses reported by a VIE. A VIE that is expected to be profitable under virtually all circumstances still has ELs,[11] because its profits will be less under certain conditions than under others. ELs and ERRs are to be determined based on probability-weighted expected cash flows. Appendix A of FIN46R illustrates the computation for a simple VIE.

PRIMARY BENEFICIARY

The primary beneficiary (PB) of a VIE is the holder of VIs that will absorb a majority of the ELs or receive a majority of the ERRs of such VIE. If different enterprises hold VIs representing a majority of the ELs and the ERRs, the enterprise that holds the VIs representing a majority of the ELs is the PB. Under FIN46, certain fees are not weighted for their probable variability. This unequal treatment of fees versus other elements of a VIE's profits effectively makes it more likely that a decision maker (DM) or certain guarantors will be the PB of the relevant VIE. Although the treatment of DM fees could have counterintuitive results, FASB only mitigated this treatment in FIN46R. Under FIN46R, the DM must meet certain specific requirements in order for the fees payable to the DM not to be considered a variable interest. These requirements are set forth in paragraphs B-18 through 21 of Appendix B to FIN46R and include that the DM be subject to substantive kick-out rights. As a result, for managed CDOs, if the manager is a DM (as appears likely) it may be the PB even if it does not hold a majority of the total equity. In many energy projects, there is a party that performs day-to-day operations and maintenance under an operations and maintenance agreement. If the operations and maintenance contractor is the DM of the project VIE, fees payable to such party will count disproportionately in the determination of the PB, making it more likely that the contractor will be the PB. Similarly, many equipment vendors to project VIEs will provide performance and other guarantees with respect to such equipment. If periodic fees are payable to such a vendor they will also be weighted disproportionately in the PB determination.

FIN46R includes provisions[12] that effectively aggregate the VIs of related parties for purposes of the PB determination and extend the concept of related party to "de facto agents." This will complicate the PB determination where parties share affiliation or are otherwise related or act as agents for one another.[13]

The PB of a VIE is required to consolidate the VIE. A VIE can have only one PB. Some VIEs will have no PB.

VARIABLE INTEREST ENTITIES

An entity is a VIE if by design either (1) it cannot finance its activities without additional subordinated financial support (or, stated alternately, the VIE's ELs exceed its total equity investment at risk) or (2) its equity holders, as a group, do not have the direct or indirect ability to make decisions about the VIE's activities.

Under FIN46R, an equity investment of less than 10 percent of assets is presumed insufficient, unless one of the following can be demonstrated:

- The entity has as much equity as comparable entities holding similar assets of similar quality that operate without additional subordinated financial support.
- The equity invested in the entity exceeds the entity's ELs based on reasonable quantitative evidence.
- The entity has demonstrated that it can finance its activities without additional subordinated financial support.

Note that this presumption is only negative; that is, there is no corresponding presumption if the equity investment exceeds 10 percent of assets that this is sufficient. In fact, FIN46R specifically notes that more equity will be required for entities that have riskier activities. In addition, for this purpose equity must be equity in form, must participate significantly in profits and losses (even if such equity does not have voting rights), must not have been received in exchange for subordinated interests of other VIEs, and must not have been directly or indirectly received from or financed by other parties involved with the entity. Note also that, unlike the prior EITF guidance, equity from all parties is considered. Equity owned by participants in a project may be counted in deciding whether the project SPE is a VIE.

For project SPEs, these requirements will have interesting applications. Often an investor in a project SPE receives its investment for nominal equity and in consideration for other services (for example, construction, input supply, output purchase or marketing, or operations and maintenance services) and such equity will not count for this purpose to the extent that it is received and/or financed by the transaction. In addition, in many projects interested parties will receive compensation that includes participation in profits (for example, a bonus payable to an operator for exceeding specified financial targets), which can cause the equity to have insufficient participation in profits. Similarly, in many projects, risk of loss will be borne under project contracts by third parties with the possible result that equity will not sufficiently participate in losses for purposes of FIN46R and make the project SPE a VIE thereunder.

Regarding the ability to make decisions regarding the entity's activities, this ability must be through voting or similar rights such as those of a common shareholder in a corporation or the general partner of a partnership, and such rights must be proportional to their obligation to absorb expected losses of the entity. For additional guidance regarding the required rights, some accountants have referred to the EITF Abstract 96-16[14] and the discussion therein of "participating" and "protective" rights. For project SPEs, again this will raise interesting interpretation questions. As noted earlier, projects often retain a contractor to perform day-to-day operations and maintenance—activities closely similar to those of a general partner in a partnership. Also, in a project financing the lenders are frequently given extensive rights to approve changes to project contracts and to contracting parties and other matters, and such rights may be deemed to result in the equity holders not having sufficient decision-making ability and cause the project SPE to be a VIE under FIN46R.

FIN46R DETERMINATION TIMING

The two key determinations in FIN46R are:

1. Whether an entity is a VIE.
2. If so, whether an interest holder is a PB.

The decision about whether an entity is a VIE is made at the formation of the entity (or at the adoption of FIN46R for preexisting entities). The decision is reconsidered if one of the following events occurs:

- The entity's governing documents or the contractual arrangements among the participants change.
- Some or all of the equity investment is returned to existing investors and, as a result, other parties become exposed to ELs.
- The entity becomes involved with additional activities or buys additional assets.
- The entity receives additional equity.

The decision about whether an interest holder in a VIE is a PB is made at the time the enterprise becomes a holder (or at the adoption of FIN46 for preexisting interests). The decision is reconsidered if one of the following events occurs:

- The entity's governing documents or the contractual arrangements among the participants change.
- The existing PB reconsiders its decision if it sells or disposes of part or all of its VIs.
- An interest holder who is not the existing PB reconsiders its decision if it buys new VIs in the VIE or part of the existing PB's interests.
- The VIE issues additional VIs to other holders.

REQUIRED VIE DISCLOSURE

A PB should disclose the following information about a consolidated VIE:

- The nature, purpose, size, and activities of the VIE.
- The carrying amount and classification of assets that are collateral for the VIE's obligations.
- Lack of recourse if any creditors or other interest holders in the VIE have no recourse to the PB's general credit.

These disclosures are in addition to any existing GAAP disclosures. Also, these disclosures are not required if the PB owns a majority voting interest in the VIE.

A holder of a significant VI in a VIE, other than the PB, should disclose the following information about a nonconsolidated VIE:

- The nature, purpose, size, and activities of the VIE.
- The nature of its involvement and when that involvement began.
- The holder's maximum exposure to loss as a result of its involvement with the VIE.

These disclosures are in addition to any existing GAAP disclosures.

TRANSITION

FIN46R is effective for all enterprises on or before the first reporting period that ends after March 15, 2004 (i.e., March 31, 2004, for calendar-year reporting enterprises).

PROPOSED INTERNATIONAL ACCOUNTING STANDARDS CONVERGENCE

Both the FASB and the International Accounting Standards Board (IASB) have projects to converge international accounting standards. Both the FASB and the IASB have guidance for the consolidation of SPEs. The IASB's guidance, contained in SIC-12 (issued by the IASB's predecessor, the International Financial Reporting Interpretations Committee), an interpretation of International Accounting Standard 27, *Consolidated and Separate Financial Statements*, share some similarities (both reflect the view that consolidation should not always be determined by voting control), but also are divergent in some respects and such differences can have significant consequences. While a review of SIC-12 is beyond the scope of this chapter, it would be incomplete if it did not acknowledge the stated objectives of the FASB and the IASB to reduce the differences between their respective accounting standards and that this could directly affect future developments of consolidation policy for SPEs generally and FIN46R specifically.

CONCLUSION

As the foregoing demonstrates, FIN46R likely will raise many difficult determinations in a variety of project and other structured financings—at least until the accounting profession has gained experience with the interpretation and application of this new and complex guidance. The effect of FIN46R often will be the consolidation of the VIE with the PB when this would not have occurred under previously applicable GAAP, unless a transaction can be structured (or restructured, as the case may be) to comply with FIN46R.

CHAPTER 31

Credit Derivatives, Insurance, and CDOs: The Aftermath of Enron

Alton B. Harris and Andrea S. Kramer

redit derivatives—bilateral contracts and debt securities, the values of which are linked to the credit status of a company, a debt obligation, or a pool of debt obligations—have been available since 1992.[1] The importance and frequency of use of these products, however, were transformed by the events of 2001. During that year, corporations defaulted on 211 bond issues valued at over $115 billion, a record number and dollar value.[2] More than 250 public companies filed for bankruptcy protection, a 46 percent increase over the previous year's 176, which itself had been a record.[3] And, of course, the year ended with Enron's astonishing bankruptcy, the largest in American corporate history—until it was eclipsed just eight months later by WorldCom's even more extraordinary and unanticipated collapse.

As a consequence of what Alan Greenspan referred to as a "sharp runup in corporate bond defaults, business failures, and investor losses,"[4] the

Portions of this chapter originally appeared in *Corporate Aftershock: The Public Policy Lessons from the Collapse of Enron and Other Major Corporations*, C. L. Culp and W. A. Niskanen, eds. (New York: John Wiley & Sons, 2003). © 2005 by Alton B. Harris and Andrea S. Kramer.

Mr. Harris is a partner of Ungaretti & Harris and heads the firm's Financial Practices Group.

Ms. Kramer is a partner of McDermott Will & Emery and heads the firm's Financial Products, Trading, and Derivatives Group.

use of credit derivatives grew in 2002 at a rate that "exceeded all expectations," reaching $1.6 trillion in notional value.[5] Since then, the market for global cash and structured credit products has continued its extraordinarily rapid growth. By the end of 2004, credit derivatives with a notional value of $8.42 trillion were outstanding, a 55 percent increase over the prior year.[6]

The increasing recognition of the value of credit derivatives in the post-Enron world has been accompanied by heightened attention to the different structures available for credit risk protection and a concerted effort to ensure that they perform as intended. In this chapter, we explain these different structures, contrast credit derivatives with insurance, discuss very briefly efforts currently under way to improve their documentation, and offer some predictions as to likely future developments with respect to credit derivatives. But before doing so, it may be useful first to address the deceptively simple question: Why credit derivatives?

MANAGEMENT OF CREDIT RISK

Credit risk "is the risk to earnings or capital arising from an obligor's or counterparty's failure to meet the terms of any contract . . . or perform otherwise as agreed."[7] Although the credit derivatives market is of very recent origin, the recognition that the persons with which you transact business may default on their obligations is as old as commerce itself, and the need, in appropriate circumstances, to manage or protect against credit risk is the reason for such commonplace practices as secured lending, letters of credit, financial covenants, guarantees, and margin requirements.

Yet, effectively protecting against credit risk while still continuing to conduct business can be difficult. Credit card debt cannot be secured, the full value of a loan may not be recovered on the sale of collateral, and margin may be insufficient in the event of an unexpectedly large market movement. Moreover, the established ways of transferring credit risk—for example, loan syndications and securitizations—require those assuming credit risk also to provide funding. Credit derivatives offer lenders and other credit risk counterparties an entirely new degree of flexibility in managing such risk. Many credit derivatives do not involve *ex ante* funding and require the party assuming the credit risk to make payment only *ex post* the occurrence of a credit event. Such credit derivatives, increasingly the majority, permit banks and other counterparties to manage their credit risk separately from their funding obligations. Other credit derivatives that do require *ex ante* funding permit that funding to be supplied through the capital markets from a far wider range of participants than was ever before possible.

Credit derivatives both separate credit risk from funding and commoditize such risk, transforming it into tradable market instruments. Both techniques provide the means for major financial institutions and corporations to manage their credit risk by distributing or laying off the type and amount of risk they do not wish to carry among a wide range of market participants. American banks, for example,

> *have effectively used credit derivatives to shift a significant part of the risk from their corporate loan portfolios to insurance firms here and abroad, to foreign banks, to pension funds, to hedge and vulture funds, and to other organizations with diffuse long-term liabilities or no liabilities at all. Most of these transfers were made early in the credit-granting process, and significant exposures to telecommunication firms were laid off through credit default swaps, collateralized debt obligations, and other financial instruments. Other risk transfers reflected later sales at discount prices as credits became riskier and banks rebalanced their portfolios. Some of these sales were at substantial concessions to entice buyers to accept substantial risk. Whether done as part of the original credit decision or in response to changing conditions, these transactions represent a new paradigm of active credit management and are a major part of the explanation of the banking system's strength during a period of stress.*[8]

Precisely how credit derivatives perform as "a new paradigm of active credit management" is the subject to which we turn next.

WHAT ARE CREDIT DERIVATIVES?

"Credit derivatives" refer to a variety of differently structured products that have as their common objective the protection of one party against credit risk associated with a specified third party (reference entity), the bonds or borrowings of a specified third party (reference obligation[9]), or a pool or portfolio of reference entities or reference obligations.[10] Neither party to a credit derivative needs to have any credit exposure to the reference entity or obligation. Nor does either party need to prove that it has incurred a financial loss in order to collect the payments specified in the derivatives contract. Like other securities and derivatives products, and unlike insurance contracts, payments are calculated and made pursuant to the terms of each particular credit derivative without regard to the obligations, liabilities, losses, or actual risks of the party to whom the payment is due.

Different user groups tend to utilize credit derivatives for different reasons.[11] In a recent study by Greenwich Associates, market participants reported that they use credit derivatives to increase incremental returns (50 percent); for investment in a different asset class (48 percent); to hedge bond credit risk (34 percent); to exploit arbitrage opportunities (33 percent); to hedge loan credit risk (31 percent); to achieve greater leverage (20 percent); to reduce a portfolio's capital intensity (20 percent); to hedge counterparty credit risk (18 percent); to speculate (16 percent); and for other reasons (16 percent).[12]

The various types of credit derivative used to achieve these objectives can be generally divided into those that are not funded prior to a credit event—for example, credit default swaps (CDSs), total return swaps (TRSs), and various types of options—and those that are funded *ex ante*—for example, credit-linked notes (CLNs) and collateralized debt obligations (CDOs). In what follows we describe the most basic of these credit derivatives structures. Keep in mind, however, that the recent low level of credit spreads has encouraged the development of a wide variety of new financial instruments. These include credit spread options, first and Nth-to-default baskets, constant maturity CDSs (CMCDSs), and constant maturity collateralized debt obligations (CMCDOs). The types of options currently traded (usually European-style) encompass payer and receiver swaptions and straddles on all the indexes, as well as single-name CDSs of different maturities. An investor who sells protection with CMCDSs and CMCDOs is exposed to counterparty default risk but is partially insulated from credit spread movements. The received coupon is in fact floating and periodically readjusted to reflect current spread levels of CDSs of the same maturity.

Nonfunded Credit Derivatives

Credit Default Swaps   In a CDS, one party buys credit protection (protection buyer) with either a single up-front payment or a series of fixed periodic payments for the term of the contract (the premium or the default swap spread). In return, the party selling credit protection (protection seller) agrees to pay the buyer if there is a credit event with respect to the reference entity or reference obligation. Neither the protection buyer nor the protection seller needs to have any actual credit exposure to the reference entity or obligation.[13] If a credit event occurs, the protection seller pays the buyer and the buyer continues to make any required premium payments until the contract matures. If a credit event does not occur, the protection seller never makes a payment, and the buyer makes all required premium payments.

CDSs are almost always documented with an International Swaps and Derivatives Association (ISDA) master agreement. The standard credit events that trigger payment by the protection seller are a specified price deterioration (the "materiality" standard) coupled with one of the following: bankruptcy, cross-acceleration, downgrade of reference entity or obligation, repudiation or moratorium, restructuring, payment default, or material default on a reference entity's debt obligations.[14] Depending on the terms of the CDS, upon the occurrence of a credit event, either the protection buyer will deliver to the protection seller the reference obligation and receive in return a payment equal to the notional amount of the contract (physical settlement) or the protection seller will pay the buyer the notional amount minus the then value of the reference obligation (cash settlement).[15]

CDSs can be entered into with respect to a single reference entity or obligation or with respect to a specified portfolio of reference entities or obligations. CDSs that reference a portfolio of some sort are often referred to as "basket default swaps." In a first-to-default basket swap, the default on any of the reference obligations triggers payment to the protection buyer. Other types of default basket swaps are also available, such as CDSs that provide credit protection after credit events have occurred with respect to two or more reference entities or obligations.

Total Return Swaps   A TRS (or total rate-of-return swap) on a reference obligation typically provides for both "yield payments" and "value payments." With respect to the yield payments, the total return payer (protection buyer) agrees to pay to the total return receiver (protection seller) the actual rate of return on the reference obligation, and the protection seller agrees to pay to the protection buyer a referenced interest rate (floating or fixed). With respect to the value payments, the total return payer pays the appreciation on the reference obligation, while the total return receiver periodically pays any depreciation on the reference obligation. The specified notional amount of a reference obligation is adjusted to reflect value payments.[16] Net value and yield payments can be made periodically or at the maturity or early termination of a TRS.

A total return payer that owns the reference obligation eliminates its credit exposure to the borrower without actually selling the reference obligation. While eliminating its credit exposure (to that borrower), the total return payer does not eliminate its market risk with respect to the payments from the total return receiver. A total return payer that does not own the reference obligation is synthetically transferring credit exposure on the reference obligation to the total return receiver, who is synthetically buying the reference obligation. Thus, TRSs allow counterparties to go long or short a particular credit-sensitive asset without necessarily funding the credit. A TRS—unlike a CDS—provides protection to the total return payer against loss of value irrespective of cause or the occurrence of a credit event.

Terminology   The payout of a CDS is similar to that of an option, with the protection seller receiving a premium in return for assuming the risk of having to make a payment in the event of a specified occurrence. But while CDSs share certain characteristics with options, they should not be confused with true credit options—that is, options on credit-risky instruments, such as bonds or loans, or on credit spreads. Just as receiving "fixed" in an interest rate swap is the duration equivalent of a long (financed) position in a bond, selling protection in a CDS (or, for that matter, being the total return receiver in a TRS) is the credit risk equivalent of a long (financed) position in a bond. The use of "swap" rather than "option" terminology in connection with CDSs and TRSs derives from this analogy. It is intended to convey the fact that a CDS or TRS effectively swaps the parties' positions in credit-risky assets, rather than their buying and granting options on positions in such assets. True credit options, just like other options in which the contingency is a market price development rather than a remote credit event, derive their value from the expected forward value and volatility of market prices. If an institution is capable of pricing a position in a loan or a bond, it is also capable of pricing a CDS. To price a credit option, however, additional information would be required about volatilities and implied forward credit spreads.[17]

Funded Credit Derivatives

Credit-Linked Notes   CLNs are debt securities the value of which is linked to the creditworthiness of third party reference entities or reference obligations. A CLN "represent[s] a synthetic corporate bond or loan, because a credit derivative (credit default or total rate of return swap (TROR) swap) is embedded in the structure."[18] CLNs have "principal (par value) at risk depending upon the credit performance of a reference credit."[19] CLNs are generally issued by operating companies and financial institutions, but can be issued by special purpose entities (SPEs). When CLNs are issued by an SPE, the SPE is typically "collateralized with high-quality assets to assure payment of contractual amounts due."[20]

CLNs are generally simple and flexible structures. The default contingency in a CLN can be based on a variety of underlying obligations, including a specific corporate loan or bond, a portfolio of loans or bonds, sovereign debt instruments, or an emerging markets index. It may also be based on a first-to-default CDS basket or a credit spread option. If a credit event occurs, the note typically matures, and the investor sustains a loss based on the reference obligation's loss. In effect, the investor is selling protection on the reference obligation, receiving a premium in the form of an attractive yield. The issuer of the note, in turn, is purchasing default protection on the reference obligation.

Investors find CLNs attractive for a variety of reasons. Because CLNs are on-balance-sheet assets, investors prohibited from entering into off-balance-sheet items, such as CDSs, can gain access to the credit derivatives market through CLNs. In addition, investors need not go through the ISDA documentation process. And banks can use CLNs to free up credit lines to particular borrowers, thereby providing access for non-bank investors to credit opportunities and customized maturity structures that are not otherwise available. A downside of CLNs, however, is counterparty risk.

Collateralized Debt Obligations Unlike CLNs, which are issued typically (but not exclusively) by operating companies, CDOs are always issued by an SPE. Similar in structure to collateralized mortgage obligations (CMOs), the CDO structure involves the transfer to the SPE of a portfolio of bonds, loans, or other assets; a sale by the SPE of debt securities (the CDOs) backed by the cash flows from the transferred portfolio; and a payment to the transferor of the proceeds of the CDO sale. While there are various types of CDOs (for example, arbitrage or balance sheet CDOs employing either cash flow or market value management), for purposes of this paper we view all such transactions simply as one more way to repackage and redistribute credit risk.

Key to the CDO structure is the securitization of the underlying collateral portfolio. In CDOs, just as in CMOs, the SPE holding the collateral portfolio sells several different classes or tranches of securities, each of which carries a different risk/return configuration defined by the priority and timing of the payments due on it. In other words, in a CMO structure the cash flow from the collateral portfolio is divided into a variety of principal and interest components that are allocated among the various security classes. This securitization process, known as tranching, turns the single risk/return profile of the underlying portfolio into multiple credit profiles. A CDO's tranches thus effect not only a redistribution of credit risk but a restructuring of it as well.

The risk/reward profile of the asset portfolio held by an SPE can be restructured in a variety of ways to appeal to a diverse array of investors.

The tranches of a CMO typically have credit ratings ranging from triple A to single B or unrated. Thus, despite holding a collateral portfolio that has, for example, a double B credit quality, through the use of overcollateralization and subordination an SPE may issue several tranches of significantly higher-rated debt. Whatever the precise structure of a CMO's tranches, however, this credit derivative product allows one party (protection buyer) that is holding, for example, a portfolio of high-yield corporate bonds to eliminate its credit exposure to this portfolio by transferring that risk, in restructured form, to investors.

Synthetic Collateralized Debt Obligations   While conceptually straightforward, CDOs are both complex to establish and expensive to administer. For example, it is costly to review loans or bonds for compliance with eligibility criteria, to transfer the legal title to loans, and to maintain the confidentiality of borrowers (critical in jurisdictions where this is required). To avoid the costs and legal and administrative problems of transferring loans or high-yield bonds to an SPE, banks and other sponsors have combined the securitization structure of CDOs with unfunded derivative techniques to create so-called synthetic CDOs (SCDOs).[21] In such transactions, the sponsor retains the reference obligations but transfers the credit risk of the portfolio to an SPE through a CDS. The SPE then issues tranched notes, the proceeds of which are used to purchase high-quality assets, such as government securities.

The SPE pays the purchaser of the tranched notes with the interest income from the collateral together with the swap premium paid by the sponsor. If default or loss occurs on the obligations in the reference portfolio, proceeds from the collateral are used to compensate the sponsor. Any collateral remaining at the maturity of the transaction is repaid to the note holders.

The SCDO market is dominated by three distinct products: (1) regulatory-driven balance sheet transactions, (2) tranched basket default swaps, and (3) managed arbitrage CDOs. "While balance sheet deals still represent the majority of synthetic [credit portfolio] outstandings" the largest growth has been in "tranched basket default swaps" and "managed arbitrage CDOs."[22] Even though the SCDO market is currently dominated by fixed portfolios of investment grade corporate loans and bonds, "there has been a proliferation in the use of actively managed portfolios of new collateral types."[23]

The market for synthetic credit-linked products is growing much faster than the market for cash issuance. The synthetic products are of various types but all involve capital market instruments whose payment profile is linked, typically through a derivative instrument, to the credit performance of one or more entities or obligations, but whose issuer does not necessarily own such underlying obligations. As ISDA recently stated:

> *The explosive and sustained growth of these synthetic securities (from 1997 onwards) reflects several clear market trends, including:*
>
> - *An acknowledgment by regulators worldwide of the growth of the derivatives market and of the need to address its development. In the United States, both the Board of Governors of the Federal Reserve System and the Office of the Comptroller of the Currency have issued prescriptive guidelines for credit derivatives allowing financial institutions to benefit from regulatory capital relief assuming certain conditions are met.*
> - *A shortage in the supply of primary securities and an increasing appetite by investors for structured credit products as they become more familiar with them.*
> - *The intent of financial institutions to offer investors the opportunity to take advantage of arbitrage opportunities arising from inefficiencies in the pricing of similar credit risks across different asset classes. Synthetic products allow investors to trade on specific credit profiles and take advantage of credit spreads available on the market by disaggregating credit exposure from yield.*
> - *The increasing need for investors to manage their credit exposure: a credit derivative instrument allows a corporation to voluntarily assume or transfer all the economic risks and benefits of a bond, a loan, or a portfolio of fixed-income instruments without having to actually purchase and hold the relevant asset.*
> - *The intent of investors to get exposure to new, or a variety of existing markets through the use of index-linked products in a liquid and highly transparent manner.*[24]

Indeed, this growth has led to a general increase in the variety of underlying assets and obligations. The market now references "bank loans, corporate debt, trade receivables, emerging market debt, convertible securities, project finance loans, residential mortgages, leveraged loans, indexed products as well as credit exposure generated from other derivatives linked activities."[25] Typical synthetic structures include credit-linked notes using either a "corporate structure" or a "special-purpose entity structure" (both of which place a credit seller in substantially the same position as a bond owner) and index-linked synthetic certificates (which replicate the risk profile of a portfolio of underlying assets). The important point to recognize is that both synthetic and cash securitizations achieve a transfer of risk through a structured financing that links payment on the securities offered to the performance of a definable set of assets or entities. In addition, both synthetic and cash securitizations represent a fixed income investment for which the primary risks are those associated with default by obligors on debt instruments. Synthetic securities allow the seller of protection to assume the credit or other risks associated with a reference obligation or index without directly acquiring, or being required to hold, such obligation or the assets represented by the index.

MISUSE OF CREDIT DERIVATIVES

Credit derivatives have proved to be valuable and generally dependable products. When used properly, credit derivatives can diversify risk, improve earnings, and lower a bank's or corporation's risk profile. But credit derivatives can be misused. A good example of the type of issues that can arise when credit derivatives are (allegedly) misused is the litigation growing out of a series of offerings of debt securities linked to Enron's creditworthiness (Enron CLNs).[26] In these transactions, Citigroup and Credit Suisse First Boston Corp. (collectively, Enron lenders) transferred much of their Enron credit exposure arising from loans and structured finance transactions[27] to third-party investors through variously structured CLNs issued by SPEs. Under the terms of these notes, when Enron became insolvent, investors in the Enron CLNs were left holding the bag, and the Enron lenders walked away without loss.[28]

Six separate issuances of CLNs are the subject of the *Hudson Soft* litigation,[29] but the basic structure of various transactions appears to have been much the same.[30] An SPE issued one primary class of CLNs to investors and a second, much smaller, class of notes subordinate to the first to the Enron lenders. The SPE purchased highly rated debt securities with the proceeds of the note issuance and executed a CDS with the Enron lenders linked to Enron's credit performance. The CDS provided that the reference obligations would be exchanged for the SPE's collateral portfolio in the event of specified Enron credit events.

Prior to an Enron credit event, the SPE was to pay to the Enron lenders the interest earned on its highly rated investments, and the Enron lenders were to pay to the SPE the interest owed to the holders of the CLNs plus the yield on the subordinated notes. Upon an Enron bankruptcy, the Enron lenders were to deliver to the SPE "senior obligations of

Enron that rank[ed] at least equal to claims against Enron for senior unsecured indebtedness for borrowed money" having a principal balance equal to the notional amount of the CDS. The SPE was to deliver to the Enron lenders the SPE's investments with a principal amount equal to the amount of Enron debt delivered to the SPE, plus the base amount of the subordinated notes.[31]

When Enron failed, the Enron CLNs performed precisely as they were intended, relieving the Enron lenders of all loss with respect to the reference Enron obligations up to the notional amount of the CDS. But because of the generally unanticipated and highly suspicious nature of Enron's bankruptcy, considerable criticism has been leveled at the Enron lenders for shifting their credit exposure to the capital markets. Citigroup for itself has responded that "[c]redit-linked notes are well-recognized financial instruments, widely issued and traded each year. . . . The instruments were sold to the largest, and most sophisticated, institutional investors in several Rule 144A offerings. Citi promised investors that the CLNs would perform similarly to straight Enron bonds—and they have."[32]

But the issues in the litigation over the Enron CLNs do not concern the legitimacy of the Enron CLN structure or the sophistication of the purchasers. Rather, the thrust of the litigation is that the Enron lenders were willing to lend great sums of money to Enron either without conducting appropriate due diligence or with knowledge that Enron's creditworthiness was not being accurately reported *because* they had no intention of ever being exposed to Enron's credit risk. In other words, the key allegations in the litigation involve an assertion that the Enron lenders "lent Enron more than $2.5 billion and invested at least $25 million in Enron's fraudulent partnerships in order to secure future investment banking business"[33] and that they were willing to do this because they intended "fraudulently [to] shift 100% of their risk of loss" to unknowing noteholders.[34]

Obviously, the allegations in the *Hudson Soft* litigation are just that: allegations. Nevertheless, they raise a serious issue concerning the use of credit derivatives. A credit provider intending to reduce or eliminate its credit risk through the use of credit derivatives may well have significantly more information about the reference entity or portfolio than the potential counterparty or note purchasers. The concern is that this information will not be shared either through the swap negotiation process or in the note sale disclosure documents. Certainly after Enron, counterparties to unfunded credit derivatives and investors in funded credit derivatives would do well to review carefully the representations by credit providers and all disclosures concerning the credit condition of the reference entity.

CREDIT DERIVATIVES OR INSURANCE

Credit derivatives and insurance have a number of similarities, and, indeed, credit derivatives are often characterized as functioning, in many circumstances, as the financial equivalent of indemnity contracts and financial guarantees. But functional equivalence is one thing and legal equivalence is quite another. If credit derivatives were deemed to be insurance, the consequences under state insurance law would be highly adverse for this vibrant and valuable market.

For example, a derivative that is found to be an insurance policy can be sold only by a licensed insurance broker. Thus, a protection seller found to have been selling an insurance contract would be acting unlawfully. In California, this would a misdemeanor.[35] In Connecticut, fines, imprisonment, or both can be imposed for acting "as an insurance producer" without a license.[36] Under Delaware law, a Delaware corporation can lose its "charter" to do business[37] if it acts "as an insurer" without a "certificate of authority"[38] to conduct an insurance business.[39] In New York, insurance law violations are a misdemeanor,[40] with fines increasing for subsequent violations.[41] And in Illinois, no one can "sell, solicit, or negotiate insurance" unless licensed.[42]

Because the term *insurance contract* is separately defined by each of the 50 states and the District of Columbia,[43] it becomes important for the participants in the credit derivatives market to understand and abide by clear guidelines to assure that credit derivatives—financial market transactions—are not treated as insurance, which are state-regulated service contracts.

Activities Associated with Insurance

The leading insurance treatise defines "insurance" as:

> *A contract by which one party (the insurer), for a consideration that is usually paid in money, either in a lump sum or at different times during the continuance of the risk, promises to make a certain payment, usually of money, upon the destruction or injury of "something" in which the other party (the insured) has an interest. [Cite omitted.] In other words, the purpose of insurance is to*

*transfer risk from the insured to the insurer. Insurance companies
act as financial intermediaries by providing a financial risk transfer
service that is funded by the payment of insurance premiums that
they receive from policyholders.*[44]

In evaluating which "financial risk transfer services" are insurance,
five characteristics are typically identified.

1. The insured must have an "insurable risk" (such as the risk of a financial loss on the occurrence of a disaster, theft, or credit event) with respect to a "fortuitous event" that is capable of financial estimate.[45]
2. The insured must "transfer" its "risk of loss" to an insurance company
(referred to as "risk shifting" or "underwriting"), under a contract
that provides the insured with an "indemnity" against the loss (with
the indemnity limited to the insured's actual loss).
3. The insured must pay a "premium" to the insurance company for assuming the insured's "insurable risk."
4. The insurance company typically assumes the risk as part of a larger
program for managing loss by holding a large pool of contracts covering similar risks. This pool is often large enough for actual losses to
fall within expected statistical benchmarks (referred to as "risk distribution" or "risk spreading").[46]
5. Before it can collect on an insurance contract the insured must demonstrate that its injury was from an "insurable risk" as the result of an
"insured event." In other words, the insured must demonstrate that it
has actually suffered a loss that was covered in the contract.

In general, therefore, an insurance contract covers the risk than an "insured" will suffer an "insured loss," and payment is due under the insurance contract only if there is "proof of an insured loss," and then only in
an amount equal to the lesser of the insured's actual loss or the maximum
loss covered by the contract.

Credit Derivatives Are Not Insurance

New York State is a key insurance regulator with jurisdiction over most of
the largest insurance companies in the United States. As a consequence,
New York's view of when a contract does and does not constitute insurance is highly influential. In New York, an insurance contract is defined as
an agreement under which the insurance company is obligated "to confer a
benefit of pecuniary value" on the insured or beneficiary upon the "happening of a fortuitous event in which the insured . . . has . . . a material in-

terest which will be adversely affected" by the happening of such event.[47] In determining whether a risk-shifting contract falls within this definition or outside of it, New York's basic approach is entirely consistent with the preceding discussion.

The New York Insurance Department (NYID) takes the position that derivatives contracts are not insurance contracts so long as the payments due under the derivatives are not dependent on the establishment of an actual loss. For example, in considering catastrophe options (cat options) providing for payment in the event of a specified natural disaster (such as a hurricane or major storm), the NYID stated that the cat options were not insurance contracts because the purchaser did not need to be injured by the event or prove it had suffered a loss. In reaching this conclusion, the NYID distinguished between "derivatives products," which transfer risk without regard to a loss, and "insurance," which transfers only the risk of a purchaser's actual loss.[48]

Similarly, the NYID concluded that weather derivatives are not insurance contracts under New York law because neither the amount of the payment due nor the event triggering the payment necessarily relates to the purchaser's loss.[49] And most recently, the NYID concluded that because CDSs provide that the "seller" must pay the "buyer" upon the occurrence of a "negative credit event" without regard for whether the buyer has "suffered a loss," they are not insurance contracts.[50] It appears clear, therefore, at least under New York law, that if the provisions of a credit derivative contract do not tie payment to the actual loss experience of the protection buyer, the derivative product will not be deemed an insurance contract.

Documentation Considerations

There are, nevertheless, certain conceptual overlaps between credit derivatives contracts and insurance contracts. As a consequence, care should be taken in documenting such derivatives contracts to avoid any implication that a party will receive a payment under the contract only for actual loss. To assure that credit derivatives are treated as derivatives and not as insurance, the following drafting guidelines may be helpful.

- ■ *Form of contract.* Unfunded credit derivatives should be documented with an ISDA master agreement with the specific terms of the agreement specified in the schedule, confirmations, and any credit support documents. The offering material for funded credit derivatives (notes) should specify the terms of the notes in language as similar to that of the ISDA definitions as possible.

- *Disclaimer.* The documentation for both funded and unfunded credit derivatives should include a disclaimer that the transaction is not intended to be insurance, the contract is not suitable as a substitute for insurance; and the contract is not guaranteed by any "property and casualty guaranty fund or association" under applicable state law.
- *Marketing materials.* Marketing materials for a credit derivative transaction should avoid any references to similarities between the contract and insurance and should not use words such as "indemnity," "guarantee," and "protect."

ONGOING EFFORTS TO IMPROVE DOCUMENTATION

The documentation of unfunded credit derivatives is generally done on ISDA published forms.[51] Indeed, ISDA has taken the lead in standardizing the terms of credit derivatives. In 1998, it published a model "Confirmation of OTC Credit Swap Transaction." In 1999, it published the "1999 ISDA Credit Derivatives Definitions," which were followed in 2001 by three supplements that expanded and clarified the 1999 definitions.[52] On February 11, 2003, ISDA released a comprehensive set of revised credit definitions. These definitions incorporate the three ISDA supplements issued in 2001 to the 1999 Credit Definitions, update many of the definitions, and generally bring documentation standards current with evolving market practices. The 2003 Credit Definitions as supplemented in May 2003, January 2005, and March 2005 should substantially improve documentation practices for credit derivatives.

CONCLUSION

As a result of the credit defaults during the early part of this century, the value of the credit derivatives market has become more apparent than ever. While representing a natural extension of the markets for products that unbundled risks, such as those for interest rate and foreign exchange derivatives, the credit derivatives market has provided a unique mechanism for assuming and shedding direct exposure to a reference entity's creditworthiness. As such, credit derivatives represent a unique and important development for the worldwide financial markets.

Despite concerns about the misuse of credit derivatives (as highlighted by the *Hudson Soft* litigation) and the desirability of further fine-tuning of ISDA documentation, the credit derivatives market has proven itself to be sound, effective, and vigorous through a very difficult credit period. Further, it is important to recognize that this market has developed and adapted without governmental regulation or supervision. Nevertheless, the International Monetary Fund (IMF) recently stated, "The combination of compressed risk premiums and the rapid growth of instruments that lack transparency and afford the potential for taking leveraged positions in the credit markets is a potential source of vulnerability that merits attention."[53] In particular, the IMF is concerned that otherwise normal market fluctuations could be amplified through liquidity problems.

> An increasingly relevant contributor to this liquidity risk is the recent proliferation of complex and leveraged financial instruments, including credit derivatives and structured products such as collateralized debt obligations (CDOs). While secondary trading for these products exists, these instruments still rely on quantitative models for relative value assessment, investment decisions, and pricing. Therefore, there is a risk that models that are overly similar in their construction could cause investors to rush to exit at the same time, leading to market liquidity shortages.
>
> . . .
>
> The question of liquidity shortage as a potential amplifier for market price shocks is still one of the major "blind spots" in our financial market landscape. The interactions of liquidity risk and other potential amplifiers of market shocks with changes in global capital flows will have to be at the forefront of all future effort to further improve the global financial architecture.[54]

The development of the credit derivatives markets alongside the highly regulated insurance market should also be noted. Primarily because of tax considerations, there remain enormous incentives for insurance companies to provide credit loss protection through insurance contracts. Nevertheless, we are seeing increasing intersections between the derivatives and insurance markets as the nature of the risks assumed by these markets converge. Thus, for example, more and more so-called transformer transactions are occurring whereby a financial instrument (for example a CDS) is transformed into an insurance contract, or vice versa.[55] Insurance companies, prohibited under applicable state law from entering into credit derivatives, can often assume the same economic position as if they had sold protection to a derivatives counterparty by issuing an insurance policy against a credit event specified in the derivative held by the insured. The insurance company thus assumes the economic results of holding the credit derivative while still complying with regulatory restrictions.

The expansion and strengthening of the credit derivatives market will unquestionably contribute to a more efficient allocation of credit risk in the economy. This market will allow banks efficiently to reduce undesirable concentrations of credit exposure by diversifying this risk beyond their customer base. This market should also lead to improved pricing information relating to both loans and credit exposures generally. In addition, this market will facilitate further specialization whereby financial institutions can fund participants in limited areas of commercial activity without having to bear the risk of excessive exposure to such limited sectors. Finally, by separating risk from funding obligations and original risk from restructured risk, credit derivatives offer an extraordinarily important mechanism for financial market participants to play precisely the role at precisely the risk/reward level they deem prudent and appropriate.

CHAPTER 32

Project Finance Collateralized Debt Obligations: What? Why? Now?

J. Paul Forrester

Project finance collateralized debt obligations (CDOs) will allow portfolio investors a greater opportunity to participate in power and other infrastructure debt markets and will bring additional liquidity and transparency to such markets. Project finance CDOs will also allow commercial banks, which have a long and successful history with project finance, to better manage their balance sheets and asset-liability mismatch. This article reviews the structures and features of a CDO, and why project finance debt is an attractive asset for a CDO.

WHAT?

Collateralized debt obligations (CDOs)[1] are a successful refinement and application of sophisticated securitization techniques originally

Earlier versions of this article have been published in Euromoney's *International Power Project Finance Yearbook* 2001 and in the *Journal of Structured and Project Finance* (Fall 2002).

    J. Paul Forrester is a partner of Mayer Brown Rowe & Maw LLP, an international law firm, and is based in its Chicago office. He can be reached at (312) 701-7366 and jforrester@mayerbrownrowe.com. The views and opinions expressed herein are solely the author's and should not be attributed to Mayer Brown Rowe & Maw LLP or its clients.

developed for collateralized mortgage-backed securities (MBSs) to facilitate the resolution of the savings and loan crisis in the United States in the 1980s. According to Moody's Investors Service, there were over $220 billion worth of CDOs in 2004,[2] making CDOs the second largest type of term asset-backed security (ABS), excluding MBSs, after home equity ABSs.

CDOs are widely admired for the rich and complex character of their market and their enviable success. Originally applied to bonds and loans, CDOs have since been applied to portfolios of emerging-market debt, subordinate and mezzanine ABSs and MBSs, real estate investment trust (REIT) debt, distressed debt, trust preferred securities (a debt/equity hybrid), and, most recently, to alternative investments (private equity and hedge funds), as well as to project finance loans, leases, or similar debt obligations.

The core concept of CDOs is that a pool of defined financial assets will perform in a predictable manner (that is, with default rates, loss severity/recovery amounts, and recovery periods that can be forecast reliably) and, with appropriate levels of credit enhancement applied thereto, can be financed in a cost-efficient fashion that reveals and captures the arbitrage between the interest and yield return received on the CDO's assets, and the interest and yield expense of the securities (CDO securities) issued to finance them. Each of the recognized rating agencies (Fitch, Moody's, and Standard & Poor's) has developed CDO criteria and statistical methodologies and analyses to so-called stress pools of CDO assets to determine the level of credit enhancement required for their respective credit ratings for the CDO securities to finance such pools.

Typically, CDOs require the CDO assets to meet certain eligibility criteria (including diversity, weighted average rating, weighted average maturity, and weighted average spread/coupon) in accordance with established rating-agency methodologies to ensure the highest practicable rating for the related CDO securities. A CDO allocates the interest and principal proceeds of such assets on periodic distribution dates according to certain collateral quality tests (typically an overcollateralization ratio and an interest-coverage ratio). CDO securities usually are issued in several tranches. Each tranche (other than the most junior tranche) has a seniority or priority over one or more other tranches, with tighter collateral quality tests set to trigger a diversion of interest and principal proceeds that otherwise would be allocable to more junior tranches, which then are used to redeem or otherwise retire more senior tranches. The resulting subordination of such junior tranches constitutes the required credit enhancement for the more senior tranches and allows the CDO securities of such senior tranches to receive a credit rating that reflects such seniority or priority. Some CDOs use financial guaranties or insurance for the same effect.

CDOs often allow principal proceeds to be reinvested in additional eligible CDO assets during a specified reinvestment period.

The CDO usually is managed by a collateral manager, who identifies, acquires, and monitors eligible assets for the CDO. Often a CDO allows a portion of its assets to be traded annually, which allows a collateral manager to enhance the arbitrage opportunity of the CDO through adept trading.

Generally, CDOs are either balance-sheet or arbitrage CDOs. Balance-sheet CDOs are transactions structured as sales for accounting and regulatory capital purposes but are debt for tax purposes. This linkage allows the related CDO securities to be priced at narrower spreads than are used for comparable arbitrage CDOs. Commercial banks use balance-sheet CDOs primarily for portfolio management and regulatory capital efficiency. By contrast, arbitrage CDOs are structured as sales for all purposes, including tax, and are motivated by the opportunity for arbitrage.

Arbitrage CDOs are either cash-flow CDOs or market-value CDOs, and are distinguished by an overcollateralization ratio determined by reference to the par or principal amount of the CDO assets (adjusted to the lower of the recovery or market value for defaulted CDO assets) in the case of a cash-flow CDO, or to the market value of the CDO assets in the case of a market-value CDO.

Typically, a market-value CDO requires more equity than a cash-flow CDO, but allows greater trading by the collateral manager. To allow the collateral manager to manage the capital structure of the CDO efficiently and to trade CDO assets as easily as possible, the capital structure of a market-value CDO usually includes a substantial revolving credit facility. While balance-sheet CDOs are an important portfolio management and regulatory capital tool, especially for commercial banks, the remainder of this article will discuss typical arbitrage CDOs.

The CDO issuer is usually established outside of the United States (for example, the Cayman Islands) and must not be engaged in trade or business in the United States in order to avoid U.S. taxation. The offering of CDO securities must be structured carefully to satisfy other applicable legal requirements, including (but not limited to):

- The perfection of the collateral lien on, and security interest in, the CDO assets.
- The exemption of such offering from registration requirements under applicable U.S. securities laws and similar laws of other jurisdictions in which such CDO securities are offered.

- The avoidance of registration under the U.S. Investment Company Act.
- The exemption from adverse consequences under the Employee Retirement Income Security Act (ERISA).

These requirements, together with a description of the innumerable variations of and refinements to the CDO structures described earlier, are beyond the scope of this article.

The underlying CDO assets affect the capital structure of the CDO. For example, if the underlying debt obligations are floating rate, the CDO securities also should be floating rate or must be hedged to avoid or minimize the interest-rate mismatch. If the underlying CDO assets require additional advances (e.g., they include construction or postcompletion working-capital facilities), the CDO securities should allow borrowings thereunder so that the CDO can make the required advances. Often, such CDO securities are held by commercial paper conduits that offer attractive pricing and flexible funding; however, the conduit likely will require a minimum rating of such CDO securities and the CDO will require a minimum rating of the conduit (which if lost effectively requires the conduit to find a replacement or to post collateral to cover the obligation to make borrowings). Obviously, these complex mechanics can be avoided if the CDO only holds fully funded debt obligations.

WHY?

Project finance loans, leases, and other debt obligations are regarded as attractive assets for CDOs because they have higher assumed recovery rates and shorter recovery periods than comparably rated corporate debt obligations. This allows the project finance CDO securities to be issued at a corresponding lower cost (since less credit enhancement is required to obtain the same credit ratings), which effectively expands the arbitrage opportunity for such CDO.

The higher assumed recovery rates and shorter recovery periods of project finance debt are primarily attributable to the tighter covenants and events of default under typical project finance documentation. These assumptions are intuitively reasonable and, most importantly, the rating agencies concur with them, even though there appears to be no great weight of authoritative research to support them. However, in connection with the pending capital requirements under the Bank for International Settlements (BIS)[3] proposed Revised International Capital Standards[4] (Basel II) initiative, there is ongoing research and work being undertaken to establish the appropriate capital for so-called specialized lending, which includes project finance. In response to an initial proposal by the BIS to require greater capital for project finance exposure than for comparably rated corporate exposure, a group of four active project finance banks[5] pooled their respective default and recovery data and retained Standard & Poor's Risk Solutions to analyze such data for (1) probability of default (PD) for a project finance loan; (2) loss given default (LGD), the portion of the loan principal lost in the event of a borrower default; and (3) the expected loss (EL) for project finance loans (essentially the product of PD and LGD). The analysis demonstrated lower EL and LGD for project finance exposures than for comparably rated corporate exposures.[6] Moreover, when a project event of default does occur, project participants are relatively limited in number and are highly motivated to resolve such default consensually and as expeditiously as possible.

The rating agencies also report a steady and growing amount of rated project finance bonds and other debt that can serve as a supply for project finance CDOs. For several years, issuance of rated project finance debt has exceeded $100 billion annually. The rating agencies have extensive experience with project finance and have elaborate rating methodologies and criteria for project finance debt. For example, Standard & Poor's has issued comprehensive guidance for project finance debt in its October 2001 *Debt Rating Criteria for Energy, Industrial and Infrastructure Project Finance* that is based on S&P's extensive experience in rating more than 500 projects in 35 countries and extensive specific guidance for particular types of projects. Similarly, Moody's Investors Service has published its *Project and Infrastructure Sourcebook* in December 2003.

Additionally, commercial banks and other originators of project finance debt can have their project finance portfolios "shadow" rated through a process in which the rating maps the rating system of such originator to the rating agency's own rating system and determines its rating of a particular project finance debt obligation by application of such mapping. This process requires the rating agency to undertake substantial due diligence regarding the originator's rating process (including its underwriting criteria and credit approval procedures) and historical information regarding the performance of the originator's project finance portfolio. Inevitably, this experience provides the rating agencies with a database and other information that allows the rating agencies to refine their respective project finance criteria.

Commercial banks are uniquely positioned to take advantage of the opportunity presented by CDOs of project finance debt. Commercial banks have a long history with project finance; the first project finance loan is thought to have been a nonrecourse loan made by a Dallas bank in the 1930s to finance the development of certain oil and gas properties. Generally, commercial banks are experienced and capable originators of project finance debt and have a competitive advantage over other financial institutions in their ability to provide flexible funding for a project's precommercial development, including construction during which draws may be accelerated or delayed. However, projects are usually capital intensive and project assets have long useful lives requiring a corresponding longer-tenor financing.

Commercial banks are constrained in their ability to provide such longer-tenor financing by the shorter duration of the assets on the balance sheet of a typical commercial bank (that is, such bank's demand or short-term deposits). As a result, all commercial banks closely monitor and attempt to manage this asset-liability mismatch. While a commercial bank could provide shorter-term project financing, it (and the project's owners and sponsors) would face a refinancing risk at the maturity of such financing. Other originators of project finance debt, even if not balance-sheet constrained, can benefit from project finance CDOs by the additional liquidity that a project finance CDO brings to an otherwise relatively illiquid asset class and, as noted earlier, by using a CDO to release otherwise-required regulatory capital and promote regulatory capital efficiency.

All financial institutions from time to time need to be able to satisfy regulators, rating agencies, and investors with respect to the adequacy of capital provisions, loan-loss reserves, and similar matters. The transparency of a project finance CDO, with its emphasis on the value of each underlying loan and the PD, LGD, and EL thereof (to use bank regulatory and rating agency vernacular), certainly would assist in such demonstration. Naturally, this same transparency may prevent some financial institutions from pursuing project finance CDOs, since they expose any inadequate pricing of the underlying CDO portfolio or other similar deficiencies therein. However, additional transparency will not be embraced by investors that use mark-to-market accounting, since it may result in greater volatility in affected earnings.

Historically, CDOs have dramatically affected the pre-existing markets for the underlying CDO assets. For example, collateralized bond obligations (CBOs) have added substantial liquidity to the U.S. high-yield bond market and dampened price volatility therein. Similarly, collateralized loan obligations (CLOs) have added liquidity and transparency to the U.S. leveraged loan market, and bank syndication practices have been changed to accommodate the tax requirements of most CLOs. It has been estimated that CLOs account for more than 50 percent of the syndicated loan market.

In addition, a project finance CDO allows a financial institution to better manage its exposure to particular countries, industries, and credits and may achieve better economic results than the alternative of loan sales in secondary transactions. Moreover, the sale of a project finance portfolio inevitably expands the opportunity for the selling financial institution to undertake additional project finance business, whether with favored existing clients or new exposure.

Significantly, in October 1999, S&P first issued its *Rating Considerations for Project Finance CDOs* and, in October 2001, issued its updated criteria based on its subsequent experience in rating, and evaluating for rating, several project finance CDOs.

From an investor's perspective, an investment in the CDO securities of a project finance CDO provides diversification and other portfolio management benefits, including a low correlation to the typical corporate bond portfolios held by most institutional investors. In addition, the tranched structure of a CDO allows the investor to determine its preferred risk/return investment since an investment in the junior tranches of a CDO represents a more leveraged exposure to the underlying CDO portfolio and correspondingly greater risk for the stated return.

NOW?

S&P's *Rating Considerations for Project Finance CDOs* are based on its belief that project finance CDOs will be an important step in expanding the participation of portfolio investors in the broader infrastructure debt markets. Over time, S&P expects to refine its rating methodology for project finance CDOs based on its experience with three key, inherent credit issues, namely,

1. How do postdefault recovery rates and timing compare for projects, especially in the emerging and developing countries, where project loans are increasingly being originated?
2. How diverse are project risks really likely to be across sectors and regions—particularly, should project debt experience some generic challenges such as construction, operating, or political risks across a number of countries?
3. How does default likelihood change over the life of a loan? With regard to loans, there is evidence, for example, that they are less likely to default after they have amortized a substantial amount of debt.

Notwithstanding that project finance CDOs may still be more art than science, Credit Suisse First Boston (CSFB) took two important early steps toward answering these issues in its two project funding transactions:

1. Project Funding I, a project finance portfolio of 40 loans primarily to U.S. projects that closed in December 1998.
2. Project Funding II, an international project finance portfolio of 42 loans that closed in January 2000.

Citibank has also made its contribution in this regard in its project finance securitization transaction with its Project Securitization Company I, an international project finance portfolio that closed in July 2001.

More recently, in October 2004, Depfa Bank PLC completed its innovative Essential Public Infrastructure Capital PLC (EPIC) synthetic infrastructure CDO that referenced a portfolio of U.K. public infrastructure loans.

Important prior transactions include the July 1994 Energy Investors Fund Funding transaction, a domestic portfolio of equity and equity-like interests in 13 power projects, which effectively monetized a substantial portion of the remaining economic interest of the Energy Investors Fund's investors. Another important precedent was the International Finance Corporation's IFC Latin America and Asia Loan Trust transaction that closed in June 1995 and consisted of a portfolio of 73 loans to borrowers in 11 countries in Latin America and Asia. Although the IFC is rumored to have pursued another similar transaction, that has not been confirmed.

As one might expect, applying the rating-agency requirements for diversification to a project finance portfolio can present certain challenges, including whether diversification is effectively provided across industries and/or countries, for which there usually is little (if any) empirical evidence and which, accordingly, requires educated judgments. For example, are loans to power projects in Brazil and Argentina effectively diversified given the substantial interaction between the energy sectors in these two countries?

In addition, an international project finance CDO portfolio presents substantially more difficult structuring and rating challenges, including sophisticated structural features to mitigate otherwise applicable withholding tax on the project finance debt from several troublesome jurisdictions. In this regard, it is noteworthy that the IFC Latin America and Asia Loan Trust and Citibank Project Securitization transactions used participation interests to avoid any required consent to transfer and to minimize withholding-tax consequences; however, as a result the CDO issuer is exposed to the credit risk of the seller of the participation and the CDO securities are subject to downgrade due to a decline in the rating of such seller, even if there otherwise has been no deterioration in the underlying project finance portfolio. In contrast, the Project Funding II transaction used a variety of sophisticated measures (including trusts and credit-linked notes) to minimize withholding-tax consequences of the required transfers. Notwithstanding these and other difficulties, the promise of project finance CDOs is so strong that S&P and other rating agencies report that a significant number of other financial institutions have expressed interest in, and are pursuing, possible project finance CDOs.

An unexpected incentive for project finance CDOs may be the proposed Basel II regulatory capital requirements for banks that, as currently proposed, would penalize project finance exposure by requiring greater capital therefor.

Only time will tell whether the substantial promise of project finance CDOs will be realized, but results to date are encouraging.

2004 Review of Trends in Insurance Securitization: Exploring Outside the Cat Box

Morton N. Lane and Roger Beckwith

The 2003–2004 period was something of a breakout time for insurance securitization. By our estimate $1.9 billion of securities were issued between 4/2003 and 3/2004 (our usual measuring interval). This represents a 50 percent increase over the previously most active year to date (1999). Sixteen securities, as defined herein, constitute the record issuance. But, as always, such measurements are subject to specification definition. During this period at least three other securities were issued that have not been included in this report, principally because of a lack of readily available data. Had they been included, the issuance level would have been an additional $900 million.

Several features of the year's issuance are particularly noteworthy. (See Exhibit 33.1.) First, two new types of coverage were included in the 2003 securities: Taiwan earthquake (Formosa Re) and European mortality risk (Vita Re). Other deals explored new exposures, including terrorism risk—hence the theme "exploring outside the cat box" where most

This article originally appeared in Lane Financial's *Trade Notes* and is reprinted with permission. The authors are president and vice president, respectively, at Lane Financial LLC.

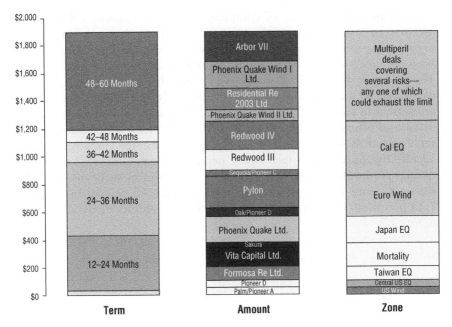

EXHIBIT 33.1 Securities Issuance, 2003–2004
Source: Lane Financial LLC.

insurance securitization has heretofore resided. Second, two of the largest of issuers (USAA and Swiss Re) introduced significantly different forms of issuance—multiyear/multiperil and medium-term note (MTN) structures—that impacted the coverage they obtain from the capital markets. The significance of these shifts is not yet widely appreciated. A third noteworthy fact is that Pylon Re provided the fourth significant example of "disintermediation" via securitization. And finally, after a gap of several years, Formosa Re provided an example of a significantly sized issue of a nonrated issue accepted by the capital markets. It also had a decidedly hairy structure.

Perhaps the single most significant feature of the year's securitizations was the fact that "life" risks were sold as securities for the first time. This story is still emerging, but mortality risk, embedded value, and life versus annuity arbitrage have all appeared on the landscape for the first time. The life market is huge relative to the catastrophe (cat) market, and inroads into life securitizations could significantly alter the insurance security landscape.

A major trend worthy of comment is price compression. Given the increase in size of issuance and absent a shift in demand, one could expect some price pressure (i.e., rising yield spreads). The opposite has been the case; spreads have begun to drop in the face of added supply. The extent of the drop is illustrated in Exhibit 33.2. It shows the average of all quoted secondary market prices quarterly since 2000. The details are shown in Exhibits 33.3 and 33.4. Clearly, some old issues have matured and others have been added, so that the index is not a consistent set. Nevertheless, it captures the large shift in average spreads over the 12 months. Spreads dropped by 25 percent. The picture is all the more dramatic considering the fact that the same series of securities actually shows a rising average of expected losses, from .88 percent in 2002 to 1.15 percent in the first quarter of 2004. Price multiples have fallen from 6.3 to 3.7.

Three explanations present themselves. Competitive fixed income spreads have collapsed, leading to more investors looking to insurance

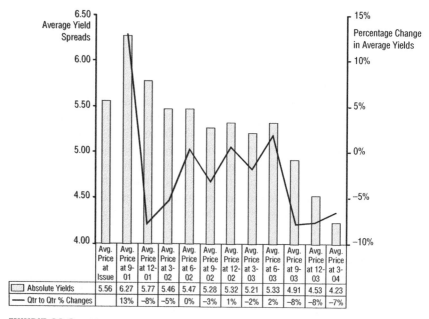

	Avg. Price at Issue	Avg. Price at 9-01	Avg. Price at 12-01	Avg. Price at 3-02	Avg. Price at 6-02	Avg. Price at 9-02	Avg. Price at 12-02	Avg. Price at 3-03	Avg. Price at 6-03	Avg. Price at 9-03	Avg. Price at 12-03	Avg. Price at 3-04
▭ Absolute Yields	5.56	6.27	5.77	5.46	5.47	5.28	5.32	5.21	5.33	4.91	4.53	4.23
— Qtr to Qtr % Changes		13%	−8%	−5%	0%	−3%	1%	−2%	2%	−8%	−8%	−7%

EXHIBIT 33.2 Changes in Average Secondary Market Cat Bond Spreads, Quarter to Quarter 2001–2003
Source: Lane Financial LLC.

securities as attractive forms of alternative risk. Second, the underlying cost of traditional reinsurance may have weakened, sending the spreads that issuers are prepared to pay lower. Anecdotal evidence suggests that, while this might begin to happen, it has not been a major trend to date. In this insurance cycle, price discipline has been pretty good (so far). Thirdly and finally, we would suggest that the universe of investors willing to accept insurance securities has expanded dramatically. Competition among a larger universe of investors for a relatively small supply of securities has pushed prices up (spreads lower).

The corollary to lower spread and greater demand for securities is that issuers should now find it much cheaper to get their coverage in the capital markets than in the traditional markets. If this market is to work like any other, increased demand will generate supply. Reinsurers (the usual issuers) need to know the coverage is now much cheaper in the capital markets.

NEW SECURITIES

The complete list of new securities is given in Exhibit 33.5. It displays the name, amount, maturity, and coupon for each of the notes. Exhibit 33.5 also shows the risk statistics provided with each offering memorandum. These are the expected loss, the probability of any loss (the attachment probability), and the probability of full loss (the exhaustion probability). Separately listed is the conditional expected loss for each deal. Regular readers will recognize this as a simple risk measure (severity of loss), which we have found useful in discriminating between deals and in fitting pricing models. A brief discussion of these price models is given later. There follows a description of the highlights of each new deal in the 2003–2004 season.

Residential Re 2003 Ltd.

USAA has been the most persistent issuer of insurance securities since the inception of the market. The 2003 Residential Re transaction was the seventh issue from USAA and we have written about it extensively elsewhere.[1] The issue was for $160 million and a three-year term. Its risk statistics were similar to previous issues—expected loss of 0.48 percent and an attachment probability of 1.1 percent.

EXHIBIT 33.3 Secondary Market Price Data

Second Quarter 2003 (6/30/03) Secondary Market Prices from Four Dealers	Issue Date	Sponsor	Issuer	Spread at Issue	Average Market Indications
	Dec-01	SCOR	Atlas Reinsurance II Class A	2.38%	1.91%
	Dec-01	SCOR	Atlas Reinsurance II Class B	6.75%	6.37%
	May-99	Oriental Land	Concentric	3.10%	3.15%
	May-02	Nissay Dowa	Fujiyama	4.00%	3.76%
	May-02	Nissay Dowa	Fujiyama Shares	7.00%	7.90%
	Nov-00	AGF	Mediterranean Re Class A	2.60%	2.10%
	Nov-00	AGF	Mediterranean Re Class B	5.85%	4.54%
	Dec-97	TokioMarine	Parametric Re	4.30%	3.90%
New Issue in Qtr.	Jun-03	Swiss Re	Phoenix Quake	2.45%	2.45%
New Issue in Qtr.	Jun-03	Swiss Re	Phoenix Quake/Wind	2.45%	2.45%
New Issue in Qtr.	Jun-03	Swiss Re	Phoenix Quake/Wind II	3.50%	3.50%
	Jun-02	Swiss Re	Pioneer A 2002-I	6.00%	6.29%
	Dec-02	Swiss Re	Pioneer A 2002-III	5.25%	6.08%
	Mar-03	Swiss Re	Pioneer A 2003-I	5.50%	6.08%
New Issue in Qtr.	Jun-03	Swiss Re	Pioneer A 2003-II	6.00%	6.08%
	Jun-02	Swiss Re	Pioneer B 2002-I	5.00%	5.26%
	Sep-02	Swiss Re	Pioneer B 2002-II	5.00%	5.21%
	Dec-02	Swiss Re	Pioneer B 2002-III	5.25%	5.21%
	Mar-03	Swiss Re	Pioneer B 2003-I	4.75%	5.21%
New Issue in Qtr.	Jun-03	Swiss Re	Pioneer B 2003-II	5.00%	5.21%
	Jun-02	Swiss Re	Pioneer C 2002-I	6.00%	6.28%
	Sep-02	Swiss Re	Pioneer C 2002-II	6.00%	6.10%
	Dec-02	Swiss Re	Pioneer C 2002-III	6.00%	6.10%
	Mar-03	Swiss Re	Pioneer C 2003-I	6.00%	6.10%
New Issue in Qtr.	Jun-03	Swiss Re	Pioneer C 2003-II	5.75%	6.10%
	Jun-02	Swiss Re	Pioneer D 2002-I	1.75%	1.90%
	Sep-02	Swiss Re	Pioneer D 2002-II	1.75%	1.85%
	Dec-02	Swiss Re	Pioneer D 2002-III	1.75%	1.85%
	Mar-03	Swiss Re	Pioneer D 2003-I	1.75%	1.85%
New Issue in Qtr.	Jun-03	Swiss Re	Pioneer D 2003-II	1.50%	1.85%
	Jun-02	Swiss Re	Pioneer E 2002-I	4.25%	5.08%
	Dec-02	Swiss Re	Pioneer E 2002-III	4.75%	4.85%
	Mar-03	Swiss Re	Pioneer E 2003-I	4.75%	4.85%
	Jun-02	Swiss Re	Pioneer F 2002-I	7.50%	7.88%

EXHIBIT 33.3 *(Continued)*

Second Quarter 2003 (6/30/03) Secondary Market Prices from Four Dealers	Issue Date	Sponsor	Issuer	Spread at Issue	Average Market Indications
	Dec-02	Swiss Re	Pioneer F 2002-III	7.50%	7.75%
	Mar-03	Swiss Re	Pioneer F 2003-I	7.50%	7.75%
	Dec-00	Munich Re	PRIME CalQuake	7.50%	6.88%
	Dec-00	Munich Re	PRIME Calquake Shares	9.00%	8.21%
	Dec-00	Munich Re	PRIME Hurricane	6.50%	9.03%
	Dec-00	Munich Re	PRIME Hurricane Shares	8.00%	12.81%
	Mar-02	Lehman Re	Redwood Capital II	3.00%	3.17%
	Mar-02	Lehman Re	Redwood Capital II Shares	4.50%	4.50%
	Jun-01	USAA	Residential Re 2001	4.99%	4.73%
	May-02	USAA	Residential Re 2002	4.90%	4.67%
New Issue in Qtr.	May-03	USAA	Residential Re 2003	4.95%	4.87%
	May-01	Swiss Re	SR Wind Class A-1	5.25%	4.68%
	May-01	Swiss Re	SR Wind Class A-1 Shares	6.75%	6.42%
	May-01	Swiss Re	SR Wind Class A-2	5.75%	5.36%
	May-01	Swiss Re	SR Wind Class A-2 Shares	7.25%	6.43%
	Apr-02	Hiscox	St Agatha Re	6.75%	6.51%
	Dec-02	Vivendi	Studio Re	5.10%	4.77%
	Dec-02	Vivendi	Studio Re Shares	8.00%	7.70%
	Jun-01	Zurich Re	Trinom Ltd Class A-1	8.00%	7.65%
	Jun-01	Zurich Re	Trinom Ltd Class A-2	4.00%	3.26%
	Jun-01	Zurich Re	Trinom Ltd Shares	10.00%	10.79%
					5.33%
			Circle Maihama Parametric Units Kelvin 1st Event Kelvin 2nd Event		

Other extant securities that may be maturing or are without any secondary prices.

	Jul-00	Vesta	NeHi	4.10%	

(Continued)

EXHIBIT 33.3 *(Continued)*

Third Quarter 2003 (9/30/03) Secondary Market Prices from Four Dealers	Issue Date	Sponsor	Issuer	Spread at Issue	Average Market Indications
New Issue in Qtr.	Jul-03	Swiss Re	Arbor Capital I	15.38%	15.31%
New Issue in Qtr.	Jul-03	Swiss Re	Arbor Capital II	1.00%	1.03%
	Dec-01	SCOR	Atlas Reinsurance II Class A	2.38%	1.46%
	Dec-01	SCOR	Atlas Reinsurance II Class B	6.75%	6.16%
	May-99	Oriental Land	Concentric	3.10%	2.70%
New Issue in Qtr.	Aug-03	Central Re	Formosa Re	3.30%	3.22%
	May-02	Nissay Dowa	Fujiyama	4.00%	3.44%
	May-02	Nissay Dowa	Fujiyama Shares	7.00%	7.75%
	Nov-00	AGF	Mediterranean Re Class A	2.60%	1.71%
	Nov-00	AGF	Mediterranean Re Class B	5.85%	4.54%
New Issue in Qtr.	Jul-03	Swiss Re	Oak Capital	4.57%	5.16%
New Issue in Qtr.	Jul-03	Swiss Re	Palm Capital	5.81%	5.14%
	Dec-97	TokioMarine	Parametric Re	4.30%	3.55%
	Jun-03	Swiss Re	Phoenix Quake	2.45%	2.25%
	Jun-03	Swiss Re	Phoenix Quake/Wind	2.45%	2.25%
	Jun-03	Swiss Re	Phoenix Quake/Wind II	3.50%	3.48%
	Jun-02	Swiss Re	Pioneer A 2002-I	6.00%	5.16%
	Dec-02	Swiss Re	Pioneer A 2002-III	5.25%	5.16%
	Mar-03	Swiss Re	Pioneer A 2003-I	5.50%	5.16%
	Jun-03	Swiss Re	Pioneer A 2003-II	6.00%	5.16%
	Jun-02	Swiss Re	Pioneer B 2002-I	5.00%	5.28%
	Sep-02	Swiss Re	Pioneer B 2002-II	5.00%	5.28%
	Dec-02	Swiss Re	Pioneer B 2002-III	5.25%	5.28%
	Mar-03	Swiss Re	Pioneer B 2003-I	4.75%	5.28%
	Jun-03	Swiss Re	Pioneer B 2003-II	5.00%	5.28%
	Jun-02	Swiss Re	Pioneer C 2002-I	6.00%	5.78%
	Sep-02	Swiss Re	Pioneer C 2002-II	6.00%	5.78%
	Dec-02	Swiss Re	Pioneer C 2002-III	6.00%	5.78%
	Mar-03	Swiss Re	Pioneer C 2003-I	6.00%	5.78%
	Jun-03	Swiss Re	Pioneer C 2003-II	5.75%	5.78%
	Jun-02	Swiss Re	Pioneer D 2002-I	1.75%	1.63%
	Sep-02	Swiss Re	Pioneer D 2002-II	1.75%	1.63%
	Dec-02	Swiss Re	Pioneer D 2002-III	1.75%	1.63%
	Mar-03	Swiss Re	Pioneer D 2003-I	1.75%	1.63%
	Jun-03	Swiss Re	Pioneer D 2003-II	1.75%	1.63%
	Jun-02	Swiss Re	Pioneer E 2002-I	4.25%	4.63%
	Dec-02	Swiss Re	Pioneer E 2002-III	4.75%	4.63%
	Mar-03	Swiss Re	Pioneer E 2003-I	4.75%	4.63%

EXHIBIT 33.3 *(Continued)*

Third Quarter 2003 (9/30/03) Secondary Market Prices from Four Dealers	Issue Date	Sponsor	Issuer	Spread at Issue	Average Market Indications
	Jun-02	Swiss Re	Pioneer F 2002-I	7.50%	6.91%
	Dec-02	Swiss Re	Pioneer F 2002-III	7.50%	6.91%
	Mar-03	Swiss Re	Pioneer F 2003-I	7.50%	6.91%
	Dec-00	Munich Re	PRIME CalQuake	7.50%	6.74%
	Dec-00	Munich Re	PRIME Calquake Shares	9.00%	9.70%
	Dec-00	Munich Re	PRIME Hurricane	6.50%	4.80%
	Dec-00	Munich Re	PRIME Hurricane Shares	8.00%	4.79%
	Mar-02	Lehman Re	Redwood Capital II	3.00%	2.70%
	Mar-02	Lehman Re	Redwood Capital II Shares	4.50%	4.35%
	Jun-01	USAA	Residential Re 2001	4.99%	3.54%
	May-02	USAA	Residential Re 2002	4.90%	3.98%
	May-03	USAA	Residential Re 2003	4.95%	4.26%
New Issue in Qtr.	Jul-03	Swiss Re	Sakura Capital	4.50%	4.63%
New Issue in Qtr.	Jul-03	Swiss Re	Sequioa Capital	5.75%	5.75%
	May-01	Swiss Re	SR Wind Class A-1	5.25%	4.88%
	May-01	Swiss Re	SR Wind Class A-1 Shares	6.75%	7.44%
	May-01	Swiss Re	SR Wind Class A-2	5.75%	4.71%
	May-01	Swiss Re	SR Wind Class A-2 Shares	7.25%	4.80%
	Apr-02	Hiscox	St Agatha Re	6.75%	6.00%
	Dec-02	Vivendi	Studio Re	5.10%	4.77%
	Dec-02	Vivendi	Studio Re Shares	8.00%	7.77%
	Jun-01	Zurich Re	Trinom Ltd Class A-1	8.00%	7.20%
	Jun-01	Zurich Re	Trinom Ltd Class A-2	4.00%	3.12%
	Jun-01	Zurich Re	Trinom Ltd Shares	10.00%	10.58%
					4.91%
			Circle Maihama Parametric Units Kelvin 1st Event Kelvin 2nd Event		

Other extant securities that may be maturing or are without any secondary prices.

	Mar-00	SCOR	Atlas Reinsurance Class A	2.70%	
	Mar-00	SCOR	Atlas Reinsurance Class B	3.70%	
	Mar-00	SCOR	Atlas Reinsurance Class C	14.00%	
	Jul-00	Vesta	NeHi	4.10%	

Source: Lane Financial LLC.

EXHIBIT 33.4 Secondary Market Price Data

Fourth Quarter 2003 (12/31/03) Secondary Market Prices from Four Dealers	Issue Date	Sponsor	Issuer	Spread at Issue	Average Market Indications
	Jul-03	Swiss Re	Arbor Capital I	15.50%	15.10%
	Jul-03	Swiss Re	Arbor Capital I-II	15.25%	15.03%
New Issue in Qtr.	Dec-03	Swiss Re	Arbor Capital I-III	15.00%	15.25%
	Jul-03	Swiss Re	Arbor Capital II	1.00%	0.98%
	Dec-01	SCOR	Atlas Reinsurance Class A	2.38%	1.18%
	Dec-01	SCOR	Atlas Reinsurance Class B	6.75%	5.51%
	May-99	Oriental Land	Concentric	3.10%	2.14%
	Aug-03	Central Re	Formosa Re	3.30%	2.63%
	May-02	Nissay Dowa	Fujiyama	4.00%	2.89%
	May-02	Nissay Dowa	Fujiyama Shares	7.00%	5.50%
	Nov-00	AGF	Mediterranean Re Class A	2.60%	1.51%
	Nov-00	AGF	Mediterranean Re Class B	5.85%	3.82%
	Jul-03	Swiss Re	Oak Capital	4.57%	4.68%
	Jul-03	Swiss Re	Palm Capital	5.81%	4.90%
New Issue in Qtr.	Dec-03	Swiss Re	Palm Capital-II	5.81%	5.35%
	Dec-97	TokioMarine	Parametric Re	4.30%	3.32%
	Jun-03	Swiss Re	Phoenix Quake	2.45%	1.94%
	Jun-03	Swiss Re	Phoenix Quake/Wind	2.45%	1.94%
	Jun-03	Swiss Re	Phoenix Quake/Wind II	3.50%	3.03%
	Jun-02	Swiss Re	Pioneer A 2002-I	6.00%	4.69%
	Dec-02	Swiss Re	Pioneer A 2002-III	5.25%	4.67%
	Mar-03	Swiss Re	Pioneer A 2003-I	5.50%	4.66%
	Jun-03	Swiss Re	Pioneer A 2003-II	6.00%	4.69%
	Jun-02	Swiss Re	Pioneer B 2002-I	5.00%	4.75%
	Sep-02	Swiss Re	Pioneer B 2002-II	5.25%	4.75%
	Dec-02	Swiss Re	Pioneer B 2002-III	5.25%	4.75%
	Mar-03	Swiss Re	Pioneer B 2003-I	4.75%	4.75%
	Jun-03	Swiss Re	Pioneer B 2003-II	5.00%	4.76%
	Jun-02	Swiss Re	Pioneer C 2002-I	6.00%	5.43%
	Sep-02	Swiss Re	Pioneer C 2002-II	6.00%	5.43%
	Dec-02	Swiss Re	Pioneer C 2002-III	6.00%	5.43%
	Mar-03	Swiss Re	Pioneer C 2003-I	6.00%	5.43%
	Jun-03	Swiss Re	Pioneer C 2003-II	5.75%	5.43%
	Jun-02	Swiss Re	Pioneer D 2002-I	1.75%	1.67%
	Sep-02	Swiss Re	Pioneer D 2002-II	1.75%	1.67%
	Dec-02	Swiss Re	Pioneer D 2002-III	1.75%	1.67%
	Mar-03	Swiss Re	Pioneer D 2003-I	1.75%	1.67%
	Jun-03	Swiss Re	Pioneer D 2003-II	1.75%	1.67%
	Dec-03	Swiss Re	Pioneer D 2003-III	1.50%	1.67%

Fourth Quarter 2003 (12/31/03) Secondary Market Prices from Four Dealers	Issue Date	Sponsor	Issuer	Spread at Issue	Average Market Indications
	Jun-02	Swiss Re	Pioneer E 2002-I	4.25%	4.43%
	Dec-02	Swiss Re	Pioneer E 2002-III	4.75%	4.43%
	Mar-03	Swiss Re	Pioneer E 2003-I	4.75%	4.43%
	Jun-02	Swiss Re	Pioneer F 2002-I	7.50%	6.37%
	Dec-02	Swiss Re	Pioneer F 2002-III	7.50%	6.37%
	Mar-03	Swiss Re	Pioneer F 2003-I	7.50%	6.37%
New Issue in Qtr.	Dec-03	Elec de Fr	Pylon A	1.50%	1.55%
New Issue in Qtr.	Dec-03	Elec de Fr	Pylon B	3.90%	3.95%
New Issue in Qtr.			Redwood III	3.85%	3.85%
New Issue in Qtr.			Redwood IV	2.30%	2.30%
	Jun-01	USAA	Residential Re 2001	4.99%	1.46%
	May-02	USAA	Residential Re 2002	4.90%	3.08%
	May-03	USAA	Residential Re 2003	4.95%	3.89%
	Jul-03	Swiss Re	Sakura Capital	4.50%	4.43%
	Jul-03	Swiss Re	Sequoia Capital	5.75%	5.41%
	May-01	Swiss Re	SR Wind Class A-1	5.25%	4.26%
	May-01	Swiss Re	SR Wind Class A-1 Shares	6.75%	6.84%
	May-01	Swiss Re	SR Wind Class A-2	5.75%	4.00%
	May-01	Swiss Re	SR Wind Class A-2 Shares	7.25%	6.00%
	Apr-02	Hiscox	St Agatha Re	6.75%	5.02%
	Jun-01	Zurich Re	Trinom Ltd Class A-1	8.00%	6.38%
	Jun-01	Zurich Re	Trinom Ltd Class A-2	4.00%	2.12%
	Jun-01	Zurich Re	Trinom Ltd Shares	10.00%	11.00%
New Issue in Qtr.			Vita Capital	1.35%	1.31%
					4.53%
			Circle Maihama Parametric Units		

Other extant securities that may be maturing or are without any secondary prices.

	Dec-00	Munich Re	PRIME CalQuake	7.50%	8.76%
	Dec-00	Munich Re	PRIME Calquake Shares	9.00%	
	Dec-00	Munich Re	PRIME Hurricane	6.50%	2.01%
	Dec-00	Munich Re	PRIME Hurricane Shares	8.00%	
	Mar-02	Lehman Re	Redwood Capital II	3.00%	3.27%
	Mar-02	Lehman Re	Redwood Capital II Shares	4.50%	4.50%
	Dec-02	Vivendi	Studio Re	5.10%	
	Dec-02	Vivendi	Studio Re Shares	8.00%	

(Continued)

EXHIBIT 33.4 *(Continued)*

First Quarter 2004 (3/31/04) Secondary Market Prices from Four Dealers	Issue Date	Sponsor	Issuer	Spread at Issue	Average Market Indications
	Jul-03	Swiss Re	Arbor Capital I	15.50%	14.55%
	Jul-03	Swiss Re	Arbor Capital I-II	15.25%	14.55%
	Dec-03	Swiss Re	Arbor Capital I-III	15.00%	14.71%
New Issue in Qtr.	Mar-04	Swiss Re	Arbor Capital I-IV	14.00%	14.00%
	Jul-03	Swiss Re	Arbor Capital II	1.00%	0.94%
	Dec-01	SCOR	Atlas Reinsurance II Class A	2.38%	0.96%
	Dec-01	SCOR	Atlas Reinsurance II Class B	6.75%	4.60%
	May-99	Oriental Land	Concentric	3.10%	2.22%
	Aug-03	Central Re	Formosa Re	3.30%	2.49%
	May-02	Nissay Dowa	Fujiyama	4.00%	2.73%
	May-02	Nissay Dowa	Fujiyama Shares	7.00%	5.25%
	Nov-00	AGF	Mediterranean Re Class A	2.60%	1.40%
	Nov-00	AGF	Mediterranean Re Class B	5.85%	3.16%
	Jul-03	Swiss Re	Oak Capital	4.75%	3.86%
New Issue in Qtr.		Swiss Re	Oak Capital—Series II	3.75%	3.75%
	Jul-03	Swiss Re	Palm Capital	5.81%	4.92%
	Dec-03	Swiss Re	Palm Capital-II	5.81%	5.32%
	Dec-97	TokioMarine	Parametric Re	4.30%	3.14%
	Jun-03	Swiss Re	Phoenix Quake	2.45%	1.84%
	Jun-03	Swiss Re	Phoenix Quake/Wind	2.45%	1.84%
	Jun-03	Swiss Re	Phoenix Quake/Wind II	3.50%	2.78%
	Jun-02	Swiss Re	Pioneer A 2002-I	6.00%	4.71%
	Dec-02	Swiss Re	Pioneer A 2002-III	5.25%	4.70%
	Mar-03	Swiss Re	Pioneer A 2003-I	5.50%	4.70%
	Jun-03	Swiss Re	Pioneer A 2003-II	6.00%	4.71%
	Jun-02	Swiss Re	Pioneer B 2002-I	5.00%	4.02%
	Sep-02	Swiss Re	Pioneer B 2002-II	5.25%	3.94%
	Dec-02	Swiss Re	Pioneer B 2002-III	5.25%	3.94%
	Mar-03	Swiss Re	Pioneer B 2003-I	4.75%	3.93%
	Jun-03	Swiss Re	Pioneer B 2003-II	5.00%	3.93%
	Jun-02	Swiss Re	Pioneer C 2002-I	6.00%	4.98%
	Sep-02	Swiss Re	Pioneer C 2002-II	6.00%	4.98%
	Dec-02	Swiss Re	Pioneer C 2002-III	6.00%	4.98%
	Mar-03	Swiss Re	Pioneer C 2003-I	6.00%	4.98%
	Jun-03	Swiss Re	Pioneer C 2003-II	5.75%	4.98%
	Jun-02	Swiss Re	Pioneer D 2002-I	1.75%	1.49%
	Sep-02	Swiss Re	Pioneer D 2002-II	1.75%	1.49%
	Dec-02	Swiss Re	Pioneer D 2002-III	1.75%	1.49%
	Mar-03	Swiss Re	Pioneer D 2003-I	1.75%	1.49%
	Jun-03	Swiss Re	Pioneer D 2003-II	1.75%	1.49%
	Dec-03	Swiss Re	Pioneer D 2003-III	1.50%	1.49%

EXHIBIT 33.4 *(Continued)*

First Quarter 2004 (3/31/04) Secondary Market Prices from Four Dealers	Issue Date	Sponsor	Issuer	Spread at Issue	Average Market Indications
	Jun-02	Swiss Re	Pioneer E 2002-I	4.25%	4.09%
	Dec-02	Swiss Re	Pioneer E 2002-III	4.75%	4.10%
	Mar-03	Swiss Re	Pioneer E 2003-I	4.75%	4.10%
	Jun-02	Swiss Re	Pioneer F 2002-I	7.50%	5.97%
	Dec-02	Swiss Re	Pioneer F 2002-III	7.50%	5.97%
	Mar-03	Swiss Re	Pioneer F 2003-I	7.50%	5.97%
	Dec-03	Elec de Fr	Pylon A	1.50%	1.32%
	Dec-03	Elec de Fr	Pylon B	3.90%	3.42%
		Swiss Re	Redwood III	3.85%	3.58%
		Swiss Re	Redwood IV	2.30%	2.09%
	Jun-01	USAA	Residential Re 2001	4.99%	1.45%
	May-02	USAA	Residential Re 2002	4.90%	3.50%
	May-03	USAA	Residential Re 2003	4.95%	4.05%
	Jul-03	Swiss Re	Sakura Capital	4.50%	4.11%
	Jul-03	Swiss Re	Sequoia Capital	5.75%	4.93%
New Issue in Qtr.		Swiss Re	Sequoia Capital—Series II	4.75%	4.75%
	May-01	Swiss Re	SR Wind Class A-1	5.25%	3.55%
	May-01	Swiss Re	SR Wind Class A-1 Shares	6.75%	5.12%
	May-01	Swiss Re	SR Wind Class A-2	5.75%	3.98%
	May-01	Swiss Re	SR Wind Class A-2 Shares	7.25%	5.11%
	Apr-02	Hiscox	St Agatha Re	6.75%	4.70%
	Jun-01	Zurich Re	Trinom Ltd Class A-1	8.00%	4.40%
	Jun-01	Zurich Re	Trinom Ltd Class A-2	4.00%	1.55%
	Jun-01	Zurich Re	Trinom Ltd Shares	10.00%	4.64%
	Dec-03	Swiss Re	Vita Capital	1.35%	1.28%
					4.23%
			Circle Maihama Parametric Units		

Other extant securities that may be maturing or are without any secondary prices.

	Dec-00	Munich Re	PRIME CalQuake	7.50%	10.12%
	Dec-00	Munich Re	PRIME Calquake Shares	9.00%	
	Dec-00	Munich Re	PRIME Hurricane	6.50%	3.33%
	Dec-00	Munich Re	PRIME Hurricane Shares	8.00%	
	Mar-02	Lehman Re	Redwood Capital II	3.00%	4.30%
	Mar-02	Lehman Re	Redwood Capital II Shares	4.50%	4.50%
	Dec-02	Vivendi	Studio Re	5.10%	
	Dec-02	Vivendi	Studio Re Shares	8.00%	

Source: Lane Financial LLC.

EXHIBIT 33.5 New Securities

SPV	Cedent	Lead Underwriters	Amount (US $Mil)	S&P Rating	Moody's Rating	Fitch Rating	Issue Date	Maturity
1. Analyzed Securities								
Arbor I Ltd.	Swiss Re	Swiss Re Cap. Mkts.	95.0	B	—	—	Jul-03	Jun-06
	Swiss Re	Swiss Re Cap. Mkts.	60.0	B	—	—	Sep-03	Jun-06
	Swiss Re	Swiss Re Cap. Mkts.	8.9	B	—	—	Dec-03	Dec-06
	Swiss Re	Swiss Re Cap. Mkts.	21.0	B	—	—	Mar-04	Mar-06
Arbor II Ltd.	Swiss Re	Swiss Re Cap. Mkts.	26.5	A+	A1	—	Jul-03	Jun-06
Formosa Re Ltd.	Central Re Corp.	Aon Capital Markets MMC Securities Corp.	100.0	—	—	—	Aug-03	Jul-06
Oak Capital Ltd.	Swiss Re	Swiss Re Cap. Mkts.	23.6	BB+	Ba3	—	Jul-03	Jun-07
			24.0	BB+	Ba3	—	Mar-04	Mar-05
Palm Capital Ltd.	Swiss Re	Swiss Re Cap. Mkts.	22.4	BB+	Ba3	—	Jul-03	Jun-07
	Swiss Re	Swiss Re Cap. Mkts.	19.0	BB+	Ba3	—	Dec-03	Dec-05
Phoenix Quake Ltd.	Zenkyoren Ins.	Swiss Re Cap. Mkts.	192.5	BBB+	Baa3	—	Jun-03	Jul-08
Phoenix Quake Wind I Ltd.	Zenkyoren Ins.	Swiss Re Cap. Mkts.	192.5	BBB+	Baa3	—	Jun-03	Jul-08
Phoenix Quake Wind II Ltd.	Zenkyoren Ins.	Swiss Re Cap. Mkts.	85.0	BBB–	Ba1	—	Jun-03	Jul-08

Pioneer 2000 Ltd. A	Swiss Re	Swiss Re Cap. Mkts.	9.8	BB+	Ba3	—	Jun-03	Jun-06
Pioneer 2000 Ltd. B	Swiss Re	Swiss Re Cap. Mkts.	12.3	BB+	Ba3	—	Jun-03	Jun-06
Pioneer 2000 Ltd. C	Swiss Re	Swiss Re Cap. Mkts.	7.3	BB+	Ba3	—	Jun-03	Jun-06
Pioneer 2000 Ltd. D	Swiss Re	Swiss Re Cap. Mkts.	2.6	BBB-	Baa3	—	Jun-03	Jun-06
	Swiss Re		51.0	BBB-	Baa3	—	Dec-03	Jun-06
Pylon Ltd.	Electricite de France	CDC IXIS Cap. Mkts.	147.0	BBB+	A2	—	Dec-03	Dec-08
	Electricite de France	Swiss Re Cap. Mkts.	85.5	BB+	Ba1	—	Dec-03	Dec-08
Redwood III	Swiss Re	Swiss Re Cap. Mkts.	150.0	BB+	Ba1	—	Dec-03	Dec-05
Redwood IV	Swiss Re	Swiss Re Cap. Mkts.	200.0	BBB-	Baa3	—	Dec-03	Dec-05
Residential Re 2003 Ltd.	USAA	Goldman Sachs BNP Paribas	160.0	BB+	Ba2	—	May-03	Jun-06
Sakura Ltd.	Swiss Re	Swiss Re Cap. Mkts.	14.7	BB+	Ba3	—	Jul-03	Jun-07
Sequoia Capital Ltd.	Swiss Re	Swiss Re Cap. Mkts.	22.5	BB+	Ba3	—	Jul-03	Jun-07
			11.5	BB+	Ba3	—	Mar-04	Mar-05
Vita Capital Ltd.	Swiss Re	Swiss Re Cap. Mkts.	150.0	BB+	Ba3	—	Dec-02	Jul-06

2. Equity Tranches of SPV—less than $10 million
None

(Continued)

EXHIBIT 33.5 (Continued)

SPV	Maturity Term	Exposure Term	Spread Premium to LIBOR (bps)	Adjusted Spread Premium (Annual)	Expected Loss (Annual)	Probability of 1st $ Loss (Annual)	Probability of Exhaust (Annual)	Expected Excess Return (Annual)	Conditional Expected Loss
1. Analyzed Securities									
Arbor I Ltd.	36	36	1550	1572	4.86%	5.9700	3.8600	1571	0.81%
	33	33	1551	1573	4.86%	5.9700	3.8600	1572	0.81%
	36	36	1500	1521	4.86%	5.9700	3.8600	1521	0.81%
	24	24	1400	1419	4.86%	5.9700	3.8600	1419	0.81%
Arbor II Ltd.	36	36	100	101	0.007%	0.0120	0.0040	101	0.58%
Formosa Re Ltd.	34	34	405	411	0.73%	0.8100	0.6600	411	0.90%
Oak Capital Ltd.	48	48	475	482	1.27%	1.5900	1.0500	482	0.80%
	12	12	375	380	1.27%	1.5900	1.0500	380	0.80%
Palm Capital Ltd.	48	48	575	583	1.28%	1.5900	0.9700	583	0.81%
	24	24	500	507	1.28%	1.5900	0.9700	507	0.81%
Phoenix Quake Ltd.	60	60	245	248	0.22%	0.2400	0.2000	248	0.92%
Phoenix Quake Wind I Ltd.	60	60	245	248	0.22%	0.2400	0.2000	248	0.92%
Phoenix Quake Wind II Ltd.	60	60	350	355	0.49%	0.5500	0.4500	355	0.89%

Pioneer 2000 Ltd. A	36	36	600	608	1.28%	1.5900	0.9700	608	0.81%
Pioneer 2000 Ltd. B	36	36	500	507	1.27%	1.5900	1.0500	507	0.80%
Pioneer 2000 Ltd. C	36	36	575	583	1.28%	1.5900	0.9800	583	0.81%
Pioneer 2000 Ltd. D	36	36	175	177	0.22%	0.2700	1.8600	177	0.81%
	33	33	150	152	0.22%	0.2700	1.8600	152	0.81%
Pylon Ltd.	60	60	150	152	0.02%	0.0400		152	0.50%
	60	60	390	395	0.54%	1.2300		395	0.44%
Redwood III	24	24	385	390	0.52%	0.7100		390	0.73%
Redwood IV	24	24	230	233	0.22%	0.3000		233	0.73%
Residential Re 2003 Ltd.	36	36	495	502	0.48%	1.1000	0.2800	502	0.44%
Sakura Ltd.	48	48	450	456	1.29%	1.5900	1.0100	456	0.81%
Sequoia Capital Ltd.	48	48	575	583	1.28%	1.5900	0.9800	583	0.81%
	12	12	475	482	1.28%	1.5900	0.9800	482	0.81%
Vita Capital Ltd.	43	42	510	517	0.65%	1.3800	0.2200	517	0.47%

The table displays securities/tranches that were issued or announced between April 2003 and March 2004. Section 1 shows 27 issues/tranches that are analyzed in this paper. Section 2 records 0 equity tranches.
Shaded columns show the date that is used in a related paper on price analysis.
All deals are converted to a 365-day year as LIBOR convention uses a 360-day year but CAT risk is a 365-day year. Adjusted spreads are therefore comparable to reinsurance pricing.
Expected Excess Return is defined as Adjusted Spread Premium less Expected Loss. Conditional Expected Loss is defined as Expected Loss divided by the Probability of First Dollar Loss.
Formosa Re spread and expected loss can vary; the indicated spread of 405 is based on the best estimate expected loss of 0.73%.
Pioneer is a shelf offering allowing quarterly offerings in each Class; in this period they issued a total of 5 times within 4 Classes.
Source: Lane Financial LLC.

The little-noted feature of the transaction that deserves further exposure is that it covers multiple perils. At one time the USAA deals were the
poster boys of single-peril bonds—they were exposed to only severe, force
3 or greater, Atlantic hurricanes for specified coastal states. The 2003
deal, however, is exposed to wind and earthquake risk anywhere in the
continental United States and Hawaii. (The addition of Hawaii first became a feature in 2002.)

The other underappreciated fact is that, while the deal is relatively
small ($160 million) its three-year structure fits with other three-year deals
from 2001 and 2002 to provide a combined coverage for the 2003 hurricane season of $435 million—the largest cover obtained by USAA in the
capital markets since 1999. Exhibit 33.6 illustrates the dovetailing nature
of the coverage.

USAA in its persistence with the capital markets has achieved
more coverage, wider coverage, and lower issuance cost than many
appreciate.

It is worth pausing here to also note the way the securities issued by

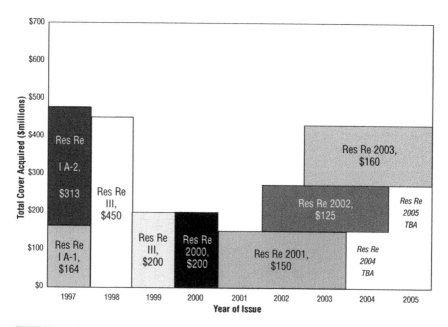

EXHIBIT 33.6   Annual Potential Recovery from USAA-Sponsored Residential Re
Securities, 1997–2003
Source: Lane Financial LLC.

USAA have traded in the secondary market. The prices are isolated in Exhibit 33.7.

The 2001 Residential Re transaction was issued at a price spread over LIBOR of 4.99 percent, the secondary prices traded in successive recent quarters at 4.73 percent, 3.54 percent, 1.46 percent, and 1.45 percent. The U.S. hurricane season starts as early as June and is usually over by mid-October. In the second quarter of 2003, the 2001 issue had only one season of exposure left (it matures in 2004). Thus the secondary price had already dropped from 4.99 percent to 4.73 percent. By the end of the third quarter, however, its exposure was significantly behind it. Its price dropped to 3.54 percent, and by year-end to 1.46 percent. As of Q2 2004, there is some chance of an early (prematurity) severe hurricane, but it is remote and the price reflects it.

The pricing of the 2002 issue is also revealing (although the numbers bounce around a little). As of the present—second quarter 2004—one season of exposure is left and yet the price is 3.5 percent. Compare this with the one-season-left price of the 2002 issue (4.73 percent) and one is led to the conclusion that this drop can only be the result of demand shift. The seasonal effects are almost absent at this time of the year so the annual rates would otherwise stay the same.

Finally, the 2003 issue has two wind seasons of exposure left, but it also has an earthquake exposure that has no seasonality to it. Its price should display much less seasonality. Its current price is again a reflection, we believe, of demand shift, but it is at least partially offset by the addition of earthquake exposure.

The foregoing is an exercise in teasing out messages from numbers that are themselves somewhat circumspect. No one would want to live or die by the precision of these secondary market prices. Nevertheless, the exercise does illustrate an issue that we have come to appreciate more and more in our attempts to craft an adequate pricing model for insurance securitizations. In pricing exercises, seasons, peril composition, and peril structure all matter. Unless expected losses are revised to match shifting exposures it is very hard to deduce how much premium over expected loss the markets are prepared to pay. Regression analyses that use only at-issue expected loss figures against current prices must inevitably be inadequate.

Pioneer and the Arboreal Series

In June 2002 Swiss Re Capital Markets introduced a new form of insurance security with its Pioneer Series. Essentially Swiss Re issued a medium-term note (MTN) program that allowed for the serial issue of several

EXHIBIT 33.7 USAA Securities—Secondary Market Prices

	Issue Price	Maturity	Q2 2003	Q3 2003	Q4 2003	Q1 2004	
Res Re 2001 Ltd.	4.99	Q2 2004	4.73	3.54	1.46	1.45	Wind Only
Res Re 2002 Ltd.	4.90	Q2 2005	4.67	3.98	3.08	3.50	Fla + Hi
Res Re 2003 Ltd.	4.95	Q2 2006	4.87	4.26	3.89	4.05	Multiperil

Source: Lane Financial LLC.

prespecified securities all from the same master document. This saved issuance costs since full documentation was required only once. Like the USAA switch to multiyear/multiperil deals to save issuer costs it has a profound impact beyond the initial concept. And like USAA, it has been dismissed as small beer and faddish. As is clear, it is neither.

The original Pioneer series was issued quarterly on demand, but all the deals were for a fixed maturity—6/15/2006. The deals covered single-exposure zones: North Atlantic hurricane, European windstorm, California earthquake, central U.S. earthquake, Japanese earthquake, and one series with a combined risk of all the preceding zones (Series F). Each was denominated in a Swiss Re–designed index, and each was attached at approximately the same probabilities. The approximate exceedance curves are shown in Exhibit 33.8.

Swiss Re continued to issue additional series through 2003 in varying amounts and prices, as shown in Exhibit 33.9. However, in mid-2003 it introduced another MTN program, the Arboreal Series, which either complements or replaces Pioneer. Each single exposure was given the name of a tree local to that zone—Palm, Oak, Sequoia, and Sakura—corresponding exactly to Pioneer Series A, B, C, and E. (Series D was dropped; no demand, no supply, or possibly no indigenous trees?) Then two other deals were added, Arbor I and Arbor II. Arbor I represents the first loss layer of a combined deal in which any of the exposures or their aggregation can exhaust the risk. Arbor II represents the third layer of a combined deal in which the aggregate loss from any of the deals can attach or exhaust the capital. Exhibit 33.10 shows a Rubik's Cube of possibilities.

A buyer could now either buy each of the four zones separately to accumulate a portfolio or purchase a layer of that risk—effectively buy-

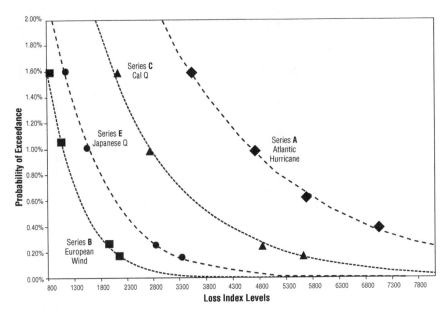

EXHIBIT 33.8 Approximate Exceedance Curves for Pioneer Risks (Market symbols represent the attachment and exhaustion points given in Pioneer prospectus)
Source: Lane Financial LLC.

ing on a leveraged basis. Twenty-five dollars invested in each of the four zones would at original issue produce a coupon income spread of 5.1875 percent. Alternatively, the investor could put $100 in Arbor I and receive a coupon of 15.5 percent together with a much higher risk. Essentially, Arbor I is the first $100 of loss from a portfolio of four $100 single-zone investments. Clearly Arbor I is a leveraged investment. The coupon on the four-deal set would be 20.75 percent, so 5.25 percent (20.75% − 15.50%) is effectively the price of the leverage. Could an investor borrow $300 on a nonrecourse basis below 5.5 percent, and have someone else take the last $300 of risk? Swiss Re is prepared to do that—at 5.5 percent.

The Arboreal Series has one other feature that is different from Pioneer. Investors can now choose the time of purchase (although they have to take Swiss Re's price at the time) and they can choose the maturity of the risk. The term has to be no greater than three years for the Arbors and four years for the trees.

EXHIBIT 33.9 Swiss Re Insurance Security Series, 2003

Pioneer Specifications

All Fixed Maturity = 6/15/2006

		Issue Date	6/26/2002	9/16/2002	12/16/2002	3/17/2003	6/17/2003	12/15/2003
		Issue Spread	L3 + Spread	L3 + Spread	L3 + Spread	L3 + Spread	L3 + Spread	L3 + Spread
N. Atlantic Hurricane	A Series	BB+	6.00%		5.25%	5.50%	6.00%	
European Windstorm	B Series	BB+	5.00%	5.25%	5.25%	4.75%	5.00%	
California Earthquake	C Series	BB+	6.00%	6.00%	6.00%	6.00%	5.75%	
Central US Earthquake	D Series	BBB−	1.75%	1.75%	1.75%	1.75%	1.75%	1.50%
Japan Earthquake	E Series	BB+	4.25%		4.75%	4.75%		
Multiperil, Any of Above	F Series	BB+	7.50%		7.50%	7.50%		

Amounts Issued $ millions

N. Atlantic Hurricane	A Series	BB+	85.00		8.50	6.50	9.75	
European Windstorm	B Series	BB+	50.00	5.00	21.00	8.00	12.25	
California Earthquake	C Series	BB+	30.00	20.50	15.70	6.50	7.25	
Central US Earthquake	D Series	BBB−	40.00	1.75	25.50	5.50	2.60	51.00
Japan Earthquake	E Series	BB+	25.00		30.55	8.00		
Multiperil, Any of Above	F Series	BB+	25.00		3.00	8.14		
			255.00	27.25	104.25	42.64	31.85	51.00

Total Issuance 511.99

	Swiss Re Index Values	Single Peril Attach	Single Peril Exhaust	Multiperil i.e. Series F Attach	Multiperil i.e. Series F Exhaust
N. Atlantic Hurricane	A Index	3546	4671	5609	7094
European Windstorm	B Index	810	955	1880	2093
California Earthquake	C Index	2098	2678	4853	5594
Central US Earthquake	D Index	—	—	—	—
Japan Earthquake	E Index	1084	1451	2803	3274
Multiperil, Any of Above	F	—	—	—	—

		Attach PFL	Exhaust PLL	Expected EL
N. Atlantic Hurricane	A Index	1.59%	0.97%	1.28%
European Windstorm	B Index	1.59%	1.05%	1.27%
California Earthquake	C Index	1.59%	0.98%	1.28%
Central US Earthquake	D Index	0.27%	0.19%	0.22%
Japan Earthquake	E Index	1.59%	1.01%	1.29%
Multiperil, Any of Above	F	1.60%	1.02%	1.31%

Components of Multiperil Series F

		PFL	PLL	EL
N. Atlantic Hurricane	A Index	*0.612%*	*0.374%*	*0.493%*
European Windstorm	B Index	*0.253%*	*0.167%*	*0.202%*
California Earthquake	C Index	*0.247%*	*0.152%*	*0.199%*
Central US Earthquake	D Index	*0.270%*	*0.190%*	*0.218%*
Japan Earthquake	E Index	*0.248%*	*0.157%*	*0.201%*
Multiperil, Any of Above	F	*1.600%*	*1.020%*	1.31%

Note: Figures in bold italic are a "best estimate" by LFC. They are not figures provided in the Pioneer Prospectus.

EXHIBIT 33.9 *(Continued)*

Arbor Specifications

Variable Maturities of 1 to 4 years

	Issue Date	7/24/2003 L3 + Spread	9/15/2003 L3 + Spread	12/15/2003 L3 + Spread	3/15/2004 L3 + Spread	
Palm Cap Ltd	BB+	5.75%	—	5.00%		N. Atlantic Hurricane
Oak Cap Ltd	BB+	4.75%			3.75%	European Windstorm
Sequoia Cap Ltd	BB+	5.75%			4.75%	California Earthquake
Sakura Cap Ltd	BB+	4.50%	—	—	—	Japan Earthquake
Arbor I Cap Ltd	B	15.50%	15.25%	15.00%	14.00%	Multiperil, Any of Above
Arbor II Cap Ltd	A+	1.00%				Multiperil, Any of Above

Amounts Issued $ millions

		7/24/2003	9/15/2003	12/15/2003	3/15/2004	
Palm Cap Ltd	BB+	22.35		19.00		N. Atlantic Hurricane
Oak Cap Ltd.	BB+	23.60			24.00	European Windstorm
Sequoia Cap Ltd	BB+	22.50	—		11.50	California Earthquake
Sakura Cap Ltd	BB+	14.70			—	Japan Earthquake
Arbor I Cap Ltd	B	95.00	60.00	8.85	21.00	Multiperil, Any of Above
Arbor II Cap Ltd	A+	26.50				Multiperil, Any of Above
		204.65	60.00	27.85	56.50	

Total Issuance 349.00

Source: Lane Financial LLC.

	Single Peril Attach	Single Peril Exhaust	Maximum Maturity	Peril
Palm Cap Ltd	3546	4671	4 Years	N. Atlantic Hurricane
Oak Cap Ltd	810	955	4 Years	European Windstorm
Sequoia Cap Ltd	2098	2678	4 Years	California Earthquake
	—	—		
Sakura Cap Ltd	1084	1451	4 Years	Japan Earthquake
Arbor I Cap Ltd	Sum of % from all four Above		3 Years	Multiperil, Any of Above
Arbor II Cap Ltd	Sum of % from Above, less 200%		3 Years	Multiperil, Any of Above

	Attach PFL	Exhaust PLL	Expected EL	Peril
Palm Cap Ltd	1.59%	0.97%	1.28%	N. Atlantic Hurricane
Oak Cap Ltd	1.59%	1.05%	1.27%	European Windstorm
Sequoia Cap Ltd	1.59%	0.98%	1.28%	California Earthquake
	—	—	—	
Sakura Cap Ltd	1.59%	1.01%	1.29%	Japan Earthquake
Arbor I Cap Ltd	5.97%	3.86%	4.86%	Multiperil, Any of Above
Arbor II Cap Ltd	0.012%	0.004%	0.007%	Multiperil, Any of Above

Maturities of	Series I	Series II	Series III	Series IV
Palm Cap Ltd	6/15/2007	12/15/2005		
Oak Cap Ltd	6/15/2007	3/15/2005		
Sequoia Cap Ltd	6/15/2007	3/5/2005		
Sakura Cap Ltd	6/15/2007			
Arbor I Cap Ltd	6/15/2006	6/15/2006	12/15/2006	
Arbor II Cap Ltd	6/15/2006		12/15/2006	3/15/2005

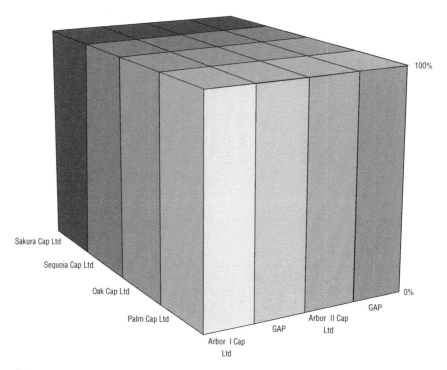

EXHIBIT 33.10   Swiss Re Insurance Security Series, 2004
Source: Lane Financial LLC.

The record of issues under both programs is shown in Exhibit 33.9. What is most remarkable about the issue record is that the additional series, whether Pioneer or Arbor, are quite small. Amounts as low as $8 million have been issued to investors, although the initial Arbor I series garnered a respectable $95 million. Clearly it was quite popular.

Because of the small size, the issue has tended to be dismissed as something of a novelty but a failure. After all, the coverage needs of the likes of Swiss Re are massive in comparison. Can this effort be worthwhile? Adherents to the world of insurance securitization know that sentiment well. But consider the result shown in Exhibit 33.11.

Because all the issues are for multiple years, the combined coverage is now considerable. For the current year each zone now has $100 million to $150 million of single-issue coverage, in addition to the combined coverage from the Arbors. When that is taken into account, coverage for this year's hurricane season is likely to approach $400 million (assuming some further issuance between now and season onset). Like USAA, Swiss Re has obtained much more from the capital markets and at much cheaper cost than the more splashy big deals. It is even possible that the cost is lower than the equivalent brokerage costs in the traditional reinsurance market. Combine that with the feature of negligible credit risk on reinsurance recoverables and it is obvious that reinsurers should pay much closer attention to securitization events.

Redwood III and IV

The Redwood transactions of 2002 matured at year-end. They were indirectly associated with the California Earthquake Authority but were rather simple in nature. The index used for loss calculation is the Property Claim Services (PCS) index so that the deals are comparable to industry loss warranty (ILW) pricing. In another demonstration of industry demand, the issue prices for Redwood III and IV are, respectively, 3.85 percent and 2.30 percent, down from 5.00 percent and 3.00 percent, respectively, in 2002.

Formosa Re

Formosa (the old name for Taiwan) Re introduced Taiwanese earthquake risk to the market. The issuer was the Taiwan Residential Earthquake Insurance Pool. Formosa Re offered a new zone of coverage and it was enthusiastically accepted in the market. The issue was nonrated but still sold $100 million. It was the first nonrated deal in quite a while, the prior received wisdom being that the imprimatur of the rating companies was a necessary endorsement of risk statistics for skeptical investors. Evidently, things change.

The reason for nonrating is obvious upon examination of the deal's specifications. The initial coupon was 3.3 percent. However, that could be adjusted quarterly and was related to the sale of underlying earthquake policies in Taiwan. If considerable numbers were sold, the coupon could eventually rise to 10.4 percent. The expected loss levels at initial issue levels are 0.5 percent. If the coupon rises to 10.4 percent, the expected loss will be 2.5 percent. In other words, from an investor perspective the deal could start as a BBB deal but migrate to a B without any significant loss activity. Hard to rate indeed!

Of course there are "best estimates" of policy sales, and taking those into account gives an average expected coupon of 4.05 percent and an expected loss of 0.73 percent. Secondary quotes are listed at 2.49 percent. One would

EXHIBIT 33.11 Swiss Re Coverages

			2002 Q1 Q2 Q3 Q4	2003 Q1 Q2 Q3 Q4	2004 Q1 Q2 Q3 Q4	2005 Q1 Q2 Q3 Q4	2006 Q1 Q2 Q3 Q4	2007 Q1 Q2 Q3 Q4
N. Atlantic Hurricane	A	109.75						
Palm Cap Ltd	I	22.35						
Palm Cap Ltd	II	19.00						
Current Q1 2004 Coverage					151.10			
European Windstorm	B	96.25						
Oak Cap Ltd	I	23.60						
Oak Cap Ltd	II	24.00						
Current Q1 2004 Coverage					143.85			
California Earthquake	C	79.95						
Sequoia Cap Ltd	I	22.50						
Sequoia Cap Ltd	II	11.50						
Current Q1 2004 Coverage					113.95			
Central US Earthquake	D	126.35						
Current Q1 2004 Coverage					126.35			
Japan Earthquake	E	63.55						
Sakura Cap Ltd	I	14.70						
Current Q1 2004 Coverage					78.25			

Arbor I Cap Ltd	I	95.00		
Arbor I Cap Ltd	II	60		
Arbor I Cap Ltd	III	8.85		
Arbor I Cap Ltd	IV	21		
Current Q1 2004 Coverage		184.85		
Multiperil, Any of Above	F	36.14		
Current Q1 2004 Coverage		36.14		
Arbor II Cap Ltd	I	26.50		
Current Q1 2004 Coverage		26.50		

TOTAL COVERAGE BY ZONE Q1 2004

N. Atlantic Hurricane	398.59	Assumes all relevant covers are triggered
European Windstorm	391.34	Assumes all relevant covers are triggered
California Earthquake	361.44	Assumes all relevant covers are triggered
Central US Earthquake	162.49	Assumes all relevant covers are triggered
Japan Earthquake	325.74	Assumes all relevant covers are triggered
Multiperil, Any Sum of Above	247.49	Assumes all relevant covers are triggered

Source: Lane Financial LLC.

have to guess that either competitive prices or slow policy sales have kept the quote that low.

Phoenix Quake Wind Ltd./Phoenix Quake Ltd./ Phoenix Quake Wind II Ltd.

Zenkyoren, the Japanese National Mutual Insurance Federation of Agriculture Co-ops, is a new sponsor of insurance securities. In 2003 it issued $470 million in securities in three separate parts. This was the largest deal of the year. The coverage was for Japanese earthquake and Japanese wind risk, particularly typhoon risk. Each maturity was for a period of five years. Incidentally, it is noticeable that nearly all Japanese deals tend to be for longer periods. This has been true ever since the first Japanese deal, Parametric Re, which was for an original 10-year maturity.

The events under the cover are mostly second events. Phoenix Quake Wind covers any typhoon losses or earthquake losses that occur after a first earthquake event. Phoenix Quake Ltd. covers specifically second event earthquake. Finally, Phoenix Quake Wind II Ltd. covers aggregate typhoon losses and aggregate earthquake losses that arise after either a typhoon or an earthquake has first occurred.

Complicating the specifications, the hurdle rate "first event" is set at a level higher than eligible coverage events in Phoenix Quake Wind and Phoenix Quake, but the threshold event is set lower in Phoenix Quake Wind II.

Notwithstanding these complications, it is clear what the cedent is after. Zenkyoren is primarily after protection from further devastation following a first big earthquake. It is concerned about severity but more importantly about frequency. It wants protection from either other earthquakes or other typhoons immediately following a very large earthquake hit. It also wants protection against several smaller, but still significant, events whether earthquake or typhoon.

Pylon Ltd.

Electricité de France issued €190 million of two tranches in December 2003. The notes were for five-year maturity and covered wind damage to its transmission and distribution lines in France. An index of wind damage was constructed, and payment was proportional to the various levels of loss on the index.

Class A issues were for the first level of loss. Class B was for subsequent losses and would be attached only if payments under A were exhausted and if a second event occurred.

Notably, Pylon was a direct issue of Electricité de France. This was not for the reinsurance of a transmission and distribution cover that had previously been insured with an insurer. As such it is an example of disintermediation, issuing directly to the capital markets rather than via the insurance markets. Previous examples of disintermediation are Tokyo Disneyland (Circle Maihama and Concentric) and Universal Studios (Studio Re).

Vita Capital Ltd.

Perhaps the most exciting transaction of 2003 was Vita Capital Ltd. It transferred excess mortality risk from the sponsor, Swiss Re, to the capital markets via an index of mortality in the United States, United Kingdom, France, Switzerland, and Italy. Original issue size was $250 million but the structure allows for up to $400 million to be issued. The maturity was for three and a half years.

The mortality risk in question was quite remote. The index had to be between 130 percent and 150 percent above normal levels at the end of 2006. The probability of attachment was .077 percent and expected loss was .016 percent. The deal was rated A+ and the coupon was a spread of 135 basis points over the London Interbank Offered Rate (LIBOR).

The risk of attachment was such that Gordon Woo of RMS in a postissue analysis suggested that "the trigger threshold for Vita Capital might thus be attained before the end of 2006 if pessimistic lethality estimates are made for both a pandemic *and* a WMD terrorist attack." In other words, in his estimation two major devastations would have to take place in three years to attach the bond. This includes estimations of either a nuclear weapon attack (dirty bomb) or a chemical or biological weapons attack (say, anthrax) by terrorists in concentrated population centers. Terrorism was clearly not excluded from the cause of loss. No doubt the SARS outbreak influenced thinking at the time of issue; however, cooler heads such as Gordon Woo's suggest it was a very good deal. More important than the note details, however, is the fact that transferring mortality risk to the capital markets is no longer a concept, but it is now a reality. More deals transferring mortality risk can be expected in the future.

Other Significant Transactions

Gordon Woo's other contribution to the 2003 securitization scene was with the "Golden Goal" transaction. This covered the cancellation risk of the soccer World Cup that is due to be held in Germany in 2006. RMS did the risk analysis for this transaction, and again it included the risk of terrorism along with natural perils. Some $260 million of the note were issued. Full details of the transaction are not included herein because of a lack of all the relevant data. Once again two events would be required to cause a loss, the first causing postponement (à la Ryder Cup), the second during the postponed event.

Another imperfectly seen transaction is the "life" transaction of Barclays

Capital. It transfers about £400 million the "embedded value" of the life portfolio of Woolwich Life, a U.K. life insurer. No mortality risk was transferred. However, by shifting the embedded value of its portfolio to investors it achieves considerable acceleration of surplus.

Life Insurance and Life Annuities-backed Charity Securities (LILACS) also made an appearance during 2003. These deals present opportunities for investors to take advantage of two phenomena. First is the assertion that term life coverage and annuity life policies are not consistently priced; arbitrage opportunities exist. Second, certain individuals do not take full advantage of the life insurance opportunities made available to them. Investors compensate the insureds for taking out such policies and making themselves the beneficiaries, then arbitrage to the annuity market. Strictly not risk transfer vehicles so much as risk arbitrage devices, they will likely come to be part of the fabric of securitization in the future. Certainly they represent another data point that the life market is finally succumbing to securitization.

These three deals represent almost another $900 million of securitization beyond the details shown in Exhibit 33.3. Risk transfer via industry loss warranties (ILWs) also represents significant transfer via quasi derivative-like instruments. Several billions are traded this way and indirectly some of these find their way into the capital markets.

Finally, rumors or at least press releases during the year suggest that certain "risk swaps" are still being traded. In particular, Swiss Re swapped $100 million of hurricane and European windstorm coverage with Mitsui Sumitomo's typhoon exposure. Other swaps were less publicized.

Interestingly, one other innovation of note was Tokio Marine's put derivative, which allows protection against too *few* typhoons. Certain insureds suffer when there is not enough demand for their reconstruction services.

Securitization—or at least alternative risk transfer—thrives.

PRICING THEORY

On the occasion of each annual review we have tried to also advance the subject of a theoretical pricing model. The Lane Financial (LFC) model has tried to show that prices are a function of frequency and severity of loss. Inevitably, perhaps, we have become more humble about the centrality of the model. We know that explaining prices by simple expected value is inadequate. So is the linkage to standard deviation. The LFC model was intended as a better mousetrap. While empirical models are useful, their application is limited.[2]

Notwithstanding, Exhibit 33.12 shows the LFC model fitted to first quarter end 2004 secondary market prices. Close inspection of the graph shows that the deviations from fitted price are at their largest either when seasonality is present, in which case expected losses should be recalculated,

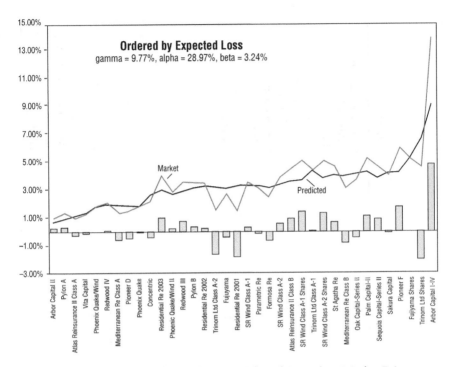

EXHIBIT 33.12 LFC Model, Fitted against Selected Secondary Market Prices, 3/31/2004
Source: Lane Financial LLC.

or when complicated structures are present. Also, as we have shown elsewhere, there is often a premium or discount for different zones of coverage. Pricing models given data and prices available must be used only with caveats. Predicted model prices are useful. They can show where inconsistent prices lie. However, price inconsistencies may not be inconsistent at all after allowance is made for features not included in the model.

OTHER TRENDS

It has been our practice in these reviews to focus also on other aspects of the current set of issues. These features are captured in the exhibits that follow. As always, the year-to-year comparisons are against a reference set of securities. The reference set is detailed in Exhibit 33.13. Comments on each of the features of this year's crop of deals follow.

EXHIBIT 33.13 Reference Set of Securities

Pre-3/98	4/98–3/99	4/99–3/00	4/00–3/01
Reliance I	Reliance IV	Juno	Alpha Wind 2000-A
Georgetown Re	XL Mid-Ocean	Domestic Re	Residential Re 2000
Residential Re I	Residential Re II	Residential Re III	NEHI
Swiss Re Cal Quake	Pacific Re	Concentric Re	Mediterranean Re
Parametric Re	Mosaic I	Mosaic II	Prime Hurricane
Trinity I	Trinity II	Gold Eagle	Prime EQEW
Reliance II	Gramercy	Namazu	Western Capital
		Atlas	Halyard Re
		Seismic	Gold Eagle 2000
		Kelvin	Sr Wind
		Halyard Re	

Note: Other deals, including contingent deals, not part of the summary analysis:

Winterthur	Reliance III Option	Circle Maihama	CEA
AIG	Allianz Option	CLOCS	West LB
Hannover	MODERNS		TokioMar/St Farm Swap
	SECTRS		Saab
			Rolls-Royce

4/01–3/02	4/02–3/03	4/03–3/04
Atlas Re II	Fujiyama	Arbor I Ltd.
Redwood Capital I	Pioneer (6 Classes	Arbor II Ltd.
Redwood Capital II	(and 4 Series)	Formosa Re Ltd.
Residential Re 2001	Residential Re 2002	Oak Capital Ltd.
Trinom	St Agatha Re	Palm Capital Ltd.
	Studio Re	Phoenix Quake Td.
		Phoenix Quake Wind Ltd.
		Phoenix Quake Wind II Ltd.
		Pioneer 2000 Ltd.
		(4 Classes with 5 Issues)
		Pylon Ltd.
		Redwood III Ltd.
		Redwood IV Ltd.
		Residential Re 2003
		Sakura Ltd.
		Sequoia Capital Ltd.
		Vita Capital Ltd.

Note: Other deals, including contingent deals, not part of the summary analysis:

K3	Golden Goal Finance
CLOCS	Barclays Life Assurance
(RBC, Michelin, MBIA)	LILACS (Life Insurance and
	Life Annuities-backed
	Charitable Securities)

Source: Lane Financial LLC.

Term

Exhibits 33.14 and 33.15 show two features that are now cemented in the market. No deals are now issued for 12-month terms! This is a significant departure from past practice. The securitization market took its original form from the traditional reinsurance market, which is entrenched in annual renewals. None of the current issuers think that is so important. Longer maturities save issuance costs and spread coverage costs. The second significant feature is the return of even longer maturities than the three years of last year.

Credit Rating

Securitizations are primarily issued with a BB rating (see Exhibit 33.16). That remains the case. However, this year saw the issue of single B deals, nonrated deals, and an A+ deal. It is clear that highly rated deals are often second event or contingent deals. Lower-rated deals are often associated with more structured transactions.

(Note that the graphic represents tranches in each category, not the dollar amount in each category.)

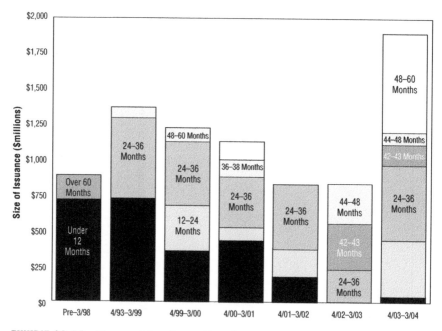

EXHIBIT 33.14   Term to Maturity and Total Amount of New Issues, 1998–2004
Source: Lane Financial LLC.

EXHIBIT 38.15 Term to Maturity

Maturity (in Months)	Amount in $Millions							
	Pre-3/98	4/98–3/99	4/99–3/00	4/00–3/01	4/01–3/02	4/02–3/03	4/03–3/04	Total
12	717.6	720.6	345.7	427	165	0	35.5	2,411.4
24	0	0	332.1	100	200	0	390	1,022.1
36	0	566.3	441.6	350	461.9	228	533.4	2,581.2
42	0	0	0	0	0	321.9	150	471.9
48	0	0	0	120	0	282.3	83.2	485.5
60	0	80	100	129	0	0	702.5	1,011.5
Over 60	168.5	0	0	0	0	0	0	168.5
Total	886.1	1,366.9	1,219.4	1,126	826.9	832.2	1,894.6	8,152.1
Average Deal Size:	127	195	111	113	138	33	70	
% Longer than 12 Months:	19%	47%	72%	62%	80%	100%	98%	
	Number of Deals							
12	5	5	3	4	2	0	2	21
24	0	0	2	1	1	0	4	8
36	0	1	5	3	3	3	11	26
42	0	0	0	0	0	13	1	14
48	0	0	0	1	0	9	4	14
60	0	1	1	1	0	0	5	8
Over 60	2	0	0	0	0	0	0	2
Total	7	7	11	10	6	25	27	93
Average Deal Size:								
% Longer than 12 Months:	29%	29%	73%	60%	67%	100%	93%	

Source: Lane Financial LLC.

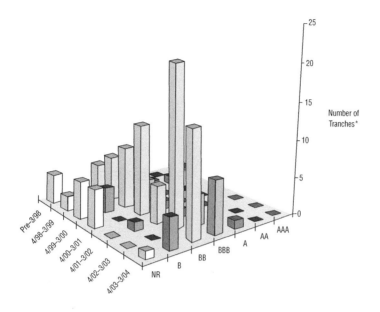

EXHIBIT 33.16   Ratings Changes over Time (by Number of Rated Tranches)
*Each issue of the Swiss Re serial transactions is considered to be a separate tranche for this graph.
Source: Lane Financial LLC.

Market Leaders

By recording whose names appear on the offering memoranda of issued deals it is possible to see who controls the market. Exhibit 33.17 shows this year's scorecard. Swiss Re is not only a believer; it looks like the *only* believer in 2003. It was cited as co-manager or sole manager on nearly all 2003 transactions. Goldman Sachs, BNP Paribas, Aon, and Marsh all appeared once, but it was Swiss Re Capital Markets that took all the Oscars. It is also notable that Swiss Re was probably the biggest sponsor of deals as well as the biggest placer of transactions.

A final question is whether the absence of investment bankers in the league tables finally indicates that they have ceded the ground to the insurers. Stay tuned.

Minor Trends

Exhibit 33.18 shows that most deals were issued as single tranches. None were "capital protected"; amazingly, also none were issued with equity

EXHIBIT 33.17 Transactions Scorecard

Co-Managers (As listed on PPM, there may be multiple co-managers for each issue)
Ranked by $ Amount of Issue for 4/03–3/04

				Amount of Issues as Co-Mgr				
	Pre-3/98	4/98–3/99	4/99–3/00	4/00–3/01	4/01–3/02	4/02–3/03	4/03–3/04	Total
Swiss Re	237	0	0	220	365	674.2	1,587.6	3,083.8
Goldman Sachs	729.1	1,176.9	1,052.4	819	300	300	160	4,537.4
BNP Paribas	0	0	0	0	0	0	160	160
CDC IXIS Cap Mkts	0	0	0	0	0	0	147	147
AON	0	80	317	67	194.9	33	100	791.9
Marsh	0	0	300	0	0	0	100	400
Lehman	477	500	450	740	515	125	0	2,807
Merrill Lynch	477	500	217	320	150	125	0	1,789
MSDW	0	0	0	0	161.9	0	0	161.9
AM Re	0	0	182.1	420	0	0	0	602.1
Blanche	0	54	45.7	90	0	0	0	189.7
Centre	83.6	56.6	0	0	0	0	0	140.2
Chase	83.6	56.6	0	0	0	0	0	140.2
DLJ	83.6	56.6	0	0	0	0	0	140.2
Zurich	83.6	56.6	0	0	0	0	0	140.2
CSFB	137	0	0	0	0	0	0	137
Lane Financial	20	10	0	0	0	0	0	30
Soc Gen	0	0	0	0	0	0	0	0
	2,411.5	2,547.3	2,564.2	2,676	1,686.8	1,257.2	2,254.6	15,397.6

(Continued)

EXHIBIT 33.17 *(Continued)*

	Pre-3/98	4/98-3/99	4/99-3/00	4/00-3/01	4/01-3/02	4/02-3/03	4/03-3/04
Goldman Sachs Share	30%	46%	41%	31%	18%	24%	7%
Lehman Bros. Share	20%	20%	18%	28%	31%	10%	0%
Reinsurers and Intermediaries	18%	10%	33%	30%	33%	56%	86%
Investment Bankers	82%	90%	67%	70%	67%	44%	14%

NUMBER OF CITATIONS AS CO-MGR

	Pre-3/98	4/98-3/99	4/99-3/00	4/00-3/01	4/01-3/02	4/02-3/03	4/03-3/04	Total
Swiss Re	2	0	0	2	2	23	25	54
Goldman Sachs	4	4	9	6	2	2	1	28
BNP Paribas	0	0	0	0	0	0	1	1
CDC IXIS Cap Mkts	0	1	0	0	0	0	1	1
AON	0	0	4	2	2	1	1	11
Marsh	0	0	2	0	0	0	1	3
Lehman	1	1	3	5	3	1	0	14
Merrill Lynch	1	1	2	2	1	1	0	8
MSDQ	0	0	0	0	1	0	0	1
AM Re	0	0	1	3	0	0	0	4

	15	13	'22	21	11	28	30	140
Blanche	0	1	1	1	0	0	0	3
Centre	1	1	0	0	0	0	0	2
Chase	1	1	0	0	0	0	0	2
DLJ	1	1	0	0	0	0	0	2
Zurich	1	1	0	0	0	0	0	2
CSFB	1	0	0	0	0	0	0	1
Lane Financial	2	1	0	0	0	0	0	3
Soc Gen	0	0	0	0	0	0	0	0
	15	13	'22	21	11	28	30	140
Goldman Sachs Share	27%	31%	41%	29%	18%	7%	3%	
Lehman Bros. Share	7%	8%	14%	24%	27%	4%	0%	
Reinsurers and Intermediaries	40%	38%	36%	38%	36%	86%	93%	
Investment Bankers	60%	62%	64%	62%	64%	14%	7%	

Source: Lane Financial LLC.

EXHIBIT 38.18 Other Trends

	Amount in $Millions							
Class by Structure	Pre-3/98	4/98–3/99	4/99–3/00	4/00–3/01	4/01–3/02	4/02–3/03	4/03–3/04	Total
Capital Protected	267.8	18	0	0	0	0	0	285.8
Single Tranche*	206	590	722.5	759.9	504	248	1,662.1	4,692.5
Multiple Tranches	388.2	758.9	465.5	335.4	307	559.2	232.5	3,046.7
"Equity" Pieces**	24	0	31.4	30.7	15.9	25	0	127
Total	886	1,366.9	1,219.4	1,126	826.9	832.2	1,894.6	8,152

*May be combined with a capital protected tranche.
**Capital in excess of 3% minimum requirement is considered to be a separate tranche.

Class by Underlying Risk	Pre-3/98	4/98–3/99	4/99–3/00	4/00–3/01	4/01–3/02	4/02–3/03	4/03–3/04	Total
Single	797.6	1200.3	667	390	482	245	1,245.7	5,027.6
Portfolio	0	0	45.7	616	194.9	158	648.9	1,663.5
Portfolio (with sublimits by line)		10	0	0	0	429.2	0	439.2
Portfolio (with sublimits by event)	0	156.6	506.7	120	150	0	0	933.3
Total	797.6	1,366.9	1,219.4	1,126	826.9	832.2	1,894.6	8,063.6
% of issues with a single risk	100%	88%	55%	35%	58%	29%	66%	

Class by Indemnity Index	Pre-3/98	4/98–3/99	4/99–3/00	4/00–3/01	4/01–3/02	4/02–3/03	4/03–3/04	Total
Indemnity	629.1	1,356.9	642.7	357	150	125	260	3,520.7
Index	257	10	576.7	769	709.9	707.2	1,634.6	4,664.4
Total	886.1	1,366.9	1,219.4	1,126	859.9	832.2	1,894.6	8,185.1
Fraction of Indemnity Deals	71%	99%	53%	32%	17%	15%	14%	

Other Deals, Including Contingent Deals	Pre-3/98	4/98–3/99	4/99–3/00	4/00–3/01	4/01–3/02	4/02–3/03	4/03–3/04	Total
Contingent: Equity (La Salle, Horace Mann, RLI)	450							
Contingent: Debt (Nationwide, Arkwright)	300		175 Maihama, REAC)	500? CLOCS (RBC, Michelin, MBIA)				
Contingent: Reinsurance (Reliance III, Allianz)		170		102 (TRINOM A2 & SHS)			582 Phoenix, Arbor II Pylon B	
	750	170	175	602			582	

(Continued)

EXHIBIT 33.18 *(Continued)*

				Number of Deals				
Class by Structure	Pre-3/98	4/98–3/99	4/99–3/00	4/00–3/01	4/01–3/02	4/02–3/03	4/03–3/04	Total
Capital Protected	4	1	0	0	0	0	0	5
Single Tranche*	5	3	7	7	3	3	26	54
Multiple Tranches	2	4	4	6	2	22	2	42
"Equity" Pieces**	1	0	4	7	3	1	0	16
Total	12	8	15	20	8	26	28	117

*May be combined with a capital protected tranche.
**Capital in excess of 3% minimum requirement is considered to be a separate tranche.

Class by Underlying Risk	Pre-3/98	4/98–3/99	4/99–3/00	4/00–3/01	4/01–3/02	4/02–3/03	4/03–3/04	Total
Single	4	4	6	2	3	3	19	41
Portfolio	0	0	1	6	2	2	8	19
Portfolio (with sublimits by line)	3	1	0	0	0	21	0	25
Portfolio (with sublimits by event)	0	2	4	1	1	0	0	8
Total	7	7	11	9	6	26	27	93
% of issues with a single risk	57%	57%	55%	22%	50%	12%	70%	

Class by Indemnity Index	Pre-3/98	4/98–3/99	4/99–3/00	4/00–3/01	4/01–3/02	4/02–3/03	4/03–3/04	Total
Indemnity	3	6	6	4	1	1	2	23
Index	4	1	5	6	5	24	25	70
Total	7	7	11	10	6	25	27	93
Fraction of Indemnity Deals	43%	86%	55%	40%	17%	4%	7%	

Other Deals, Including Contingent Deals	Pre-3/98	4/98–3/99	4/99–3/00	4/00–3/01	4/01–3/02	4/02–3/03	4/03–3/04	Total
Contingent: Equity (La Salle, Horace Mann, RLI)	3							
Contingent: Debt (Nationwide, Arkwright)	2		2		3			
Contingent: Reinsurance (Reliance III, Allianz)		2			1		3	
	5	2	2		4			

Source: Lane Financial LLC.

pieces. This may be because of the geographical location of the issuers, but it shows that accounting issues and issuer acceptance is less a barrier than it once was. Perhaps the old categorizations are also obsolete. The MTN programs started by Swiss Re may be replicated by others, in which case it could be a new standard of issue.

Exhibit 33.18 shows a swing back to single risk—66 percent of issuance compared to 29 percent last year. Again, credit must go to the MTN form and the cafeteria style available to investors. Just as the 12-month deal seems to have disappeared, so is the indemnity deal disappearing. Only 14 percent of the transactions this time were based on indemnity losses.

Finally, note that although there were no contingent equity or debt deals this year, several deals can be described as contingent reinsurance deals whose recovery feature depends on some preceding event or condition being satisfied. All the Phoenix deals depend on a prior event before they go on risk. Similarly, the senior tranche of Pylon must be preceded by a first event. Finally, as Gordon Woo has argued, it should be noted that both Golden Goal and Vita are implicitly second-event covers, given how remotely they are drawn. While we agree with the spirit of the idea that the markets are ripe for multiple-event covers, we feel that explicit contingencies are rich in possibilities without stretching the definition of remote triggers as being "contingent." We keep promising ourselves that we will write

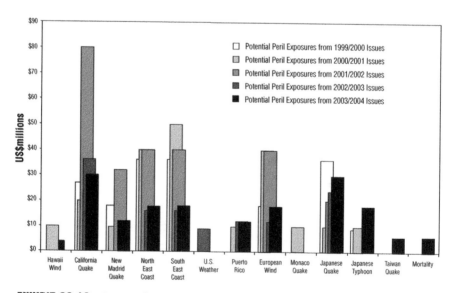

EXHIBIT 33.19   Potential Perils
Source: Lane Financial LLC.

up, in one framework, all the contingent possibilities seen or contemplated. Maybe this will be the year.

CONCLUDING REMARKS

The subtitle of this review is "Exploring Outside the Cat Box." Hopefully, that has been amply demonstrated—new zones and new exposures were the hallmark of this year's issues (see Exhibit 33.19). In one sense our continued review of events in this space confirms our long-held prejudice that more innovation and issuance is at hand. One can conceive of a day, perhaps, when all reinsurers will have a capital market window and several MTN programs available to investors. As the reinsurers accumulate their assumed risks they could vary the price quoted at the window to encourage or discourage investors. Once the concept is investor-accepted the problem will only be setting the right price, not establishing demand. Competition between both issuers and investors should also make for a tight, transparent market. Reinsurers and insurers in this worldview will become factories manufacturing risk for investors rather than warehouses of risk for somewhat more remote capital suppliers. As the old saw goes, insurers will be in the moving business rather than the storing business. Again, maybe this will be the year.

CHAPTER 34

Enterprise Risk Management: The Case of United Grain Growers

Scott E. Harrington, Greg Niehaus, and Kenneth J. Risko

For many corporate risk managers, *risk management* refers to the management of so-called pure risks, such as losses arising from property damage, liability suits, and worker injuries. These risks are typically managed individually through a combination of loss control (efforts to reduce the likelihood or magnitude of losses) and loss financing (either with internal funds or through the purchase of insurance). To many *financial* managers, however, risk management refers to the management of *price* risks, such as exchange rate risk, interest rate risk, commodity price risk, and credit risk. These risks are usually managed through derivatives contracts, such as options, forwards, futures, and swaps. Most corporations manage financial risks separately from pure risks, often within different depart-

Reprinted with permission from the *Journal of Applied Corporate Finance* 14, No. 4 (Winter 2002). The authors appreciate the information and time provided by managers at United Grain Growers (especially Mike McAndless and Peter Cox) and Willis Group Ltd. (Jim Davis, Michelle Bradley, and John Bugalla); the research assistance from Tae Ho; and the travel support from the Spencer Educational Foundation.

Messrs. Harrington and Niehaus are professors of insurance and finance at the University of South Carolina's Moore School of Business.

Mr. Risko is a senior vice president at Willis Risk Solutions.

ments, and the terminology and methods used in price risk management differ from those used in pure risk management.

In the latter part of the 1990s, however, many consultants and risk management professionals began to question this silo approach to risk management. They argued that a firm should identify and (when possible) measure *all* of its risk exposures—including operational and competitive risks—and manage them within a single *unified* framework. This idea came to be known as enterprise risk management (ERM). To facilitate ERM, some corporations established a new position—the chief risk officer.[1]

United Grain Growers (UGG), based in Winnipeg, Manitoba, was one of the first corporations to change its risk management practices to reflect ERM. UGG provides commercial services to farmers, and markets agricultural products worldwide. Although UGG hedged most of its currency and commodity price risk and purchased insurance against property and liability losses, its earnings continued to exhibit substantial volatility. After an extensive risk identification and measurement process, UGG's managers found that the firm's earnings volatility was largely attributable to volatility in the volume of grain that it shipped, which in turn was heavily affected by variation in weather. The firm considered using weather derivatives to hedge the risk, but instead entered into an insurance contract that provided payment to UGG if its grain volume was unexpectedly low in a given year. The innovative structure of this contract mitigates moral hazard by basing payoffs not on UGG's grain shipments but on industry grain volume. In addition, the contract bundles UGG's grain volume coverage with its traditional insurance coverages. In this fashion, UGG integrated its insurance coverage for pure risk with a previously unhedged operational risk.

In the next section, we discuss the potential advantages and disadvantages of ERM. We then go on to describe the ERM process at UGG and the initial outcome of the ERM process—UGG's innovative insurance transaction. We conclude with a discussion of the lessons to be learned from UGG's experience with ERM, and of the extent to which the approach used by UGG could prove useful in other contexts and in other firms.

ENTERPRISE RISK MANAGEMENT

Before discussing the potential advantages and disadvantages of ERM, it is useful to step back and review why risk reduction can increase value for well-diversified shareholders—investors for whom a loss in one investment is generally offset by a windfall in another. The well-known Modigliani and Miller proposition tells us that in a perfect capital market the method used to finance losses—whether it be internal funds, new equity capital, new debt capital, insurance indemnity payments, or payoffs from derivatives contracts—does not affect firm value. The explanation for how risk reduction can add value must be found in the various market imperfections faced by firms, principally transaction costs, taxes, and the costs of financial distress.

Modern risk management theory posits that risk reduction can add value to well-diversified shareholders in three ways: (1) by reducing the likelihood that the firm will have to raise costly external capital, which in turn can influence investment decisions; (2) by reducing expected tax payments because of different marginal tax rates at different levels of income or because certain institutions are taxed differently (such as insurers versus noninsurers); or (3) by reducing the likelihood of financial distress, which in turn can improve contractual terms with other parties such as employees, suppliers, debtholders, and customers.[2] These explanations for why risk reduction adds value do not depend on the source of risk. The theory holds regardless of whether the variation in cash flows or earnings arises from pure risks, price risks, or some other type of risk.

To illustrate, consider the first reason for risk reduction listed in the preceding paragraph: the desire to avoid raising costly external capital. Assume that a firm has an investment project that requires an initial investment of $50 million and that the project has a net present value of $5 million if financed with internal funds. Suppose, however, that the cost of raising external capital (transaction costs and underwriter underpricing costs) would exceed the net present value of the project. Without available internal funds, the firm might forgo the project.

Now step back in time and consider the firm's decision to hedge its currency risk or liability risk exposures. The managers know that an unexpected reduction in internal funds might cause the firm to forgo the new project, regardless of whether the reduction in funds arises from a judgment in a liability suit or a change in exchange rates that has caused lower than expected cash flows. Consequently, if an unexpected reduction in internal funds occurs, shareholders would experience a loss beyond the direct cash flow loss; they would also lose the net present value of the new project. For this reason, reducing the likelihood of large losses (by purchasing liability insurance and by hedging currency exposures) can increase shareholder wealth, although the cost of insuring or hedging the risk must be factored in.

THE SILO APPROACH CAN BE INEFFICIENT

While the previous discussion implies that risk reduction can be value en-hancing, insuring or hedging each risk exposure separately can be ineffi-cient. Under some circumstances, companies would be better off insuring (hedging) *bundles* of exposures.

Saving on Transaction Costs

Negotiating, writing, and purchasing insurance and derivatives contracts involve transaction costs for both the provider and the purchaser of the hedging vehicle. If there are fixed costs associated with this process, then using a single contract that covers multiple sources of risk can reduce transaction costs.

Bundling exposures for risk transfer purposes can also reduce *proportional* transaction costs, although the argument is slightly more complex. To illustrate with a simple example, suppose that a firm's cash flows are subject to two uncorrelated sources of variability—liability risk and ex-change rate risk. The distribution for liability losses is:

$$\text{Liability Loss} = \begin{array}{l} \$50 \text{ million with probability } 0.02 \\ \$25 \text{ million with probability } 0.04 \\ \$\ 0 \text{ million with probability } 0.94 \end{array}$$

For simplicity, assume that the losses from exchange rate risk have the same distribution:

$$\text{Exchange Rate Loss} = \begin{array}{l} \$50 \text{ million with probability } 0.02 \\ \$25 \text{ million with probability } 0.04 \\ \$\ 0 \text{ million with probability } 0.94 \end{array}$$

To capture the idea that corporate hedging programs are designed mainly to avoid large losses, assume that the managers do not want total retained losses to exceed some critical value, say $40 million (perhaps be-cause the firm would then violate a debt covenant or be forced to raise costly external capital).[3] The firm can insure or hedge the loss exposures to achieve its objective, but assume that the contracts are priced so that the firm must pay 120 percent of the contract's expected payout, implying a 20 percent loading or transaction cost. This transaction cost can make the cost of separately managing each exposure greater than the cost of manag-ing the bundled exposure.

If the firm hedges each exposure separately, it can achieve its objective (total retained losses less than $40 million) by purchasing a contract on each exposure that reimburses the firm for losses in excess of $20 million.[4] In insurance jargon, the firm would want to purchase $30 million of coverage excess of $20 million. In the language of options, the firm would want to purchase an option spread—that is, buy a call option with an exercise price of $20 million and sell a call option with an exercise price of $50 million. The expected payout on either contract equals

$$(\$30 \text{ million} \times 0.02) + (\$5 \text{ million} \times 0.04) = \$600,000 + \$200,000$$
$$= \$800,000$$

Therefore, the transaction costs on each policy would equal $160,000 (0.2 × $800,000).

Table 34.1a summarizes the results of purchasing separate contracts on each exposure. The first four columns list all the possible combinations of outcomes and the associated probabilities. The later columns indicate the coverage provided by the separate contracts. Recall that the firm was willing to retain losses of up to $40 million. If the coverage provided by the separate contracts results in a payout from the counterparty (insurer or option writer) and retained losses are less than $40 million, then the firm has purchased coverage that, after the fact, it did not really need. For example, if there is a $50 million liability loss and no exchange rate loss, the insurance company pays $30 million and the firm absorbs $20 million. But the firm was willing to absorb $40 million, so it paid for $20 million in redundant coverage—coverage that was not really required. The final column indicates the amount of redundant coverage. Since there are positive transaction costs associated with purchasing the coverage, the extra coverage is an unnecessary expense.

Now suppose that the firm could purchase a contract that would indemnify the firm based on *total* losses. To achieve its objective of absorbing losses of only up to $40 million, the firm could use one contract with an aggregate retention level of $40 million and an aggregate limit of $60 million. The outcomes with this contract are summarized in Table 34.1b. With such a contract, there is no redundant coverage. The expected payout on such a policy is $472,000, which makes transaction costs equal to $94,400 (0.2 × $472,000). The firm achieves its desired coverage, but at a lower cost ($94,400 vs. $320,000) when total losses are indemnified in aggregate versus indemnifying individual losses separately.

This example illustrates that an important benefit of viewing all the firm's exposures in the same framework and structuring contracts based on

TABLE 34.1a Outcomes from Hedging Two Exposures with Separate Contracts ($millions) (Retention for Each Exposure Is $20 Million and Coverage Is $30 Million)

Liability Loss	Exchange Rate Loss	Total Loss	Probability	Liability Coverage	Exchange Rate Coverage	Total Coverage	Total Retention	Redundant Coverage
0	0	0	0.8836	0	0	0	0	0
25	0	25	0.0376	5	0	5	20	5
50	0	50	0.0188	30	0	30	20	20
0	25	25	0.0376	0	5	5	20	5
25	25	50	0.0016	5	5	10	40	0
50	25	75	0.0008	30	5	35	40	0
0	50	50	0.0188	0	30	30	20	20
25	50	75	0.0008	5	30	35	40	0
50	50	100	0.0004	30	30	60	40	0
Expected Value				0.8	0.8	1.6	2.4	1.128

749

TABLE 34.1b Outcomes from Hedging Two Exposures with One Contract ($millions) (Aggregate Retention Is $40 Million and Aggregate Coverage Limit Is $60 Million)

Liability Loss	Exchange Rate Loss	Total Loss	Probability	Combined Coverage	Total Retention	Redundant Coverage
0	0	0	0.8836	0	0	0
25	0	25	0.0376	0	25	0
50	0	50	0.0188	10	40	0
0	25	25	0.0376	0	25	0
25	25	50	0.0016	10	40	0
50	25	75	0.0008	35	40	0
0	50	50	0.0188	10	40	0
25	50	75	0.0008	35	40	0
50	50	100	0.0004	60	40	0
Expected Value				0.472	3.528	0.0

aggregate exposures is that the firm purchases better coverage; that is, the firm is less likely to purchase costly redundant coverage.[5]

Moral Hazard

A completely bundled policy would have only an aggregate retention level and an aggregate limit; consequently, the source of a loss would not matter for the contract's payoff. The problem with such a policy, however, is that once a firm's aggregate retention level were reached, any additional loss (up to the aggregate limit) would be covered. Such a policy would therefore greatly minimize the insured's incentive to minimize additional losses once the retention level was reached. (An aggregate deductible would create the same problem.) Incorporating deductibles for each type of loss exposure would mitigate this moral hazard problem.

Costs Associated with a More Complex Contract

A disadvantage of bundling multiple exposures into one contract is that the parties need to have an understanding of all of the risk exposures *and* their correlations. For several reasons, the cost associated with performing this analysis can increase the transaction costs relative to those on separate contracts for each type of exposure. Since only a limited number of counterparties are likely to have the expertise to price a complicated bundled contract, the lack of competition could increase the cost of a bundled policy.

Also, institutions that possess the modeling expertise to price such a policy may not have expertise in other areas, such as loss control and claims processing. A bundled policy could therefore result in a lower quality of service. Finally, there is a large body of insurance contract law that has the effect of reducing the transaction costs associated with settling coverage disputes and claims for standard policies. Until a similar body of law is developed for bundled policies, transaction costs for these policies could be higher.

Understanding Risk Exposures

Perhaps the most valuable aspect of enterprise risk management is as a source of information about the firm's operating environment. Proponents of enterprise risk management suggest that the exercise of identifying and measuring all of a firm's risk exposures is useful in and of itself. It provides managers with a better understanding of their business and events that can prevent the firm from accomplishing its strategic objectives. Thus, another potential benefit of ERM is that managers will make better operating decisions as a result of having a better understanding of the firm's risk.

Consistent with this logic, several organizations concerned with corporate governance have recommended that companies engage in a comprehensive risk assessment process and manage their risks appropriately. For example, both the 1994 Dey Report issued by the Toronto Stock Exchange and the 1999 Turnbull Report issued by the London Stock Exchange recommended that boards of directors of listed corporations identify the corporation's principal risks and implement appropriate systems to manage those risks.[6]

ENTERPRISE RISK MANAGEMENT AT UGG

UGG, with 1999 revenues of $209 million (Canadian), was founded in 1906 as a farmer-owned cooperative, and became a publicly traded company on the Toronto and Winnipeg stock exchanges in 1993. Although UGG is a public company, it retains some of its farmer cooperative roots. The company has both members and shareholders. Members are generally farmers who do business with UGG. Although a member is not entitled to share in any profit or distribution by the company (unless the member is also a shareholder), members have control rights. Of the 15 people on UGG's board of directors, 12 must be elected by delegates representing members from various geographical regions.

UGG has four main business segments: Grain Handling Services, Crop Production Services, Livestock Services, and Business Communications. UGG's four business units help farmers plan, produce, and market their products. Exhibit 34.1 shows earnings before interest and taxes

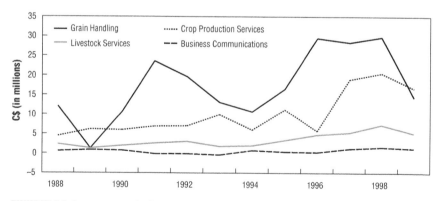

EXHIBIT 34.1 Earnings before Interest and Taxes (EBIT) By UGG Business Unit

(EBIT) for each of the business units over time. The two largest segments, Grain Handling Services and Crop Production Services, typically account for more than 80% of UGG's earnings in a given year. The chart also illustrates the substantial earnings volatility in the main business segments.

The role of UGG's Grain Handling Services unit is to identify sources of grain and oilseeds and deliver them to exporters and to domestic end users, such as food processors. In 1999, UGG was the third largest provider of grain handling services in western Canada, with about a 15 percent market share. Grain handling involves the operation of grain elevators to which farmers bring their production of grain and oilseeds. From the elevator, the product is shipped to a domestic consumer (a mill, for example) or to an export terminal. UGG historically owned hundreds of relatively small "country" elevators, but began replacing them in the 1990s with a smaller number of large, high-throughput, more efficient elevators.

The farming industry in Canada is heavily regulated by several government agencies. The Canadian Wheat Board (CWB) markets human-consumable grains on behalf of farmers. About 85 percent of the wheat and 45 percent of the barley produced in Canada is sold through the CWB. The CWB must ensure that the sales it has arranged are available to customers at the agreed-upon site and date. Thus, the CWB contracts with companies like UGG to collect, store, and deliver grains. About 60 percent of UGG's grain handling unit's business is on behalf of the CWB. The prices paid to farmers and the prices for storage and transportation of "board grains" are determined by the CWB. Thus, to some extent, regulation reduces volatility in the prices that UGG receives for its services, although it does pose risk associated with changes in regulation or the regulatory process.

Table 34.2 contains selected information from UGG's balance sheet, income, and cash flow statements. Note that UGG increased capital expenditures substantially in 1998 and then again in 1999. Most of these expenditures were for the large, high-throughput grain elevators mentioned earlier. Also, the percentage of the firm's total assets financed with debt increased in 1999 with the issuance of another $50 million in long-term debt.

ERM PROCESS AT UGG

Several factors led UGG to investigate enterprise risk management. The previously mentioned listing requirement of the Toronto Stock Exchange

TABLE 34.2 UGG Consolidated Financial Highlights[a]

	1994	1995	1996	1997	1998	1999
Operating						
Gross Profit and Revenue from Services	$156,030	$185,637	$198,749	$216,260	$224,953	$209,227
Earnings before Interest, Taxes, and Depreciation	25,538	30,573	40,198	54,788	60,577	42,423
Operating Income	12,612	15,151	24,090	38,452	43,335	21,636
Earnings before Income Taxes and Unusual Items	3,772	282	8,065	24,744	31,926	8,067
Net Earnings	153	–7,385	5,851	9,059	16,332	3,575
Cash Flow Provided by Operations	12,533	16,177	21,322	32,770	35,871	29,853
Capital Expenditures and Business Acquisitions	27,725	43,894	26,826	21,904	53,760	91,002
Financial						
Working Capital	$ 75,028	$ 44,573	$ 71,557	$101,790	$136,155	$119,249
Net Investment in Capital Assets	153,228	182,079	190,308	193,323	226,304	287,442
Total Assets	564,043	544,284	531,416	489,214	515,209	554,322
Shareholders' Equity	140,516	130,620	133,694	161,290	234,611	233,182
Ratios						
Total Debt to Net Assets	59.11%	57.72%	55.36%	36.01%	26.24%	36.76%
Return on Average Common Equity, before Unusual Items	0.06%	–2.20%	4.30%	8.51%	8.69%	1.17%
Per share						
Earnings (Loss), before Unusual Items (Net of Taxes)	$0.01	–$0.024	$0.45	$0.89	$0.91	$0.15
Cash Flow from Operations	1.30	1.47	1.94	2.66	2.08	1.72

[a]For the years ended July 31; amounts are in thousands of Canadian dollars except per share amounts.

was one factor. Other factors included increased requirements for disclosure of risk exposures, increased emphasis on risk management by credit rating agencies, and UGG's perception that equity analysts' recommendations were sensitive to earnings results that deviated from forecasts.

UGG started by forming a risk management committee, which consists of the CEO, chief financial officer (CFO), risk manager, treasurer, compliance manager (for commodity trading), and manager of corporate audit services. This committee, along with a number of UGG employees, then met with a representative from Willis Group Ltd., a major insurance broker, for a brainstorming session to identify and qualitatively rank the firm's major risks. This process identified 47 exposure areas, from which the top six were chosen for further investigation and quantification. The six risks were (1) environmental liability, (2) the effect of weather on grain volume, (3) counterparty risk (suppliers or customers not fulfilling contracts), (4) credit risk, (5) commodity price and basis risk, and (6) inventory risk (damage to products in inventory).

Willis Risk Solutions, a unit of the Willis Group Ltd., took on the task of gathering data and estimating the probability distribution of and correlations among losses from each of the six risk exposures. These probability distributions were then used to quantify the impact of each source of risk, both alone and in combination, on several measures of UGG's performance, including return on equity (ROE), economic value added (EVA), and earnings before interest and taxes (EBIT).

The analysis conducted by Willis Risk Solutions led to the conclusion that, of the six risks originally identified, UGG's main source of unmanaged risk was weather. Willis and UGG therefore focused their energies on understanding how weather affected UGG's performance. More specifically, they conducted an in-depth regression analysis of data from the period 1960–1992 on how crop yields in each province of western Canada were influenced by temperature and precipitation. Among the monthly temperature and precipitation variables, the average temperature in June and the average rainfall in July were the most significant. Of course, crop yields have increased over time, reflecting productivity gains. These three factors (June temperatures, July rainfall, and time trends) explain roughly 60 to 70 percent of the annual variation in assorted crop yields in the various provinces (see the appendix at the end of this chapter).

The next step in Willis's analysis was to estimate the relationship between crop yields and UGG's grain volume. It found that UGG's grain volume in any given year was highly correlated with overall crop yields in the previous year, due to the natural time lag between grain growing and harvesting as well as UGG's July 31 fiscal year-end. Using UGG's internal data

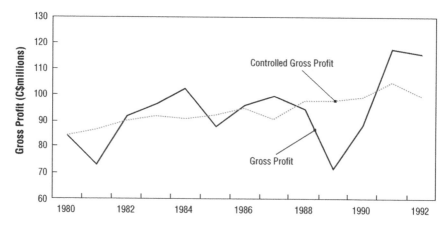

EXHIBIT 34.2   The Impact of Weather on UGG Earnings Volatility
Source: Willis Risk Solutions.

on gross profit per ton of grain shipments, the analysts could then link profits to grain volume.

To summarize, the analysis established a relationship between weather and UGG's gross profit by linking weather to crop yields, crop yields to grain volume, and grain volume to profit:

Weather → Crop Yields → UGG's Grain Volume → UGG's Profit

Using these estimated relationships, Willis illustrated UGG's results by graphing its actual gross profit over time and what gross profit would have been with the effects of weather removed. Willis's graph, which is reproduced in Exhibit 34.2, shows clearly the impact of weather on UGG's earnings volatility.

UGG'S DECISION ON MANAGING WEATHER RISK

UGG considered three options for managing its weather risk. One approach was to maintain the status quo and simply retain the exposure, thus subjecting earnings to large swings due to weather variation. Accepting this volatility had several disadvantages. First, UGG planned to continue making large investments in high-throughput grain elevators. The ability to finance these capital expenditures from internally generated funds would allow the firm to avoid the costs associated with raising external capital.

To the extent external capital would be needed, the rate that the firm would have to pay on borrowed funds would likely be higher if it retained the weather risk. Also, since greater earnings volatility reduces the optimal proportion of the firm financed with debt, retention would prevent UGG from using more debt financing and therefore prevent it from gaining additional interest tax shields.

Although much of UGG's current business could be characterized as a commodity business, UGG tries to distinguish itself from competitors by creating products with brand names and by providing ongoing services to customers. Stability in the firm's cash flows would increase the likelihood of being able to capitalize on past investments in brand-name products and customer service. In addition, the importance of supplier and customer relationships is likely to increase in the coming years as the marketplace for agricultural products adjusts to scientific advances. Analysts have predicted that over the next decade, food producers will demand specific genetically engineered crops, which in turn would require farmers to plant specific seeds. The coordination of these activities between farmers and food producers would require a sophisticated information, storage, and transportation network. Stability and experience would enhance UGG's attractiveness as a provider of these intermediary services to end users and producers.

The disadvantages of risk retention led UGG to consider hedging its exposure using weather derivatives. In 1999, the weather derivatives market was beginning to emerge. Several dealers, including Goldman Sachs, Merrill Lynch, Enron, and Duke Energy, were willing to take on weather-related risks. However, most of the existing weather derivatives deals involved utilities and were based almost exclusively on heating and cooling degree days, or deviations in average daily temperature above and below 65 degrees Fahrenheit, respectively. Since UGG's needs would require contracts designed specifically for UGG, the costs of hedging with derivatives would likely be high and the contracts would be illiquid. In addition, basis risk was a concern. The statistical relationships linking weather variables to UGG's profit were significant, but measurement error and unexplained variation still remained.[7]

After many months of analyzing how weather affected UGG's profit, the CFO and risk manager considered an alternative approach. They reasoned that weather was important because it affected the amount of grain produced and therefore the amount of grain that UGG shipped. Therefore, perhaps it would be better to design a contract that directly reimbursed UGG when its grain shipments were lower than expected.

The obvious problem with such a contract is the moral hazard problem arising from the fact that grain shipments are in part a function of

UGG's pricing and service. The solution to the moral hazard problem was to use industry-wide grain shipments as the variable that would trigger payments to UGG. Industry shipments were highly correlated with UGG's shipments, implying relatively low basis risk. In addition, relative to a contract based on weather, a contract based on grain shipments had the advantage of hedging against nonweather risks that might affect grain volume (such as regulatory policies and exchange rates). And because of its relatively low market share, UGG's shipments would have minimal effect on the value of industry-wide shipments, thus significantly reducing the moral hazard problem.

As in the case of weather derivatives, a contract based on industry grain volume would have to be designed and priced, which would be costly. One of the CFO's objectives was to manage the weather/grain volume exposure without substantially increasing the firm's risk management costs. UGG therefore considered integrating its grain volume coverage with its other traditional property and liability coverages to take advantage of the potential efficiencies from an aggregate deductible and an aggregate limit (discussed earlier). UGG asked Willis to design a risk transfer vehicle with the desired structure and to obtain proposals from several major insurers on a bundled policy.

THE CONTRACT

Grain Volume Coverage

UGG eventually entered into an integrated policy contract with Swiss Re. According to the terms of the contract, a grain volume loss occurs, and UGG receives a payment from Swiss Re, if industry grain volume in a given year is lower than the average industry grain volume over the previous five-year period. Thus, the contract is essentially a put option on grain volume.

To specify the grain volume loss to UGG, the difference between the industry grain volume in the current year and the five-year average industry grain volume is multiplied by 15 percent, which was UGG's approximate market share. (The contract adjusts for changes in UGG's market share over time.) To translate the volume number into a dollar figure, the volume differential is multiplied by UGG's gross margin per ton of grain shipments.

Integration of Coverages

The grain volume coverage was integrated with a number of UGG's other property and liability insurance coverages. The policy has an annual aggregate retention and limit and a term aggregate limit for the three-year policy period. Without disclosing the actual figures, the policy takes the following form: In the event UGG incurs either a property, liability, or grain volume loss, Swiss Re is obligated to compensate UGG for annual losses of up to $35 million after retention, regardless of whether the loss was a property loss, a liability loss, or a grain volume loss. The term aggregate limit provides for Swiss Re to pay losses of up to $80 million over the three-year period.

For reasons discussed earlier, the policy also specifies per-occurrence limits and retentions. Each of the separate property coverages (property in transit, extra expense, boiler and machinery) and each of the separate liability coverages (environmental impairment liability, charterer's liability) have a per-occurrence sublimit. The grain volume coverage (for which an occurrence is defined as the annual loss) has a per-occurrence (annual) limit and retention as well as a term limit. The combined property coverages also have an annual retention, as do the combined liability coverages. Within the property coverages and liability coverages, there are maintenance deductibles if the annual retentions are reached.

Exhibit 34.3 presents a conceptual view of how the insurance coverage was changed. Instead of separate retention levels and limits for each type of coverage, the new policy has retentions based on aggregate property losses and aggregate liability losses. The new policy also incorporates coverage for grain volume losses. In addition, there is an annual aggregate limit and a term aggregate limit for all the coverages.

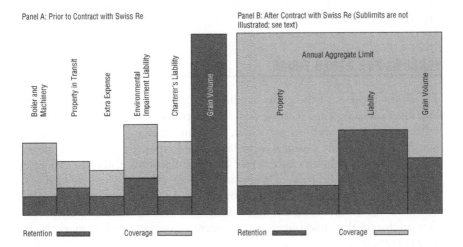

EXHIBIT 34.3　Coverage under the Old and New Programs

BENEFITS TO UGG

UGG managers continue to work on an enterprise approach to risk management. They view the insurance contract entered into with Swiss Re as the initial step in an ongoing process. They continue to evaluate other exposures with an eye toward integrating coverage for these exposures into their insurance contracts.

Despite its ongoing nature, UGG's initial foray into the enterprise risk management area has yielded several benefits. The insurance contract provided coverage for a risk that the firm previously did not (and could not) hedge. By hedging this risk, UGG is more likely to have the internal funds necessary to carry out its capital expenditure plan and to establish itself as a leading intermediary between farmers and end users. Also, it is in a better position to borrow additional capital and to increase its debt-to-equity ratio, and thereby benefit from additional tax shields.

These benefits were achieved without increasing the firm's cost of risk, as measured by the sum of insurance premiums and expected retained losses. The integration of the firm's insurance coverages with the grain volume coverage allowed the firm to rearrange its coverages and keep its cost of risk roughly constant.

Finally, discussions with UGG's managers clearly indicate that they found the risk identification and measurement *process* highly valuable in itself, quite apart from the decision to hedge the firm's grain volume coverage and integrate that coverage with the firm's other coverages. The managers feel that the process has given them a better understanding of the firm's risks and that communication about such risk exposures has improved within the firm.

LESSONS FOR OTHER FIRMS

The characteristics of the grain handling business that make UGG's multi-line insurance coverage a value-adding strategy are likely to be present in other industries as well. In particular, the grain handling business is a low-margin, high-volume business with large fixed costs. In such cases, unexpected drops in volume can severely hamper the firm's ability to generate revenue to cover total costs. This problem is exacerbated when the firm has large capital expenditures, because unexpected drops in volume can prevent a firm from financing the investment with internal funds, forcing it either to forgo the investments or to access external capital markets at inopportune times.

In designing a program like UGG's, however, a key consideration is whether there are industry volume indexes that are sufficiently highly correlated with the firm's own volume but that cannot be substantially influenced by the firm that is seeking the coverage (in other words, the firm has a relatively low market share). Whether industry indexes with these properties exist for other high-volume, low-margin businesses is an empirical question, but our own intuition suggests that industries like retailing and stock brokerage are potential candidates.

Discussions with UGG's managers indicate that an enterprise risk management approach requires cooperation from many individuals across the firm. To achieve this cooperation, top managers must buy into the idea and demonstrate their support. Enterprise risk management can also take time and patience to implement. UGG spent more than three years from the initial brainstorming session to the signing of the insurance contract. To be sure, subsequent enterprise risk management endeavors undertaken by Willis have taken considerably less time (on the order of 6 to 12 months), but the need for top-level buy-in and firmwide cooperation remains unchanged.

Technical expertise is also important. Someone must estimate the probability distributions of various exposures (and how they are related) and also quantify how the exposures affect the firm's results. Although the complex statistical and actuarial analyses can be provided by consultants and brokers, internal managers must be knowledgeable enough to provide input and to interpret the output. Nonetheless, the approach underlying UGG's grain volume coverage is likely to be applicable to other firms.

APPENDIX TO CHAPTER 34

Examples of the regression analysis conducted by Willis are presented in Table 34.3. The table provides the results of estimating a regression equation where the dependent variable is the crop yield (bushels per acre) for either wheat or oats, and the explanatory variables are a time trend (to capture productivity increases over time), the average June temperature, and the average July precipitation. The analysis was conducted using data from 1960 to 1992 for the provinces of Alberta, Manitoba, and Saskatchewan. These results are similar to the actual results obtained using stepwise regression where temperature and precipitation readings from each month were considered. In general, among all the monthly temperature and precipitation variables considered, June average temperature and July average precipitation were the most statistically significant. A similar analysis was also conducted for other grains and seeds.

To illustrate the results, consider the first row of Table 34.3. The

TABLE 34.8 Results of Selected Regression Analysis of Crop Yields (Bushels per Acre) and Weather Conditions in Three Canadian Provinces Using Data from 1960 to 1992

Dependent Variable			Independent Variables				
Province	Crop		Time Intercept	Avg. June Trend	Avg. July Temp.	Precip.	R²
Alberta	Wheat	Coef:	59.88	0.33	−0.76	2.70	0.68
		t-stat:	4.49	6.19	−3.19	2.63	
Manitoba	Wheat	Coef:	79.34	0.42	−0.98	1.00	0.65
		t-stat:	5.70	5.94	−4.38	0.95	
Saskatchewan	Wheat	Coef:	55.60	0.19	−0.69	4.80	0.61
		t-stat:	4.02	2.65	−3.01	4.44	
Alberta	Oats	Coef:	43.53	0.69	−0.17	4.70	0.72
		t-stat:	1.89	7.59	−0.41	2.71	
Manitoba	Oats	Coef:	121.02	0.65	−1.50	5.30	0.64
		t-stat:	4.89	5.16	−3.77	2.96	
Saskatchewan	Oats	Coef:	74.07	0.24	−0.76	9.30	0.56
		t-stat:	2.93	1.91	−1.82	4.70	

Temperature is measured in degrees Fahrenheit and precipitation in inches. The time trend variable equals (year − 1960); thus, for the year 2000 the time trend equals 40.

positive and statistically significant coefficient on the time trend variable indicates that Alberta wheat yields have increased over time. The negative and statistically significant coefficient on the average June temperature variable indicates that wheat yields in Alberta are negatively related to the average June temperature. Finally, the positive coefficient on the average July precipitation variable indicates that crop yields increase, on average, with rainfall in July. The R2 indicates that about 68 percent of the annual variation in Alberta wheat yields is explained by these three variables. Although there are some exceptions, the remainder of Table 34.3 indicates that the regression results just described hold for other crops and provinces.

Representations and Warranties Insurance and Other Insurance Products Designed to Facilitate Corporate Transactions

Theodore A. Boundas
and Teri Lee Ferro

A s the volume of corporate transactions surged in the 1990s, major insurance companies realized that risks inherent in corporate transactions called for innovative insurance solutions. Corporate transactions, including mergers and acquisitions (M&A), depend on the services of a variety of professionals, such as investment bankers, accountants, and lawyers, to assess the actual and potential exposures inherent in a transaction, orchestrate financing options for the transaction, and document the understanding of the parties and the terms of their agreement. Within the past few years, insurers actively entered the market for insurance products designed to facilitate business transactions. This chapter examines some of the insurance products designed to facilitate business transactions. Generally, these products are referred to as M&A insurance because they developed in response to the tremendous volume of merger and acquisition activity in the late 1990s. These products, however, are not limited to use in M&A transactions; some

Mr. Boundas and Ms. Ferro are principals with Boundas, Skarzynski, Walsh & Black, LLC, a law firm internationally recognized as a leader in insurance law that provides sophisticated worldwide legal and consulting services with a special emphasis on the risk management, insurance, and financial services industries.

of them also are used to facilitate other types of transactions, such as financing arrangements. While insurance nomenclature is far from standard, most insurance professionals consider a variety of products, such as representations and warranties (R&W) insurance, tax opinion or tax indemnity insurance, aborted bid insurance, and loss mitigation products (LMPs), as examples of M&A insurance products. Since these products all share the common purpose of facilitating business transactions, including but not always limited to mergers and acquisitions, we refer to them generally as transactional insurance products (TIPs).

In this chapter, we examine the most prevalent forms of TIPs and explore the market for TIPs. In our exploration of the TIPs market, we consider whether TIPs are traditional insurance products or alternative risk transfer (ART) insurance products; discuss how TIPs represent the continued convergence of the insurance, banking, and finance industries; and examine the future prospects for TIPs.

PRODUCTS DESIGNED TO FACILITATE MERGERS, ACQUISITIONS, AND OTHER TRANSACTIONS

Essentially, TIPs transfer an unknown or unwanted exposure from the parties in a transaction or from a company's balance sheet to a third party insurer for a price. It appears that TIPs were originally used by private equity partnerships and private businesses that wanted to eliminate or minimize postclosing problems, disputes, and liabilities. However, the market for TIPs has expanded to reach all types of businesses entities, including public corporations. The reality facing any public corporation is that bad news can severely impact the market valuation of its shares and ultimately its balance sheet. In fact, the failure to meet earnings projections or Wall Street's "whisper number" by even a nominal amount can have severe consequences for public corporations and their shareholders. A contingent tax liability or an actual or potential securities or environmental problem, for example, could cast a cloud over a company's stock price or impede its ability to obtain financing or capital. Likewise, such issues could drive down a purchase price or derail a merger or an acquisition. A variety of TIPs, particularly R&W insurance, tax opinion or indemnity insurance, aborted bid cost policies, and LMPs, allow businesses to diminish the impact of an actual or potential exposure associated with a specific event or sequence of events by removing the liability from a company's balance sheet or guaranteeing the payment of an unrealized but actual or potential future risk.

Even after a transaction closes, TIPs can be useful where a party later recognizes a problem and decides to implement an insurance solution to manage an exposure that could otherwise present difficulties. Usually, TIPs are tailored to defined risks and issues in the transaction and often require the insurer to conduct its own due diligence and risk assessment in consultation with its own lawyers, economists, and other experts. TIPs can be purchased by the buyers or sellers in a transaction and are usually based on negotiated issues, legal opinions, or representations and warranties involved in the transaction. The insured may not be the party paying the premium and the responsibility for financing the premium, much like the allocation of all other responsibilities in the transaction itself is often a negotiated item. Additionally, tax benefits may be gained by placing exposures into TIPs instead of holding reserves for them on a company's balance sheet or holding funds in escrow after the closing of a transaction. Aside from potential tax benefits, the premiums for TIPs may be a cost-effective alternative to the usual mechanisms for dealing with the potential risks associated with representations and warranties in transactions, such as holding money in escrow or otherwise reflecting the risk in the purchase price.

The key to finding the right solutions for business risks is to help clients identify and evaluate complex business risks and create the most appropriate insurance or financial solutions that generate the most value for the insured while utilizing accurate pricing methodologies for the insurer. The placement of TIPs into corporate transactions is not as linear a process as that of traditional insurance products that are placed by insurers directly or through brokers and agents. The attorneys, bankers, accountants, and other professionals integral to the deal-making process and the parties to the transaction itself may not be aware of or open to the use of TIPs to facilitate the deal.[1] Some early industry observers commenting on TIPs noted concerns expressed by bankers and consultants that insurers could not be "responsive in the heat of the deal"[2] or that TIPs might be used to substitute for conducting sufficient due diligence.[3]

Insurers and their advisers who are experienced in the use, placement, drafting, and pricing of TIPs, however, typically have a ready source of professionals, such as consultants, lawyers, and economists, prepared to quickly assess and underwrite deals. As such, these concerns have diminished as the marketplace for TIPs has become defined and supported by professionals experienced in the underwriting and pricing of such insurance products. In order to craft a product that addresses specified risks, these professionals independently evaluate the specified risk in the transaction and often review and augment the due diligence otherwise conducted in connection with the transaction. Particularly in transactions involving intellectual property rights, environmental, and securities exposures, insurers will utilize the services of expert consultants with substantial experience in both evaluating these specialized risks and designing insurance products for these specialized risks. Experienced insurers and their advisers, working in tandem with other professionals integral to the deal, can add value by assisting with the process of articulating and addressing the risks inherent in the transaction.

The following sections discuss some of the most popular TIPs available in the market today. While these TIPs are often marketed as distinct products, they all are used to transfer identified risk to facilitate a transaction and may, in certain situations, be interchangeable solutions for a problem.

Representations and Warranties Insurance

R&W insurance insures specified representations and warranties, and corresponding indemnity obligations, in corporate transactions. It is "sleep" insurance for parties to a transaction who want to eliminate potential risk from future disputes arising out of representations or warranties in a transaction. Basically, sellers will represent and warrant a variety of things about the business, assets, or liabilities involved in a transaction to augment the due diligence and other information exchanged in connection with the transaction. Representations and warranties will vary depending on the type of transaction (e.g., a stock or asset sale) and the type of entities involved in the transaction. The representations may involve a variety of issues including but not limited to ownership in the business or its intellectual property, size of inventories, cash flows, tax issues, known litigation, and products liability or environmental concerns. Parties extensively negotiate the scope, breadth, and materiality of representations and warranties because these declarations often concern the assets, liabilities, and financial condition of the business and influence the purchase price. Additionally, broader representations and warranties benefit the buyer and allocate more risk and responsibilities to the seller. Therefore, the seller typically attempts to narrow the representations and warranties so future events not specifically addressed in the agreement cannot constitute a breach of a representation or warranty.

In connection with the representations and warranties, transactional agreements usually impose an indemnification obligation upon the seller to provide the buyer with recourse against the seller for liabilities or losses that occur after the transaction closes. The indemnification obligation may also require that a portion of the sale proceeds be set off or held back or otherwise placed into escrow to secure the seller's indemnification obligations in the event a representation or warranty is later found to be untrue. The seller usually negotiates limits on any indemnification agreement so that it is enforceable only for a set period of time and only up to an agreed-upon amount.

Although R&W insurance can cover all representations and warranties in a corporate transaction, it is not uncommon for such policies to cover only very specific or narrowly defined risks, such as specified intellectual property rights, environmental issues, existing claims or litigation and contingent tax liabilities. Any potential uncertainty that could impact the value of a transaction or require the seller to make certain representations and warranties about the state or condition of the potential risk or liability can be addressed in an R&W insurance policy. Of course, the price of the policy should reflect the nature and magnitude of the risk, and some risks may be too expensive or risky for the insured and/or the insurer. We suspect that R&W insurance, and all TIPs in general, are most effective and better priced when tailored to address narrowly defined risks.

R&W insurance products can cover the buyer and/or the seller as insureds. R&W insurance policies covering sellers offer third-party coverage to secure the seller's indemnity obligations. In exchange for an insurance premium, a seller could avoid posting a portion of the sale proceeds in escrow and shift all or a portion of its indemnification obligation to a third-party insurer. A buyer could utilize R&W insurance where it does not want to accept the risk, cost, and expense of pursuing the seller if a breach of a representation or warranty occurs and where the buyer may be concerned about timing issues associated with a future pursuit of the seller in the event of such a breach. If the buyer does not have adequate resources to pursue the seller or the seller is not financially viable, indemnity obligations may not help the buyer recover its losses in a timely fashion. A buyer's R&W insurance policy would operate as first-party insurance, much like a fidelity bond, in that the insured is both the policyholder and the claimant. Such a policy allows the buyer to recover the loss at issue from the insurer if it is unable to obtain recovery from other available sources such as the seller. R&W insurance, particularly for a buyer, can limit uncertainties in the deal that necessitated the insured representations and warranties in the first place.

R&W insurance products are particularly useful in transactions involving companies in the high-technology industry because their values are usually very dependent upon intellectual property rights that can be difficult to assess or may be subject to ownership disputes. We expect that R&W insurance will continue to play an important role in transactions involving intellectual property rights and that the value of intellectual property rights will continue to be an important component of the total value of many companies.[4] Two notable examples of this from our experience in assisting R&W insurers involved the multibillion-dollar acquisitions of an

Internet professional services firm and a telecommunications technology firm. In both transactions, the buyers insisted upon seller warranties concerning the ownership of certain intellectual property, particularly business methods patents, crucial to the economic viability of the involved businesses. The underwriting centered on an assessment of the actual warranties given and the potential scope and magnitude of the types of claims that could implicate the indemnity obligations associated with the representations and warranties and, ultimately, the R&W insurance policy.

Of course, representations and warranties are used in a variety of transactions, and often they are used to allocate risks and responsibilities between the parties. For example, in a transaction involving the sale of a theme park, the buyer did not want to assume the liability for the retention obligation in the seller's existing liability policy. Based on an analysis of the potential exposure from our firm and other consultants, the insurer decided to underwrite the buyer's exposure for the retention on the liability policy. Therefore, for a set premium, both the buyer and the seller were relieved of this obligation to pay the retention on the liability policy and that responsibility was no longer an issue that needed to be allocated between the parties. The matter of which party was obligated to pay the premium, however, remained an issue open for negotiation.

In one particularly novel transaction, a lender sought an insurance solution to secure a loan obligation to finance the multibillion-dollar acquisition of a business dependent upon gambling revenues. As in the case of technology companies that have a substantial portion of their value tied to intellectual property, a substantial portion of the value of the company depended on its ability to continue to operate a certain type of gambling establishment in a jurisdiction with some noted opposition to the gambling industry. Essentially, the transaction rested in part upon certain representations about the ability of the business to continue its gambling operations in the relevant jurisdiction. After investigation, we determined that the uncertainty the parties were trying to transfer to an insurance solution was legislative in nature and examined the likelihood of adverse legislative or governmental action that could impair or diminish the ability of the company to obtain sufficient revenue to service the debt that would be created by the acquisition. Contrary to the expectations of the parties, the analysis indicated that the potential risk was within a level the lender was willing to assume as part of the pricing structure for the loan obligation.

Many potential purchasers of R&W insurance question the utility of such coverage if most sellers and buyers already have a variety of insurance coverages in place, most notably directors and officers liability insurance and usually some other form of professional liability insurance. R&W insurance policies specifically cover representations and warranties and the parties making such representations and warranties. Therefore, the R&W insurance policy would be considered more specific, and therefore primary, if other coverage arguably was available under a more general coverage like a directors and officers policy. A typical directors and officers policy, however, may not cover a breach of a representation or warranty in a corporate transaction.

Consider the situation where sellers breach representations and warranties and the buyer pursues a cause of action against the sellers. While many sellers may be directors, most sellers will be shareholders. The usual directors and officers policies will not cover directors acting in their capacities as shareholders. Therefore, the directors and officers policy should not extend coverage to shareholders, and to the extent the directors made the representations or warranties at issue, there could be an issue as to whether they did so in their capacities as directors or as shareholders. Even if some other type of professional liability coverage were available, professional liability policies generally cover claims arising out of the insured's rendering of professional services to third parties in the regular course of conducting its business. As such, the sellers' professional liability policy would not cover claims against the sellers arising out of the sale of their business.

These same considerations apply to R&W insurance purchased by the buyer. No buyer's professional liability policy would provide first-party insurance to cover loss associated with the buyer's purchase of a business. Even if the buyer sued the seller and then sought to collect under the sellers' directors and officers liability or professional liability policies, as explained earlier, the sellers' policies probably would not cover the exposure arising from the breach of representations and warranties by the sellers in connection with the sale of its business. Therefore, R&W insurance creates more certainty for sellers and buyers because it specifically addresses this type of exposure whereas other coverages not otherwise designed for this purpose probably will not provide any coverage (or questionable coverage, if any) for these exposures.

Tax Opinion or Tax Indemnity Insurance

Tax contingencies are often the subject of representations and warranties and could be addressed in an R&W insurance policy. However, many companies separately offer tax opinion or tax indemnity insurance to insure against the adverse consequences that a particular tax treatment or position might be incorrect. These policies insure the risk of a successful Internal Revenue Service (IRS) challenge of the intended tax consequences of a transaction as, for example, where a spin-off of a subsidiary is intended to be a tax-free event. Tax issues, similar to securities, antitrust, environmental, and intellectual property issues, can present a significant impediment in a transaction and may not be covered by other traditional insurance products. Even if the particular tax treatment has been approved in a formal legal opinion, a buyer may not be willing to sustain the financial impact resulting from incorrect tax treatment. If the questioned tax treatment might cause the buyer to lose interest in the deal, reduce the purchase price, or require the seller to place a portion of the sale proceeds in escrow, the buyer and/or the seller may find that transferring the uncertainty associated with the questioned tax treatment to a third-party insurer is worth the premium associated with such a policy. Tax opinion and tax indemnity insurance policies can insure the buyer and/or the seller, depending on how the parties address the tax issues in the transaction documents and who will bear the responsibility for any future adverse tax consequences.

Aborted Bid Insurance—Coverage for the Costs of the Uncompleted Transaction

Aborted bid insurance covers the external third-party fees and costs incurred in connection with a transaction that fails for reasons beyond the control of the insured company or a party. Merger attempts can be very costly and often involve the fees of a variety of professional advisers, including lawyers, accountants, investment bankers, stockbrokers, management consultants, lobbyists, proxy solicitors, and public relations consultants. Typically, the policy defines the specific trigger for the coverage, such as loss of financing, failure to obtain regulatory approval, a failure to obtain shareholder approval, or the effective withdrawal of the other party to the transaction (not the insured). Such coverage generally does not apply to so-called breakup fees. Another similar product provides reimbursement for the third-party costs incurred in the defense of a hostile takeover bid and/or proxy contest. The existence of a policy to cover the costs of defending a hostile bid could be an effective negotiating tool for a company that is concerned that it could be a takeover target.

Loss Mitigation Products— Coverage for Existing Claims

LMPs are smoothing mechanisms similar in concept to the smoothing function of finite risk insurance products[5] except that finite risk finances exposure over time whereas LMPs effectuate the transfer of risk above certain levels of retained, insured, or financed risk. LMPs limit or cap the uninsured, underinsured, or contingent exposure of a known claim by transferring the specified risk to a third-party insurer for a fixed price.

LMPs transfer actual or contingent risk exposures associated with known claims. They are an effective tool for limiting a company's exposure to liability arising out of a significant claim, such as a securities class action lawsuit, antitrust litigation, or a long-tail environmental claim, because these types of exposures could fall outside of the parameters of a business entity's insurance program or the magnitude of the potential exposure may exceed available insurance program limits. To the extent an unresolved claim can dampen the financing and acquisition abilities and strategies of a business entity or impact its valuation, an LMP can limit the exposure presented by an unresolved claim to the self-insured portion of the risk (plus any insurance premiums for the LMP).

In the context of an acquisition, an LMP can allow the seller to avoid posting sale proceeds in escrow or retaining any liability or indemnity obligation to the buyer for a known claim. Even beyond the financial certainty the seller and buyer can obtain by using an LMP to limit the exposure arising out of a known claim, LMPs allow the parties to the transaction to define and limit the magnitude of the exposure associated with the known claim and reduce further transaction costs associated with that claim. Probably the most publicized LMP involved Oxford Health Plans. Oxford, an HMO, was a defendant in class action litigation involving patient billing practices. The program took the form of an LMP that would pay 90 percent of any adverse judgment over $175 million up to a $200 million cap in exchange for a premium in the amount of $24 million.[6]

DEVELOPMENT OF THE MARKET FOR TIPS

While an active market for TIPs is relatively new, insurance products that facilitate business transactions have been in existence for many years. In the early 1980s, for example, underwriters at Lloyd's of London offered tax insurance policies for risks associated with the legal uncertainty surrounding the tax treatment of certain equipment leasing transactions.[7] Although there is little statistical data tracking the volume and growth of TIPs in the insurance industry, an active market for such products developed over the past few years in connection with the increased volume of corporate transactions in the late 1990s.[8] For example, R&W insurance has been offered in the worldwide insurance market for many years. However, the market for this product in the United States is still in its incipient stage of development, and the vast majority of R&W policies underwritten have been placed within the last two years.[9] Likewise, the market for LMPs was nonexistent before 2000, and industry observers predict that premiums for these products should exceed $500 million in 2001 (at the time this essay was originally written).[10] Even though the increased activity in the TIPs market appears to coincide with the high volume of corporate transactions in the late 1990s, TIPs were utilized in a relatively small portion of the numerous corporate transactions conducted during that period.

Another factor limiting the development of the TIPs market was the reluctance of many insurers to underwrite very significant TIPs after the disastrous experience of insurers in the property and casualty markets in the 1980s. Over the past few years, insurers have become more open to underwriting these products because the TIPs market is more developed and insurance professionals have more experience assessing transactional exposures as well as drafting and pricing the appropriate policies to address such exposures. Of course, the ability of any insurer to underwrite an insurance product depends on the state of the insurance market and the availability of reinsurance. If the insurance market hardens, insurers have less access to the capital that supports their underwriting efforts. Additionally, the ability of insurers to market TIPs will depend on the level of corporate transactions sustainable by market conditions. During the first half of 2001, the volume of worldwide merger and acquisition activity decreased nearly 54 percent during the first half of 2001 from levels reported the prior year.[11] Although a decrease in the volume of corporate transactions may limit the opportunities for insurance companies to place TIPs, the economic slowdown could well increase the demand and utility for such products. Weak economic conditions generally increase the risk associated with transactions and could provide the impetus for parties and their advisers to seek insurance solutions like TIPs.

Although the market for TIPs is becoming more established with each passing year, we suspect that the use of TIPs has not become more prevalent because many insurance practitioners and deal makers are not familiar with these products. Indeed, within the insurance industry, there exists some confusion surrounding the classification of TIPs. Many insurers and insurance commentators categorize the various forms of TIPs as alternative risk transfer (ART) insurance products. Putting aside the issue of what properly should be considered under the rubric of ART, the insurance industry offers a variety of products and programs under the broad classification of ART, and there exists a divergence throughout the industry on the types of products classified as ART. The acronym ART is not used uniformly and may encompass almost any insurance product not defined as a traditional insurance product regardless of whether the product actually transfers risk or operates as a smoothing mechanism for financing retained risk and reducing the impact of losses on corporate results.[12] In their varied forms, many insurance products classified as ART represent the evolution of traditional insurance into a wide range of products that allow insurers greater and more direct participation in the goals and results of their clients. Many of these nontraditional insurance products, regardless of whether they are true ART products, finance rather than transfer risk and represent the convergence of the insurance, banking, and finance industries.

Of course, this begs the question of whether the TIPs described in this chapter are ART insurance products. They are not true ART insurance products because they do not contain a mechanism for profit or loss sharing between the insurer and the insured, an important hallmark of an ART insurance product. Although one could characterize TIPs as traditional insurance contracts, they remain distinguishable from traditional insurance products. Quite simply, traditional insurance products are the commonly available insurance products that are well established in the industry by insurers, insureds, the public, and the legal system. The use, acceptance, and understanding of traditional insurance products, such as commercial general liability, employment liability, or directors and officers liability products, are built upon years of underwriting, claims, and coverage experience. To the extent TIPs are sometimes treated as ART products, the TIPs discussed in this article have fallen into the ART rubric because they do not otherwise fall into the rubric of traditional insurance products commonplace in the market. Therefore, they are not considered traditional because they are relatively new products covering nontraditional risks for a new market. Stripped of their novelty in this regard, these products otherwise function like traditional insurance contracts, and their form of contract is often derivative of standard insurance contracts used for directors and officers liability insurance products. Even though they are basically traditional insurance products, TIPs are distinguishable from traditional insurance products because they not only transfer risk like a traditional insurance product but transfer risk for the explicit purpose of facilitating a business transaction. Viewed in this light, these products, much like many true ART insurance products, also represent the convergence of the insurance, banking, and finance industries.

Even outside the insurance industry, deal makers have been slow to warm to the prospects offered by TIPs products. Throughout this chapter, we have explained how TIPs facilitate business transactions. Used to complement other banking and financing services, TIPs represent one of many crossroads in the financial services sector where the insurance, banking, and finance industries converge. This convergence of separate industries within the financial services sector has both limited and frustrated the development of a market for TIPs. Although the insurance, banking, and finance industries deal with similar concepts and goals, they developed along different paths and remain somewhat insular, in large part because of differences in terminology[13] and access to capital. As such, while the forms of a variety of insurance, banking, and finance products appear very different, substantively they may be very similar, and practitioners within these respective industries may not be aware of services and products in other industries that are identical or complementary to products and services in their own industries. Without common experience and terminology, deal makers and insurers continue to face a learning curve as they become accustomed to the integration of insurance solutions into business transactions.

Of course, the trend toward continued convergence among the insurance, banking, and financing industries is inescapable. Just consider the expansion of commercial banks into consumer insurance products and the expansion of investment banks into the business of transferring bundled insurance risks into the capital markets by issuing catastrophe bonds. In response to the competitive threat presented by the convergence of the insurance, banking, and finance industries, insurers became interested in leveraging their capital resources and knowledge to enter into markets traditionally serviced by the banking and finance industries and developed products to facilitate business transactions and operations. Insurers realized offering products that transfer or finance risk, as a strategic business tool or as part of a risk management program, could help them remain competitive with the banking and finance segments of the financial services sector.[14]

The competition from banking and financial institutions is only one of the catalysts propelling insurers to expand into the types of business transactions traditionally serviced by commercial and investment banks. But whatever the impetus, insurers and their advisers are becoming more adept at assessing opportunities to utilize the capital of insurers to facilitate business opportunities for a price. The access to capital and risk evaluation services provided by insurers who underwrite TIPs usually complement the professional services provided by investment bankers and other professionals involved in corporate transactions. Insurers often use brokers, lawyers, economists, and other consultants to conduct independent due diligence assessing the risk exposure it may underwrite in connection with a transaction and to structure appropriate TIPs to address the specific nuances of transactions. It is not uncommon for insurers and their advisers to help recast a transaction because they may approach the risk or transaction from a different perspective or present options not otherwise contemplated by the parties. Therefore, TIPs are not a replacement for the professional services offered by investment bankers and other professionals. In this regard, the convergence of insurance, banking, and finance has increased competition as well as cooperation among insurers, bankers, and financiers,[15] and this convergence should continue to foster opportunities for insurers to market TIPs as a mechanism for facilitating business transactions.

Capital Structure Irrelevance

The 1958 paper by Franco Modigliani and Merton Miller (M&M), "The Cost of Capital, Corporation Finance, and the Theory of Investment," is almost universally regarded as having created the modern theory of corporate finance. As Ross (1988) says, "If the view of the progress of science that interprets it as one of changing paradigms has merit, then surely the work of Miller and Modigliani provides a laboratory example of a violently shifted paradigm" (p. 127).

Prior to M&M, the conventional belief was that because debt was cheaper than equity, a firm's value should rise with increased leverage, at least up to some threshold level of debt beyond which a company would have difficulty servicing.[1] Consequently, the average cost of capital for a firm was thought to *fall* for increases in debt, as long as the firm avoided truly excessive leverage. M&M showed that this conventional wisdom was wrong, at least under certain assumptions.

The four assumptions under which the three M&M "irrelevance propositions" hold are:[2]

1. *Perfect capital markets.* Capital markets are perfect in the sense of no taxes, no transaction costs, no institutional frictions (e.g., short selling restrictions on securities), no costs of bankruptcy or financial distress, and no unexploited riskless arbitrage opportunities.
2. *Symmetric information.* All investors and managers have the same information about the quality of a firm's investments *and* have identical (as well as correct) perceptions concerning the impact of new information on the prices of all financial instruments, including securities.
3. *Equal access.* Firms and individuals can issue the same securities in the capital markets on exactly the same terms.[3]
4. *Given investment strategies.* Investment decisions by firms are taken as a given.

When these assumptions hold, M&M demonstrated that a firm's value is driven solely by its investment decisions and that the purely financial decisions made by the firm are irrelevant to the value of the firm. Such decisions will, of course, generally affect the *relative* welfare of the firm's different security holders, but they will not affect the *total* wealth of all investors combined.

Many question the need to study the M&M irrelevance propositions, arguing that the assumptions underlying the propositions are so unrealistic as to render the M&M world irrelevant in the real world. For some, perhaps that is true. But for those uninitiated in the modern theory of corporation finance, the M&M world provides a very useful starting point. The M&M propositions essentially give us a "laboratory control" of corporate financing decisions, or a base case against which alternatives that *do* involve deviations from the M&M world can be compared. As Miller aptly put it, "[S]howing what *doesn't matter* [in corporate finance] can also show, by implication, *what does*" (Miller 1988).

Nevertheless, this discussion is relegated here to an appendix. The chapters in the main body of our text—especially in Part One—assume that readers are thoroughly familiar with the M&M assumptions and what they imply. If you are, then feel free to skip this appendix. But if not, this short summary of one of the fundamental works of academic finance theory should provide an adequate introduction.

PROPOSITION I: CAPITAL STRUCTURE

The most important implication of the M&M assumptions is that the value of a firm and its cost of capital depend entirely on the *real assets* that the firm owns, and the firm's financial capital structure cannot ever impact the market value of those real assets. We saw in Chapter 1 when we looked at the economic balance sheet of the firm that the market value of a firm's assets is always equal to the aggregate value of its financial capital, and that will continue to be true. What we essentially want to explore now is why the value of a package of real assets *does not depend on the firm that owns them.*

M&M referred to capital structure irrelevance as their Proposition I, which in their original paper stated that "the market value of any firm is independent of its capital structure and is given by capitalizing its expected return at the rate P_k appropriate to its [risk] class" (M&M 1958, p. 268). So, the value of an unleveraged firm should be the same as the value of a leveraged firm holding the same assets.

To prove Proposition I, M&M argued that investors need not invest in leveraged firms to take whatever advantage leverage itself might have. Instead, investors could invest in unleveraged firms and borrow on their own account to manufacture "homemade leverage." If the assets held by the leveraged and unleveraged firm are identical, then both strategies will yield the same payoff as long as the M&M assumptions hold. To preclude the existence of riskless arbitrage opportunities, the costs of the strategies thus must be the same, and, hence, the values of the leveraged and unleveraged firms must be equal.[4]

M&M also stated their Proposition I in terms of the firm's cost of raising capital by issuing debt and equity securities: "The average cost of capital to any firm is completely independent of its capital structure" (M&M 1958, p. 268).

M&M showed that the conventional wisdom that the average cost of capital for a firm would fall for increases in debt was wrong, at least under their four assumptions. Instead, the firm's average cost of capital depends entirely on the risk of the *real assets* owned by the firm and the expected return on those assets. The risk of those real assets, moreover, does not depend on the firm that owns them—at least not in an M&M world.

When M&M were writing, the modern theory of finance was not yet well developed. Terms like *systematic* and *idiosyncratic* were not to be found in the tools of the trade that M&M had to work with.[5] Today, we can be much more general in stating Proposition I and say that the firm's average cost of capital depends *only* on the systematic risks facing the firm. The reason? In an M&M world of perfect markets, symmetric information, and equal access, investors can eliminate all firm-specific or idiosyncratic risks through portfolio diversification decisions. So, the firm's average cost of capital is the capitalization rate for the firm's assets, or the expected return on the assets the firm owns.

PROPOSITION II: WEIGHTED AVERAGE COST OF CAPITAL

M&M Proposition I told us that the value of the firm did not depend on its leverage. In Proposition II, M&M showed that the expected return on a share of stock increases as a firm's leverage ratio increases, and this increased expected return is exactly offset by *increasing risk* that causes shareholders to demand a higher expected return on their equity capital.

M&M argued that "[a] number of writers have stated close equivalents to our Proposition I although by appealing to intuition rather than by attempting a proof. . . . Proposition II, however, so far as we have been able to discover is new" (M&M 1958, p. 271). Proposition II holds that "the expected yield of a share of stock is equal to the appropriate capitalization rate for a pure equity stream in that [risk] class, plus a premium related to financial risk equal to the debt-to-equity ratio times the spread between [the capitalization rate for the pure equity stream] and [the interest rate on the firm's debt]." Formally, Proposition II can be written as

$$E(R_j^S) = E(R^A) + [E(R^A) - R_j^D]\frac{D_j(t)}{S_j(t)} \tag{A.1}$$

where R_j^D and R_j^S represent the return on firm j's debt and equity (respectively) from time t.[6]

Equation (A.1) is often rewritten to express the firm's weighted average cost of capital (WACC):

$$E(R_j^{WACC}) = \frac{S_j(t)}{S_j(t) + D_j(t)} E(R_j^S) + \frac{D_j(t)}{S_j(t) + D_j(t)} R_j^D = E(R^A) \tag{A.2}$$

An inspection of equation (A.2) immediately confirms what we saw in Proposition I—that the firm's WACC is equal to the expected return on the assets held by the firm (appropriately adjusted for systematic risk) and does not depend on the relative proportions of debt and equity issued by the firm.

Note in particular in (A.2) that the WACC of firm j carries the subscript j, whereas the expected return on the assets owned by firm j does not. This is an immediate implication of Proposition I—that the expected return on the assets owned by the firm does not depend on the particular firm that owns them.

We have assumed for simplicity that the firm's debt has a constant interest rate and is riskless. Exhibit A.1 may provide some insight into the intuition underlying M&M Proposition II when we allow for the possibility that debt holders may not receive a full or even partial repayment. The flat heavy black line is the expected return on the firm's assets, which does not depend on the firm's capital structure—Proposition I. This is also the firm's WACC. If the firm has no debt, the expected return on the firm's equity—in that case also the firm's WACC—is equal to the expected return on the assets held by the firm.

Assume that the debt issued by the firm becomes risky at leverage ratio $D^*/(S + D)$ in Exhibit A.1. For levels of debt below that point, bondholders have a constant expected return equal to the stated interest rate on the debt. But once leverage rises to the point that debt holders are exposed to

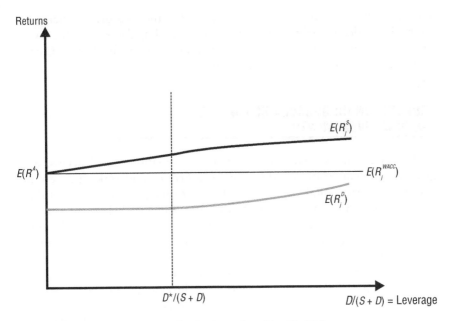

EXHIBIT A.1   The Invariance of WACC to Firm-Specific Risk

the risk of default, bondholders will demand a higher expected return. This increase in expected returns on debt, moreover, occurs at an increasing rate. As the firm builds up more and more leverage, bondholders bear more and more relative risk of the firm's assets.

Now look at the expected return on equity in Exhibit A.1. For low levels of leverage at which the firm's debt is default risk-free, the expected return on equity increases proportionately with the firm's leverage, just as Proposition II tells us. At leverage ratio $D^*/(S + D)$, the increase in expected returns demanded by stockholders begins to level off. Because debt holders now bear some of the asset risk, stockholders no longer require the same compensation for increased leverage as they did when debt was default risk-free and equity was bearing *all* the asset risk.

Importantly, notice how leverage affects the two classes of securities in the context of Proposition II, which tells us that the WACC of the firm is invariant to leverage. As long as debt is default risk-free, all of the increased risk of leverage is borne by equity holders. But the WACC does not change because the increased risk to equity is directly proportional to the change in the values of the firm's outstanding securities. When debt becomes risky, the premium demanded by bondholders is then just offset by a lower premium demanded by stockholders. In other words, the increased return demanded by debt is offset by a corresponding decrease in the leverage risk premium demanded by equity, again leaving the firm's WACC constant and equal to the expected return on the firm's assets.

PROPOSITION III: SOURCES OF FINANCE FOR NEW INVESTMENTS

With perfect capital markets, symmetric information, equal access, and given investment strategies, the value to a firm of undertaking a new investment in real capital, a new growth opportunity, or a new project does not depend on how the investment or project is financed. This is known as M&M Proposition III: "The cut-off point for investment . . . will be completely unaffected by the type of security used to finance the investment" (M&M 1958, p. 288).

Our model follows closely the original work of M&M (1958), modified primarily to adopt the notation used throughout this book. Specifically, consider a capital investment project that generates a single cash flow at time $t + 1$ in the amount $X(t + 1)$. This cash flow is realized only if the firm makes a one-time investment of $I(t)$ at time t. The return on this investment is defined as

$$\rho(t) = \frac{E[X(t + 1)] - I(t)}{I(t)}$$

We assume only a single cash distribution and a single investment cost purely to reap the gains from working with a two-period model. In fact, this is still a completely general representation. If future expenditures are required to maintain the project, for example, $I(t)$ is then just the present value of those expenditures expressed in time t dollars. Similarly, any cash distributions beyond time $t + 1$ would just be reflected in $X(t + 1)$ on a discounted expected present value basis. So, we get to work here with such a simple model with absolutely no loss of generality.

M&M Proposition III says that the hurdle rate for all capital investments is the expected return on the assets of the firm, or the firm's WACC. Specifically, a firm should undertake a capital investment project if

$$\rho(t) \geq E(R^A)$$

This criterion is not affected by the means used by the firm to finance the investment in an M&M world.

Suppose for simplicity that the firm has no growth opportunities and has only ssets in place. The value of the firm prior to undertaking the new investment project is then:

$$V(t) = \frac{E[X(t+1)]}{1 + E(R^A)} \qquad (A.3)$$

where $X(t + 1)$ denotes the net cash flows on the firm's existing assets in place before the new project. Again we are assuming a two-period model, so that any future net cash flows are subsumed into $X(t + 1)$ on a discounted present value basis. So, the value of the firm at time t is equal to the expected net cash flow on the firm's assets in place at time $t + 1$ discounted at the expected return on those assets.

Project Financed with a New Debt Issue

Suppose first that the firm considers the new project financed exclusively with a new debt issue. Prior to undertaking the project, the market value of the firm's common stock is

$$S(t) = V(t) - D(t) \qquad (A.4)$$

If the firm borrows $I(t)$ to finance a new project with a return $\rho(t)$, the value of the firm next period will be

$$V(t+1) = \frac{E[X(t+1)] + I(t)[1+\rho(t)]}{1 + E(R^A)} V(t) + \frac{I(t)[1+\rho(t)]}{1 + E(R^A)} \qquad (A.5)$$

If the new project is accepted, the time $t + 1$ value of the firm's stock will be

$$S(t+1) = V(t+1) - [D(t) + I(t)] = V(t) + \frac{I(t)[1+\rho(t)]}{1 + E(R^A)} - [D(t) + I(t)] \quad (A.6)$$

Using equation (A.4), equation (A.6) can be re-written as

$$S(t+1) = S(t) + \frac{I(t)[1+\rho(t)]}{1 + E(R^A)} - I(t) \qquad (A.7)$$

From equation (A.7), we can see that the project will raise the value of the firm's stock only if

$$\rho(t) > E(R^A)$$

and will reduce the value of the firm's equity otherwise. Because the debt issued to finance the project is issued at a fair market price, the value of the firm will rise if the value of the stock rises and conversely fall if the value of the stock falls.

Project Financed with Retained Earnings

Now suppose the firm's assets in place have generated surplus cash in an amount exactly equal to $I(t)$ as of time t. The firm can either pay a dividend to stockholders or use the cash to finance the new project.

If the firm distributes the cash to stockholders at time t, we can write the time t shareholder wealth as

$$W^S(t) = S(t) + I(t) = \frac{E[X(t+1)]}{1 + E(R^A)} - D(t) + I(t) \tag{A.8}$$

If instead the firm retains the cash $I(t)$ and uses that cash to finance the new project, the firm's shareholder wealth at time $t + 1$ is then

$$\begin{aligned} W^S(t+1) = S(t+1) &= \frac{E[X(t+j)] + I(t)[1+\rho(t)]}{1 + E(R^A)} - D(t) \\ &= S(t) + \frac{I(t)[1+\rho(t)]}{1 + E(R^A)} \end{aligned} \tag{A.9}$$

As in the debt financing case, shareholder wealth increases when the firm accepts the new project only if

$$\rho(t) > E(R^A)$$

Project Financed with a New Equity Issue

Finally, suppose the firm raises funds $I(t)$ to fund the new project by issuing new stock. Suppose further that prior to the project, the firm had N shares of common stock outstanding with a price per share of $s(t) = S(t)/N$. At that price per share, the firm needs to issue M new shares to fund the investment:

$$M = \frac{I(t)}{s(t)} \tag{A.10}$$

If the firm accepts the project, the total value of the firm's equity at time $t + 1$ (including the newly issued stock) is now

$$
\begin{aligned}
S(t+1) &= \frac{E[Q(t+j)] + I(t)[1+\rho(t)]}{1+E(R^A)} - D(t) = S(t) + \frac{I(t)[1+\rho(t)]}{1+E(R^A)} \\
&= Ns(t) + \frac{I(t)[1+\rho(t)]}{1+E(R^A)}
\end{aligned}
\tag{A.11}
$$

and the new price per share is

$$s(t+1) = \frac{S(t+1)}{N+M} = \frac{1}{N+M}\left\{ Ns(t) + \frac{I(t)[1+\rho(t)]}{1+E(R^A)} \right\} \tag{A.12}$$

Using equation (A.10), we can simplify equation (A.12) to

$$s(t+1) = s(t) + \frac{1}{N+M}\left\{ \frac{[\rho(t)-E(R^A)]}{1+E(R^A)} \right\} I(t) \tag{A.13}$$

from which we can see once again that the project only makes sense if

$$\rho(t) > E(R^A)$$

Risk-Based Capital Regulations on Financial Institutions

The M&M assumption of perfect capital markets can be violated by the existence of costly and/or distortionary taxes, subsidies, and regulations. Among those regulations that may affect the capital structure of a firm are the capital requirements imposed on certain types of firms by their regulators. In this appendix, we summarize very broadly the capital requirements that affect the major types of financial intermediaries today—specifically, banks, broker/dealers, and (re)insurance companies.

BANK CAPITAL AND THE BASEL ACCORD

The Committee on Bank Supervision of the Bank for International Settlements (BIS) promulgated in 1988 the Basel Capital Accord (hereinafter "Accord" or "Basel I") primarily to strengthen bank safety and soundness and level the international playing field. Together with its five substantive amendments, the Accord specifies minimum capital requirements for internationally active banks in the G-10 industrialized countries. Some other countries have also adopted the Basel requirements, and, although it is aimed exclusively at *internationally active* banks, some national banking regulators have chosen to apply it to *all* banks in their jurisdiction.

The Accord essentially requires that banks hold enough capital at all times to weather losses related to certain types of risk that they might assume. We discuss the Accord in brief in terms of what risks it covers, how banks can satisfy their capital requirements for those risks, and what changes in the Basel framework lie on the horizon. Readers desiring a more detailed account of the Basel Accord should see Matten (2000) or Crouhy, Galai, and Mark (2001), or should visit the BIS web site at www.bis.org for a listing of the Bank's own extensive library of resources and reports.

Scope of Basel I

In its original form, banks must hold enough capital to cover the risks of certain on- and off-balance-sheet assets and liabilities. Importantly, a bank's compliance with its capital requirements is *aggregate*, so that the bank either *is* or *is not* compliant at any given time. But compliance itself is determined by adding up the so-called risk weights assigned to assets and liabilities with different risk characteristics.

On-Balance-Sheet Credit Risks   The main body of Basel I applies to the credit risk banks incur from their assets. The capital a bank must hold to cover its credit risk for most balance sheet assets is determined by multiplying the book value of the asset times a pre-defined risk weight, where risk weights may be 0, 10, 20, 50, or 100 percent of the asset's value. Table B.1 gives an example of the assignment of risk weights by asset type.

On-balance-sheet assets and liabilities can sometimes be netted for the purpose of calculating capital requirements, provided the netting is backed by a legal opinion concluding that netting is very likely to be legally enforceable. In addition, the maturity of the liability (e.g., term deposit) must be no less than the maturity of the asset (e.g., loan) against which it is netted, and the positions to be offset must have the same currency denomination. Finally, the bank must manage the net position on a consolidated basis.

Off-Balance-Sheet Credit Risks   The credit risks of off-balance-sheet assets are also covered by Basel I. Such assets usually fall into one of two categories: contingent claims or derivatives. Contingent claims are usually assigned a risk weight based on their asset-equivalent position. To arrive at

TABLE B.1   Credit Risk Weights for Major Balance Sheet Assets under Basel I

Asset Type	Risk Weight
Cash	0%
Sovereign Debt Issued by OECD Countries	0
Claims on Government-Sponsored Enterprises	10
Claims on Banks Located in OECD Countries	20
Claims on OECD Securities Firms with Banklike Capital Requirements	20
Claims on Non-OECD Banks with Less than a Year to Maturity	20
Residential Mortgages	50
All Private Nonbank Lending	100
All Claims on Non-OECD Banks with More Than a Year to Maturity	100
All Other Assets	100

an asset equivalency, the BIS specifies "conversion factors" that amount to assumptions about how much of the contingent facility is presumed to be fully drawn. A conversion requirement of 100 percent for a letter of credit (LOC), for example, means that the bank must treat the LOC as if it were an existing loan. An undrawn standby credit facility made to a firm to support its trading operations, by contrast, has a 20 percent conversion requirement, which means that a $1 million contingent facility would be assessed the capital charge for the underlying loan but only on a $200,000 principal amount.

Table B.2 summarizes the conversion weights used to transform some of the most popular contingent claims into asset equivalents.

Derivatives are assigned credit risk capital requirements based on current exposure of the transaction plus an add-on for potential exposure (reflecting maturity and type). If the transaction is out-of-the-money there is no credit exposure. But if it is in-the-money, the BIS requires a conversion of the position to an asset equivalent by adding the current market value (i.e., current replacement cost in the event of a default today) and an add-on. The add-on reflects the potential exposure of the deal, or the possibility that the asset may become a bigger asset in default at some point over its remaining life. The add-on amount is based on the notional size of the transaction and the add-on factors listed in Table B.3.

After the asset-equivalent amount has been calculated as current exposure plus the add-on, the normal asset risk factor is used to compute the capital required on the deal. A six-month interest rate swap with a notional principal of $200 million and a current exposure of $100,000, for example, has a zero add-on and an asset-equivalent exposure of $100,000.

TABLE B.2 Conversion Weights for Contingent Claims under Basel I

Asset Type	Conversion
Guarantees	100%
Standby Facilities and Letters of Credit	100
Repurchase Agreements	100
Forward Agreements	100
Performance Bonds	50
Transaction-Specific Contingencies	50
Note Issuance Facilities	50
Documentary Credits	20
Standby Facilities for Trading with Maturities over One Year	20
Standby Facilities for Trading with Maturities Less Than One Year That May Be Canceled Prior to Drawdown	0

TABLE B.3 Potential Exposure Add-On Factors for the Credit Risk of Derivatives

	≤ 1 Year	> 1 Year and ≤ 5 Years	> 5 Years
Interest Rate	0%	0.5%	1.5%
Exchange Rate and Gold	1	5	7.5
Equity	6	8	10
Precious Metals (Not Gold)	7	7	8
Other Commodities	10	12	15

An otherwise identical two-year swap is asset-equivalent to $1.1 million (i.e., $100,000 current exposure plus 0.5% × $200,000,000). If the swap is with a non-OECD bank, the risk weight of 100 percent is applied to the asset-equivalent amount to derive the total capital charge.

Some limited netting is allowed for derivatives following a 1995 amendment to the Accord.

Market Risk Apart from the aforementioned capital requirements for credit risk, the "market risk amendments" to the Accord of 1996 also require banks to hold additional capital against the risk of market price fluctuations in the values of certain assets, such as equities or derivatives. Banks can choose among several different methods to determine these risk weights.

Of particular significance in the market risk amendments was the decision by the BIS to let banks opt to use their own internal models to calculate their capital charges for market risk. The BIS still specifies the basic methodology, but the acknowledgment by the BIS that internal models could be used for capital requirement calculation was a major step forward in modernizing the Accord.

Compliance with Basel I

Bank capital is classified into three categories or tiers by the BIS for the purpose of assessing capital adequacy. Tier I capital includes mainly fully paid-up and issued equity, noncumulative perpetual preferred stock, disclosed reserves, and minority equity interests in subsidiaries that are consolidated upon the bank holding company's balance sheet.[1] Tier II capital includes undisclosed and revaluation reserves, general loan-loss reserves, hybrid securities, and subordinated debt. Finally, Tier III capital includes debt with original maturities of at least two years that contains lock-in provisions allowing the bank to suspend interest and/or principal payments if the total capital of the bank falls below its required minimum.

A bank's total *regulatory capital* must equal at least 8 percent of the sum of its risk-weighted assets at all times (i.e., the sum of 8 percent of the values of the bank's assets), where risk weights are determined in the manner described in the prior section. At least 50 percent of the ratio of the bank's total regulatory capital to the sum of its risk-weighted assets (i.e., the *total capital ratio*) must be in the form of Tier I capital. In addition, subordinated debt cannot exceed more than 50 percent of the Tier I capital amount. Tier III capital can be used *only* to meet the market risk requirements, and may not exceed 250 percent of the Tier I capital that is allocated to market risk.

Basel II[2]

International banking regulators announced in 1999 a plan to revise the Accord, often referred to as Basel II. The revision contains three "pillars," the first of which is risk-based capital requirements. The updated Accord is a recognition of several major shortcomings with the original Accord. Among other things, Basel II contemplates tightening the link between the credit risk of bank assets and the capital that regulators require internationally active banks to hold against those assets. In particular, the current "standard model" for capital charges does little to distinguish between differences in credit quality. Capital held against corporate loans, for example, barely depends on the creditworthiness of the borrower; the distinction between Organization for Economic Cooperation and Development (OECD) and non-OECD, for example, is widely regarded as excessively coarse.

Acknowledging the limitations of the Accord, the BIS considered three alternative capital adequacy calculation schemes in its concept release. The first ties capital requirements when possible to ratings published by external credit assessment institutions or bodies like export insurance agencies. Transactions with relatively good credits will generally require less capital than before, and conversely for high-risk borrowers. Loans to corporations, for example, have a lower capital charge if the borrower is rated AAA to AA– and a higher charge if the borrower is rated below B–.

The second method links capital charges to banks' *internal* credit ratings. A capital scheme based on banks' internal ratings would rely on information that banks themselves collect about borrower credit risk. Banks have always been acknowledged to have comparative advantage in the acquisition and analysis of credit information about their own customers. Because external ratings tend to lag more than lead firms' actual financial conditions, an internal ratings approach thus may be preferable for promoting bank safety and soundness. Relying on internal ratings for capital charge calculations, moreover, would *not* penalize banks for dealing with firms that have chosen to remain unrated by external credit assessment institutions.

Internal ratings do not, however, allow banks to take into consideration portfolio effects arising from multiple credit exposures. A third alternative thus was explored by the BIS that would allow banks to use internal portfolio-based credit evaluation models for capital measurement in the same spirit as the 1996 market risk amendments. Although only a handful of sophisticated banks would find this alternative palatable in the short run, those banks could benefit greatly from an internal model-driven approach.

Basel II also goes well beyond simply making marginal changes to the capital that banks must hold against credit risk. Indeed, Basel II is intended to create a "whole capital charge" that reflects *all* the major risks facing banks, including the interest rate risk of the banking book and operational risk as well as the usual credit and market risk. Operational risk, in particular, has been contentiously debated—that is, little agreement exists on how the BIS should require firms to allocate capital to operational risks. Some argue for a "loss distributions" approach based on actual operational loss data, whereas others argue for more of a "basic indicators" approach or an "internal rating" approach. As of this writing, the final implementation date for all aspects of Basel II still remains an open question.

The second and third pillars of Basel II—apart from the first pillar of revised risk-based capital requirements—are supervisory review and market discipline, respectively. The supervisory review pillar emphasizes the importance of examiner discretion in assessing a bank's total capital requirements. The market discipline pillar emphasizes the importance of enhanced risk disclosures and transparency by banks.

SECURITIES BROKER/DEALERS

The capital requirements to which international securities firms are subject are a bit different than the BIS risk-based capital standards for banks. The Basel Accord is primarily concerned with ensuring that banks have enough capital to absorb losses and remain in business, in large part to ensure that "systemic stability" is not threatened by the failure of a major bank. Capital requirements imposed on securities participants like broker/dealers take a very different approach and are intended not to prevent a failure, but rather to protect customers in the event of a failure. These requirements specify capital the firm must hold to ensure that it can be liquidated in an orderly and nondisruptive manner if the need arises.

The SEC Net Capital Rule

Capital requirements imposed on securities firms are exemplified by the U.S. Securities and Exchange Commission (SEC) "net capital rule" of 1975.[3] Under the net capital rule, firms are required to hold enough regulatory capital so that they can be liquidated in an orderly manner if they fall below minimum capital levels. Importantly and quite differently from the capital requirements imposed on banks, the net capital rule can be satisfied only with *liquid* capital, and the required minimum level is thus also aimed only at firms' *liquid* capital assets.

The actual minimum liquid asset requirement imposed on a broker/dealer depends on many factors—the size of the firm, whether it manages customer funds and/or issues securities, the other activities of the firm, and the like.

Despite the heterogeneity of the minimum capital requirement, the way that firms *satisfy* these requirements is the same across all firms. Specifically, to calculate minimum capital levels, securities firms take the market values of their current securities holdings and multiply them by asset-specific risk factors that are set by the SEC to reflect the credit, market, and liquidity risk of the securities. The resulting so-called haircuts are then subtracted from the net worth of the institution for comparison to the firm's minimum capital level.

Haircuts   For equity securities, U.S. firms may choose between the "basic standard" and "alternative standard" approaches. The former specifies a 30 percent haircut and a requirement that aggregate indebtedness cannot exceed 15 times net capital. The latter requires firms to hold a capital cushion equal to 2 percent of customer and customer-related receivables, and imposes a 15 percent haircut with some added complications. Almost all large firms today opt for the alternative standard method.

Under the alternative standard method, the net capital rule specifies a haircut based on the following calculation:

$$\text{Haircut} = 0.15\max(L, S) + 0.15\max[0, \min(L, S) - 0.25\max(L, S)]$$

where L and S denote the market values of the broker's long and short positions, respectively. This is confusing, so let us take an example. Suppose a broker/dealer has long positions in the common stock of Firm Dracula worth $200,000 and short positions in the same common stock worth $15,000. The long exposure is the greater of the two, so the haircut is

$$\text{Haircut} = 0.15(\$200,000) + 0.15\max[0, \$15,000 - 0.25(\$200,000)]$$

The last term is negative and thus vanishes, so the broker/dealer's haircut on its Dracula holdings is

$$\text{Haircut} = 0.15(\$200,000) = \$30,000$$

Now suppose the long positions of the firm are worth $200,000 and the short positions worth $250,000. The short positions now represent the maximum exposure, and the haircut is

$$
\begin{aligned}
\text{Haircut} &= 0.15(\$250,000) + 0.15\max[0, \$200,000 - 0.25(\$250,000)] \\
&= \$37,500 + 0.15\max(0, \$200,000 - \$62,500) \\
&= \$37,500 + 0.15(\$137,500) \\
&= \$37,500 + \$20,625 = \$58,125
\end{aligned}
$$

In other words, if *both* positions are big enough, *both* enter the haircut calculation. The 25 percent multiplier in the last term reflects the fact that netting is only partially credited in this calculation—but that is still more than in the basic standard method.

Haircuts on debt securities are based on the credit quality of their issuer and the maturity of the claim, both of which materially impact the volatility of the security. Table B.4 shows the current haircut amounts by issuer and maturity.

Derivatives Policy Group Voluntary Reporting Framework   In March 1995, the six largest U.S. securities participants in over-the-counter derivatives activity—Goldman Sachs, Credit Suisse First Boston, Merrill Lynch, Morgan Stanley, Salomon Brothers, and Lehman Brothers—released a *Framework for Voluntary Oversight* intended to provide guidance for capital allocation to the risks of derivatives. Known as the Derivatives Policy Group (DPG), these six firms agreed to report their activities in derivatives to the SEC voluntarily.

In addition, the DPG members agreed to use proprietary statistical models to measure the capital at risk on their derivatives activities using a mutually agreed-upon reporting framework.[4] The DPG participants calculate the risks of their interest rate, equity, foreign exchange, and commodity swaps; over-the-counter options; and foreign exchange forwards under

TABLE B.4   Haircuts for Debt Instruments Under the SEC Net Capital Rule

Maturity	Government[a]	Municipal[b]		High-Grade Debt[c]	Others (Liquid)[d]	Others (Illiquid)[e]
0–1 Months	0%		0%			
1–3 Months			⅛%			
3–6 Months	0.5%	1%	¼%	2%		
6–9 Months	0.75%		⅜%			
9–12 Months	1%		½%			
1–2 Years	1.5%	2%	¾% / 1%	3%	30% (15%)[f]	40%
2–3 Years	2%	3%		5%		
3–5 Years	3%	4%		6%		
5–7 Years	4%	5%		7%		
7–10 Years		5.5%				
10–15 Years	4.5%	6%		7.5%		
15–20 Years	5%	6.5%		8%		
20–25 Years	5.5%	7%		2.5%		
Over 25 Years	6%			9%		

[a]Includes securities issued or guaranteed by the U.S. government, government-sponsored enterprises, or the Canadian government.
[b]The second column applies to municipal securities with less than 732 days to maturity at issue, and the first column applies to all other municipal securities.
[c]The debt must be nonconvertible and have a rating in one of the top four rating categories of a recognized rating agency.
[d]Three or more market makers.
[e]One or two market makers.
[f]Alternate method in parentheses.

two different scenarios: a large shock of a size to be determined by the member firms, and a shock to several predefined "core risk factors" specified by the SEC.

The DPG participants report these results to the SEC but may *not* use these calculations as a substitute for the regular net capital requirements. The SEC appears to use the information mainly to monitor how a correlated shock to major risk factors would affect all firms at the same time.

Internal Models   The SEC has shown much greater reluctance than the BIS in allowing firms to use their own internal models for capital requirement calculation purposes. In February 1997, the SEC took its first step in this direction by agreeing to let broker/dealers calculate the haircut on their listed equity, equity index, and currency options positions using models.

Broker/dealers must report their positions to a "third-party source" that maintains generally accepted option pricing models and that is subject to supervision by a "designated examining authority." The third party revalues the broker's options under 10 specified valuation scenarios. The broker then downloads the changes in option values under these scenarios and applies these changes to its own proprietary and market maker positions. The maximum loss at each of the 10 scenarios is the haircut.

The SEC is currently considering an approach more like the one embodied in Basel II, especially with respect to allowing large derivatives participants to rely on internal models for the calculation of their haircuts.

IOSCO International Guidance

Securities regulation can differ quite a lot across international borders. The International Organisation of Securities Commissions (IOSCO) has attempted to promulgate some cross-border uniformity, and one area of particular interest to IOSCO has been the harmonization of international minimum capital requirements on securities broker/dealers. The Technical Committee of IOSCO worked on a document articulating its views on minimum capital requirements from July 1987 to June 1989.

The resulting *Capital Adequacy Standards for Securities Firms* sets forth a framework that is broadly similar to the SEC's net capital rule. Firms are expected to have sufficient liquid assets to meet their obligations given the risks to which they are subject. The liquid capital of broker/dealers is expected to exceed the sum of risk-based requirements imposed on assets in a manner analogous to SEC haircuts.

INSURERS AND REINSURERS

The regulation of insurance and reinsurance suppliers is complicated and disparate. Some countries are much more lenient than others, and some countries—including the United States—leave regulation to individual region or state insurance commissions and chartering agents.

Nevertheless, most countries do specify minimum capital requirements for insurance underwriters and sometimes for reinsurers. Some examples of these capital requirements are detailed in the following subsections, but readers should keep in mind that, unlike the BIS that applies to all internationally active G-10 banks, insurance capital requirements can vary widely by jurisdiction.

The U.S. NAIC Risk-Based Capital Standards for Insurers

Although American states are ultimately allowed a large amount of discretion in their implementation of minimum capital requirements, the National Association of Insurance Commissioners (NAIC) has developed a set of risk-based capital (RBC) standards in an effort to promote conformity. The NAIC RBC standards attempt to require insurers to hold an amount of capital deemed adequate to cover most of their major risks. As in the Basel Accord, risk weights are defined for all risky assets, liabilities, and premium writings. The size of the exposure is adjusted with a risk weighting factor, and the aggregate weighted risk exposure defines an insurer's *authorized control level* (ACL).

The total adjusted capital (TAC) of insurers is then compared to their ACLs to determine capital adequacy. Insurers may satisfy their TAC requirement with statutory capital, voluntary reserves, and certain premium surpluses. Companies with a TAC-to-ACL ratio of 200 percent or more are typically left alone. Insurers with a TAC-ACL ratio of between 150 percent and 200 percent often must submit an "RBC Plan" to their home state regulators proposing the corrective actions they will take to move their ratio in the right direction. And so on. Table B.5 summarizes the usual implications for insurance writers based on their TAC-ACL ratios.

TABLE B.5 NAIC RBC TAC-ACL Minimum Capital Ratio Triggers

Ratio of TAC to ACL	Action
≥ 200%	No action
≥ 150% and < 200%	RBC Plan must be submitted to state proposing specific corrective actions
≥ 100% and < 150%	RBC Plan as above *plus* regulatory agency-mandated corrective actions
≥ 70% and < 100%	Discretionary seizure of firm *allowed*
< 70%	Closure and seizure of firm *required*

Solvency Margins in the European Union for Insurers

In the European Union (EU), capital requirements for insurance underwriters are usually based on a *solvency margin*, defined broadly as the minimum relation required between capital (called *surplus*) and premiums written and either claims incurred (nonlife) or mathematical reserves (life). As early as 1946, for example, the United Kingdom required that the total assets of a nonlife insurer exceed total liabilities by 20 percent of the premiums written.[5]

Note that we encounter here an important industry distinction that arises repeatedly in the book: the distinction between *life* and *nonlife* insurance lines. Nonlife may include property and casualty, professional indemnity, directors and officers, and other types of insurance. The two types of insurance lines have been separated by historical convention for many years, many because the nature of the liabilities and the actuarial models required to manage the liabilities are inherently different. Most specifically, it is possible for a nonlife policy to never result in a claim, whereas life policies *always will* because everyone dies eventually.

An EU directive sets forth minimum solvency margins based on the general type of insurance line. Nonlife lines, for example, must have capital that is equal to the greater of (1) 18 percent of written premiums or (2) 26 percent of average net claims paid over the prior three to seven years. Adjustments are allowed in both cases for reinsurance.

Capital Requirements for Reinsurers[6]

As is the case with insurance companies, capital requirements on reinsurers can vary widely across countries and legal jurisdictions. Unlike insurers, however, solvency concerns with reinsurers are widely regarded as less of a public policy problem for the simple reason that insurers deal directly with members of the public and reinsurers do not. Accordingly, the solvency of a reinsurer is typically regarded as a concern only to the extent that it might affect the solvency of an insurer.

Reinsurance capital requirements may target companies' technical reserves and/or solvency margins. In the United States, for example, reinsurers must maintain the same technical reserves as insurers for similar lines. Other countries like the United Kingdom rely on surplus margins in excess of reserves instead of just absolute reserves.

Whether or not credit is given to primary insurers for reinsurance in the calculation of their own capital and reserve requirements depends in part on how the reinsurers are regulated. In the United States and within Lloyd's, for example, there is no real distinction between insurers and reinsurers, and any firm purchasing insurance from another firm can deduct that cover from its own capital requirement. In France, by contrast, no reserve requirement is imposed on reinsurers, *but* primary insurers are not allowed to deduct insurance from their own technical reserve requirements. In other words, France enforces a "gross reserving" environment in which reinsurers are essentially unregulated, but insurers are not allowed to show the benefits of reinsurance in their own capital regulations.

Risk Capital

Risk capital is financial capital allocated or assigned to absorb specific risks and/or to guarantee performance on specific portfolios. Mechanically, risk capital is essentially cash set aside in a loss reserve with the specific purpose of providing a cushion against losses that may arise in a particular business line or asset/liability portfolio.

Risk capital and risk capital allocation have limited applications for nonfinancial corporations. Few corporate treasurers think about allocating capital to risks. As discussed in Chapters 6 and 7, much more common for corporations is to think about protecting net profits, cash flows, or earnings. Nevertheless, risk capital is a conceptually important ingredient of any complete risk management discussion. Also, risk capital does *sometimes* matter to nonfinancial corporates. For these reasons, it is worth some attention here.

RISK CAPITAL: WHO NEEDS IT?

Many argue that risk capital matters only for financial institutions and not for nonfinancial corporations. The Basel Capital Accord of 1988, for example, requires that banks allocate financial capital to certain risks (e.g., the credit risk of loans and the market risks of long-term derivatives) in order to promote the safety and soundness and the fair competitiveness of the global financial system. For all financial institutions that are not overcapitalized relative to these regulatory minimums, this creates a sort of artificial scarcity in certain types of financial capital that must be addressed through risk capital allocation. Appendix B provides a brief summary of risk-based capital requirements faced by banks, securities broker/dealers, and (re)insurance companies.

In addition, some financial institutions issue liabilities that are intended *only* to be funding instruments and that are *not* intended to help disperse the risks of the firm to those claim holders. Specifically, banks and insurance companies incur liabilities as part of their core business activities, and these firms may not wish to have the holders of those liabilities incur the same firmwide credit risk to the issuer as the holder of, say, an unsecured debenture. The institution must allocate risk capital to guarantee or self-insure the firm's ability to repay those so-called customer liabilities.

Nonfinancial corporations do not have financial capital that also represents customer liabilities, and this is the main reason why risk capital allocation may make sense for financial firms even when it does not make sense for most corporations. Yet, the need to allocate risk capital to specific liabilities is not limited to corporate securities. Corporations regularly enter into long-dated *commercial* contracts that are or can represent liabilities, and the counterparties on the other side of those deals may demand more than just a promise of the firm's ability to honor the contracts. In commercial contracts, this often goes well beyond just a question of credit risk—customers do not just want to know the firm will be around; they also want what the contracts promise them.

The need for risk capital associated with customer contracts is well illustrated by the example of the extremely long-dated customer contracts offered by MG Refining & Marketing, Inc. (MGRM), in the early 1990s discussed by Culp and Miller (1995). These contracts allowed commercial customers to lock in the price of gasoline or heating oil on monthly deliveries of product *out to 10 years*. At the height of its program, MGRM had sold forward the equivalent of 150 million barrels of oil in these contracts to customers ranging from mom-and-pop gas stations to local fuel distributors like Thornton Oil and corporate end users like Chrysler Corp. and Browning-Ferris Industries Corp (Culp and Miller 1995).

MGRM's contracts were guaranteed by MGRM's highly rated and stalwart parent Metallgesellschaft AG (MG AG). At the end of 1992, MG AG was one of the largest industrial conglomerates in Europe—a century-old industrial conglomerate with 251 subsidiaries around the world involved in trade, engineering, and financial services activities. MG AG was owned largely by institutional investors, including Deutsche Bank, Dresdner Bank, Daimler-Benz, and the Kuwait Investment Authority, and Deutsche Bank and Dresdner Bank were also its primary creditors. Given the backing of MGRM and MG AG, it's not surprising that most market participants viewed the firm is nearly indestructible. As one swap dealer commented, "[T]here was a feeling in the market that [MGRM] was the Bundesbank: the Bundesbank would bail out Deutsche Bank, which stood behind MG. The ultimate risk was the country."[1]

This was not enough for customers. Customers also wanted to ensure that they would get their oil and gas. In fact, MGRM's contracts with its customers required MGRM to remain 100 percent hedged *at all times* against its future customer delivery obligations.[2] And this apparently worked. MGRM's program was terminated in December 1993 by the supervisory board of MG AG, its required hedges liquidated and its customer contracts canceled with no payment required by either party. As it turned out thanks to a precipitous decline in oil prices, the customer contracts were major *asset* for MGRM when the program was terminated. Yet, at least one of MGRM's big customers sued the firm to get its contract back. True, the contract was a then-current liability for the customer, but that firm had evidently resold the product using similar long-dated contracts with *its* customers. *It needed the oil.*

This example also illustrates an extremely fundamental point. Namely, hedging with derivatives or buying insurance can provide off-balance-sheet risk capital to a firm. In some cases, derivatives and insurance can be even more attractive. Paid-up risk capital is pledged to honor specific projects, but merely raising cash and setting it aside provides outsiders with no real guarantee of how those funds will actually be used. Nor can firms always account for such reserves in a way that reflects the true reduction of risk in a firm's earnings. Derivatives and insurance, by contrast, can be tied to specific transactions so that cash inflows do not occur until there is a specifically associated cash outflow first.[3] This can both increase transparency and allow firms to achieve a more accurate earnings disclosure relative to the true risk of the project in question.

THE NATURE OF RISK CAPITAL

Risk capital may be defined most generally as financial capital or cash allocated or assigned to a risky portfolio of assets and certain liabilities to help absorb potential shortfalls in net asset value. A risky portfolio could be a specific investment project, an operating division of a firm, an entire firm, and so on.

Consider a single project with a useful life of T periods that requires an up-front investment at time t of $I(t)$ and that will generate future net cash flows denoted $X(t + j)$ for any period $t + j$. Following our discussion in

Chapter 1, the value of this project at time t—call it $V^A(t)$—can be expressed *without any risk capital* as

$$V^A(t) = \sum_{j=1}^{T} \frac{E_t[X(t+j)]}{[1 + E(R^A)]^j} - I(t) \qquad (C.1)$$

where $E(R^A)$ is our expected return on the assets underlying this particular project as per Chapter 5. Let's assume for simplicity that this expected return is constant.

We also suppose that this single project is the only asset held by a firm—a special purpose entity (SPE) whose sole purpose is to finance, build, and operate this project. The firm is set up at time $t - 1$ and capitalized with a new issue of stock, the proceeds of which are held in a cash account until the project is acquired at time t.

With this framework in mind, the next two subsections now discuss the two popular ways of viewing risk capital.

Risk Capital as a Cushion Against Catastrophic Loss

The first conception of risk capital is essentially synonymous with the use of some kind of funded loss reserve or cash cushion against future possible catastrophic losses. The cleanest way to view this type of risk capital is just to imagine that a firm computes what it considers to be a reliably conservative estimate of its "maximum reasonable loss" on the project and then either issues new equity or diverts retained earnings to invest in cash that is then set aside in escrow to absorb that loss. The cash earns the risk-free rate over the life of the project and reverts to the firm's general funding if the potential loss never occurs. If the loss does occur, it is paid for directly from the cash account so that the *combined* value of the project and the cash cushion never falls below a specified minimum value.

The notion of a maximum potential loss is essentially what risk managers know as *value at risk* (VaR). The VaR of any project is the maximum reasonable loss the project may experience over a fixed time period, where "maximum reasonable" is defined in probabilistic terms based on a fixed, desired level of confidence or conservatism. A project with a $1 million one-day VaR at the 99th percentile, for example, is expected to experience a one-day loss of more than $1 million only 1 percent of the time (i.e., the project loss will be less than $1 million 99 percent of the time).[4]

VaR is principally used to measure market risk. To measure the analogous *capital at risk* (CaR) in a project, we also want to include other risks (both financial and non-financial). But apart from that, this first interpretation of risk capital essentially *is* capital at risk defined in VaR-like terms.

The period of time over which a firm will compute the maximum potential loss or CaR for a project is not necessarily the whole length of the project. This time period, known as the risk horizon, depends on why the firm is holding risk capital for the project. If the goal is to guarantee some liability associated with the project whose maturity is shorter than the tenor of the project, the debt maturity will provide us with the relevant risk horizon. But for now, let's assume we are concerned with the CaR on the project over its entire life.

The firm must also select the percentile or confidence level for its CaR estimate. This depends mostly on the degree of conservatism with which the firm wants to guarantee the project's net asset value. A firm cannot know, of course, what its true maximum loss is for a wide range of project types. If the project involves a short exposure of some kind, the maximum loss is theoretically unbounded. But even if the project involves a traditional long position in a real or financial asset, the potential for the price of the asset to decline to zero may be unreasonable. So, firms often settle for percentiles to try to approximate what they call a "maximum potential loss." The 99th percentile and 99.9th percentile are popular choices.

Having specified a risk horizon and given level of probabilistic confidence, the rest is pure numerical methods. Returning to equation (C.1) and assuming each period in the life of the project is a month, we can essentially simulate a sample path of net cash flows up to the end of the risk horizon, which we will assume is the end of the project at date $t + T$. Denote one of these sample paths of net cash flows $X^{(1)} = X^{(1)}(t + 1)$, $X^{(1)}(t + 2)$, ..., $X^{(1)}(t + T)$. We can then do the same thing again to generate a second possible sample path of net cash flows, $X^{(2)} = X^{(2)}(t + 1)$, $X^{(2)}(t + 2)$, ..., $X^{(2)}(t + T)$. And again and again, until we have generated M sample paths (where M may be around 10,000) corresponding to M different risk scenarios.

Let's now assume for the purpose of our example that the firm does not know which value will be realized from this distribution of risk scenarios and possible cash flow paths. Assume, however, that the firm is either unconcerned about losses occurring at any time prior to $t + T$ or that a catastrophic loss, if it occurs, will occur for sure at time $t + T$. We can then compute the time $t + T$ value of the project using our distribution of time $t + T$ cash flows $[X^{(1)}(t + T), \ldots, X^{(M)}(t + T)]$. The present value of the time $t + T$ value of the project along sample path m, for example, is just

$$V^{A(m)}(t) = \sum_{j=1}^{T} \frac{X^{(m)}(t+j)}{[1 + E(R^A)]^j} - I(t) \tag{C.2}$$

so that one point in our change of value distribution is

$$\Delta V^{A(m)}(t) = V^A(t) - V^{A(m)}(t)$$

expressed in time t dollars. Any positive change in value is of no interest to us here, so we collect all the *negative* values of $\Delta V^{A(m)}(t)$ to generate a distribution of project losses. In this example we have looked at losses over all T periods in the project. We may prefer, of course, to look only at losses over the next month or year. Amassing all the losses and associating them with probabilities generates a figure like Exhibit C.1.

For a chosen probability level that indicates our desired definition of maximum reasonable loss, we can compute L^* in Exhibit C.1 as the total loss per period that leaves the desired percentage of probability in the tail. If we define maximum reasonable loss to be the loss that occurs 99 percent of the time, L^* will be the loss that leaves 1 percent of the probability distribution uncovered. This is the area under the curve in Exhibit C.1 *above* L^*. So, you don't expect to lose more than L^* 99 percent of the time.

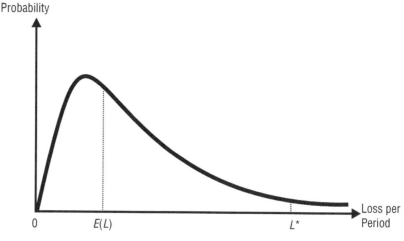

EXHIBIT C.1 Distribution of Potential Losses per Period

L^* may *not*, however, be our measure of capital at risk. The reason is that many projects give rise to *expected losses*. If we *expect* a loss to occur, however, that needs to be treated as a *cost* of the project, not a *risk* of the project. You set aside cash in advance to cover this expected loss in a loss reserve. A corporation that routinely expects to lose 10 percent of its trade receivables to trade credit defaults should treat that expected loss as a known cost of investing in the business. The risk capital is then the distance between the *expected* loss and L^*. That amount *plus* the expected loss reserve is the size of the cash cushion the firm needs to hold to ensure that the project is essentially riskless.

So, our risk capital in this case is

$$K^* = L^* - E(L)$$

Remember, moreover, that this is expressed in time t dollars. The amount K^* will be invested at the riskless rate and grow to $K^*(1 + R_f)^T$ by time $t + T$.

A popular way of simplifying the measurement of a loss distribution rather than simulating cash flows as we have just done is to assume that per-period changes in the value of the assets underlying the project in question are normally distributed. In this case, we can use the properties of a normal distribution to infer the CaR threshold. Suppose, for example, we want a CaR that covers our project against 99 percent of the losses it may generate over the next T periods. We know that 99 percent of the normal distribution falls above a value that is 2.33 standard deviations below the mean. If we assume a zero mean for simplicity, the 99th percentile risk capital that should be allocated to a project with a current value of $V(t)$ for a risk period from t to $t + T$ is just

$$K^* = V(t)2.33\sigma\sqrt{T} \tag{C.3}$$

Risk Capital as Net Asset Insurance

Merton and Perold (1993) define risk capital as "the smallest amount that can be invested to insure the value of the firm's net assets against a loss in value relative to a risk-free investment." As they define it, the firm's net assets are its gross assets minus customer liabilities *assuming* the customer liabilities are default risk-free. We can generalize that for our purposes here and say that net assets are the firm's gross assets minus *any* liabilities or contracts that the firm chooses to offer on a risk-free basis. At any time t, net assets thus have a value of $A(t) - L(t)$.

Using Merton and Perold's definition of risk capital, we want to avoid a *shortfall* of net assets relative to the riskless return on those assets. The actual shortfall at some time $t + T$ can be expressed as

$$\underbrace{[A(t)-L(t)](1+R_f)^{T-t}}_{\substack{\text{Starting Value of Net Assets Invested} \\ \text{at the Risk-Free Rate until } T}} - \underbrace{[A(t+T)-L(t+T)]}_{\text{Value of Net Assets at } T}$$

To absolutely eliminate any risk of a shortfall, we can characterize the risk capital like an insurance or option contract with the following payoff at time $t + T$:

$$\max\{[A(t) - L(t)](1 + R_f)^{T-t} - [A(t + T) - L(t + T)], 0\} \qquad (C.4)$$

which is the same as the payoff on a put option written on the project's net assets with a strike price equal to the floor on the net assets we have required (i.e., the starting value of net assets invested for T periods—from t to $t + T$—at the risk-free rate).

If we assume changes in asset values are normally distributed and liabilities are either fixed or nonexistent, Merton and Perold remind us that the properties of the Black-Scholes option pricing formula allow us to approximate the value of the aforementioned "risk capital option" as

$$K^* = A(t)0.40\sigma\sqrt{T} \qquad (C.5)$$

where $A(t)$ is the current asset price and σ the volatility of changes in that price. Comparing (C.5) to (C.3), 5.825 times the price of option in (C.5) gives us the 99th percentile risk capital in (C.3). We can always scale (C.5) up or down to the appropriate number of standard deviations we want to recover (C.3).

RISK CAPITAL ALLOCATION

In a Modigliani and Miller (M&M) world when systematic risk is the only risk affecting the prices of a firm's securities, the risk capital assigned to specific projects inside a portfolio or firm will be additive; that is, the sum of the risk capital amounts allocated to each project will always equal the total risk capital for the portfolio of projects. But when risk capital has deadweight costs arising from idiosyncratic risks, risk capital is no longer additive across projects and business lines. The correlations across projects and the combination of projects pursued by the firm will affect the capital budgeting decision. We can see this most clearly if we separate the risk budgeting process into two stages: defining the aggregate CaR available for allocation in a risk budget, and actually assigning the capital to projects or activities within the firm.

Defining the Risk Capital Available in a Risk Budget

Any business unit or project K can be assigned a risk capital allocation in a risk budget. The main distinction between different measures of *aggregate* risk capital and how that capital is allocated to business units is how correlations are taken into account *across* business units. If correlations across business units are not taken into account, the business-unit-level risk capital is called its stand-alone or undiversified capital at risk (CaR), denoted CaR_j^U for any business unit j. The sum of the stand-alone CaRs for all K business units in a firm is called its *undiversified total CaR*:

$$CaR^U = \sum_{j=1}^{K} CaR_j^U$$

The aggregate CaR of the firm inclusive of cross-business-line correlations, by contrast, is called the *enterprise-wide CaR*, or CaR^E. Undiversified total CaR is not equal to enterprise-wide CaR unless the returns on different business units are perfectly correlated. Otherwise, enterprise-wide CaR is less than undiversified total CaR.

Undiversified and enterprise-wide CaR are both measures of *total* capital at risk. Alternatively, a corporation can measure the *marginal* contribution of a business to enterprise-wide VaR. The marginal CaR of a business line is the difference between enterprise-wide CaR with and without that business line, or CaR_j^M.

Interactions between business units can impact enterprise-wide CaR differently depending on the specific combination of businesses in the total firm. Consequently, the sum of marginal CaRs is less than enterprise-wide CaR if changes in cash flows are imperfectly correlated across business lines. The following relation thus generally holds:

$$\sum_{j=1}^{M} CaR_j^M \leq CaR^E \leq CaR^U$$

Apportioning Allocatable Risk Capital to Projects or Units

Firms may define allocatable enterprise-wide CaR using any of four different methods, each of which defines an allocatable CaR.[5]

Method I: Pro Rata Allocation   Method I for capital allocation allocates undiversified total CaR pro rata across business units. Each unit receives an allocation of undiversified total CaR based on the share of its stand-alone CaR in the total amount. If the allocation of capital to business unit j is denoted δ_j, Method I defines that proportion as

$$\delta_j = \frac{CaR_j^U}{CaR^U}$$

Method I thus evaluates each business in isolation and takes into consideration no interactions between business units.

Method II: The Splitting Method of Allocation   Method II for capital allocation incorporates cross-business correlations by allocating enterprise-wide CaR. Called the "splitting method," this approach allocates to each business unit a proportion of its stand-alone CaR, where the proportion is equal to the ratio of enterprise-wide CaR to total undiversified CaR.[6]

$$\delta_j = \frac{CaR^E}{CaR^U}$$

The resulting allocation is called the diversified CaR for business unit j and is

$$CaR_j^D = \delta_j CaR_j^U$$

If enterprise-wide CaR is 20 percent less than undiversified CaR, for example, Method II will allocate to each business unit 20 percent of its stand-alone CaR. This method thus assumes—incorrectly—that each business unit contributes equally to enterprise-wide risk diversification.

Consider, for example, a multinational firm with three existing business units: chocolate sales, cocoa sales, and espresso/coffee machine sales. Table C.1 shows the correlations in returns across these business units and how Method II would be used to apportion capital across them.

TABLE C.1 Allocating Capital in a Multinational Firm by Method II

	1—Chocolate Sales	2—Cocoa Sales	3—Machine Sales
Correlation with 1	1	0.8	−0.1
Correlation with 2	0.8	1	0.65
Correlation with 3	−0.1	0.65	1
CaR_i^U	\$500 million	\$400 million	\$700 million
δ_i	77.9%	77.9%	77.9%
CaR_i^D	\$384 million	\$308 million	\$538 million

The total undiversified CaR is \$1,600 million (\$500mn + \$400mn + \$700mn), and the total diversified CaR taking correlations into account is \$1,230 million. The resulting adjustment factor is the ratio of the latter to the former, or 0.769. That adjustment factor applied to each unit's undiversified CaR yields the diversified CaR for each unit. Notice in Table C.1 that the sum of the diversified CaRs equals the enterprise-wide diversified CaR. In other words, Method II allocates the risk capital of the firm fully.

Because the sum of *marginal* CaRs does not equal enterprise-wide CaR, however, Method II allocates risk capital in a manner that does not reflect the true marginal contribution of each business to the total risk of the firm. In extreme cases, the overinvestment of risk capital to some businesses—which is costly for the businesses—can cause new investment opportunities to be rejected when they should actually be accepted. In other words, Method II can lead to underinvestment problems.

Method III: Marginal CaR Allocation Method III allocates capital based on the marginal CaR of a business unit. This method takes into account the specific contribution of each business unit to firmwide CaR in the allocation scheme and has the added benefit of being naturally comparable to the standard investment criterion of investing capital up to the point where its marginal benefit equals its marginal cost.

Table C.2 shows how Method III would be implemented at the multinational. The first row shows the enterprise-wide diversified CaR for only two business units, assuming the omitted unit does not exist. The marginal CaR allocated to a given business unit is then the *total* enterprise-wide diversified CaR of \$1,230 million minus the diversified CaR of the two remaining units. In the case of unit 1, for example, the marginal CaR of chocolate sales is \$223 million, or \$1,230 million minus the \$1,007 million CaR that results when only cocoa and espresso machine sales are considered.

TABLE C.2 Allocating Capital in a Multinational Firm by Method III

	Unit 2+3	Unit 1+2	Unit 1+3
CaR^D for given business units	$1,007 million	$819 million	$854 million
Excluded Unit	1	3	2
CaR_j^M of Excluded Unit	$223 million	$411 million	$376 million
CaR_j^M/CaR_j^U	0.45	1.03	0.54

Note from Table C.2 that the sum of the marginal CaRs is $1,011 million, or about $200 million less than total enterprise-wide diversified CaR. Method III thus does not fully allocate enterprise-wide capital as long as business line returns are imperfectly correlated. Merton and Perold (1993) characterize this implication of Method III as a type of "positive intrafirm externality" in which different businesses de facto insure one another and, in the process, reduce the total economic risk of the firm.

Method IV: Internal Beta Allocation Method IV allocates enterprise-wide CaR based on the "internal beta" of each business unit. Internal beta is defined for any business line as the covariance of its returns with the returns on the whole firm scaled by the variance of firmwide returns. Each business line is assigned such a beta and then allocated a fraction of diversified enterprise-wide CaR based on that beta in a manner similar to the capital budgeting rule of thumb in which positive net present value (NPV) projects competing for scarce funding capital are selected based on their internal beta ranks.

Unlike Method III, Method IV fully allocates enterprise-wide capital. The weighted average of all internal betas is equal to one, which means that the sum of the weighted CaR allocations to each business unit will exactly equal enterprise-wide CaR.

Interpretation

Methods I and II can clearly lead to inappropriate capital allocation decisions, whereas Methods III and IV can both be appropriate. Differentiating between Methods III and IV, however, is no easy task. Both have economic intuition behind them, as well as practical appeal. For those who believe the Merton and Perold (1993) story that risk capital diversification effects create a firmwide externality, unallocated enterprise-wide CaR should not be a concern. But for those who believe unallocated risk capital is a wasting asset, the internal beta approach likely will be preferred to the marginal CaR allocation rule.

ECONOMIC COST OF RISK CAPITAL AND "RISK CAPITAL STRUCTURE"

As long as a firm "gets what it pays for," there is no economic cost to raising risk capital. In an M&M world, a firm should be able to procure risk capital in unlimited quantities by issuing new corporate securities. This may change the relative values of its existing securities, but, as we know, it will neither change the value of the firm nor give rise to any need for internal capital allocation or capital rationing. The reason is simply that the only risk in an M&M world is systematic, and this risk is fully reflected in the prices of any securities issued.

In considering the value of risk capital, we also need to remember that issuing risk capital creates an *economic asset* for us. To see this, let's suppose we have a single project with fixed assets that cost $I(t)$ to acquire at time t that will generate risky cash flows over the next T periods with a discounted present value of $V^A(t)$. Assume there are no liabilities that we need to keep riskless so that risk capital is the amount of capital required to ensure that the assets of the project are worth at least $V^A(t)(1 + R_f)^T$ at time $t + T$ when the project ends. Our risk capital thus is equivalent to a put with the following payoff at time $t + T$:

$$p(t + T) = \max[V^A(t)(1 + R_f)^T - V^A(t + T), 0] \qquad \text{(C.6)}$$

In an M&M world, the actuarially fair price of that option will just be the discounted present value as of date t of the expiration value of the option:

$$p(t) = PV_{t,t+T}\{E_t[p(t + T)]\} \qquad \text{(C.7)}$$

We can now write the NPV of the project as of date t as the gross present value of the *insured* project less the *total* investment expenditure:

$$V(t) = \left(\underbrace{V^A(t)}_{\text{Traditional}} + \underbrace{[PV_{t,t+T}(E_t\{\max[V^A(t)(1+R_f)^T - V^A(t+T), 0]\})]}_{\text{Insurance}} \right)^{\overbrace{}^{\text{Gross PV}}}$$

$$\underbrace{- [I(t) + p(t)]}_{\text{Investment Cost}}$$

which we can rearrange into the traditional project NPV plus the NPV of the risk capital:

$$V(t) = \overbrace{[V^A(t) - I(t)]}^{\text{Traditional NPV}}$$

$$+ \overbrace{[PV_{t,t+T}(E_t\{\max[V^A(t)(1+R_f)^T - V^A(t+T), 0]\}) - p(t)]}^{\text{NPV of Risk Capital}}$$

(C.8)

In an M&M world, the last term is clearly zero—the price of the risk capital that the firm *pays* will result in the acquisition of an economic asset that has exactly the same current market value as the price paid. The NPV of the risk capital may not be zero *ex post*, of course, but equation (C.8) is an *ex ante* present value.

Things look similar if we use a VaR approach to risk capital measurement. Assume we compute our maximum reasonable loss on the project in time t dollars as

$$K^* = V(t)2.33\sigma\sqrt{T}$$

This represents the cash cushion or loss reserve—the amount of cash we must raise now and invest in order to guarantee a riskless return on the project's assets. The project's NPV becomes

$$V(t) = \overbrace{[V^A(t) - I(t)]}^{\text{Traditional NPV}} + \overbrace{[(V^A(t)2.33\sigma\sqrt{T})(1+R_f)^T - V^A(t)2.33\sigma\sqrt{T}]}^{\text{NPV of Risk Capital}}$$

Again we see that the true economic cost is zero; the firm raises just as much as it needs at a fair price and then earns the riskless return on cash until that cash is needed to cover a contingent loss.

The existence of idiosyncratic risks that can neither be fully diversified away by a firm's shareholders nor be separately traded by a firm's customers and counterparties gives rise to certain deadweight costs of risk capital. These costs we *cannot* ignore. If a firm pursues a project, for example, that requires $25 million of risk capital *and* that capital has deadweight costs accompanying it, we have to charge those costs against the project. Otherwise, the firm could pursue projects that are positive NPV excluding the deadweight costs of risk capital but that are negative NPV when the deadweight costs of risk capital are taken into account.

Merton and Perold (1993), Froot and Stein (1998), and Perold (2001) all articulate the need to take into account the deadweight costs of risk capital arising from the inability of shareholders to diversify away all the risks of the firm. In some cases, those risks are simply not separately tradable—for example, the credit risk of a counterparty default in a swap transaction if there are no credit derivatives available on the counterparty's name. In other cases, the risks may be tradable but not with perfect observability and not with equal access of all participants to the same markets and prices.

The deadweight cost of risk capital depends on whether the capital is paid-in or contingent. We discuss the distinction between the costs associated with the two different possible sources of risk capital in the next two subsections.

Deadweight Costs of Paid-In Risk Capital

Paid-in risk capital is just financial capital issued specifically to raise cash that is set aside by firms to cover specific risks. Raising paid-in risk capital enables a firm to assign a cash cushion to specific risks, business activities, projects, operating units, or contractual liabilities using an internal risk capital allocation system. In this sense, risk capital might appear to be similar to collateral. Unlike true collateral, however, the cash has simply been set aside to help the firm absorb the risks from the position or activity; it has not been pledged.

Upon closer inspection, moreover, risk capital and collateral are *not* substitute forms of credit enhancement from the perspective of the firm. To see why, recognize that customers and counterparties of a firm care about their credit risk to the firm, which is a function of both the probability of default and the loss given default (LGD). Collateral is cash or a cash equivalent pledged to a counterparty to credit enhance a transaction or security, thereby reducing the expected cost of default from the counterparty's perspective *by reducing its LGD*. In the event the firm defaults, the counterparty keeps the collateral. Assigning risk capital to the very same transaction will *also* reduce the counterparty's expected default, but *by reducing the probability of default*.

The firm may not be indifferent between these two choices. Because financial distress is costly, a failure to honor a transaction could precipitate a ratings downgrade, trigger cross-default provisions in other contracts, give rise to adverse reputation effects, and the like. As a result, all else being equal, a firm will prefer to reduce the probability of a default, thereby decreasing customer credit risk *and* decreasing its own expected costs of financial distress.

Reducing the probability of default on a specific risk by assigning risk capital to that risk, however, comes at a cost. Specifically, when a firm sets aside cash to cover a risk, the firm has raised its cash balances and thus could experience agency costs of free cash flows. The more opaque the firm and the harder it is for outsiders to verify how it uses its cash, the bigger the agency cost.

Firms relying on risk capital may also face credibility problems. Because the cash has merely been allocated to internally maintained and monitored economic risk reserves, investors may worry that the firm will treat these reserves as a so-called cookie jar. In other words, what is to stop the firm from tapping into these risk reserves to finance subsequent but currently unanticipated investment expenditures? Even if the firm reaches into its risk reserve cookie jar to finance genuinely positive NPV projects, it is *not* in that case using the cash for its intended purpose as a cushion against unexpected losses. This can badly exacerbate the adverse selection costs already associated with new securities issues.

Deadweight Costs of Contingent Risk Capital

As we have said, if a firm "gets what it pays for" then the economic cost of risk capital is zero. In the context of *contingent* risk capital, this means that fairly priced derivatives and insurance contracts should not impose any net economic benefits or costs on the firm; the value of the insurance will just be offset by the price paid for it.

Merton and Perold (1993), Froot and Stein (1998), and Perold (2001) remind us, however, that contingent risk capital is indeed costly in an economic sense in a non-M&M world. As we argued in Chapter 4, certain sources of capital are less susceptible to the *adverse selection* costs arising from information asymmetries. We argued that these sources of capital generally engaged in more careful credit risk evaluations of the firm, better due diligence, and more ongoing monitoring. But all of those activities are also costly. Guarantors and other providers of risk capital will increase the prices of their external capital to reflect these monitoring costs.

In addition, contingent risk capital is subject to *moral hazard*, or the potential for the existence of the risk capital facility to abrogate the firm's risk management and risk mitigation practices. External providers of risk capital will, to the extent possible, try to mitigate moral hazard contractually using features like deductibles and co-insurance, all of which is explained in more detail in Chapters 9 and 10. But in the end, the external capital provider will still probably remain worried about moral hazard and thus will charge a markup to cover the monitoring costs and risks to which moral hazard gives rise.

Optimal Risk Capital Structure

The deadweight costs of contingent risk capital and paid-in risk capital are very unlikely to be completely independent of each other. For any given amount of risk capital L^* that a firm needs to assign to a project, there *may* be a specific mixture of contingent and paid-in risk capital that minimizes the total deadweight cost of risk capital.[7] If so, firms should choose this. And if we extend our project perspective to the whole firm—and we know from Chapters 1 and 5 that we can easily do that – there may also be an optimal *risk capital structure* for the firm; that is, some unique blend of contingent risk capital (including insurance and derivatives) and paid-in risk capital (retained cash reserves) may well minimize the total deadweight costs of risk capital for the firm.

A concrete example of this is provided by Perold (2001). He assumes that paid-in risk capital that allows the firm to create a cash cushion of $C(t)$ causes "leakage" in the firm's net asset value proportional to some rate d. The term d is driven by the agency costs of outside equity, the agency costs of free cash flow, the adverse tax effects of excess cash subject to the double taxation of corporate income, and so on. If $V^\circ(t)$ is the net asset value of a project or firm at time t excluding risk capital, the deadweight costs of risk capital required to insure $V^\circ(t)$ thus is $(1 - d)V^\circ(t)$.

Similarly, Perold (2001) assumes that contingent risk capital imposes adverse selection and monitoring costs on the firm at some rate m. If the actuarially fair price of contingent capital is the theoretical price of asset insurance or a put required to ensure that net assets are worth at least their current value grossed up at the risk-free rate in the future—we called it $p(t)$ in equations (C.6), (C.7), and (C.8)—then the net cost to the firm of asset insurance is $(1 + m)p(t)$. The variable m will be a function of external monitoring and verification costs, signaling costs, adverse selection costs, and the like.

In Perold's formulation, the deadweight costs of paid-in and contingent capital both are dependent on the total cash cushion the firm holds, $C(t)$. The more paid-in risk capital and the larger a cash cushion a firm has, the higher its net asset value leakage rate d. At the same time, the larger cash cushion increases the transparency of the firm, making it easier for outsiders to monitor the firm's investments and thus reducing continent risk capital deadweight costs m.

The deadweight cost $\varphi^*(t)$ is the *minimum* deadweight cost of risk capital—the deadweight cost of capital conditional on an optimal mixture of contingent and risk capital. The mixture of contingent and paid-in risk capital that yields cash cushion $C^*(t)$ and total deadweight risk capital cost $\varphi^*(t)$ is the risk capital structure for the firm.

Notice that we use the variable $\varphi^*(t)$ to indicate the firm's minimum cost of risk capital. This now allows us to more meaningfully reinterpret the project NPV as:

$$V^A(t) = V^\circ(t) - K^*\varphi^*(t) \qquad (C.9)$$

where

$$V^\circ(t) = \sum_{j=1}^{T} \frac{E_t[X(t+j)]}{[1+E(R^A)]^j} - I(t)$$

Equation (C.9) is fundamentally important. It tells us that whether we are evaluating a project or valuing a whole firm, we need to adjust the net present value to take into account the *net deadweight cost* of risk capital as an additional investment expenditure of sorts. In turn, the cost of risk capital is equal to the price of a put option written on the net assets of the project or firm (and struck at the forward price of those net assets) multiplied by the deadweight cost of risk capital *assuming an optimal mixture of contingent and paid-in risk capital.*

Structured Finance and the Cost of Risk Capital

Structured finance is a way of reducing the deadweight costs of risk capital. In essence, structured finance seeks to chop up the assets of a firm into small pieces, place those pieces in essentially separate legal entities, and then fund those assets using a much more narrowly defined set of financial capital claims than the general corporation has issued. Suppose, for example, we consider an aircraft manufacturer that enters into long-term, capital-intensive contracts with airlines for new planes. A typical aircraft manufacturer also may be active in other high-tech businesses, such as satellite communications, weapons production, and the like. If the firm is attempting to allocate risk capital to its customer contracts to help convince customers of its long-term delivery capabilities, just changing the seniority of the firm's general claims will not do it. But structuring a financial solution *will*.

Suppose the firm houses a new aircraft in a subsidiary. For now, suppose the equity in the subsidiary is 10 percent of its assets and is retained by the aircraft company. The remaining 90 percent of the assets are financed with debt. Subordination now *can* be used to create different risk exposures to the performance of the underlying asset pool without commingling the other risks of the company.

In addition, moving the aircraft project into a separately financed entity also reduces the agency costs of risk capital allocation. A cash cushion set aside in the new firm is specifically earmarked as a cushion against the risks of the aircraft project. Because the sole purpose of the subsidiary is to complete that project, the cookie jar problem basically goes away. This not only allows the firm to more credibly allocate cash reserves to risk than when the project was housed along with all the other projects of the firm, it also likely will reduce the adverse selection costs of the securities issued by the special purpose entity.

In short, we can use structured financing solutions to significantly reduce the costs of asymmetric information associated with nontradable, nondiversifiable risks. We reduce the agency costs of free cash flow problem, as well as the adverse selection costs, both of which arise primarily from the potential for a firm to spend cash on projects for which the cash was not intended. In the structured finance case, there is one project and one set of project risks, so the concerns about how the cash will be used essentially disappear.

Insurance, Alternative Risk Transfer, Hedging, and the Cost of Risk Capital

Because we know there may be an optimal mixture of contingent and paid-in risk capital that minimizes the deadweight costs of risk capital for the firm, this implies that contracts like insurance, alternative risk transfer (ART) forms, and derivatives may be valuable to firms *for reasons other than the usually stated goals of simply reducing expected distress costs.*

It is well established that risk transfer using these kinds of products can increase the value of a firm when they are used to help reduce expected distress costs, smooth out a convex tax schedule, mitigate underinvestment problems, and the like.[8] But these traditional justifications for risk management products do not always take into account the issues we have raised here.

Consider, for example, an AAA-rated firm with a very low market leverage ratio. Such a firm is likely to question the value of insurance and perhaps even of derivatives. We might promote the use of these contracts in the context of surgically eliminating a very specific risk exposure that the firm doesn't like, but it would be hard to promote a comprehensive insurance or hedging program motivated solely by these traditional considerations.

Now reconsider this same firm in light of the discussion here. Even AAA-rated firms with low leverage may have a demand for risk capital—for example, to assure delivery on long-term customer contracts or to reduce the risk of a specific liability issued to a targeted group of customers or investors. If the firm has a need for risk capital, then it may very well be the case that using only paid-in cash reserves as a source of risk capital is *not* the most efficient solution. If the firm is relatively opaque and heavily invested in intangible assets, for example, it may experience relatively high adverse selection costs and agency costs of outside equity. It may be *cheaper* and *more efficient* for the firm to procure risk capital through insurance and derivatives or by utilizing the structured financing methods discussed in the last section to obtain its optimal risk capital structure.

In other words, *no firm—regardless of size or credit rating—can ignore the issues we are raising in this appendix.*

CAPITAL BUDGETING WITH COSTLY RISK CAPITAL

Now that we have formally developed the concept of risk capital and risk capital structure and we have developed a concrete understanding of the true economic cost of risk capital, the next logical step is to consider how these variables affect the project selection, performance evaluation, and capital budgeting decisions we reviewed in Chapter 5. We begin by discussing how the costs of risk capital affect the hurdle rates we developed for project evaluation and performance measurement in Chapter 5. We then discuss the problem of allocating risk capital to specific projects in a firm when we have capital rationing. That process is widely known as *risk budgeting.*

Hurdle Rates, Project Selection, and Performance Evaluation Revisited

Risk-adjusted return on capital (RAROC) is the most common measure of return per unit of risk capital in use by firms today in the risk capital budgeting process. RAROC is defined as the net economic income of a project, activity, or business line scaled by its economic capital at risk:

$$\text{RAROC} = \frac{\text{Economic Net Income}}{\text{Risk Capital}}$$

Economic net income is the economic revenue less the economic costs of the activity over some measurement period, where the period is based on the frequency of capital allocations and rebalancing. Costs may include funding costs, operating costs, bonuses, salaries, and other costs of doing business for the unit. Economic net income should also include a subtraction of *expected losses* as a cost to the business unit of normal operations. We use the adjective *economic* to emphasize that we are not talking about accounting net income; it is crucial to include off-balance-sheet items in this calculation, as we shall see.

The other component of RAROC is risk capital. As a measure of risk-adjusted return, RAROC is appealing because it can be consistently applied to and compared across business units, regardless of the nature of the businesses. RAROC provides a common yardstick, for example, to compare a derivatives desk with a trade finance or construction project. RAROC also has some very intuitive interpretations as the basis for measuring shareholder value added (SVA).

Hurdle Rates in an M&M World   It will help us understand what we are looking at if we return for a moment to the M&M world. In addition to the four M&M assumptions listed in Appendix A, assume all returns on projects, investments, and the like are distributed multivariate normal. In that case, all the firm's idiosyncratic risks will be diversified away and the only risk that will affect expected project returns is systematic risk.

If the capital asset pricing model (CAPM) holds, we saw in equation (5.7) in Chapter 5 that the expected return on any bundle of assets or cash flows can be expressed as

$$E(R) = R_f + \beta[E(R_m) - R_f] \qquad (\text{C.10})$$

where R_f is the risk free rate, R_m is the return on the market portfolio, and β is the covariance of returns on the assets or cash flows with the return on the market portfolio, reflecting how the systematic risk of the market is reflected in the return on the specific assets in question.

We know from Chapter 1 that the weighted average cost of capital (WACC) for the firm in the M&M case is determined solely by systematic risk and is equal to the expected return on the firm's assets. From equation (C.10), this implies that

$$E(R^A) = E(R^{WACC}) = R_f + \beta_{A,m}[E(R_m) - R_f] \qquad (C.11)$$

where

$$\beta_{A,m} = \frac{\sigma_{A,m}}{\sigma_m^2} = \frac{\rho_{A,m}\sigma_A\sigma_m}{\sigma_m^2} = \frac{\rho_{A,m}\sigma_A}{\sigma_m}$$

where $\sigma_{A,m}$ = covariance between asset returns and returns on the market

σ_m^2 = variance of returns on the market

σ_A = standard deviation of asset returns and returns on the market

ρ_m^2 = correlation between asset returns and returns on the market

Using these definitions, we can rewrite the CAPM relationship between the return on the firm's assets (excess of the risk free rate) and the excess return on the market as:

$$\frac{E(R^A) - R_f}{\rho_{A,m}\sigma_A} = \frac{E(R_m) - R_f}{\sigma_m} \qquad (C.12)$$

Equation (C.12) is sometimes called the *marginality condition* for the CAPM. It tells us that if we begin with a portfolio consisting of only investments in the market, we are indifferent at the margin between subtracting a small amount of the market and adding a small amount of the asset *in a proportion that satisfies equation (C.12)*. Specifically, we are willing to give up a small unit of market Sharpe ratio—the right-hand side of (C.12)—in exchange for a small unit of the asset, where the amount of the asset that makes us indifferent is proportional to the Sharpe ratio of the asset scaled by the inverse of the correlation between that asset and returns on the market.

Equation (C.12) can be rewritten in the form of a hurdle rate as in Chapter 5. Beginning with the market portfolio, we are willing to add a small amount of a new asset or project to our portfolio as long as

$$\frac{1}{\rho_{A,m}} SR^A \geq SR^m \qquad \text{(C3.13)}$$

where SR^A and SR^m denote the Sharpe ratios of our asset and the market, respectively, and where the Sharpe ratio is just the expected excess return divided by volatility.

In a CAPM world, the hurdle rate decision rule in equation (C.13) is a sufficient criterion to assess new investments. This hurdle rate tells us that the expected excess return on a new asset or project must exceed the WACC of the firm as determined by the CAPM. As long as we adhere to this, we will fully and accurately allocate our risk capital.

Firms using RAROC generally present equation (A3.13) in a slightly different form, so that any project should be taken if:

$$RAROC > E(R^{WACC}) \qquad \text{(C.14)}$$

where $RAROC$ is the RAROC of the project or business line being evaluated. If the risk-adjusted return on capital for the business line is above the firm's weighted average cost of capital, the decision rule says to accept the project.

What equation (C.14) essentially tells us in the context of the foregoing discussion is that capital at risk has no unique meaning when systematic risk is all that matters. Capital at risk *is* the capital required to support the systematic risk of a project. In a CAPM world, beta thus fully characterizes capital at risk.

RAROC and EVA Recall from Chapter 5 one of the decision rules we reviewed was based on economic profits or economic value added (EVA). Specifically, we saw that a project should be accepted if the EVA spread or residual return on capital is positive; that is,

$$ROI > E(R^{WACC}) \qquad \text{(C.15)}$$

where ROI in EVA-land is defined as

$$ROI = \frac{NOPAT - I(t)}{I(t)} \tag{C.16}$$

We can reinterpret equation (C.16) in EVA language as

$$RAROC = ROI = \frac{NOPAT - I(t)}{I(t)} = \frac{NOPAT - L^*}{L^*} \tag{C.17}$$

The investment in the project $I(t)$ is just the project's capital at risk in a RAROC world. In other words, if we define our investment in the project as the project's capital at risk, *the following three decision rules are perfectly equivalent:*

1. Accept a project when its ROI (defined in EVA terms, as opposed to book or cash flow terms) exceeds the firm's WACC.
2. Accept a project when its EVA economic profit is positive.
3. Accept a project when its RAROC exceeds the firm's WACC.

Hurdle Rates and the Deadweight Costs of Risk Capital—CAREVA

The RAROC framework and RAROC-like hurdle rates are fairly general and do not in and of themselves presume that the CAPM holds or that we live in a world where idiosyncratic risk is entirely diversified away. In other words, we can salvage the RAROC framework in a non-M&M world if we just ensure that capital at risk is defined to take account of the deadweight costs of capital.

Recall from equation (C.9) that we can write the NPV of a project that requires both a financial investment expenditure $I(t)$ and an investment at time t in risk capital of K^* as

$$V^A(t) = \sum_{j=1}^{T} \frac{E_t[X(t+j)]}{[1 + E(R^A)]^j} - I(t) - K^* \varphi^*(t) \tag{C.18}$$

Our capital budgeting criterion thus should be that equation (C.18) be positive in order for the project to add value to the firm. If we reexpress the discounted expected cash inflows and the investment expenditure in (C.18) as an "annualized NPV" (using the EVA language we adopted in Chapter 5), we can rewrite equation (C.18) as

$$\text{Expected Net Income} - K^* \varphi^*(t)[1 + E(R^A)] > 0 \qquad (C.19)$$

We might call this the *capital-at-risk*-adjusted *economic value added* or "CAREVA" of a project.

As we emphasized in Chapter 5, a big problem with implementing hurdle rates and value-based management systems is their heavy reliance on data and information technology (IT) systems. Especially if a firm is tracking its information in a purely accounting context, translating that data into the economic data required to compute EVA or SVA is not trivial.

We can see from equation (C.19) that we now face an even bigger problem. To get an estimate of CAREVA that is reliable, we need to come up with values to plug into the last term in addition to the other terms that we already had to estimate. Numerous different specific assumptions can be made that allow us to make more precise characterizations of any given firm's deadweight costs of risk capital, optimal risk capital structure, and the amount of risk capital to hold. The answer for one firm may not be the same as the answer for another. Some differences may arise from the way firms measure the risk capital required,[9] whereas other differences may arise from the precise method that a firm uses to compute the deadweight costs of contingent and paid-in risk capital. Even if two firms face substantially the same deadweight cost structure, *estimates* of those cost functions may differ.

Two different firms, moreover, may well specify similar deadweight costs in entirely different ways. In this appendix, we have only focused on specific examples of factors that give rise to deadweight costs. There are doubtless many others factors that we have not discussed. Just exactly how to come up with deadweight cost curves like those shown in Exhibit C.2 also remains an open question for individual firms to address, perhaps with the aid of specialized consultants.

In Exhibit C.2, for example, we assumed that the deadweight costs of contingent and paid-in risk capital were mutually interdependent through a common dependence on the amount of cash held by the firm. Yet we could imagine a situation where the amount of cash *does* affect the deadweight costs of paid-in capital but does *not* mitigate monitoring and adverse selection costs of contingent capital. We then would need to specify some measurable function to help us quantify both deadweight costs, and then to specifically map those estimates into a final estimate of $\varphi^*(t)$. Froot and Stein (1998) and Perold (2001) are but two examples of efforts to specify such functions.

Commonly Used Abbreviations

ABCP	Asset-backed commercial paper program
ABS	Asset-backed security
ADC	Adverse development cover
ADS	Asset default swap
APV	Adjusted present value
ART	Alternative risk transfer
BI	Business interruption (insurance)
BOT	Built-operate-transfer (project management model)
CaR	Capital at risk
CCA	Cash collateral account
CDO	Collateralized debt obligation
CDO^2	CDO of CDOs
CDS	Credit default swap
C/E	Credit enhancement
CFO	Collateralized fund obligation
CFROI	Cash flow return on investment
CLN	Credit-linked note
CMCDS	Constant maturity credit default swap
CPN	Capital-protected note
CSO	Collateralized synthetic obligation
D&O	Directors and officers (insurance)
DCF	Discounted cash flow
DSCR	Debt service coverage ratio
E&O	Errors and omissions
EDO	Equity default obligation
EDS	Equity default swap
ELN	Expected loss note
EM	Emerging market
EN	Extendable note
EPS	Earnings per share
EVA	Economic value added
FI	Fidelity (insurance)
HY	High yield
IBNR	Incurred but not reported

I/C	Interest coverage (ratio or test)
IP	Intellectual property
IRR	Internal rate of return
IT	Information technology
LAE	Loss adjustment expense
LGD	Loss given default
LOC or L/C	Letter of credit
LPT	Loss portfolio transfer
MBS	Mortgage-backed security
NOPAT	Net operating profits after taxes
NPV	Net present value
O&M	Operation and maintenance
O/C	Overcollateralization (amount, ratio, or test)
P&C	Property and casualty (insurance)
P&I	Principal and interest
PB	Primary beneficiary (of a VIE under FIN46R)
PE	Private equity
PI	Professional indemnity (insurance)
PV	Present value
QSPE	Qualified special purpose entity (FIN46R)
QST	Quota share treaty
RAL	Retrospective aggregate loss cover
ROA	Return on assets
ROE	Return on equity
ROI	Return on investment
RROC	Residual return on capital
RXL	Retrospective excess of loss cover
SCDO	Synthetic collateralized debt obligation
SME	Small-to-midsize enterprise
SST	Surplus Share Treaty
STSCDO	Single-tranche collateralized debt obligation
SVA	Shareholder value added
UPR	Unearned premium reserve
VI	Variable interest
VIE	Variable interest entity
WACC	Weighted average cost of capital
XOL	Excess of loss
XS	Excess of loss attachment point—A XS B is $A of coverage above lower attachment point $B, and the upper attachment point is A + B

Notes

CHAPTER 1 Real and Financial Capital

1. Jensen and Meckling (1976) first described the firm as a "nexus of contracts." Numerous other depictions of the firm can also be found, of course.
2. Myers (1977) draws the distinction between "assets in place" and "growth opportunities," both of which correspond to our definition of a real asset. Think of a growth opportunity just as the opportunity to acquire or develop a real asset in the future.
3. "Use value," of course, also corresponds to "market value" or "exchange value," to use the classical economic terminology.
4. We adopt the terminology suggested by Myers (1977).
5. The governance rights of debt holders increase as the firm approaches insolvency.
6. The reason for the "and/or" here is that some debt securities are originally issued at a discount and then appreciate over time to their face value, thus embedding the interest in the original discounted price. Other debt securities pay interest explicitly.
7. As we will see in Chapter 14, corporate debt with a floating interest rate is actually fixed-rate debt plus a derivatives contract.
8. Suspending a preferred dividend may well get you downgraded, however.
9. Even in this case, the term "junk bond" is misleading. Better to call it "high-risk venture debt."
10. Exceptions tend to be related to corporate actions or to regulations. As an example of the former, firms that amass more than a certain amount of an open corporation's stock must declare their intent to initiate a bid for control of the company if that is their goal. As an example of the latter, bank holding companies and their affiliates in the United States are not allowed to hold more than a certain percentage of the outstanding stock an open corporation has issued.
11. Subtract $A(T) - FV$ from the expression and then add it back to both terms in the maximand and you can see that the equations are the same.
12. This depends very critically on the kinds of costs reflected in our calculation of net asset value.

CHAPTER 2 Risk and Risk Management

1. See Outreville (1998).
2. Our categorization of financial risk is based on the Global Derivatives Study Group (1993). See also Culp (2001).

3. Settlement risk is sometimes called "Herstatt risk," so named from the failure of Bankhaus Herstatt in Germany in 1974. The convention in most foreign currency markets is for settlement two days after a spot transaction is consummated or a forward contract matures. A number of New York banks had initiated payments to Herstatt on their side of a bunch of spot and forward currency trades, and Herstatt failed *after* those payments were initiated from New York but *before* any reciprocal payments were initiated from Germany. The New York banks suffered considerable principal losses.
4. This list is a hybrid from several sources, but mainly Outreville (1998) and Doherty (2000).
5. These examples are based on the sample data entry form for the British Bankers' Association operational risk and loss database.
6. For those who have read my 2004 book, "risk neutralization" here represents an amalgamation of what I called "consolidation" and "reduction." The discussion in Culp (2004) is significantly more detailed as well.
7. A firm might not act *entirely* on its own. Consultants, for example, may come in handy. The important point here is that a firm engaged in risk neutralization as we are defining the term is not reducing its risks by transferring them to another firm.
8. J. Diamond (1997) and F. L. Smith (1992, 2003) provide additional interesting historical examples.
9. Any counterparty to any financial transaction can always sue to try to get its money back, but this is a different kind of risk than an *ex ante* refusal to pay.

CHAPTER 3   Leverage

1. For a survey of the major optimal capital structure theories, see Harris and Raviv (1991).
2. For a summary, see Swoboda and Zechner (1995).
3. We could also imagine that $V_j(t)$ and $V_k^F(t)$ are two different firms j and k, provided they each hold identical assets.
4. This analysis is based on the example given in Brealey and Myers (2000).
5. Miller (1977) argues, however, that the optimal capital structure choices depicted in Table 3.1 do not represent an equilibrium and that the original M&M result of capital structure irrelevance in fact still holds under taxation as long as taxes on equity are well below taxes on debt and all firms face the same marginal corporate tax rate.
6. See, for example, Davis and Pacelle (2001).
7. Formally, $F(A \leq Y) < F(A \leq Z)$ for any $Y < Z$ because $F(A)$ is a strictly nondecreasing function, where $F(A)$ is the cumulative distribution function corresponding to density $f(A)$, or

$$F(A \leq X) = \int_0^X f(A)dA$$

for any X.

8. See Myers (1977). See Culp (2001, 2002a) for a summary of the Myers model.
9. For an analysis of bond covenants, see Smith and Warner (1979).
10. Note that $B(t) \equiv B(L(t))$ and $C(t) \equiv C(L(t))$.

CHAPTER 4　Adverse Selection and Corporate Financing Decisions

1. See, for example, Masulis and Korwar (1986), Smith (1986a), and Eckbo and Masulis (1995).
2. See Linn and Pinegar (1988).
3. See, for example, Vermaelen (1981).
4. See Masulis (1980).
5. See, for example, Smith (1986a).
6. See, for example, Mikkelson and Partch (1986).
7. See, for example, Shyam-Sunder (1991).
8. See, for example, Eckbo (1986), Smith (1986a), and Fama and French (1998). Shyam-Sunder (1991) finds that the fact that debt issues do not produce a stock price response statistically distinguishable from zero holds regardless of the risk of the debt.
9. This is at least one plausible interpretation of the results in Fama and French (1998).
10. See Palmer (2003).
11. See Diamond (1984, 1991).
12. See James (1987).
13. See Diamond (1991).
14. See, for example, Smith (1986a).
15. A key assumption in Ross's analysis is that firms' return distributions are distinguished by "first order stochastic dominance." Otherwise, it would not necessarily be true that better firms have lower expected financial distress costs *at all debt levels.*

CHAPTER 5　Capital Budgeting, Project Selection, and Performance Evaluation

1. Mutually exclusive projects also necessitate choosing among competing projects and have a similar effect as capital rationing.
2. See the essays in Part I of Culp and Niskanen (2003)—especially Bassett and Storie (2003).
3. There are numerous variations on this theme—for example, including interest in the numerator.
4. See, for example, Rappaport (1998).
5. See, for example, Bassett and Storie (2003).

6. Portions of this section appeared in Culp (2001), although the section has been modified and greatly shortened.
7. The NPV rule says that firms should accept *all* positive NPV projects, so we don't want to get into the habit of choosing projects by comparing NPVs and then simply picking the highest. But the example here is an important exception—namely, when the two projects are mutually exclusive and cannot both be chosen. Because we are talking about the same project accepted at two different times, we cannot possibly accept both, and thus can compare the two NPVs directly to decide what to do.
8. *Other People's Money* was a successful play before it was a film, but it was DeVito who made the buggy whip speech a classic finance speech in film right up there with Michael Douglas's "Greed is good" speech in *Wall Street* and Alec Baldwin's "Do I have your attention?" speech in *Glengarry Glen Ross.*
9. For an excellent discussion of the use of real options at Airbus Industrie and one of the best real options case studies around, see Stonier (1999).
10. This assumes that beyond the forecast period, the firm invests only in zero NPV projects and has no growth opportunities. This is not a very realistic assumption on its own, but becomes especially troublesome if our forecast period is chosen to be the useful life of a project—which may or may not correspond to the "value growth" period of the firm. For now, however, let's just assume T represents both the life of the project and the firm's value growth period, after which the firm's growth stabilizes at a constant expected annual cash flow.
11. EVA® Stern Stewart & Co.
12. CFROI® Holt Value Associates, LP.

CHAPTER 6   Risk Transfer

1. In an M&M world, earnings are not relevant because the symmetric information assumption means that everyone already perceives corporate profits on the same basis. And cash flows are not relevant because firms can also incur new debt to create liquidity at a fair market price.

CHAPTER 7   Risk Finance

1. The "cover period" is likely to be a much shorter time period than the maturity of the debt issued to fund the retention.
2. A firm may use risk finance *improperly* to try and disguise a loss, but this is an inappropriate and illegitimate use of risk finance. Accordingly, we do not consider this a benefit of risk finance. On the contrary, we consider it an *abuse* of risk finance. We will revisit this issue again in Chapter 24.

3. The theoretical argument is advanced especially well by Froot, Scharfstein, and Stein (1993), and an excellent practical version of the same argument can be found in Lewent and Kearney (1990).
4. This example is based on an analogous one presented in Froot, Scharfstein, and Stein (1994).

CHAPTER 8   Insurance

1. An insurable interest is not always required for life insurance, provided the insured gives written consent to defining a different beneficiary.
2. See Borch (1990) and Outreville (1998).
3. See Outreville (1998).
4. In life insurance, reserves are known as policy or mathematical reserves. Because the bulk of this book does not involve life products, readers are referred to Outreville (1998) for a discussion of life reserve management, which is omitted here for brevity.

CHAPTER 9   Reinsurance

1. Indeed, reinsurance is sometimes called re*assurance*, and the purchaser of reinsurance called the re*assured*. See Kiln (1991).
2. The reinsurer in a quota share treaty usually also bears a fixed proportion of any loss adjustment expenses. See Kiln (1991) and Phifer (1996).
3. This is extremely unusual. One reason surplus treaties are used is to allow the retention to vary by policy.

CHAPTER 10   Credit Insurance and Financial Guaranties

1. See Remy and Grieger (2003).
2. The reason for the inability of most insurers to make payments extremely rapidly (e.g., within 24 hours of receiving a claim) is their lack of access to central bank payment systems.
3. Culp (2004) explains the mechanics of achieving irrevocability and finality in fund transfers in more detail.
4. New York Insurance Law §6902.
5. New York Insurance Law §1102(b).
6. New York Insurance Law §1106(f).
7. New York Insurance Law §1113(a)(16).
8. New York Insurance Law §6901(a).

9. State of New York Insurance Department, *Opinion Re "Lease Bond" as Financial Guaranty Insurance* (May 4, 2004).
10. See *JPMorgan Chase Bank v. Liberty Mutual et al.*, U.S.D.C. S.D.N.Y. 01 Civ. 11523 (JSR) Amended.
11. See *Defendants' Memorandum of Law in Opposition to Plaintiff Motion for Summary Judgment* (February 11, 2002).
12. The facts of this case are based on the excellent article by Ballantine (2001b).
13. Quoted in Ballantine (2001b), p. 29.
14. Howard (2001).
15. Quoted in Ballantine (2001b), p. 29.
16. See "CSFB and JLT Join Film Dispute," *Reactions* (September 2001).
17. Standard & Poor's, *Financial Enhancement Ratings Help Reconcile the Cultural Differences Between Multiline Insurers and Financial Guarantors* (April 24, 2002).
18. Margin calls on a securities exchange are designed to reduce the settlement risk on transactions that have been executed but have not settled. In a T+3 settlement system, for example, margin calls would cover some of the replacement cost risk that could arise if the price of a stock rises (or falls) after a trade and the seller (or buyer) defaults. The Zürich coverage is intended to substitute for such margin calls.

   Margin deposits required to be posted on futures exchanges like the Sydney Futures Exchange, by contrast, are performance bonds designed to mitigate the exposure in the event of a default on a futures or options transaction. Because of the different nature of the risk exposure of the clearinghouse, guarantees provided to futures and options exchanges usually supplement rather than replace margin requirements.

CHAPTER 11   Derivatives

1. Much of this section is adapted from Culp (2001, 2002a) and Culp and Overdahl (1996).
2. Exchange-traded derivatives have a variety of definitions under the law, but these definitions have evolved over time as a contentious amalgam of international case law and national statutes and regulations. The definition of "futures" under the law is anything but clear.
3. The "building block" approach was pioneered by Smithson (1987). The "cash flow diagrams" in this chapter are also based on Smithson's (1987) framework, which is now virtually "industry-standard."
4. In practice, the "trade date" may be the date on which the terms of the transaction are *confirmed* rather than first negotiated.
5. Technically, the put writer's liability is limited by the fact that the asset price cannot fall below zero, whereas the call writer's liability is *truly* unlimited. For most assets, however, the probability of a price decline to zero is negligible.
6. A "realized" price may be restricted to certain types of prices (e.g., closing prices, transaction prices, etc.).

CHAPTER 12   Credit Derivatives and Credit-Linked Notes

1. Fitch Ratings Special Report, *Global Credit Derivatives Survey* (September 7, 2004).
2. Culp (2004) explores the distinctions between over-the-counter and exchange-traded derivatives.
3. In some cases, the calculation may specify a different "strike price" than the par amount of the reference security.
4. See Whetten and Jin (2005).
5. For a good overview of this issue, see Lucas and Thomas (2003).

CHAPTER 13   The Structuring Process

1. This and later similar diagrams relating loss distributions to capital structure and credit ratings are inspired by the graphic design adopted by Merrill Lynch in much of its structured products research literature. See, for example, Batchvarov, Davletova, and Davies (2004) and Hawkins (2004). In this book, I have modified the graphs to suit the specific examples and applications being discussed, but credit for the "idea" behind these and other similar graphs belongs to Merrill Lynch and the authors just noted.

CHAPTER 14   Hybrids, Convertibles, and Structured Notes

1. See Lerner (2000b).
2. See, for example, Chapman Tripp (1998).
3. BKD *Financial Alert* (March 28, 2005).
4. McEntee (2004) offers a good discussion of the various benefits of TruPS for BHCs.
5. PERCS have so many different names and acronyms that it's hard to keep track. Indeed, almost all the products discussed in this chapter have a large number of potential names.
6. Portions of this section rely heavily on Culp, Furbush, and Kavanagh (1994) and Culp and Mackay (1997).
7. More detailed discussions of interest-rate-linked notes can be found in any of several books on structured notes—for example, Knop (2002).
8. Rate swaps are "settled in arrears." The floating interest payable on any settlement date thus was the floating rate *set* on the *previous* reset/settlement date. Consider, for example, a swap that settles semiannually each June 15 and December 15 between 2004 and 2008. Interest payable on December 15, 2008, on the floating leg of the swap thus will be the six-month LIBOR prevailing on June 15, 2008 (and corresponding to a CD that matures on December 15, 2008).
9. See Smith (1988).
10. For details, see Falloon (1993).

CHAPTER 15   Contingent Capital

1. Portions of this chapter are drawn from Culp (2002b).
2. If the contingent capital facility calls for a hybrid or equity-like capital infusion, the facility may need to specify alternative redemption methods for the capital provider. For example, the facility may contain a provision that allows the capital supplier/contingent investor to convert its financial capital claim on the borrowing firm into traded securities issued by the borrowing firm, thereby facilitating the sale of those securities if the investor so desires. If the underlying contingent capital is straight debt, special redemption provisions are not necessary; the capital provider is just repaid when the debt matures.
3. As discussed in Chapter 7, providers of these facilities will anticipate their exercise on a postloss basis and will price the programs accordingly. The use of contingent capital for preloss finance thus is not necessarily a way to save money on the new security issue, although locking in a financing cost and eliminating the *risk* of obtaining postloss finance can lead to an increase in the value of the firm for other reasons. Again, see Chapter 7.
4. This first trigger condition is not usually defined as an explicit part of the committed capital agreement. Nevertheless, the firm that has bought an option on paid-in capital will clearly not exercise that option unless the intrinsic value is positive. If the firm can obtain equivalent capital more cheaply from some other source, it will simply let the committed capital option expire out-of-the-money and worthless. Assuming optimal exercise behavior on the part of contingent capital purchasers, we can view the option's "moneyness" as functionally equivalent to a first trigger.
5. See Mayers (2000).
6. See Froot (1999).
7. The structures shown are those reported by S&P in Mischel et al. (2004).
8. *Aon Insights* (Edition 4, 1999).
9. This section merely summarizes the salient features of this deal. For a more in-depth analysis of the structure, see Lane (1999).
10. The reported loss numbers on which these exposures were based was the loss reported by *Sigma*, a publication (and loss index) of Swiss Re. In most of the risk categories, losses on the Reliance III notes were based on a schedule rather than a complete loss of 20 percent principal if the trigger was activated. Property losses, for example, were tied to the 20 percent principal at risk in the optionable note as follows: a 5 percent principal reduction for any loss in 1998 over $6.5 billion, with the proportion of principal reduction increasing up to a maximum of 20 percent for a US$15 billion or greater loss. See Lane (1999) for all the details.
11. Do not confuse this with a *letter* of credit, discussed in Chapter 10.
12. A typical credit line, moreover, may include a material adverse change (MAC) clause that prevents the borrower from drawing on the line if it has experienced a material adverse change in its financial condition or credit quality.
13. The RBC deal is discussed in Banham (2001).

14. The C$200 million would result in Swiss Re owning about 1 percent of the firm's total equity if the facility was exercised, which means that neither Swiss Re nor RBC had to worry that Swiss Re would be running the company because of RBC's exercise of the facility. The small size of the deal relative to RBC's total equity also kept moral hazard problems to a minimum.
15. Banham (2001).
16. The details of the Michelin deal are discussed in "Swiss Re and SocGen in $1bn Loan," *Reactions* (September 2000); Schenk (2000); and Banham (2001).
17. See "Allied-Lyons Trombone Issue to Accommodate EC Ruling," *Practical Law Company* (May 1994).
18. For some examples, see Credit Lyonnais, *A Practical Guide to Reverse Convertibles on Shares and Indices* (2002).
19. See Topatigh (1999).
20. The descriptive parts of this case are based on the fascinating article by Chacko, Tufano, and Verter (2002). The authors analyze the merits and drawbacks of Cephalon's program in much more detail than we do here, and interested readers would certainly find a review of their article a worthy expenditure of time.

CHAPTER 16 Securitization

1. Fees and expenses of the SPE are differentiated as being either *senior* or *subordinated*. Senior fees and expenses are paid off the top of the cash flow waterfall on the underlying assets. These fees and expenses might include fees and expenses for the trustee, structuring agent, custodian, law firm, rating agency, and so on, as well as any fees associated with external credit and liquidity risk management. Subordinated fees, by contrast, are sometimes paid to those who assist the structuring process on an incentive basis, such as a structuring agent responsible for selecting collateral across multiple originators that expects a portion of its fees to be based on its capacity to select superior credits for the securitization structure.
2. When a single firm provides liquidity and credit support, that firm runs the risk that it may have to consolidate the structure. See Chapter 30 by Forrester and Neuhausen.
3. If you want, you can also assume various other features we have discussed (e.g., diversion of excess spread into I/C and O/C reserves, an asset swap to smooth any cash flow and maturity mismatches, etc.). But we don't really need to complicate matters with these other features.

CHAPTER 17 Cash Collateralized Debt Obligations

1. Moody's, *2004 U.S. CDO Review/2005 Preview* (February 1, 2005).
2. Murphy (2003).

3. The chart shows only traditional CDOs and omits synthetic CDOs.
4. All of the exhibits in this chapter are simplified. We show only those parts of the deal that are essential to understanding the basic structure of the deal.
5. This assumes the other credit enhancements are applied to the cash flow waterfall between the residual and subordinated tranche. If they instead enhance the senior tranche directly, we can no longer interpret the C/E as a pure deductible—just the residual plays that role. But we can still interpret it as a *retention* by the originator, albeit at a higher loss layer than the deductible.
6. Readers should note that rating agency guidance for this and other structures can be obtained by the general public through the S&P, Moody's, and Fitch web sites. In addition, Goodman and Fabozzi (2002) and the essays in Perraudin (2004) provide especially good summaries of the various rating agency criteria for different types of CDOs.
7. Do not confuse the terms *cash CDO* and *cash flow CDO*. The former is any CDO in which the collateral assets are acquired with a cash payment. The latter is a specific type of arbitrage CDO in which cash P&I on the collateral pool are used to finance the interest and principal waterfall (as opposed to liquidations of collateral on the market).

CHAPTER 18 Synthetic Collateralized Debt Obligations

1. Note that the x-axis labels stop when the total loss reaches around 50 percent. In fact, the capital structure of the SPE in a fully funded instrument extends all the way up to 100 percent of the portfolio, despite not being shown. In future graphs when we wish to indicate that the capital structure covers losses up to 100 percent, we do as we have done here and extend the capital structure up to the arrow on the x-axis (instead of terminating it somewhere corresponding to the drawn distribution).
2. Fitch Ratings, *Single-Tranche Synthetic CDOs* (June 13, 2003).
3. If not AAA-rated, then it is AAA-equivalent quality.
4. See Hay (1999).
5. Hay (1999).
6. Fitch Ratings, *Single-Tranche Synthetic CDOs* (June 13, 2003).
7. Many originators delta hedge their retained exposure on these deals. This allows them to reduce hedging costs, but it does create basis risk in the hedges.
8. See Murphy (2003) and D. Smith (2003).
9. This section is based on the insightful commentary in Forrester (2003).

CHAPTER 19 Structured Synthetic Hybrids

1. For the details, see Weidner, De Melo, and Williams (2005).
2. See Moody's Investors Service, CEDO I Plc Pre-Sale Report (April 8, 2005).
3. See Weidner, De Melo, and Williams (2005).

4. See Moody's Investors Service, Chrome Funding Limited ACEO Series Zoom-3, Pre-Sale Report (September 2, 2004).
5. See Davletova, Batchvarov, and Davies (2004).
6. See Weidner, De Melo, and Williams (2005).
7. The mechanics and analysis of this structure are based on Batchvarov, Davletova, and Davies (2004) and Davletova, Batchvarov, and Davies (2004).
8. Assuming equal recoveries under the EDS and CDS, an EDS is exactly equal to an insolvency-triggered CDS if the EDS has a zero strike price.

CHAPTER 20 Securitizing Private Equity and Hedge Funds

1. This list of hedge fund strategy types is not intended to be exhaustive.
2. This deal is analyzed in more detail in L'Habitant (2002).
3. See Forrester (2005).
4. See the pre-sale credit reports from the three agencies for more details.

CHAPTER 21 Project and Principal Finance

1. For details, see Standard & Poor's, Eiffel FTC, Pre-Sale Report (October 19, 2004).
2. For details, see Standard & Poor's, Essential Public Infrastructure Capital PLC, Pre-Sale Report (September 24, 2004).
3. See Heberle (2003).
4. Standard & Poor's, Punch Taverns Finance PLC Transaction Update (May 3, 2005).
5. See Standard & Poor's, The Main Legal and Analytical Rating Issues of Pub Securitizations (October 11, 2004).
6. See Standard & Poor's, South East Water (Finance) Ltd., Pre-Sale Report (July 2, 2004).
7. The theory here was that rate-regulated businesses like water had growth rates comparable to the inflation rate.
8. Tax issues also played a significant role in the Bowie bond issue.
9. Questions about moral hazard inevitably come up here—for example, if Mr. Bowie had decided to criticize his prior works as inferior to new works. But this seems a long stretch; few artists would have much incentive to deliberately devalue the value of their prior artistry. Quite the contrary, it seems.
10. See the essays contained in Culp and Niskanen (2003) for more details.
11. See *JPMorgan Chase Bank v. Liberty Mutual et al.*, U.S.D.C. S.D.N.Y. 01 Civ. 11523 (JSR) Amended.
12. See *Defendants' Memorandum of Law in Opposition to Plaintiff Motion for Summary Judgment* (February 11, 2002).

CHAPTER 22   Risk Securitizations and Insurance-Linked Notes

1. No partially funded risk securitizations have been done . . . yet.
2. See, for example, Lane (1998b); Parkin (1998); and Canter, Cole, and Sandor (1999).
3. See, for example, Gerling Global Financial Products, Inc. (2000).
4. See Bernero (1998).
5. The details of these transactions are discussed in Bernero (1998).
6. The use of a parametric trigger in a cat bond was pioneered by Goldman Sachs in a November 1997 cat bond issue for Tokio Marine.
7. For the details, see Lane and Beckwith (2003).
8. The trustee also has a reserve requirement to which surpluses must be applied in the event the collateral account becomes deficient relative to claims obligations to TMCC.
9. Bernero (1998).
10. Most of this section is based on Culp (1996), a small portion of which appeared also in Culp (2001).
11. Over time, the CBOT has considered a number of such insurance-based derivatives contracts. See Cox and Schwebach (1992), D'Arcy and France (1992), and Niehaus and Mann (1992).
12. Recall that because the premium pool for the ISO index is known at time t, the change in the loss index is the only factor that affects the settlement price of the futures contract. A 5 percent increase in the loss index results in a 5 percent increase in the value of the futures contract.

CHAPTER 23   Captives, Protected Cells, and Mutuals

1. We explored contingent debt in Chapter 15 as a form of postloss risk finance. Although usually offered by (re)insurance companies, this is not strictly an insurance product and thus was discussed in the structured finance section of the book. Nevertheless, corporations seeking postloss risk finance should remember that contingent capital is a very good alternative to the structures discussed herein. Also, contingent capital can be used *in conjunction with* the solutions discussed in this chapter quite effectively.
2. See Outreville (1998) and Trieschmann, Gustavson, and Hoyt (2001).
3. See, for example, Myers (2000).
4. Although the notion that captives could serve as separately capitalized "risk management service centers" for their sponsors, actual captive use remains largely confined to insurance solutions.
5. See Myers (2000).
6. All of the captive diagrams used here are based on those presented in the marketing materials prepared by Zürich Financial's Corporate Customer Financial

and Risk Services (Zürich CH-8085, www.zurichbusiness.ch/art). See also Wöhrmann (1998).
7. See Kloman (1998).
8. See Wöhrmann and Bürer (2001) for a discussion of PCCs.
9. Zürich Financial, for example, requires a minimum premium payment of CHF250,000 per annum in its Rent-a-Captive program. See the previously cited (note 6) marketing materials for Zürich Financial.
10. See Sullivan (1995).
11. See Rogers, Sargeant, and Osborne (1996).
12. In turn, the law of large numbers tells us that the mean of the (approximately normal) distribution of the sum of a large number of i.i.d. random variables is the same as the mean of the underlying distributions from which the samples were drawn.
13. See Sullivan (1995).

CHAPTER 24   Finite Risk

1. See Dyson (2001).
2. Shimpi (2001) and Swiss Re, *Sigma* No. 5 (1997).
3. See Carter, Lucas, and Ralph (2000), Gerling Global Financial Products, Inc. (2000), and Shimpi (2001).
4. This represents a contingent asset that may cause the insurance purchaser some tax and accounting headaches.
5. Background for this example was obtained from Lenckus (2000).
6. The settlement is still subject to a federal court approval.
7. See Gerling Global Financial Products, Inc. (2000).
8. Ibid.
9. For a discussion of Frontier's situation and the finite structure it adopted, see "Frontier Gets a New Lifeline," *Reactions* (November 2000).
10. This case is based on information presented in Raybin (2003).

CHAPTER 25   Multiline and Multitrigger Insurance Structures

1. Part II of Culp (2001) discusses the benefits and practices of EWRM.
2. This terminology and the ensuing discussion are based on Hoffman (1998).
3. I first encountered this analogy to the London Underground in a presentation by Tom Skwarek. He deserves full credit for connecting "mind the gap" to ART forms.
4. See, for example, Lonkevich (1999).
5. See Banham (2000).
6. Ibid.

7. See Young (1996).
8. See Banham (2000).
9. Gerling Global Financial Products, Inc. (2000).
10. This example is adapted from Schienvar (2003).
11. Quoted in Butt (2003), p. 21.
12. This section is based on information contained in a Case Studies document published in 2002 by Zurich Corporate Solutions.
13. AIG *Risk Finance Review* Vol. 1, No. 1 (Spring 2002).
14. Ibid.
15. This case study is based on McGinnis (2004).
16. This example is similar in spirit to the one presented in Schön, Bochicchio, and Wolfram (1998).
17. For a description, see Imfeld (2000).
18. See Banham (1999).
19. This section is based on information contained in a Case Studies document published in 2002 by Zurich Corporate Solutions.
20. FASB, *Statement 133 Implementation Issue No. B26* (2001).
21. See also Zurich Corporate Solutions, *Flash Report* (April 2001).

CHAPTER 27   The Emerging Role of Patent Law in Risk Finance

1. Merges (1999).
2. See Culp (2001), Ch. 26.
3. The '045 patent is described at Investors Guaranty Fund, Ltd.'s home page at http://styx.forgedesign.com/domains/igf/pages/home/home.html.
4. The quoted language was found at www.financialpatents.com/Whyus.html.
5. *Diamond v. Diehr*, 450 U.S. 175, 182 (1981) (quoting a 1952 Senate Report)
6. The patent laws contain severe restrictions on the patentability of inventions that were in public use or on sale during times prior to application. For example, one U.S. District Court recently held that a company's demonstrations of its computer software to nonemployees without assurances of confidentiality could be such a public use.

CHAPTER 28   Critical Distinctions between Weather Derivatives and Insurance

1. Weather risks are based on daily climate fluctuations rather than unexpected events, such as hurricanes, major storms, or other catastrophes.
2. Chicago Mercantile Exchange, *Weather Futures & Options on Futures*, available at www.cme.com/trading/prd/env/abtwthder2766.html web site visited February 10, 2005. Many industries, including energy utilities and distributors, are sensitive to weather conditions.

3. Cal. Ins. Code §1633 (2001).
4. Conn. Gen. Stat. §38a-704 (2001). The penalty for acting as an insurance producer without a license is a fine of not more than $500 or imprisonment of not more than three months or both. An "insurance producer" is defined at Conn. Gen. Stat. § 38a-702(1) (2001).
5. 18 Del. C. §505(c) (2001).
6. 18 Del. C. §505(a) (2001).
7. 18 Del. C. §505(b) (2001).
8. New York CLS Ins. §109(a) (2002).
9. New York CLS Ins. §1102(a) (2002).
10. 215 ILCS 5/500-15(a) (2002).
11. Exchange-traded weather futures and options on futures began trading at the Chicago Mercantile Exchange (CME) in September of 1999. CME weather contracts are currently offered for more than 20 cities in the United States, Europe, and Japan. See "CME Achieves Record Weather Futures Volume," CME News Release, December 20, 2004, available at www.cme.com web site visited February 10, 2005. In October of 2001, the London International Financial Futures and Options Exchange announced that it would offer exchange trading in weather futures and currently offers weather contracts for London, Paris and Berlin. See Euronext.liffe Weather Indices, available at www.liffeweather.com web site (visited February 11, 2005).
12. When addressing temperature changes, HDDs and CDDs are typically used as the way to measure how far a temperature varies from the designated baseline over the time period specified in the contract. Because many people set their thermostats at 65 degrees Fahrenheit, 65 degrees is usually the baseline used for HDDs and CDDs.
13. A commodity is defined in CEA §1(a)(4) as certain enumerated agricultural products and "all goods and articles . . . and services, rights, and interests in which contracts for future delivery are presently or in the future dealt in."
14. New CEA §2(g) was enacted by the Commodity Futures Modernization Act of 2000, which was signed into law on December 21, 2000.
15. An eligible swap participant includes banks and certain financial institutions, insurance companies, certain employee benefit plans, certain entities registered with either the Securities and Exchange Commission or the CFTC, and corporations with total assets exceeding $10 million or with net worth of $1 million.
16. 67 Fed. Reg. 64067 (October 17, 2002).
17. The "insured" must be able to demonstrate that it has both an economic and a legal connection to the asset or subject matter of the risk. Financial Services Authority, "Discussion Paper: Cross-Sector Risk Transfers" (May 2002) at Annex B1.
18. Because most business relationships involve risks and the assumption of risk, the key here is that an insurance company spreads or distributes the risks among a pool of contracts covering similar risks. See Amerco v. Comm'r, 96 T.C. 18 (1991), aff'd 979 F. 2d 192 (9th Cir. 1992). See also Comm'r v. Treganowan, 183 F. 2d 288 (2nd Cir. 1950).

19. See, for example, Union Labor Life Ins. Co. v. Pireno, 458 U.S. 119, 128-29 (1982), and Group Life & Health Insurance Co. v. Royal Drug Co., 440 U.S. 205, 210-17 (1979).

20. New York Ins. Law §1101(a)(1) (LEXIS through Ch. 14, 3/16/2004, with the exception of Chs. 1–3 and 12). Key to this definition is the notion that the insured will be adversely affected by the fortuitous event specified in the contract. In other words, insurance requires the establishment of actual loss.

21. NYID, Letter to F. Sedgwick Brown re: Catastrophe Options, dated June 25, 1998, available at www.ins.state.ny.us/nyins.htm web site visited April 13, 2004.

22. NYID, "Weather Financial Instruments (Derivatives, Hedges, Etc.)," *Office of General Counsel Informal Opinion* (February 15, 2000), available at www.ins.state.ny.us/rg000205.htm web site visited April 13, 2004.

23. The Weather Derivatives Opinion points out that NYID has not ruled out the "possibility" that a contract or transaction might have unique circumstances (not addressed in this opinion) so that "NYID would deem certain weather derivatives to be insurance contracts."

24. NYID, letter dated June 16, 2000, addressing a credit default option facility, available at www.ins.state.ny.us/nyins.htm web site visited April 13, 2004.

25. See, for example, Cal. Ins. Code §22 (LEXIS through 2004 Supplement); Conn. Gen. Stat. §38a-1(10) (LEXIS through January 6, 2003 Special Session); *Griffin Systems, Inc. v. Washburn*, 505 N.E. 2d 1121 (Ill App. Ct. 1987); Ind. Code §27-1-2-3(a) (LEXIS through 2004 Special Session); Neb. Rev. Stat. Ann. §44-102 (LEXIS through 2003 Regular Session).

26. Crop Insurance Working Group, Property and Casualty Committee, NAIC, "Weather Financial Instruments (Temperature): Insurance or Capital Markets Products?," September 2, 2003, working draft.

27. The NAIC is a quasi-trade association for insurance regulators. Its mission is to assist insurance regulators to protect the public interest; promote competitive markets; facilitate the fair and equitable treatment of insurance consumers; promote the reliability, solvency and financial solidity of insurance institutions; and support and improve state regulation of insurance. The NAIC mission statement is available at www.naic.org/about/mission.htm web site visited January 25, 2004.

28. Crop Insurance Working Group, Property and Casualty Committee, NAIC, Weather Financial Instruments (Temperature): Insurance or Capital Markets Products?," September 2, 2003, working draft, at 2.

29. Ibid., at 8.

30. Ibid.

31. Ibid.

32. See "Weather Risk Firms Hit Back," *Insurance Day* (January 30, 2004); Meg Fletcher, "Status of Weather Hedges Debated," *Business Insurance* (February 9, 2004), at 4. See also, Letter from Valerie B. Cooper and Brian D. O'Hearne, Weather Risk Management Association, to Rob Esson and Ernst N. Csiszar, NAIC, dated January 23, 2004, available at www.wrma.org web site visited April 13, 2004; letter from Robert G. Pickel, ISDA, to Ernst N. Csiszar and Robert Esson, NAIC, dated February 23, 2004, available at www.isda.org web

site visited April 13, 2004; letter from Mike Moriarty, NYID, to Rob Esson, NAIC, dated January 22, 2004.

33. The International Swaps and Derivatives Association (ISDA) has developed standard agreements that have been widely adopted by parties to derivative contracts. The ISDA website is at www.isda.org. ISDA Master Agreements that are typically used to document weather derivatives transactions include the 1992 Master Agreement (Multicurrency-Cross Border) and the 1992 ISDA Master Agreement (Local Currency—Single Jurisdiction). The 2002 ISDA Master Agreement is increasingly being used. Use of an ISDA Master Agreement is not required, however, and the parties to derivatives contracts can enter into customized (often referred to as "home grown") agreements.

34. Confirmation of OTC Weather Index Swap Transaction; Confirmation of OTC Weather Index (Put Option/Floor); Confirmation of OTC Weather Index (Call Option/Cap); Form of Weather Index Appendix for CPD (Critical Precipitation Day) Weather Index; Form of Weather Index Appendix for CDD (Cooling Degree Day) Weather Index; Form of Weather Index Appendix for HDD (Heating Degree Day) Weather Index; Form of Definitions Appendix for Weather Index Derivative Confirmation, all available at www.isda.org. Sample confirmations for weather derivatives can also be found at the web site for the Weather Risk Management Association at www.wrma.org.

35. 11 U.S.C. §§362(b)(17) and 560.

36. 11 U.S.C. §362(b)(6).

37. For a detailed discussion of possible tax treatments of weather derivatives, see Andrea S. Kramer, *Financial Products: Taxation, Regulation, and Design*, 3d ed. (CCH, 2000), at §§6.07, 35.03[D], and 80.05. See also Andrea S. Kramer and William R. Pomierski, "The Tax Angle on Weather Derivatives," *Risk Desk* (October 2001), at 1.

38. IRC §1221(b)(2)(A)(iii).

39. Weather Risk Management Association, Comments to the Treasury Regarding Proposed Hedging Regulations, Code Section 1221(a)(7), April 25, 2001, available at http://64.125.144.31/librarydocs/bc51_wrma/public/file110.doc web site visited February 10, 2005.

40. IRC §162.

41. IRC §4371.

42. See Helvering v. Le Gierse, 312 U.S. 531, 539 (1941), rev'g 110 F.2d 734 (2nd Cir. 1940), 39 B.T.A. 1134 (1939).

43. See *Allied Fidelity Corp. v. Comm'r*, 66 T.C. 1068 (1976), aff'd 572 F.2d 1190 (7th Cir. 1978).

CHAPTER 29   Is Insurance a Substitute for Capital under the Revised Basel Accord?

1. Bank for International Settlements, *International Convergence of Capital Measurement and Capital Standards: A Revised Framework* (Basel, June 2004), p. 137.

2. The following itemization and attendant explanation draws heavily on the Basel Committee on Banking Supervision's "Working Paper on the Regulatory Treatment of Operational Risk," Annex 2, September, 2001. However, these same categories and descriptions can be found in related materials published by other sub-groups under the BIS such as RMG (Risk Management Group).
3. Additional criteria may be assigned by local regulatory authorities as Basel II is implemented within each nation. The criteria listed herein are major points in the Basel II accord only.

CHAPTER 30   Is My SPE a VIE under FIN46R, and, If So, So What?

1. In the Second Interim Report, dated January 21, 2003, by Neal Batson, the court-appointed examiner *in re Enron*, the examiner reviews several SPE transactions used by Enron that in 2000 accounted for over 95 percent of Enron's reported net income and over 105 percent of Enron's reported funds from operations and avoided recording debt of $11.9 billion.
2. The Financial Accounting Standards Board (FASB) has a controversial history with its consolidation policy, causing one structured finance wit to proclaim that if consolidation policy were human it would be old enough to vote. FASB has been debating consolidation policy for over 15 years and had released two prior exposure drafts (EDs)—one in 1995 and another in 1997—each becoming embroiled in substantial disagreement regarding the bright-line benefits and certainty of a voting test versus the more discretionary and subjective concept of control. In 1999, FASB suspended its consideration of the 1997 ED after being unable to reach critical consensus and scheduled to take its consideration back up in the first quarter of 2001 after a scheduled change of FASB members (that presumably was expected to allow consensus to form).
3. The FASB "Staff Position" was introduced in February 2003 by the FASB. These are positions developed by the FASB staff and published for comment. After comment and appropriate modification, they become final. For more information see www.fasb.org/fasb_staff_positions.
4. See FSP FIN46(R)-1 thru -3 and proposed FSP FIN46(R)-b available at www.fasb.org/fasb_staff_positions.
5. The EITF was unable to resolve the issue and the FASB has addressed it in proposed FSP FIN 46(R)-c.
6. Described in EITF Issue 90-15.
7. See Ernst & Young's "Consolidation of Variable Interest Entities: A Summary of FASB Interpretation 46," April 2003.
8. For example, Deloitte & Touche's "A Roadmap to Applying the New Consolidation Guidance" re FIN46R, containing 140 pages, and Ernst & Young's "Financial Reporting Developments" re FIN46R, comprising 386 pages.
9. See Paragraph 4 of FIN46R.

10. In June, FASB released an Exposure Draft, *Qualifying Special-Purpose Entities and Isolation of Transferred Assets*, that proposes to amend FAS140 to substantially restrict the permitted activities of a QSPE. If adopted as proposed, many structures currently considered QSPEs would instead be VIEs subject to FIN46R.

11. Specifically confirmed by the FASB staff in FSP FIN46(R)-2.

12. See paragraphs 16 and 17 of FIN46R.

13. Specifically addressed as "implicit" VIs by the FASB staff in proposed FSP FIN46(R)-b.

14. "EITF Abstract 96-16 "Investor's Accounting for an Investee When the Investor Has a Majority of the Voting Interests but the Minority Shareholder or Shareholders Have Certain Approval or Veto Rights," in which a distinction is drawn between protective rights and participating rights and stating that the existence of protective rights does not disturb the normal consolidation when there is a majority voting interest (since these protective rights have little or no impact on the control by the majority voting interest), while the existence of participating rights must be considered in determining whether the majority voting interest is a controlling interest that requires consolidation. Examples of protective rights are (1) a veto over liquidation or bankruptcy, (2) a veto over pricing for transactions between the investee and the majority voting interestholder, (3) a veto over amendment of organization documents of the investee or the issuance or repurchase of equity interests, and (4) a veto over acquisitions or dispositions of over 20 percent of the investee's total assets. Examples of substantive participating rights that would overcome the normal presumption requiring the majority voting interest to consolidate the investee are (1) selecting, terminating and setting compensation of management responsible for implementing the investee's policies and procedures, and (2) establishing operating and capital decisions of the investee, including budgets, in the ordinary course of business. These same concepts have also surfaced in the proposed FSP SOP78-9-a that would amend AICPA Statement of Position 78-9, *Accounting for Investments in Real Estate Ventures*, to be consistent with the tentative conclusions reached by the EITF in Issue 04-5.

CHAPTER 31   Credit Derivatives, Insurance, and CDOs: The Aftermath of Enron

1. It has been reported that the International Swaps and Derivatives Association (ISDA) first used the term *credit derivatives* in 1992. "Evolution of Credit Derivatives," available at www.credit-deriv.com/evolution.htm (visited November 4, 2002).

2. Li (2002).

3. Ibid.

4. Remarks by Alan Greenspan, chairman, Board of Governors of the U.S. Federal Reserve System, at the Institute of International Finance, New York (via videoconference), (April 22, 2002), available at www.federalreserve.gov/boarddocs/speeches/2002/20020422/default.htm (visited October 16, 2002).

5. ISDA, News Release, "ISDA 2002 Mid-Year Market Survey Debuts Equity Derivatives Volumes at $2.3 Trillion; Identifies Significant Increase for Credit Derivatives" (September 25, 2002), available at www.isda.org/press/index .html (visited October 22, 2002).
6. ISDA, News Release, "Credit Derivatives Surge 55 Per Cent." ISDA Year End 2004 Market Survey (March 16, 2005), available at www.isda.org (visited April 13, 2005).
7. Office of the Comptroller of the Currency, "OCC Bank Derivatives Report, Second Quarter 2002," available at www.occ.treas.gov/ftp/deriv/dq202.pdf (visited October 14, 2002), 1.
8. Greenspan Remarks, op. cit.
9. Reference obligations are also referred to in discussions of credit derivatives as "reference assets" or "reference credits."
10. In fact, the 1999 ISDA Credit Derivatives Definitions simply define a "Credit Derivative Transaction" as "any transaction that is identified in the related Confirmation as a Credit Derivative Transaction or any transaction that incorporates these Definitions." 1999 Credit Definitions, § 1.1.
11. See D'Amario (2002).
12. Ibid.
13. Banking or insurance regulations may require a bank or insurance market participant to own a reference obligation, but that is not a requirement for entering into a CDS.
14. 1999 Credit Definitions, 16–18.
15. For example, if after a credit event a reference obligation is valued at $3 million and the notional amount specified in the contract is $10 million, the protection seller must pay the protection buyer $7 million. Alternatively, the protection seller may be required to pay a predetermined sum (a "binary" settlement) regardless of the then value of the reference obligation.
16. Board of Governors of the Federal Reserve System, "Supervisory Guidance for Credit Derivatives," *SR Letter 96-17* (August 12, 1996), Appendix.
17. JPMorgan (1998).
18. Ibid. "Depending upon the performance of a specified reference credit, and the type of derivative embedded in the note, the note may not be redeemable at par value. . . . For example, the purchaser of a credit-linked note with an embedded default swap may receive only 60 percent of the original par value if a reference credit defaults."
19. Ibid.
20. Office of the Comptroller of the Currency (OCC), OCC Bulletin 96-43, "Credit Derivatives Description: Guidelines for National Banks," available at www.occ.treas.gov/fh/bulletin/96-43.txt (visited November 26, 2002).
21. Goodman and Faozzi (2002), pp. 60–61. SCDOs are referred to as "synthetic" because the credit exposure is created by the derivatives contract and not with an actual obligation of, or relationship with, the reference portfolio.
22. Lang Gibson, "Synthetic Credit Portfolio Transactions: The Evolution of Synthetics," available at www.gtnews.com/articles/3918.pdf (visited October 1, 2002).

23. Ibid.
24. ISDA Comment Letter to the Securities and Exchange Commission, March 8, 2005.
25. Ibid.
26. *Hudson Soft Co. Ltd. et al. v. Credit Suisse First Boston Corp. et al.*, Civil Action 02-CV-5768 (TPG) (October 8, 2002) (Amended Complaint).
27. We use the phrase "structured finance transactions" as it is used in Kavanagh in Chapter 8 as any transaction that makes use of an SPE or special purpose vehicle (SPV).
28. *Newby v. Enron Corp. (In re Enron Corp., Securities Litigation)*, Civil Action No. H-01-3624, 206 F.R.D. 427.
29. *Hudson Soft* Class Action Amended Complaint, supra note 26, pp. 44–58.
30. On November 4, 1999, Yosemite Securities Trust I 8.25 percent Series 1999-A Linked Enron Obligations in the aggregate amount of $750 million were issued. On August 25, 2000, Enron Credit Linked Notes Trust issued Enron CLNs in the aggregate amount of $500 million. On May 24, 2001, three separate Enron CLNs were issued: (1) Enron Euro Credit Linked Notes Trust 6.5 percent notes in the aggregate amount of EUR200 million; (2) Enron Sterling Credit Linked Notes Trust 7.25 percent notes in the aggregate amount of £125 million; and (3) Enron Credit Linked Notes Trust II 7.3875 percent notes in the aggregate amount of $500 million. On October 18, 2001, Credit Suisse First Boston International JPY First-to-Default Credit Linked .85 percent notes were issued in the aggregate amount of ¥1.7 trillion.
31. S&P Corporate Ratings, "New Issue: Enron Credit Linked Notes Trust, $500 million Enron Credit Linked Notes" (October 9, 2000), available at www.standardandpoors.com (visited November 26, 2002). Senate Permanent Subcommittee on Investigation, Appendix D, Citigroup Case History. See also, Opening Statement of Rick Caplan before the Senate Permanent Subcommittee on Investigations, July 23, 2002 (Caplan Opening Statement) available at www.senate.gov/~gov_affairs/072302caplan.pdf (visited October 22, 2002).
32. Statement of Rick Caplan, supra note 31.
33. *Hudson Soft* Class Action Amended Complaint, supra note 26, pp. 153–156.
34. Ibid., pp. 157–162.
35. Cal. Ins. Code §1633 (2001).
36. Conn. Gen. Stat. §38a-704 (2001). The penalty for acting as an insurance producer without a license is a fine of not more than $500 or imprisonment of not more than three months or both. An "insurance producer" is defined at Conn. Gen. Stat. §38a-702(1) (2001).
37. 18 Del. C. §505(c) (2001).
38. 18 Del. C. §505(a) (2001).
39. 18 Del. C. §505(b) (2001).
40. New York Ins. Law §109(a) (2002).
41. New York Ins. Law §1102(a) (2002).
42. 215 ILCS 5/500-15(a) (2002).
43. McCarron-Ferguson Act, 15 U.S.C. §1011–1015.
44. 67 Fed. Reg. 64067 (October 17, 2002).

45. The "insured" must be able to demonstrate that it has both an economic and a legal connection to the asset or subject matter of the risk. Financial Services Authority, *Discussion Paper: Cross-Sector Risk Transfers* (May 2002) at Annex B1.

46. Because most business relationships involve risks and the assumption of risk, the key here is that an insurance company spreads or distributes the risks among a pool of contracts covering similar risks. See *Amerco v. Comm'r*, 96 T.C. 18 (1991), *aff'd* 979 F.2d 192 (9th Cir. 1992). See also *Comm'r v. Treganowan*, 183 F.2d 288 (2nd Cir. 1950).

47. New York Ins. Law §1101(a)(1) (LEXIS through Ch. 221, 8/29/2001). Key to this definition is the notion that the insured will be adversely affected by the specified fortuitous event. In other words, insurances require the establishment of actual loss.

48. NYID, "Catastrophe Options," *Office of General Counsel Informal Opinion* (June 25, 1998).

49. NYID, "Weather Financial Instruments (Derivatives, Hedges, Etc.)" *Office of General Counsel Informal Opinion* (February 15, 2000), available at www.ins.state.ny.us/rg000205.htm.

50. NYID, Letter dated June 16, 2000, addressing a credit default option facility, available at www.ins.state.ny.us.

51. The ISDA has developed standard agreements that have been widely adopted by parties to unfunded derivative contracts. The ISDA web site is at www.isda.org. Although CLNs, CDOs, and SCDOs are credit derivatives, we do not discuss their documentation in this chapter. CLNs, CDOs, and SCDOs are typically documented as privately placed notes.

52. Restructuring Supplement to the 1999 ISDA Credit Derivatives Definitions (May 11, 2001); Supplement to the 1999 ISDA Credit Derivatives Definitions Relating to Convertible, Exchangeable or Accreting Obligations (November 9, 2001); Commentary on Supplement Relating to Convertible, Exchangeable, or Accreting Obligations (November 9, 2001); Supplement Relating to Successor and Credit Events to the 1999 ISDA Credit Derivatives Definitions, (November 28, 2001).

53. International Monetary Fund, "Global Financial Stability Report, Market Developments and Issues" (April 2005), p. 9.

54. Ibid., p. 3.

55. *Discussion Paper: Cross-Sector Risk Transfers* (U.K. May 2002), supra note 45, Annex A: Transformers, available at www.fsa.gov.uk/pubs/discussion/index-2002.html. Press Release, "Risk Transfer: Benefits and Drawbacks Need Careful Balancing," May 3, 2002, available at www.fsa.gov.uk/pubs/press/2002/049.html (visited September 16, 2002).

CHAPTER 32 Project Finance Collateralized Debt Obligations: What? Why? Now?

1. CDOs include collateralized bond obligations (CBOs), collateralized fund obligations (CFOs), collateralized loan obligations (CLOs), and collateralized swap

Notes 851

obligations (CSOs). CDO market convention categorizes a CDO by primary collateral type. For example, a CLO would usually have loans as the primary collateral, but might include high-yield bonds or other debt or other securities within the CDO's portfolio.

2. See "2004 U.S. CDO Review/2005 Preview: Record Activity Levels Driven by Resecuritization CDOs and CLOs," Moody's Investors Service, February 1, 2005.
3. See www.bis.org.
4. See www.bis.org/publ/bcbsca.
5. The four banks were ABN Amro, Citibank, Deutsche Bank, and Société Générale.
6. The study was described in greater detail in "Credit Attributes of Project Finance" by Chris Beale, Michel Chatain, Nathan Fox, Sandra Bell, James Berner, Robert Preminger, and Jan Prins, in the *Journal of Structured and Project Finance* (Fall 2002).

CHAPTER 33 2004 Review of Trends in Insurance Securitization: Exploring Outside the Cat Box

1. See "USAA and the Magnificent Seven," Lane Financial *Trade Notes* (August 2003).
2. These observations were discussed in "Rationale and Results with the LFC Cat Bond Pricing Model," Lane Financial *Trade Notes* (December 2003).

CHAPTER 34 Enterprise Risk Management: The Case of United Grain Growers

1. Examples include St. Paul, Duke Energy, and Credit Agricole Indusuez; see Lam (2001), pp. 16-22.
2. For further discussion, see Froot, Scharfstein, and Stein (1994) and Stulz (1996). Efficiencies associated with bundling risk-bearing services with other services (such as loss control and claims processing) can also be a source of value creation; see Doherty and Smith (1993).
3. More generally, managers could be assumed to have some value-at-risk constraint, as when they want the probability that losses exceed $40 million to be less than 1 percent.
4. Other combinations of contracts would also achieve the stated objective, but the point of the example would be unchanged.
5. Obtaining the desired coverage using separate insurance policies is analogous to purchasing a portfolio of two separate options, and obtaining the desired coverage using one bundled insurance policy is analogous to purchasing one option

on the portfolio of risks. The option on the portfolio will have lower volatility and therefore have a lower price (expected payout is lower). With proportional transaction costs, the firm is better off purchasing the option on the portfolio as opposed to the portfolio of options.

6. See Lam (2001) for further discussion.

7. Also, UGG's managers were concerned about the accounting treatment of the derivatives contracts. If the values of the derivatives contracts were marked to market at UGG's fiscal year-end, July 31, then the derivatives could actually increase the volatility of reported earnings. To illustrate, suppose that the derivatives contracts were based on weather conditions in June and July. Also suppose that in a particular year, the weather in these months indicated that crop yields would be poor and therefore that the weather derivatives contract would have a positive payoff. The increased value of the derivative contract as of July 31 would then be recognized in earnings. However, the lower crop yields as a result of the bad weather in June and July would not affect operating earnings until the next fiscal year when the crops were harvested and shipped. Thus, if UGG hedged using the weather derivative, its earnings would increase in one fiscal year and decrease in the subsequent fiscal year relative to expected earnings. If UGG were unhedged, then its earnings would have dropped only in the subsequent fiscal year, leading to lower earnings volatility.

CHAPTER 35   Representations and Warranties Insurance and Other Insurance Products Designed to Facilitate Corporate Transactions

1. M. J. Auer with J. Berke, "Risk Management—Insuring the Deal," The Daily Deal.com (April 28, 2000) (updated November 8, 2000).

2. Ibid.

3. Banham (1999).

4. One commentator observed that mergers and acquisitions activity has become riskier not only because of slowing economic conditions, but also because of the increasing trend toward cross-border transactions involving intellectual property assets, as differences in laws, legal systems, and cultures increase the risk associated with such deals. See Hansen (2001).

5. Generally, finite risk insurance is considered a smoothing mechanism that spreads losses over long periods, usually 5 to 10 years, to eliminate peaks and valleys from a company's earnings statements, thereby smoothing the financial impact of adverse developments.

6. R. G. Mullins, "Boxing the Unknown Exposure" (January 24, 2001), at www.erisk.com.

7. Auer, op. cit.

8. See, for example, Auer, op. cit. (quoting estimates from AIG that premiums for M&A products written between 1998 and 1999 increased 50 percent, from $400 million to $600 million).
9. Hansen (2001) and Auer, op. cit.
10. Mullins, op. cit.
11. Hansen (2001) (quoting Thomson Financial).
12. See, for example, Loh (2000).
13. See Booth (2001).
14. See Sammer (1999).
15. See Booth (2001). See also P. C. Bernstein, "Hidden Linkages: Risk Management, Financial Markets, and Insurance," American Academy of Actuaries (November/December 2000) (discussing the convergence of insurance, financial services, and finance and commenting that insurance companies transform "damaging consequences into manageable consequences" is an observation that is equally applicable to all hedging strategies).

APPENDIX A   Capital Structure Irrelevance

1. M&M characterize what happens (according to the conventional view) when a firm reaches its threshold leverage ratio as follows: "Beyond [the threshold], the [expected stock return] will presumably rise sharply as the market discounts 'excessive' trading on the equity" (M&M 1958, p. 277). Today, proponents of a leverage threshold argue that this threshold kicks in when the increased probability of financial distress created by high leverage levels offsets the other benefits of debt. See, for example, Myers (1984) and Culp (2002a) for an explanation of this trade-off theory of optimal capital structure.
2. These actually are not the original assumptions as presented by M&M, but rather are based on the slightly simpler version presented in Fama (1978). Nothing is lost by working with this version of the assumptions. These assumptions are basically the same ones under which put-call parity holds. True, we argued that we needed only the principle of no arbitrage to get put-call parity, but that was *already* assuming certain things to be the case (e.g., that firms and individuals could issue securities we viewed as options on the same terms).
3. Fama (1978) shows that this assumption can be relaxed if it is replaced with the assumptions that no firm is a monopolistic supplier of any security *and* firms all maximize their total market value at whatever prices are given from a perfectly competitive securities market.
4. Grundy (2002) notes that for irrelevance to hold, arbitrage can be carried out by individual investors, by intermediaries acting on behalf of investors (e.g., investment banks), or by supply adjustments within the corporate sector as a whole. See also M&M (1959), Fama and Miller (1972), and Fama (1978). If, say, taxes or transaction costs interfere with arbitrage by one of these groups, either of the other two could take its place and the same irrelevance result would

obtain. How taxes affect the M&M propositions has received considerable attention, including by M&M themselves in their famous 1963 "correction" paper. See also Miller (1977, 1988) and Modigliani (1982, 1988).

5. For a precise definition of systematic risk in the context of modern asset pricing theory, see Cochrane (2001) and Cochrane and Culp (2003).

6. For most of our discussion, we are treating the interest rate on the firm's debt as given. Of course we would just replace this term with the expected return on the firm's debt if debt is risky.

APPENDIX B   Risk-Based Capital Regulations on Financial Institutions

1. Disclosed reserves must meet certain criteria for their inclusion. In addition, Tier I capital also requires the deduction by the bank of "unamortized goodwill," such as the goodwill capital created for some U.S. banks during the savings and loan crisis of the 1980s.

2. This section is based largely on Culp (1999).

3. 17 C.F.R. 240.15c3-1 (U.S. Code)

4. The methodology was value at risk with a 99 percent confidence level and two-week risk horizon. See Chapter 10 for a further discussion of value at risk, as well as Culp (2001).

5. See Skipper (1998).

6. See Kiln (1991).

APPENDIX C   Risk Capital

1. Quoted in Shirreff (1991), pp. 42–43.

2. For those who followed the major debate over MGRM's program in the mid-1990s, this 100 percent hedge requirement was a major reason that MGRM did not adjust its hedge ratios and opted for a one-to-one hedge. For those who have no idea what I am talking about but are curious, the major issues raised by the MGRM debacle—including this one—are surveyed in the papers collected in Culp and Miller (2000).

3. This is not true, for example, of programs like "macro hedges," which may still be perfectly useful but may be little different from paid-in risk capital in terms of their impact on earnings.

4. Whether the probability level chosen in the VaR calculation is interpreted to mean that there is a X percent chance of a larger loss or a larger loss will occur in X of the next 100 time periods depends on whether we assume the probability distribution used to compute the VaR is stable over time.

5. These four methods are reviewed in Saita (1999), Perold (2001), Smithson (2003), and elsewhere.

6. See Saita (1999).

7. There also may *not* be a well-defined optimum. It depends on what precisely we use to estimate the costs of contingent and paid-in risk capital.

8. This is well-covered ground in other books (including my own previous works). We don't get into the same level of detail here.

9. If the put option method is used to compute the amount of risk capital, there is still the open question of which model to use. And if the VaR-like empirical approach is chosen, there is even more room for differences arising from choices about data frequency, length of time series, estimation method, distributional assumptions, and the like.

References

Akerlof, G. A. 1970. "The Market for 'Lemons': Quality Uncertainty and the Market Mechanism." *Quarterly Journal of Economics* 84, No. 3 (August).

Allen, F., and G. R. Faulhaber. 1989. "Signaling by Underpricing in the IPO Market." *Journal of Financial Economics* 23.

Allen, F., and R. Michaely. 1995. "Dividend Policy." *Handbooks in OR & MS 9.* Amsterdam: Elsevier.

Allen, F., and A. Winton. 1995. "Corporate Financial Structure, Incentives and Optimal Contracting." *Handbooks in OR & MS 9.* Amsterdam: Elsevier.

Ballantine, R. 2001a. "Deals That Fly." *Reactions* (April).

Ballantine, R. 2001b. "Not Like It Is in the Movies." *Reactions* (August).

Banham, R. 1999. "Two for the Money." *Journal of Accountancy* (November).

Banham, R. 2000. "Rethinking the Future." *Reactions* (April).

Banham, R. 2001. "CLOCS Ticking to New Market." *Reactions* (April).

Banz, R. W. 1981. "The Relationship between Return and Market Value of Common Stocks." *Journal of Financial Economics* 9.

Barclay, M. J., and C. W. Smith, Jr. 1996. "On Financial Architecture: Leverage, Maturity, and Priority." *Journal of Applied Corporate Finance* 8, No. 4 (Winter).

Barclay, M. J., and C. W. Smith, Jr. 1999. "The Capital Structure Puzzle: Another Look at the Evidence." *Journal of Applied Corporate Finance* 12, No. 1 (Spring).

Bassett, R., and M. Storrie. 2003. "Corporate Accounting After Enron: Is the Cure Worse Than the Disease?" In *Corporate Aftershock.* C. L. Culp and W. A. Niskanen, eds. New York: John Wiley & Sons.

Batchvarov, A., J. Collins, and W. Davies. 2003. "Considerations for Dynamic and Static, Cash and Synthetic Collaterised Debt Obligations." In *Credit Derivatives: The Definitive Guide.* J. Gregory, ed. London: Risk Books.

Batchvarov, A., A. Davletova, and W. Davies. 2004. *CDO Compendium.* Merrill Lynch (December 15).

Belonsky, G., D. Laster, and D. Durbin. 1999. "Insurance-Linked Securities." In *Insurance and Weather Derivatives.* H. Geman, ed. London: Risk Books.

Bernero, R. H. 1998. "Second-Generation OTC Derivatives and Structured Products: Catastrophe Bonds, Catastrophe Swaps, and Insurance Securitizations." In *Securitized Insurance Risk.* M. Himick, ed. Chicago: Glenlake Publishing Company, Ltd.

Black, F., and M. Scholes. 1973. "The Pricing of Options and Corporate Liabilities." *Journal of Political Economy* 81, No. 3: 637–654.

Booth, G. 2001. "Needed: A Common Language of Risk." *MMC Views* (November 1).

Borch, K. H. 1990. *Economics of Insurance*. Amsterdam: North-Holland.

Brealey, R. A., and S. C. Myers. 2000. *Principles of Corporate Finance*. 6th ed. New York: Irwin McGraw-Hill.

Brennan, M. J., and E. S. Schwartz. 1988. "The Case for Convertibles." *Journal of Appled Corporate Finance* 2, No. 1 (Summer).

Butt, V. 2003. "Integrated Risk: Heyday or Gone Away?" *Risk & Insurance* (March 3).

Canter, M. S., J. B. Cole, and R. L. Sandor. 1999. "Insurance Derivatives: A New Asset Class for the Capital Markets and a New Hedging Tool for the Insurance Industry." In *Insurance and Weather Derivatives*. H. Geman, ed. London: Risk Books.

Carow, K. A., G. R. Erwin, and J. J. McConnell. 1999. "A Survey of U.S. Corporate Financing Innovations: 1970–1997." *Journal of Applied Corporate Finance* 12, No. 11 (Spring).

Carter, R., L. Lucas, and N. Ralph. 2000. *Reinsurance*. 4th ed. London: Reactions Publishing Group in association with Guy Carpenter & Company.

Chacko, G., P. Tufano, and G. Verter. 2002. "Raising Contingent Capital: The Case of Cephalon." *Journal of Applied Corporate Finance* 15, No. 1 (Spring).

Chapman Tripp. 1998. "Mezzanine Finance: One Person's Ceiling Is Another Person's Floor." *Finance Law Focus* 11 (November).

Chen, N., R. Roll, and S. Ross. 1986. "Economic Forces and the Stock Market." *Journal of Business* 59.

Choudhry, M. 2004. *Structured Credit Products*. Singapore: John Wiley & Sons (Asia) Pte Ltd.

Cifuentes, A., I. Efrat, J. Gluck, and E. Murphy. 1998. "Buying and Selling Credit Risk: A Perspective on Credit-Linked Obligations." *Credit Derivatives: Applications for Risk Management, Investment, and Portfolio Optimisation*. London: Risk Books.

Cochrane, J. H. 1991. "Production-Based Asset Pricing and the Link Between Stock Returns and Economic Fluctuations." *Journal of Finance* 46.

Cochrane, J. H. 1996. "A Cross-Sectional Test of an Investment-Based Asset Pricing Model." *Journal of Political Economy* 104.

Cochrane, J. H. 2001. *Asset Pricing*. Princeton, NJ: Princeton University Press.

Cochrane, J. H., and C. L. Culp. 2003. "Equilibrium Asset Pricing and Discount Factors: Overview and Implications for Derivatives Valuation and Risk Management." In *The Growth of Risk Management: A History*. P. Field, ed. London: Risk Books.

Corrigan, E. G. 1990. "Perspectives on Payment System Risk Reduction." In *The U.S. Payment System: Efficiency, Risk, and the Role of the Federal Reserve*. D. B. Humphrey, ed. Boston: Kluwer Academic Publishers.

Cox, S. H., and R. G. Schwebach. 1992. "Insurance Futures and Hedging Insurance Price Risk." *Journal of Risk and Insurance* 59, No. 4.

Coxe, T. A. 2000. "Convertible Structures: Evolution Continues." In *Handbook of Hybrid Instruments*. I. Nelken, ed. New York: John Wiley & Sons.

Crouhy, M., D. Galai, and R. Mark. 2001. *Risk Management.* New York: McGraw-Hill.

Culp, C. L. 1996. "Relations between Insurance and Derivatives: Applications from Catastrophic Loss Insurance." In *Rethinking Insurance Regulation,* Vol. 1: *Catastrophic Risks.*Y. B. McAleer and T. Miller, eds. Washington, DC: Competitive Enterprise Institute.

Culp, C. L. 1999. "Wettbewerbsnachteile für Schweizer Banken? Konsultativpapier des Basler Ausschusses mit Schwächen." *Neue Zürcher Zeitung* (October 15).

Culp, C. L. 2000. "Revisiting RAROC." *Journal of Lending and Credit Risk Management* (March).

Culp, C. L. 2001. *The Risk Management Process: Business Strategy and Tactics.* New York: John Wiley & Sons.

Culp, C. L. 2002a. *The ART of Risk Management: Alternative Risk Transfer, Capital Structure, and the Convergence of Insurance and Capital Markets.* New York: John Wiley & Sons.

Culp, C. L. 2002b. "Contingent Capital: Integrating Corporate Financing and Risk Management Decisions." *Journal of Applied Corporate Finance* 15, No. 1: 9–18.

Culp, C. L. 2002c. "The Revolution in Corporate Risk Management: A Decade of Innovations in Process and Products." *Journal of Applied Corporate Finance* 14, No. 4: 8–26.

Culp, C. L. 2004. *Risk Transfer: Derivatives in Theory and Practice.* Hoboken, NJ: John Wiley & Sons.

Culp, C. L., D. Furbush, and B. T. Kavanagh. 1994. "Structured Debt and Corporate Risk Management." *Journal of Applied Corporate Finance* 7, No. 3 (Fall).

Culp, C. L., and B. T. Kavanagh. 1994. "Methods of Resolving Over-the-Counter Derivatives Contracts in Failed Depository Institutions: Restrictions on Regulators from Federal Banking Law." *Futures International Law Letter* 14, Nos. 3–4 (May/June).

Culp, C. L., and R. J. Mackay. 1997. "An Introduction to Structured Notes." *Derivatives* 2, No. 4 (March/April).

Culp, C. L., and M. H. Miller. 1995. "Metallgesellschaft and the Economics of Synthetic Storage." *Journal of Applied Corporate Finance* 7(4).

Culp, C. L., and M. H. Miller. 2000. *Corporate Hedging in Theory and Practice: Lessons from Metallgesellschaft.* London: Risk Publications.

Culp, C. L., and A. M. P. Neves. 1998a. "Credit and Interest Rate Risk in the Business of Banking." *Derivatives Quarterly* 4, No. 4 (Summer).

Culp, C. L., and A. M. P. Neves. 1998b. "Financial Innovations in Leveraged Commercial Loan Markets." *Journal of Applied Corporate Finance* 11, No. 2 (Summer).

Culp, C. L., and W. A. Niskanen, eds. 2003. *Corporate Aftershock: The Public Policy Lessons from the Collapse of Enron and Other Major Corporations.* New York: John Wiley & Sons.

Culp, C. L., and J. A. Overdahl. 1996. "An Overview of Derivatives: Their Mechanics, Participants, Scope of Activity, and Benefits." In *The Financial Services Revolution.* C. Kirsch, ed. Chicago: Irwin Professional Publishing.

Cummins, J. D., and H. Geman. 1995. "Pricing Catastrophe Insurance Futures and Call Spreads: An Arbitrage Approach." *Journal of Fixed Income* (March).

Daniel, K., and S. Titman. 1995. "Financing Investment under Asymmetric Information." *Handbooks in OR & MS 9*. Amsterdam: Elsevier.

D'Amario, P. B. 2002. "North American Credit Derivatives Market Develops Rapidly." *Greenwich Associates* (January 9).

D'Arcy, S. P., and V. G. France. 1992. "Catastrophe Futures: A Better Hedge for Insurers." *Journal of Risk and Insurance 59*, No. 4.

Davidson, A., A. Sanders, L. Wolff, and A. Ching. 2003. *Securitization: Structuring and Investment Analysis*. New York: John Wiley & Sons.

Davis, A., and M. Pacelle. 2001. "Covad to Pay Its Bondholders Before Default." *Wall Street Journal* (August 8).

Davletova, A., A. Batchvarov, and W. Davies. 2004. "Application of Traditional Structuring Techniques to the Creation of New Hybrid Products (Case Studies)." In *Hybrid Products: Instruments, Applications and Modelling*. A. Batchvarov, ed. London: Risk Books.

Deacon, J. 2004. *Global Securitisation and CDOs*. West Sussex, England: John Wiley & Sons, Ltd.

DeAngelo, H., and R. W. Masulis. 1980. "Optimal Capital Structure under Corporate and Personal Taxation." *Journal of Financial Economics 8*.

Diamond, D. 1984. "Financial Intermediation and Delegated Monitoring." *Review of Economic Studies 51*.

Diamond, D. 1989a. "Asset Services and Financial Intermediation." In *Financial Markets and Incomplete Information: Frontiers of Modern Financial Theory*, Vol. 2. S. Bhattacharya and G. Constantinides, eds. Savage, MD: Rowman & Littlefield Publishers.

Diamond, D. 1989b. "Reputation Acquisition in Debt Markets." *Journal of Political Economy 97*.

Diamond, D. 1991. "Monitoring and Reputation: The Choice between Bank Loans and Directly Placed Debt." *Journal of Political Economy 99*.

Diamond, D. 1993. "Seniority and Maturity of Debt Contracts." *Journal of Financial Economics 33*.

Diamond, D., and R. Verrecchia. 1982. "Optimal Managerial Contracts and Equilibrium Security Prices." *Journal of Finance 37*.

Diamond, J. 1997. *Guns, Germs, and Steel*. London: Chatto & Windus.

Doherty, N. A. 2000. *Integrated Risk Management*. New York: McGraw-Hill.

Doherty, N. A., and C. W. Smith Jr. 1993. "Corporate Insurance Strategy: The Case of British Petroleum." *Journal of Applied Corporate Finance 6*, No. 3 (Fall).

Dyson, B. 2001. "Striking the Vital Balance." *Reactions* (January).

Eckbo, B. E. 1986. "Valuation Effects and Corporate Debt Offerings." *Journal of Financial Economics 15*.

Eckbo, B. E., and R. W. Masulis. 1995. "Seasoned Equity Offerings: A Survey." *Handbooks in OR & MS 9*. Amsterdam: Elsevier.

Erhart, B. 2002. "Contingent Cover." In *Alternative Risk Strategies*. M. N. Lane, ed. London: Risk Books.

Falloon, W. 1993. "Fairway to Heaven." *Risk 6*, No. 12.

Fama, E. F. 1978. "The Effects of a Firm's Investment and Financing Decisions on the Welfare of Its Security Holders." *American Economic Review* 68, No. 3.

Fama, E. F., and K. R. French. 1992. "The Cross-Section of Expected Stock Returns." *Journal of Finance* 47.

Fama, E. F., and K. R. French. 1993. "Common Risk Factors in the Returns on Stocks and Bonds." *Journal of Financial Economics* 33.

Fama, E. F., and K. R. French. 1995. "Size and Book-to-Market Factors in Earnings and Returns." *Journal of Finance* 50.

Fama, E. F., and K. R. French. 1996. "Multifactor Explanations of Asset Pricing Anomalies." *Journal of Finance* 51.

Fama, E. F., and K. R. French. 1997. "Industry Costs of Equity." *Journal of Financial Economics* 43.

Fama, E. F., and K. R. French. 1998. "Taxes, Financing Decisions, and Firm Value." *Journal of Finance* 43, No. 3.

Fama, E. F., and K. R. French. 1999. "The Corporate Cost of Capital and the Return on Corporate Investment." *Journal of Finance* 54, No. 6.

Fama, E. F., and K. R. French. 2002. "Testing Trade-Off and Pecking Order Predictions about Dividends and Debt." *Review of Financial Studies* 15, No. 1: 1–33.

Fama, E. F., and K. R. French. 2004. "Financing Decisions: Who Issues Stock?" Working Paper, Graduate School of Business, University of Chicago, Center for Research in Security Prices.

Fama, E. F., and M. H. Miller. 1972. *The Theory of Finance.* New York: Holt, Rinehart, & Winston.

Fenn, G. W., N. Liang, and S. Prowse. 1995. *The Economics of the Private Equity Market.* Research Paper, Board of Governors of the Federal Reserve System (December).

Finnerty, J. D. 1996. *Project Financing: Asset-Based Financial Engineering.* New York: John Wiley & Sons.

Forrester, J. P. 2003. "Synthetic Resecuritizations: A Step Too Far?" *International Financial Law Review* (December).

Forrester, J. P. 2004. "CDOs and CFOs: UFOs or WFMD?" Speech before Structured Finance and ART MBA Class (Prof. C. Culp), Graduate School of Business, University of Chicago (December).

Forrester, J. P. 2005. "Project Finance." Speech before Alternative Risk Transfer Executive Education Seminar, Graduate School of Business, University of Chicago (April).

Frank, M. Z., and V. K. Goyal. 2003. "Testing the Pecking Order Theory of Capital Structure." *Journal of Financial Economics* 67.

Frank, M. Z., and V. K. Goyal. 2004. "The Effect of Market Conditions on Capital Structure Adjustment." Finance Research Letters1.

Froot, K. A. 1999. *The Financing of Catastrophic Risk.* Chicago: University of Chicago Press.

Froot, K. A., D. S. Scharfstein, and J. C. Stein. 1993. "Risk Management: Coordinating Investment and Financing Policies." *Journal of Finance* 48, No. 5.

Froot, K. A., D. S. Scharfstein, and J. C. Stein. 1994. "A Framework for Risk Management." *Harvard Business Review* (November–December).

Froot, K. A., and J. C. Stein. 1998. "Risk Management, Capital Budgeting, and Capital Structure Policy for Financial Institutions: An Integrated Approach." *Journal of Financial Economics* 47.

Geman, H. 1999. *Insurance and Weather Derivatives*. London: Risk Books.

Gergen, M. P., and P. Schmitz. 1997. "The Influence of Tax Law on Securities Innovation in the United States, 1981–1997." *New York University Tax Review*.

Gerling Global Financial Products, Inc. (GGFP). 2000. *Modern ART Practice*. London: Euromoney Institutional Investor.

Global Derivatives Study Group. 1993. *Derivatives: Practices and Principles*. Washington, DC: Group of Thirty.

Goodman, L. S., and F. J. Fabozzi. 2002. *Collateralized Debt Obligations: Structures and Analysis*. Hoboken, NJ: John Wiley & Sons.

Graham, J. R. 1996. "Debt and the Marginal Tax Rate." *Journal of Financial Economics* 41.

Grant, J. L. 2003. *Foundations of Economic Value Added*. 2nd ed. New York: John Wiley & Sons.

Grantham, R. J. 2004. "Innovations to Give Issuers Flexibility in Equity-Linked Funding." In *Hybrid Products: Instruments, Applications and Modeling*. A. Batchvarov, ed. London: Risk Books.

Green, P. 2001. "Risk Management Covers Enterprise Exposures." *Global Finance* (January).

Gregory, J., ed. 2003. *Credit Derivatives: The Definitive Guide*. London: Risk Books.

Grinblatt, M., and C. Y. Hwang. 1989. "Signaling and the Pricing of New Issues." *Journal of Finance* 44.

Grundy, B. D. 2002. "Preface." In *Selected Works of Merton H. Miller, A Celebration of Markets*, Vol. 1: *Finance*. B. D. Grundy, ed. Chicago: The University of Chicago Press, xv–xxviii.

Hansen, F. 2001. "The M&A Triple Threat." *Business Finance* (October).

Hardy, C. O. 1923. *Risk and Risk-Bearing*. 1999 ed. London: Risk Books.

Harris, M., and A. Raviv. 1990. "Capital Structure and the Informational Role of Debt." *Journal of Finance* 45.

Harris, M., and A. Raviv. 1991. "The Theory of Capital Structure." *Journal of Finance* 46, No. 1.

Hart, O., and J. Moore. 1990. "A Theory of Corporate Financial Structure Based on the Seniority of Claims." NBER Working Paper 343 (September).

Hay, J. 1999. "A Veteran Investor Ups Tempo." *Structured Finance International* No. 2 (June 1).

Hayre, L. S., C. Mohebbi, and T. A. Zimmerman. 1995. "Mortgage Pass-Through Securities." In *The Handbook of Fixed Income Securities*. F. J. Fabozzi and T. D. Fabozzi, eds. Chicago: Irwin Professional Publishing.

Heaton, J. B. 2000. "Patent Law and Financial Engineering." *Derivatives Quarterly* 7, No. 2.

Heaton, J. B. 2004. "Deepening Insolvency." *Journal of Corporate Law*.

Heberle, M. 2003. "Introduction to Emerging Market Future Flow Securitizations." *Wachovia Securities Structured Products Research* (November 20).

Hicks, J. R. 1989. *A Market Theory of Money.* London: Oxford University Press.

Himick, M., ed. 1998. *Securitized Insurance Risk.* Chicago: Glenlake Publishing Company, Ltd.

Hoffman, W. 1998. *Multiline Multiyear Agreements: A Guide for the Drafter and Negotiator.* Zürich: Swiss Re New Markets.

Howard, L. S. 2001. "Movie Bonds Get Bad Review After AIG Declines Coverage." *National Underwriter Online News* (February 9).

Hull, J. C. 2003. *Options, Futures, and Other Derivatives.* Upper Saddle River, NJ: Prentice Hall.

Ibbotson, R. G., and J. R. Ritter. 1995. "Initial Public Offerings." *Handbooks in OR & MS 9.* Amsterdam: Elsevier.

Imfeld, D. 2000. "Keeping an Eye on Interruption Risk." *Alternative Risk Strategies: Special Supplement to Risk Magazine* (December).

Ingersoll, J., and S. Ross. 1992. "Waiting to Invest: Investment and Uncertainty." *Journal of Business* 65, No. 1 (January).

ISDA/BBA/RMA. 1999. *Operational Risk: The Next Frontier.* New York: International Swaps and Derivatives Association, British Bankers' Association, and Risk Management Association.

Jagannathan, R., and Z. Wang. 1996. "The Conditional CAPM and the Cross-Section of Expected Returns." *Journal of Finance* Vol. 51.

James, C. 1987. "Some Evidence on the Uniqueness of Bank Loans." *Journal of Financial Economics* 19.

Jensen, M. C. 1986. "Agency Costs of Free Cash Flows, Corporate Finance and Takeovers." *American Economic Review* 76.

Jensen, M. C., and W. H. Meckling. 1976. "Theory of the Firm: Managerial Behavior, Agency Costs and Ownership Structure." *Journal of Financial Economics* 3, No. 4.

John, T. A., and K. John. 1991. "Optimality of Project Financing: Theory and Empirical Implications in Finance and Accounting." *Review of Quantitative Finance and Accounting* 1 (January).

JPMorgan. 1998. *Credit Derivatives: A Primer.* New York: JPMorgan.

Kat, H. M. 2002. *Structured Equity Derivatives.* New York: John Wiley & Sons.

Katz, D. M. 1999. "Banks Gain Entry into Insurance via Captives." *National Underwriter* (March 15).

Kavanagh, B., T. R. Bohemio, and G. A. Edwards Jr. 1992. "Asset-Backed Commercial Paper Programs." *Federal Reserve Bulletin* (February).

Kiln, R. 1991. *Reinsurance in Practice.* London: Witherby & Co. Ltd.

Kloman, H. F. 1998. "Captive Insurance Companies." In *International Risk and Insurance: An Environmental-Managerial Approach.* H. D. Skipper, ed. New York: Irwin McGraw-Hill.

Knop, R. 2002. *Structured Products.* New York: John Wiley & Sons.

Lam, J. 2001. "The CRO is Here to Stay." *Risk Management* (April).

Lane, M. N. 1998a. "AQS: Accelerated Quota Share." *Trade Notes.* Sedgwick Lane Financial (December 23).

Lane, M. N. 1998b. "Price, Risk, and Ratings for Insurance-Linked Notes: Evaluating Their Position in Your Portfolio." *Derivatives Quarterly* 4, No. 4 (Summer).

Lane, M. N. 1999. "An Optionable Note: The Reliance III Case Study." *Trade Notes*. Lane Financial LLC (www.lanefinancialllc.com).

Lane, M. N. 2000. "CDOs as Self-Contained Reinsurance Structures." *Trade Notes*. Lane Financial LLC (www.lanefinancialllc.com) (December 10).

Lane, M. N., and R. G. Beckwith. 2003. "2003 Review of Trends in Insurance Securitization." *Trade Notes*. Lane Financial LLC (April 25).

Leland, H. E., and D. H. Pyle. 1977. "Information Asymmetries, Financial Structure, and Financial Intermediation." *Journal of Finance* 32, No. 2 (May).

Lenckus, D. 1997. "Self-Insurance Expanding Its Reach: Risk Management Takes Sophisticated Turn." *Business Insurance* (February 17).

Lenckus, D. 2000. "Finite Risk Superfund Deal Set." *Business Insurance* (November 6).

Lerner, J. 2000a. *Venture Capital*. New York: John Wiley & Sons.

Lerner, J. 2000b. "Where Does State Street Lead? A First Look at Finance Patents, 1971–2000." Working Paper 01-005, Harvard Business School.

Lev, B. 1989. "On the Usefulness of Earnings and Earnings Research: Lessons and Directions from Two Decades of Empirical Research." *Journal of Accounting Research* 27, Supplement.

Lewent, J. C., and A. J. Kearney. 1990. "Identifying, Measuring, and Hedging Currency Risk at Merck." *Journal of Applied Corporate Finance* 1.

L'Habitant, F.-S. 2002. *Hedge Funds: Myths and Limits*. New York: John Wiley & Sons.

Li, M. Y. 2002. "Transfer That Risk." *U.S. Banker* (March).

Linn, S. C., and J. M. Pinegar. 1988. "The Effect of Issuing Preferred Stock on Common and Preferred Stockholder Wealth." *Journal of Financial Economics* 22.

Loh, J. 2000. "Alternative Risk Transfers: What Managers Need to Know Separating Hype from Facts, and Is It Right for You?" *Asia Insurance Review* (December 5).

Lonkevich, D. 1999. "Integrated Risk Products Slow to Catch On." *National Underwriter* (April 12).

Lucas, D. 2001. *CDO Handbook*. New York: J. P. Morgan Securities, Inc.

Lucas, D., and A. Thomas. 2003. "Nth Toe Default Swaps and Notes: All About Default Correlation." In *Credit Derivatives: The Definitive Guide*. J. Gregory, ed. London: Risk Books.

Mackie-Mason, J. K. 1990. "Do Taxes Affect Corporate Financing Decisions?" *Journal of Finance* 45.

Maksimoic, V. 1995. "Financial Structure and Product Market Competition." *Handbooks in OR & MS* 9. Amsterdam: Elsevier.

Masulis, R. W. 1980. "The Effects of Capital Structure Changes on Security Prices: A Study of Exchange Offers." *Journal of Financial Economics* 8.

Masulis, R. W., and A. W. Korwar. 1986. "Seasoned Equity Offerings: An Empirical Investigation." *Journal of Financial Economics* 15.

Matten, C. 2000. *Managing Bank Capital*. 2nd edition. New York: John Wiley & Sons.

Mayers, D. 2000. "Convertible Bonds: Matching Real Options with Financial Options." *Journal of Applied Corporate Finance* 13, No. 1 (Spring).

McDonnell, E. 2002. "Industry Loss Warranties." In *Alternative Risk Strategies*. M. N. Lane, ed. London: Risk Books.

McEntee, J. J., III. 2004. "Trust-Preferred Securities Enhance Investor, Issuer Opportunities." In *Hybrid Products: Instruments, Applications and Modeling*. A. Batchvarov, ed. London: Risk Books.

McGinnis, D. 2004. "Creating Solutions to Preserve Business Relationships." *AIG Risk Finance Review* 3, No. 1.

Merges, R. P. 1999. "As Many As Six Impossible Patents Before Breakfast: Property Rights for Business Concepts and Patent System Reform." *Berkeley Technology Law Journal* 14.

Merton, R. C. 1974. "On the Pricing of Corporate Debt: The Risk Structure of Interest Rates." *Journal of Finance* 29.

Merton, R. C. 1993. "Operation and Regulation in Financial Intermediation: A Functional Perspective." Working Paper 93-020, Harvard Business School.

Merton, R. C., and A. F. Perold. 1993. "Management of Risk Capital in Financial Firms." In *Financial Services: Perspectives and Challenges*. Boston: Harvard Business School Press.

Mikkelson, W. H., and M. M. Partch. 1986. "Valuation Effects of Security Offerings and the Issuance Process." *Journal of Financial Economics* 15.

Miller, M. H. 1977. "Debt and Taxes." *Journal of Finance* 32, No. 2: 261–275.

Miller, M. H. 1986. "Financial Innovation: The Last Twenty Years and the Next." *Journal of Financial and Quantitative Analysis* 21.

Miller, M. H. 1988. "The Modigliani-Miller Propositions After Thirty Years," *Journal of Economic Perspectives* 2, No. 4: 99–120.

Miller, M. H. 1991. "Leverage." *Journal of Finance* 46, No. 2: 479–488.

Miller, M. H. 1997. *Merton Miller on Derivatives*. New York: John Wiley & Sons.

Miller, M. H., and K. Rock. 1985. "Dividend Policy under Asymmetric Information." *Journal of Finance* 40, No. 4 (September).

Miller, M. H., and M. S. Scholes. 1982. "Dividends and Taxes: Some Empirical Evidence." *Journal of Political Economy* Vol. 90, No. 6.

Mischel, H., R. P. Smith, R. E. Green, D. S. Veno, and V. Orgo.2005. *S&P Bond Insurance Book 2005*. New York: Standard & Poor's.

Modigliani, F. 1982. "Debt, Dividend Policy, Taxes, Inflation and Market Valuation." *Journal of Finance* 37, No. 2: 255–273.

Modigliani, F. 1988. "MM—Past, Present, Future." *Journal of Economic Perspectives* 2, No. 4: 149–158.

Modigliani, F., and M. H. Miller. 1958. "The Cost of Capital, Corporation Finance, and the Theory of Investment." *American Economic Review* 48, No. 3: 261–297.

Modigliani, F., and M. H. Miller. 1959. "The Cost of Capital, Corporation Finance, and the Theory of Investment: Reply." *American Economic Review* 49, No. 4: 655–669.

Modigliani, F., and M. H. Miller. 1961. "Dividend Policy, Growth, and the Valuation of Shares." *Journal of Business* 34, No. 4: 411–433.

Modigliani, F., and M. H. Miller. 1963. "Corporate Income Taxes and the Cost of Capital: A Correction." *American Economic Review* 53, No. 3: 433–443.

Monti, R. G., and A. Barile. 1995. *A Practical Guide to Finite Risk Insurance and Reinsurance.* New York: John Wiley & Sons.

Murphy, E. 2003. "Overview of the CDO Market." In *Credit Derivatives: The Definitive Guide.* J. Gregory, ed. London: Risk Books.

Myers, G. 2000. "The Alternative Insurance Market: A Primer." White Paper, Munich Re/America Re (June 30).

Myers, S. C. 1977. "The Determinants of Corporate Borrowing." *Journal of Financial Economics* 5.

Myers, S. C. 1984. "The Capital Structure Puzzle." *Journal of Finance* 39, No. 3.

Myers, S. C., and N. S. Majluf. 1984. "Corporate Financing and Investment Decisions When Firms Have Information That Investors Do Not Have." *Journal of Financial Economics* 13.

Nelson, P. 1970. "Information and Consumer Behavior." *Journal of Political Economy* 78.

Nelson, P. 1974. "Advertising as Information." *Journal of Political Economy* 81.

Niehaus, G., and S. V. Mann. 1992. "The Trading of Underwriting Risk: An Analysis of Insurance Futures Contracts and Reinsurance." *Journal of Risk and Insurance* 59, No. 4.

Ogden, J. 1987. "An Analysis of Yield Curve Notes." *Journal of Finance* (March).

Outreville, J. F. 1998. *Theory and Practice of Insurance.* Boston: Kluwer.

Pacelle, M., and S. Young. 2001. "Bondholders Press Telecom Firms to Halt Spending Sprees." *Wall Street Journal* (July 2).

Palmer, P. 2003. "The Market for Complex Credit Risk." In *Corporate Aftershock.* C. L. Culp and W. A. Niskanen, eds. New York: John Wiley & Sons.

Parkin, A. 1998. "Catastrophic Risk as an 'Alternative Investment.'" In *Securitized Insurance Risk.* M. Himick, ed. Chicago: Glenlake Publishing Company, Ltd.

Perold, A. F. 2001. "Capital Allocation in Financial Firms." Harvard Business School Working Paper 98-072 (February).

Perraudin, W. 2004. *Structured Credit Products: Pricing, Rating, Risk Management, and Basel II.* London: Risk Books.

Peterson, M. 2001. "Master Chefs of the Credit Market." *Euromoney* (June).

Peterson, P. P., and F. J. Fabozzi. 2002. *Capital Budgeting: Theory and Practice.* New York: John Wiley & Sons.

Phifer, R. 1996. *Reinsurance Fundamentals: Treaty and Facultative.* New York: John Wiley & Sons.

Rajan, R. G. 1992. "Insiders and Outsiders: The Choice between Informed and Arm's-Length Debt." *Journal of Finance* 47.

Rajan, R. G., and L. Zingales. 1995. "What Do We Know About Capital Structure? Some Evidence from International Data." *Journal of Finance* Vol. 50.

Rappaport, A. 1998. *Creating Shareholder Value.* 2nd ed. New York: Free Press.

Raybin, P. 2003. "When One Door Closes . . ." *AIG Risk Finance Review* 2, No. 2.

Remy, U. E., and D. Grieger. 2003. "Industry-Specific Practices and Solutions: Credit Solutions Provided by Insurance Companies." In *Alternative Risk Strategies.* M. Lane, ed. London: Risk Books.

Reoch, R. 2003. "Credit Derivatives: The Past, the Presemt and the Future." In *Credit Derivatives: The Definitive Guide.* J. Gregory, ed. London: Risk Books.

Roach, R. 2002. *Testimony Before the Permanent Subcommittee on Investigations on The Role of Financial Institutions in Enron's Collapse* (July 23).

Rogers, M. T., A. Sargeant, and G. Osborne. 1996. "Insurance Captives Offer Buoyant Risk Financing." *Corporate Cashflow* (April).

Ross, S. A. 1988. "Comment on the Modigliani-Miller Propositions." *Journal of Economic Perspectives* 2, No. 4: 127–133.

Rothschild, M., and J. Stiglitz. 1976. "Equilibrium in Competitive Insurance Markets." *Quarterly Journal of Economics* 90.

Saita, Francesco. 1999. "Allocation of Risk Capital in Financial Institutions." *Financial Management* 28, No. 3 (Autumn).

Sammer, J. 1999. "Brave New Business Risks." *Business Finance* (December 1999).

Schenk, C. 2000. "Michelin: Setting the Standard." *Alternative Risk Strategies: Special Supplement to Risk Magazine* (December).

Schienvar, S. 2003. "Structure Puts Cost Relief in Sight." *AIG Risk Finance Review* 2, No. 1 (Spring).

Schön, E., V. Bochicchio, and E. Wolfram. 1998. *Integrated Risk Management Solutions.* Zürich: Swiss Re New Markets.

Sclafane, S. 1996. "Product Liability Plan Taps Capital Market." *National Underwriter* (April 22).

Scordis, N. A., and M. M. Porat. 1998. "Captive Insurance Companies and Manager-Owner Conflicts." *Journal of Risk and Insurance* 65, No. 2.

Senbet, L. W., and J. K. Seward. 1995. "Financial Distress, Bankruptcy, and Reorganization." *Handbooks in OR & MS 9.* Amsterdam: Elsevier.

Shepheard-Walwyn, T., and R. Litterman. 1998. "Building a Coherent Risk Measurement and Capital Optimisation Model for Financial Firms." *FRBNY Economic Policy Review* (October).

Shimpi, P. 2001. *Integrating Corporate Risk Management.* New York: Texere.

Shirreff, D. 1991. "Dealing with Default." *Risk* 4, No. 1.

Shyam-Sunder, L. 1991. "The Stock Price Effect of Risky versus Safe Debt." *Journal of Financial and Quantitative Analysis* 26, No. 4.

Shyam-Sunder, L., and S. C. Myers. 1999. "Testing Static Tradeoff Against Pecking Order Models of Capital Structure." *Journal of Financial Economics* 51.

Sick, G. 1995. "Real Options." *Handbooks in OR & MS 9.* Amsterdam: Elsevier.

Skipper, H. D. 1998. "The Nature of Government Intervention into Insurance Markets: Regulation." In *International Risk and Insurance: An Environmental-Managerial Approach.* H. D. Skipper, ed. New York: Irwin McGraw-Hill.

Smith, C. W., Jr. 1986a. "Investment Banking and the Capital Acquisition Process." *Journal of Financial Economics* 15.

Smith, C. W., Jr. 1986b. "On the Convergence of Insurance and Finance Research." *Journal of Risk and Insurance* 53, No. 4.

Smith, C. W., Jr., and R. M. Stulz. 1985. "The Determinants of Firms' Hedging Policies." *Journal of Financial and Quantitative Analysis* 20, No. 4: 391–405.

Smith, C. W., Jr., and J. Warner. 1979. "On Financial Contracting: An Analysis of Bond Covenants." *Journal of Financial Economics* 7.

Smith, D. 1988. "The Pricing of Bull and Bear Floating Rate Notes: An Application of Financial Engineering." *Financial Management* 17, No. 4.

Smith, D. 2003. "CDOs of CDOs: Art Eating Itself?" In *Credit Derivatives: The Definitive Guide*. J. Gregory, ed. London: Risk Books.

Smith, F. L. 1992. "Environmental Policy at the Crossroads." In *Environmental Politics: Public Costs, Private Rewards*. M. Greve and F. Smith, eds. New York: Praeger.

Smith, F. L. 2003. "Cowboys versus Cattle Thieves: The Role of Innovative Institutions in Managing Risks Along the Frontier." In *Corporate Aftershock*. C. L. Culp and W. A. Niskanen, eds. New York: John Wiley & Sons.

Smithson, C. W. 1987. "A LEGO Approach to Financial Engineering." *Midland Corporate Finance Journal* 4.

Smithson, C. W. 1998. *Managing Financial Risk*. 3rd ed. New York: McGraw-Hill.

Smithson, C. W. 2003. *Credit Portfolio Management*. New York: John Wiley & Sons.

Smithson, C. W., and D. H. Chew Jr. 1992. "The Uses of Hybrid Debt in Managing Corporate Risk." *Journal of Applied Corporate Finance* 4, No. 4 (Winter).

Solow, R. 1956. "A Contribution to the Theory of Economic Growth." *Quarterly Journal of Economics* 70.

Spence, M. 1973. "Job Market Signaling." *Quarterly Journal of Economics* 87.

Stonier, J. 1999. "Airline Long-Term Planning Under Uncertainty: The Benefits of Asset Flexibility Created Through Product Commonality and Manufacturer Lead Time Reductions." In *Real Options and Business Strategy: Applications to Decision Making*. L. Trigeorgis, ed. London: Risk Books.

Stulz, R. 1990. "Managerial Discretion and Optimal Financing Policies." *Journal of Financial Economics* 26.

Stultz, R. 1996. "Rethinking Risk Management." *Journal of Applied Corporate Finance* Vol. 9 (Fall).

Sullivan, A. 1995. "A Sprung Trap." *Airfinance Journal* (July/August).

Swoboda, P., and J. Zechner. 1995. "Financial Structure and the Tax System." *Handbooks in OR & MS* 9. Amsterdam: Elsevier.

Tavakoli, J. M. 1998. *Credit Derivatives*. New York: John Wiley & Sons.

Tavakoli, J. M. 2003. *Collateralized Debt Obligations and Structured Finance: New Developments in Cash and Synthetic Securitization*. Hoboken, NJ: John Wiley & Sons.

Thompson, R. E., Jr., and E. F. J. Yun. 1998. "Collateralized Loan and Bond Obligations: Creating Value Through Arbitrage." In *Handbook of Structured Financial Products*. F. J. Fabozzi, ed. New Hope, PA: Frank J. Fabozzi Associates.

Topatigh, C. 1999. "Reverse Convertibles." *Swiss Derivatives Review*.

Trieschmann, J. S., S. G. Gustavson, and R. E. Hoyt. 2001. *Risk Management and Insurance*. Cincinnati, OH: South-Western College Publishing.

Trigeorgis, L. 1995. "Real Options; An Overview." In *Real Options in Capital Investment: Models, Strategies, and Applications.* L. Trigeorgis, ed. New York: Praeger.

Trigeorgis, L. 1996. *Real Options: Managerial Flexibility and Strategy in Resource Allocation.* Cambridge, MA: MIT Press.

Trigeorgis, L. 1999. *Real Options and Business Strategy.* London: Risk Books.

Tufano, P. 1989. "Financial Innovation and First-Mover Advantages." *Journal of Financial Economics* 25.

Vermaelen, T. 1981. "Common Stock Repurchases and Market Signaling: An Empirical Study." *Journal of Financial Economics* 9.

Weidner, N. J., J. De Melo, and P. J. Williams. 2005. "Equity Default Swaps and Their Use in CDO Transactions." *Capital Markets Report.* Cadwalader, Wickersham & Taft (Winter/Spring).

Welch, I. 1989. "Seasoned Offerings, Imitation Costs, and the Underpricing of Initial Public Offerings." *Journal of Finance* 44.

Whetten, M., and W. Jin. 2005. "Constant Maturity CDS—A Guide." *Nomura Fixed Income Research* (May 5).

Williams, C. A., M. L. Smith, and P. C. Young. 1995. *Risk Management and Insurance.* 7th ed. New York: McGraw-Hill.

Winston, P. D. 2000. "Seeing Insurance as Capital Rather Than Cost." *Business Insurance* (November 27).

Wöhrmann, P. 1998. "Swiss Developments in Alternative Risk Financing Models." *European America Business Journal* (Spring).

Wöhrmann, P. 1999. "Finite Risk Solutions in Switzerland." *European America Business Journal* (Spring).

Wöhrmann, P. 2001. "Alternative Risk Financing—Developing the Market Potential of Small and Medium-Sized Companies." *European America Business Journal* (Spring).

Wöhrmann, P., and C. Bürer. 2001. "Instrument der Alternativen Risikofinanzierung." *Schweizer Versicherung* 7.

Young, J. B. 1996. "Alternative Risk Financing: The Calm Before the Storm." Manuscript, Alternative Risk Solutions, Inc.

Index

Printed and bound by CPI Group (UK) Ltd, Croydon, CR0 4YY

23/04/2025

14660999-0005